Beyond Lex Loci Delicti

About the author:

Ted M. de Boer was born in 1943 in Uithoorn (the Netherlands). In 1969, he graduated from the University of Utrecht with the degree of Master of Laws. Having received the degree of Master of Comparative Jurisprudence from New York University School of Law in 1972, he joined the Faculty of Law of the University of Amsterdam, where he teaches private international law at the Center for Foreign Law and Private International Law. In 1985, he was appointed as a (part-time) judge in the Court of Alkmaar. This book was submitted to the University of Amsterdam as his doctoral thesis.

Beyond Lex Loci Delicti

Conflicts methodology and multistate torts
in American case law

Th. M. de Boer

Kluwer Law and Taxation Publishers
Deventer – Antwerp – London – Frankfurt – Boston – New York

Distribution in USA and Canada
Kluwer Law and Taxation Publishers
101 Philip Drive
Norwell, Massachusetts 02061 U.S.A.

Library of Congress Cataloging in Publication Data

Boer, Th. M. de.
  Beyond Lex Loci Delicti.

  Bibliography: p. 513
  Includes index.
  1. Conflict of laws–Torts–United States. 2. Conflict of laws–Lex loci delicti–United States. I. Title.
  KF418.T6B64 1987   340.9'3   86-21299
  ISBN 90-6544-276-6

This book was originally submitted as a doctoral thesis to the University of Amsterdam, on January 9, 1987.

© 1987, Th.M. de Boer, The Netherlands
Cover design: © 1987, Dick Elffers, The Netherlands

All rights reserved. No part of this publication may be reproduced, stored in a retrieval system, or transmitted in any form or by any means, mechanical, photocopying, recording or otherwise, without prior written permission of the author.

Acknowledgments

Five years ago, when I started doing research for this book, somebody asked me, rather skeptically, how many people would want to read a Dutch dissertation on American choice of law methodology. Considering the small number of conflicts adepts in the Netherlands, I realized that my prospective readers would be a very select group indeed – unless the book were written in a more accessible language than Dutch. In the course of the past years, I have had many moments to regret my boldness. The task I had assigned myself put a much greater tax on my mental and physical resources than I had anticipated, and for more than just linguistic reasons. Although I consulted my Webster more frequently than any treatise on conflicts law, it is in the nature of academic writing that the substance of my book, not its form, style or language, caused me most of my sleepless nights. If it were not for the kindness of friends and colleagues, I would never have known the relief I feel now, while writing these final words. I thank them all for their sympathy, their encouragement, their patience, and their help.

I am indebted to Dr. Norman Herzig for his punctilious correction of a large part of the manuscript. Thanks to his efforts, there are fewer misspelled words, clumsy expressions and punctuation errors than there would have been without his help.

Jeanne Wennekers, Tineke Kerstens and Margreet Kroon checked the manuscript for various other kinds of lapses, while Johan Westenberg helped with the proof-reading. I thank them for their accuracy and perseverance, but most of all for their encouragement in times of stress, exhaustion, or despair. Among my moral supporters I also count Pieter Beelaerts, my long-time friend, confidant and morale booster; my father, who, from the moment I finished the first chapter, kept urging me to write the last page straight away; and my friend Rob, who, despite his periodic grumblings about late hours and lack of companionship, did show an amazing tolerance for the self-absorbed lifestyle I assumed after I started writing in earnest.

Much work, even beyond the call of duty, has been done by Kees van Ophem, student-assistant at the Center for Foreign Law and Private

International Law, who took care of the table of cases, the index of names, the list of abbreviations and the bibliography. I have much appreciated his critical questions and keen observations, as well as his cheerful readiness to check and re-check the ever-increasing number of footnotes.

Adèle Stuijfzand is a dear friend who, despite her busy life, found time to relieve me of a number of chores requiring accuracy and patience, two of the many virtues for which I admire her. Thanks to her, I feel reasonably secure that the full manuscript can now be seen in print, without a paragraph or footnote missing.

Another close friend, Marjolein van der Tweel, took charge of the production process; she conducted most of the negotiations with typesetters and printers and proved to be an expert overseer, troubleshooter and production manager. Without her efficiency, the publication of this book would certainly have been delayed for several months.

I owe a special debt of gratitude to Dick Elffers, who designed the cover. When I asked him for the names of some of his less well-known colleagues, he kindly offered to do the design himself. The result is a perceptive interpretation of the theme of this book: the contrast between the straight lines of traditional allocation and the policy-oriented slant of modern American choice of law. I salute him for his artistry and thank him for his kindness.

Financial help came from two Dutch organizations. The stipends of the Netherlands Organization for the Advancement of Pure Research (Z.W.O.) and of the Foundation for the Advancement of Research in Private International Law (S.T.I.P.) enabled me to do most of my research in New York, first during a period of four months in 1982, and a second time for two months in the late fall of 1984. In this connection, I should like to mention that, by courtesy of New York University School of Law, I could make use of its well-stacked library and other facilities for research.

I am proud to acknowledge the intellectual support I received from Professor Herman Schoordijk, and the benefit I derived from Professor Luc Strikwerda's prompt reactions and constructive criticism. I am grateful to my *promotor*, Professor Hans Ulrich Jessurun d'Oliveira, for leaving me ample room to shape this book in my own fashion and, after I finished the first draft, for coping with my opinionated attitude during the long hours we spent discussing the manuscript. His exacting scholarship and fastidious attention to detail were a constant challenge to my sense of perfection and kept me on my toes whenever I was about to sit back. Thanks to his suggestions, I have learned a lot about subjects I had not even contemplated, some of which I included at his behest. I am sure that our debates have resulted in improvements, and that is, after all, what counted most to both of us.

My final words of gratitude go to the one who deserves them more than anyone else: my friend and colleague Roelof Kotting. For the past five years, I have pestered him with my monomaniacal interest in the methodology of conflicts law. But for this very paragraph, he has read every sentence in this book, in all of its various drafts. No page was rewritten without the benefit of his opinion, no chapter was shown to others without his blessing. I have greatly profited from his perceptive criticism, his extraordinary editorial gift, and, above all, his generous friendship and dedication. No word in any of the dictionaries and thesauruses I used captures the profundity of my thankfulness. A heart-felt "*dank!*" will have to do.

Amsterdam, January 1987   Ted M. de Boer

Contents

Acknowledgments   v
Abbreviations and miscellaneous remarks   XI

Points of Departure   1

Part One: The Bounds of Tradition   17

Chapter 1   Transitions in European conflicts law   19
                 1 The Dutch perspective   19
                 2 Proper law notions and
                    "semi-open conflicts rules"   25
                 3 Functional allocation   42
                 4 Favor concepts   53
                 5 "Priority rules"   75

Chapter 2   The "pervasive problems" of conflicts law revisited   92
                 1 Characterization   95
                 2 Renvoi   117
                 3 Public policy   139
                 4 Notice and proof of foreign law   174

Part Two: Beyond Lex Loci Delicti   187

Introduction: Is there a "crisis" in American conflicts law?   189

Chapter 3   The most significant relationship approach   198

Chapter 4   Interest analysis   227
                 1 False conflicts and no-conflicts   233
                 2 False conflicts   239
                 3 The unprovided-for case   252
                 4 True conflicts   271
                    a Weighing conflicting interests   274
                    b Comparative impairment analysis:
                      the California answer   282
                    c Territorial solutions   302

Chapter 5	Leflar's choice-influencing considerations	323
Chapter 6	The comeback of lex loci delicti: the New York experience	348
Chapter 7	Beyond interest analysis: the supremacy of lex fori	373

Part Three: The Viability of Policy-oriented Choice of Law 395

Introduction 397

Chapter 8	The guest statute problem	403
	1 Guest statute policies	408
	2 The spatial reach of a guest statute	426
	3 A systematic survey of policy-oriented guest statute decisions	440
Chapter 9	The ambiguities of policy-oriented choice of law	457

Conclusion 485

Summary	499
Samenvatting	503
Bibliography	513
Names	546
Cases	555
Index	568

Abbreviations

A.	Atlantic Reporter
A.Ae.	Ars Aequi
Abb. N. Cas.	Abbot's New Cases
A.D.	Appellate Division Reports
aff'd	affirmed
All E.R.	All England Law Reports
A.L.R.	American Law Reports
Am.J.Comp.L.	American Journal of Comparative Law
Am. Rep.	American Reports (Selected Cases)
Am. U. L.Rev.	American University Law Review
Ark. L.Rev.	Arkansas Law Review
Asser	Kaartsysteem T.M.C. Asser Instituut
BGH	Bundesgerichtshof
Calif. L.Rev.	California Law Review
Can. B.Rev.	Canadian Bar Review
Cass. Civ.	Cour de Cassation, chambre civile
C.D.	Central District
cert. den.	certiorari denied
CIEC	Commission Internationale de l'Etat Civil
Cir.	Circuit (Federal Court of Appeals)
Clunet	Journal du droit international
Col. J.Transn.L.	Columbia Journal of Transnational Law
Col. L.Rev.	Columbia Law Review
concurr. op.	concurring opinion
Const.	Constitution(al)
Curr. Legal Probl.	Current Legal Problems
D.	District
D.C.	District of Columbia
Dec.	Decision(s)
diss. op.	dissenting opinion
Doc.	document(s)
Duke L.J.	Duke Law Journal
E.D.	Eastern District
E.E.C.	European Economic Community
Eng. Rep.	English Reports
F.	Federal Reporter
FamRZ.	Zeitschrift für das gesamte Familienrecht
F.R.D.	Federal Rules Decisions
F.Supp.	Federal Supplement

Harv. Int.L.J.	Harvard International Law Journal
Harv. L.Rev.	Harvard Law Review
HR	Hoge Raad der Nederlanden
I.C.J.	International Court of Justice
I.C.L.Q.	International & Comparative Law Quarterly
Ill.App.	Illinois Appellate Court Reports
Ill.Dec.	Illinois Decisions
Ind.App.	Indiana Court of Appeals (prior to 1972, Appellate Court) Reports
IPRax	Praxis des Internationalen Privat- und Verfahrensrechts
J.Z.	Juristenzeitung
Ky. L.J.	Kentucky Law Journal
L. & C.P.	Law & Contemporary Problems
L.Ed.	Supreme Court Reports, Lawyers' Edition
L.J.	Law Journal
Lloyd's Rep.	Lloyd's List Law Reports
L.Q.	Law Quarterly
L.Q. Rev.	Law Quarterly Review
L.Rev.	Law Review
M.& W.	Meeson & Welsby Exchequer Cases
Marq. L.Rev.	Marquette Law Review
M.D.	Middle District
Med. N.V.I.R.	Mededelingen van de Nederlandse Vereniging voor Internationaal recht
Mich. L.Rev.	Michigan Law Review
Misc.	New York Miscellaneous Reports
Mod. L.Rev.	Modern Law Review
Mo. L.Rev.	Missouri Law Review
N.C. L.Rev.	North Carolina Law Review
N.D.	Northern District
N.E.	Northeastern Reporter
N.I.L.R.	Netherlands International Law Review
NIPR	Nederlands Internationaal Privaatrecht, Repertorium op verdragenrecht, wetgeving, rechtspraak en literatuur
NJ	Nederlandse Jurisprudentie
N.J.B.	Nederlands Juristenblad
N.J.W.	Neue Juristische Wochenschrift

N.T.I.R.	Nederlands Tijdschrift voor Internationaal Recht
N.V.I.R.	Nederlandse Vereniging voor Internationaal Recht
N.V.R.V.	Nederlandse Vereniging voor Rechtsvergelijking
N.W.	Northwestern Reporter
N.W.U. L.Rev.	Northwestern University Law Review
N.Y.S.	New York Supplement
N.Y.U. L.Rev.	New York University Law Review
Ohio St. L.J.	Ohio State Law Journal
OLG	Oberlandesgericht
Or.App.	Oregon Reports, Court of Appeals
Or. L.Rev.	Oregon Law Review
P.	Pacific Reporter
P.O.D.	Proposed Official Draft (Restatement 2d Conflict of Laws)
Pres. Rb.	President Arrondissementsrechtbank
Publ. EEC	Official Journal of the EEC
RabelsZ.	Rabels Zeitschrift für ausländisches und internationales Privatrecht
Rb.	Arrondissementsrechtbank
Rec. des Cours	Recueil des Cours
reh. denied	rehearing denied
Rest.	Restatement of the Law
rev'd	reversed
Rev. Crit. d.i.p.	Revue Critique de droit international privé
RG	Reichsgericht
RGZ	Entscheidungen des Reichsgerichts, Zivilsachen
R.M. Themis	Rechtsgeleerd Magazijn Themis
Rptr.	Reporter
Rut. Cam. L.J.	Rutgers-Camden Law Journal
Rv.	Wetboek van Burgerlijke Rechtsvordering
RvdW/KG	Rechtspraak van de Week/Kort Geding
R.W.	Rechtskundig Weekblad
S&S	Schip en Schade
Schw.Jb.I.R	Schweizerisches Jahrbuch für Internationales Recht
S.C. L.Rev.	South Carolina Law Review
S. Ct.	Supreme Court Reporter
S.E.	Southeastern Reporter

So.	Southern Reporter
So. Cal. L.Rev.	Southern California Law Review
Stanf. L.Rev.	Stanford Law Review
StaZ.	Das Standesamt
Stb.	Staatsblad van het Koninkrijk der Nederlanden
Super. Ct.	Superior Court
S.W.	Southwestern Reporter
Syr. L.Rev.	Syracuse Law Review
Tex. L.Rev.	Texas Law Review
transf'd	transferred
Tr. Law. Guide	Trial Lawyer's Guide
Trb.	Tractatenblad van het Koninkrijk der Nederlanden
Tul. L.Rev.	Tulane Law Review
UCC	Uniform Commercial Code
U.C. Davis L.Rev.	U.C. Davis Law Review
U. Chi. L.Rev.	University of Chicago Law Review
U.C.L.A. L.Rev.	University of California at Los Angeles Law Review
U. Colo. L.Rev.	University of Colorado Law Review
U. Fla. L.Rev.	University of Florida Law Review
U. Pa L.Rev.	University of Pennsylvania Law Review
U.S.	United States Supreme Court Reports
U. San Fr. L.Rev.	University of San Francisco Law Review
U.S.C.	United States Code
U. Toronto L.J.	University of Toronto Law Journal
Va. L.Rev.	Virginia Law Review
Vand. L.Rev.	Vanderbilt Law Review
V.R.	Verkeersrecht
W.	Weekblad van het Recht
W. & M. L.Rev.	William & Mary Law Review
Wash. U. L.Q.	Washington University Law Quarterly
W.D.	Western District
West.St.U. L.Rev.	Western State University Law Review
W.L.R.	Weekly Law Reports
W.P.N.R.	Weekblad voor Privaatrecht, Notariaat en Registratie
Zeitschr. Ausl. I.P.	Zeitschrift für ausländisches und internationales Privatrecht
Z.f.Rv.	Zeitschrift für Rechtsvergleichung

Miscellaneous remarks

- All quotations from non-English sources have been translated into English.

- Unless otherwise stated, citations and footnotes have been omitted from quotations.

- Quotations from cases have generally been taken from the last source cited.

- References to "Restatement" or "Restatement Second" are to the Restatement of the Law (Second), Conflict of Laws.

- References to Dutch courts are either to the "Hoge Raad" (Supreme Court), a "hof" (court of appeal), a "rechtbank" (district court), or a "kantongerecht" (small claims court).

- Footnotes are numbered per chapter; page numbers are preceded by the chapter number (*e.g.*: 2–97 = chapter 2, page 97). Footnotes in the introductory section entitled "Points of Departure" are assigned to chapter 1, footnotes in the "Conclusion" to chapter 9.

- Where appropriate, the words "he" or "his" should be understood to include "she" or "her".

- Generally, the terms "domicile" and "residence" are meant to denote a more or less durable connection between an individual and his "home state"; unless expressly stated, no attempt has been made to differentiate between the two concepts. In the context of American case law, "citizens" can generally be equated with "domiciliaries".

Points of Departure

"Gone are the days when the choice of law in tort cases was relatively definite and simple." Embarking on a laborious analysis of policies and interests in a fairly straightforward guest statute case, the author of these words[1] must have felt a twinge of nostalgia. Before him was a case involving an automobile guest passenger who had his home in the forum state, Oregon, and a host driver hailing from the Canadian province of British Columbia, where the accident had occurred. On their way from Oregon to Canada, the parties had been travelling through the night, when the host fell asleep at the wheel and lost control of the car. Seeking damages for personal injuries, the plaintiff contended that British Columbia law governed his action, which would entitle him to full recovery. The defendant host, on the other hand, relied on the Oregon guest statute which did not impose liability on host drivers unless the guest could establish gross negligence. The trial court had found for the defendant, but the Oregon Court of Appeals reversed, holding that British Columbia law ought to be applied. It did not arrive at this result by blind jurisdiction-selection, as prescribed by traditional conflicts law and its abstract "place of wrong" criterion for torts. Instead, the court's choice of law approach entailed the determination of the policies underlying Oregon's guest statute and British Columbia's recovery rule, followed by an evaluation of the interests which each jurisdiction might have in the resolution of this particular case. This process is much more complicated than the ordi-

---

1 Judge Butler writing for the majority in *Fisher v. Huck* 50 Or.App. 635, 624 P.2d 177 at 178 (1981).

nary subsumption required by the traditional allocation method,[2] and, as the Oregon appellate court noted with resignation, judicial performance is seldom beyond criticism: " ... the endeavor, in many instances, is like skeet shooting with a bow and arrow: a direct hit is likely to be a rarity, if not pure luck. With that chance of success in mind, we nock the arrow and draw the string."[3]

This example may serve to introduce the problem to be tackled in the following chapters. Basically, this book is not about tort choice of law but about choice of law method. Its main theme is the question whether the choice of law approach that seeks to solve conflicts of law by a relative evaluation of substantive laws is a preferable alternative to the method of abstract coordination. While the latter approach still prevails in most legal systems in the world today, American conflicts law has undergone fundamental changes since the highest court of New York, the Court of Appeals, decided to adopt a policy-oriented choice of law method in the early 1960's. *Babcock v. Jackson*[4] may not have been the first American case in which the conceptualistic precepts of traditional conflicts law were rejected,[5] but it did mark the beginning of a methodological revolution which still divides the scholars of contemporary conflicts law as it continues to convert the American courts. Most of the battle was fought in the field of multistate torts, and that is the reason why this subject figures so prominently in the title and contents of this book. "Beyond *lex loci delicti,*" I found a number of alternative solutions to the problem of multistate torts which have in common that, to a greater or lesser extent, they take

2 This term – or the more common expression "jurisdiction-selection" – denotes the choice of law method by which the applicable law is selected by reference to (usually predetermined) geographical aspects of multistate cases. Still the prevailing choice of law method of today, at least outside the United States, it was conceived in the 1840's by the German Romanist Friedrich Carl von Savigny. In the United States, it was championed by Joseph H. Beale, the author of the 1934 Restatement of Conflict of Laws.
3 *Ibid.* Obviously, Judge Butler would have preferred the traditional approach: from the time the Oregon Supreme Court abandoned it, in *Casey v. Manson Construction Company* 247 Or. 274, 429 P.2d 898 (1967), "the choice of law has been based upon somewhat amorphous considerations, the evaluation of which depends in large measure on the semantics used by the court making the particular decision. Regardless of whether that approach represents progress, it was new and different when adopted, and is now with us."
4 *Babcock v. Jackson* 12 N.Y.2d 473, 240 N.Y.S.2d 743, 191 N.E.2d 279 (1963).
5 See *infra* chapter 8, note 1.

account of the contents and purposes of the substantive laws involved. With one exception,[6] their scope is not limited to tort choice of law; even though their impact might have been most powerful in the tort area, these are integral techniques designed to solve any choice of law problem, regardless of its classification.

The prototype of these policy-oriented approaches, loosely denominated by the term "neo-statutism",[7] is interest analysis.[8] Most eloquently described and advocated by one of the keenest minds in twentieth century conflicts law, Professor Brainerd Currie, this method approaches the choice of law problem as a potential *conflictus legum*, to be discovered by an assessment of the policies behind the relevant rules of law in their relation to the facts. Several offshoots of this theory have come into their own as solutions to the perplexing *true conflict* dilemma, the Gordian knot of Currie's choice of law conception. Important contributions in this category are the "comparative impairment" approach, devised by Professor William Baxter,[9] and the "principles of preference", developed by one of the first champions of policy-oriented choice of law, Professor David Cavers.[10] In a class by itself is the set of "choice-influencing considerations", proposed by Professor Robert Leflar.[11] At the same time descriptive and normative, these principles were meant to elucidate the workings of the choice of law process, and to guide judicial and legislative decision-makers to sensible results. Some of Leflar's considerations embody choice of law policies and have little bearing on the purposes of substantive law, but at least two of them contain direct references to the contents of the domestic laws at issue, and in that respect they belong to the ambit of neo-statutism. The same can be said of the choice of law principles laid down in the Restatement Second of Conflict of Laws, the brainchild of Professor Willis Reese.[12] This unofficial codification of the "national" conflicts law of the United States, which has proved to be an influential source of law in a number of jurisdictions, couples jurisdiction-selection on the basis of a neutral "proper law"

6 *Viz.*: the "Fuld principles"; see text accompanying note 13 and, *infra* chapter 6.
7 I owe the phrase to Ehrenzweig (1967-1) *passim*. Although it sounds like a typical Ehrenzweig expression, I am not sure whether he used it first.
8 *Infra* chapter 4.
9 *Infra* chapter 4, section 4(b).
10 *Infra* chapter 4, section 4(c).
11 *Infra* chapter 5.
12 *Infra* chapter 3.

standard with several policy-oriented criteria. This hybrid approach allows the courts to justify their choice of law decisions either by reference to geographical factors, or by an evaluation of the contents and objectives of domestic law. Finally, there are two other solutions I think should be included in this survey, even though they hardly qualify as policy-oriented techniques. Forming neither method nor approach, the three rules known as the "Fuld principles" or "Neumeier rules" were conceived specifically for the solution of multistate tort problems.[13] Distilled from the policy-oriented choice of law experience the New York Court of Appeals had gained in the field of guest statute litigation, they embody an abstracted policy evaluation, and for that reason they merit a closer look. Even less deserving of a neostatutist classification is the *lex fori* approach that has emerged in Kentucky and, more recently, in Michigan.[14] However, since this solution could not come about without a policy-oriented background and since it still leaves room for policy evaluation in close cases, it will be reviewed as one of the alternative solutions "beyond *lex loci delicti.*"

While the winds of change gathered their main force in the United States, the innovations in American choice of law methodology were keenly monitored in Europe, almost from the beginning. One of the earlier descriptions of the "New Trends in American Conflicts Law" was published in Switzerland by Dr. Anton Heini in 1962.[15] A critical account of Currie's governmental interest analysis and Ehrenzweig's *lex fori* approach formed the substance of Professor Gerhard Kegel's lectures on "The Crisis of Conflict of Laws" at the Hague Academy of International Law in 1964.[16] At the same time, the new approaches won the support of several young academicians, some of whom had completed graduate studies in the United States. Their publications greatly contributed to the discovery of American conflicts law by European conflicts scholars, awakening them to the shortcomings of mechanical jurisdiction-selection and kindling a lively interest in the possibilities of adaptation or reform. Among the first European authors who referred to the American developments in their criticism of traditional conflicts law for its abstract dogmatism were H.U. Jessurun

---

13 *Infra* chapter 6.
14 *Infra* chapter 7.
15 Heini (1962) offering an articulate presentation of mid-century American conflicts theory, notably the contributions of Cavers, Currie, and Ehrenzweig.
16 Kegel (1964) p. 97–207.

d'Oliveira and J.E.J.Th. Deelen in the Netherlands,[17] Peter Max Gutzwiller in Switzerland,[18] and Christian Joerges in Germany,[19] to name just a few authors who advocated reflection on the subliminal substantive law factor for the resolution of choice of law problems.[20] Numerous other books and law review articles, far too many to list here, have continued to keep Europe well informed on the state of affairs of American choice of law methodology. It may be doubted if the reverse is also true: in the course of my research in the United States, I could not escape the impression that American conflicts writers have very little interest in European legal literature, which could be attributed either to linguistic obstacles, or to a complacent conviction that European conflicts law is lagging behind and has little to offer.[21]

My own interest in the methodology of conflicts law was aroused in 1970, when I became a student of Professor Michael A. Schwind of New York University's Institute of Comparative Law. An inspiring teacher with a vast knowledge of both the law of conflicts and comparative law, he took our class of foreign graduates on a brisk *tour d'horizon* of American choice of law methodology, guiding us to an unbiased appreciation of the merits and drawbacks of each approach.

17 H.U. Jessurun d'Oliveira, *Internationale Verkeersongevallen, het slagveld van een grondslagenstrijd in het IPR*, (International Traffic Accidents, the Battleground of a Fundamental War in Private International Law), 1965; J.E.J.Th. Deelen, *De blinddoek van Von Savigny* (Von Savigny's Blindfold), inaugural lecture, 1966.
18 *Von Ziel und Methode des IPR* (The Objectives and Method of Private International Law), 25 *Schweizerisches Jahrbuch für internationales Recht* 161 ff. (1968).
19 *Zum Funktionswandel des Kollisionsrecht, Die "Governmental Interest Analysis" und die Krise des Internationalen Privatrechts* (The Changing Function of the Law of Conflicts, Governmental Interest Analysis and the Crisis of Private International Law), 1971.
20 An early plea for "substantive law solutions to multistate conflicts" is found in Ernst Steindorff's *Sachnormen im internationalen Privatrecht*, 1958. Even earlier, in 1947, Professor L.I. de Winter published a seminal article on the "social function" of law as a decisive choice of law factor: De Winter (1947); see also *infra* chapter 4, section 4(b), note 191.
21 European immigrants, notably Ehrenzweig, Baade and Juenger, have consistently tried to bridge this gap. It should be noted that, on either side of the Atlantic, attention mostly focuses on the developments in the Western world. Relatively little is known, either in Europe or in the United States, on the conflicts laws of Eastern Europe, Asia or Africa. I am therefore liable to use "European" conflicts law as my frame of reference when contrasting traditional method with the new approaches in the United States.

Upon my return to the Netherlands, as a newly appointed member of the University of Amsterdam Law Faculty, I set out to discover the philosopher's stone of conflicts law, fairly sure that it was waiting to be found somewhere in the orbit of neo-statutism. The first thing to do, however, was to examine the evolution of traditional choice of law in Europe and to compare theoretical dogma with the law in action. In the early 1970's, Dutch conflicts law was still in a state of flux and the debate on fundamental change, initiated in the 1960's, was still continuing. Fresh from New York and convinced by the American choice of law experience, I soon joined the critics of traditional jurisdiction-selection in their efforts to expose the deficit of a fossilized method. At the Center for Foreign Law and Private International Law of the University of Amsterdam, the intellectual atmosphere proved most congenial in this respect. At that time, we set great store by the doctrine of the rules of immediate application, the narrow European counterpart of interest analysis. Used as a device to escape the rigors of impartial conflicts law in deference to a rule of law of exceptional socio-economic importance, this doctrine was believed to open up a new general approach to choice of law and to achieve the long awaited rejuvenation of the law of conflicts.[22] In 1978, Luc Strikwerda, another Dutch Fellow of New York University's Institute of Comparative Law, published his dissertation on "Rules of quasi-public law in the conflict of laws." He contended that traditional conflicts law, which is premised on the dichotomy between public and private law, is unable to accommodate the needs of the modern welfare state in which "the fundamental distinction between state and society and consequently between public and private law" has lost its former significance, particularly as a point of departure in choice of law.[23] Instead, he argued, an adequate choice of law model should be based on an appreciation of the function of law in society, regardless of the classification of the conflicting rules as public, private or "quasi-public" law. In short, Strikwerda advocated an integral choice of law solution along the lines of the "special allocation doctrine"[24] and, more specifically, Currie's version of interest analysis. He is therefore one of the few European conflicts theorists who support policy-oriented choice of law as a desir-

22 *Infra* chapter 1, section 5.
23 Strikwerda (1978) p. 199.
24 This is the literal translation of the German term "Sonderanknüpfung", also known as the doctrine of the "règles d'application immédiate"; see *infra* chapter 1, section 5.

able alternative to the allocation method. Strikwerda's book is an impressive contribution to the theory of conflicts law in Europe, and it is a pity that the Dutch language in which it was written makes its contents inaccesible to most foreign scholars.

Despite the wealth of information on the development of American conflicts *theory*, little was known in Europe about the way the new approaches functioned in actual *practice*. Invariably, European writers would discuss *Babcock v. Jackson, Dym v. Gordon, Reich v. Purcell, Tooker v. Lopez* and the like, usually to demonstrate the flaws of interest analysis in contrast to good old-fashioned jurisdiction-selection.[25] On the whole, supporters and opponents kept to the continental tradition of approaching legal topics from a theoretical angle, a manner which encourages deductive argumentation and relegates case law to the lesser plane of illustration. For that reason, I was generally intrigued, but never convinced by those monographs in which the author, citing just a few telltale examples, sets out to prove why policy-oriented choice of law rests on unsound theory and cannot possibly produce a workable solution. If I had any objections to the new approaches at all, they were of a practical nature and concerned the difficulties of assessing policies and interests, but I had no quarrel with the logic of a theory which approaches the main issue of choice of law as a potential conflict of interests. The practical problems, I felt, might be slightly more complicated than those encountered under the traditional approach, but since the American courts apparently managed to solve them, it was clear to me that in the debate on the fundamentals of conflicts law practical considerations were not decisive.

It was with this idea in mind that I started doing the research for this book. Not the theory behind policy-oriented choice of law, but its application in judicial practice would be my subject. I wanted to examine the modern approaches in the context of social reality, not as abstract intellectual constructs but as operative solutions to actual problems. For a number of reasons I decided to concentrate on their functioning in the area of multistate torts. Over the years, tort choice of

---

25 See, *e.g.*, Loussouarn (1973) p. 342 ff.; Jayme (1974) p. 583 ff.; Ferrer Correia (1975) p. 72 ff.; Kegel (1979) p. 622 ff.; Vitta (1982) p. 4; Patocchi (1985) p. 153 ff.

law had become one of my pet subjects.[26] It is a fairly clearcut topic which lends itself well to a comprehensive presentation of the conundrum of conflicts law to the beginning student. The daily news offers a large variety of dramatic illustrations, ranging from airplane crashes to environmental disasters, which can be used to broach a discussion on the objectives and methods of conflicts law. In the second place, tort choice of law is the field where the neo-statutist solutions have achieved most of their (American) success. In matters of family law, they are virtually unknown.[27] Generally speaking, the applicable law here is the domiciliary law of one or both of the parties, in many cases coinciding with the *lex fori* as a consequence of jurisdictional criteria. In this area, little can be found in American cases or comments to help us understand modern choice of law methodology.

In contracts, most American courts now follow the most significant relationship test proposed in the Restatement Second of Conflict of Laws,[28] but since the bulk of contract cases is governed by the Uniform Commercial Code, adopted nationwide, interstate conflicts problems are generally limited to the question which version of the Code applies.[29] Furthermore, the American approach to multistate contracts is carried by two major considerations which do not come into play in tort choice of law and tend to preclude a full-scale evaluation of policies and interests. Party autonomy is approved by both the Restatement and the Uniform Commercial Code and, provided the parties' choice is reasonably related to their contract, sustained by most courts. In torts, on the other hand, the parties are unlikely to forestall

---

26 I have covered it extensively in my lectures at the University of Amsterdam and in several publications, notably my *Alternatieven voor de lex loci delicti* (1982). Since 1977, I am in charge of the conflicts of law section of *Onrechtmatige daad*, a looseleaf publication on the Dutch law of torts. This authoritative publication, whose chief editor is Huib Drion, a renowned scholar (*infra* chapter 7, note 6) and former *Hoge Raad* Justice, derives its principal value from its regular and accurate updates.
27 Notable exceptions are a few New York cases at the interface of family law and the law of property and succession. See: *Wyatt v. Fulrath* 16 N.Y.2d 169, 264 N.Y.S.2d 233, 211 N.E.2d 637 (1965); *In re Estate of Crichton* 20 N.Y.2d 124, 281 N.Y.S.2d 811, 228 N.E.2d 799 (1967). *Cf.* Strikwerda (1978) p. 165 ff.
28 The basic provision for contracts is found in § 188. *Cf.* Leflar (1977-1) p. 306 ff.
29 Leflar, *ibid.* p. 303. Weintraub (1980) p. 453 ff. (on commercial property transactions). In § 1–105 (1) UCC, the forum is allowed to apply its own version of the Code if the transaction bears "an appropriate relation" to the forum, a solution most courts are likely to seize upon.

judicial determination of the choice of law issue by a post-factum agreement on the applicable law. Another consideration, also pertinent to contracts rather than torts, is the *favor validitatis*, which could be seen as an expression of a forum policy of furthering the convenience and reliability of international and interstate commerce.[30] Since most states have this basic policy in common, choice of law in contracts is relatively bland. For these reasons, I prefer the field of multistate torts, where conflicts are more acute, solutions more spectacular, the methodology more varied and therefore more instructive. In theory and in practice, American tort choice of law proves to be the richest source of information.

The various principles of policy-oriented tort choice of law can be surveyed from different angles. The legal historian may delve into the past, tracing the origin of Leflar's better law concept to Aldricus, or contrasting medieval statutism with Currie's interest analysis. The scholar of comparative law may embark on a state-by-state survey of choice of law methodology, comparing Kentucky's *lex fori* postulate with New York's more ambiguous forum bias, or studying the differences between the proper law criteria prevailing in several states or nations. One could choose to describe case law past or present, or prefer to concentrate on doctrinal alternatives. By themselves or in combination, all these approaches, and more, are feasible and valid, depending on the purpose of the description. Since I was more interested in the practical aspects of policy-oriented choice of law than in the theoretical merits of each of its varieties, it was obvious that my research should focus on case law, while doctrinal sources would be the whetstone of my interpretation. Within the confines of American tort choice of law, the number of reported cases was still formidable enough to make me realize that a strict classification scheme was imperative. Assuming that a study of methods required a methodological grouping of cases, I first discarded the many *lex loci delicti* decisions containing no information on policy-oriented choice of law, and then attempted to arrange the remaining cases in a number of classes, labeled "Restatement Second", "interest analysis", "Leflar approach" and so forth. I soon discovered, however, that a methodological map of the sundry choice of law approaches to torts can be drawn in

---

30 *Cf.* Leflar (1977-1) p. 304 ff.; for citations in regard of the "rule of validation" see: Weintraub (1980) p. 372, note 77.

more than one way, and only by approximation. As policy-oriented solutions tend to overlap one another, or blend into combinations, thus fitting into more than one category, their contours remain somewhat hazy and no classification of the relevant case law will prove completely unassailable.[31]

Aware of possible objections, I collected some 600 multistate tort decisions[32] in which the choice of law solution was somehow "policy-oriented", and ranged them in five major categories, according to the approach the court in question had chosen as a point of departure. Most difficult to classify were those cases in which reference was made to the Restatement Second of Conflict of Laws. To the extent that these decisions are predicated on an assessment of the policies and interests of the jurisdictions involved, they belong to the category of interest analysis; the emphasis on the geographical aspects, on the other hand, suggests a different classification. Similar problems arose when I tried to grasp the development of New York's tort choice of law since the early 1970's: vacillating between *lex loci delicti*, interest analysis, forum preference, and a factual center of gravity test, the New York approach turned out to be so eclectic, to put it mildly, as to warrant a separate classification. Easier to deal with were those cases in which the court purported to rely on Leflar's choice-influencing considerations, or on the *prima facie* applicability of forum law.

To further organize the collected material, I thought of several possible subcategories, but the most functional subdivision would be the

---

31 Several American authors have noted that contemporary choice of law is characterized by eclecticism: " ... it appears that the various scholarly views concerning choice of law, developed during the last couple of decades, are being accepted by the courts as though they constituted one somewhat multi-faceted approach to the subject." Leflar (1977-1) p. 197 ff., at p. 219. See also: Westbrook (1975) *passim*; Reppy (1983) *passim*; Rosenberg (1980) p. 444, p. 455.

32 Since no law library in the Netherlands stacks a complete collection of federal and state reporters, I had to go elsewhere. I am indebted to the S.T.I.P. (Foundation for the Advancement of Research in Private International Law) and Z.W.O. (Netherlands Organization for the Advancement of Pure Research) whose financial support helped me to conduct most of my "American" research in the library of N.Y.U. Law School, initially from January to June 1982, and subsequently, to conclude my investigations, from October to December 1984. As I do not have the opportunity to check alternative sources, I will generally quote from one reporter only, citing other sources without references to the exact page number of the quotation.

one that answered to the methodological character of my research. For that reason, I sorted the cases of each major category according to their methodological peculiarities rather than their chronological, geographical or factual distinctions. Classification by issue, another possibility, proved to be less enlightening than might be expected. In several areas of tort law, the number of available choice of law cases was too small, and the various choice of law approaches too distinct, to allow any comparison but one of material results. A more systematic analysis could be made of the cases turning on much-litigated issues, such as those involving guest statutes, punitive damages, or wrongful death limitations; in these areas, enough cases can be found which have not only their issue but also a particular choice of law approach in common. Still, considering that I was studying the merits of policy-oriented choice of law in general, I decided against an issue-by-issue presentation of the various approaches, as it would detract from the methodological panorama displayed by the ensemble of assorted cases. To test the impact of policy-oriented choice of law on the adjudication of a particular issue, I felt, an analysis of the case law on a single topic should suffice.[33]

When gleaning, selecting and sorting the cases that appeared to be relevant to my subject, I noticed a recurring mention of traditional conflicts doctrines, such as characterization, renvoi and public policy. This struck me as odd, since the champions of policy-oriented choice of law had virtually ignored these subjects in their writings, making me believe the new theories had no further use for these outworn doctrines, with the possible exception of public policy. Yet, in more instances than I expected, the author of a judicial opinion, while clearly embracing the principles of post-Bealian choice of law, would refer to the remedy of public policy, take into account a foreign conflicts rule, or distinguish between substance or procedure. I had already decided that this intriguing phenomenon needed to be examined more thoroughly, when I came across an article by Professor Russell Weintraub in which he described the "pervasive problems" of conflicts law and appraised "the effect that change from a territorial to a functional method of choice-of-law analysis will have upon these problems."[34] His observations on characterization, renvoi, the public policy excep-

---

33 *Infra* chapter 8.
34 Weintraub (1968) p. 817 = Weintraub (1980) p. 48.

tion, and notice and proof of foreign law[35] proved to be an inspiring point of departure for my own investigations. In line with the overall conception of this book, my treatment of the pervasive problems[36] covers judicial practice rather than legal theory, and the cases discussed mainly involve tort issues. In this perspective, the problem to be dealt with is the question whether policy-oriented choice of law, as practiced in the courts, still needs the doctrines that were designed and used as appropriate tools of the jurisdiction-selecting method, but were often deployed by the courts as devices to circumvent the rigid neutrality of traditional conflicts law.

Having announced the major topics to be discussed, I should also mention some of the problems that will be left out. As I pointed out before, I have concentrated on multistate tort cases to appreciate the value of policy-oriented choice of law as applied to one particular category of conflicts of law. Consequently, the focus of the following chapters is on method, not on torts. For that reason, one should not expect an exhaustive discussion of tort choice of law as such. Since this book was not meant to be an all-inclusive chatechism of the law of multistate torts, I refrained from describing the more traditional solutions to tort conflicts. In my opinion, the ubiquitous *lex loci delicti* rule, the English double actionability rule, and the alternative reference rules of the two relevant Hague Conventions have been explained and evaluated sufficiently in textbooks, articles, or explanatory reports to warrant their exclusion here. For similar reasons, little will be said about those problems which are incidental to the traditional *locus delicti* criterion, such as the dichotomy of place of wrong and place of injury, the multilocal wrong, the *locus sine lege* dilemma,[37] or the very question whether the old *lex loci* rule is still an appropriate choice of law standard for every tort issue arising today. Also, there will be no systematic information on the subjects of adjudicatory jurisdiction or the recognition of foreign judgments, nothing on intertemporal problems or the idiosyncrasies of American civil procedure. In these areas, the problems are too far beyond *lex loci delicti* to claim our attention. One

---

35 In the latest edition of his textbook, Weintraub included dépeçage as an additional pervasive problem: Weintraub (1980) p. 72 ff.
36 *Infra* chapter 2.
37 In American conflicts law, collisions at sea and other maritime torts are treated as a separate choice of law category, decided by admiralty courts, and often acccording to federal law. See: Ehrenzweig (1967-1) p. 196 ff.; Leflar (1977-1) p. 287 ff.

more limitation should be mentioned. Since I have chosen case law as my primary source of information, the emphasis will be on judicial application of policy-oriented approaches, not on their underlying theories. Assuming that those who take an interest in the subject matter of this book are familiar with the basics of policy-oriented choice of law, I did not see fit to rehash the doctrinal arguments for or against each theory.

There is one theme I originally wanted to pursue further but eventually decided to curtail. Being a Dutch lawyer teaching Dutch private international law at a Dutch University, I intended to contrast the American developments with recent choice of law trends in the Netherlands, from which comparison a survey of American-Dutch conflicts methodology would emerge. Gradually, I realized that the gap between the American choice of law revolution and the slow mutation of conflicts law in Europe was too wide to make such comparative efforts worthwhile. A detailed description of Dutch tort choice of law[38] does not give us much of an insight into the relation between substantive law and conflicts law, the main theme of this book. While the trend in American case law is openly policy-oriented, the Dutch courts generally rely on outwardly neutral conflicts rules and seldom acknowledge the substantive law factors that have influenced their decision. Yet, the existence of these hidden determinants is unmistakable, and in some areas they have even been allowed to surface. In this respect, the development of conflicts law in the Netherlands[39] has been more progressive, I feel, than that in other European countries, which is one reason to depict its main features. Furthermore, the recent trend in Europe to take account of substantive law factors stems from the same dissatisfaction with blind jurisdiction-selection that gave rise to America's more radical solutions. What prompted me to go beyond *lex loci delicti* and explore the frontiers of American tort choice of law was the ultimate question whether we, conflicts lawyers in Europe, should finally stop trying to mend the worn choice of law model Savigny gave us, and adopt one of the new American ap-

---

38 This can be found in the loose-leaf edition *Onrechtmatige daad* (Drion/De Boer), mentioned *supra* note 26.
39 In an article on the development of Dutch conflicts law in the 1970's, I charted the symptoms of a trend towards the "socialization of private international law." I used this expression to denote the gradual adjustment of traditional conflicts law to the legal ideals of the contemporary social welfare state. De Boer (1980).

proaches instead. Since the answer to that question not only depends on the results of American pioneering but also on the quality of the repairs done in Europe, a brief description of the most effective attempts to rejuvenate European conflicts law will precede my reflections on the vital force of the American renaissance.[40]

---

40 *Infra* chapter 1.

Part One

The Bounds of Tradition

Chapter 1

Transitions in European Conflicts Law

1 The Dutch perspective

An unchauvinistic appreciation of the world abroad is part of Dutch culture. More receptive to foreign influences than most of our fellow Europeans, we have a way of thinking in the Netherlands that does not hold with patriotism or national pride, but favors the cachet of foreign ways and tastes. We hardly acknowledge the achievements of Dutch artists abroad, but in our theaters we applaud German dancers, British opera singers, and American actors. In our cinemas, we see the latest French film, with the original soundtrack. Our bookstores are crammed with books by foreign authors, either in translation or in the original language. On the Dutch radio, an endless stream of English and American pop songs can be heard, while our television programmers seem to have a penchant for American soap operas and German "Krimis". A restaurant offering Dutch specialties is hard to find anywhere in Holland, as most of them are bent on serving French, Italian, Spanish, or Oriental food. At school, we learn to express ourselves in several foreign languages, spending more time and energy on mastering English, French or German than on the principles of Dutch grammar and orthography, learning more about sociopolitical structures in the third world than about our own cultural heritage. This international orientation might have helped us to adjust more readily to the impact of large-scale immigration than other Europeans have been able to. There is no cause for self-congratulation in this respect, not as long as there are symptoms of discrimination, but, on the whole, the Dutch have been relatively quick to learn that ethnic differences must be taken for granted, and the prevalent reaction to signs of racism or xenophobia is indignation.[41]

From the time our country became too small for our ambitions, we developed a merchant tradition that brought us into contact with every nation in the world. Travelling to the four corners of the earth, Dutch settlers laid the foundations of a colonial empire that has sustained the economic prosperity of the Netherlands for centuries. Always active participants in international commerce, the Dutch do business in many countries of today's world, feeling at home wherever the pursuit of profit takes them. Due to its geographic position, the Netherlands channels a large volume of international trade, and a great many travellers choose our country for a convenient stop-over on their way to or from Europe. All these factors have contributed to an international way of thinking that welcomes extraneous impulses and allows the integration of domestic and foreign ideas. It keeps track of developments abroad and seeks to discover correlations. Fostering a climate of tolerance, it encourages an open-minded apperception of the values cherished by others. It has given the Dutch a front-rank window on the world.

Given this international spirit, it is not surprising that Dutch jurists have played an important part in the development of both the law of nations and the law of conflicts of law. The independence of the Republic of the United Netherlands, near the end of the 16th century, marked the beginning of an extremely creative period in the history of Dutch law. Often regarded as the founder of modern international law, the Dutchman Hugo Grotius (1583–1645) "exercised influence of a sort which no writer could hope to exercise nowadays."[42] While Grotius still adhered to the principles of natural law, his compatriot Cornelis van Bynkershoek (1673–1743) was the first influential advocate of a positivist approach to international law. At the same time, a new era of the law of conflicts of law began. Lead by Christiaan Rodenburg (1618–1668), Paulus Voet (1619–1667), his son Johannes Voet (1647–1714) and Ulricus Huber (1636–1694), the "Dutch

---

41 Cf. the reports on clashing cultures and racism in Europe by Jacob Young, Edward Behr and others, entitled "Europe's New face: A growing minority population falls victim to a rising tide of racial hatred" in contrast to "The Dutch Model": *Newsweek* January 27 1986, p. 14–19.
42 Akehurst (1984) p. 13, p. 37.

School" gave conflicts law the comity doctrine, which justified the application of foreign law on the grounds of international deference and convenience.[43] Huber's influence on the development of Anglo-American conflicts law has been substantial. His work is generally acknowledged as a major source of inspiration to the American Joseph Story (1779–1845), the "father of the conflict of laws" in the Anglo-American world.[44] Further Dutch contributions to the development of public and private international law were to follow. Towards the end of the 19th century, several initiatives were taken in restoring legal unity in a rapidly diverging world. One of the driving forces behind this internationalist movement was the Dutchman Tobias M.C. Asser (1838–1913). His efforts helped to establish the *Institut de Droit International* in 1873, and led to the creation of the Permanent Court of Arbitration in 1899.[45] In the field of conflicts law, Asser's major accomplishment was the first assembly of the Hague Conference on Private International Law. For several decades, the unification of private international law in Europe had been advocated by Asser and other prominent jurists, notably the Italian Pasquale Mancini. Their endeavors met with success in 1893, when thirteen European states convened in The Hague for the first Hague Conference on Private International Law, which would become an international organization that is active to this day. It was only natural that Asser, a man of great international prestige among diplomats, politicians and members of the legal profession, became its first president. One of his most proficient successors was Louis I. de Winter, another Dutch jurist who has won international renown for his allegiance to the cause of unification of conflicts law. President of the Hague Con-

---

43 On the subject of comity, the teachings of Huber cannot be fully identified with those of Paulus and Johannes Voet. In Huber's perception, the *comitas gentium* has its roots in the law of nations (*ius gentium*), which creates a binding obligation to take account of foreign law. To the Voets, comity depended more on courtesy and good will than on a binding relationship between nations. See: Kollewijn (1937) p. 83 ff.; p. 114 ff.; Kosters/Dubbink (1962) p. 38 ff.; for further references, see: Ehrenzweig (1967-1) p. 50, note 17. See also: *Hilton v. Guyot* 159 U.S. 113 (1895).
44 Lorenzen (1947-4) p. 202. Huber is called Story's "idol" by Ehrenzweig (1967-1) p. 54. See also: Cavers (1965) p. 4; Cramton/Currie/Kay (1981) p. 2 ff.; Yntema (1953) p. 306 ff. It should be noted, however, that Story's concept of comity was based on courtesy rather than obligation; in this respect, he was the spiritual heir of the Voets rather than Huber: Story (1834) § 33; Kosters/Dubbink (1962) p. 65.
45 For this achievement Asser received the Nobel Peace Prize in 1911, together with the Austrian A.H. Fried.

ference on Private International Law from 1966 to his death in 1972, De Winter was a persuasive advocate of international cooperation and contributed greatly to the conclusion of some of the most successful Hague Conventions.

Modern Dutch conflicts law reflects the international spirit that has permeated the cultural tradition of the Netherlands for centuries. Hardly a book or article on private international law is written by a Dutch author in which foreign sources are not cited extensively. New developments abroad are noticed, discussed and evaluated, in a continuing effort to bring out the merits and demerits of our own system of conflicts law. As a result, Dutch private international law rests on a blend of theories, mostly imported from Germany, France, Switzerland, and even England. So used are we to foreign legal thought that we have not even invented Dutch names for some of the doctrines we adopted, or, if some Dutch equivalent is suggested at all, we still use it interchangeably with the foreign expression. In Dutch conflicts literature, one encounters artless references to the validity of the *Grundsatz der engsten Beziehung* and the desirability of *Entscheidungseinklang*, to the intricacies of *renvoi*, the difficulty of a *conflit mobile* and the spatial reach of a *règle d'application immédiate*, to the unmistakable *homeward trend* or *Heimwärtsstreben* and to the reprehensible use of *escape devices*. We know the difference between *Schuldort* and *Erfüllungsort* in the theory of the characteristic performance, as well as the difference between *Handlungsort* and *Erfolgsort* in torts. We teach our students about *forum shopping* and *proper law*, about *traités doubles* and *mariages mixtes*, about *Dauerstatute* and *Näherberechtigung*. At least in its terminology, Dutch private international law is truly international.

On the other hand, our receptive attitude towards foreign ways of thinking has given Dutch conflicts law an eclectic nature. Methodologically, it is based on a combination of abstract jurisdiction-selection, proper law considerations, functional analysis, and a fairly liberal acceptance of party autonomy. At the surface, it is not much different from what it was some decades ago and its structure is still very much the same as that of the other systems of conflicts law of continental Europe. Yet, an unmistakable transition has taken place which, starting in the 1960's, has mitigated the rigidity of traditional jurisdiction-selection and left more room for result-selective reasoning than orthodox theory allowed. The aspirations for neutral allocation, serving the utopian ideal of uniformity of decision, gave way to notions that had influenced the development of substantive law all along. Gradually, it was acknowledged that conflicts law was, or should be, more than a mechanical coordination technique and that it could no longer be blind to the substantive rules of decision eligible for application. Clearly, this transition did not just occur in the Netherlands. The symptoms of change were everywhere, and they gave rise to scholarly debate all over Europe. As a result, an innovative mood started to pervade the discussions of the Hague Conference on Private International Law, at the same time encouraging the bold approach that characterized the preliminary draft of the EEC Convention on Obligations. Still, it is my impression that the transition to a more result-oriented conflicts law was more readily accepted in the Netherlands than it was in other European countries, and, also, that its impact on Dutch conflicts law has been more profound than it seems to be elsewhere. I have no intention to attempt a comparative analysis of result-selective trends in European conflicts laws. Such an endeavor would go far beyond the limits of this book. What I propose to examine in this chapter are some of the solutions we have worked out in Europe to meet the objections against blind jurisdiction-selection without abandoning the allocation method altogether. While Dutch conflicts law will serve as my frame of reference, I do not mean to suggest that the result-oriented development of choice of law is limited to the Netherlands. The result-oriented features to be discussed are also found in other European choice of law systems, particularly those of Germany and Switzerland. They are apparent in the (preliminary) draft of the EEC Convention on Obligations as well.[46] Hence, my Dutch perspective encompasses more than choice of law evolution in the Netherlands alone, and what I have to say about recent trends in my own country will, to a large extent, apply to other European countries as well. Thus, occasional excursions to foreign legal systems are meant to broaden our view.

Within the bounds of traditional allocation, the transition from mechanical to result-oriented choice of law is carried by several factors,

---

46 The preliminary draft covered both contractual and non-contractual obligations. Although the provisions on delictual obligations are no longer included in the convention's final version, they will be examined in this chapter as symptoms of the trend towards a more flexible choice of law philosophy.

linked by the trend towards the achievement of "just" results. To circumvent the disagreeable outcome which orthodox allocation would prescribe, the courts first resorted to the ingenious use of various choice of law doctrines generally conceived for other purposes than that of result-selection. The most notorious of these "escape devices" are characterization, renvoi and public policy, which have been widely used in both Europe and the United States to alleviate the strictures of the traditional method. Belonging to the "pervasive problems" of conflicts law, they will be discussed in a separate chapter on their present-day function in European and American conflicts law, with emphasis on tort choice of law.[47] Of more recent date are four other phenomena that, each in a slightly different way, contribute to the result-oriented development of conflicts law in Europe. The first one is the emergence of a new type of jurisdiction-selecting rule in which an abstract connecting factor is combined with "proper law" considerations, resulting in structured, yet flexible rules, which I have ventured to call "semi-open conflicts rules."[48] Another type of rule that still fits in with the principles of jurisdiction-selection but is geared to the requirements of result-oriented choice of law is the "functional conflicts rule" in which the connecting factor is derived from the function attributed to the corresponding substantive law.[49] The third phenomenon to be described is the growing influence of *favor* considerations. Derived from substantive law, these notions have been acknowledged as valid choice of law criteria in certain areas in which a sound material result is deemed to be of greater importance than the values of impartial jurisdiction-selection.[50] Finally, there is the doctrine of the *règles d'application immédiate*, the European counterpart of interest analysis which has achieved most of its success, it seems, in the Netherlands.[51] Based on an assessment of legislative policies and their (presumptive) spatial reach, this neo-statutist theory contrasts sharply with the tenets of the traditional allocation method. In that respect, it differs from the other result-oriented tendencies described in this chapter. However, since this doctrine is generally perceived and applied as a corrective

47 *Infra* chapter 2.
48 *Infra* section 2, text accompanying notes 52–110. The topics to be discussed in this chapter have been summarized in: De Boer (1980); Strikwerda (1986).
49 *Infra* section 3, text accompanying notes 111–138.
50 *Infra* section 4, text accompanying notes 139–199.
51 *Infra* section 5, text accompanying notes 200–237, under the heading "priority rules."

device, not as an alternative choice of law approach, I feel justified in discussing it in the context of what may be termed "rational jurisdiction-selection."

2 Proper law notions and "semi-open conflicts rules"

Shortly after the second world war, Professor E.M. Meijers, one of the Netherlands' most prominent scholars of the first half of this century, was commissioned by the Dutch government to draft a new civil code.[52] As a kind of drafting exercise, Meijers quickly proposed a set of choice of law rules, complete with explanatory report, which were to be the substance of a Uniform Law on Private International Law for the three Benelux countries. In 1951, the Netherlands, Belgium and Luxemburg signed a treaty to the effect that each country would adopt the Uniform Law, to replace the few antiquated provisions which thus far constituted the body of their choice of law legislation. Yet, ratification was held up in Belgium and in the Netherlands, and the new conflicts rules never entered into force. Mounting criticism of Meijers' choice of law concept, increasing discrepancies between Dutch and Belgian conflicts practices, a growing aspiration for the unification of *European* conflicts law – these and other factors had a crippling effect on the Benelux efforts.[53] A new treaty and a revised Uniform Law were signed in 1969, but by that time, the premises of traditional conflicts law were already under attack, and academic support of the Benelux project was rapidly dwindling.[54] A last revision of the Uniform

52 Meijers' efforts did result in the recodification of some portions of Dutch civil law, but after his death in 1954, the post-war zeal for replacing the obsolete Civil and Commercial Codes of 1838 gradually vanished. At this time, enactment of the "New Civil Code" is not expected until the 1990's.
53 *Cf.* Jessurun d'Oliveira (1975-2) p. 224 ff.
54 In 1971, the revised Uniform Law was the subject of virtually unanimous criticism at the annual meeting of the Netherlands Association for International Law. *Ontwerp Benelux-verdrag houdende eenvormige wet betreffende het internationaal privaatrecht van 3 juli 1969, Discussienota's*, Med. N.V.I.R. No. 63 (1971) and: *Verslag van de algemene ledenvergadering*, Med. N.V.I.R. No. 64 (1971). Jessurun d'Oliveira (1975-2) p. 227, has pointed out that the Uniform Law received far more attention in the Netherlands, both from scholars and the courts, than it did in Belgium. As a contribution to the development of conflicts law, the debate on ratification and, generally, on the premises of modern private international law has probably had its greatest impact in the Netherlands.

Law, in 1973, had little chance of success in view of the anticipated EEC unification. By then, it was abundantly clear that the Benelux project was no longer viable.[55] Since the publication of the first Uniform Law almost a quarter of a century had passed. In retrospect, we can appreciate that this was a period of transition, surely not the right time for the preservation of conflicts law in uniform rules. Yet, the debate on the merits of the Uniform Law has undoubtedly contributed to the modernization of conflicts law, as yet unwritten, in the Netherlands.

The provisions of the Uniform Law, even in subsequent versions of the draft, generally reflect the uncompromising aspiration for uniformity of result that characterizes traditional jurisdiction-selection. Choice of law is made dependent on single connecting factors, and even in those articles in which an alternative reference is provided, the circumstances allowing the exception are narrowly defined. Two of the proposed choice of law rules, however, are based on a different concept. In article 17 (of the 1951 version), contracts are subjected to the law of the jurisdiction with which they are "so closely connected, that they must be deemed to belong predominantly to the legal sphere of that jurisdiction."[56] The same article, paragraph 2, explains that –apart from the place of contracting and the place of performance– the nationality and domicile of either party, as well as "any other relevant fact" may be taken into account as indications of a close connection. When in doubt, the court should apply the *lex loci contractus*. In the revised version of 1969, in which article 17 was renumbered to article 13, party autonomy has become the first criterion for contracts choice of law, while the objective standard determines the applicable law by a simple reference to "the law of the jurisdiction with which the contract has the closest connection." The other provision which leaves ample room for *ad hoc* choice of law, is the draft's conflicts rule for torts. Article 18 of the 1951 version –renumbered to 14 in the version of 1969, its text otherwise unchanged– provides that a wrongful act is governed by the *lex loci delicti*, unless "the consequences belong to the

---

55 In 1975, it was officially abandoned: *19e Rapport Commun des Gouvernements belge, néerlandais et luxembourgeois au Conseil interparlementaire consultatif de Benelux au sujet de la coopération entre les trois états en matière d'unification de droit,* Doc. 159/1, and the *Annexe*.

56 In the 1951 version, party autonomy was given minimal effect: the parties' choice was not allowed to replace the *ius cogens* of the otherwise applicable law.

legal sphere of another jurisdiction than the one where the wrong occurred, in which case the obligations to which the wrong gave rise shall be determined by the law of that other jurisdiction."[57] Whether an act or omission constitutes a tort – thus the draft's tort provision can be paraphrased – is an issue that is invariably answered by the *lex loci delicti*, but all other issues shall be determined by the law of the jurisdiction most closely connected.

The "legal sphere" doctrine underlying the contract and tort provisions of the Benelux Uniform Law was a departure from the prevailing choice of law principles in the Netherlands, but it was not unknown to Dutch conflicts scholars. In a uniquely personal treatise on the "pervasive problems of private international law," published in 1937, Professor I. Henri Hijmans of the University of Amsterdam had advocated a sociological theory of law by which he sought to explain the phenomenon of law, especially private law, "not as a force that exists outside the community of man, or one that soars above it and to which mankind must submit, but as the Law of Reality which is entrenched in the community of man and in its ever changing relations."[58] In Hijmans' perception, the law is – and statutory law should be – a reflection of the dynamic reality of human relations. Conflicts law, having as its main source the reality of *international* human relations, should therefore focus on the actual contacts between the legal relationship at issue

---

57 According to Kollewijn, Meijers' original text did not include an exception to the traditional place of wrong rule. The flexible "legal sphere" formula seems to have been suggested by the Belgian delegate E. van Dievoet: Kollewijn (1967) p. 287. Curiously, there seem to be no direct sources confirming this proposition. Erauw (1982-1) p. 105, cites Kollewijn, who probably based his statement on a personal recollection. Sauveplanne (1982) p. 66, on the other hand, refers to a lecture Van Dievoet held in 1941. In this lecture, published posthumously in 1967 (E. van Dievoet, De taak van de rechtsgeleerde, *Tijdschrift voor Privaatrecht* 1967, p. 327–338), Van Dievoet briefly mentioned the shortcomings of *lex loci delicti* as exemplified by a collision in Germany between two Belgian cars: "Clearly, application of the local law in this case must be considered the wrong solution in every respect, morally and psychologically." *Ibid.* p. 334. See also: Erauw (1982-2) p. 2522.
Whatever Van Dievoet's contribution may have been, the Belgian judiciary was not convinced. In 1957, the highest court refused to take account of the "legal sphere", thus confirming the primacy of *lex loci delicti* in Belgian choice of law: Cour de Cassation 17 May 1957, *Clunet* 1958, p. 1158; *Rev. Crit. d.i.p.* 1958, p. 339 (*Bologne v. Sainte*). Since then, nothing seems to have changed: *cf.* Erauw (1982-2) p. 2519 ff.
58 Hijmans (1937) p. 4.

and the "legal sphere" of one or more communities.[59] As to torts, Hijmans categorically rejected the prevailing place of wrong standard, and propounded his basic contacts-grouping approach instead: "All kinds of circumstances should be considered: the mutual relationship of the parties concerned, their nationality and domicile, the circumstances accompanying the infliction of damages. More than ever, the actual case should be taken into account: in this area, reality takes on such a multi-faceted appearance that it is impossible to formulate a general rule."[60] Writing in 1937, Hijmans was probably the first European conflicts scholar who professed himself a fervent supporter of legal realism and sociological jurisprudence. In perceiving the choice of law process as an *ad hoc* and issue-by-issue evaluation of actual facts he was certainly ahead of his time. The practical merits of his approach were virtually ignored until the 1950's, when the time proved to be ripe for several theories that were premised on the "proper law" principle.

The most authoritative proponent of the proper law doctrine as a solution to tort conflicts was, no doubt, the English conflicts scholar J.H.C. Morris. In England, the courts had applied the doctrine to contracts conflicts as early as 1865.[61] In his celebrated Harvard Law Review article, published in 1951,[62] Morris suggested that this approach, by which proper weight could be attributed to the constantly varying significance of the actual circumstances of a particular case, would be suitable to torts as well. Its flexibility, he claimed, would enable the courts to distinguish between tort categories as well as between tort issues, thus "achiev[ing] socially desirable results."[63] The

59 *Ibid.* p. 61 ff.
60 *Ibid.* p. 93.
61 Morris, J. (1951) p. 881, note 3, cites *Lloyd v. Guibert*, L.R. 1 Q.B. 115, 122; 122 Eng. Rep. 1134, 1136 (1865). Dicey, *Conflict of Laws*, 6th ed., 1949, p. 579, described the proper law of a contract as " ... the law, or laws, by which the parties intended, or may fairly be presumed to have intended, the contract to be governed." In this respect, the doctrine closely resembles the German theory of the *hypothetischer Parteiwille* (presumed parties' choice): Kegel (1985) p. 382 ff.; Neuhaus (1976) p. 263 ff. In Dicey/Morris (1980) vol. 2, p. 747, a more realistic definition is found: "The 'proper law of a contract' means the system of law by which the parties intended the contract to be governed, or, where their intention is neither expressed nor to be inferred from the circumstances, the system of law with which the transaction has its closest and most real connection."
62 An earlier publication – 12 *Mod. L.Rev.* 248 (1949) – held the same proposition.
63 Morris, J. (1951) p. 884.

emphasis on significant "social factors" in Morris' article is echoed in other writings on tort choice of law of this period. In Germany, Heinz Binder argued that the rigid place of wrong rule should be "loosened up" in those cases in which the tort is entrenched in a different "social environment" than the one in which the wrong occurred.[64] In France, Pierre Bourel adopted the same *milieu social* criterion in a curious attempt to save the traditional rule by giving the term *locus delicti* a dynamic, non-geographical meaning.[65] Variations on the "social environment" theme can be found in the publications of subsequent writers favoring some kind of exception from the place of wrong rule.[66] The main difference between Morris and other proponents of a more flexible approach to tort choice of law is the total absence of predetermined criteria in the proper law doctrine, which leaves the courts free to take account of any "social factor" involved, including "policy factors."[67] Morris' comments on two well-known American cases make it clear that his proper law concept involves more than mere contacts-counting: the purpose of the rule at issue[68] and the interest of a concerned state[69] are possibly even more significant than the geographical aspects of the case.

In their interpretation of the "legal sphere" formula of the Benelux Uniform Law, the Dutch courts never went so far as to discuss policies

64 The German term is *soziale Umwelt*, as opposed to the *örtliche Umwelt* or "local environment". Binder (1955) p. 480 ff., discussing the *soziologische Einbettung* ("sociological entrenchment") of a tort.
65 Bourel (1961) p. 45 ff, p. 54 ff.
66 Notably Kahn-Freund (1968) p. 86 ff. and Kropholler (1969) p. 617 ff. *Cf.* Jessurun d'Oliveira (1965) p. 1 ff.; Duintjer Tebbens (1979) p. 178 ff.; De Boer (1982) notes 126–142 and accompanying text.
67 Morris, J. (1951) p. 887 ff.: "If we adopt the proper law of the tort, we can at least choose the law which, *on policy grounds*, seems to have the most significant connection with the chain of acts and consequences in the particular situation before us." Emphasis added.
68 In *Alabama Great Southern R.R. v. Carroll* 97 Ala. 126, 11 So. 803 (1892), the Alabama Supreme Court "should have inquired whether the Alabama Employers Liability Act modifying the common law fellow-servant rule was intended to apply" to the case at bar. Morris, J. (1951) p. 889.
69 E.g. Connecticut in *Levy v. Daniels' U-Drive Auto Renting Co.*, 108 Conn. 333, 143 A. 163 (1928): " ... might it not have been said that Connecticut had sufficient interest in the business of renting cars in Connecticut to justify the application of Connecticut law, that the place where the car was rented was of more significance than the place where the accident happened, and that therefore Connecticut was the proper law of the tort?" Morris, J. (1951) p. 890.

or interests. Deference to legislative intent would be at variance with the impartial allocation method and jeopardize its ideal of decisionial harmony. Instead, they set out to explore and delimit the flexibility of the new conflicts rules, gradually reducing the relevant circumstances to a single connecting factor. In torts, the first major decision along these lines was rendered by the Appellate Court of The Hague. In *De Beer v. De Hondt*,[70] a Dutch woman had been injured in an automobile accident in France while riding as a guest in the car of defendant, another Dutch woman. Both parties were domiciled in the Netherlands. There was no conflict between French and Dutch law as to the standard of conduct; otherwise, the court noted, French law would apply as *lex loci delicti*. With regard to the real issue in this case, the extent of defendant's liability, the "legal sphere" proviso of the Benelux Uniform Law was used as an escape from the traditional rule. Listing as relevant factors the nationality of the parties, their domicile, and the place where they had arranged their trip, the court was satisfied that Dutch law was the proper law of the "legal consequences" in this case. The reverse law-fact pattern was presented by *Backx v. Franssen*, decided by the Court of Breda,[71] involving two Belgian automobile drivers who had collided in the Netherlands. This time, Belgian law was applied on the grounds that both parties were Belgians, living in Belgium. Gradually, the courts turned the elastic "legal sphere" formula into a fixed criterion: the common denominator of all decisions in which it was applied is the common domicile of the parties.[72] At present, the general criteria for tort choice of law[73] in

70 Hof The Hague 10 June 1955, *NJ* 1955, 615.
71 Rb. Breda 2 October 1962, *NJ* 1963, 109; *VR* 1969, 11.
72 In some cases, the courts reinforced their decision by adding one or two other factors that pointed to the *lex domicilii communis*, such as: the nationality of the parties, the place of registration of their vehicle(s) or vessel(s), the place of business of the insurance corporation(s) involved, or the fact that the parties were bound by a legal relationship of a different order (usually a contract) governed by the same law as their delictual relationship. *Cf.* De Boer (1982) p. 13; Morse (1978) p. 101 and p. 106, note 63.
    While Dutch tort choice of law received little doctrinal attention in the years between the publication of Dubbink's dissertation (1947) and Jessurun d'Oliveira's monography (1965), the few commentators of this period did endorse application of the *lex communis*. See: Erades (1960) p. 93 ff.; Slagter (1961) *passim*; both authors seem to place some extra weight on the common nationality.
73 That is: outside the area of traffic accidents and products liability, as these topics are now governed by the criteria laid down in the Hague Conventions. Furthermore, Dutch tort choice of law supports the principle of party autonomy: Rb. Rotterdam 8 —

the Netherlands seem to be well-settled: the *lex domicilii communis* applies if the parties have their home in another state than the one where the wrong occurred; in all other cases, *lex loci delicti* applies.[74]

Since the Dutch courts have sealed the open-ended tort conflicts rule of the Benelux Uniform Law with a predetermined connecting factor, no room is left for an assessment of relevant policies or interests. It could be argued, however, that the common domicile criterion is compatible, *qua* outcome, with a predetermined interest analysis, giving the presumed interests of the parties' home state priority over the interests, if any, of the *locus* state. And even in cases in which the wrong occurred in the home state of one of the parties, whether tortfeasor or victim, the then applicable *lex loci delicti* rule could be construed, none too subtly, as a predetermined true conflict solution, based on the assumption that either of the domiciliary states will generally have an interest in the application of its law.[75] However, in cases in which three different states are involved (because the parties do not live in the same state and the wrong occurred in yet another state), the place of wrong rule is nothing but a catch-all formula enabling the courts to cut the Gordian knot of allocation without regard to any policy or interest, not even *in abstracto*. For these cases, I submit, the flexible "legal sphere" approach could be used as a stepping-stone to attain a more rational solution than the one dictated by the blind *lex loci* rule. It would allow the courts, for instance, to displace the *lex loci delicti* in case the respective domiciliary laws are substantially the same. It could also be used as a way to assess the relevance of the "policy factors" that Morris included in his proper law concept. However, the development of Dutch tort choice of law does not suggest that the "legal sphere" approach will be expanded beyond the common domicile situation.

January 1979, *NJ* 1979, 119, *A.Ae.* 1980, p. 788, note Jessurun d'Oliveira (*French Potassium Mines II*). *Cf.* Drion/De Boer, no. 57 b; De Boer (1982) p. 27 ff.

74 There is still some doubt regarding the question whether the "unlawfulness" issue is invariably governed by the law of the place of wrong, even if the law of common domicile applies to other issues. This subject is further discussed, *infra* chapter 2, section 1, text accompanying notes 16–22.

75 More on the presumed interests of the domiciliary jurisdictions, *infra* chapter 4, section 3, text accompanying notes 112–119; chapter 8, sections 2 and 3, *passim*; chapter 9, text accompanying notes 39–52.

In one area, though, it has gained unexpected support from the highest court in the Netherlands, the *Hoge Raad*. For tortious events occurring in a legal vacuum, such as collisions at sea, the Dutch courts had traditionally used the *lex fori* solution, for want of a territorial *lex loci delicti*. In the 1970's, several such cases had been decided by application of Dutch law, not *qua* forum law but because of the close connection between the event and the Netherlands.[76] Since the only extraneous element in these cases was the extraterritorial place of wrong, application of Dutch law was the obvious solution. A collision on the North Sea between a British ferry and a Dutch Navy vessel provided an excellent testcase to confirm the new trend. The main issue in *Free Enterprise/Brielle* was the question whether the Dutch government, more than two years after the occurrence, had timely filed suit against the British shipowners.[77] The lower courts had applied Dutch domestic law, allowing the action. According to the British defendant, however, they should have followed the two-year limitation prescribed by the Brussels Convention on Collisions at Sea, or, alternatively, by English substantive law.[78] The *Hoge Raad*, in a brief opinion, affirmed the lower courts' "legal sphere" approach: since the collision had caused damage to a *Dutch* ship, which had been repaired in a *Dutch* harbor, at the cost of the *Dutch* government, Dutch law applied as the law of the jurisdiction most closely connected to the occurrence and its consequences. In his advisory opinion,[79] Attorney-General Franx pointed out that the *legal* consequences[80] of the collision were in equal balance, affecting both the Netherlands and England. The *factual* consequences, however, indicated a closer connection with the Netherlands. Among these, the fact that the damage was

---

76 Rb. The Hague 16 June 1976, *S&S* 1976, no. 77, *aff'd* Hof The Hague 11 May 1978, *NJ* 1979, 108; *S&S* 1979, no. 41 (*Cornelia Wilhelmina/Panter*). Hof The Hague 24 December 1976, *S&S* 1977, no. 21, *rev'd on other grounds* HR 26 May 1978, *NJ* 1978, 615 (note J.C. Schultsz); *S&S* 1978, no. 63 (*Gaasterdijk/Zuidpool*).
77 HR 16 March 1979, *NJ* 1979, 540 (note J.C. Schultsz); *S&S* 1979, no. 63.
78 In Dutch conflicts law, the question which statute of limitations applies is considered a substantive issue, not a matter of procedure.
79 A member of the Public Prosecutor's office, the *Procureur-Generaal* or *Advocaat-Generaal*, submits an opinion on the juridical merits of each case before the *Hoge Raad*. As an independent legal advisor, whose opinions are not binding on the *Hoge Raad*, he could be considered as a full-time *amicus curiae*.
80 By the "consequences" of a tort, a term first used in article 14(2) of the Benelux Draft, we generally mean its "legal consequences", covering both the tortfeasor's liability and the victim's right to recovery.

done to a Dutch ship seemed to be predominant; if both ships had been damaged, the Attorney-General hypothesized, the factual consequences would have been in balance as well, in which case application of forum law might be warranted for want of a better solution. Although I have no quarrel with the actual result in *Free Enterprise/ Brielle*, I am not particularly impressed by its underlying choice of law reasoning. In my view, the Attorney-General's seemingly neutral reference to the factual consequences of the tort (*i.e.* actual damage or injury) concealed a result-selective approach. The wrong occurred on the high seas, and it was there, not on Dutch territory, that the damage was done. In that sense, the collision had its major factual consequence at sea. Its impact, however, was felt in the Netherlands, where repairs had to be made at the cost of the Dutch government. If these factors are considered decisive, the factual consequences of a tort will be most closely connected, usually, with the state of the victim's domicile. Unless the place where the damage has been repaired (or the place of hospitalization or recuperation in case of physical injury) is deemed relevant, there is no difference, I submit, between the legal sphere of a tort's *factual* consequences and the jurisdiction where the victim's *legal* right to recovery can be situated: his home state.[81] I would not be surprised if the Dutch courts, when dealing with collisions at sea and other extraterritorial events, would gradually narrow the now prevailing "legal sphere" approach to a more abstract solution. If the factual consequences of such a tort are to be localized there where the after-effects of harmful conduct are mostly felt, the domicile of the victim is an obvious and suitable connecting factor, and definitely a less ambiguous choice of law standard than the "legal sphere of a tort's factual consequences."[82]

Proper law notions have contributed greatly to the modernization of European conflicts law. In the 1970's, a new type of choice of law rule has emerged which combines an *ad hoc* center of gravity approach with predetermined connecting factors. I have ventured to call these rules "semi-open conflicts rules," because they are usually based on an

---

81 In a few cases, in which the term "consequences" in article 14(2) of the Benelux Draft was (mis)read as "*factual* consequences", the courts listed a series of "after-effects" of the tortious occurrence and allocated them promptly to the victim's home state. *Cf.* Rb. Amsterdam 30 November 1971, *NJ* 1972, 474, note Hijmans van den Bergh; Rb. Maastricht 11 November 1982, *Asser* 13 487.
82 *Cf.* De Boer (1982) p. 18 ff.; p. 54 ff.

open-ended proper law formula, restricted by a presumption as to the normally applicable law.[83] In the Netherlands, the *Hoge Raad* established such a rule for contracts. While the Benelux Uniform Law, in article 17 (in the 1951 version) and in article 13 (in the text of 1969), contained open-ended rules, requiring an *ad hoc* examination of relevant contacts to determine the "legal sphere" of a contract or, in article 13, the jurisdiction with which the contract was most closely connected, the Dutch courts obviously felt a need for a more structured approach. Using the proper law theory as a point of departure, the Appellate Court of Amsterdam, faced with a contract of agency between a Dutch agent and a German principal,[84] discarded the "more or less fortuitous circumstances" of the case as insignificant, and focused on the "nature of the contract" as the major source of relevant contacts. In fact, the court expressly adopted the theory of the "characteristic performance," advocated by the Swiss Professors Adolf F. Schnitzer and Frank Vischer.[85] According to this theory, a contract generally gives rise to two obligations: one that is "characteristic" for that particular type of contract, and one that is not.[86] This distinction affords the formulation of a choice of law rule which generally refers to the domicile or place of business of the party carrying out the characteristic obligation, *e.g.* the seller, the landlord, the employee, the insurer, the bailee, etc. In *NAP v. Christophery*, the Amsterdam Appellate Court therefore applied Dutch law as the law

---

83 In this respect, they are similar to those rules of the American Restatement (Second) of Conflict of Laws that call for the application of the local law of a certain state "unless, with respect to the particular issue, some other state has a more significant relationship ..." See, *e.g.* § 146 ff. It should be noted, however, that the Restatement, by its constant reference to § 6, leaves ample room for the consideration of all kinds of policy factors, pertaining to both choice of law and domestic law. The European "semi-open conflicts rule" is supposed to reveal the most significant connection in a detached, geographical sense; theoretically, it remains blind to the contents or purposes of substantive law. See also, *infra* notes 109–110 and accompanying text.
84 Hof Amsterdam 1 April 1970, *NJ* 1971, 115 (*NAP v. Christophery*).
85 Schnitzer (1957) vol. I, p. 52 ff., vol. II, p. 639 ff.; Vischer (1962) p. 108 ff. In the Netherlands, the theory has been sharply criticized by Jessurun d'Oliveira (1975-1) p. 94 ff. Among its supporters are: Lemaire (1968) p. 269 ff.; De Winter (1971) p. 367 ff.; Haak (1975) p. 54 ff.
86 This is true for so-called "bilateral" or "mutual" contracts, such as a contract for sale, or transportation, or insurance. In "unilateral" contracts, such as gifts, the characteristic obligation is carried out by the one party obliged to perform (e.g. the *donor*). For certain kinds of contracts, such as barter or compromise, no distinction can be made between characteristic and non-characteristic obligations.

of the state where the agent had his principal place of business. This approach was endorsed by the *Hoge Raad* in three subsequent decisions, but in each of them the court emphasized that there might be cases in which other circumstances could prove to be more relevant than the domicile of the party carrying out the characteristic performance.[87] Thus, the *Hoge Raad* created a "semi-open conflicts rule" in which the domicile of the "characteristic performer" functions as the predetermined connecting factor, complemented by a proviso for atypical situations.

I would not have paused to mention the development of the Dutch conflicts rule for contracts, if it did not fit in with a general trend. Since the 1960's, a willingness to loosen the bonds of traditional jurisdiction-selection seems to pervade conflicts law in Europe and elsewhere. In a resolution on tort choice of law, the Institute of International Law, at its Edinburgh session in 1969, adopted the rule that "on principle" the law of the place of wrong should govern delictual liabilities. The members did acknowledge, however, that "the application of the law of the place of the delict should be subject to exceptions where that place is merely fortuitous and where the social environment of the parties differs from the geographical environment of the delict."[88] The pre-

---

87 The *Hoge Raad* never mentioned the technical term. In *Neska v. de Beijer*, HR 27 October 1972, *NJ* 1973, 121 (note Hijmans van den Bergh), the court referred to the place of business of a transporter as a particularly relevant contact; in *Topsøe v. Del Prado*, HR 6 April 1973, *NJ* 1973, 371 (note Hijmans van den Bergh), the place of business of a commercial agent was considered conclusive, "in the absence of circumstances which create such contacts with the law of another country – whether the country where the principal is established, or any other country – that the law of this other country should govern the contract." Finally, in *Mackay v. American Express II*, HR 8 June 1973, *NJ* 1973, 400 (note Hijmans van den Bergh), the applicable law was found by reference to the place where an employee generally carries out his duties, or, if his employment takes him to more than one country, the place where he is stationed. The "place of duty" criterion for employment contracts is an exception to the general rule, which is predicated on the domicile of the party carrying out the characteristic performance rather than the place where the characteristic performance is carried out. *Cf.* Schnitzer (1957) vol. II, p. 647 ff.; Vischer (1962) p. 112 ff.

88 Resolution on delictual obligations in private international law, 53 *Annuaire de l'Institut de Droit International, Session d'Edimbourg* vol. II, p. 386 (1969). Hence, article 3 provided that "[i]n the absence of any substantial connection between the issue to be determined and the place or places at which the delict has been committed ... that law is to be applied which is indicated by a special relation between the parties or between the parties and the occurrence ..." *Ibid.* p. 388 ff. See also the preliminary draft, prepared by Professor J. Offerhaus, and the draft resolution, prepared by Professor O. Kahn-Freund: *Ibid.* vol. I, p. 342, and p. 472.

liminary draft of the EEC Convention on the Law Applicable to Contractual (and Non-Contractual) Obligations mitigated the regime of *lex loci delicti* by allowing an exception from the general rule for torts, though subject to a double restriction. Under article 10, a tort would be governed by *lex loci delicti*, unless "on the one hand, no significant link exists between the situation which has caused the damage and the State in which that event occurred and, on the other hand, such situation has a predominant connection (*connection prépondérante*) with another State."[89] The double restriction – apparently the result of a compromise between those in favor of flexibility, and those preferring a hard and fast rule –[90] is followed by the direction that "[n]ormally, such a connection must be based on a connecting factor common to the victim and the author of the damage ... ," such as a common nationality or domicile, and, arguably,[91] a pre-existing contractual or social relation between the parties.

The controversial contents of the preliminary draft's tort provision may have contributed to the decision to reduce the scope of the convention to contracts.[92] Destined to further the unification of conflicts law within the EEC, the Convention on the Law Applicable to Contractual Obligations 1980[93] reflects the moderate approach to choice of law which most European conflicts specialists now endorse. Remaining within the bounds of tradition, the new conflicts rules for contracts demonstrate a trend towards differentiation, and away from abstract jurisdiction-selection. Apart from consumer transactions and contracts of employment, which are covered by two separate provisions,[94] contractual obligations are governed by the law chosen by the parties,

89 Article 10(2). This is the English translation as published in 21 *Am.J.Comp.L.* 587 ff. (1973); it is slightly different in: *European Private International Law of Obligations*, ed. Ole Lando, Bernd von Hoffmann and Kurt Siehr, Tübingen, 1975, p. 230 ff.
90 Siehr (1975) p. 52, refers to the background information given by one of the members of the EC working group of experts, Jenard, describing the "difficult birth of art. 10 of the Draft Convention."
91 *Cf.* Siehr (1975) p. 53; Fallon (1975) p. 90 ff. Article 13 of the preliminary draft, covering non-contractual obligations other than those arising from torts, also contained an exception clause premised upon a common connecting factor, but without the two restrictive conditions of article 10.
92 *Cf.* Haak (1980) p. 866.
93 Publ. EEC, no. L 266, 9 October 1980; explanatory report by Giuliano/Lagarde: Publ. EEC, no. C 282, 31 October 1980.
94 To be discussed *infra* section 3, text accompanying notes 121–124.

or, in the absence of such a choice, by the law of the country with which the contract is most closely connected.[95] This proper law approach is combined with the presumption that, generally, the closest connection will be found in the country in which the party carrying out the characteristic performance has his habitual residence. The relation between this predetermined connecting factor and its proper law prelude is not very clear, particularly in view of the provision in paragraph 5: if it cannot be established which obligation must be deemed characteristic, or if the contract is more closely connected to some other country, the presumptions of the preceding paragraphs will not apply. Is the "closest connection" of article 4(1) to be taken as the primary criterion? Or should it be reserved for exceptional cases, such as those in which a characteristic performance cannot be established?[96] If it should be understood as a "general guideline" which has been transformed to a fixed criterion in the second paragraph, it could have been omitted. If the proper law approach of paragraph 1 was meant to be the main rule, the fifth paragraph would seem to be redundant. Judicial practice indicates that, in the Netherlands at least, the problem might be more academic than real. When choosing the applicable contracts law, the Dutch courts generally refer to the place of business of the party carrying out the characteristic performance. Despite the leeway afforded by the *Hoge Raad* examples, or by the flexible formula of the EEC Convention, which is cited more and more often as an unofficial, but persuasive source of law,[97] the courts seldom indulge in the sort of contacts-juggling the advocates of hard and fast rules seem to fear so much. In my opinion, it is only natural that the courts make use of a presumptive connecting factor and consider the proper law provision as a tool of last resort. If they would proceed the other way around, first establishing the closest connection, then checking the result against the presumption, their task would be unnecessarily laborious. For that reason, I predict, European judicial practice is bound to choose the second paragraph of article 4 as the

---

95 Party autonomy is covered by article 3. The subjective choice of the applicable law is restricted to international contracts; in a domestic situation, the parties' choice will not be allowed to displace the *ius cogens* of the law that would apply otherwise (article 3, paragraph 3). Article 4 covers the "objective" choice of law.
96 *Cf.* the discussion reported by Von Hoffmann (1975) p. 10.
97 See, *e.g.*, Pres. Rb. The Hague 17 September 1982, *RvdW/KG* 1982, 167 (*C.E.P. v. Sensor*); Rb. Maastricht 1 November 1984, *NIPR* 1985, no. 404 (*Fransbergen v. ENCI*); Rb. Arnhem 31 January 1985, *NIPR* 1985, no. 413 (*Kuipers–Denmark v. Van Wetten*).

main rule,[98] thus affirming the redundance of the article's open-ended introductory clause: the "closer connection" exception in paragraph 5 lends enough flexibility to the article as a whole to give it the quality of a "semi-open conflicts rule."[99]

In other legislative products, the combination of proper law notions and abstract conflicts rules gives rise to similar questions in respect of their interrelation. The very first paragraph of the Austrian federal law on private international law,[100] for instance, wants conflicts cases to be governed by the law of the jurisdiction with which they have the "strongest connection." This *Grundsatz der stärksten Beziehung* must be considered as the statute's basic allocation principle. Thus, the opening section continues, all of the subsequent choice of law rules should be understood as specific expressions of this general guideline. In other words, the evaluation of the "strongest connection" has been incorporated in each of the statute's predetermined connecting fac-

---

98 According to one British author, however, "the presumptions are to be applied only in cases where the various connecting factors are so diffuse or evenly balanced that a sufficiently paramount connection between the contract and a particular country cannot be found. Their importance is therefore far less than would appear at first sight. Accordingly, the presumptions fail in their objective, namely that of promoting certainty." Williams P. (1986) p. 15. This interpretation of article 4 may be inspired by the English tendency "against the use of presumptions, preferring instead to consider all the factors of the case, weighing them against each other and so (purportedly) finding an implied intention or closest connection." *Ibid.* p. 17. If this is true, the English courts will only resort to the presumptions of article 4 "when a closest connection cannot be found." *Ibid.* p. 15. A Dutch court, on the other hand, is likely to follow the presumptions, only resorting to the proper law escape when it is obvious that there is a closer connection with another country.

99 Whether the proper law principle should be viewed as "main rule" or not, is, at least from a practical point of view, a question of semantics. Although I am convinced that most courts will first refer to a predetermined criterion, it could still be argued that exceptions from such a rule are derived from the "main" proper law principle. Thus, Jessurun d'Oliveira (1965) p. 12, submitted that, from a logical perspective, the main rule of the torts provision of the Benelux Uniform Law (*supra* text accompanying note 57 and notes 70–72) is its "legal sphere" criterion; as an expression of this principle, the *locus delicti* is normally a suitable choice of law standard, only to be displaced in atypical cases.

100 Bundesgesetz vom 15. Juni 1978 über das internationale Privatrecht (IPR-Gesetz), *Bundesgesetzblatt* 1978/304; Alfred Duchek/Fritz Schwind, *Internationales Privatrecht, Das IPR-Gesetz vom 15. 6. 1978 samt einschlägigen sonstigen Rechtsvorschriften und zwischenstaatlichen Abkommen mit ausführlichen Erläuterungen*, Vienna, 1979.

tors, precluding an *ad hoc* determination of the proper law.[101] This interpretation is confirmed by the torts provision, § 48, which requires application of *lex loci delicti*, unless both parties have a stronger connection to the law of another jurisdiction. Such a proper law exception would be superfluous if § 1 was meant to function as a general escape clause.[102]

Before long, Switzerland will also have its code of private international law.[103] Drafted by a number of teams comprising virtually all of Switzerland's experts in conflicts law, the text is a model example of meticulous legislation, covering judicial jurisdiction, choice of law, and recognition of judgments, as well as arbitration and matters of international procedure. Modern in spirit and expression, it combines various kinds of jurisdiction-selecting rules with a number of general provisions enabling the courts, at least theoretically, to decide each case with regard to relevant facts, policies, and interests. In its last version, article 14 allows the displacement of the designated law in exceptional situations, "when it is obvious, in view of all circumstances, that the case has but a tenuous link with the designated law, at the same time having a much closer connection with the law of some other jurisdiction." The final report of the experts committee[104] implies that the provision is not meant as an excuse for *ad hoc* adjudica-

---

101 The commentary by Duchek and Schwind tends to confirm that in each of the statute's conflicts rules, the "strongest connection" is preconceived. They note that the allocation principles are not predicated on spatial factors alone, but that relevant *interests* have been (and in case of a statutory lacuna should be) evaluated and taken into account as well. *Ibid.* p. 8.
102 According to Duchek and Schwind, *ibid.* p. 5, the practical significance of § 1 is limited to those situations for which the legislature did not want to include a specific provision and those which it did not foresee. The "closest connection" principle could then be used to fill the gap. In short, § 1 should be understood as no more than an explanatory opening statement; its normative effect, limited to the occasional lacuna, seems negligible. *Cf.* Patocchi (1985) notes 266–273 and accompanying text.
103 The draft's final text, dated November 10, 1982, has been published in: *Bundesblatt* 1983, vol. I, no. 4, p. 263–519: *Botschaft des Schweizerischen Bundesrates zum Bundesgesetz über das internationale Privatrecht (IPR-Gesetz); Message concernant une loi fédérale sur le droit international privé (loi de DIP)* du 10 novembre 1982, no. 82.072, p. 1–255.
104 *Bundesgesetz über das internationale Privatrecht (IPR-Gesetz); Schlussbericht der Expertenkommission zum Gesetzesentwurf*, Zürich, 1979.

tion, legal certainty being one of the objectives of codification. It should therefore be used sparingly, for instance in case of a legislative lacuna or in exceptional situations in which the predetermined solution is altogether unsatisfactory: "The draft's choice of law rules – unlike those of the American 'Restatement' for instance – are not 'open-ended' on principle, *i.e.* they should have more than just *prima facie* authority. Rather, the draft is binding as a matter of principle, and there should be no departures from its solutions except in extreme cases."[105] Such exceptions might be present if the parties could reasonably expect that another than the designated law would govern their relationship, if the predetermined criterion happens to refer to an isolated factor in space or time, or if the prescribed solution would actually frustrate decisional harmony.[106]

It is obvious that European choice of law is changing. In several countries, the inflexible regime of predetermined jurisdiction-selection is being mitigated by proper law notions. While such relaxation may further realistic allocation, *i.e.* designation of the legal system in which the legal relationship at issue has its true "*Sitz*" or "center of gravity", many Europeans, both scholars and practitioners, seem to be fretting about the uncertainty such an approach entails. In my opinion, these fears are greatly exaggerated. Legal certainty might be a cornerstone of the law, but its worth is relative. To all those believing that choice of law problems should be resolved by hard and fast rules to safeguard legal certainty I put the same question that Peter Max Gutzwiller asked some twenty years ago: "Would it not be another certainty, one that should be valued at least as highly, to know that the court will do anything possible to find and apply the 'most just' law (*sit venia verbo!*), despite the prevailing system of multilateral, mechanical conflicts rules?"[107] It should be clear that proper law notions, such as the "legal sphere" criterion or the principle of the closer (or closest) connection, do not furnish the courts with a license to indulge in *Kadi-*

---

105 *Ibid.* p. 29, p. 59 ff.
106 *Ibid.* p. 60. In the final version of article 14, a second paragraph has been added which excludes application of the escape clause in case the parties have chosen the applicable law. *Cf.* Patocchi (1985) p. 75. Other restrictions have been suggested by Professor K. Kreuzer and questioned by others at an international symposium in Lausanne: *Lausanner Kolloquium über den deutschen und den schweizerischen Gesetzentwurf zur Neuregelung des Internationalen Privatrechts*, Zürich, 1984, p. 14 ff., p. 49 ff. See also: *Message* (*supra* note 103) p. 17, p. 46 ff.
107 Gutzwiller (1968) p. 188.

Justiz. The European choice of law tradition hardly encourages the liberal use of factual criteria. When open-ended choice of law standards are incorporated in legislative projects, they either take the form of a declaratory statement with little normative import, or they are formulated as an exception to the normally applicable conflicts rule. Combining a preconceived connecting factor and an open-ended exception clause, the "semi-open conflicts rule" represents a compromise between certainty and flexibility. If the Dutch experience is any indication, there is little cause for anxiety about judicial contacts-juggling.

Without doubt, the proper law doctrine has relaxed the bonds of traditional jurisdiction-selection in the Netherlands and elsewhere. In most areas of Dutch conflicts law, particularly contracts, torts and domestic relations,[108] it has encouraged the courts, at least in atypical cases, to determine the applicable law by reference to real rather than formal connections. In that respect, the allocation process has regained some of the credibility it had lost during a prolonged period of stagnancy. The flexibility afforded by open and semi-open conflicts rules has greatly reduced the misuse of traditional doctrines, such as characterization, renvoi, public policy and the like, since such devices are no longer needed to correct the mechanical operation of rigid conflicts rules.[109] Whether the proper law escape is being used in recognition of actual policies or interests, or just because of a "closer connection" in geographical terms, is debatable. As a rule, the Dutch decisions suggest that the choice of the "proper law" is based on factual contacts only; no reference is made to the contents of the competing substantive laws before the choice of law issue is settled. However, such silence hardly proves that the courts do not take a surreptitious peek from under Savigny's blindfold.[110] On the other hand, it could be argued that they seldom need to do so, as a preponderance of geographical contacts will often be indicative of a state's preponderant interest in the application of its law. Either way, the (semi-)open con-

---

108 In the Netherlands, the gradual decline of the nationality principle in family law and succession is largely due to judicial acceptance of proper law notions. They are instrumental in determining the "national law" of a person with dual nationality or hailing from a state with more than one legal system. In the field of divorce, the parties' national law will not be applied, unless the parties expressly elect its application, if one of them no longer has a "true social connection" with the country of their common nationality. *Cf. infra* note 149.
109 *Cf.* Strikwerda (1986) p. 9.
110 *Cf.* the title of Professor Deelen's inaugural lecture: *supra* note 17.

flicts rule calls for an evaluation of relevant circumstances. In deciding what is "relevant" and what is not, the courts are likely to look beyond a given geographical fact pattern, and to measure the weight of each contact by result-oriented standards.

3 Functional allocation

In April 1942, in the middle of the second world war, the Dutch *Hoge Raad* ruled on the formal validity of a gift inter vivos.[111] The suit was brought by the disappointed promisee, a domiciliary of the Netherlands who, some thirty years earlier, had been the private tutor of defendant's children. The promisor was a wealthy Dutchman living in London. The promised sum amounted to 4000 guilders, which plaintiff had requested from his former employer as a contribution towards the expenses of his divorce and subsequent marriage. The question which law applied arose when the promisor, rather unexpectedly, announced that religious scruples about divorce prevented him from keeping his promise, and refused to pay on the more technical ground that, under Dutch law, promise and acceptance of a gift should have been recorded in a notarial document to constitute a binding contract. In first instance, the Court of Arnhem agreed and rejected plaintiff's claim, but the Appellate Court, applying what it thought to be English law,[112] reversed. Addressing the question which law governed the substantive aspects of the gift, as required by the *favor negotii*,[113] the *Hoge*

---

[111] HR 2 April 1942, *NJ* 1942, 468 (*Jurgens Verbruggen v. Van Heesch*). The promise had been made before the war, in 1938, and the court of first instance ruled on the matter in March 1940, just two months before the Netherlands was occupied by the Nazis.

[112] In fact, the promisor would not be bound under English law either. Unless it is made by deed under seal, a gift promise can generally be revoked until delivery has taken place. *Cf. Crossley Vaines' Personal Property*, 5th ed. by E.L.G. Tyler and N.E. Palmer, London, 1973, p. 305 ff. See also: René David, *Les contrats en droit anglais*, Paris, 1973, nos. 70, 73 and 145, explaining that English law does not treat the gift as a contract but as a transfer of property. The conclusion of the Appellate Court as to the contents of English law was described as "erroneous" by D.J. Veegens, *Cassatie in burgerlijke zaken*, 2d ed., Zwolle, p. 142.

[113] *Infra* section 4, text following note 142. The *Hoge Raad* took the opportunity to declare that the formal validity of legal transactions need not be measured exclusively by the time-honored *locus regit actum* principle, which had prevailed in the Netherlands thus far.

Raad created a brand-new conflicts rule for inter vivos gifts. As a connecting factor the court chose the domicile of the donor, explaining this choice by referring to legislative objectives. In the Netherlands and elsewhere, the court observed, it is the donor rather than the donee whose interests are the focal point of legislative protection. In view of this legislative concern, the law of the donor's home country should be given priority over the law of the domicile of the donee. Since the *Hoge Raad* traditionally abstained from reviewing foreign law, it did not question the Appellate Court's assumption that English law –if not as *lex loci actus*, then as *lex causae*– would uphold the formal validity of the gift promise.[114] Thus, appellant's motions were dismissed and the donee prevailed.

This decision is a good example, I think, of a choice of law phenomenon which is hardly ever mentioned as such in conflicts literature and consequently lacks an official name.[115] I like to call it "functional allocation", a term meant to convey that we are dealing with a particular mode of abstract jurisdiction-selection.[116] Structurally identical to

---

114 Since 1963, article 99 of the Judicial Organization Act (*Wet op de Rechterlijke Organisatie*) does not allow the *Hoge Raad* to reverse on the grounds of erroneous interpretation of foreign law. The original text of article 99 was less explicit in respect of foreign law, but a narrow interpretation of its substantive reach excluded foreign law all the same. *Cf.* Jessurun d'Oliveira (1971) p. 124 ff. See, generally, *infra* chapter 2, section 4.

115 In contemporary German and Swiss conflicts literature, the *Schutz des schwächeren Partei im IPR* (protection of the weaker party in private international law) is a much-discussed topic. *Cf.*, for instance, Lando (1974); Von Hoffmann (1974); Kropholler (1978); Keller (1983). Generally, the authors focus on contracts choice of law, proposing restrictions on party autonomy in case of unequal bargaining power. One of the alternatives, to some of them, is allocation on a functional basis. Yet, this approach is seldom presented as a distinct methodological phenomenon.

116 Since functional allocation is generally inspired by a protective policy of the corresponding substantive law, some authors prefer the term "protection principle". Cohen Henriquez (1980) p. 164 ff.; Strikwerda (1986) p. 4 ff. and *passim*. As long as we know what is meant by it, I have no fundamental objection against this expression. Out of context, "protection principle" seems a rather ambiguous phrase; as demonstrated by the *Hoge Raad* decision just discussed, the "protection principle" happened to be useless to the party to be protected, the donor. Furthermore, functional allocation is only one of various ways to take account of the interests of the weaker party; in that respect, it is a narrower concept than the one covered by the term "protection principle". See *infra* note 121.

the traditional choice of law rule, a "functional" conflicts rule is characterized by its connecting factor, which is not conceived as an abstract expression of the factual center of gravity of a legal relationship, but as a criterion which predetermines the closest connection in a "functional" way, *i.e.* by taking account of the function of substantive law. In traditional conflicts law, the center of gravity metaphor expresses the presumption that the legal relationship at issue has preponderant factual contacts with the designated legal system. When proper law notions are allowed to replace the presumption, the applicable law is still determined, as a rule, by a preponderance of (actual) geographical contacts. A conflicts rule based on functional allocation, on the other hand, is not designed to establish the factual center of gravity. Instead, its connecting factor focuses on the party whose interests have been deemed to warrant protective legislation. This is generally the party whose social condition is structurally weak, as in relationships between employers and employees, vendors and consumers, landlords and tenants, parents and children, possibly husbands and wives. In the modern welfare state, efforts have been made to counterbalance the inequalities characteristic of these types of legal relationships. This concern for the weaker party is reflected in the substantive laws of these states. Functional allocation then translates the protective function of substantive law into a connecting factor that points to the law of the jurisdiction which is presumed to be most concerned with the party in need of protection, as a rule the country of his domicile. Thus, one could say that the center of gravity, when defined in terms of functional allocation, is established by some sort of *a priori* policy assessment. To appreciate the merits of this proposition we will need to examine a few more examples of functional conflicts rules.

In the Hague Convention on the Law Applicable to Maintenance Obligations in Respect of Children, concluded in 1956, article 1 provides that the law of the child's habitual residence governs the issue if, to what extent, and from whom a child may claim maintenance. Professor L.I. de Winter, writing for the *Commission Spéciale*, pointed out that this conflicts rule would afford maximum protection of the child's interests –this being the main purpose of the Convention– as local authorities are in the best position to issue rules on children's maintenance in accordance with the prevailing socio-economic circumstances in their country.[117] For the same reason, the Hague Convention of the Law Applicable to Maintenance Obligations of 1973 focuses on "the person in need, the main interested party, the 'centre of gravity' of the maintenance relationship."[118] The substantive law of maintenance, the Special Commission observed, is generally based on a "social policy" of providing for the needs of the maintenance creditor, "who by hypothesis is in a weaker position than the debtor."[119] This explains why the habitual residence of the maintenance creditor was chosen as the primary connecting factor: " ... the aim of the maintenance obligation is to protect the creditor. As he is the focal point of the institution, he must be considered in the reality of his daily life and not in the purely legal attributes of his person, as he will use his maintenance to enable him to live. Indeed in this field it is wise to appreciate the concrete problem arising in connection with a concrete society: that in which the petitioner lives and will live. Secondly, this system facilitates a degree of harmonization within each State: all maintenance creditors living in that State will be put on the same footing."[120] In other words, since the substantive law of maintenance has made the maintenance creditor the "focal point of the institution," choice of law should focus on "the reality of his daily life." On the assumption that the legal standards of the country where he lives reflect the local socio-economic circumstances, he will be awarded support in accordance with the local law of maintenance. If the award is less than it would be under another law, he should not complain, for he will get no less than other creditors in the country where he lives; if it is more, he will need it to live. Thus, the conflicts rule for maintenance is based on a ra-

---

117 *Actes et Documents de la 8e Session de la Conférence de La Haye, 2 au 24 Octobre 1956*, vol. II, p. 127 (*Rapport de la Commission Spéciale par L.I. de Winter*). As *Justice* De Winter, the same author has unmistakably written the opinion for the Appellate Court of Amsterdam in a case concerning the maintenance claim of a child living in Czechoslovakia against its Dutch father: Hof Amsterdam 9 June 1964, *NJ* 1966, 68. The court's main consideration is an almost literal translation o. the relevant paragraph in the Special Committee's report.
118 *Actes et Documents de la 12e Session de la Conférence de La Haye, 2 au 21 Octobre 1972*, vol. IV, p. 101, no. 14 (Report of the Special Commission by Michel Verwilghen). It should be noted that article 8, calling for application of the *lex divortii* to questions of maintenance between ex-spouses, has a different rationale. See also: HR 4 May 1979, *NJ* 1979, 547, particularly the advisory opinion by Attorney-General Franx, *ibid.* at p. 1836 ff., p. 1842 ff.
119 *Ibid.* p. 107, no. 29–32.
120 *Ibid.* p. 117, no. 58. *Cf. ibid.* p. 441, no. 138 (Explanatory Report by Michel Verwilghen).

tionale of abstract protection; what it achieves is equal treatment of all local creditors.

The same line of reasoning applies to an increasing number of conflicts rules in the field of contracts. In several European countries, functional allocation is now being used as a choice of law instrument to take account of the interests of specific classes of contracting parties. Article 5 of the EEC Convention on the Law Applicable to Contractual Obligations provides that, absent a choice of law by the parties[121] and provided that certain conditions are met, consumer transactions will be governed by the law of the consumer's habitual residence. Since the substantive law of the modern welfare state generally tends to protect consumers as a class of structurally weak contracting parties, the predominant choice of law consideration must be for the consumer, who may expect to be protected according to the legal standards prevailing in the country of his residence. To him, the international aspects of his contract are irrelevant: application of the law of his habitual residence entitles him to the same protection (or the lack of it!) as extended to any consumer living in that country. Again, functional allocation results in equal treatment rather than optimal protection. Similarly, article 6 of the Convention, concerning contracts of employment, focuses on the employee: if the parties have not agreed upon the applicable law, their contract will be governed by the law of the country in which the employee habitually carries out his work. Here, too, allocation is inspired by the function of substantive law, which is translated into a connecting factor providing abstract protection of the weaker party. Thus, the principle of the closest connection is implemented with regard to the objectives of substantive law rather than those of traditional conflicts law.[122] While the Convention's choice of law solution for employment contracts had already

---

121 To protect consumers and employees, articles 5 and 6 lay down restrictions on the principle of party autonomy. See *infra* section 4, text preceding note 160.

122 However, article 6 contains an escape clause enabling the courts to take account of other relevant circumstances which make it clear "that the contract [of employment] is more closely connected with another country." Such a "proper law escape" is not provided in article 5, dealing with consumer transactions.

123 Franz Gamillschegg, *Internationales Arbeitsrecht (Arbeitsverweisungsrecht)*, Berlin/Tübingen, 1959, p. 125 ff.; p. 141 ff. See also: *Cf.* Lando (1975) p. 139. In the Netherlands, the *Hoge Raad* affirmed the prevailing judicial and doctrinal trend in *Mackay v. American Express II*, HR 8 June 1973, *NJ* 1973, 400 (note Hijmans van den Bergh); see also *supra* note 87.

found favor with the courts in several countries,[123] its recognition of consumer contracts as an independent choice of law category and the choice of a functional allocation criterion will be new to most of Europe's conflicts laws.[124]

In the original draft of the Swiss statute on private international law, protection of the weaker party was mentioned as one of the major choice of law considerations in the area of contracts.[125] Article 122 listed four specific classes of contracting parties entitled to special protection: the purchaser paying in installments, the debtor of a small money loan, the surety in case of non-commercial guarantees, and, in contracts of employment, the employee. Without much explanation, however, these provisions have been deleted from the final draft, to be replaced by specific conflicts rules for consumer contracts and contracts of employment. Still the same are the connecting factors that had been chosen for these categories: for employment contracts the criterion is the place where the employee generally carries out his work, whereas consumer contracts are governed by the law of the consumer's habitual residence. Thus, on the choice of law level, the protection of the weaker party is abstracted from its substantive law setting and made dependent on the applicable law. This is not necessarily the most favorable law, nor the law with which the contract is most closely connected, but the predetermined law of the "contractual sphere of the weaker party,"[126] as determined by his habitual residence, his place of work, or some other fixed criterion, depending on the type of contract.

---

124 More on these two provisions can be found in: Ian F. Fletcher, *Conflict of Laws and European Community Law, With Special Reference to the Community Conventions on Private International Law*, Amsterdam/New York/Oxford, 1982, p. 165 ff.: P.M. North (ed.), *Contract Conflicts, The E.E.C. Convention on the Law Applicable to Contractual Obligations: A Comparative Study*, Amsterdam/New York/Oxford, 1982, p. 111 ff. (by T.C. Hartley) and p. 143 (by C.G.J. Morse); Haak (1980) p. 900 ff.

125 Article 120(2): "The closest connection can be determined specifically by the characteristic performance, the special need for protection of one of the parties, or an unequivocal territorial connection of the contract."

126 Kropholler (1978) p. 644, the German phrase being *Vertragssphäre des Schwächeren*. As another example of "weak party contracts", Kropholler mentions the relationship between landlord and tenant, to be governed by the law of the *situs* of the rented property. *Ibid.* p. 642. For some insurance contracts, the applicable law could be determined either by the "place of the risk" or the residence of the insured. *Ibid.* p. 644. All these connecting factors are selected on a functional basis.

Both in the European Convention and in the Swiss draft, the theory of the characteristic performance has been endorsed as a catch-all solution to contracts choice of law. Apart from the relatively few cases in which the result turns on functional allocation or proper law considerations, most contracts will be governed by the law of the country where the party who is to effect the characteristic performance has his habitual residence, its central administration, or its (principal) place of business.[127] There would be no need to discuss this criterion here, if the authors of the theory, Schnitzer and Vischer, had not emphasized the "functional" aspects of their approach. The "essential" distinction between the characteristic and non-characteristic performances, they claim, depends on the economical or sociological function which a specific type of contract fulfills in any country's social system.[128] One of the objections raised by Professor Jessurun d'Oliveira in his eloquent critique of the theory tackles the muddled references to both functional and ontological factors: " ... it is difficult to perceive how a *rattachement fonctionnel* in terms of economics and sociology could also affect the 'essence' of the legal relationship. We are used to associate the concept of 'essence' with the notion of stability, while the expression 'function' enhances the aspect of changeability. Thus, the amalgamation of essence and function gives rise to either the paradox of a mutable essence (la donna è mobile) or the one of an immutable function."[129] It will be clear that the characteristic performance theory has nothing to do with functional allocation in the sense here described. It does not focus on any basic policy of the substantive law of contracts, it does not reflect the substantive law's concern for either of the contracting parties, and, contrary to its economical or sociological pretense, its allocation criteria are not inspired by an estimate of presumptive interests.

A better example of functional allocation is found in the Hague Convention Concerning the Jurisdiction of Authorities and the Applicable

---

127 Article 4(2) EEC Convention on the Law Applicable to Contractual Obligations. *Cf.* article 114 (formerly article 121) of the Swiss Draft Statute on Private International Law. Judicial practice in the Netherlands has adopted the same rule for most contracts: *cf. supra* note 87.
128 Schnitzer (1957) vol. II, p. 640; p. 645; Vischer (1962) p. 108.
129 Jessurun d'Oliveira (1975-1) p. 100. Apart from the theory's premise that the function of contract would not be susceptible to change (the alternative being too implausible to consider), there are other flaws, notably the authors' gratuitous statements on a contract's "economical" or "sociological" function. *Ibid.* p. 101.

Law Regarding the Protection of Minors, concluded in 1961. Strictly speaking, it is not the applicable law but adjudicatory jurisdiction which is determined here on a functional basis: while article 1 grants jurisdiction to the authorities in the country of the child's habitual residence, article 2 requires them to apply their own law. But even if allocation is coupled to a jurisdictional standard, it is still –indirectly– predicated on functional considerations. According to the explanatory report, this solution comports with the basic objective of the convention: the protection of minor children. That purpose is best served by an approach that correlates jurisdiction and applicable law, since "the authorities of the State of the habitual residence ... are generally in a better position to appreciate the minor child's actual situation and the appropriate protective measures in the instant case."[130] The Convention thus reflects the trend of modern legislation on the relationship between parents and children, which has focused increasingly on the protection of the minor's interests. In many countries, government agencies, invested with considerable authority, are charged with the task of safeguarding the child's welfare. Their intervention may involve investigations into the family situation, compulsory counseling, or even termination of the parents' natural guardianship. In this area, government interference is not only justified by a policy of protecting the individual child but also by the community's interest in being protected "against dangers resulting from improper upbringing, inadequate hygiene, or moral corruption of young people."[131] To take account of this mixture of public interest and individual protection, the correlation of *forum* and *ius* –neatly expressed in the German term *"Gleichlauf"* – is an effective choice of law device. Since protection of minors is an area of the law where the traditional distinction between public and private law is rapidly fading, any other solution would pose insurmountable adaptation problems. The Convention's *Gleichlauf* approach calls for an integral application of forum law, which precludes a precarious distinction between public and private

---

130 *Actes et Documents de la 9e Session de la Conférence de La Haye, 5 au 26 octobre 1960*, vol. IV (*Rapport explicatif de M. W. Steiger*), p. 221, p. 226.
131 International Court of Justice 28 November 1958, Reports of Judgments 1958, p. 55 (*Re Marie Elisabeth Boll*). Inspired by the theories of Pillet, the court distinguished between the aim of "individual protection" which warranted application of Dutch law as the child's national law, and the aim of "social guarantee" which called for application of Swedish law as the law of the child's residence.

law.[132] Its jurisdictional criterion eliminates the difficulties inherent in applying foreign law. To the extent that the child's protection is made dependent on the substantive law of its habitual residence, all minors living in that country are treated equally. This way, the Convention achieves a result which is no different from functional allocation. Unfortunately, its functional approach is compromised by various provisions based on the nationality principle. While these were meant to give the child the added protection of its national law, the overlapping jurisdiction of local and national authorities tends to produce incompatible decisions. Due to this ambivalent conception, the Convention has proved to be a source of confusion and uncertainty, despite the clarity of its first two provisions.

It would be wrong to equate functional allocation in European conflicts law with the various approaches to "functional choice of law" which now prevail in the United States. While the American solutions emphasize the particularities of the individual case and the contents of the relevant rules, functional allocation is still a fairly crude technique of jurisdiction-selection. Its criteria are predicated on "basic policies underlying a particular field of law", to borrow a phrase from the Restatement Second.[133] Whether these basic policies are actually at stake in an individual case, is a question they ignore. In other words, they leave no room for an evaluation of possibly conflicting *interests*. Furthermore, it is highly unlikely that the basic policies which inspired the

---

132 For the same reason, Kropholler (1978) p. 641, recommends functional allocation for employment contracts, as it precludes an unwanted dichotomy between the *lex contractus* and the (public) law of labor relations in force in the country where the employee performs his duties. See also: Kegel (1985) p. 387: "With regard to employment contracts, it is difficult to separate the rules of private law, which should be taken from the law governing contractual obligations, from the rules of public law, which should really be taken from the law of the place of employment." *Cf.* Gamillschegg, *supra* note 123, p. 187 ff. I should like to add that a separate choice of law treatment of public and private law is apt to cause problems in all areas in which legal relationships of a private law nature are affected by public law. However, if the coordination of public and private law is not coupled to jurisdictional criteria as well, the forum may be confronted with foreign rules of public law which cannot be applied in any jurisdiction but the one in which they are in force, for instance a rule calling for the offices of a specific government agency.

133 Restatement Second, § 6(2e). Comment h explains that "[t]his factor is of particular importance in situations where the policies of the interested states are largely the same but where there are nevertheless minor differences between their relevant local rules."

creation of a functional conflicts rule are shared by all other legal systems. Since functional allocation is as blind to the contents of the applicable law as any other form of abstract jurisdiction-selection,[134] it may refer to a foreign law which happens to pursue a policy of a different order. In such cases, the translation of substantive law policy into a functional allocation standard loses much of its meaning. The weaker party, for whose benefit the forum adopted a functional conflicts rule, falls victim to a choice of law paradox whenever the applicable law, presumed to be most interested in his welfare, displays a greater concern for his juridical counterpart. Conversely, the interests of the latter could be given an unexpected and undeserved boost: the paradox of functional allocation requires that the protective foreign law be applied regardless of its actual claim to application.[135]

On the other hand, functional allocation does have an important aspect in common with most of the "functional" choice of law alternatives that have emerged in the United States in that it is premised on the function and the objectives of substantive law. Its choice of law standards are attuned to policies which are embodied in the law of the forum and likely to be pursued in most jurisdictions with which the forum maintains steady relations. Whereas the American approaches require an *ad hoc* identification of interests, a functional conflicts rule is based on the presumption that the jurisdiction to which it refers will have an interest in the application of its law,[136] and, conversely, that other jurisdictions involved must be disinterested. As far as *forum* interests are concerned, this presumption is likely to be sound. Inferred from the policy of forum law, it establishes when the forum will have an interest in the application of its law, and when it will not. In each case in which the focal point of the forum's legislative concern happens to be centered in the forum state, the forum may be presumed to have such an interest, and vice versa. Usually, the required connection is established by a domiciliary criterion, but if forum policy

---

134 *Cf.* Strikwerda (1986) p. 11 ff., p. 16, note 46.
135 If the weaker party is living in the country protecting the stronger party, and vice versa, this type of situation comes close to what is called an "unprovided-for case" in modern interest analysis: neither of the jurisdictions involved has an interest in the application of its law. More on this subject, *infra* chapter 4, section 3.
136 *Cf.* Lando (1974) p. 54 = Lando (1975) p. 153: "In the contracts mentioned the legal system interested in [the weaker party's] protection will also be the proper law of the contract ..."

focuses on a public interest, such as labor relations or housing accommodation, another connecting factor may have been chosen. If functional allocation were used as a unilateral choice of law technique, I submit, its result would not greatly differ from those of interest analysis.[137] Demarcating the scope of a specific portion of forum law, its rules would claim its application in one case and declare the forum's lack of interest in another. However, functional conflicts rules are generally bilateral. Whenever they refer to foreign law, they express –correctly at least in theory– the forum's lack of interest in the application of its law, but they may be wrong in their implicit assumption that the forum's lack of interest must entail the foreign law's claim to application. Since functional allocation is deployed in those areas in which there is considerable international consensus on the purpose of the underlying substantive law, this flaw might be less serious than it seems to be from a dogmatic point of view.[138] As long as the relevant policies of all jurisdictions involved are the same, there is a good chance that functional allocation will achieve by and large the same results that American courts would reach in what they would call "false conflict" situations. However, even if we are willing to view functional allocation as a preconceived and streamlined variant of interest analysis, we will have to admit that it suffers from its inherent abstraction, particularly in those cases in which an *ad hoc* approach would reveal competing interests. The basic policy of the underlying field of law might be a suitable foundation for a functional conflicts rule, but if it is contradicted by a more specific policy embodied in the substantive law of a concerned jurisdiction, functional allocation becomes a parody of policy-oriented choice of law.

---

137 *Cf.* Keller (1983) p. 179: "Consideration of this [functional] aspect in the creation of conflicts rules can be viewed as a way to make use of the American policy-weighing method within the confines of our rule-oriented approach to law."
138 Keller (1983) p. 182, is probably a little over-optimistic in his assertion that "nowadays, virtually all States have enacted, in one way or another, protective laws for the benefit of the socially weak." I suppose that there is still quite a gap, in this respect, between social welfare states and most third world countries.

4 Favor concepts

"As private international law merely refers to the applicable substantive law or to a specific substantive rule by way of abstract connecting factors, it is much less influenced by social values than any other area of law," wrote Konrad Zweigert in 1973, in a seminal article on "The Dearth of Social Values in Conflict of Laws."[139] To bridge the widening gap between impartial conflicts law and value-oriented substantive law, he suggested a subsidiary "better rule" approach, to be used in case the relevant conflicts rule, invoked by either of the parties, suffers from ambiguity and therefore fails to achieve its primary goals of legal certainty and uniformity of result. While Zweigert's better law idea as such has not had much of an impact on European conflicts thinking, there is a growing willingness in Europe to integrate social values into the various systems of conflicts law. Increasingly, normative notions inherent in a legal system's substantive law are transplanted to its choice of law rules, gradually changing the blunt features of the neutral allocation method. The substantive law values supported by contemporary conflicts law in Europe are generally, but not necessarily, of a social nature. Most of them point to the social disadvantages peculiar to certain groups, roughly the same ones we encountered in the section on functional allocation: children, maintenance creditors, consumers, employees. On a different plane, there are values that have a wider dimension, reflecting a community's sense of morality or justice. In the law of conflicts, some of these substantive law notions have been recognized as relevant factors in the determination of the applicable rule of law. To the extent that they support application of the law that conforms most to the legal ideal in question, they can be classified as "*favor* concepts." Their choice of law expression can range from an alternative reference rule to a conditional better law approach. Some of them favor members of the forum community only, some benefit anyone in need of protection, while other ones express humanitarian or cultural convictions held by the forum community. In conflicts law, *favor* concepts are hardly less diverse in meaning and expression than the values that dominate substantive law. What they have in common, though, is their result-selective pur-

---

139 Zweigert (1973) p. 443; the English translation has been borrowed from the summary at p. 452.

pose: meant to further substantive law policies, they take precedence over traditional choice of law values such as uniformity of result or the avoidance of international friction.[140]

Not all *favor* concepts encountered in the law of conflicts have their origin in the policies of substantive law. Some of them owe their existence to the very condition that gave rise to conflicts law itself: the need to reconcile the ideal of international harmony with the reality of discordant legal systems.[141] While modern conflicts law is gradually re-establishing its relation with substantive law, it still pursues specific choice of law objectives. To further international intercourse, conflicts law not only aspires to accommodate the differences between legal systems, but it also tries to remove some of the national obstructions that threaten the stability of international relations. In this light, the protection of justified expectations is not only a substantive law value of universal caliber, but an autonomous conflicts policy as well. One of the oldest and most effective devices for its implementation is the *favor* construction. The *favor recognitionis*, for instance, calls for a recipient attitude towards foreign judgments, as it is generally deemed unjust that a litigant who has won his case abroad should be obliged to go through the whole adjudicatory process again, now in another country.[142] Similarly, the *favor negotii*, which subjects a transaction to the law upholding its formal or even its substantive validity, is meant to mitigate the negative effect which the discrepancies between national laws may have on the stability of international legal relationships. In this respect, it expresses a characteristic choice of law value which is not echoed in substantive law. In modern European conflicts

140 *Cf.* Reese (1983-2), discussing various *favor* concepts embodied in the Swiss draft statute on private international law: "What is particularly striking in the articles on choice of law is the effort that was so clearly made to tailor rules to further fundamental substantive policies in those situations where the existence of such policies can be perceived." *Ibid.* at p. 292.
141 *Cf.* Strikwerda (1986) p. 8, note 23. According to Neuhaus (1976) p. 178 ff., the only justification for result-selective allocation is the promotion of supranational values. Consequently, he rejects any *favor* concept which is predicated on substantive law considerations.
142 *Cf.* article 23 of the Hague Convention on the Recognition and Enforcement of Decisions Relating to Maintenance Obligations (1973), allowing application of other standards of recognition than those laid down in the Convention "for the purposes of obtaining recognition or enforcement of a decision or settlement." See also: article 11 of the Hague Convention on the Recognition and Enforcement of Decisions Relating to Maintenance Obligations in respect of Children (1958).

law, the statutist maxim *locus regit actum*, which defined the scope of formal requirements as territorial, has lost most of its imperative suggestion, and is generally construed as a rule which permits rather than commands compliance with local formalities. If the formal validity of the act or transaction is upheld by another law, notably the law governing its substantive aspects, the (invalidating) local law should be ignored.[143] Much more could be said about the *favor negotii*, but since its relation with substantive law is relatively weak,[144] I will now turn to those *favor* concepts which primarily reflect domestic values.

One example is the *favor divortii*, which is gradually being accepted as a valid choice of law consideration in several European countries. It expresses the notion that a marriage need not be continued if either of the spouses, or both of them, wishes its dissolution. While there may be some truth in Kegel's proposition that "international marriages break down most easily, hence their dissolution should be facilitated,"[145] I do not believe that this is the only motive supporting the

---

143 The largest range of alternatives from which the validating law may be selected, it would seem, is found in the Hague Convention on the Conflicts of Laws Relating to the Form of Testamentary Dispositions, concluded in 1961. Article 1 declares a testamentary disposition valid if its form complies with the law of the place where it was made, the law of the testator's nationality, domicile or habitual residence (either at the time when he made the disposition or at the time of his death) or, in relation to immovable property, the law of the situs.

144 To be sure, the *favor testamenti* and other *favor negotii* variants also reflect a general presumption of validity underlying substantive law. *Cf.* Batiffol's explanation of the *favor testamenti* in the Hague Convention, *Actes et Documents de la 9e Session de la Conférence de La Haye, 5 au 26 octobre 1960*, vol. III, Explanatory Report by Henri Batiffol, at p. 165: " ... the law governing form should reflect above all a predisposition to defer to the wish of the testator." One of the objectives which conflicts law has in common with substantive law, obviously, is the protection of justified expectations. In this respect, the *favor validitatis* in conflicts law supports the same values as those permeating substantive law.

145 Kegel (1985) p. 508, quoted (from the third edition) approvingly by Neuhaus (1976) p. 179. In the Netherlands, this consideration may have contributed to a liberalization of divorce *jurisdiction* in 1970. *Cf.* Wendels (1983) p. 18 ff. Article 814 of the Code of Civil Procedure now couples jurisdiction to either party's domicile in the Netherlands. Thus, a Dutch citizen remigrating to the Netherlands following the breakdown of his/her marriage can bring a divorce action in a Dutch court against the spouse still living abroad. A Dutch couple living abroad can bring proceedings before the court at The Hague. In this respect, article 814 is an expression of the *favor divortii* in jurisdictional terms.
In the following discussion, the term "divorce" stands for all legal means of loosening the bonds of matrimony, including the various forms of separation.

favor divortii in choice of law. It also reflects a cultural attitude which considers divorce not as a threat to society's moral fibre but as an indispensable means to end an irremedial disruption of family relations.[146] In many countries, this attitude has led to the liberalization of divorce by the adoption of an elastic "breakdown" criterion, either as a general principle, or complementing a range of traditional divorce grounds. In the Netherlands, "lasting disruption of the marriage" is the sole ground for divorce since 1971. The concept of fault, which used to be an overriding factor, was largely abandoned. At the same time, Dutch conflicts law started to change. In the 1970's, proper law notions encouraged the courts to substitute domicile for nationality in cases in which the parties no longer had a significant connection with the country of their common nationality, while the once predominant role of forum law[147] was reduced to that of a last resort solution. Since the exercise of divorce jurisdiction is tied to domiciliary criteria, the only choice of law cases that did not end in an actual divorce under Dutch law were those, generally, in which foreign spouses, despite their domicile in the Netherlands, had not sufficiently assimilated to warrant the displacement of their national law prohibiting divorce. In 1981, a new statute on divorce conflicts further expanded the *favor divortii* in Dutch choice of law.[148] In addition to a reformulation of the

---

146 *Cf.* Wolfgang Friedmann, *Law in a Changing Society*, 2d ed., 1972, p. 238 ff., distinguishing between the "essentially religious" principle of the permanency of the marriage union, the individualistic philosophy which postulates "the right to cast off a burden that has become intolerable," and the social philosophy which is concerned with the negative effects an unhappy marriage may have on the family, hence on society.
In countries in which the ideal of the permanency of marriage is premised on religious or moral precepts, the substantive law of divorce, if it exists at all, will be restrictive. It is unlikely that *favor divortii* will dominate the conflicts law of such a country. *Cf.* Strikwerda (1986) p. 20.
147 Originally, the dissolution of marriage was treated as a matter of public policy, calling for application of Dutch law under any circumstances. Both the Hague Convention on Divorce of 1902 and the original version of the Benelux Uniform Law required cumulative application of the parties' national law and forum law, hardly in tune with the emerging *favor divortii* in Dutch substantive law.
148 *Wet Conflictenrecht Echtscheiding* of March 25, 1981, *Staatsblad* 1981, 166. The statute was enacted in connection with the ratification by the Netherlands of the Conventions of Luxemburg (1967) and The Hague (1970) concerning the recognition of divorces and legal separations. Hence, it also covers recognition.

established judge-made law in this area, the statute contains a provision allowing the parties to opt for application of Dutch law.[149]

By comparison, the approach to international divorce in other European countries is more conservative. In Germany, the new statute on private international only allows the foreign law of common nationality to be substituted by German law if the plaintiff is or was a German citizen and the foreign law would prohibit the divorce.[150] The Swiss draft, on the other hand, calls for application of Swiss law, unless the spouses have a common foreign nationality and only one of them is domiciled in Switzerland. In that case the national law prevails, subject to another *favor divortii* proviso: if the national law does not allow the divorce, or if it only allows it on exceptionally harsh grounds, Swiss law will be applied if one of the spouses is also a Swiss citizen or has at least two years' residence in Switzerland.[151] As in the Netherlands, the combination of jurisdictional criteria and choice of law rules is such that it will be a rare case in which a divorce will be denied on account of a foreign law less liberal than forum law. Inher-

---

149 Article 1(4), which Van Rooij (1981) p. 423, has called the statute's "hidden main rule". If the parties are foreign nationals, the law of their common nationality will be applied, unless one of them "apparently lacks a true social connection with the country of common nationality." Nevertheless, the parties may restore the national law to its primary position by another option: article 1(2).
To the extent that both parties may choose either Dutch law or the law of their common nationality, the statute supports limited party autonomy. Contrary to the principle of party autonomy in contracts choice of law, however, an uncontested choice by one of the parties is valid as well. To the extent that forum law may be chosen in any case, the result comes close to "facultative choice of law": *infra* chapter 2, section 4, note 291. *Cf.* Strikwerda (1986) p. 7, note 17.

150 Article 17 of the German Act on the Reform of Private International Law (*Gesetz zur Neuregelung des Internationalen Privatrechts*) of 25 July 1986, amending several rules of private international law of the Federal Republic, in force since September 1, 1986: text in *Bundesgesetzblatt* 1986, I, 1142; 5 *IPRax* 322–330 (1986), See also: Erik Jayme, *Das neue IPR-Gesetz – Brennpunkte der Reform*: 5 *IPRax* 265–270 (1986). The primary reference is to the law governing the "general effects of matrimony" determined in article 14. The latter provision calls for application of the law of the spouses' common nationality, to be replaced by the law of their habitual residence in case they are nationals of different countries. A residuary solution is application of the law of the country with which both spouses have the most significant relationship.

151 Article 59(3). A similar provision was included in the original draft (article 61), but the primary conflicts rule was more conservative: article 60 called for application of the law of the parties' common domicile, followed by the law of the common nationality, or, ultimately, *lex fori*.

ent in this *favor divortii* is an overriding forum bias, which is totally incompatible with the principles of neutral allocation. Its ultimate justification is a preference for the forum's "divorce-friendly" substantive law, considered to be the better law *per se*.[152]

Similar preconceived better law notions support several *favor* concepts in regard to children. Best known, probably, is the *favor legitimitatis*, calling for application of the law that establishes a family relationship between a child born out of wedlock and its putative father.[153] Again, the result-selective choice is inspired by a substantive law tendency: in those countries in which illegitimacy has ceased to rouse society's moral indignation, the concomitant legal discrimination of illegitimate children is gradually disappearing. Thus, contemporary law increasingly supports the notion that "bastards" should not be punished for the "sin" of their parents.[154] Whereas legislative efforts have been made to reduce the differences between legitimate and illegitimate children on the level of substantive law, conflicts law has followed the trend by expanding the *favor* solution. The Swiss draft allows an "acknowledgment" in Switzerland under the law of the child's habitual residence, or the law of either parent's domicile or nationality. The same criteria apply to the recognition of an "acknowledgment" or legitimation which took place abroad.[155] Modelled upon

---

152 *Cf.* Strikwerda (1986) p. 17 ff. It should be noted that these *favor* constructions transpose substantive law values to the plane of abstract allocation. Whether forum values are actually promoted depends on the availability of a "favorable" law, which in turn depends on the coincidence of actual facts and predetermined connecting factors. Unless the choice of forum law is one of the available *favor* alternatives, there is no guarantee that domestic policy prevails in the jurisdiction-selecting process.

153 Since there are vast differences between the domestic laws on the subject, this *favor* concept is hard to define. Essentially, it is related to the child's status, established by legitimation, voluntary recognition or "acknowledgment", and perhaps affiliation. To the extent that paternity actions are meant to establish maintenance obligations, they are of a different order.

Taken literally, the phrases *"favor legitimationis"* and *"favor legitimitatis"* are too restrictive, as they tend to express a preference for legitimacy and ignore other ways to legalize a father-child relationship. Less common are the expressions *favor paternitatis* and *favor agnitionis* used by some authors.

154 *Cf.* Mühl (1982) p. 106 ff.; Ehrenzweig (1962) § 142.

155 Articles 69–72 (articles 71–73a in the original draft). In 1976, Switzerland abolished legitimation as a means of establishing family ties between father and child. Hence, the scope of article 72 is restricted to recognition of foreign legitimations.

the CIEC Convention on Legitimation by Subsequent Marriage, concluded in 1970, § 22 of the Austrian statute provides that such legitimation depends on the national law of the parents, or, if they have different nationalities, on the national law "which is more favorable to the child's legitimation." In the Netherlands, where the courts used to subject issues pertaining to the father-child relationship to the law of the father's nationality, a general *favor pueri* has caused a shift towards application of Dutch law to achieve the desired change of the child's status. In these cases, an exception from the traditional rule is justified by a number of contacts with the Netherlands, such as the nationality and domicile of the child and its mother, sometimes combined with the domicile of the father and his decreasing "social connection" with the country of his nationality. It is quite obvious, generally, that the choice of law result is directly determined by the social values which underlie the Dutch substantive law in this area.[156]

In the two Hague Conventions on the Law Applicable to Maintenance Obligations, the *favor* idea has been expressed in a system of primary and subsidiary conflicts rules. Article 3 of the Convention on child maintenance of 1956 prescribes application of the forum's municipal conflicts rule should the law of the child's habitual residence withhold maintenance altogether.[157] This solution is of little help if the forum's national conflicts rule is identical to the one laid down in the Convention, but in 1956, when the nationality principle was still firmly established in international family law, it might have been a true alternative in most European member states. The Maintenance Convention of 1973, conceived as a set of rules with a universal scope, was meant to replace the "domestic" conflicts rule on maintenance entirely. Hence, the former system of reciprocity was abandoned, and

---

156 Most explicit was the Court of Zwolle deciding on the validity of a prenatal "acknowledgment" by an American. Confirming that "on principle" these matters are governed by the father's personal law, here Missouri law, the court saw "no compelling reason to enforce this general conflicts rule in those instances in which the child's interest clearly refers to a different legal system, provided there is a sufficient connection with that other system," in this case the Netherlands. Rb. Zwolle 7 March 1983, *NIPR* 1983, no. 194. See also: Hof Amsterdam 27 January 1984, *NIPR* 1984, no. 18.
157 The original text provided that this renvoi-like solution should be used whenever its result would be "more favorable" to the child, but several delegations objected to this arbitrary formulation and the proviso was amended to its present "anything or nought" standard.

alternative connecting factors were substituted for the *favor* reference to municipal conflicts law. The Convention's main rule, article 4, provides that maintenance obligations are governed by the law of the creditor's habitual residence, a good example of functional allocation.[158] The *favor creditoris* is articulated in two subsidiary conflicts rules, articles 5 and 6, offering the creditor a second, possibly a third chance if the law of his habitual residence leaves him empty-handed. The first alternative calls for application of the law of the parties' common nationality, the second one refers to forum law. In many cases, the creditor will have just one alternative, or none at all: if the parties have different nationalities, article 5 will be of no avail, while article 6 has nothing to offer if the creditor has his habitual residence in the forum state. Furthermore, as in the Child Maintenance Convention, subsidiary allocation on a *favor* basis is only allowed if the creditor obtains no maintenance at all under the law of primary reference. The law of his habitual residence might allow him no more than a pittance, but the fact that it does not prohibit maintenance altogether precludes recourse to more rewarding options. This implies that the court is bound to the allocation order the Convention prescribes: the law of the habitual residence comes first, then the parties' common national law, and finally *lex fori*. Here, the implementation of the *favor* concept seems less liberal than it is in other areas, in which the order of *favor* alternatives is not hierarchic, but this has more to do with the character of maintenance obligations than with the Convention's underlying philosophy. Repeatedly, the Explanatory Report emphasizes the need to protect the maintenance creditor, "who is regarded as being in a weaker situation than the debtor."[159] In maintenance proceedings, two major issues must be decided: first, it should be asked whether the claimant is entitled to maintenance at all; the second question concerns the modalities of the maintenance obligation. The first issue which requires a simple "yes or no" answer could be subjected to any of the eligible laws, just as the question whether a divorce may be granted or not, or whether the status of an illegitimate child may be altered or not, is governed by the law which brings about the desired result. It is quite easy to determine which law is "more favorable" when the difference between all or nothing is at stake. A

---

158 *Supra* section 3, text accompanying notes 111–138.
159 *Actes et Documents de la 12e Session, 2 au 21 octobre 1972*, vol. IV, Explanatory Report by M. Verwilghen, p. 444, no. 144.

decision on the terms of a maintenance obligation, on the other hand, entails a much more difficult choice in which arbitrary factors (how much? how long?) come into play. If the Convention would allow a free choice of the most favorable law on this score, it would support the courts' natural inclination to apply their own law, which, in turn, encourages forum shopping and frustrates the goal of decisional harmony. Thus, the hierarchy of the Convention's *favor* alternatives reflects the antagonism between substantive law values and the objectives of traditional conflicts law.

While the Maintenance Conventions preclude a choice on a "better or worse" basis, the provisions on consumer transactions and employment contracts in the EEC Convention on Contractual Obligations require a relative evaluation of the better law in case the contract contains a choice of law clause. As in the Maintenance Conventions, the *favor* approach is inspired by the same substantive law notion that supports functional allocation in these areas, *viz.* protection of the weaker party. Article 5(2) and article 6(1) provide that "a choice of law made by the parties shall not have the result of depriving the consumer [respectively the employee] of the protection afforded to him by the mandatory rules of the law" which would govern the contract without such a choice. Limitations on party autonomy, serving to counteract the unwanted consequences of the parties' disparate bargaining power, have been advocated by many writers.[160] If the parties' right to choose the applicable law stems from the freedom of contract prevailing in substantive law, it follows that restrictions on that freedom extend to conflicts law as well and militate against unfettered party autonomy.[161] Whereas the draftsmen of the EEC Convention have opted for a *favor* approach, calling for application of the more favorable law, other legislators have either excluded or reduced the parties' choice of law freedom in respect of specific "weak party" contracts. The Swiss draft, for instance, does not allow a choice by the parties in consumer contracts, and limits their choice of law options in employment contracts to the law of the employee's habitual residence, or that of the employer's place of business, domicile or habitual

---

160 Notably Lando (1974); Von Hoffmann (1974) p. 398 ff.; Kropholler (1978) p. 644 ff.
161 Hartley (1982) p. 111 ff.; p. 125; Morse (1982) p. 150 ff.; De Boer (1974) p. 64. ff.

residence.[162] In fact, the Swiss solution eliminates all *favor* alternatives: functional allocation should suffice to protect the consumer, even if the parties' chosen law would be more favorable, whereas employment contracts may be subjected by the parties to a limited number of laws, regardless of the degree of protection they afford. Thus, the courts are spared the precarious task of ascertaining the more favorable law in the instant case. The EEC Convention, on the other hand, requires a *favor* decision on a comparative basis. Contrary to the other *favor* concepts we encountered, the protective policy underlying articles 5 and 6 is not expressed in a clearcut "yes or no" standard which would enable the courts to measure the eligible substantive laws against specific objectives. The only clue these rules contain as to the result to be achieved is a reference to the *degree* of protection each of the eligible laws affords the weaker party. The comparative evaluation this solution requires comes close to Zweigert's "*bessere Regel*" or Leflar's "better law consideration."[163] Although I do not think that the courts will actually have great problems deciding which law affords the best protection, there might be a tinge of arbitrariness in such comparisons, particularly when both laws protect the weaker party, but in different ways.[164]

Lest we forget that this book focuses on choice of law methodology in the field of torts, I will conclude this survey with some examples of the

162 Articles 117(3) and article 118(3), respectively. In the original draft, article 117(2) provided in general that "one of the parties' special need for protection" (*das besondere Schutzbedürfnis einer Partei*) would override the principle of party autonomy. *Cf.* Von Overbeck (1982) p. 272 ff. See also: section 27(2) of the British Unfair Contract Terms Act 1977, discussed by Hartley (1982) p. 121. In the Austrian statute on private international law, party autonomy is limited in respect of consumer contracts (§ 41), agreements concerning the lease of real property (§ 42), and employment contracts (§ 44), in each case depending on the "disadvantage" of the chosen law for the weaker party.
163 Zweigert's three-layered choice of law system was briefly mentioned *supra* text following note 139; Leflar's "choice-influencing considerations" will be discussed in more detail, *infra* chapter 5.
164 A plausible example is given by Morse (1982) p. 152: " ... let us assume that the chosen law entitles an employee to reinstatement (but no compensation) after a wrongful dismissal, whereas the law which would have been applicable pursuant to Article 6(2) would permit only compensation on such an event." It can hardly have been the intention of the draftsmen to afford "international" employees a double protection to which no "domestic" employee in any country would ever be entitled. See also: Von Overbeck (1982) p. 273, for an example in the area of consumer contracts.

favor laesi in European conflicts law. The notion that tort victims deserve preferential treatment is not new. As early as 1887, the German *Reichsgericht* adopted an alternative reference rule favoring the victim in those cases in which the place of wrong does not coincide with the place of injury.[165] In such situations, application of the *lex loci delicti* rule is impracticable as it does not distinguish between the place where the wrongful act occurs and the place where the harm is done. American choice of law used to refer to the place of injury, pursuant to a subsidiary "last event rule". The European solutions, supported by a variety of theories, range from (cumulative) application of *lex loci actus* and/or *lex loci iniuriae* to victim-oriented allocation, which either calls for application of the plaintiff's domiciliary law or allows the choice of the most favorable law.[166] This lack of consensus might be explained from the limited experience of the courts in deciding "bilocal" (or even "multilocal") tort problems. Apart from the occasional defamatory letter, the musty textbook example, it seems that most wrongs used to cause damage or injury there where they were committed.[167] Modern technology has provided conflicts scholars with ample material to test their theories on bilocal torts. Products liability is one choice of law area in which the place of injury is apt to differ from the place of wrong, environmental damage another. Not surprisingly,

---

165 Hohloch (1984) p. 104, note 273, cites RG 23 September 1887, *RGZ* 19, 382, complemented by RG 20 November 1888, *RGZ* 23, 305, which case is also cited by Strömholm (1961) p. 119, and Neuhaus (1976) p. 177. In the second case, the *favor laesi* was justified by the "ubiquity rule", *viz.* the construction that any place in which one of the facts constituting a tort occurs qualifies as *locus delicti*. *Cf.* Strömholm (1961) p. 119 ff.; Kegel (1985) p. 306 ff.; Duintjer Tebbens (1979) p. 192; Mühl (1982) p. 103 ff.

166 See: Dubbink (1947) p. 81 ff.; Binder (1955) p. 474 ff.; Strömholm (1961) p. 116 ff.; Ehrenzweig (1980) no. 39 ff.; De Boer (1982) p. 35 ff.; Hohloch (1984) p. 105, note 275. See also: Mühl (1982) p. 104, citing a German case (OLG Saarbrücken 22 October 1957, *NJW* 1958, 752) in which the reference to France's more favorable *lex loci actus* was subjected to a renvoi test, in a rather superfluous attempt to reinforce the decision to apply French law. In my opinion, renvoi is totally incompatible with the *favor laesi* said to support the choice of the more favorable law. In his summary of the case, Rest (1980) p. 33, p. 69, does not mention this particular aspect.

167 Dubbink (1947) p. 81, summarizing the pre-war state of affairs, noted that, in most countries, case law was either non-existent or inconclusive on this point, except in Germany and the United States. According to Strömholm (1961) p. 120, the German courts gained most of their experience in the area of unfair competition.

the few legislative efforts to reconcile the new reality of bilocal torts with the traditional *lex loci delicti* standard have focused on these topics. A prominent feature of the approach to this type of conflicts is the *favor laesi*.

In the Hague Convention on Products Liability, which does not expressly address the problem of bilocal torts, the only article expressly favoring the victim is article 6. Ordinarily, either the place of injury or the habitual residence of the victim will be decisive, provided they coincide with some other factor. If they do not, article 6 allows the plaintiff to choose between the *lex loci iniuriae* and the law of the state where the defendant has his principal place of business. Since articles 4 and 5 list no less than five different pairs of predetermined contacts, it is unlikely that the option of article 6 will be readily available, and even then it may be of little value to the plaintiff.[168] The Swiss draft provided a more generous option: article 133 allowed the claimant in a products liability case to choose between the law of the place of business of the person claimed to be liable, and, subject to certain conditions, the law of the state in which the product was acquired or the law of the victim's habitual residence. In effect, this triple option would include both the law of the place of acting and the law of the place where the damage occurred in most cases in which they do not coincide, as the *locus iniuriae* is likely to be situated there where the product is acquired or the victim has his home. However, in the final text of what is now article 131, the third alternative was deleted. Instead, a new paragraph provides that, in case the claim is governed by foreign law, no other damages may be awarded in Switzerland than those that would be granted under Swiss law. Thus, the original *favor laesi* has been reduced considerably, apparently for the benefit of Swiss manufacturers against whom no foreign measure of damages can be invok-

---

168 *Cf.* Duintjer Tebbens (1979) p. 192, note 135 and accompanying text, and p. 344/345, noting that "the suggestion to favour one party met with little enthusiasm among the Continental delegations." Article 7 reduces the option of article 6 to zero if defendant establishes that he could not reasonably have foreseen that the product would be marketed in the state of the place of injury. In that case, the *lex loci iniuriae* is no longer eligible, which leaves the plaintiff without a choice.

ed which would be deemed excessive by Swiss standards.[169] To some extent, the Swiss limitation on damages in products liability cases echoes the defendant-protective policy embodied in article 12 of the German *Einführungsgesetz*, a provision which controls German tort choice of law in general. If the tort is governed by foreign law, the liability of a German national can extend no further than German law allows. In other words, both the existence of a right of action and the maximum liability which German tort-feasors incur are controlled by German law. Here, too, the *favor*-inspired alternatives, available in case of bilocal torts, are subject to the maxima of forum law. The effect of such provisions, by which forum law "is superimposed, as it were, as an ultimate control over the material result obtained by application of the foreign rules,"[170] is an abstract reduction of the *favor laesi* to the level of forum justice. At the same time, the protection of forum interests is guaranteed.

In the largely judge-made law of multistate torts of the Netherlands, *favor* notions are conspicuously absent. Plaintiffs are granted no options, and hardly a trace of result-selective allocation can be spotted. To some degree, this dispassionate approach to multistate torts can be explained by the courts' displacement of the *lex loci delicti* in those cases in which the parties are domiciled in the same state, whether the Netherlands or a foreign country.[171] Application of the law of their common domicile neither benefits the victim nor hurts the tort-feasor any more than it would benefit or hurt them in a domestic case. On the other hand, since most multistate tort cases arise from traffic accidents, they are subject to the Hague Convention of 1971, which

---

169 *Cf.* Patocchi (1985) p. 172, noting that the consumer's choice of law options have been criticized for putting Swiss manufacturers at a disadvantage: the limitation of article 131(2) "purports to restore the equality of the parties, *viz.* between the tort-feasor and the victim, which would be jeopardized without it." In Patocchi's opinion, the limitation is dispensable, as excessive awards under foreign law could just as well be parried by public policy.
Article 133 (formerly article 135) dealing with restraint of trade, contains a similar limitation, meant to exclude exemplary damages or any other award exceeding compensatory damages. *Cf.* the *Schlussbericht*, *supra* note 104, p. 247.
170 Strömholm (1961) p. 84. See also: Mühl (1982) p. 105 ff.; Hohloch (1984) p. 100, p. 204.
171 *Supra* section 2, text accompanying notes 70–74.

–apart from its provision on direct actions–[172] does not support a plaintiff-protective policy. As to collisions at sea, for which the place of wrong rule is inconclusive, I have already noted that the *Hoge Raad* has endorsed a proper law solution which focuses on the tort's factual effects, hence primarily on the position of the victim.[173] Structured along proper law lines, and functional in effect, this approach cannot be equated with the *favor* constructions here discussed.

Confronted with the problem of applying *lex loci delicti* to bilocal torts, the Dutch courts have adopted various solutions, emphasizing either the place of acting or the place of injury, or resorting to a center of gravity approach,[174] but a reference to the most favorable law will not be found. From the few doctrinary sources no consensus comes to light either. Although there seems to be a growing acceptance of the notion that a policy-oriented approach to bilocal torts warrants application of the law of the place of injury, possibly the law of the victim's domicile, most writers are unwilling to support a direct *favor laesi*.[175] Professor Jessurun d'Oliveira, who seems to be the only Dutch author squarely favoring an option for the victim, has written extensively on environmental torts, and most of his arguments were made in that context.[176] There would seem to be no compelling reason, however, why he would not extend the right to choose the most favorable law to the victim of *any* bilocal tort. In the actual conflict

---

172 Article 9 allows the *action directe* against the liability insurer if such an action is allowed by either the *lex loci delicti*, the law governing the contract of insurance, or the law of the state of registration of the vehicle if it applies pursuant to article 4. On the Convention's underlying philosophy, see Strikwerda (1980).
173 HR 16 March 1979, *NJ* 1979, 540 (*Free Enterprise/Brielle*); *supra* note 77 and accompanying text.
174 For a survey of relevant case law, see: Drion/De Boer, no. 58.
175 Dubbink (1947) p. 87, rejected an option on principle and advocated application of the *lex loci actus*, unless the tort-feasor caused the transnational harm intentionally. In that case, he must be deemed to have exposed himself to the sanctions of the foreign law. Only then would Dubbink grudgingly allow the plaintiff the choice of the most favorable law. *Ibid.* p. 89, note 81 and accompanying text. Lemaire (1968) p. 278, suggested an *ad hoc* approach, but rejected the possibility of an option. To Van Rooij (1979) p. 258, the practical and theoretical merits of a *favor* option in torts are patently insufficient.
176 Jessurun d'Oliveira (1978); *id. A.Ae.* 1980, p. 791 ff. *Accord*: Francescakis, *Rev. Crit. d.i.p.* 1979, p. 266 ff., p. 268. *Contra*: Van Rooij (1979) p. 258; De Boer (1982) p. 36 ff. For a comparative survey of the *favor laesi*, particularly in the area of environmental torts, see: Rest (1980) p. 20, p. 58.

that prompted D'Oliveira's *favor* plea, the much-discussed "Rhine pollution case", the choice of law issue turned out to be moot, as the parties eventually agreed to have Dutch law applied.[177] In Switzerland, the victims of pollution would have the option of article 134 of the future Swiss conflicts statute, providing that they may choose either the law of the state from which the polluting substance was emitted or the law of the state where the injury occurred.[178]

Many authors, both in the Netherlands and elsewhere, have raised practical and theoretical objections against *favor* concepts in choice of law, particularly against those requiring a comparative evaluation of the better or more favorable rule of law. In a lucid essay on the *loi la plus favorable*,[179] the Dutch comparatist Kisch has made a distinction between *favor* concepts according to the formulation of the conflicts rules in which they are expressed. On the one hand, there are rules containing alternative references to any law which achieves the desired result, whether it is validation of a testamentary disposition or the dissolution of a marriage. On the other hand, there are conflicts rules which permit the choice of any law supporting a "more favorable" result. Rules of this type call for an exhaustive comparison of all the legal systems to which they refer alternatively and do not allow a simple "yes" or "no" resolution in answer to the question which law should be applied. Kisch concluded that a comparison of substantive laws is impracticable in any case in which their contents are not com-

---

[177] The case arose in the early 1970's and concerns the question whether the defendant, a French mining industry, is liable to the Dutch plaintiffs, a group of nursery gardeners, for the damage resulting from defendant's pollution of the Rhine. After the European Court decided that the Court of Rotterdam had adjudicatory jurisdiction pursuant to a liberal interpretation of article 5(3) of the EEC Convention on Jurisdiction and Enforcement – European Court 30 November 1976, case 21/76, *NJ* 1977, 494 – the case drags on in the Dutch courts due to defendant's delaying tactics. The decision of the Rotterdam Court to uphold the parties' choice of law – Rb. Rotterdam 8 January 1979, *NJ* 1979, 119, *A.Ae.* 1980, p. 788 (note Jessurun d'Oliveira), *aff'd* Hof The Hague 10 September 1986, no. 65 R/84 (as yet unpublished) – confirmed the acceptance of party autonomy in Dutch tort choice of law.
[178] Apart from the special categories of products liability, environmental torts and public defamation, bilocal torts are subject to the provision of article 129(2), which calls for application of the *lex loci actus*, unless the defendant could foresee the harmful effect of his act in another state.
[179] Kisch (1959) p. 373 ff., criticizing article 9(3) of the Benelux Uniform Law (draft of 1951), which referred to the more favorable law in respect of child maintenance.

mensurable.[180] In other words, it is impossible to determine which of the eligible laws is the more favorable one if each of them strikes the balance between the interests of the parties in a different way.[181]

The objection is akin to the one raised against the "better law" idea in general, with the notable difference that *favor* constructions are embodied in conflicts rules in which either the result to be achieved or the beneficiaries of a comparative evaluation are specified. Analyzing the difference between the *favor* principle and the better law guideline, Professor Strikwerda seems to limit his definition of *favor* concepts to those of the first type, those which require allocation on a "yes" or "no" basis. In his opinion, all *favor*-inspired conflicts rules rest on a double abstraction: "In the first place, the question which set of rules is 'better' has been settled *a priori* by the conflicts rule." Second, pursuant to the *favor* principle, " ... the comparative evaluation of concurrent rules of substantive law is carried out without regard to the fairness of the ultimate result of allocation."[182] The better law theory, on the other hand, is said to be much less abstract, as it expects the court to render "super-value judgments" on what it deems to be the better law in the individual case, without the support of predetermined legislative preferences. To Strikwerda and other critics, this is also the theory's biggest flaw: judicial pronouncements on the quality of domestic or foreign legislation are based on supranational pretensions and may run counter to the forum's constitutional principles.[183]

---

180 *Ibid.* p. 390.
181 *Cf.* Morse (1982) p. 152; Von Overbeck (1982) p. 273; De Boer (1982) p. 49 ff. In countries in which conflicts law is applied *ex officio*, the question *who* is to decide which law is more favorable, the plaintiff or the court, turns on the formulation of the *favor*-inspired conflicts rule. The evaluation is delegated to the plaintiff if the rule allows him an option. Articles 5(2) and 6(1) of the EEC Convention on Contractual Obligations, on the other hand, leave it to the court to determine which law is more favorable to consumer or employee.
182 Strikwerda (1986) p. 17 ff. At this point it will be useful to know that the "better law" criterion is one of five "choice-influencing considerations" advocated by the American scholar Robert Leflar. The "Leflar methodology" will be discussed in greater detail in chapter 5.
183 Strikwerda (1986) p. 22. A similar argument is voiced by Baxter (1963) p. 5 ff.; Westbrook (1975) p. 461 (see also *infra* chapter 5, text accompanying note 42). Other scholars have objected to the lack of objective standards by which the quality of substantive law can be measured in an international context. *Cf.* Gutzwiller (1968) p. 188 ff.; Kegel (1974) p. 35 ff.; Neuhaus (1976) p. 86; Keller (1983) p. 178; Patocchi (1985) p. 245; *contra*: Zweigert (1973) p. 441.

Since *favor* constructions articulate the legislature's ideas on the choice of the better law, the courts are spared the dubious task of measuring substantive rules by a "better" or "worse" standard. In that respect, Strikwerda contends, the *favor* principle cannot be faulted. Not only is the legislature entitled to lay down choice of law criteria which, in the abstract, support application of what it deems to be the better law, it is also capable of determining which legal values, policies, or objectives ought to be promoted in choice of law. However, the preconceived better law notions embodied in *favor*-expressing conflicts rules are necessarily colored by forum bias, as legislatures are unlikely to disavow their own normative beliefs in deference to the values of foreign jurisdictions.[184]

I agree with Strikwerda that some forms of *favor*-defined allocation release the courts from the responsibility of passing the kind of "super-value judgments" required by an indeterminate better law approach. The *favor divortii* in the Dutch statute on divorce conflicts, the *favor legitimitatis* in the Swiss draft, the choice of law alternatives in the Hague Conventions on Maintenance Obligations, all of them express legislative "principles of preference" which can be implemented without a judicial assessment of the quality of substantive law, or even without judicial mediation at all. Other *favor* constructions, however, do not fit the mold of self-sufficient conflicts rules. Provisions such as articles 5(2) and 6(1) of the EEC Convention on Contractual Obligations, as well as those allowing one of the parties to claim application of the more favorable law, are conflicts rules embodying *favor* concepts which are less abstract than those defined by Strikwerda, yet traditional in expression and therefore not to be equated with the better law approach. Here, the question which law is deemed to be better has *not* been settled in advance: the conflicts rule just delegates the answer to the court or to the plaintiff, in either case compelling the parties to go to law.[185] If the more favorable law is to be ascertained by

---

184 Strikwerda (1986) p. 20, note 54 and accompanying text. The same argument applies, Strikwerda contends, to *favor* constructions in international conventions: as the contracting states are apt to hold compatible normative beliefs, the *favor* effect will be most apparent in case the law of a non-contracting state is involved.

185 Reese (1983-2) p. 290, prefers delegation of the choice to the plaintiff for practical reasons: not only does it relieve the court of the burden of investigating the content of all possibly applicable laws, it also eliminates the possibility that the court's choice of law decision will be subject to appeal.

the court, the *favor* construction comes close to the better law approach. Still, there is a difference. The *favor* solution suggests a choice of the *more favorable law* in the interest of the favored party, not an evaluation of the intrinsic quality of the rules involved. The *better law* theory, on the other hand, requires a normative evaluation of the conflicting laws, and subordinates the interests of the individual litigants to the choice of the better law *per se*.[186] In that respect, judicial determination of the the most favorable law is theoretically less objectionable than a quasi-supranational evaluation of the better law.

That leaves us with the *favor* solutions which delegate the choice of the more favorable law to one of the parties. Most of these options are to be found in tort choice of law, as expressions of the *favor laesi*. Characteristic of this particular *favor* concept is the tort victim's autonomy to choose from a limited range of alternatives the law which affords him the best protection. It does not require defendant's express or implicit assent, nor does it allow the court to interfere in any way with plaintiff's choice of law. This raises the practical question what ought to be done if the plaintiff refrains from designating the more favorable law. In any legal system in which the maxim "*da mihi facta, dabo tibi ius*" dominates civil proceedings, the conclusion seems inescapable that the court should then make the choice on plaintiff's behalf, unless one is willing to accept the anomalous proposition that the case should be dismissed because the party to be protected has posited insufficient "facts" to deserve any protection at all. As a matter of *principle*, I fail to see any justification for the excessive *favor laesi* these options embody. True, the victim in a products liability case will most often be the consumer, who may be assumed to be the weaker party against the more powerful manufacturer. Similarly, the victims of environmental torts will often come up against corporate en-

---

186 If this is a valid distinction, it has escaped Dr. Rest, who endorsed the choice of the more favorable law, particularly in the area of environmental torts, as "a means of strengthening the protection of the individual." Referring to Zweigert's three-layered choice of law system (*supra* note 139), he contends that "the judge ... should apply the better solution by following the more favourable law principle; the better solution will be the rule which most effectively protects the legal interest in question." Rest (1980) p. 79. In the German text (*ibid.* p. 42), the *bessere Regelung* is described as "*die Norm, die das betroffene Rechtsgut am wirksamsten schützt.*"

terprises for which litigation does not hold the same threat as it does for the individual.[187] In contracts, however, disparities in the parties' socio-economic circumstances have not been considered sufficient reason, obviously, to allow the weaker party to opt for the more favorable law.[188] Neither do other beneficiaries of *favor*-inspired choice of law enjoy the right to determine which law serves their interests best: no options are granted to the claimant in maintenance proceedings, or to the child seeking recognition of a family relationship, or to the parties in a divorce case.[189] Liberal though it may be, the *favor laesi* option is limited to specific torts or specific tort problems. In the Swiss draft, its availability depends on the type of tort and, implicitly, on the policies underlying the corresponding substantive law. In products liability cases and actions for defamation, a limited choice mainly purports to reinforce the position of the structurally weaker party, *viz.* the consumer against the manufacturer, the individual against the media. A slightly different function is said to be the "advancement of the law" (*Rechtsfortbildung*), predicated on the notion that a legislative endorsement of plaintiff's choice of the better

---

187 On the other hand, defective products, as well as environmental pollution, can cause damage on such a large scale that the individual victims are apt to pool their resources in a class action. Support from consumer organizations or environmental defense leagues, in some cases joined by a concerned governmental agency, may tip the procedural scales in favor of the plaintiffs.

188 In the absence of a choice by *both* parties, the employee will just have to accept the applicability of the law of his place of work, according to article 6(2a) of the EEC Convention on Contractual Obligations, or article 118(1) of the Swiss draft. Consumers will have to be content with the law of their habitual residence, pursuant to article 5(3) of the Convention or article 117(1) of the Swiss draft. The *favor* constructions in articles 5(2) and 6(1) of the Convention only apply in case of a contractual choice of law clause, and even then they leave the decision to the courts, not to the consumer or employee.

189 In these cases, the "better law" is predetermined by the conflicts rule; *supra* note 152 and text accompanying note 182. That is why it would not make much of a difference if the plaintiff were allowed to choose one of the prescribed alternatives. See, however, *supra* text following note 158, on the hierarchy of articles 4, 5 and 6 of the Hague Maintenance Convention 1973.
In the Netherlands, the statute on divorce conflicts (*supra* note 148) allows a choice between either Dutch law or the law of the parties' common nationality, against the law that would apply otherwise. Yet, this is not a true option, as it can be disputed by the other spouse.

law will lead to reform of the laws dismissed. This dubious choice of law objective,[190] the only one the draftsmen could think of to support the *favor laesi* in the provision on environmental torts, would justify an option in any area of choice of law.[191] While the policies behind the Swiss tort options may be debatable, particularly in contrast to the absence of any pro-plaintiff bias in the basic tort article,[192] the rationale of the German *favor laesi* is anybody's guess. The German approach to bilocal torts benefits any plaintiff "lucky" enough to be the victim of wrongful conduct causing damage across the border. If the solution must be taken as an expression of the *favor laesi*, it is hard to perceive why it is restricted to bilocal torts, and why the benefit of the more favorable law should not be granted to other tort victims as well.[193] This disparity suggests that simplification of the judicial task rather than a concern for the tort victim has motivated the German solution to bilocal torts.[194]

---

190 It is unlikely that such a policy would be pursued if the forum state were not convinced that its own substantive law is beyond criticism. Not only do I dislike the "holier-than-thou" attitude this policy reflects, I also wonder if its implementation by way of an option will have the desired effect. Furthermore, I believe that there are more appropriate means of persuading foreign legislatures to change their laws. *Cf.* De Boer (1982) p. 41 ff.

191 The *Schlussbericht* (*supra* note 104), p. 244 and 248, emphasizes the plaintiff-protective character of the provisions on products liability and defamation, adding the "advancement of the law" as an extra argument. The option in the provision on environmental torts is motivated by its *"rechtsfortbildende Funktion"* alone.

192 Article 129 is based on the traditional *lex loci delicti* principle, subject to exceptions in case the parties are domiciled in the same country or agreed on the applicability of Swiss law. *Cf.* Reese (1983-2) p. 292, suggesting that the draftsman of the Swiss tort articles might well "have gone further than he did in singling out torts where the choice-of-law rule should favor the plaintiff."

193 For a long time it has remained unclear whether the choice of the more favorable law could be left to the plaintiff or should be made by the court. *Cf.* Hohloch (1984) p. 105, note 275. According to Rest (1980) p. 22, p. 60, the plaintiff is no longer entitled to an option: "The *Bundesgerichtshof* has in recent times expressly made it plain that the German judge must always consider the foreign legal system *ex officio*."

194 *Cf.* Neuhaus (1976) p. 178, rejecting the notion that the German *favor laesi* is carried by sympathy for the victim, but accepting it here as an adequate solution ("for want of a better one") as it reflects, to some extent, the developments of the substantive law of torts. To Kegel (1985) p. 407, "rationalization is difficult", but sympathy for the victim is decisive. See also: Mühl (1982) p. 103, combining the plaintiff-protective and admonitory policies of modern tort law in explanation of the German solution.

My chief objection against the *favor laesi* – whether the choice of the more favorable law is made by the court or by the plaintiff – is the "bonus" it presents to the victim of a (particular kind of) multistate tort, in so far as it grants him the benefit of a better law than his own. I fail to see why the victim of an international tort should be entitled to a higher degree of protection than the claimant in a domestic case, who will have to be satisfied with the application of domestic law. I fail to see any justification for choice of law windfalls bestowed upon the consumer in a products liability case and denied to the victim of fraudulent misrepresentation. I fail to see a compelling reason why the plaintiff-protective policy of the substantive law of torts should be translated into a comparative allocation criterion which can be found in no other area of choice of law.[195] In my view, the *favor* constructions encountered in tort choice of law go way beyond their plaintiff-protective purpose. To implement a policy of shielding the innocent victim in multistate situations, I submit, it suffices to grant him the benefit of his domiciliary law, no more and no less. Compensation according to the delictual standards prevailing in the plaintiff's home state puts him in no better or worse position than the one he would have in a domestic case. Dependent on the happenstance of the law-fact pattern, the *favor laesi* could provide him with a more attractive alternative not available to domestic tort victims. I can think of no reason why such discrimination is more acceptable – even more commendable – in the area of multistate torts than it is, for instance, in the area of consumer contracts or maintenance, where protective policies are translated into a domiciliary standard and where a rule supporting equal rather than preferential treatment has been approved as a most suitable standard. Furthermore, why should a tort victim complain about the ap-

---

195 It will be recalled that no other *favor* construction permits the beneficiary to choose the "best" of the eligible laws. The alternatives in the Hague Convention on Maintenance Obligations 1973, as well as those expressing a *favor legitimitatis*, permit selection of the law which achieves the predetermined result. They do not support an approximate choice of the more favorable law. The same applies to the *favor divortii*. The predetermined result to be achieved here is divorce; there can be no question of a divorce which is "more favorable" to one of the parties. Even if the plaintiff is entitled to opt for a "favorable" divorce law, as he is in the Netherlands, the choice is subject to defendant's agreement.

plication of his home state law?[196] Since he did not expect to be wronged at all, he could not possibly have anticipated a windfall due to the *favor laesi* in choice of law. What he is likely to expect – after the fact, of course – is compensation according to standards which are considered normal in the social environment of his daily life, certainly nothing less, probably nothing more. To the extent that the *favor* alternatives permit the choice of any law which affords plaintiff the same degree of protection as he would normally expect, I have no objection against the outcome, but I do question the technique. Functional allocation would be a more equitable way, in my opinion, to buttress the position of the plaintiff in multistate tort litigation.

Said to be supported by policy considerations, *favor* constructions in choice of law do not necessarily further the objectives of the forum's substantive law. If, as the expression suggests, the *favor laesi* is rooted in the plaintiff-protective, and therefore compensatory policy of the forum's substantive tort law, one can hardly be satisfied with the finding that even the best law available affords the plaintiff less protection than he would be entitled to under either the law of his domicile or forum law.[197] If, on the other hand, the choice of the more favorable law should be viewed as an instrument of deterrence, it is equally possible that none of the eligible laws holds the defendant to more exacting standards than his own.[198] Unless the forum's conflicts law and its substantive law are totally disconnected, they are bound to be based on the same set of values. It must be assumed, therefore, that any policy underlying a *favor*-expressing conflicts rule is pursued in

---

196 These days, each major disaster which can be linked somehow to an American corporation (Lockheed, McDonnell-Douglas, Union Carbide and the like) seems to attract a host of American attorneys descending on potential plaintiffs anywhere in the world to lure them with the suggestion of limitless compensation by American standards. I have no doubt that the professional fervor of these international ambulance-chasers would rapidly disappear if compensation were to be measured by the foreign victim's domiciliary law.

197 For instance: if, in the area of products liability, the Swiss draft permits a choice between the law of defendant's principal place of business and the law of the place where the product was acquired, a Swiss plaintiff might still receive less compensation than he would get under Swiss law.

198 For instance: if the German solution to bilocal torts should be based on a policy of deterrence, the choice between the law of the place of conduct and the law of the place of injury does not guarantee application of the law which best serves that policy.

the forum's substantive law as well. It follows, then, that a *favor* construction which excludes *lex fori* from the range of eligible alternatives, as most of them do, does not guarantee achievement of the purpose it serves. A choice of law solution said to express a concern for the weak or the innocent is rather ambiguous, I feel, if the weak and the innocent are not allowed, on principle, to take advantage of the one law that may be presumed to afford them a most adequate protection.[199] Since the range of *favor* alternatives is usually limited to a lesser number of laws than that of the states involved, they are tainted by an inherent discrepancy between the substantive law values on which they rest and the abstract allocation formula in which they are expressed. Thus, the *favor laesi* may either fail to protect the tort victim at all, or it may gain him a windfall beyond the compensatory policy it is said to support. As a tool of deterrence it may or may not achieve its admonitory purpose, depending on the availability of a law less clement than defendant's own. If the results of *favor*-inspired allocation are dictated by chance rather than policy, we had better find a different way of attuning our choice of law criteria to the values we claim to support.

5 "Priority rules"

Beyond the bounds of tradition, no doubt, is a European conflicts doctrine which answers to a variety of unattractive names. Emphasizing its methodological aspects, the Germans call it the theory of the *Sonderanknüpfung*, which literally means "special allocation". The French generally refer to the *lois d'application immédiate* (rules of immediate application), an expression denoting the type of substan-

---

[199] While it is not always clear why forum law is not included in the range of *favor* alternatives, one reason may be that the forum state has wanted to strike a balance between choice of law objectives and substantive law values. In other words, it has created reasonable preconditions for the advancement of its domestic policy, but it does not insist on implementation absent a more or less substantive connection between the actual dispute and the forum state.

tive law rules deemed to deserve special treatment.[200] In the Netherlands, where the doctrine has found considerable favor with the courts, the term *voorrangsregels* ("priority rules") is used occasionally, but most Dutch writers seem to favor one of the French names.[201] Just for the sake of brevity, I prefer the expressions "special allocation" and "priority rules". While methodologically different from traditional jurisdiction-selection, the special allocation doctrine answers to the same result-oriented description that fits the other choice of law concepts discussed in this chapter. On the other hand, its technique is basically the same as that of interest analysis, to be surveyed and evaluated in the second and third parts of this book. Still, inasmuch as the doctrine is conceived as an exception to ordinary allocation, it differs from the integral approaches advocated in the United States. The peculiar problems inherent in the methodological bifurcation thus created warrant a brief discussion of this European choice of law phenomenon in the context of this chapter. Since there is a wealth of literature on the subject,[202] I will confine myself to a description of the theory's main features, a survey of its development in Dutch judicial practice, and an appraisal of its viability in European choice of law.

---

200 French and German authors would hesitate to equate the doctrine of the *lois d'application immédiate* with *Sonderanknüpfung*. While the former theory would give priority to rules of forum law only, most variants of the *Sonderanknüpfung* extend this choice of law privilege to foreign rules as well. *Cf.* Schurig (1981) p. 39 ff. See also: Schwander (1975) p. 199 ff. In my opinion, there are no fundamental differences between the *methodological* principles of the various doctrines, since they are all premised on the notion that application of the substantive rule in question depends on the interrelation between its content and the multistate circumstances. See also *infra*, notes 205–206 and accompanying text.

201 Schwander (1975) p. 248 ff., offers the following terminological catalogue: règles d'application immédiate, lois de police, normas de aplicación necesaria, norme sostanziali funzionalmente limitate, norme sostanziali spazialmente (de-)limitate, norme sostanziali autolimitate, norme con apposita sfera di efficacia, räumlich bedingte Sachnormen, international absolut zwingende Rechtssätze, spatially conditioning rules, peremptory norms, and more. Obviously, literary beauty was not what the authors of these phrases tried to achieve.

202 Suffice it to list some of the principal publications on the subject since 1950. In French: Neumayer (1957); Francescakis (1958); De Nova (1960); Toubiana (1972); Deby-Gérard (1973); Mayer (1981); Patocchi (1985). In German: Neumayer (1963); Vogel (1965); Schwander (1975); Bucher (1975). In English: Mann (1971) p. 157 ff.; Lipstein (1977); Van Hecke (1977); Schultsz (1983). In Dutch: De Winter (1964); Deelen (1965); Van Rooij (1976); Strikwerda (1978); Kotting (1984).

In 1966, the Dutch *Hoge Raad* ruled on the validity of a choice of law clause included in a bill of lading. Until then, the lower courts had held that such agreements were invalid in so far as they excluded the mandatory rules of the law that would apply without the parties' choice. In its celebrated *Alnati* decision,[203] the *Hoge Raad* overruled this narrow interpretation of the doctrine of party autonomy, holding that, in principle, Dutch private international law permits the parties to an international contract to substitute the law of their choice for the law that would otherwise apply, regardless of the mandatory or non-mandatory character of the rules of law thus displaced. Hidden in the paragraph on full freedom of choice, however, was a cryptic proviso hinting at possible statutory restraints on the principle of party autonomy. More explicit is a further passage in the opinion, in which it is suggested that *foreign* rules should be given priority over the law of the parties' choice, provided that foreign interests of such importance are at stake that they warrant displacement of the chosen law. From this circular description the commentators inferred that the *Hoge Raad* had endorsed the special allocation theory, as advocated in the Netherlands by De Winter and Deelen.[204] Principal characteristic of this approach is its substantive law perspective: contrary to the traditional allocation method, which ignores the contents of substantive law until the applicable law has been selected, the special allocation doctrine calls for an assessment of the spatial reach of any rule of substantive law which could be thought to claim application. To verify such claims, it will be necessary to examine the contents of the rule in question so as to determine whether its (extra)territorial scope has

---

[203] HR 13 May 1966, *NJ* 1967, 3 (note Hijmans van den Bergh). Law review comments: L.I. De Winter, *NJB* 1966, p. 933; A.V.M. Struycken, *Rev. Crit. d.i.p.* 1967, p. 522; J.E.J.Th. Deelen, *N.T.I.R.* 1968, p. 82; W.C.L. van der Grinten, *A.Ae.* 1968, p. 342. For further references, see Strikwerda (1978) p. 76, notes 363 and 367.

[204] De Winter (1940); *id.* 1964; Deelen (1965). *Cf.* Strikwerda (1978) p. 59 ff; p. 76 ff. In the 1969 version of the Benelux Uniform Law, *supra* note 54 and accompanying text, the *Alnati* ruling was codified in article 13(2), providing: "Where the contract is manifestly connected with a particular country, the intention of the parties shall not have the effect of excluding the provisions of the law of that country which, by reason of their special nature and subject-matter, exclude the application of any other law." *Cf.* Strikwerda (1978) p. 99 ff., discussing the many objections raised by Dutch commentators against this awkward and misleading formulation.

been demarcated by the legislature,[205] or, if not, to deduce its spatial dimensions from its rationale in relation to the actual circumstances. Apart from the obvious pertinence of geographical contacts, I fail to perceive any similarity between this rule-oriented approach and the one that selects the applicable law by matching the facts against a predetermined connecting factor. Therefore, I reject the proposition that the doctrine rests on essentially the same methodological premises as those underlying traditional allocation.[206]

Since none of the various doctrines of "spatially conditioned rules" was meant to replace the traditional choice of law technique, each of them has its own criteria to distinguish between substantive rules which are eligible for special treatment and those which are not. Thus, the French concept of *lois d'application immédiate*, as described by Francescakis, is limited to rules of *forum* law reflecting an element of

---

[205] In some publications on the special allocation phenomenon, the authors appear to discuss statutory delimitations of substantive law ("scope rules") instead of substantive rules claiming "immediate application." See: De Nova (1966); Kelly (1969). To prevent confusion, I suggest the following classification of the various kinds of rules in force in one legal system and to be used or considered in the choice of law process: (1) traditional allocation rules ("conflicts rules"); (2) statutory scope rules, demarcating the spatial reach of a specific rule or set of rules of the enacting state's substantive law; (3) mandatory rules of substantive law; (4) non-mandatory rules of substantive law. The rules we are concerned with in this section are part of the third category. A scope rule *as such* is not a "rule of immediate application"; it just contains legislative directions concerning the spatial reach of the rule of substantive domestic law to which it refers. The scope rule laid down in the American Export Administration Regulations, to be discussed *infra* note 225 and accompanying text, would be a good example if it did not refer to export restrictions enforced by penal sanctions.

[206] Toubiana (1972) p. 227 ff., p. 232; Deby-Gérard (1973) p. 55; Bucher (1975) p. 89 ff.; Patocchi (1985) p. 224. *Contra*: Strikwerda (1978) p. 98/99. Discussing articles 17(2) and 18(1) of the Swiss draft at the Freiburg colloquium, Professor Rigaux expressly mentioned (and criticized) the *dualité des méthodes* underlying the draft. On the one hand, there is Savigny's method, having as its point of departure the legal relationship it is meant to localize. On the other hand, articles 17(2) and 18(1) embody a bilateral version of the special allocation doctrine, a method that "starts with the rules in conflict and searches for the one that has the best title to application. This is the statutist method, the method of 'interest analysis'." F. Rigaux, *Freiburger Kolloquium über den schweizerischen Entwurf zu einem Bundesgesetz über das internationale Privatrecht*, Zürich, 1979, p. 82.

"state organization" (*organisation étatique*).[207] More liberal is the German theory which does not restrict the *Sonderanknüpfung* to rules of forum law and gradually expands its reach, it seems, to mandatory rules of a socio-economic nature.[208] In the Netherlands, a "priority rule" is, at least theoretically,[209] any mandatory rule of domestic or foreign, public or private law, meant to protect a significant political, cultural, social or economical interest of the enacting state. The one clear-cut conclusion that can be drawn from these descriptions reveals one of the doctrine's inherent flaws: conceived as a means to by-pass the ordinary process of jurisdiction-selection in case national interests are at stake, the theory calls for a distinction between rules that do and rules that do not claim priority, but it fails to define criteria which are sufficiently distinctive to determine the methodological choice its limited scope entails. While the difference between public and private law might have been an obvious dividing line to those following the Romanist tradition, it is a dubious standard in the modern welfare state where the protection of collective interests and the promotion of social justice account for all kinds of encroachments upon the autonomy of private law.[210] Francescakis' reference to the *organisation étatique* is no less vague than the allusion to a state's "considerable interests" by which the Dutch *Hoge Raad* delineated the new concept in the *Alnati* decision. Most authors seem to concur in the proposition that a rule of immediate application must be mandatory, as it is hard to conceive a non-mandatory rule claiming application on the strength of its underlying policy. However, if special allocation was meant to be an exceptional choice of law technique, it must be assumed that relatively few mandatory rules qualify for the special status the doctrine affords, which implies that most of them remain subject to the ordinary process of jurisdiction-selection. In the absence of more precise criteria, however, the courts are left to their own devices when it comes to a choice between the two methodological alternatives.

207 Francescakis (1968) p. 480 nos. 124 and 125; *id.* (1966) p. 12/13. *Contra*: Toubiana (1972) p. 233; Deby-Gérard (1973) p. 55, both being in favor of bilateralization. *Cf.* Strikwerda (1978) p. 92 ff.; p. 96 ff.
208 Schurig (1981) p. 41. See also: Strikwerda (1978) p. 90 ff., noting that the courts in Germany do not seem to support the doctrinal views in this respect.
209 *Cf.* the tentative descriptions by Van Rooij (1976) p. 139; Sauveplanne (1982) p. 34 ff.; *id.* (1986) p. 95; Kotting (1984) p. 119. See also the advisory opinion by Attorney-General Franx in *Saudi Independence*: HR 16 December 1983, *NJ* 1985, 311 at p. 1095.
210 *Cf.* Strikwerda (1978) p. 136 ff.; Rehbinder (1973) p. 154 ff.

Following the *Alnati* decision, in which the Dutch variant of the special allocation doctrine was approved but not applied, the first test case before the *Hoge Raad* concerned a contract of employment between American Express Inc., a New York corporation, and one of its European executives, a Dutchman by the name of Mackay, who had performed most of his duties in the Netherlands.[211] Central issue in this case was the applicability of a Dutch decree prohibiting the termination of employment contracts without prior leave of a governmental labor agency.[212] Mackay asserted that American Express should have obtained the Dutch permit when it decided to dismiss him. American Express, on the other hand, claimed that the contract was governed by New York law, and that no permit was required. The *Hoge Raad* affirmed the decisions of the courts below, holding that the applicability of the decree depended solely on the legislative objectives it embodied. Whether the employment contract as such would be governed by Dutch law or any other law was totally irrelevant: what mattered was the purpose of the rule in question, *viz*. the "regulation of socio-economic relations in the Netherlands, particularly the regulation of Dutch labor relations." Thus, ordinary jurisdiction-selection was subordinated to an *ad hoc* evaluation of a Dutch priority rule: since it was meant to control the employment situation in the Netherlands and since Mr. Mackay's dismissal affected that situation, application of the rule was warranted by its purpose, no matter which law governed the contract. Interestingly, the controversy between Mackay and American Express led to a second *Hoge Raad* decision, in which it was held that the employment contract was subject to Dutch law.[213] Characteristic of the special allocation doctrine, however, is the disconnection between the identification of a priority rule and the selection of

211 HR 8 January 1971, *NJ* 1971, 129 (*American Express v. Mackay I*).
212 Article 6 *Buitengewoon Besluit Arbeidsverhoudingen 1945* ("Special Decree on Labor Relations") or *B.B.A.*. The decree was issued shortly after the second world war and was meant, originally, to control Dutch labor relations in the interest of post-war reconstruction. For that reason, both employers and employees were required to obtain a permit to terminate the employment contract. Gradually, the decree became a dead letter in respect of the duty of the employee, turning more and more into an instrument to prevent unreasonable dismissal. In view of the changing character of the decree, it can be asked whether the *Hoge Raad* correctly assessed the legislative objective of article 6. *Cf.* Jessurun d' Oliveira (1976) p. 21; Van Maanen (1981) p. 810 ff.
213 HR 8 June 1973, *NJ* 1973, 400, note Hijmans van den Bergh (*American Express v. Mackay II*).

the *lex causae*. By itself, the fact that the contract is governed by Dutch law does not entail application of the *B.B.A.* In *Landhuis v. Nederlandse Zeeboormij.*, concerning another unauthorized dismissal, the Court of The Hague first ruled on the *B.B.A.*'s applicability, then on the question which law applied to the employment contract as such.[214] Although the contract was most closely connected with the Netherlands, justifying the choice of Dutch law as *lex causae*, the court saw no reason to hold the employer to the requirement of article 6. Mr. Landhuis had been living in Canada, the United States and Spain before he was employed by the Dutch defendant to work on an offshore drilling rig in Spain; after his dismissal, he returned to Canada. In other words: since the termination of the employment contract did not in any way affect labor relations in the Netherlands, there was no point in applying article 6. Even though the decree was part of the Dutch *lex causae*, it could not be said to claim immediate application.

These two cases involved a rule of (semi-)public law which was not difficult to classify as a potential *règle d'application immédiate*. More controversial are the decisions, mostly rendered by courts of first instance, in which the special allocation doctrine was employed to resolve typical private law issues. Most of them concern an accessory claim in divorce proceedings pertaining to the continued occupancy of the matrimonial home. Article 165 (book 1) of the Dutch Civil Code provides that spouses who have no title to stay in the matrimonial home following divorce – since ownership or tenancy is in the name of the other spouse – can obtain a judicial order permitting them to continue living there for a period not exceeding six months. In view of the housing shortage in the Netherlands, such an order affords a reprieve to the claimant or petitioner faced with the problem of finding another place to live. In the late 1970's, the courts of Amsterdam and Alkmaar were the first to abstract this question from the process of ordinary allocation, either by a blunt assertion that article 165 should be treated

---

214 Rb. The Hague 18 May 1972, *NJ* 1973, 259. As a rule, the autonomous applicability of the *B.B.A.* seems to depend on the question whether the employee is likely to look for a new job in the Netherlands or not. *Cf.* Rb. The Hague 17 December 1981, *NIPR* 1983, 333, *rev'd on other grounds* HR 15 April 1983, *NJ* 1983, 697 (note J.C. Schultsz). *Cf.* Van Maanen (1981) p. 796. See also: Rb. Alkmaar 17 February 1983, *NIPR* 1983, 226 and Rb. The Hague 13 April 1983, *NIPR* 1985, 155, both verifying whether the dismissed employee did or did not have recourse to Dutch social security, and using the answer as an additional argument for or against immediate application of the *B.B.A.*

as a priority rule,[215] or, more subtly, by an assessment of the relevant circumstances supporting application of the rule in the light of its policy.[216] Nowadays, these are standard decisions in Dutch divorce practice. Less convincing was a ruling of the Amsterdam court announcing that, "in view of their mandatory contents, the Dutch provisions concerning minors apply as *règles d'application immédiate*, even if the relevant conflicts rule would subject the legal relationship [between the child and his parents] to some other law than Dutch law."[217] This particular extension of the special allocation doctrine has not found much of an echo, not even within the Amsterdam court itself, but it illustrates the difficulties of the methodological bifurcation created by the *Alnati* decision. If the radius of the new doctrine is to be determined by such hazy notions as the "important social policy" or the "socio-economic relations" the rule is meant to protect, one is inclined to believe Professor Jessurun d'Oliveira's prediction that the use of the traditional method is bound to be relegated to that of a residuary conflicts solution, since *any* mandatory rule of private law could claim application on the strength of a compelling policy.[218]

215 Rb. Amsterdam 17 May 1978, *NJ* 1979, 562. See also: Rb. Roermond 10 November 1983, *NIPR* 1984, 259; Rb. Utrecht 14 March 1984, *NIPR* 1985, 101.
216 *E.g.* Rb. Alkmaar 20 December 1979, *Asser* 11.834: "In view of the fact that the matrimonial home is situated in the Netherlands, and both of the parties – since they are not likely to leave the Netherlands following their divorce – will have to depend on the Dutch housing market, only the Dutch legal order is concerned with the claim for continued occupancy of the matrimonial home ..."
217 Rb. Amsterdam 13 October 1975, *Asser* 9719. See also: Rb. Alkmaar 16 February 1984, *NIPR* 1984, 183, concerning the nullity of a bigamous marriage between a Spanish man and a Dutch woman. Article 33 (book 1) of the Dutch Civil Code, prohibiting such marriages, was said to claim application "in respect of any marriage concluded in the Netherlands, regardless of the nationalities of the parties."
218 Jessurun d'Oliveira (1975-1) p. 114; *id.* (1976) p. 21 ff: "But – and this consideration would seem to strike at the root of the conflicts rule – is it not true that 'governmental policies and interests' can also be identified in major parts of what is usually called pure private law?" *Cf.* Strikwerda (1978) p. 136 ff.
According to Professor Deelen the switch from traditional to special allocation depends on the mandatory character of the rule *in its international context*. This relative cogency should be measured along a sliding scale, indicating the intensity of the enacting state's interest in the actual dispute. Deelen (1965) p. 168/169; *id.* (1971) p. 73 ff.; (1980) p. 21. *Accord*: Haak (1984) p. 689. In my opinion, a distinction between international and domestic mandatory rules, dependent on an *ad hoc* correlation of the rule's policy with the actual circumstances, hardly solves the problem of methodological bifurcation. On any sliding scale, there is a stretch of indefiniteness between the upper and lower standards. Deelen's suggestion is of little help when it comes to narrowing this gap.

Dutch literature on the special allocation doctrine is characterized by its authors' liberal attitude towards foreign *règles d'application immédiate*. Whether such a rule belongs to the *lex causae* or not, its potential claim to priority should be evaluated by the same standard that is used to gauge the assertions of a domestic rule. On this score, the *Alnati* decision left no doubt: the Dutch variant of the special allocation doctrine is multilateral. It is surprising, therefore, that there is virtually no Dutch decision to date in which a foreign rule was allowed to take precedence over the *prima facie* applicable law. One *Hoge Raad* decision, turning on the applicability of the Surinam Currency Control Regulation, has given rise to much speculation on the question why the court refused to grant the Surinam rule the priority it unmistakably claimed. The case concerned a transaction between the brothers Sewrajsing, involving the sale of a house situated in the Netherlands Antilles. The buyer was a domiciliary of Surinam, the seller lived in Curaçao. Surinam law voided the purchase of foreign real estate if it entailed the unauthorized transfer of Surinam currency to creditors abroad. When the seller's wife invoked the nullity of the transaction, Surinam had just become an independent republic, no longer part of the Kingdom of the Netherlands. This implied that Surinam's interest in the application of its currency regulation qualified as the kind of foreign interest to which Dutch courts, pursuant to the *Alnati* decision, should defer if it is likely to be furthered by application of the foreign rule. While it could hardly be denied that the Surinam rule did claim application in the instant case,[219] the Appellate Court of the Netherlands Antilles and the *Hoge Raad* gave short shrift to the special allocation argument.[220] Quoting directly from the *Alnati* opinion, the Appellate Court suggested that Surinam's interest in controlling its monetary resources would not be furthered appreciably by the nullification of this particular contract, and that, therefore, the

---

219 In his advisory opinion, Attorney-General Van Oosten took a different view. To him, the spatial reach of the Surinam decree was territorial, precluding its application outside of Surinam. This narrow view denies the very purpose of currency regulations. *Cf.* Jessurun d'Oliveira, *A.Ae.* 1980, p. 257; Van Rooij, *Rev. Crit. d.i.p.* 1980, p. 76.

220 HR 12 January 1979, *NJ* 1980, 526, note J.C. Schultsz (*Sewrajsing Bros.*); *A.Ae.* 1980, p. 254 (note Jessurun d'Oliveira); *Rev. Crit. d.i.p.* 1980, p. 68 (note Van Rooij). For further comments, see: Schultsz (1983) p. 277 ff.; Haak (1984) p. 694; Kotting (1984) p. 120 ff. It should be noted that the *Hoge Raad* acted as the highest court of the Netherlands Antilles. Antillean law was therefore both *lex causae* and *lex fori*.

Antillean *lex causae* applied. The *Hoge Raad* affirmed. Virtually ignoring Surinam's interest, it held that "the considerable interest of the Netherlands Antilles in safeguarding the stability of transactions concerning real estate in the Netherlands Antilles does not allow the acceptance there of the nullity of the sale as prescribed by Surinam law." In my opinion, it is impossible to give a plausible explanation of this holding. Since the Surinam Currency Regulation 1947 was a carbon copy of the Dutch version dating from 1945, it could not be thought to violate Dutch public policy. Surinam's interest in its application was undeniable, and the Appellate Court's implication that the amount of Surinam currency involved was so insubstantial that its unauthorized transfer would not really hurt Surinam, is clearly erroneous. The only sound argument in justification of the decision would seem to be the proposition that a preponderant interest of the Netherlands Antilles tipped the scales against application of Surinam's priority rule.[221] However, the *Hoge Raad* was singularly nonspecific in its allusion to the Antillean interest in the stability of its real estate transactions, omitting any reference to a particular Antillean provision supporting that interest. In the light of *Sewrajsing*, the *Alnati* promise to consider foreign interests seems little more than a mirage.

Subsequent Dutch decisions on foreign priority rules are equally restrained. In *Hubers v. Kaak*, the issue turned on the applicability of a German decree prohibiting a tort action between fellow employees. The parties were Dutch citizens living in the Netherlands, travelling back and forth to Germany where they worked for a German employer. Due to defendant's negligence, plaintiffs were injured in Germany while riding home from work as passengers in defendant's car. Having received workmen's compensation under German law, they brought an action for additional damages. In first instance, Dutch law was held to apply and plaintiffs prevailed. On appeal, however, the Appellate Court of Arnhem referred to the policy behind the German decree, said to be the maintenance of peaceful working conditions (*Aufrechterhaltung des Betriebsfriedens*).[222] This rationale, the court opined, required its "immediate application" to any tort action be-

---

221 *Cf.* Jessurun d'Oliveira, *A.Ae.* 1980, p. 259; Van Rooij, *Rev. Crit. d.i.p.* 1980, p. 77; Kotting (1984) p. 121. Haak (1984) p. 694, seems to be convinced by this explanation: "I see no deviation from the *Alnati* doctrine."
222 Hof Arnhem 24 June 1980, *NJ* 1982, 263. The German decree at issue was the *Reichsversicherungsordnung*, more particularly §§ 636 and 637.

tween fellow employees working in Germany. Even if the extent of defendant's liability would be subject to Dutch law, the question whether he could be sued in tort by his fellow employees should be decided under the German decree, now that the occurrence could be characterized as a "traffic accident" and a "business accident" at the same time. The *Hoge Raad*, advised by Attorney-General Franx, did not see it that way and reversed.[223] Doubting that the court below had indeed resorted to the doctrine of the *règles d'application immédiate* instead of ordinary characterization, the Attorney-General disputed Germany's actual interest in the maintenance of peaceful working conditions in one of its corporations, considering that the real parties in interest in this case were the Dutch insurance companies rather than the litigating co-employees. The *Hoge Raad* agreed, emphasizing the tenuous link between the accident and the parties' employment situation: it had been a typical traffic accident, in no way connected with the operation of the employer's enterprise; it occurred when the parties were on their way home; no other (German?) fellow employees were involved; the parties had started working in Germany only a few days before the accident, and their employment ended immediately after the occurrence. Under these circumstances, the *Hoge Raad* concluded, the German rule did not take precedence over the applicable Dutch law. Since the opinion explicitly acknowledges the possibility of a different result if there were a closer relation between the accident and the employment situation, it would seem that the *Hoge Raad* is still willing to uphold the *Alnati* doctrine, even though it did not mention it expressly.[224]

---

223 HR 18 December 1981, *NJ* 1982, 263, note J.C. Schultsz, *Hubers v. Kaak*. *Cf.* Duintjer Tebbens, *W.P.N.R.* 1985, p. 421 ff.
224 It could be argued that the *Hoge Raad* did not hint at the special allocation doctrine at all. Its assessment of the connection between the accident and the parties' employment could be understood as part of the ordinary process of characterization and jurisdiction-selection. *Cf.* R. Kotting, *Med. N.V.I.R*, no. 90, 1985, p. 15/16. However, the opinion is couched in such ambiguous language that it supports both a neo-statutist and a traditional interpretation: having balanced Dutch against German contacts, the *Hoge Raad* concluded that, as such, the connection with Germany did not carry sufficient weight to compel the court "to accept that the *prima facie* applicable law would have to *yield* in this case to the *rules* of German law just mentioned." The words I emphasized do not sit well with the principles of neutral allocation. *Accord*: P. Vlas, *Med. N.V.I.R.*, no. 90, 1985, p. 13.

One more decision should be mentioned here, as an example of a case in which the interest of the foreign jurisdiction in the application of its substantive law can be inferred from a statutory scope rule. I am referring to the *Sensor* case, which centered on the applicability of the American Export Administration Regulations. These rules prohibited the unauthorized export of goods destined for the exploitation of natural resources in the Soviet Union. In June 1982, President Reagan expanded the prohibition to "non U.S. goods" exported by "any person subject to the jurisdiction of the United States," including any entity, wherever organized or doing business, which is "owned or controlled" by an American corporation, citizen, domiciliary, or resident.[225] Sensor B.V. was a Dutch company, established in the Netherlands, but ultimately controlled by a Texas corporation. Shortly before the Reagan embargo, it had entered into a contract with a French company, involving the sale of equipment destined for the Soviet Union. When Sensor refused to perform, on account of the American prohibition, the French buyer applied to the President of the Court of The Hague for an injunction.[226] In a rather confusing decision, the President first determined that Dutch law, more particularly the Dutch version of the Uniform Sales Act, applied to the contract as such. He then proceeded to examine whether the Export Administration Regulations, despite the applicability of Dutch law, provided Sensor with a valid excuse for its breach of contract. Inasmuch as the decree's spatial reach extended to a Dutch company controlled by an American corporation, its scope rule was deemed to violate the principles of public international law, and for that reason it was held that the American embargo would not be heeded. As if that were not enough, the opinion ends with an *obiter dictum* paraphrasing the *Alnati* doctrine: despite the applicability of Dutch law, the Dutch courts must sometimes give priority to foreign mandatory rules, depending on the circumstances. One of these circumstances is the condition that there be a substantial connection between the transaction at issue and the enacting state. In the instant case, the President held, this requirement had not been met.

---

225 Export Administration Regulations § 385.2(c).
226 Pres. Rb. The Hague 17 September 1982, *RvdW/KG* 1982, 167 (*Compagnie Européenne des Pétroles v. Sensor*). *Cf.* De Boer/Kotting (1982); *id.* (1984); Basedow (1983); Kotting (1984) p. 140 ff.

The decision illustrates some of the difficulties inherent in the ambiguous position of public law in the choice of law process. In the first place, since the Export Administration Regulations imposed penal rather than private law sanctions, its scope rule is in reality a rule of criminal (rather than private) international law. The substantive law for which it claims priority is criminal law, which implies that the claim is moot: as a rule, national courts will not impose foreign penal sanctions, least of all in civil proceedings. Thus, the Export Administration Regulations do not qualify as rules of immediate application; at best, they are *data* in the evaluation of the defense of *force majeure*.[227] In the second place, if the Regulations would have contained a private law sanction, let us say nullity of the contract, their scope rule would have been a clear indication of an American interest in their enforcement abroad. Such an interest must be taken for granted, I submit, whenever the foreign legislature has explicitly delineated the (extra)territorial reach of its substantive law.[228] Right or wrong, such rules demarcate the spatial dimensions of legislative concern: within the limits of the scope rule, the foreign substantive law was *meant* to protect the interest in question. Thus, the "substantial connection" requirement in the *Sensor* opinion, while (perhaps) justified in the absence of legislative delimitation, ignores the predetermined radius of foreign interests. This is not to say that the forum should meekly yield to any priority claim asserted by a foreign scope rule. As illustrated by *Sensor*, such a claim may be preposterous in the light of public international law or the forum's public policy. This may be sufficient reason to *ignore* the foreign state's interest, but not to *deny* its existence. Whether we approve or not, the foreign state does assert an interest in the application of its substantive law whenever its scope rule insists on it.

In the E.E.C. Convention on Contractual Obligations, the special allocation doctrine is embodied in article 7. Compared with its original text in the preliminary draft, the provision has been mitigated consid-

---

227 *Cf.* De Boer/Kotting (1982) p. 1179 ff; *id.* (1984) note 15 and accompanying text.
228 *Cf.* De Boer/Kotting (1982) p. 1185; *id.* (1984) note 23 and accompanying text. *Contra*: Basedow (1983) p. 158/159; Schultsz (1983) note 73 and accompanying text.

erably.[229] The final version no longer requires that priority rules "shall be taken into account", but suggests that "effect may be given" to them. To let the foreign rule take precedence over the *lex causae*, the court must check if, and to what extent, it would have priority status in the enacting state itself, it must consider the "nature and purpose" of the rule, and it must envision the consequences of its application and non-application. If all these requirements were not enough to discourage any consideration of third-country mandatory rules, article 7 also stipulates "a close connection".[230] Formulated more clearly than its counterpart in the E.E.C. Convention, article 18 of the Swiss draft contains similar conditions for situations in which "legitimate and manifestly preponderant interests" claim application of a foreign rule. Here, too, the court is asked to consider the purpose of the rule and the consequences of its application, and to establish that there is a "sufficiently close connection" between the enacting state and the case at issue.[231] If these combined requirements are meant to ensure a proper identification of the foreign state's interest, I have nothing against them, considering that Currie described interests as "the product of (a) a governmental policy and (b) the concurrent existence of an appropriate relationship between the state having the policy and the transaction, the parties, or the litigation."[232] What bothers me,

229 Moreover, as provided by article 22 in the Convention's definitive version, any contracting state may reserve the right not to apply article 7(1), covering foreign priority rules. In the report by Mario Giuliano and Paul Lagarde, reprinted in *Contract Conflicts, The E.E.C. Convention on the Law Applicable to Contractual Obligations, A Comparative Study* (ed. P.M. North), p. 355 ff., the reservation is explained by "the novelty of the provision and the fear of the uncertainty to which it could give rise, [which] have led some delegates to ask that a reservation may be entered." *Ibid.* p. 382.
230 In the preliminary draft, *a* connection was deemed sufficient. This was first changed to "significant connection", later to "close connection". *Cf.* Philip (1982) p. 103. See also: Drobnig (1975) p. 83 ff., submitting "that only a *close* connection of the legal relationship with the other country would justify the intervention of the latter's mandatory rules."
231 The same requirement is laid down in some of the recent Conventions of the Hague Conference on Private International Law featuring a provision on foreign mandatory rules. See *e.g.* article 16 of the Convention on the Law Applicable to Agency 1978; article 16 of the Convention on the Law Applicable to Trusts and Their Recognition 1984.
232 Currie (1963-1) p. 621. *Cf.* Leflar (1977-1) p. 210: "A governmental interest in a choice of law case, in its simpler sense, is discoverable by putting together (a) the reasons supporting the rule of law in question, and (b) the state's factual contacts with a case, or the issue in a case, to see if they match."

however, is a sneaking suspicion that these European demands for a "close connection" have less to do with interest *identification* than with interest-*weighing*. Why does the Swiss draft postulate a "legitimate, manifestly preponderant interest" as well as a "sufficiently close connection"? Why did the draftsmen of the E.E.C. Convention find it "essential that there be a genuine connection with the other country," and why is it that "a merely vague connection is not adequate"?[233] Why was a "substantial connection" required in the *Sensor* case, despite the interest the United States unmistakably asserted in the application of its Export Administration Regulations? If the demand for a connection between the enacting state and the actual circumstances is meant to establish the *existence* of an interest, it is clearly redundant: to deserve priority status, a mandatory rule must satisfy a number of other conditions, pertaining to its purpose and the consequences of its application, specifically meant to identify the enacting state's actual interest. Besides, without any connection there can be no interest; the fact that there is an interest implies that there is also a connection. Thus, there must be another motive for this "redundant" condition. As indicated by the adjectives "close", "sufficient", "substantial" and the like, the genuine link requirement does not prescribe that a foreign interest should be *present*, but that it should be *strong enough* to warrant displacement of the applicable law. In other words, in the absence of a "sufficient connection", it must be assumed that the other state has an "insufficient interest" in the application of its mandatory rule, and vice versa. This implies that the interest of the enacting state is not *established by* that state's connection to the actual circumstances, but *weighed according to* the closeness of the connection.[234]

I would not have dwelled on what may seem a mere quibble, if the "substantial connection" requirement had not exposed the am-

---

233 Mario Giuliano and Paul Lagarde, Report on the Convention on the Law Applicable to Contractual Obligations, *supra* note 229, p. 381.
234 In this perspective, the decisions by the Dutch *Hoge Raad* in both *Sewrajsing*, *supra* note 220, and *Hubers v. Kaak*, *supra* note 223, could be said to be in tune with the special allocation doctrine. *Cf.* Van Rooij, *Rev. Crit. d.i.p.* 1980, p. 78: drawing a parallel between the "substantial connection" requirement and the relativity concept in the doctrine of public policy (*infra* chapter 2, section 3), he suggests that the clue to *Sewrajsing* can be found in the weak link the transaction at issue had with Surinam. "Only, the *Hoge Raad* keeps absolute silence on this point." In my opinion, the fact that the buyer was domiciled in Surinam and had to transfer the purchase price from Surinam constituted anything but a weak link.

bivalence of the special allocation doctrine as its most serious flaw. On the one hand, it recognizes that a specific kind of rule should be allowed to take precedence over the *lex causae*, provided that such priority is warranted by an actual interest of the enacting state. On the other hand, it recognizes the primary applicability of the *lex causae*, and does not allow its displacement by a priority rule until the enacting state's legitimate interest in its application has been measured against the weight of factual connections. In other words, the special allocation doctrine aspires to be an interest-oriented approach, but, since it is grafted upon the method of impartial jurisdiction-selection, it actually induces a weighing process between interests and contacts.[235] Wavering between jurisdiction-selection and interest analysis, it balances an asserted interest of one state against an impassive involvement of another state.[236] Since it does not ask if any interests of the *lex causae* state will be furthered by application of its law, its purported yardstick is indistinctive, its "substantial connection" criterion nothing but an empty phrase. Despite their hairsplitting formulation, the various legislative provisions on foreign mandatory rules say little more than that the courts, when considering a foreign rule's priority claim, should use their own discretion and exercise a maximum of restraint.[237] If the Dutch experiments with foreign priority rules are any indication, it must be feared that the development of the bilateral variant of the special allocation doctrine, from its promising inception

---

235 As we shall see, *infra* chapter 4, section 4(a), American courts practicing interest analysis sometimes resort to interest-weighing to solve true conflicts. While this approach has been criticized on several grounds, it measures the strength of one interest against another, and cannot be faulted for comparing values which are incomparable *per se*.

236 *Cf.* Strikwerda (1978) p. 101 ff. and p. 110: "On the one hand, [the proponents of the 'close connection' requirement] are willing to endorse the claim to application of a semi-public law precept outside of the *lex causae*, while, on the other hand, they hasten to minimize this concession by imposing a restriction derived from the Savignian choice of law model, a restriction which, on closer inspection, turns out to be arbitrary and redundant."

237 By contrast, the provisions on the priority of the *forum*'s mandatory rules are couched in much less stringent language. Article 7(2) of the E.E.C. Convention does not impose any restrictions on the precedence of forum rules: "Nothing in this Convention shall restrict the application of the rules of the law of the forum in a situation where they are mandatory irrespective of the law otherwise applicable to the contract." Similarly, article 17 of the Swiss draft affords priority to "the rules of Swiss law which, by reason of their particular purpose, claim application irrespective of the designated law." No (close or sufficient) connection is required.

in *Alnati* to its controversial inclusion in the E.E.C. Convention, has come to a standstill. This apprehension is born out by the European doubts and reservations on the wording and adoption of article 7(1), which seems to be destined to become a typical example of a dead letter.

Chapter 2

The "Pervasive Problems" of Conflicts Law Revisited

"An important test of the desirability of any proposed method of conflict of laws analysis is the degree to which it eliminates or provides satisfactory answers to the 'pervasive problems' of the conflict of laws."[1] Fascination with the mind-numbing complexities of traditional conflicts law, characteristic of conflicts theory in the first half of this century, has gradually ebbed away. Nowadays the very premises and methods of conflicts law are scrutinized, and less attention is paid to the trappings of a method whose objectives and mode are no longer taken for granted. Nevertheless, a few of these "technical problems"[2] are still exhaustively treated in the textbooks on the law of conflicts. Not peculiar to the conflicts law of any particular country, they are "pervasive" in the sense that they belong to the general part of conflicts law and cannot be classified as typical of any of its categories. The four major topics in this notorious batch are in my opinion: characterization, renvoi, public policy, and the status of foreign law.

It is the thesis of this chapter that under a policy-oriented approach to torts choice of law, characterization and renvoi could be dispensed with altogether, whereas the role of public policy could be reduced to virtual non-existence. I submit that these doctrines are peculiar to the traditional method of jurisdiction-selection in which, paradoxically, they have become tools to correct the unhappy results of the very conceptualism that produced them. Even though I am convinced that

---

1 Weintraub (1968) p. 839 = (1980) p. 89. See also: Scoles/Weintraub (1972) chapter 3.
2 Cramton/Currie/Kay (1981) p. 379 ff.

the jurisdiction-selecting method is much less indifferent, at least in practical application, to the interests of the parties and the jurisdictions involved than it is said to be, its technique is definitely not designed to induce a comparative evaluation of substantive law solutions. Apparently, the doctrinal attempts to justify this method's possibly unjust results (by ranking so-called "conflicts justice"[3] as the supreme interest of conflicts law, for instance) have never quite succeeded in pacifying judicial practice, as can be inferred from the clever ways the courts have found to dodge the dictates of mechanistic choice of law rules. Fittingly called "escape devices," the doctrines of characterization, renvoi, and public policy have proved particularly helpful in covering up choice of law decisions a strict application of the traditional method[4] would not have allowed. Supporting the shift from a preconceived nexus to the actual center of gravity, they might even conceal "an unconscious judgment as to the relative worth and importance of competing legislative grounds."[5]

Functional and result-selective approaches to the choice of law problem being openly concerned with policies and interests, there is no need, it would seem, for manipulative devices to sway the choice of the applicable rule of law, or to preclude its application. The friction between "conflicts justice" and substantive law justice, produced by over-abstract choice of law rules and assuaged by means of a conscious

---

3 Since 1953, the German conflicts authority Professor Gerhard Kegel has advocated a distinction between "substantive justice" and "conflicts justice" as the respective goals of substantive law and conflicts law. While substantive law aims at solutions which are considered the most "just" in a direct, material sense, conflicts law is not supposed to achieve the best material result (by choosing *das sachlich beste Recht*). Instead it is meant to further "conflicts justice" by designating the "spatially most appropriate law" (*das räumlich beste Recht*). Kegel (1953) p. 259 ff.; *id.* (1964) p. 184 ff.; *id.* (1985) p. 71 ff. and p. 70/71 for further references. See also: Dubbink (1973, p. 63 ff. *Contra:* Juenger (1982) p. 11: " ... [some scholars] believe the conflict of laws to exist in a rarefied atmosphere of 'conflicts justice,' far removed from the concerns of ordinary mortals."
4 The more flexible contacts-grouping approach, which is one of the varieties of jurisdiction-selection, is usually capable of designating the "proper law" without the help of these gimmicks, but might still depend on them for the purpose of achieving "proper results", that is: results that satisfy the court's notions of substantive rather than conflicts justice. But then, to this end a selective emphasis on certain contacts appears to be just as effective, so the stratagems of traditional conflicts law might no longer be needed here. *Cf. supra* chapter 1, section 2.
5 Hancock (1961) p. 366.

misapplication of general principles, is not likely to occur under an approach that measures possibly competing rules of law by their respective claims to application and selects as the "proper law" the law of the jurisdiction whose interests are at stake.[6] If the "Sitz" or "center of gravity" metaphor of traditional conflicts law could be adapted for the imagery of functional approaches, it would stand for the jurisdiction with the most cogent claim on the application of its rule. Whatever objections may be raised against such methods, in order to achieve "justice in the individual case" the rule-selecting techniques should have no need for the artful pretexts that the courts have been able to find in the general part of conflicts law. Whether judicial practice bears out this contention will be examined in this chapter.

If characterization, renvoi and public policy can be ruled out as escape devices, as pervasive problems of the conflict of laws they still deserve an answer. It will be seen that some proponents of policy-oriented approaches have tried to give new meaning to characterization and renvoi, but in my opinion modern choice of law theory can well do without the questionable services these timeworn doctrines could possibly render. As to public policy, that most pliable and elusive device of the law of conflicts is hardly ever used for the purpose it is meant to serve, which is the displacement of a foreign rule of law on account of its inferior quality. Irrespective of the preferred choice of law approach, public policy ought to retain precisely that function. As it is, judicial indignation against "pernicious and detestable"[7] foreign law very seldom rings true. This implies that public policy is frequently invoked for the wrong purpose, so it could be dispensed with if that purpose were to be achieved by different means, in a forthright manner. Yet, the doctrine cannot be discarded altogether, as public policy is still the proper tool for an assessment of the quality of foreign law. Contrary to characterization and renvoi, I submit, public policy cannot be eliminated from the general part of policy-oriented conflicts law, for it is a necessary last resort under any approach allowing a foreign rule of law to decide the issue. In torts choice of law, however, the quality of foreign law is seldom so unsavory as to warrant public policy's intervention. Its proper function in this field should therefore remain largely theoretical.

6 True conflicts and unprovided-for cases do give rise to complications, however. See *infra* chapter 4, sections 4 and 3 respectively.
7 Goodrich (1938) p. 33/34; *infra* note 188.

The last topic in Weintraub's discussion of pervasive problems is notice and proof of foreign law. At first blush, one would think that methodological preferences have no bearing on this particular problem. In other words, the answer to the question whether the content of foreign law should be determined by the court or be proved by the parties does not depend, it would seem, on the prevailing choice of law method. Considering that the subject is hardly discussed in the literature on policy-oriented choice of law – even Weintraub gave it a cursory treatment – I was inclined to ignore it altogether. On reflection, however, I realized that the answer to this problem is vital to the credibility of any choice of law approach that is based on an assessment of the policies of substantive law and an evaluation of possible interests. Although the doctrine of notice and proof of foreign law differs from characterization, renvoi and public policy in that it is a procedural point of departure and hardly serves as a manipulative device, it will be included in this chapter as a truly pervasive problem.

1 Characterization

The first of the "pervasive problems" encountered in the choice of law process is characterization. The area of torts choice of law is no exception. Theoretically, a real characterization dilemma is presented by the traditional conflicts rule that submits the question whether a tort has been committed to the *lex loci delicti*. Especially older writers[8] have theorized on the relation characterization establishes between choice of law concepts and those of substantive law. Their thoughts on the subject can be summarized as follows. Before the relevant conflicts rule can be selected, the problem presented by a certain fact pattern must be characterized: the actual dispute is shaped into a legal abstraction as embodied in one of the forum's conflicts rules, so as to permit subsumption. Essentially, characterization is a process of juridification, which in choice of law can be performed in a number of ways, since reference can be made to more than one set of rules. Possible modes of characterization are: (1) with reference to the concepts of the substantive law of the forum; (2) with reference to those of the

---

8 Notably Kahn (1891); *id.* (1896); Bartin (1897); Lorenzen (1947-2); Falconbridge (1937); Robertson (1940). Further references in Leflar (1977-1) p. 174, note 2.

substantive law designated by the forum's conflicts rule; or (3) with reference to concepts of the forum's conflicts law itself.[9] The first approach, if applied to the letter of forum law, could lead to cumulation,[10] since a fact pattern is first subjected to forum law and subsequently to the applicable law designated by the conflicts rule for which the fact pattern has been fitted. For the decision whether a seemingly tortious occurrence may properly be labeled a (multistate) tort the facts are subjected to the notions of the forum's substantive law of torts, and if the forum's tort label can be affixed to the occurrence, the *lex loci delicti* rule may put it to the test of a foreign substantive law of torts. The Dutch writer Dubbink has summed up the problem quite succinctly: in this theory of characterization, "the lex loci delicti can only be applied if its definition of a tort is covered by that of the lex fori."[11] If cumulation of applicable laws is rejected, which it is if choice of law focuses on the *lex loci delicti* alone, this method of characterization cannot be right. The second approach, characterization by reference to the legal concepts of the *lex causae* is tainted by its underlying circular reasoning: characterization is made dependent on the substantive law designated by one of the forum's conflicts rules, whereas the selection of this conflicts rule depends on characterization. The only way out of this maze seems to be the third approach which, scholarly altercations notwithstanding, sensible courts have followed all along. This mode of characterization makes use of rather loose choice of law headings ranging over a wider variety of fact patterns than those covered by the forum's substantive law concepts. In this approach, the conflicts rules of the forum are construed independently from both the forum's substantive law and the *lex causae*. A "tort" in the *lex loci*

---

9 To the extent that the latter approach interprets choice of law concepts on a comparative basis, it comes close to Rabel's theory of "comparative characterization." One of Rabel's major contributions to conflicts theory was his proposition that "[i]t is not the forum's substantive law, but its conflicts law which determines the characterization." In his view, the scope of choice of law rules should be construed with the help of comparative law, which could point out common "legal phenomena" regardless of their denomination. Rabel (1931); *id.* (1958) p. 54 ff. See also: Kropholler (1975) p. 329 ff.; Neuhaus (1976) p. 130 ff.; Kegel (1985) p. 193 ff.

10 Not unlike the results of English torts choice of law: Dicey/Morris (1980) vol. 2, p. 927 ff. See, however, Dubbink (1947) p. 78, pointing out that characterization *lege fori* always entails cumulation if the conflicts rule refers to foreign law, while the English cumulation rule only applies to torts. In other words, the two forms of cumulation are totally unrelated.

11 Dubbink (1947) p. 63.

delicti rule is a conflicts law concept not covered by any substantive law definition. Whether a fact pattern may be labeled a tort for choice of law purposes is largely answered by elimination of other possibilities, resulting in the conclusion that the occurrence is a "tort-something" rather than a "contract-something" or a "family relationship-something".[12] The presence of relatively few conflicts rules addressing fairly broad categories of fact patterns facilitates proper characterization, although it must be conceded that there are cases in which more than one conflicts rule is eligible for application.[13] On the whole, however, characterization has proved to be an academic rather than a practical problem: the less choice of law categories are created, the less confusion will arise about the scope of conflicts rules. Furthermore, as Dubbink has pointed out, even characterization with reference to the forum's substantive tort definition would not cause any real difficulty if the forum's concept of a tort is wider than that of the *lex causae*.[14] Since the Dutch definition of a tort is loose enough to cover a very extensive range of conduct resulting in damages,[15] the method of characterization has hardly been at issue in the Dutch case law on multistate torts.

---

12 Sedler (1970) p. 48 ff. In the EEC Convention on Judicial Jurisdiction and the Recognition and Enforcement of Foreign Judgments, article 5, paragraph 3, a tort is neutrally described as a "damage-producing fact" (*fait dommageable*) thus covering the Dutch "onrechtmatige daad", the German "unerlaubte Handlung", the French "acte illicite", the English "tort" etcetera.
13 In the United States, the interspousal or parental immunity issue, for instance, gave rise to the precarious choice between family law and tort law. See *e.g. Algie v. Algie* 261 S.C. 103, 198 S.E.2d 529 (1973): matter of tort law; *Koplik v. C.P. Trucking Corporation* 37 N.J. 1, 141 A.2d 34 (1958): matter of family law. Even more difficult proved the characterization problem in case of a combined contractual and delictual relationship between the parties, particularly in workmen's compensation cases: *Witherspoon v. Salm* 251 Ind. 575, 243 N.E.2d 876 (1969): matter of contract law; *Masera v. Trans World Airlines, Inc.* 492 F.Supp. 950 (1980): matter of tort law. In the Netherlands, the *Saudi Independence* case, *infra* note 23 and accompanying text, posed the question whether the (un)lawfulness of a strike should be characterized as a matter of contract, one of tort, or as a problem *sui generis*.
14 Dubbink (1947) p. 77/78.
15 The concept of tort, as embodied in article 1401 of the Dutch Civil Code, was restated by the *Hoge Raad* in its landmark decision *Lindenbaum v. Cohen* (HR 31 January 1919, *NJ* 1919, p. 161, *W.* 10365): "A tort should be understood as any act or omission that either infringes upon someone else's right, or contravenes the actor's legal duty, or violates either good morals or the duty of care which befits in social intercourse in respect of someone else's person or property."

In recent times, the doctrinal debate on characterization has all but subsided, as have most discussions on the tenets of traditional choice of law, such as renvoi, the incidental question, or *conflits mobiles*. Yet, an actual problem is posed by issue-splitting, or *dépeçage*. This is illustrated by the dichotomy introduced by article 14 of the Benelux Uniform Law on Private International Law.[16] This provision distinguished between the question whether there is wrongful conduct ("unlawfulness"), to be governed by the law of the place of the wrong, and on the other hand all sequential tort issues, such as (vicarious) liability, the measure of damages, capacity to sue, prescription or limitation, etcetera, to be decided by the proper law of the tort. Phrased as a "legal sphere" exception to the *lex loci delicti* rule in the first paragraph of article 14, the second paragraph served in practice to support the application of the law of the parties' common domicile, sometimes reinforced by references to other factors pointing to the same law, such as their nationality, the place of registration of their vehicle(s), or the business seat of their insurance company.

The distinction in article 14 between the issue of "unlawfulness" and all remaining issues has revived the characterization dilemma, as it calls for a precise determination of issues in those cases in which the parties are domiciled in the same state. This is especially difficult if the dispute centers around the question whether defendant's conduct amounts to a tort. For instance: is *fault* a component of "unlawfulness," to be measured against the standards of the *lex loci delicti*, or should it be regarded as one of the issues governed by the parties' domiciliary law? Two Dutch cases are in direct contrast in this respect. In the first one,[17] a Dutch domiciliary driving at night through a Belgian enclave in the south of Holland collided with a tree which had fallen across the road. Although the tree had grown on Belgian territory and was Belgian public property, Dutch regional authorities were responsible for the maintenance of the road and its adjoining trees. They were sued by the owner of the damaged car, a Dutch corporation. Deciding that the proper law of the tort was Dutch law since both plaintiff and defendant were Dutch corporate entities established in the Netherlands, whereas the car was registered and insured in the Netherlands as well, the court nevertheless held that the issue of fault

---

16 On the ill-fated history of this Benelux project, see *supra* chapter 1, section 2.
17 Rb. 's-Hertogenbosch 8 February 1980, *NJ* 1981, 86 (note J.C. Schultsz).

as a possible prerequisite for liability was governed by the Belgian *lex loci delicti*. The second case[18] concerned the fault of a minor who had wrecked his father's car while driving it without his consent in Spain. Having compensated the father for his damages, the insurance company sued the son by virtue of subrogation. All parties were domiciled in the Netherlands. As to the question whether the son's conduct constituted a tort, Spanish law applied. But the matter of fault, as a prerequisite for the son's liability, was relegated to Dutch law as the law most closely connected. The two cases demonstrate the hazards of issue-splitting along the hazy delineations of "unlawfulness". In the Dutch substantive law of torts, this concept covers both the notion of a tort as such ("unlawful act") and one of its components (unlawfulness, fault, causality and damage being the principal ones). As a choice of law concept, it has such a strong substantive law connotation that cumulation of the applicable law and *lex fori* is hard to avoid, which brings us back to the rejected method of characterization referring to the forum's substantive law concepts.

The problem the drafters of article 14 tried to escape by isolating the "unlawfulness" issue and putting it to an exclusive *lex loci delicti* test was caused by the possible displacement of local rules of conduct. Without a special *lex loci* provision, they must have thought, the "legal sphere" criterion could deprive the victim of a cause of action, or the tort-feasor of a defense, which they would have had under the law of the place of wrong. For instance: two Dutch automobile drivers sue each other in the Netherlands for damages arising from a frontal collision in England. The accident was caused by defendant who had forgotten he had left the continent and continued to drive on the right-hand side of the road. Under the "legal sphere" approach of article 14, the proper law of the tort would be Dutch law, and, according to Dutch traffic regulations, it would be the plaintiff rather than defendant who committed the tort by driving on the left. To prevent such absurdities, the Benelux Uniform Law retained *lex loci delicti* for the "unlawfulness" issue. A better way to take account of local standards of conduct, however, is shown in the Hague Convention on the Law Applicable to Traffic Accidents. The "basis and extent of liability" is governed by whatever applicable law, not necessarily the law of the place of the wrong, but "in determining liability account shall be taken

18 Rb. Alkmaar 17 April 1980, no. 245/1979, *Asser* 11973.

of rules relating to the control and safety of traffic which were in force at the place and time of the accident."[19] These rules come into play as local data,[20] with resort to factual information embodied in local rules of conduct. There will be much less confusion as to the question what exactly constitutes an "unlawful act", and which prerequisites for a "tort" must be taken from what law. Because the Benelux Uniform Law has never been enacted, and the Dutch courts have been free to retain from its provisions those elements that have proved serviceable, it may be expected that the dichotomy of article 14 will fade into legal history and cease to be a problem. Commenting on the case of the fallen tree, the conflicts law annotator of the Dutch Law Reports, Professor J.C. Schultsz, has renounced the dichotomy as obsolete, since most case law based on article 14 was concerned with traffic accidents, and in this area the solution of article 14 was superseded by the Hague Convention with its much less ambiguous approach.[21]

Even though the dichotomy of article 14 has required the Dutch courts to differentiate between precariously close issues, at least if the proper law of the tort did not coincide with the *lex loci delicti*, it may have alleviated the characterization problem at the same time. Because the most significant relationship principle of paragraph 2 was taken to support the application of the law of the parties' common domicile, the courts when deciding tort actions between parties related to one another by contractual or family ties may have been spared the need to resort to manipulative characterization. In many of these cases, the parties were domiciled in the same country, so a tort characterization would produce the same outcome as a characterization in contract or family law, for in these areas, too, domicile is one of the predominant connecting factors. A case involving a Dutch domiciliary who as a guest in her friend's car was injured in France could therefore be classified as tortious and still be governed by Dutch law, since the defendant friend had her home in the Netherlands as well. In an attempt to

---

19 Article 7. A similar provision is included in the Hague Convention on the Law Applicable to Products Liability, article 9.
20 The concept of "nonchoice" by reference to local or moral data has been advocated most eloquently by Ehrenzweig (1967-1) p. 77 ff., p. 83 ff. The same result could be achieved by treating local rules of conduct or safety as *règles d'application immédiate*; see *supra* chapter 1, section 5.
21 Annotation to Rb. 's-Hertogenbosch 8 February 1980, *NJ* 1981, 86, *supra* note 17 and accompanying text.

reinforce its decision,[22] the court did mention the Dutch-based contract between the two women in respect of their vacation trip, but it emphasized the tort features of the case and proceeded to apply the proper law of the tort as provided in article 14, paragraph 2. But for paragraph 2, a contractual characterization might have been the only way to reach the obvious result.

Yet, result-selective characterization of cases *prima facie* sounding in tort is not unknown in the Netherlands. In a recent case concerning a strike aboard a Saudi Arabian vessel when it happened to be docked in a Dutch harbor, the issue whether the strike was lawful or not was submitted to Philippine labor law, this being the law the strikers and their (Greek) employer had agreed upon in their employment contracts.[23] As I see it, the Appellate Court of The Hague characterized the problem before it as one of contract. The court started out by stating that international strikes should be regarded as labor disputes. If they take place on board a sea-going vessel they are governed, as a rule, by the law of the flag, in this case Saudi Arabian law. However, as the parties had actually chosen Philippine law to apply to their contractual relationship, the law of the flag was displaced. This is an odd conclusion insofar as the Saudi Arabian ship-owners and the Greek employer brought their action not only against the Philippine employees of the latter but also against the Dutch branch of an international labor union. While it had incited the strike, it could hardly be said to be in any contractual relationship with any of the plaintiffs. Although it is generally hard to tell why a case is characterized differently from what it appears to be at first sight, I cannot help but feel that here the court refused to label the case unequivocally[24] as one

---

22 Hof The Hague 10 June 1955, *NJ* 1955, 615, *De Beer v. De Hondt*. See also: *supra* chapter 1, section 2, text accompanying note 70.

23 Hof The Hague 23 April 1982, *S&S* 1982, no. 79, *aff'd* HR 16 December 1983, *NJ* 1985, 311 (note J.C. Schultsz), *S&S* 1984, no. 25 *Saudi Independence*.

24 In his advisory opinion to the *Hoge Raad*, Attorney-General Franx acknowledged that the Appellate Court chose to apply the *lex contractus*, but in his view this choice of law was not preceded by a contractual characterization. This assertion is founded on an ingenious construction: as Dutch choice of law theory does not object to party autonomy in torts, the parties' choice of Philippine law should be understood as a deliberate choice of law meant to govern not only the contractual relationship but also any delictual relationship that might arise between them. Whether a strike is characterized as a matter of contract or a matter of tort, is then irrelevant, because that question is precluded by the parties' choice of law. In my opinion, this line of →

sounding in tort. The latter characterization would have obliged the court to apply the Dutch *lex loci delicti*, probably resulting in a decision for the strikers. The main reason why the court decided otherwise, it seems, is one of choice of law policy. To uphold the legality of a strike that was barely connected with the Netherlands would run counter to the first and foremost aspiration of traditional conflicts law: determining the closest connection.[25]

All in all, characterization does not seem to be a real bone of contention in the Dutch conflicts law of torts. Practice has largely overcome theoretical ambiguities by referring to a broad concept of international torts, or, put another way, by extending the scope of the conflicts rules for torts beyond the narrow limits of substantive law definition. The Hague Conventions on Traffic Accidents and Products Liability will help to expel the dubious distinction between unlawfulness and other tort issues introduced by article 14 of the Benelux Uniform Law, so the scope of the two delictual conflicts rules will hopefully cease to cause confusion. Furthermore, the leeway of the proper law approach, which is now firmly established in the Dutch conflicts law of torts, has served to relax the inflexible regime of *lex loci delicti* which, in other systems of conflicts law, has compelled the courts to have recourse to manipulative characterization. In the past, when characterization was much more a focal point of doctrinal attention than it is now, it does not seem to have been a vexed question for the Dutch courts. It is even less likely that it will come to be one in the near future. Therefore, I feel justified in refraining from further elaboration on characterization in the Dutch conflicts law of torts. Its American counterpart requires some closer scrutiny, however, as judicial practice in the United States reveals some peculiar characterization problems.

---

reasoning only succeeds by virtue of the close connection between labor contracts and labor disputes settled by strikes. If anything, the construction could be classified as an accessory choice of law. I fail to see much practical difference between a straight characterization in contract and a construction by which the parties' contractual choice is given controlling effect over a non-contractual relationship.

25 See also: *infra* notes 173–174 and accompanying text. As to the subject of international strikes, their characterization and the applicable law, see: J. van Schellen (1983). See also: Ter Kuile (1983) p. 92 ff.; A. Korthals Altes (1983) p. 104 ff.

In American conflicts law, characterization has been employed especially in the field of torts as a device to evade the application of undesirable substantive rules dictated by a strict and, therefore, inadequate *lex loci delicti* rule. Many cases can be listed to exemplify how characterization functioned as a result-selective technique before more subtle choice of law approaches succeeded in displacing the mechanical subsumption method of the Restatement First. As to torts, the New Hampshire Supreme Court noticed in 1966, "Some jurisdictions, experiencing the same dissatisfaction [as ours] with the mechanical place of wrong rule, have substituted a straight characterization approach."[26] This manipulative (rather than "straight") characterization was practiced in cases that can be grouped according to their typical fact situations and resulting issues: they center on intrafamily immunity, the influence of a concomitant contractual relationship, and the notorious substance/procedure dichotomy. The *Haumschild* decision[27] may serve as an example of cases in which the defense of interspousal or intrafamily immunity under the *lex loci delicti* was construed away by a non-tort characterization.[28] In *Haumschild*, a Wisconsin wife sued her (former) husband for injuries she had suffered through his negligent driving in California. California law denied spouses the right to sue one another, whereas the law of the parties' domicile, Wisconsin, allowed such suits. Incapacity to sue because of marital status was held to be a matter of family law rather than tort law, so the forum law of Wisconsin governed the immunity issue, even though the court cautioned that "the instant case should not be interpreted as a rejection by this court of the general rule that ordinarily the substantive rights of parties to an action in tort are to be determined in the light of the law of the place of the wrong."[29]

The escape from the *lex loci delicti* afforded by a contractual characterization is demonstrated in the well-known decision of *Levy v.*

---

26 *Clark v. Clark* 107 N.H. 351, 222 A.2d 205 at 207 (1966).
27 *Haumschild v. Continental Casualty Co.* 7 Wis.2d 130, 95 N.W.2d 814 (1959).
28 On the characterization of the interspousal immunity issue as a matter of family law, see also: *Aurora National Bank v. Anderson* 268 N.E.2d 552 (Ill. App. 1971); *Balts v. Balts* 273 Minn. 419, 142 N.W.2d 66 (1966); *Flogel v. Flogel* 257 Iowa 547, 133 N.W.2d 907 (1965); *Koplik v. C.P. Trucking Corporation* 27 N.J. 1, 141 A.2d 34 (1958).
29 *Haumschild v. Continental Casualty Co.* 7 Wis.2d 130, 95 N.W. 814 at 819 (1959).

Daniels' U-Drive Auto Renting Co.[30] To justify the application of a Connecticut statute imposing (vicarious) liability upon the defendant renting company for injuries a Connecticut resident sustained in a Massachusetts accident as a passenger in the rented car, the Connecticut court characterized defendant's liability as contractual and applied Connecticut law as the law of the place where the contract had been made, thus evading Massachusetts law which did not impose liability on the lessor. The decision may be criticized for being silent on the court's true motives for switching labels.[31] It is also true that the contractual characterization of the relationship between the plaintiff and the bailor was at best tenuous.[32] Yet, it is hard to see by which other means a court in 1928 could have avoided the unhappy result of the place of wrong rule.

The distinction between substance and procedure has probably produced the hardest characterization problems and the most disingenuous and arbitrary solutions.[33] Much confusion could have been avoided, it seems, if the American courts would have reserved the characterization process, even as a manipulative device, for its primary function which is the conflicts denomination of the issues presented by a given set of facts. Instead, many courts found themselves entangled in the snarls of what is known in Europe as "secondary characterization". This exercise in quasi-logic centers on the question

---

30 *Levy v. Daniels' U-Drive Auto Renting Co.* 108 Conn. 333, 143 A. 163 (1928). More recent examples are found in: *Stacey v. Greenberg* 9 N.J. 390, 88 A.2d 619 (1952); *Kline v. Wheels by Kinney, Inc.* 464 F.2d 184 (1972, diss. op. *per* Butler, C.J.); *Snow v. Bayne* 449 N.E.2d 296 at 299 (Ind. App. 1983).
31 Weintraub (1980) p. 295: "There was a passing reference in *Daniels' U-Drive* to the purpose of the Connecticut bailor's liability statute as 'providing an incentive to him who rented motor vehicles to rent them to competent and careful operators ...' Aside from this remark, there is little or no indication in *U-Drive ...* that the switch in labels was keyed to underlying domestic purposes or was other than an arbitrary, although serendipitous, occurrence."
32 Weintraub (1980) p. 294. In *Kline v. Wheels by Kinney, Inc.* 464 F.2d 184 (4th Cir. [N.C. transf'd to Va.] 1972), the same issue was characterized as sounding in tort, resulting in a decision for defendant.
33 *Cf. Woodward v. Stewart* 243 A.2d 917 at 920 ff. (R.I. 1968). Rejecting the traditional place of wrong rule, the Rhode Island Supreme Court emphasized the "subjective" substance/procedure characterization as one of the main reasons why *lex loci delicti* never provided the expected uniformity of result in tort choice of law. See also: *Wilcox v. Wilcox* 26 Wis.2d 617, 133 N.W.2d 408 at 412 (1965).

"how much of the law of the selected jurisdiction should apply,"[34] and is concerned with the classification of statutes rather than problems.[35] Both primary and secondary characterization may be expedient in a result-selective approach[36] and the substance/procedure dichotomy has been instrumental in either of them. The notorious *Kilberg* case[37] is a good example of manipulative characterization of the *issue*. Having rejected plaintiff's contention that his cause of action arose out of the contractual relationship between his intestate and the defendant airline company, the New York Court of Appeals held that the measure of damages recoverable in tort was a "procedural or remedial question controlled by our State policies," thus escaping the limitation on wrongful death damages imposed by the Massachusetts *lex loci delicti*. The measure of damages, deemed to be "the only controversy" in this case, was thus classified beyond the scope of New York's place of wrong rule and within the scope of its procedural conflicts rule.[38]

Secondary substance/procedure characterization, on the other hand, does not refer to the scope of the forum's conflicts rule but to that of the domestic rules of the jurisdiction selected by the forum's conflicts rule. It does not classify the issue but the rule of decision.[39] This technique, which was more prevalent in American than in European practice, is a sequence to primary characterization: if the action is characterized as sounding in tort, the conflicts rule for torts must be applied and a foreign jurisdiction may be selected as the source of applicable law. At this stage, secondary characterization is performed on the foreign rule of decision: it is either said to be substantive, in which case it will be applied, or it is deemed procedural, in which case it will be

---

34 Şedler (1970) p. 36/37.
35 Rheinstein (1962) p. 659.
36 Leflar (1977-1) p. 176 ff., discussing characterization as a "gimmick" and giving examples of both types of characterization.
37 *Kilberg v. Northeast Airlines, Inc.* 9 N.Y.2d 34, 172 N.E.2d 526 (1961).
38 See also: *Papizzo v. O. Robertson Transport, Ltd.* 401 F.Supp. 540 at 542 (E.D. Mich. 1975): "It is the opinion of this court that a consideration of the recoverable elements of damage goes to the issue of remedy, not to the substance of the right." On the other hand, see *e.g.*: *Bruck v. Eli Lilly & Co.* 523 F.Supp. 480 (S.D. Ohio, transf'd from Mich., 1981): under Michigan choice of law principles, Ohio law would apply to the issue of the measure of damages. See also: *McDaniel v. Sinn* 194 Kan. 625, 400 P.2d 1018 (1965): " ... the measure, extent, or amount of damages for wrongful death pertains to a matter of the substance of the right to recovery ..."
39 *Cf.* Robertson (1940) p. 118: " ... the judge has to determine exactly how much of the foreign law is to be applied to the case before him."

displaced. Characterization of the foreign rule of decision as being either substantive or procedural has its roots in the distinction between rights and remedies, and this dichotomy, in turn, may go back to the writ system in which a plaintiff did not have a cause of action unless recognized procedure afforded a remedy ("remedies precede rights"). Obviously, the rationale of the substance/procedure dichotomy in conflicts law is to prevent the "unreasonable burden on the judicial machinery of the forum"[40] which would arise if the entire foreign law including its procedural law should be applied. The courts in one state may not be equipped to give effect to procedural provisions applying elsewhere. As Leflar has put it: "It would be utterly impractical and unrealistic to expect judges, lawyers, juries, bailiffs, court clerks, reporters, and other judicial functionaries to master and apply an entire new system of judicial procedure for each out-of-state case that comes to trial in their courts. That fact justifies the rule that a forum court applies its own procedure."[41] This being so, American courts have addressed the problem in various, highly inconsistent ways. The most obvious approach would be primary characterization of the issue, e.g. the decision whether the measure of damages in torts is a substantive matter to be subjected to the *lex loci delicti*, or a matter of procedure calling for the application of forum law.[42] Even though the courts may be divided about the answer to this question, the approach appears to be sound, at least more so than secondary characterization directed at the (foreign) rule of decision. Yet, this is the road that many American courts have followed. Statutes of limitations have been, and still are, the object of secondary characterization in

40 *Bournias v. Atlantic Maritime Co., Ltd.* 220 F.2d 152 (2d Cir. 1955), with reference to Restatement First, Introductory note to Chapter 12.
41 Leflar (1977-1) p. 240. Yet, secondary characterization could cause considerable complications. In *Mudd by Mudd v. Goldblatt Bros., Inc.* 118 Ill.App.3d 431, 73 Ill.Dec. 657, 454 N.E.2d 754 (1983), the issue turned on proof of contributory negligence on the part of the victim, who had been injured in Indiana. Under the law of Illinois, the forum state, the plaintiff would have to prove he was free of contributory negligence, while under the law of the state where the wrong had occurred, Indiana, defendant had to prove plaintiff's contribution. Quoting from the Restatement Second (§ 133), the Appellate Court characterized the Indiana rule as one of procedure, since it was satisfied that its primary purpose was not "to affect the decision of the issue [but] to regulate the conduct of the trial." Thus, the Illinois evidence rule (also deemed procedural) was applied. The cases to be discussed *infra* notes 45–47 and accompanying text, demonstrate what could have happened if the *Mudd* court had classified its own rule as substantive.
42 As exemplified by *Kilberg v. Northeast Airlines, Inc.*, *supra* note 37.

many cases. Instead of characterizing the issue of time limitation as substantive or procedural, calling for the application of *lex causae* or *lex fori* respectively, many courts have indulged in resilient characterization exercises. In *Lillegraven v. Tengs*, the Supreme Court of Alaska submitted the statute of limitations of British Columbia, where the tort at issue had occurred, to a substance/procedure test and concluded it was procedural, so it could be replaced by the longer Alaska statute. The court did admit its decision would have been different if it had construed "the limitation as being directed so specifically to the right of action as to warrant saying that it qualifies or is made a condition of the right."[43] Along the same line of reasoning, the District Court for the District of Maryland reached the opposite result. In *President and Directors of Georgetown College v. Madden*, a case involving breach of contract and negligence by the architects, engineers and contractors of a defective building in Washington D.C., the (shorter) statute of limitations of the place of the wrong was applied: "As a general rule, a statute of limitations is considered procedural ... However, when the statute of limitations bars the right and not merely the remedy, an exception to the general rule applies and the statute of limitations is considered substantive."[44] As opposed to the Maryland statute, the Washington D.C. limitation was deemed to operate as a grant of immunity to builders and therefore held to be substantive.

In these cases attention was focused on the characterization of the foreign statute. Dizzying results are achieved when secondary characterization is directed at the forum law as well. Such was the case in *Nelson v. Eckert*.[45] In a car accident in Texas, the occupants, Arkansas residents all of them, were killed. A wrongful death action was brought in Arkansas, but not until more than two years had passed since the occurrence, so the special statute of limitations for wrongful death actions of both Texas and Arkansas had run. This did not daunt

---

43 *Lillegraven v. Tengs* 375 P.2d 139 at 141 (Alaska 1962), quoting from the Restatement First and the *Bournias* opinion (*supra* note 40.). See also: *Hansen v. Sears, Roebuck & Co.* 574 F.Supp. 641 (E.D. Mo. 1983): since Indiana's "statute of repose" (limiting the time during which a cause of action accrues) was characterized as procedural, the Missouri *lex fori* applied to the issue whether plaintiff's action was barred.
44 *President and Directors of Georgetown College v. Madden* 505 F.Supp. 557 at 571 (D. Md. 1980).
45 *Nelson v. Eckert* 231 Ark. 348, 329 S.W.2d 426 (1959).

the Arkansas court when it decided that the Texas limitation was not part of the Texas wrongful death act, and therefore procedural and inapplicable in an Arkansas court, whereas the Arkansas limitation was part of the Arkansas wrongful death act, therefore substantive and only applicable to wrongful deaths occurring in Arkansas. According to the general Arkansas statute of limitations, substituted for both the rejected Texas and Arkansas wrongful death limitations, the action was not barred. The case echoes the much-criticized decision in *Marie v. Garrison*,[46] or the notorious holding of the German *Reichsgericht*,[47] both dating from an era that seems long past. Their common feature is the finding that the rule of decision of the *lex causae* does not apply since it is held to be procedural, whereas its counterpart in the *lex fori* does not apply since it is held to be substantive, which leaves the courts free to look for yet another solution. In all three cases the result was different from what it would have been under either the *lex fori* or the *lex causae*. The impression that secondary characterization was often used, and still is, as a quasi-dogmatic device to influence the outcome of the case is hard to escape.

Secondary characterization has been denounced as "a remnant of statutist thinking."[48] If it is remembered that it has as its object rules or statutes instead of issues or problems, this technique does indeed evoke the statutist approach of classifying statutes to ascertain their claim to application. On the other hand, it should not be forgotten that secondary characterization is employed as a stratagem of the objective allocation method which is not concerned with policies or objectives of conflicting substantive rules, but with a neutral and mechanical determination of the applicable law. In this method, secondary characterization purports to delimit how much of the applicable law should be applied, and it may do so without investigating the objectives of the rule in question: "the judge's attention is diverted from the problems

---

46 *Marie v. Garrison* 13 Abb. N. Cas. 210 (N.Y. Super. Ct. 1883). The case concerned the validity of an oral contract made in Missouri. Under the respective Statutes of Frauds of New York and Missouri, the only states involved, the contract was void. Still, its validity was upheld by a procedural characterization of the Missouri rule, while the New York rule was said to be substantive and, therefore, equally inapplicable.
47 *J. v. H.* 7 RGZ 21 (1882). The case turned on the statutes of limitations of Tennessee (procedural) and Germany (substantive). Neither of them being applicable, plaintiff's claim became perpetual.
48 Rheinstein (1962) p. 661.

of policy posed by the facts and the alternative solutions suggested by the dispositive rules to the remote and taxonomic issue of assigning the dispositive rules to some general rubric of the law."[49] That is not to say that a court in trying to establish the borderline between substance and procedure will never touch on the purpose of the rule in question, but usually the delimitation is arrived at by a less sophisticated classificatory approach. In this respect secondary characterization may connote renvoi in that the forum will sometimes follow the substance/procedure characterization of the foreign jurisdiction.[50]

If it is true that under the traditional choice of law method characterization has become a manipulative device, it might be interesting to know if there is still a need for it under the modern, policy-oriented approaches that claim to remedy the ills of mechanical subsumption. It should be established at the outset that characterization, understood as the juridification of a fact pattern to suit it to the choice of law process, will be indispensable under any approach. The difference must lie in the purpose of characterization and in the way it is best achieved. Its purpose under the traditional method was supposed to be the classification of the case according to the scope of the forum's various conflicts rules. We have seen that in some cases several specious characterizations could be distinguished, leaving room for the court to maneuver the outcome of the litigation toward the result desired. Furthermore, the deceptive concept of secondary characterization added to the result-selective predisposition of the courts confronted with an inflexible method. The modern choice of law approaches boasting flexibility and rationality have been criticized by some for their lack of "rules" and their emphasis on case-by-case adjudication, to the extent they may not even be called "methods". One would surmise that characterization has no place in such unsystematic schemes. However, if it is understood that the new approaches have in common that they are not jurisdiction-selecting but rule-selecting processes, by which conflicting rules of domestic law are tested for their functionality in the individual case, it will become clear that the first step in any of them is to identify the issue or issues dividing the parties

---

49 Hancock (1961) p. 369.
50 American courts are apt to cite relevant decisions from sister states as (persuasive) authority. Secondary characterization must be much more hazardous if the rule in question hails from abroad.

in dispute.⁵¹ For without a proper definition of the issue, the search for the relevant rule of decision in each possibly interested jurisdiction may be fruitless. This process may be called characterization if it is borne in mind that here it is essentially the same form of "low-level labeling"⁵² any court practices when dealing with domestic cases, only differing in this respect that under the new choice of law approaches it may have to be repeated as many times as there are concerned jurisdictions.

As a specific tool of the conflict of laws, however, and particularly as a manipulative device, characterization might no longer be required. This assumption is affirmed by several writers. Admitting that "the problem of characterization is ubiquitous in the law and can never wholly be avoided," Currie is confident that "[w]ithout choice of law rules, however, there would be no occasion for the specialized function of characterization as the mode of discriminating among the available prefabricated solutions of a problem; juridical gymnastics of the sort displayed in *Levy v. Daniels' U-Drive Auto Renting Co.* would be beside the point."⁵³ From Hancock's rejection of the "classificatory approach" it follows that characterization is incompatible with the functional or result-selective approaches he advocates.⁵⁴ Weintraub believes that "[a] method of resolving conflicts problems which focuses directly on the domestic rules in putative conflict and on their underlying policies does not require a substantive characterization of

---

51 *Cf.* Strikwerda (1978) p. 144 ff. *Acme Circus Operating Co., Inc. v. Kuperstock* 711 F.2d 1538 at 1540 (11th Cir. [Cal. transf'd to Fla.] 1983): "The first step in the choice of law analysis is to ascertain the nature of the problem involved, i.e. is the specific issue at hand a problem of the law of contracts, torts, property etc." *Hurtado v. Superior Court of Sacramento County* 11 Cal.3d 574, 114 Cal.Rptr. 106, 522 P.2d 666 at 672/673 (1974): "In making a choice of law, these three aspects of wrongful death [*viz.* compensation for survivors, deterrence of conduct, and limitations upon recoverable damages] must be carefully separated. The key step in this process is delineating the issue to be decided."
52 Cramton/Currie/Kay (1981) p. 97. Leflar (1977-1) p. 177: "It is an essential early step in almost any legal analysis, but the step is one that can serve the purposes of the legal artist as well as those of the legal logician."
53 Currie (1963-1) p. 184.
54 Hancock (1961).

those rules,"⁵⁵ at least in cases involving false conflicts. In Ehrenzweig's view, "the concept of characterization will have lost both its promise and its threat" if his approach to the choice of law problem is adopted.⁵⁶

In a lengthy article, Professor Sedler claims that "[i]t is obvious that the premises upon which the traditional characterization process rested are totally inapplicable to a policy-oriented approach." Yet, he introduces a similar concept "which has great utility in assisting a court to arrive at sound decisions based upon considerations of policy and fairness."⁵⁷ This concept, called "identification of the problem area", will guide the court to the "state of primary reference", this being the state which seemingly has an interest in implementing the policy behind its substantive law. In immunity cases, such as *Haumschild*,⁵⁸ this would mean, for instance, that the problem area would not be identified as "tort" but "with reference to the policy behind the granting of immunity; *i.e.* as a problem of decedents' estates, charitable associations, family law, automobile liability insurance, and the like."⁵⁹ Much as I appreciate Sedler's writings, I cannot help feeling that the notion of neo-characterization suffers from a certain circularity in that it depends on an assessment of the policy behind substantive rules of a foreign state, *e.g.* the state where the plaintiff was injured, before the state of primary reference, *e.g.* the state of the family domicile, can be identified. This is, of course, a procedure quite compatible with interest analysis, but I fail to see the added advantage of "identification of the problem area" if anything more than a correct formulation of the issue is meant. Faced with the facts in *Haumschild* a court devoted to interest analysis would have to phrase the issue along these lines: "Can a wife sue her husband for injuries she suffered as a result of his reck-

---

55 Weintraub (1968) p. 819 = Weintraub (1980) p. 51, distinguishing between primary ("substantive") characterization, "characterization of the choice of law rule" and secondary characterization ("how much of the law selected by the choice-of-law rule should be applied"). Defining the meaning of the choice of law rule or method to be applied will remain a problem, according to Weintraub, under any approach. In my opinion, this is a problem of interpretation, for which the term "characterization" is hardly fitting.
56 Ehrenzweig (1961) p. 408.
57 Sedler (1970) p. 41 and p. 17 respectively.
58 *Haumschild v. Continental Casualty Co.* 7 Wis.2d 130, 95 N.W.2d 814 (1959), discussed *supra* notes 27–29 and accompanying text.
59 Sedler (1970) p. 60.

less driving?" It should then proceed to determine the policies behind the conflicting California and Wisconsin substantive rules, which might evince a false conflict. Identification of the problem area is a device that reverts to *a priori* rules, such as: (non)immunity is usually the concern of the parties' home state, and therefore that state's law has a *prima facie* claim to application. Thus coupled, identification of the problem area pointing to a state of primary reference might induce the courts to be less exacting in the determination of policies and interests of other states, gratefully taking the shortcut implied in this approach. Sedler's theory might be helpful in a transitional period during which the vestiges of traditional conflicts thinking still influence the "mind-set" of judges dealing with multistate problems, as it may make them conscious of the policies and interests involved and of the jurisdictions possibly concerned. However, from identification of the problem area and the state of primary reference it takes but a short step to "neo-conflicts rules" predicated on policy considerations. This may not have been Sedler's intent, since he emphasizes the need to consider the policies and interests of other concerned states, but this new face of characterization might once again conceal the really decisive factors in the outcome of conflicts cases. I think this danger outweighs the possible advantages of Sedler's proposition.[60]

Turning to recent American case law displaying a willingness to adopt the modern choice of law approach of interest analysis, one will still find anomalous results caused by the lingering influence of the doctrine of characterization. To be sure, in the area of torts primary characterization has ceased to pose most of the classificatory problems (and their amenability to manipulation) it caused under the traditional approach, such as the classification of an issue as sounding in tort, in contract, or in family law.[61] On the other hand, the dichotomy between substance and procedure has continued to confound the courts.

60 In practice, litigants are apt to draw the court's attention to any relevant rule of substantive law that might help their case. In this light, the value of Sedler's construction (and of my objection) appears to be largely academic.
61 Weintraub (1980) p. 53: "Labels were switched in the best now-you-see-it-now-you-don't tradition of that most skilled of all prestidigitators, the common law judge who has decided on the correct result and is seeking a way to get there. What was a 'tort' problem was changed before your eyes by the incantation 'administration of decedents' estates' or 'family law' or 'contract' or, most powerful conjuring word of them all, 'procedural'. The results, though wondrous, seemed arbitrary and unpredictable."

Most writers agree that it should not, since "interest analysis and the distinction between substance and procedure are fundamentally irreconcilable."[62] They advocate an outright application of interest analysis to all issues including seemingly procedural ones. The overriding interest the forum has in applying its own procedural rules is the efficiency of its judicial machinery. In the absence of such an interest a foreign jurisdiction may supply the rule of decision, even if it is couched in procedural language. "A true interest analysis approach would examine each procedural rule to determine whether a given state has an interest in having the rule applied. In making the decision, a court would take into account the impact of such a ruling on the operation of its own judicial machinery," Twerski and Mayer observed.[63] Some courts have chosen this integral approach.

In *Heavner v. Uniroyal*,[64] the New Jersey Supreme Court applied the North Carolina statute of limitations, barring the action. New Jersey was said to have no substantial interest in the matter, as the cause of action arose in North Carolina and the parties were all present in and amenable to the jurisdiction of that state. In effect, the statute of limitations issue was held to be substantive, but the court did not need to go into primary or secondary characterization as it established that North Carolina was the only state having an interest in the application of its statute of limitations. In a federal case brought before the District Court sitting in the District of Columbia where interest analysis had been adopted in *Gaither v. Myers*,[65] the purpose of time limitations was analyzed and the issue decided thus: "The purpose of both the Virginia and District of Columbia statutes of limitations is to protect domiciliaries from the prosecution of stale claims ... The District of Columbia has no relation to the plaintiff, a Virginia resident, and no person or property in the District of Columbia has been adversely affected by the alleged act of negligence which occurred in Virginia ...

---

62 Milhollin (1975) p. 10.
63 Twerski/Mayer (1979) p. 784 note 15. In this light, it is hard to see why the Illinois Appellate Court in *Mudd by Mudd v. Goldblatt Bros., Inc.* 118 Ill.App.3d 431, 73 Ill.Dec. 657, 454 N.E.2d 754 (1983), discussed *supra* note 41, discarded the Indiana evidence rule for being procedural. The efficiency of the Illinois "judicial machinery" would not have suffered either way.
64 *Heavner v. Uniroyal* 63 N.J. 130, 305 A.2d 412 (1973).
65 404 F.2d 216 (D.C. Cir. 1968). *Tramontana v. S.A. Empresa de Viaçao Aérea Rio Grandense* 350 F.2d 468 (D.C. Cir. 1965), despite its reference to Brazil's "substantial interests", is less explicit in this respect.

Thus there is no interest of the District of Columbia which compels the application of its statute. Virginia is the only jurisdiction whose interest would be served by the application of its laws."[66]

Other courts have stuck to the substance/procedure dichotomy. In *Klingebiel v. Lockheed Aircraft Corporation*, a products liability case, the widows of German air force pilots brought an action for wrongful death against the California-based manufacturer of the allegedly defective plane in which their husbands had crashed in Germany. The German statute of limitations being three years, it had not yet run when the action was brought, but the statute of limitations of the California forum barred an action after one year. In *Reich v. Purcell*[67] interest analysis had been introduced into California's choice of law, but not for all issues, according to the federal District Court in *Klingebiel*: "While the court agrees with the plaintiffs' contention that the principle of 'interest analysis' enunciated in *Reich* will probably lead to the application of the German substantive law to their causes of action, the court does not agree that *Reich* requires this court to apply the German statute of limitations. The cases cited by plaintiffs do not support the assertion that the principle of 'interest analysis' also applies to the choice of 'procedural' law."[68] This decision was affirmed by the Ninth Circuit, with the difference that in a concurring opinion Chief Judge Wright made it known that in his opinion "California's new interest balancing approach to conflict of laws problems, announced in *Reich v. Purcell* ... , was intended to be applicable alike to substantive and procedural choice of law problems," in this case still resulting in the application of the California statute.[69]

To a large extent the problem we are here confronted with is caused by the widespread enactment of so-called "borrowing statutes", chang-

---

66 *Farrier v. May Dep't Stores Co.* 357 F.Supp. 190 at 193 (D. D.C. 1973).
67 *Reich v. Purcell* 67 Cal.2d 551, 63 Cal.Rptr. 31, 432 P.2d 727 (1967).
68 *Klingebiel v. Lockheed Aircraft Corporation* 372 F.Supp. 1086 at 1088/1089 (N.D. Cal. 1971), *aff'd* 494 F.2d 345 (9th Cir. 1974). For similar decisions in relation to other modern approaches, see *e.g.*: *Gordon v. Gordon* 387 A.2d 339 (N.H. 1978); *Hines v. Tenneco Chemicals, Inc.* 546 F.Supp. 1229 (S.D. Tex. 1982); *Horvath v. Davidson* 148 Ind. App. 203, 264 N.E.2d 328 at 334 (1970): "The so-called 'center of gravity' theory approved in Barber v. Hughes [223 Ind. 570, 63 N.E.2d 417 (1945)] and the New York cases cited does not carry over automatically to statute of limitation problems ..."
69 *Klingebiel v. Lockheed Aircraft Corporation* 494 F.2d 345 (9th Cir. [Cal.] 1974).

2 – 114

ing the traditional common law rule that the forum apply its own statute of limitations. They are inspired by various policies,[70] one of the best reasons for their enactment probably being the "policy against prolonging the period of limitations because of the defendant's absence from a jurisdiction where there was no reason to expect him to be present,"[71] a possibility created by so-called "tolling statutes".[72] Borrowing statutes come in many variations but mostly they "borrow" the statute of limitations of a foreign jurisdiction to the effect that the action will be barred by either, whichever is shorter, the statute of limitations of the forum or the statute of limitations of the state where the cause of action "arose", or "accrued", or "originated". These words recall the vested rights theory and, as to torts, the place of the wrong rule, and this is apparently the construction some courts have deemed proper when dealing with time limitations and borrowing statutes. A case in point is *Gross v. McDonald*, in which the plaintiff was a student in Kentucky who had been injured in Indiana when riding as a guest in the car of defendant who at that time resided in Kentucky as well. When suit was brought in Pennsylvania defendant was a temporary resident of that state. Indiana had a guest statute and a statute of limitations with a two year limit. Kentucky had no guest statute and a one year limitation. The federal district court sitting in Pennsylvania, where interest analysis had been adopted in *Griffith v. United Airlines, Inc.*,[73] decided the case by performing what one commentator has dubbed "a most peculiar feat of interest analysis calisthenics."[74] It found that "Indiana had no interest in this suit at all and Kentucky has a strong nexus; hence displacement of Indiana's guest rule will advance relative substantive law purposes without impair-

---

70 *Cf.* Ester (1962) p. 40 ff.
71 *George v. Douglas Aircraft Co.* 332 F.2d 73 at 78 (2d Cir. [N.Y.] 1964), *cert. den.* 379 U.S. 904 (1964). See also: *Rhoades v. Wright* 622 P.2d 343 at 351 (Utah 1980), *cert. denied* 454 U.S. 897 (1981): Utah's borrowing statute "serves the purpose of preventing forum shoppers from flocking to Utah to take advantage of a larger limitation period ..."
72 *Cf.* Leflar (1977-1). p. 256 ff. These statutes generally provide that the period of the forum's statute of limitations shall not run in favor of a debtor who is "absent from" or "not a resident of" the forum state. Cramton/Currie/Kay (1981) p. 190: they were meant to "assure that statutes of limitation would not deprive the plaintiffs of a reasonable opportunity to sue defendants who were beyond the reach of service of process."
73 *Griffith v. United Airlines, Inc.* 416 Pa. 1, 203 A.2d 796 (1964).
74 Wurfel (1974) p. 565.

ment of the working of the multi-state system."[75] As to the time limitation, the court was faced with the Pennsylvania borrowing statute referring to the laws of the state or country in which the cause of action "arose"; if this law would bar the action, such bar would be a complete defense in Pennsylvania. Surprisingly, the court held that the cause of action "arose" in Indiana rather than Kentucky, and since the Indiana time limit had not yet run, the borrowing statute had no effect. Consequently, the Pennsylvania statute of limitations, allowing the action, was held to apply. In a comment on this case, Professor Wurfel summed up this line of reasoning: "Thus the court of a 'disinterested' forum held the substantive law of Indiana insignificant and inapplicable but at the same time looked to Indiana lex loci as most 'significant' in determining the effect of the Pennsylvania borrowing statute. This ingenious dichotomy of reasoning richly rewarded resourceful forum shopping."[76]

Twerski and Mayer noted that "[t]hose courts that have been called upon to interpret borrowing statutes have been faced with a dilemma. The statutes call for the application of the shorter statute of limitations of the state in which the cause of action 'arose' or 'accrued'. The question arises how the statutory language should be interpreted after a state has adopted interest analysis. The terms 'arose' and 'accrued' were meaningful when First Restatement territorial concepts prevailed, but are decidedly out of step with modern interest analysis. The better reasoned decisions have read interest analysis into the old statutory language ... Nonetheless, given the statutory emphasis on the place where the cause of action arose or accrued, a court may not be free to perform an interest analysis on the statute of limitations issue alone, but may be required to tie the result to the substantive law which governs the case."[77] Obviously, borrowing statutes, and other conflicts of law statutes for that matter,[78] phrased in terms and style of the traditional conflicts rules do cause discrepancies if they are to be interpolated in the process of interest analysis. Depending on the approach, the relevance of geographical factors is assessed differently, which compels a strained interpretation of notions such as "the state

75 *Gross v. McDonald* 354 F.Supp. 378 at 381 (E.D. Pa. 1973).
76 Wurfel (1974) p. 565/566.
77 Twerski/Mayer (1979) p. 785 note 16; *cf.* Milhollin (1975) p. 53.
78 *Cf.* Brilmayer (1980). See also, on related difficulties in connection with the Federal Tort Claims Act, *infra* notes 95–105 and accompanying text.

where the cause of action arose" if the forum's choice of law approach is based on interest analysis. Once this approach is adopted, there is no reason to except certain issues from its scope. This entails a functional rather than territorialist construction of the language of borrowing statutes, as long as they have not been abolished. If they were designed to "combat the procedural characterization of limitations"[79] they must be dispensable from the moment the issue of limitations, as all other issues, is to be resolved according to the policies of the statutes in conflict. Thus, the confusing distinction between substance and procedure and the characterization puzzles and ploys it brought forth should gradually disappear and become one of the oddities of the history of conflicts law.

2 Renvoi

Traditionally, the doctrine of renvoi has never been very popular in the Netherlands. It was rejected by most of the prominent Dutch scholars of the first half of this century.[80] Even when the Draft Uniform Benelux Law, in article 11, introduced a limited variety of renvoi, the courts remained reluctant to put the theory into practice. Confusion and inconsistency resulted. Apart from obsolete arguments pertaining to international law, particularly in respect of legislative jurisdiction and the limits of sovereignty, the main purpose and justification of renvoi is said to be the reconciliation between the reality of divergent choice of law rules and the traditional method's postulate of uniformity of decision.[81] Whether renvoi could possibly achieve uniformity of result and counteract forum shopping remains extremely doubtful, however. If the foreign choice of law principles, arrived at by one or more choice of law detours, point back to forum law, the vicious circle thus created is usually broken by application of the forum's domestic law. For instance, if we assume that Dutch choice of law principles in matters of succession refer to the law of the deceased's nationality, and Danish choice of law to the law of the de-

---

79 Milhollin (1975) p. 53.
80 *Cf.* Kosters/Dubbink (1962) p. 287/288.
81 Kosters/Dubbink (1962) p. 280/281; Kropholler (1975) p. 335. See also: Von Mehren (1961) p. 384; Restatement Second, § 8, comment h; Leflar (1977-1) p. 9 ff.; Cramton/Currie/Kay (1981) p. 74.

ceased's domicile, renvoi would compel a Dutch court to apply Dutch substantive law to the question of distribution of the estate of a Dane living in Holland, whereas a Danish court would apply the domestic law of Denmark.[82] For a Dutch court would first be referred to Danish choice of law, and from there, by the doctrine of renvoi, back to the (conflicts) law of the domicile, resulting in the application of Dutch substantive law, whereas a Danish court would be referred to the conflicts law of decedent's domicile, and hence, again due to renvoi, to the law of his nationality, resulting in the application of Danish substantive law. Without renvoi, a Dutch court would apply the Danish substantive law of decedent's nationality, whereas a Danish court would subject the issue to Dutch domestic law, being the law of decedent's domicile. This example illustrates Lorenzen's objection to the doctrine: "Personally I cannot approve of a doctrine which is workable only if the other country rejects it."[83]

The real reason behind renvoi might therefore be different from the advocated decisional harmony. From the haphazard way renvoi is employed it might be inferred that it rather serves as a device to escape the rigors of traditional conflicts law. An example is presented by a Dutch succession case concerning the estate of a former Dutch national who had acquired the Estonian nationality for what seemed to be opportunistic reasons. Unlike Dutch law, it was assumed, the Estonian law of succession allowed a testator to exclude his children from his will, which was one of the purposes the deceased had wanted to achieve by changing nationalities. As Dutch choice of law generally submits matters of succession to the law of the decedent's last nationality, Estonian law would apply to the validity of the will, and the claims of the children would be defeated. However, the Appellate

---

82 This example is derived from an actual case involving a Danish decedent who had his last domicile in Belgium. The Dutch *Hoge Raad* rejected plaintiffs' contention that Belgian law should have been chosen by means of renvoi: HR 8 January 1943, *NJ* 1943, 202 (*Reijers v. Coert*).
83 Lorenzen (1947-3) p. 127. This statement is generally true in all cases in which, at one point or another, the chain of references to (foreign) conflicts rules becomes a circle. If all choice of law systems would apply renvoi, the doctrine will only fulfill its promise in the exceptional situation in which the last link of the chain is a conflicts rule that refers to its own legal system. Put another way, renvoi will only work if all connecting factors encountered are different.

Court of Amsterdam was obviously unconvinced that Estonian law would be the proper law in this case. Listing a number of reasons why Dutch substantive law should be applied, it further reinforced its decision by using renvoi as an incidental argument: it was held that Estonian choice of law would refer to the law of the decedent's domicile, another reason for the court to apply its own law.[84] Since in Dutch conflicts law renvoi is usually rejected, it is obvious that in this case the court availed itself of the doctrine – rather superfluously at that – for the sole reason that it wanted to redress an injustice which it felt would result from application of Estonian substantive law, or, to put it in more general terms, an injustice induced by the abstractions of traditional choice of law. As contemporary Dutch choice of law has achieved considerable flexibility in the jurisdiction-selecting process,[85] renvoi and other doctrines fashioned into escape devices may have become dispensable. This presumption seems to be confirmed by the paucity of recent Dutch cases in which renvoi is still resorted to.

As far as Dutch *torts* choice of law is concerned, renvoi was and is conspicuously absent, both in case law and in theory. This is hardly surprising, since the doctrine is usually discussed in the context of family law and succession, where divergent connecting factors – nationality and domicile – frustrate uniformity of decision more than in any other category of conflicts law. In these areas, renvoi is usually recommended as a proper way to achieve decisional harmony, but actually used as a device to circumvent inappropriate choice of law results. While it could serve the latter purpose in any area of conflicts law suffering from inflexible jurisdiction-selecting rules, its mechanics do not allow an escape if the conflicts rule in question is universal. In the field of torts the *lex loci delicti* rule used to be the global choice of law standard, and even today, in spite of refinements and exceptions, it is still the prevailing conflicts rule for torts in most countries, with the notable exception of the majority of the jurisdictions in the United States. For that reason renvoi could hardly be considered as pertinent to torts choice of law, not even in jurisdictions whose conflicts laws

---

84 Hof Amsterdam 11 July 1946, *NJ* 1947, 66, *aff'd* HR 21 March 1947, *NJ* 1947, 382 (*Estlandse nalatenschap*).
85 *Cf. supra* chapter 1.

support renvoi in other areas. Conversely, it might be speculated that – in its "official" and therefore largely theoretical function – renvoi could become more relevant in respect of multistate torts when more jurisdictions abandon the universal *lex loci delicti* standard and replace it by various, diverging choice of law rules. However, since it might be expected that the rigid *lex loci* standard will be replaced, if at all, by rules which are more pliable and therefore more conducive to just results, and since uniformity of result does no longer seem to be the foremost concern of conflicts law, it is not very likely that renvoi, in either of its functions, will make an appearance in the law of multistate torts. An examination of some American renvoi cases might help to test this hypothesis.

In American torts choice of law, renvoi has not achieved great popularity, but it is not totally absent, either. In some cases the courts, obviously prompted by one of the litigants, have flatly rejected the doctrine. Most explicit was the Wisconsin Supreme Court in *Haumschild v. Continental Casualty Co.*: "The reason why authorities on conflict of laws almost universally reject the renvoi doctrine ... is that it is likely to result in the court pursuing a course equivalent to a never ending circle."[86] Other courts, while rejecting renvoi, perfunctorily refer to foreign choice of law principles apparently to buttress other arguments for their decisions. An example of such corroborative renvoi is *Hawley v. Beech Aircraft Corp.*[87] in which case the Tenth Circuit had to decide whether the longer Kansas or the shorter California statute of limitations applied to a wrongful death action arising from an aircraft crash in California. As Kansas, the forum, had a borrowing statute barring a tort action brought by a non-resident if the statute of limitations of the *locus delicti* had run, the California *lex loci delicti* was held to be controlling. The plaintiff, however, urged the court to apply the "whole law" of California, including its choice of law principles. For the sake of argument the court did follow this suggestion, but the conclusion was the same: California's borrowing statute would be operative only if the statute of limitations of the other

---

86 *Haumschild v. Continental Casualty Co.* 7 Wis.2d 130, 95 N.W.2d 814 at 820 (1959); see also: *Aurora National Bank v. Anderson* 268 N.E.2d 552 (Ill. App. 1971); *Patch v. Stanley Works (Stanley Chemical Company Division)* 448 F.2d 483 at 492 (2d Cir. [Conn.] 1971); *Maroon v. State, Dept. of Mental Health* 411 N.E.2d 404 (Ind. 1980).
87 *Hawley v. Beech Aircraft Corp.* 625 F.2d 991 (10th Cir. [Kansas] 1980).

state (Kansas) was shorter than California's, so even with the use of renvoi the plaintiff did not prevail. In *Tramontana v. S.A. Empresa de Viação Aérea Rio Grandense*, Brazilian law was applied, on the basis of interest analysis, to the issue of wrongful death limitations.[88] Although plaintiff had not hinted at the possible applicability of Maryland law, the law of her and her deceased husband's domicile, the court *sua sponte* referred to Maryland's *lex loci* rule and concluded that a Maryland court would have reached the same choice of law result under its more traditional conflicts rule. This is quasi-renvoi at best,[89] since the *Tramontana* court had already decided that Brazilian law applied, ignoring Brazilian conflicts law, and only looked into Maryland choice of law because Maryland was one of the jurisdictions possibly concerned.[90] A rather silly example of corroborative renvoi can be found in *Saharceski v. Marcure*.[91] A Massachusetts resident had been injured in the course of his employment in Connecticut, due to the negligence of his fellow-employee, also a Massachusetts resident. Massachusetts law, contrary to the law of Connecticut, barred an action against fellow-employees if workmen's compensation had been collected. Relying heavily on the parties' expectations, the Supreme Judicial Court of Massachusetts decided Massachusetts had the greater interest, in line with the choice of law approach it had adopted in *Pevoski v. Pevoski*.[92] For some reason, however, the court felt obliged to pursue a different approach as well. Connecticut law being the *lex loci delicti*, renvoi was thrown in as an extra argument. The court concluded that a Connecticut court would probably have characterized the facts of the case "as involving principally a contractual relationship under Massachusetts and not simply a tort claim under Connecticut law." To top it all, the court expressed the opinion that

---

88 *Tramontana v. S.A. Empresa de Viação Aérea Rio Grandense* 350 F.2d 468 (D.C. Cir. 1965), *cert. denied*, 383 U.S. 943 (1966).
89 For a different construction, see *infra* notes 124–125 and accompanying text.
90 The same happened in *DeVane v. United States* 259 F.Supp. 18 (D. Puerto Rico 1966), an action for personal injuries sustained by a Florida domiciliary in a Puerto Rico accident. The District Court held Puerto Rico law to apply as *lex loci delicti* but added that "even if renvoi would be employed," Florida choice of law rules would refer to Puerto Rico law as well.
91 *Saharceski v. Marcure* 373 Mass. 304, 366 N.E.2d 1245 (1977).
92 *Pevoski v. Pevoski* 371 Mass. 358, 358 N.E.2d 416 (1976).

Connecticut would not have "a strong public policy in support of authorizing suits against fellow employees."[93] Not only is the use of (quasi)renvoi in these cases gratuitous, as it serves no other purpose than the confirmation of the court's principal choice of law decision and would probably have been omitted if its result had been incompatible, but in their wavering between rejecting and acknowledging the doctrine the opinions are rather inconclusive as well. A firm and consistent denial of renvoi would have been preferable.[94]

The clumsy formulation of a federal *lex loci delicti* rule has added to the confusion surrounding renvoi. In *Richards v. United States*,[95] the U.S. Supreme Court endorsed the doctrine in applying the Federal Tort Claims Act. Pursuant to this statute, the U.S. government is held liable for tortious conduct committed by its employees "under circumstances where the United States, if a private person, would be liable to the claimant *in accordance with the law of the place where the act or omission occurred.*"[96] Petitioners in this case were the personal representatives of passengers who had been killed in an airplane crash in Missouri, while *en route* from Oklahoma to New York. It was alleged that the Federal Aviation Agency had been negligent, so suit was filed against the U.S. government. Having received from the airline company the maximum amount of damages the Missouri Wrongful Death Act allowed, petitioners sought additional damages under the Federal Tort Claims Act and argued that Oklahoma law –which did not limit the amount of recovery– should be applied as the law of the state where the negligence had occurred. The Supreme Court agreed, but

---

93 *Saharceski v. Marcure* 373 Mass. 304, 366 N.E.2d 1245 at 1251 (1977). See also: Egnal (1981) p. 278 ff., calling the *Saharceski* approach a "perversion" of renvoi: "This is traditional renvoi at its worst, in a fact pattern where no authority would support its use."
94 By using renvoi to reinforce a choice of law decision, the courts in effect resort to a similar technique as the one sometimes used in "no-conflict situations," when the choice of *substantive* law is immaterial to the outcome of the case. Here, the *choice of law* conclusion is the same under the conflicts law of each concerned jurisdiction. For a discussion of this "anti-choice" solution as applied to no-conflict situations, see *infra* chapter 4, section 1, text following note 28.
95 *Richards v. United States* 369 U.S. 1 (1962).
96 28 U.S.C. §§ 1291 ff.; § 1346 b; emphasis added.

with a twist. Although the anomalous[97] standard of the Federal Tort Claims Act –the place of conduct rather than the place of harmful impact– was acknowledged, the Court apparently wished to circumvent the results this connecting factor would produce and to realign federal tort conflicts law with traditional practice. It did so by resorting to renvoi. It was held that the Federal Tort Claims Act did not refer to the *internal* law of "the place where the acts of negligence took place", but to the *whole law* of that state including its choice of law principles. Since most states in the days of the *Richards* decision still adhered to the place of injury rule, decisional harmony was restored even in federal tort cases. *Richards v. United States* was decided by application of Missouri law *via* Oklahoma's choice of law rule, and the lower courts' decisions were affirmed.

Later cases involving the Federal Tort Claims Act are curiously inconsistent, despite the Supreme Court's ruling. The Rhode Island District Court seemed to ignore the *Richards* holding altogether when it decided a malpractice suit against a U.S. Navy hospital in Pennsylvania by applying Pennsylvania domestic law: "There is no dispute that the tort in this case took place in Pennsylvania, thus, the applicable law is that of Pennsylvania."[98] The interest analysis approach Pennsylvania adopted in *Griffith v. United Air Lines, Inc.*[99] was totally disregarded, which would suggest that the court was unwilling to employ renvoi. The same happened in *Pierce v. United States*,[100] involving the negligence of government employees at a flight service station in Indiana. Plaintiff, whose plane had crashed in Tennessee during a thunderstorm, claimed that the accident would not have happened but for the inaccurate weather information the station relayed to him. The Sixth Circuit agreed with the district court in Tennessee that Indiana

---

97 The orthodox rule for torts and crimes having their impact in another state than the one where the act or omission occurred dictated application of the law of the place "where [the act] first takes harmful effect or produces the result complained of": Leflar (1977-1) p. 267 ff. with citations. *Cf.* § 377 Restatement First: "the state where the last event necessary to make an actor liable for an alleged tort takes place." It seems that the draftsmen of the Federal Tort Claims Act, enacted in 1946, were mistaken as to the contents of the standard rule: Goodrich (1950) p. 894/895; Leflar (1977-1) p. 201.
98 *Foskey v. United States* 490 F.Supp. 1047 at 1057 (D. R.I. 1979).
99 *Griffith v. United Air Lines, Inc.* 416 Pa. 1, 203 A.2d 796 (1964).
100 *Pierce v. United States* 679 F.2d 617 (6th Cir. [Tenn.] 1982), *aff'd* 718 F.2d 825, *reh. denied* 722 F.2d 289.

law applied, since the acts or omissions that would have caused the accident occurred at the Indiana flight service station. No mention was made of Indiana choice of law principles.[101] Other courts have been more conscientious. In *White v. Trans World Airlines, Inc.*, an action in which the United States was a co-defendant under the Federal Tort Claims Act, the District Court of the Southern District of New York obediently cited *Richards v. United States* and proceeded to apply New York conflicts law, for it was alleged that New York air traffic controllers had been negligent. Without much further inquiry it was held, in a footnote, that "[u]nder New York law, the law of the place of the tort governs the issue of liability," resulting in the application of New York's domestic law.[102] A district court in California carefully examined numerous Nevada choice of law cases in order to determine whether Nevada, as the state where tortious conduct under the Federal Tort Claims Act had occurred, had or had not substituted the *lex loci delicti* rule for the most significant relationship approach of the Restatement Second.[103] Another case, arising from a mining accident in Tennessee, was decided by reference to Tennessee conflicts of law

101 Indiana abandoned the place of wrong rule in *Witherspoon v. Salm* 142 Ind.App. 655, 237 N.E.2d 116 (1968), *rev'd on other grounds*, 251 Ind. 575, 243 N.E.2d 876 (1969).
More difficult to interpret is *Edwards v. United States*, 497 F.Supp. 379 (M.D. Alabama 1980), a malpractice suit against a Veterans' Administration Hospital in Alabama. In a footnote the court remarked that "[t]he applicable law for a case brought under this [Federal Tort Claims] Act is the law of the state in which the alleged negligent act took place." No reference was made to Alabama choice of law principles, possibly because Alabama still adhered to the traditional rule, or because the case had no significant connection with any other jurisdiction.
102 *White v. Trans World Airlines, Inc.* 320 F.Supp. 655 at 657, footnote 3 (1970), citing *Babcock v. Jackson* as authority. As the issue centered on "breach of duty", application of the *lex loci delicti* may have been warranted, but in its terminology the court seemed hardly inspired by the nuances of the *Babcock* approach. See also: *Ins. Co. of North America v. United States* 527 F.Supp. 962 (E.D. Ark. 1981), in which case the court referred to the *lex loci* rules of Tennessee and Arkansas.
103 *Southern Pacific Transp. Co. v. United States* 462 F.Supp. 1227 (E.D. Cal. 1978). See also: *Ducey v. United States* 713 F.2d 504 at 508 (9th Cir. [Nev.] 1983), divining Nevada's "appropriate choice of law principles for tort cases," after the district court – *Ducey v. United States* 523 F.Supp. 225 (D. Nev. 1981) – had bluntly held that "this Court must apply Nevada [substantive] law." The Ninth Circuit, in *Broudy v. United States* 722 F.2d 566 at 569 (9th Cir. [Cal.] 1983), had no patience to indulge in choice of law niceties: "Rather than examining the law of the other circuits or the common law of torts, the district court should determine whether an actionable duty exists by applying the law of the state where the act or omission occurred."

rules calling for an "allusion" to the substantive law of Tennessee.[104] Although the *Richards* decision removed any doubt[105] on the use of renvoi in connection with the Federal Tort Claims Act, the mixed results of the cases just mentioned tend to show that the doctrine has failed, even in this area, to contribute to the uniformity of decision it was meant to further.

Even more confusion is likely to result from the questionable status of renvoi outside the sphere of federal torts. On the whole, however, renvoi is mercifully absent from tort choice of law. When directed by their own choice of law principles to apply the law of another jurisdiction, the courts in most cases do follow the prevailing doctrine and apply the local law of that state, just as the Restatement Second recommends in § 8(1) and § 145 comment h. Yet, there are some exceptions. A new kind of renvoi seems to have been given a boost by the policy-oriented approaches, although their authors, notably Currie and Cavers, did not exactly approve of the doctrine.[106] Its new function is summarized quite adequately in the Restatement Second, where it says: "It should be reiterated that in the torts area the forum will not apply the choice-of-law rules of another state. The forum will *consult* these rules, however, for whatever light these rules may shed upon the extent of the other state's *interest* in the application of its relevant local law rule."[107] The idea that renvoi could be effective in ascertaining the claim to application of the foreign state's rule of decision may perhaps be attributed to Professor Von Mehren's article on "The Renvoi and Its Relation to Various Approaches to the Choice-of-Law Problem."[108] Although he has little use for renvoi if the fo-

---

104 *Mosley v. United States* 456 F.Supp. 671 (E.D. Tenn. 1978).
105 However, in *Caban v. United States* 728 F.2d 68 (2d Cir. [N.Y.] 1984), the Second Circuit suggested that the "whole law" of the place where the incident took place would mean a combination of state and federal law. No reference was made to New York choice of law principles. See, however, *Bowen v. United States* 570 F.2d 1311 (7th Cir. [Ill.] 1978).
106 Currie (1963-1) p. 184: " ... it seems clear that the problem of renvoi would have no place at all in the analysis that has been suggested."; Cavers (1965) p. 103 ff.; *cf.* Cramton/Currie/Kay (1981) p. 399.
107 Restatement Second § 145 comment h; emphasis added. See also: § 8, comment k.
108 Von Mehren (1961). Before him, in 1946, Professor Freund had already advocated a "technique bearing some resemblance to the renvoi" as a means of "harmonizing conflicting interests." This approach would entail an examination of "not merely the policy but the conflict-of-laws delimitation of each [competing] law." Freund (1946) p. 1217/1218.

rum's conflicts rule refers to a jurisdiction where the mechanical jurisdiction-selecting approach still prevails, he hopes for a better future in which choice of law rules everywhere will be based on functional analysis. By that time, Von Mehren suggests, the choice of law rules of interested states "should state fairly precisely whether the jurisdiction wishes to regulate a given issue at all, and, if so, under what conditions."[109] Professor Weintraub tends to agree, with the same reservation in respect of mechanical conflicts rules: "There are times, however, when it would be wrong to attempt to derive any functional information from the foreign choice-of-law rule. This is [likely to be] so if the foreign choice-of-law rule is cast in a rigid territorial mold."[110] Since this type of conflicts rule selects the applicable law without reference to its content, it does not convey any information on the underlying policies of the designated law. Neither, I should like to add, does it shed any light on the possible interests of the jurisdiction whose mechanical conflicts rule is followed.

At this point, I must take issue with those advocates of policy-oriented choice of law who are willing to invest the doctrine of renvoi with a new, informative function. In my opinion, the examination of foreign choice of law decisions as a means to identify the foreign state's possible interests has nothing to do with renvoi. For one thing, the 19th century doctrine is based on unequivocal jurisdiction-selection, whereas the new choice of law approaches are predicated on rule-selection. A true renvoi approach is premised on total impartiality and allows foreign choice of law principles to take full charge of the allocation process, even to a quadratic degree. Still, there is only one jurisdiction eventually providing the rule of decision. Under a rule-selecting approach, on the other hand, "renvoi" is meant to examine the spatial scope attributed to the substantive law of *all* jurisdictions involved. If the results of such a survey would prove to be incompatible, a likely enough prospect, the choice of the applicable rule of law is not dictated by any of the foreign conflicts laws, as the doctrine of renvoi

---

109 Von Mehren (1961) p. 393.
110 Weintraub (1968) p. 832 = Weintraub (1980) p. 70/71. The words in parentheses were added in the 1980 text. However, the territorial choice of law rule of the foreign jurisdiction may be considered "when the forum is neutral, having no policy of its own to advance." *Ibid.* p. 71. See also: Weintraub (1980) p. 276.

would have it, but by the choice of law principles of the forum.[111] Traditional renvoi presupposes the forum's readiness to *apply* a foreign choice of law principle, while informative renvoi is a process allowing the forum to browse through foreign conflicts case law without any obligation. The rule embodied in the foreign choice of law decision is not *applied*, but treated as *datum*; to the forum, it has no normative strength or status. Characteristic of renvoi is the chain of references it creates, each of them linked to another until the circle is closed or until the last link refers to itself. "Modern" renvoi, on the other hand, does not establish any serial connection between the jurisdictions involved; operating in a parallel way, it collects a bundle of separate references to the informative sources of each possibly interested state. I would prefer to call this process "one of construction and interpretation"[112] and reserve the expression "renvoi" for its traditional function.

To Professor Egnal, a champion of the "essential role of modern renvoi in the governmental interest approach," renvoi connotes "[a]ny reference to a choice of law decision of another jurisdiction."[113] Covering both the traditional doctrine and its modern, informative variant, this description brings up a problem which demonstrates the hazards of interpolating a doctrine of traditional conflicts law in modern methodology. I am referring to the dubious status of foreign scope

---

111 *Cf.* Egnal (1981) p. 246: "The essential distinction between traditional and modern renvoi is that, in traditional renvoi, reference to the choice of law decision of another state involves a total relinquishment of the choice of law decision." Modern renvoi "involves reference to the choice of law decisions of another state for the purpose of learning more about that state's interest. The forum retains control over all aspects of the choice of law decision." See also: Kotting (1984) p. 136.

112 Currie (1963-1) p. 183/184: The identification of interests "is essentially the familiar one of construction and interpretation. Just as we determine by that process how a statute applies in time, and how it applies to marginal domestic situations, so we may determine how it should be applied to cases involving foreign elements in order to effectuate the legislative purpose." Here, Currie described the assessment of *forum* interests, but the same process will serve to identify foreign interests: "If necessary, the court should *similarly* determine the policy expressed by the foreign law, and whether the foreign state has an interest in the application of its policy." Emphasis added.
It is significant that Cavers discussed "the other state's choice-of-law rules" in the context of his chapter on "the ordinary processes of construction and interpretation." Cavers (1965) p. 88 ff., p. 102 ff.

113 Egnal (1981) p. 246.

rules, which can be described as rules by which the foreign legislature has demarcated the spatial reach of a specific portion of its substantive law. Assuming that the expression "choice of law decisions" in Egnal's renvoi definition not only comprises judicial contributions to conflicts law, but enacted choice of law rules as well, I wonder how he would view the "essential role of modern renvoi" in relation to scope rules. Should they be taken as expressions of a foreign jurisdiction's preconceived interest, precluding the forum from probing the foreign law's actual claim to application? Should they be regarded as sources of useful but not necessarily conclusive data, which can be set off against other information on the interests of the state in question? Or should they be ignored altogether, on the assumption that the foreign legislature when enacting the scope rule was "not motivated by a desire to achieve acceptable choice of law solutions, but, more likely, by an understandable, yet objectionable urge to secure for its own product the largest possible reach."[114] As I see it, foreign interests should be identified by a process of construction and interpretation. I agree with Egnal that the forum should go beyond "armchair speculation"[115] about the extent of the other jurisdiction's interest. I have no quarrel, at least not in theory,[116] with the proposition that, in the process of construction and interpretation of the foreign law's spatial reach, the

---

114 Strikwerda (1978) p. 155. A provocative example is § 385.2(c) paragraph 2 of the Export Administration Regulations, as amended by President Reagan by order of June 22, 1982. The new Regulations expanded the prohibition of unlicensed export of "goods of U.S. origin" destined for the Soviet Union to the export of "non U.S. goods." They were declared binding upon "any person subject to the jurisdiction of the United States," including *foreign* corporations owned or controlled by American persons or corporate entities. In *Compagnie Européenne des Pétroles v. Sensor Nederland B.V.*, discussed *supra* chapter 1, section 5, text accompanying notes 225–228, the President of the Court of The Hague doubted whether the Export Administration Regulations, by their terms, were applicable at all. But even if defendant, a Dutch corporation controlled by a Texas holding company, would come within the scope of § 385.2(c), paragraph 2, it was held, a Dutch court would not be obliged to give priority to the foreign rule absent a close connection between the contract at issue and the foreign jurisdiction in interest. Pres. Rb. The Hague 17 September 1982, *RvdW/KG* 1982, no. 167. See: De Boer/Kotting (1982); Basedow (1983); De Boer/Kotting (1984); Kotting (1984) p. 140 ff. and p. 147 note 46 for further references.
115 Egnal (1981) p. 248 and *passim*, borrowing the expression from Weintraub (1980) p. 68 ff.
116 In practice, the informative value of foreign choice of law decisions based on one of the new approaches is greatly reduced by their inherent parochialism. More on this subject, *infra* text following note 140.

forum will have recourse to the choice of law sources of the state concerned, as long as they contain reliable information on the scope of that state's substantive law. The most explicit information in this respect can be gained from a scope rule. Expressing preconceived interests, such a rule asserts an interest of the foreign jurisdiction whenever the fact pattern fits its description. As far as that jurisdiction is concerned, I submit, no more data are needed.[117] However, since there are more states whose interests may be at stake, the process of interest identification must go on, and, until the forum has completed its inventory of interests, it will heed none of the choice of law dictates encountered, as it would when using renvoi. For that reason I would prefer another label for policy-oriented data-collecting than "renvoi", but as long as we know what we are talking about, the terminology is not essential.

Thus, I have no objection to "informative renvoi", not on principle at least, if it yields *reliable* information on the postulated spatial reach of foreign substantive law or, in the absence of scope rules, on the interests of the foreign jurisdiction, as inferred from its choice of law decisions. Unfortunately, the meaning of the word "reliable" is susceptible to different interpretations. As we have seen,[118] both Professor Von Mehren and Professor Weintraub tended to reject a consideration of foreign choice of law decisions if they were based on *lex loci delicti*. It was obvious to them, as it is to me, that the information these decisions contained had no bearing on the presence or the intensity of the interests of the jurisdiction concerned. Precisely for this reason the New Jersey Supreme Court in *Pfau v. Trent Aluminum Company* refused to follow defendants' suggestion to take account of a foreign conflicts rule. Having found that Iowa, the state of the *locus delicti*, did not have an interest in the application of its guest statute to a tort involving a Connecticut guest and a New Jersey host, the court concluded that the case presented a no-conflict situation, as the substantive laws of Connecticut and New Jersey were identical. But even if Connecticut law were to apply, the court added, its choice of law rule (referring to the Iowa *lex loci*) would not be followed: "To do so would frustrate the very goal of governmental interest analysis. Connecticut's choice-of-law rule does not identify that state's interest with the

---

117 *Cf.* De Boer/Kotting (1984) p. 112, note 23 and accompanying text.
118 *Supra* text accompanying notes 108–110.

matter. *Lex loci delicti* was born in an effort to achieve simplicity and uniformity and does not relate to a state's interest in having its law applied to given issues in a tort case."[119]

A different opinion was expressed by Professor Seidelson.[120] In cases in which two or more states have substantial interests in the issue, he argued, the forum should examine the "indicative law" (*i.e.* choice of law rules) of each competing jurisdiction in order to find out whether that jurisdiction would apply its own law if the action had been brought there. In Seidelson's view, choice of law rules are indicative of an "enhanced" or, as the case may be, "diminished" interest on the part of that particular state in the issue before the court. It does not make much of a difference whether the foreign conflicts rule is based on functional analysis or rooted in the traditional method. There is one exception, however. The words "enhanced" and "diminished" imply that Seidelson's renvoi test measures interests by degree. Indeed, the foreign state's *lex loci delicti* rule yields little information on the intensity of that state's interests, if the highest appellate court of that state "hasn't resolved a choice-of-law problem for twenty years." Conversely, "[i]f the highest appellate court of State A expressly rejects interest analysis and decides to retain lex loci delicti, it cannot come as an unfair surprise to that court if another forum reads the result achieved as evidencing State A's interest in the issue." In the latter situation, renvoi would be a legitimate means of assessing the intensity of State A's interest.[121] From the fact that a jurisdiction re-

---

119 *Pfau v. Aluminum Trent Company* 55 N.J. 511, 263 A.2d 129 at 137 (1970). *Contra*: Egnal (1981) p. 260 ff., blaming the *Pfau* court for refusing to take guidance from Connecticut's place of wrong rule, and for deciding that Iowa would not have had an interest in a guest statute case involving a driver and a victim who were Iowa *residents*. While it may be granted that the parties involved in the Iowa accident were students in Iowa, the owner of the car, defendant Trent Aluminum Company, was a New Jersey corporation and it had its car garaged and insured in New Jersey. It is hard to see why Iowa would be interested in having its guest statute applied for the benefit of a New Jersey defendant and its insurance carrier. On the various policies and interests in guest statute litigation, see *infra* chapter 8.
120 Seidelson (1973). See also: Egnal (1981).
121 Seidelson (1973) p. 290. *Cf.* Egnal (1981) p. 267/268, rejecting the distinction as "an exercise in futility."
I cannot think of any state retaining *lex loci delicti* just because its highest appellate court "hasn't resolved a choice-of-law problem for twenty years." Montana perhaps?

jects interest analysis in favor of the *lex loci delicti* rule Seidelson infers a conscious decision of that jurisdiction to sacrifice the protection of its domiciliaries to the presumed advantages of the retention of *lex loci delicti*, at least in those cases in which the foreign jurisdiction's conflicts rule would refer to another state's substantive torts law.[122] Turning the *Pfau* case into a true conflict between Iowa and Connecticut by pretending that Iowa did have an interest in the application of its guest statute, whereas Connecticut rather than New Jersey would have an interest, *viz.* in the protection of the Connecticut plaintiff, Professor Seidelson would have wanted the New Jersey Supreme Court to heed the Connecticut *lex loci delicti* rule as evidence of Connecticut's diminished interest in the protection of the plaintiff.[123] As support for "the proposition that the indicative law of an interested state may enhance or diminish that state's interests in the issue to be resolved, even if the indicative law be lex loci delicti," Seidelson cites the *Tramontana* decision.[124] In his opinion, the court looked into Maryland's conflicts law "to gain additional insight into the degree of Maryland's interest,"[125] and found that its *lex loci* rule indicated a diminished interest in the issue. My objection to this interpretation is based on the structure of the opinion: whereas much thought is given to Brazil's interest and the absence of any interest on the part of the forum, the reference to Maryland's law is rather perfunctory, and hardly a word is said on the contents of its substantive law or on its possible claim to application. But apart from speculation on the true motives of the *Tramontana* court, Seidelson's renvoi solution, insofar as it takes account of the traditional conflicts rule as indicative of "enhanced" or "diminished" interests, fails to convince me on principle. The place of wrong rule is predicated on considerations of certainty, ease of application and pre-

---

122 Seidelson (1973) p. 290. Egnal (1981) p. 257 ff. takes the same view, but has none of Seidelson's reservations on the informative value of foreign *lex loci* decisions.
123 Seidelson (1973) p. 290. Egnal (1981) p. 260 ff., claiming that Iowa did in fact have an interest, did not need Seidelson's hypothesis to conclude that *Pfau* presented a true conflict between the laws of New Jersey and Iowa.
124 Seidelson (1973) p. 297. *Tramontana v. S.A. Empresa de Viaçao Aérea Rio Grandense* 350 F.2d 468 (D.C. Cir. 1965), *cert. denied*, 383 U.S. 943 (1966).
125 Seidelson (1973) p. 297. Since Maryland's law, contrary to Brazilian law, had no ceiling on recovery, Maryland was said to have "a substantial interest in the plaintiff, a Maryland domiciliary." Seidelson (1973) p. 296. The result is a true conflict between Brazilian and Maryland interests, to be solved by way of renvoi.

dictability,[126] not on interest analysis. The reasons why a *"lex loci state"* rejects a functional approach can be manifold, but I fail to see how it could be taken to mean a "conscious decision" on the interests of that state and its domiciliaries. For in practice, so Seidelson's proposition implies, it will depend on the place of the wrong – within the forum state or without it – whether an enhanced or a diminished interest should be ascribed to the *lex loci* state. For that decision, I feel, the capricious *locus* is not a proper criterion.

Nevertheless, to support the application of forum law, some courts have considered the foreign *lex loci* rule. Such was the case in *Forsyth v. Cessna Aircraft Company*,[127] a strict liability action brought in Oregon, surprisingly,[128] by a resident of the state of Washington against a Kansas airplane manufacturer. Applying Oregon's version of the most significant relationship test,[129] the Ninth Circuit decided that Kansas did not have an interest since a Kansas court would have applied Washington law as *lex loci delicti*. As there was no conflict between the laws of Washington and Oregon, both permitting strict liability actions, Oregon law was applied as *lex fori*.[130] In my opinion,

---

126 *Cf. Babcock v. Jackson* 12 N.Y.2d 473, 240 N.Y.S.2d 743, 191 N.E.2d 279, at p. 281 (1963). Seidelson (1973) p. 290/291, admits that a state's conscious decision to retain the traditional rule may be inspired by advantages which "are stated in terms of ease of application or certainty of result."
This is not the place to trace the history of the *lex loci delicti* rule. Suffice it to say that the original rationale of the rule is related to notions of territorial sovereignty and vested rights. *Cf.* Morse (1978) p. 23 ff., p. 80 ff. If the place of wrong rule expresses any interest at all, it would be a state's interest in local conduct: *cf.* Dubbink (1947) p. 49 ff. That would seem to be insufficient reason to retain it as the single choice of law standard for all (other) tort issues. There are even less grounds, I submit, to read it as evidencing an enhanced or diminished interest of the *"lex loci* state" in its domiciliaries.
127 *Forsyth v. Cessna Aircraft Company* 520 F.2d 608 (9th Cir. [Or.] 1975).
128 As Washington was the state where the airplane crash-landed, it is not quite clear why the action could be brought in Oregon. One can only surmise that Cessna was somehow subject to Oregon's "long arm" statute, but that does not explain why plaintiff preferred this forum.
129 Adopted in *Casey v. Manson Construction and Engineering Co.* 247 Or. 274, 428 P.2d 898 (1967) and refined in *Erwin v. Thomas* 264 Or. 454, 506 P.2d 494 (1973).
130 In the same vein, but more bluntly, renvoi was used in *Panter v. Marshall Field & Co.* 646 F.2d 271 (7th Cir. [Ill.] 1981). This was a class action for intentional interference with prospective advantage, brought by the shareholders against a Delaware corporation having its principal office in Illinois, and its directors. Although the court noted that the substantive laws of Delaware and Illinois in this kind of action were the same, it felt compelled to refer to Delaware conflicts law: "Dela- →

the case demonstrates the peculiar results of Professor Seidelson's renvoi theory. It is fairly obvious that Kansas as the state where the plane had been manufactured and sold *did* have an interest in the application of its rule disallowing strict liability actions, just as much as Washington could be said to have an interest in the application of its strict liability rule on behalf of one of its residents. This true conflict is construed away by a questionable[131] reference to the Kansas conflicts rule supposedly demonstrating a "diminished interest" on the part of Kansas. Why, then, is Washington's conflicts law – just breaking away from the traditional approach –[132] ignored? Besides, should not the court pursue the renvoi technique all the way, taking into account not only the choice of law principles of all jurisdictions concerned but their respective positions on renvoi as well?[133]

ware courts hold that the law of the place of the tort governs actions for interference with prospective economic advantage ... We therefore look to Illinois law ..." (*ibid.* p. 298, note 10).
131 In *Vrooman v. Beech Aircraft Corp.* 183 F.2d 479 (10th Cir. [Kansas] 1950) it was held that Kansas law applied as *lex loci delicti* to a personal injuries action arising out of an air crash in Indiana due to negligence of the manufacturer in Kansas. The case has been described as "a mistake", however: Case note, 78 *Harv. L.Rev.* 1452, 1457 note 48 (1965); *cf.* Ehrenzweig (1960-2) p. 797; Duintjer Tebbens (1979) p. 234.
132 *Potlatch No. 1 Federal Credit Union v. Kennedy* 76 Wash.2d 806, 459 P.2d 32 (1969) In *Johnson v. Spider Staging Corporation* 555 P.2d 997 (Wash. 1976) the most significant relationship rule was adopted, with emphasis on the "consideration of the interests and public policies of potentially concerned states"; in that case the Washington Supreme Court noted that "our recent decisions have rejected the lex loci delicti choice-of-law rule."
133 A fearsome example of "total renvoi" can be found in *Tyminski v. United States* 481 F.2d 257 (3d Cir. [N.J.] 1973). This case involved an action under the Federal Tort Claims Act for medical malpractice and recovery of the value of nursing services. Plaintiff's deceased (her husband) was a veteran who had received medical treatment in a Veterans' Administration Hospital in New York. At the time of his death, the couple lived in New Jersey. The Third Circuit applied New York's conflicts law, in accordance with *Richards v. United States* (*supra* note 95), and found that New York would apply the substantive law of New Jersey, allowing recovery. Urged by defendant to take account of New Jersey's conflicts law, the court added that under New Jersey's interest analysis approach the same result would be reached, but "even were we to find that New Jersey would apply New York law, New Jersey in turn would apply New York's choice of law rule," so it would apply its own local law. This, it would appear, is triple renvoi on a hypothetical basis: first there is a reference to New York's conflicts law (1), as prescribed by *Richards*; New York conflicts law would refer to New Jersey's whole law; on the strength of New Jersey's hypothetical conflicts rule (2), New York's choice of law (3) is revisited, which now refers to New Jersey's substantive law.

Professor Egnal would dismiss such a suggestion for being a "perversion" of the "modern renvoi" he deems "so obvioulsy appropriate to interest analysis."[134] Going two steps further than Seidelson, Egnal maintains that a foreign *lex loci* rule, whether expressly retained or not, should always be taken as a sign of a *diminished* interest of the *lex loci* state, even if the tort occurred in that state. While I do not agree with Seidelson's proposition that a *lex loci* state demonstrates a diminished interest if it is willing to apply a foreign *lex loci delicti* to a tort that occurred elsewhere, I can at least understand his argument. Egnal's ideas escape me completely. In his version, as in Seidelson's, renvoi is meant to inform the forum on the extent of foreign interests. Thus, it covers all references to foreign choice of law decisions, including those of *lex loci* jurisdictions.[135] Yet, while foreign states devoted to interest analysis provide the forum with data about their interests, Egnal unexpectedly turns a blind eye to the information coming from *lex loci* jurisdictions: "If, however, the other state adheres to *lex loci*, it will provide no data. As a result, adherence to *lex loci* is a disservice to a national drive toward a coherent choice of law system, and it is, therefore, proper to deny a *lex loci* state the benefit of any doubt concerning the strength of its interest in conflicts cases. Although this approach may work as a penalty on *lex loci* states, it is a justifiable penalty if the goal is a coherent choice of law system."[136] Egnal's discussion of *Rosenthal v. Warren*[137] as one of the cases in which his renvoi technique would have worked wonders if only the courts would have thought of it, exemplifies this ingenious line of reasoning. *Rosenthal* was a malpractice suit brought by a New York citizen against a Massachusetts hospital and a Massachusetts surgeon to recover for the death of plaintiff's husband following an operation. By way of "mod-

---

134 Egnal (1981) p. 252: " ... the real question is not whether to use it, but rather why it is so little used by the courts which have adopted interest analysis."
135 This idea has some support in comment k to § 8 of the Restatement Second. Yet, the Restatement does not distinguish between "interest analysis states" and "*lex loci* states." It does say: " ... the fact that a state's choice-of-law decisions call for the application of *its own local rule* may provide some evidence of the existence of an interest on the part of the state in the application of its rule in the resolution of the particular issue." Emphasis added.
136 Egnal (1981) p. 272.
137 *Rosenthal v. Warren* 475 F.2d 438 (2d Cir. [N.Y.] 1973), *cert. denied* 414 U.S. 856 (1973).

ern renvoi", Egnal suggests, the Second Circuit could have buttressed its holding that New York law rather than the Massachusetts *lex loci delicti* applied, despite the strong Massachusetts interests involved: " ... Massachusetts' adherence to *lex loci* suggested that its interests in protecting the doctor and the hospital were not very strong since it had chosen to emphasize the place of injury over such defendant-protecting considerations. The inclusion of such a point in the *Rosenthal* opinion, if erroneous, would have invited correction by the Massachusetts courts or legislature, a service to interest analysis."[138] Now this is what *I* would call a "perversion of renvoi."

An inherent danger of renvoi is the possibility that foreign choice of law principles are misinterpreted, adding to the already existing hazards of dealing with foreign substantive law. Even the hard and fast *lex loci* rule suffers from ambiguity if the place of conduct does not coincide with the place of injury,[139] and it would seem that the risk of misinterpretation increases with the subtlety of the foreign jurisdiction's choice of law approach.[140] The very flexibility of the modern approaches may tempt a forum to follow the "homeward trend" and to indulge in a little teleology when interpreting foreign conflicts law. This might have been the case in *Griggs v. Riley*.[141] The action arose out of a car accident in Missouri and involved an Illinois host and guest, as well as a Missouri third party defendant. The Missouri Court of Appeals saw fit to apply its own compensatory law rather than the Illinois guest statute by denying any interest Illinois might have in the issue. First, it examined the contacts listed in § 145(2) Restatement Second, and came to the obvious conclusion that the domicile of the parties and the place where their relationship centered – § 145 para-

---

138 Egnal (1981) p. 274.
139 *Cf. Forsyth v. Cessna Aircraft Company*, discussed *supra* note 127.
140 In *Bowen v. United States* 570 F.2d 1311 (7th Cir. [Ill.] 1978) it was maintained that Indiana still adhered to *lex loci delicti*. See, however, *Watts Pioneer Corn Co.* 342 F.2d 617 (7th Cir. [Ind.] 1965), in which the Seventh Circuit referred to the proper law approach in *W.H. Barber v. Hughes* 223 Ind. 570, 63 N.E.2d 417 (1945), a contract case. *Witherspoon v. Salm* 142 Ind.App. 655, 237 N.E.2d 116 (1968), *rev'd on other grounds* 251 Ind. 575, 243 N.E.2d 876 (1969) marked the end of the *lex loci delicti* era in Indiana.
141 *Griggs v. Riley* 489 S.W.2d 469 (Mo. App. 1972).

graph 2(c) and (d)– "would, if considered alone, require that Illinois law governing the relationship be applied."[142] The court then took refuge in the "basic principles" of § 6, and embarked on an assessment of Missouri and Illinois interests by way of "renvoi". Acknowledging that Illinois had adopted the most significant relationship approach,[143] the court opined that an Illinois court would apply the Missouri *lex loci delicti*, as Illinois' interest in guest-host relationships would extend no further than its borders. "We are not constrained to afford Illinois hosts greater protection than Illinois courts would afford them, particularly when to do so conflicts with the policy of this state," the court concluded,[144] and Missouri law was applied. Whatever valid reason the court may have had to apply its own law –as a proper way to solve a true conflict between Missouri and Illinois law, or as the better law,[145] or on any other motive– I do not think that the decision was sound insofar as it was based on the presumption that Illinois would not have asserted an interest in an Illinois host-guest relationship. Illinois multistate tort cases involving Illinois residents strongly suggest the contrary.[146] Since the courts have a natural tendency to favor their own substantive law, it is understandable, though not beyond doctrinal reproach, that the reference to foreign conflicts law is not always handled in the most objective manner. Paradoxically, some courts seem to seize upon the intrinsic impartiality of renvoi to satisfy a concealed forum bias: professing a willingness to abide by the foreign jurisdiction's choice of law principles they create an impression of objectivity, but a self-serving interpretation of foreign choice of law or foreign

---

142 *Ibid.* p. 473.
143 *Ingersoll v. Klein* 46 Ill.2d 42, 262 N.E.2d 593 (1970).
144 *Griggs v. Riley* 489 S.W.2d 469 at 473 (Mo. App. 1972).
145 As the Wisconsin Supreme Court did in *Conklin v. Horner* 38 Wis.2d 468, 157 N.W.2d 579 (1968), when it applied Wisconsin's "better law" to a guest statute issue between Illinois residents who hadbeen involved in a Wisconsin car accident.
146 Among the Illinois cases decided in the two years that separate *Griggs* from *Ingersoll*, I have not been able to find any choice of law decision turning on the Illinois *guest statute*, and involving Illinois residents and a foreign *locus*; a prudent Illinois plaintiff would probably look around for a "guest-friendly" forum, such as Missouri. In *Ingersoll v. Klein* 46 Ill.2d 42, 262 N.E.2d 593 (1970) and *Aurora National Bank v. Anderson* 268 N.E.2d 552 (Ill. App. 1971), Illinois was said to have a more significant relationship with the (Illinois) parties and the occurrence than the state where the wrong occurred. According to the Missouri Court of Appeal, however, Illinois continued to apply *lex loci delicti* in guest statute cases despite the *Ingersoll* ruling.

interests is apt to tip the scale in favor of forum law again.[147] The irony of such a renvoi construction lies in the presumption that the foreign jurisdiction is *actually* as impartial towards its own law as the forum itself *pretends* to be in respect of forum law.

For that reason I do not have much confidence in Professor Von Mehren's optimistic suggestion that by the use of renvoi "[t]he difficult problem posed by a functional analysis –understanding the application that another jurisdiction would wish to give in a multijurisdictional situation to rules largely or wholly developed for domestic situations– would largely be solved," at least by the time functional analysis prevails in all concerned jurisdictions.[148] On a theoretical level it is hard to disagree with the thesis that "[i]n a fully developed system of functional choice-of-law rules much vital information would be stated in a jurisdiction's choice-of-law rules,"[149] for it would seem that that jurisdiction is in the best position to determine under what circumstances its own substantive law has a claim to application. In practice, however, the foreign choice of law experience might prove to be less persuasive if the foreign courts have not consistently resisted a natural preference for their own law, or were quick to assume that an interest of their own jurisdiction was at stake. Under a functional approach renvoi could be a useful tool provided that forum bias is absent in all jurisdictions concerned. As will be seen in the next chapters, this condition has hardly been fulfilled in modern American conflicts law.

In American torts choice of law, (traditional) renvoi is rarely used, with the exception of cases decided under the Federal Tort Claims

---

147 To me, one of these cases is *Gagne v. Berry* 112 N.H. 125, 290 A.2d 624 (1972). The action arose from a car accident in New Hampshire, involving Massachusetts domiciliaries who had been on their way to a funeral in Maine. The issue turned on the applicability of the Massachusetts guest statute. The New Hampshire Supreme Court, deciding the case with the help of Leflar's choice-influencing considerations, speculated that Massachusetts courts would refuse to apply their own guest statute, not only because of Massachusetts' continued adherence to *lex loci delicti*, but also because they were anticipating the repeal of the statute. The fact that Massachusetts, prior to the final decision in *Gagne*, did abolish its guest statute was advanced as another argument in favor of application of New Hampshire law. *Ibid.* p. 627. The decision demonstrates the interplay of substantive law and choice of law considerations in the process of construction and interpretation.
148 Von Mehren (1961) p. 393.
149 *Ibid.*

Act. Not even within that limited area are all decisions consistent. If renvoi is to prevent forum shopping and to further uniformity of decision, the doctrine must fail if it is not followed scrupulously by all courts. The *Tyminski* decision[150] exemplifies the formidable difficulties a conscientious court may even then encounter, and how easy it is to reach an opposite result.[151] In the few instances outside the sphere of federal torts in which the courts have been willing to heed foreign choice of law principles they did so either "for the sake of argument", or in order to corroborate a choice of law decision they had arrived at on the strength of more compelling arguments. None of these cases would have been decided differently, it would appear, if the renvoi argument had been left out. In multistate torts practice, I submit, renvoi lacks an autonomous function, so the doctrine might as well be abandoned altogether. On the other hand, if taken as a reference to foreign choice of law decisions in which the underlying policies of the foreign jurisdiction's substantive law are discussed, "modern renvoi" is a legitimate step in the process of construction and interpretation the forum follows when assessing interests. In this conception its function is informative instead of decisive, and I would hesitate, therefore, to equate it with the traditional doctrine. Even so, the benefits of "informative renvoi" should not be overestimated, as the foreign court's natural forum bias may have colored its evaluation of domestic interests. As far as the technique is used to establish a methodological link between a functional approach and the mechanical jurisdiction-selecting rule (Professor Seidelson's proposition and an unexpected consequence of the *Richards* ruling), I feel it should be rejected on principle, since the traditional conflicts rule for torts was not conceived to convey reliable information on the interests of the jurisdiction adhering to it, and –in case the wrong occurred elsewhere– even less on those of the jurisdiction to which the rule then refers. On the whole, the doctrine of renvoi hardly fulfills its promise in American torts choice of law. Given its relatively infrequent, haphazard and inconsis-

150 *Supra* note 133.
151 If the Supreme Court wanted to read renvoi into the Act's conflicts rule in order to mitigate the irregularity of its connecting factor, it might be asked what useful purpose renvoi could serve if the conflicts law of the jurisdiction where "the act or omission occurred" is based on principles which are radically different from the traditional place of wrong criteria. Under such circumstances renvoi may breed more confusion and disharmony than could have been caused by a conflicts rule referring to the substantive law of the *locus actus*, especially in cases in which the places of conduct and injury coincide.

tent application in this field, it should be considered obsolete and, except as an incentive to investigate foreign policy evaluations, without merit.

3 Public policy

In the methodology of conflicts law, the concept of public policy has taken on various meanings, from an excuse to bar any dissimilar rule of foreign law[152] to a device for the promotion of the better law.[153] In its best known forms, the doctrine operates either positively to warrant application of forum law, or, in a negative way, to exclude an offensive rule of foreign law.[154] Essentially, public policy is a tool to remedy the unwanted consequences of our willingness to apply foreign law. As such, it gauges and resolves the possible friction between certain paramount interests the forum's substantive law is meant to protect, and on the other hand the interests with which the forum's conflicts law is concerned. Since both kinds of interests are variable in time and

---

152 *E.g.* in the "dissimilarity doctrine", *infra* text accompanying notes 181–186.
153 *Cf.* Hanotiau (1979) p. 318/319.
154 Much confusion has been caused by Mancini's "Italian School" and its unsuccessful attempts to classify national rules of substantive law into rules pertaining to the nation's *ordre public*, or public interests, and rules pertaining to private interests, the difference being decisive for their (extra)territorial reach. *Cf.* Kosters/Dubbink (1962) p. 332 ff.; Van Rooij (1976) p. 47; Strikwerda (1978) p. 25 ff.; Kegel (1985) p. 110 ff. None of Mancini's followers, not even the influential French scholar Antoine Pillet, succeeded in defining a viable standard for this distinction. As a result, public policy could serve to justify the claim to application of practically any rule of substantive law, be it a rule of public or private, domestic or foreign law. The distinction between public and private law did not become a bone of contention until the rise of the twentieth century welfare state, so it was in the area of private law that the proponents of the Italian School had their main battle. According to some of them, all mandatory rules (*ius cogens*) of private law belonged to the ambit of public policy; others divided private law into rules pertaining to "internal" and "international" public policy respectively. The concept of territoriality in a formal sense implied that public policy dictated priority of *forum* law only, as foreign rules of public policy could not be applied by the forum, and vice versa. To some writers, however, territoriality meant the territorial scope of a substantive rule of law. In their view the forum should heed the principle of territoriality in a material sense, and follow the dictates of (foreign) public policy if the facts of the case fell under the scope of the rule in question, regardless of its origin. See generally: Van Rooij, (1976) p. 47 ff.; Strikwerda (1978) p. 25 ff.

space, the doctrine of public policy must be versatile and allow for policy shifts in either area. For that reason its function is adaptable and its meaning elusive, covering both an "aggressive" promotion of forum interests and a "defensive" rejection of foreign law.

Modern European conflicts law, still dominated by the influence of Savigny's impartial jurisdiction-selecting method, generally views public policy as a corrective exception to the principle that, in respect of content and source, all legal systems are interchangeable. Whether or not the conflicts rule appoints *lex fori* to be the applicable law, and whether or not the application of foreign law produces a gratifying result, the traditional method's premise of neutrality must be safeguarded if its ideal of decisional harmony is to be attained at all. This being the first and foremost concern of Savigny-inspired conflicts laws, it is considered an interest of a superior order which is generally allowed to take precedence over the interests of forum law.[155] As an exception to the rule, however, this supranational interest must sometimes yield to values treasured by the community of the forum and protected by its substantive law. When application of a foreign rule of law would result in an intolerable encroachment upon the forum's interest in upholding and pursuing these values, public policy is deployed to ward off its threat, at the loss of uniformity of result. Not surprisingly, proponents of the traditional method have been shy of acknowledging public policy as a helpful instrument of the law of conflicts.[156] Still exhorting the courts to circumspection and restraint in

---

155 This is the premise underlying Kegel's distinction between *internationalprivatrechtliche Interessen* and *materiellprivatrechtliche Interessen* and, consequently, the cornerstone of his thesis that conflicts law should designate *das räumlich beste Recht* instead of *das sachlich beste Recht*. Kegel (1985) p. 71 ff. See also: *supra* note 3.
156 This reluctance resulted, *e.g.*, in a very narrow public policy clause in the Hague Convention Governing Conflicts of Laws Concerning Marriage (1902), which excluded application of the doctrine on non-religious grounds (articles 2 and 3). In several instances it gave rise to the dilemma of adherence to the Convention or denunciation of the applicable, yet intolerable national law, such as the Nazi laws on interracial marriage. A more recent example of an attempt to curb public policy escapes is found in the CIEC Convention on Legitimation by Subsequent Marriage of 1970, articles 2 and 3.

wielding the "blunt ax of public policy", modern writers nevertheless accept the doctrine as a legitimate escape from the blind neutrality of the jurisdiction-selecting method.[157]

Using public policy as a shield is a discretionary exercise requiring great judicial wisdom and legal skill. Not only does it assume a valid interpretation of foreign law and a fine-tuned appreciation of the priorities lodged in forum law, it also relies on a keen perception of the intensity of the forum's connection to the multistate case at issue. The latter aspect of the public policy doctrine – usually referred to with the bland term "relativity"– is fraught with uncertainty. Properly understood,[158] the concept of relativity in the doctrine of (negative) public policy calls for moderation in asserting that foreign law is unacceptable, in proportion to the strength of the forum connection. The demands on the quality of foreign law should be adjusted to the degree of *Inlandsbeziehung* (or "forum connection") displayed by a particular multistate fact pattern. In short, the public policy test should be performed along a sliding scale.[159]

However, there is a limit to our tolerance. Application of foreign law will be refused if its quality, hence its result, does not measure up to a

---

157 Since 1956, the Conventions of the Hague Conference on Private International Law try to inhibit recourse to public policy by the phrase "manifestly incompatible with public policy," which suggests an inducement to even greater caution than the courts should exercise outside the Convention. The same phrase has been adopted in recent EEC and CIEC Conventions. See also the Swiss (Draft) Conflicts Statute, article 17. Whether the courts are willing to adhere to stricter public policy standards when deciding a case under one of these Conventions rather than their national conflicts law, is an open question. See: Jessurun d'Oliveira (1968) p. 283 ff.; Kropholler (1975) p. 340 ff.
158 Verheul (1979) p. 109, distinguishes three functions of the relativity rule, the first one requiring that public policy evaluates the foreign law not in the abstract but in view of its "result in the concrete case." In this sense, relativity is deemed a "misleading description." The second and third functions, predicated either on *boni mores* or on state interests, refer to "the intensity of the relationship between the case and the country of the forum." As will be seen, Verheul would like to reserve the relativity concept for the latter function of public policy.
159 Lemaire (1968) p. 405; Deelen (1971) p. 72. *Contra*, Verheul (1979) p. 118: " ... there is no continuum, but a caesura."

minimum standard of justice, regardless of any *Inlandsbeziehung*.[160] Such a standard can hardly be defined, as it may vary in time and space, but at its core there seems to be a notion of some supranational morality, as embodied in the Universal Declaration of Human Rights, for instance.[161] In a series of decisions concerning an American prohibition against gold clauses,[162] the Dutch *Hoge Raad* attempted to circumscribe the ambit of this criterion by linking it to "principles of decent legislation", as perceived in the Netherlands on the assumption the Dutch legislature would have to address an issue similar to the subject matter of the foreign rules.[163] The standard is vague, of course, and conveys the impression that the Dutch sense of justice is controlled by politicians. Concepts like "justice," "decency," "equity" or "morality" may be universal,[164] but when applied in practice, notably in public policy assessments, they are apt to display national or temporal peculiarities. Nowadays, laws condoning racial discrimination are denounced in most countries for being morally repulsive. Yet, racial discrimination was quite acceptable in some of the United States until the Civil Rights Act of 1964, and in South Africa *apartheid* is even now defended on moral grounds. Surely, the courts of a "civilized nation"[165] would refuse to apply foreign law if it were conducive to racial discrimination, *e.g.* a statute disallowing interracial marriage. But how about other forms of discrimination, on account of religion,

---

160 This might not be a generally accepted view. In German conflicts theory, for instance, the relativity of the *Vorbehaltsklausel* is treated as impregnable dogma, even in connection with constitutional rights. *Cf.* Neuhaus (1976) p. 367 ff., p. 381; Kegel (1985) p. 307 ff. However, relativity is a very elastic concept, so it should not be too difficult for judicial practice to establish that the forum is sufficiently connected (possibly on the merest jurisdictional grounds) to warrant the displacement of detestable foreign law.
161 *Cf.* Verheul (1978) p. 10 ff; Verheul (1979) p. 112 ff., discussing the relation between public policy and morality: "Here, no relativity!"
162 Joint Resolution of June 5, 1933.
163 HR 11 February 1938, *NJ* 1938, 787 (*Dollar debentures City of Rotterdam*). In earlier decisions the *Hoge Raad* had used the expression "contrary to what is decent and permissible in legislation, according to the views held in the Netherlands": HR 13 March 1936, *NJ* 1936, 280 and 281 (*Vereeniging voor de Effectenhandel v. Kon. Ned. Mij. tot Exploitatie van Petroleumbronnen in Ned.-Indië* and *Vereeniging voor de Effectenhandel v. Bataafsche Petroleum Maatschappij* respectively). By virtue of the relativity rule, the American prohibition against gold clauses was deemed contrary to public policy in the first of these two cases, not in the second one.
164 *Cf.* Verheul (1978) p. 10; Verheul (1979) p. 112.
165 *Cf.* Article 38(1) of the Statute of the International Court of Justice. See also *infra* note 217.

gender, nationality and the like? In some Western countries where the modern feminist movement has asserted itself, the notion that men and women should have equal rights has slowly gained acceptance even if it has not been fully implemented in legislation; in other cultures the strong forces of religion or tradition preclude any inroads on male dominance. Legal equality of the sexes is considered a fundamental principle of Dutch law. For that reason, the Court of Maastricht, in a divorce case, refused to follow the applicable Belgian law, as it purportedly made the husband's adultery more difficult to prove than that of the wife.[166] In this case the Dutch forum nexus was probably strong enough to warrant interposition of public policy under the relativity rule alone, but that does not answer the question whether sex discrimination is unacceptable *per se*. It does not seem likely that a Dutch court would offhandedly dismiss foreign law supporting this kind of inequality if it were to apply the standard of "decent legislation" in the perspective of prevailing cultural conditions in the country concerned. In striking a balance between national notions of what is just and equitable a court may be hard put to steer clear of the lure of cultural imperialism.[167] The wider the culture gap between the forum state and the foreign jurisdiction involved, the greater the restraint to be exercised in judging foreign law. Even a "minimum standard" of public policy, I submit, is subject to some sort of relativity.

At this point, there is no need to dwell on public policy's minimum standard.[168] In torts choice of law, public policy is indeed an *exceptional* device, probably more so than in the area of multistate family law. Since the law of torts, like contracts, mainly addresses questions of pecuniary import, it is less imbued with morality, or "universal" justice, or other unmanageable notions on which the doctrine of public policy supposedly relies.[169] Consequently, it is hard to imagine a substantive rule of torts which could be said to violate human rights, or

166 Rb. Maastricht 11 January 1968, *NJ* 1969, 64 (*Belgian adultery*).
167 *Cf.* Jessurun d'Oliveira (1975-3) p. 256 ff.
168 See, however, *infra* text following note 252, for a discussion of its residual function in modern choice of law methodology.
169 *Cf.* Dubbink (1947) p. 138/139: "In this area, it is submitted, public policy should not be resorted to too soon. We are dealing here with the pecuniary interests of the individual, hardly a concern that will affect the fundamental principles of the legal order."

to be inherently immoral regardless of the multistate context in which it is to be applied. In other words: if in this area public policy is to be invoked at all, it is not because the foreign rule is intolerable *per se*, but because the instant case is so substantially connected to the forum state that the foreign law's infringement of forum values cannot be tolerated. Foreign law will be rejected if its application to the case at bar would be hurtful to the community of the forum state. Conversely, if the outcome of the case does not affect the forum community, there is no need to invoke public policy. Thus, the relativity concept tends to encourage the use of public policy as "a choice of law principle, imprecise, uncertain of application, but nevertheless discharging a choice of law function."[170] The inadequacy of the forum's conflicts rule, more than the quality of the applicable foreign law, is at issue. It would follow, then, that the need for public policy's service as "a provisional and fuzzy explanation of intuitive *ad hoc* solutions to new problems, a secret laboratory where new rules crystallize,"[171] must dwindle if the choice of law process were controlled either by more sophisticated jurisdiction-selecting rules or by an approach that calls for a structured interest evaluation in the individual case. Under such conditions, I submit, the function of public policy could be reduced to that of *ultimum remedium* in case the properly designated rule of foreign law, or its result, is intolerable *per se*. Such public policy decisions should not be affected by considerations of relativity, as this notion rightly belongs to the realm of choice of law in the sense of allocation.

In practice, public policy has proved itself worthy of its "unruly horse" epithet. Even though its appearance might be expected to be less frequent in the area of multistate torts than it is in other corners of conflicts law,[172] virtually all of the doctrine's variants are represented

---

170 Paulsen/Sovern (1956) p. 981.
171 Verheul (1979) p. 118. The same idea, it would seem, has been articulated by Franz Kahn as early as 1898: "What is often summed up in expressions such as 'laws pertaining to the public order,' 'public poliy exception' and the like, is usually the unexplored, still unfinished part of conflicts law. Every exception to the prevailing rule, every conflicts rule which is just emerging as a new and more specific principle, every departure from or modification of an existing principle is apt to be introduced with that passe-partout of public policy." Kahn (1898) p. 251.
172 In Europe, public policy is seldom applied in this field: Dubbink (1947) p. 139; Morse (1978) p. 99. While the lower courts in France have attempted to avoid a foreign *lex loci delicti* by invocation of public policy, the *Cour de Cassation* has →

here, notably in American case law. The few Dutch decisions to be found need not be discussed in detail insofar as they summarily *refuse* to sustain a public policy argument. The most interesting case in this category would appear to be the *Saudi Independence* decision,[173] as it concerned the right to strike, an issue that might come close to fundamental principles of Dutch law. As we have seen, the *Hoge Raad* affirmed the lower court's decision to apply the law of the Philippines, governing the employment contracts of the Philippine crew, and to displace the Dutch *lex loci delicti*. Since Philippine labor law would not allow a strike which had not been authorized by a Philippine government agency, the strike was deemed unlawful. In a very short statement, the Hoge Raad confirmed the opinion of the Appellate Court of The Hague which held that this particular provision of the Philippine Labor Code did not violate Dutch public policy. Attorney-General Franx, in his scholarly advisory opinion, pointed out that public policy should generally function as an *ultimum remedium*, and that it can only be invoked in a Dutch court "if the interests of the Dutch legal order are sufficiently involved in the litigation." He conceded that there is also an *absolute* standard of public policy which relies on supranational principles, but in this case the grounds for its intervention were insufficient. Even though the right to strike is protected by the European Social Charter, its provisions do not cover strikes of a political nature (as the one in dispute could be thought to be), which would suggest that the principle underlying the right is somewhat less than fundamental. Even if one were to take a different view, the opinion goes on, the minimum standard of public policy would only apply if the restrictions on the right to strike were so stringent that "actually very little would be left of it." However, from the information available it could not be inferred that Philippine law does indeed impose such restrictions. Thus, appellants' public policy plea was dismissed

---

overruled several of these decisions, notably in *Lautour v. Guiraut*, Cass. Civ. 25 May 1948, 1949 Rev. Crit. d.i.p. 89 (note Batiffol) and *Kieger v. Amigues*, Cass. Civ. 30 May 1967, 1967 Rev. Crit. d.i.p. 728, 1969 Rev. Crit. d.i.p. 512 (note Bourel); 1967 Clunet 622 (note Goldman). *Cf.* Morse *ibid.*; Duintjer Tebbens (1979) p. 304.; Batiffol/Lagarde (1983) vol. II, § 557, note 5.

173 Hof The Hague 23 April 1982, *S&S* 1982, no. 79, *aff'd* HR 16 December 1983, *NJ* 1985, 311 (note J.C. Schultsz), *S&S* 1984, no. 25. *Supra* notes 23–25, and accompanying text.

with the help of the relativity rule: although the strike on board the *Saudi Independence* happened to be called in the Netherlands and might have elicited the solidarity of the Dutch unions and the International Transport Workers Federation, in the eyes of the Attorney-General the Dutch legal order was not sufficiently touched by these contacts to warrant interposition of public policy. In effect, his public policy exposé does not so much address the quality of foreign law as it confirms an acceptable *choice of law* result: in the instant case the conflicts rule accurately[174] referred to a jurisdiction more closely connected with the case than the forum state.

The Dutch multistate tort decisions that *allow* public policy's intervention are few and far between. One focused on assignment rather than tort and was reversed.[175] One held Dutch law to apply anyway, in view of the many contacts with the Netherlands, but added *ex hypothesi* that public policy would prohibit application of German law if that law would condone the wartime conduct of a Dutch informer to the Nazis, which it probably would not.[176] One concerned the slipshod way a French court had calculated damages to be paid by a Dutch defendant to a German plaintiff injured in France, but in correcting the outcome, the Dutch court relied on French law – as it should have been applied in France.[177] The remaining cases seem to be more principled, yet their present-day import is negligible since they deal with breach of promise of marriage. A tort according to some, to others a matter of family law, breach of promise is not recognized in Dutch law as a cause of action, apart from specific material loss. In the Dutch conflicts cases, the issue has been treated in several ways, but generally the action has been dismissed, either by way of characterization or with the help of public policy. The latter approach seems to verge on the doctrine of "positive public policy", in that the multistate aspects of the case are

---

174 To be sure, the court below had resorted to what could be seen as a nifty characterization trick. See *supra* section 1, text following note 23. If it would have characterized the issue of a strike's (un)lawfulness as sounding in tort, a tenable enough proposition, application of the Dutch law of torts as *lex loci delicti* would have been warranted by the prevailing conflicts rule. Instead, the Appellate Court preferred a contractual characterization. Whether the Attorney-General's choice of law construction qualifies as "accurate", is a matter of opinion. *Cf. supra* note 24.
175 Rb. The Hague 19 April 1971 *rev'd* Hof The Hague 12 April 1973, *NJ* 1973, 428.
176 Hof Amsterdam 6 June 1957, *aff'd* HR 18 April 1958, *NJ* 1958, 308.
177 Rb. The Hague 14 January 1960, *VR* 1961, 42.

subordinated to the paramount principle of Dutch law that warrants complete freedom of marriage.[178] The Appellate Court of 's-Hertogenbosch[179] held that article 113 Civil Code pertained to "public policy and *boni mores*" which was obviously sufficien reason to deny the claim for damages of a German woman against a Dutch defendant. Less straightforward was the Rotterdam Court[180] when it applied Dutch law as the law of defendant's nationality adding that, even if Belgian law were to apply as *lex loci,* "the action would be such an infringement of the Dutch legal order that it could not be brought in a Dutch court." Decided before the second world war, when marriage was deemed more sacrosanct than it is now, these cases are hardly illuminating. In our efforts to unravel the mysteries of public policy we might find the American case law to be more instructive.

It can hardly be denied that on occasion American courts managed to forge public policy into a xenophobic jack-in-the-box, springing the brusque displacement of the applicable foreign law for what would seem untenable reasons. Such practice was given a semblance of theoretical merit by the adoption of the "dissimilarity rule" in some jurisdictions.[181] According to this rule, a foreign statute – whether in force

---

178 Kosters/Dubbink (1962) p. 340. This principle is safeguarded by article 49 (formerly 113) of the Dutch Civil Code: breach of a promise of marriage does not create a cause of action, except that an action for specific material losses may be allowed under certain conditions. *Cf.* F.T. Oldenhuis, Enkele opmerkingen naar aanleiding van een verbroken verloving, *W.P.N.R.* 1978, p. 1–6; p. 17–19.
179 Hof 's-Hertogenbosch 5 January 1932, *NJ* 1932, 1336. See also: Rb. Rotterdam 12 May 1922, *NJ* 1923, 48.
180 Rb. Rotterdam 27 July 1932, *NJ* 1933, 311.
181 The origins of the rule are obscure. Paulsen/Sovern (1956) p. 975, note 24, in reliance on Hancock's *Torts in the Conflict of Laws* (1942), cite *Leonard v. Columbia Steam Nav. Co.* 84 N.Y. 48 (1881) as its source, but in *Loucks v. Standard Oil Co. of New York* 224 N.Y. 99, 120 N.E. 198 (1918), *in fine,* Cardozo J. doubted if the "test of similarity ... has ever been accepted here."
According to Morse (1978) p. 13, note 71, the earliest case in which the notion of similarity appeared would be a decision of the Georgia Supreme Court in *The Selma, Rome and Dalton Railroad Co. v. Lacy* 43 Ga. 461 (1871).
Texas and Maryland seem to have retained the dissimilarity doctrine longer than any other state: Maryland until 1937 (Paulsen/Sovern (1956) p. 975, note 26), Texas until 1979. Leflar (1977-1) p. 90, note 3, cites *Flaiz v. Moore* 359 S.W.2d 872 (Tex. 1962) as the decision in which Texas rejected the rule, but this is contradicted by *Gutierrez v. Collins* 583 S.W.2d 312 (Tex. 1979), to be discussed *infra* notes 184–186 and accompanying text.

in a sister state or abroad– would not be applied if it were "substantially dissimilar" to the forum statute covering the same subject matter.[182] In Texas the doctrine has proved particularly persistent. Established in two nineteenth century cases, *Texas & Pacific Ry. Co. v. Richards* and *Mexican Nat. R.R. v. Jackson*,[183] it was not abolished until 1979, when the Supreme Court of Texas in *Gutierrez v. Collins* re-examined its rationale and found it wanting. In the *Jackson* case, as summarized by the *Gutierrez* court, "[t]here was the practical problem of obtaining translations of Mexican statutes and judicial opinions. It was thought that the paucity of translated material might lead to incorrect interpretations of Mexican law by Texas courts, which would be unfair to the parties. Finally, several features of the laws of Mexico were considered to be so dissimilar to the laws of this state that they should not be enforced."[184] As a solution to the problem of inaccessible foreign law, application of *lex fori* is not uncommon and, in my opinion, not unwarranted.[185] But this argument is of another order than dissimilarity *per se*, which presupposes a comparison between the actual contents of the applicable foreign law and *lex fori*. It is here that public policy comes into play as an instrument of evaluation. After dismissing the possibility of incorrect interpretation and application of foreign law as sufficient justification of the dissimilarity doctrine, the Texas Supreme Court proceeded to reduce its scope to that of the usual public policy exception: "Texas courts will not enforce a foreign law that violates good morals, natural justice or is prejudicial to the

---

182 Leflar (1977-1) p. 90; Morse (1978) p. 12 ff. In *Bruck v. Eli Lilly & Co.* 523 F.Supp. 480 (S.D. Ohio, 1981), a federal court in Ohio, upon transfer of the case to its jurisdiction, had to apply Michigan choice of law principles. In an awkward public policy definition the court seemed to hint at the dissimilarity doctrine when it stated: " ... a public policy question exists if the law of the other state provides plaintiffs with a cause of action which does not exist in Michigan; such a cause of action will not be recognized by the Michigan courts." *Cf.* the differences with § 90 Restatement Second: "No action will be entertained on a foreign cause of action the enforcement of which is contrary to the strong public policy of the forum."
183 *Texas & Pacific Ry. Co. v. Richards* 68 Tex. 375, 4 S.W. 627 (1887); *Mexican Nat. R. Co. v. Jackson* 89 Tex. 107, 33 S.W. 857 (1896).
184 *Gutierrez v. Collins* 583 S.W.2d 312 at 320 (Tex. 1979).
185 De Boer (1979) p. 28 ff., p. 30 ff. See also: BGH 26 October 1977, *NJW* 1978, 496; *StAZ* 1978, 98; *FamRZ* 1978, 979.

general interests of our own citizens ... , a limitation recognized by all jurisdictions."[186]

Yet, in spite of the implication that public policy, especially under the dissimilarity rule, may have been abused as "a substitute for thinking",[187] or, to put it more charitably, as an escape from the inconvenience of applying foreign law, most courts must have had worthier motives for resorting to this *ultimum remedium*. The best motive, of course, lies in the sheer offensiveness of the rule to be applied, for the doctrine of public policy is generally perceived as a defense against repulsive foreign law.[188] Naturally, if it comes to the quality of law, evaluation is highly subjective and the standards are vague.[189] For all its literary beauty, little guidance is offered by Cardozo's classic de-

---

186 *Gutierrez v. Collins* 583 S.W.2d 312 at 321 (Tex. 1979). See also: *Robertson v. McKnight* 609 S.W.2d 534 at 537 (Tex. 1980), repeating the *Gutierrez* description of public policy in the context of interspousal immunity.
Several courts in other jurisdictions have made it clear that "[o]ne state's law does not violate another state's public policy merely because the laws of the two states differ." *Delhomme Industries, Inc. v. Houston Beechcraft* 669 F.2d 1049 (5th Cir. [La.] 1982), with reference to § 90 Restatement Second. See also: *Jeffrey v. Whitworth College* 128 F.Supp. 219 (E.D. Wash. 1955); *Maroon v. State, Dept. of Mental Health* 411 N.E.2d 404 (Ind. App. 1980).
187 Paulsen/Sovern (1956) p. 987.
188 *Cf.* Goodrich (1938) p. 33/34: "the foreign law ... must appear 'pernicious and detestable'"; the phrase stems from *McGirl v. Brewer* 132 Or. 422, 280 P. 508 (1929). Lorenzen (1947-1) p. 13; Paulsen/Sovern (1956) p. 1015; Ehrenzweig (1962) § 120; Ehrenzweig (1967-1) p. 153 ff.
189 A curious example is *Holzer v. Deutsche Reichsbahngesellschaft* 277 N.Y. 474, 14 N.E.2d 798 (1938). Plaintiff was a German national, who had been hired in 1932 by defendants' German corporation. The contract provided that plaintiff would be entitled to the sum of 120,000 marks if he would become unable, without any fault on his part, to perform his services to defendants during a stipulated three-year period. In 1933, plaintiff was incarcerated in a concentration camp. Before his release, defendants discharged him from his obligations on the sole ground that he was a Jew. In New York, plaintiff claimed damages for breach of contract, as well as the promised 120,000 marks. Considering the first claim, the New York Court of Appeals found that defendants had not breached their contract, as German law, "however objectionable," had forced them to discharge plaintiff. The applicable German law was *not* deemed to violate New York's public policy: "It cannot be against the public policy of this State to hold nationals to the contracts which they have made in their own country to be performed there according to the laws of that country." 14 N.E.2d at 800. On the other hand, plaintiff was entitled to the contractual compensation of 120,000 marks, since he had become unable to perform his services "without any fault on his part." *Cf.* Cramton/Currie/Kay (1981) p. 142.

scription of public policy, echoes of which still ring in the *Gutierrez* opinion: "[The courts] do not close their doors, unless help would violate some fundamental principle of justice, some prevalent conception of good morals, some deep-rooted tradition of the common weal."[190] Given such latitude to gauge the quality of foreign law the courts can hardly be blamed for occasional lapses. However, most of the objectionable public policy decisions seem to have been inspired by another motive than that of safeguarding the forum's sense of justice from odious foreign law. In those cases public policy does not function to keep out substandard foreign law but to correct a substandard rule of forum law itself: the conflicts rule that inappropriately displaces substantive forum law.[191] According to Lorenzen, the doctrine of public policy owes its very existence to "[t]he notion that the rules of the Conflict of Laws can be derived from some general formula or theory ..." and Ehrenzweig contends: "Reliance on ordre public or public policy for application of the law of the forum has always been the last resort of any court faced with an overgeneralized rule of choice of law."[192] The same notion is expressed by Paulsen and Sovern: "The overwhelming number of cases which have rejected foreign law on public policy grounds are cases with which the forum had some important connection," which implies that it is the forum's conflicts rule rather than the quality of the applicable foreign law which is wanting.[193]

190 *Loucks v. Standard Oil Co. of New York* 224 N.Y. 99 at 111, 120 N.E. 198 at 202 (1918). See also: *Champagnie v. W.E. O'Neil Construction Co.* 77 Ill.App.3d 136, 32 Ill.Dec. 609, 395 N.E.2d 990 at 992 (1979): " ... a court should not refuse to apply the law of a foreign state, however unlike its own, unless it is contrary to pure morals or abstract justice, or unless the enforcement would be of evil example and harmful to its own people." Measured against this standard, a New Jersey law allowing gambling transactions did not pass muster in Illinois: *Resorts International, Inc. v. Zonis* 577 F.Supp. 876 (N.D. Ill. 1984).
191 Paulsen/Sovern (1956) p. 981: "The objection of the forum, thus, is not to the content of the foreign law but to its own choice of law." Verheul (1979) p. 117 ff., discussing the Dutch "gold clause decisions" (*supra* notes 162–163 and accompanying text), comes to a similar conclusion: "What the Hoge Raad did in fact was look for a new conflict rule, a sub-rule, covering only the currency aspect of the relationship and thus amounting to an exception to the *lex causae* ... What appeared, in the context of public policy, as 'relativity' turned out to be nothing but the connecting factor, a necessary element in any conflict rule."
192 Lorenzen (1947-1) p. 12; Ehrenzweig (1967-1) p. 153.
193 Paulsen/Sovern (1956) p. 981. See also: Morse (1978) p. 100; Weintraub (1968) p. 833 ff. = (1980) p. 82 ff.

In this light, the rejection of foreign law by recourse to public policy may be less parochial or mindless than it is often said to be. The strictures of a rigid "*a priori* mode of reasoning",[194] such as the vested rights theory in the United States or the products of Savigny's teachings in Europe, may have left the courts no choice but to denounce a dissimilar foreign law in order to circumvent an uncompromising conflicts rule. A much-criticized case in point is *Mertz v. Mertz* turning on interspousal immunity. The spouses were domiciled in New York. The wife sued her husband for injuries she sustained in a Connecticut car accident due to his negligent driving. Plaintiff relied on the Connecticut *lex loci delicti* which permitted interspousal suits, but the New York Court of Appeals refused to apply Connecticut law on the grounds of public policy: "The law of this state ... recognizes the wrong, but denies remedy for such wrong by attaching to the person of the spouse a disability to sue. No other state can, outside of its own territorial limits remove that disability or provide by its law a remedy available in our courts which our law denies to other suitors."[195] A rule of law which permits recovery in interspousal suits can hardly be called "pernicious or detestable", but obviously Judge Lehman saw no compelling reason to apply the law of a jurisdiction whose only connection to the case was the happenstance that the accident occurred there. So on what other pretext save public policy could the court have bypassed the *lex loci* rule, given its disposition to do so? It could have characterized the issue as one of family law or capacity to sue, to be subjected to the law of the spouses' domicile,[196] which might have been a more elegant[197] yet equally artful construction. The best justification for

194 Lorenzen, (1947-1) p. 14.
195 *Mertz v. Mertz* 271 N.Y. 466 at 473, 3 N.E.2d 597 at 600 (1936).
196 As the decision in *Emery v. Emery* 45 Cal.2d 421, 289 P.2d 218 (1955) is generally understood; see however *infra* chapter 4, section 2, text accompanying notes 49–52. In *Haumschild v. Continental Casualty Co.* 7 Wis.2d 130, 95 N.W.2d 814 at 819 (1959), the same issue was characterized as a question of family law. The concurring opinion (*ibid.* at 821) would have preferred renvoi or a procedural characterization, either approach warranting the same result anyway.
197 The opinion in *Mertz* did try to employ characterization as a second ground for the rejection of the Connecticut rule, but it is unclear what precisely the court had in mind. According to Morse (1978) p. 155, the characterization was probably procedural, but "the result in *Mertz v. Mertz* would be more defensible" had the court applied New York law as the law of the common domicile of the spouses, *viz.* by characterizing the matter as one of family law. Paulsen and Sovern (1956) p. 995, on the other hand, have no doubts: "the opinion characterizes the question as a family law matter appropriately referred to the law of the domicil." Whether →

applying *lex fori* in this case would have been an admission of the inadequacy of "overgeneralized rules of choice of law," but *Mertz v. Mertz* was decided in 1936 and conflicts law had still a long way to go before the shortcomings of abstract allocation would be acknowledged in a less roundabout way than by resort to public policy, characterization and the like. It does not seem quite fair, then, to suggest, as Leflar does, that the *Mertz* court reverted to the provincialism of the dissimilarity rule, which "Cardozo's enlightened hospitality to extra-state causes of action" had dispelled in *Loucks*.[198] In my opinion, Cardozo's liberal attitude in respect of foreign law must be linked to his ardent support of the vested rights theory, which could only tolerate intervention by public policy as the rarest exception to the rule. His universalism demanded strict impartiality in choice of law, at the possible cost of justice in the individual case. This tenet of traditional conflicts law is still very much at the heart of the *Mertz* opinion, where it says: "The courts of the State of New York are not concerned with the wisdom of the law of Connecticut or of the internal policy back of that law. They must enforce a transitory cause of action arising elsewhere ..."[199] But in *Mertz* the balance shifted from universalist

    characterization, as an escape device, should be preferred to public policy, is obviously a matter of taste: in the opinion of Neuhaus (1976) p. 375, invocation of public policy to support the priority of forum law is a "lesser evil" than "unreasonable characterization." See *infra* note 251.

198 Leflar (1977-1) p. 91. It might be thought that Cardozo rejected defendant's invocation of public policy against application of the Massachusetts *lex loci* so as to allow the New York plaintiffs to recover. But the Massachusetts wrongful death statute, other than New York's law, had a limitation on recovery. Currie (1963-1) p. 630, wrote on this aspect: "[Cardozo's] highly regarded opinion in *Loucks v. Standard Oil Co.*, while almost piously liberal by comparison with some of the precedents, seems completely insensitive to the possibility that the New York dependents of the New York decedent might have been given the full protection provided for them by New York law ... ," adding in a footnote "in fairness to Cardozo" that plaintiffs for some reason did not invoke New York law. Thus, in *Mertz v. Mertz* as well as *Loucks v. Standard Oil Co. of New York*, both cases involving New York plaintiffs and defendants, the outcome was (relatively) unfavorable for the plaintiffs.

199 *Mertz v. Mertz* 3 N.E.2d 597, 271 N.Y. 466 at 470 (1936). The sentence then continues with the public policy exception: " ... unless enforcement is contrary to the law of this State."
    The accusation of provincialism may be traced to an awkward definition of the public policy concept. Having quoted Cardozo's adage in *Loucks v. Standard Oil Co.*, Judge Lehman ad-libbed: " ... a state can have no public policy except what is to be found in its Constitution and laws" (*ibid.* at 472, 3 N.E.2d at 599), thus →

dogma to what might have been an apprehension of its fallibility and an urge to reverse the outcome of its relentless rule. Today, courts and scholars in various countries would confidently choose the law of the parties' common domicile as the "proper law" for tort issues, especially if it happens to be the law of the forum. If, in the *Mertz* opinion, public policy was used as a pretext for dodging an inappropriate choice of law, all courts and commentators who have strived to loosen the *lex loci* rule may be accused of provincialism, though theirs is wrapped in theories and principles more sophisticated than the one Judge Lehman had on hand.

Even more attention was attracted by another New York case, aptly labeled by Weintraub[200] as one of "the half-articulated forerunners of current functional analysis": *Kilberg v. Northeast Airlines, Inc.*[201] As far as multistate torts are concerned, the case marked the end of the vested rights doctrine, or what remained of it, in the Court of Appeals of New York: its next prominent torts decision was to be *Babcock v. Jackson*. At stake was, in fact, the issue whether the defendant airline company had failed to fulfill its contractual obligation to transport Mr. Kilberg, a New York resident, safely from New York to his destination in Massachusetts. If so, plaintiffs might have been entitled to full recovery, including the loss of prospective earnings of their deceased. In spite of the trial court's decision to the contrary, the Appellate Division and the Court of Appeals agreed that plaintiffs' cause of action sounded in tort rather than in contract, to be governed by the law of the place of the wrong. As the plane in which Mr. Kilberg met his death crashed in Massachusetts, the applicable law would be Massachusetts' wrongful death statute which limited the amount of recovery to a maximum of $ 15,000. The Court of Appeals could have left it at that, since only the nature of wrongful death actions was on appeal,

evoking the dissimilarity doctrine once more. *Cf.* Weintraub (1968) p. 834 = (1980) p. 83. See also: *Branyan v. Alpena Flying Service, Inc.* 236 N.W.2d 739 at 743 (Mich. App. 1975): "The public policy of a state is fixed by its constitution, its statutory law and the decisions of its courts; and when the Legislature enacts a law within the limits of the constitution, the enactment insofar as it bears upon the matter of public policy is conclusive."

200 Weintraub (1968) p. 835 = (1980) p. 85. In the latter version, Weintraub added the Michigan Supreme Court's decision in *Sweeney v. Sweeney* 402 Mich. 234, 262 N.W.2d 625 (1978) as another example.

201 *Kilberg v. Northeast Airlines, Inc.* 9 N.Y.2d 34, 172 N.E.2d 526, 211 N.Y.S.2d 133 (1961).

whereas the measure of recoverable damages under Massachusetts law had not been argued. Inviting the vehement protest of the minority and subsequent law review commentators,[202] the court decided to rule on that question all the same. Having stressed the fortuity of the place of the wrong in transportation accidents, Chief Judge Desmond was looking for a way to protect his "own State's people against unfair and anachronistic treatment of the lawsuits which result from these disasters." He found one in public policy: "There is available, we find, a way of accomplishing this conformably to our State's public policy and without doing violence to the accepted pattern of conflict of law rules."[203] Since the New York Constitution prohibited any limitation on death action damages,[204] full recovery was deemed to be New York's "basic law." On these grounds, a strong argument could be made in this case for the interposition of public policy between New York's conflicts rule and the Massachusetts limitation, not so much correcting a malfunctioning conflicts rule as dismissing an "absurd and unjust" rule of foreign substantive law.[205] Yet, there are some indications that moral indignation against the Massachusetts rule was not the true motive for the use of public policy.[206] First, Judge Desmond

202 For an anthology of criticisms, see Currie (1963-1) p. 696 ff.
203 *Kilberg v. Northeast Airlines, Inc.* 9 N.Y.2d 34, 211 N.Y.S.2d 133, 172 N.E.2d 526 at 528 (1961).
204 N.Y. Const. (1894), art. I, § 18. This provision is often invoked in support of an affirmative New York policy of compensation. *Cf. Rosenthal v. Warren* 475 F.2d 438 at 443 (2d Cir. [N.Y.] 1973): "This review of the relevant case law leaves us with the overwhelming conclusion that ... the strong New York public policy against damage limitations has triumphed over the contrary policies of sister states in every case where a New Yorker brought suit. This conclusion is particularly striking in wrongful death actions where the New York policy, embedded in a state constitutional prohibition against damage limitations, has without exception been applied in suits brought for New York decedents since *Kilberg*."
205 The court did not stop there. A second argument was found in a procedural characterization of the measure of damages. In the light of New York precedent, this approach was questionable at best: see Judge Froessel's concurring opinion, *Kilberg v. Northeast Airlines, Inc.* 9 N.Y.2d 34, 211 N.Y.S.2d 133, 172 N.E.2d 526 at 532 (1961); Currie (1963-1) p. 694. It was soon to be retracted: *Davenport v. Webb* 11 N.Y.2d 392, 183 N.E.2d 902 (1962).
206 No such indignation influenced the court, obviously, in *Loucks v. Standard Oil Co.*, but Judge Desmond gave short shrift to that case: "the [Loucks] court was merely deciding that the minimum set for recovery in the Massachusetts wrongful death statute did not make it a 'penal statute' unenforceable here because contrary to our public policy." *Kilberg v. Northeast Airlines, Inc.* 9 N.Y.2d 34, 211 N.Y.S.2d 133, 172 N.E.2d 526 at 529 (1961).

wanted to "provide protection of our own State's people" which implies that, *ceteris paribus*, non-resident plaintiffs would not readily be shielded from *lex loci* limitations. The reservation is repeated in a crucial passage: "For our courts to be limited by this damage ceiling (*at least as to our own domiciliaries*) is so completely contrary to our public policy that we should refuse to apply that part of the Massachusetts law."[207] Furthermore, the court noted that Massachusetts courts would likewise apply *lex loci delicti* in wrongful death cases, "unless public policy forbids."[208] Finally, there was the (questionable) procedural characterization of the measure of damages,[209] indicating that public policy alone did not quite support the rejection of the Massachusetts limitation. Why did Judge Desmond attempt to take the sting out of his ruling? If the applicable law were as "arbitrary," "absurd," "unjust," "anachronistic," or "completely contrary to our public policy" as alleged, would it then acquire a different quality if the courts of the foreign jurisdiction were less fastidious in their evaluation of questionable New York law, or if the victim of wrongful death hailed from another state?[210] Or could it be that public policy was used, again, as a device to achieve a more appropriate choice of law result?

It is not too difficult to explain the *Kilberg* decision in terms of a functional approach. In Currie's analysis, *Kilberg* is a true conflict, to be resolved by application of the law of the interested forum: "Mas-

---

207 *Kilberg v. Northeast Airlines, Inc.* 9 N.Y.2d 34, 211 N.Y.S.2d 133, 172 N.E.2d 526 at 528 (1961); emphasis added. In *Gore v. Northeast Airlines, Inc.* 373 F.2d 717 (2d Cir. [N.Y.] 1967), the restriction was somewhat mitigated: *infra* note 216.
208 *Kilberg v. Northeast Airlines, Inc.* 9 N.Y.2d 34, 211 N.Y.S.2d 133, 172 N.E.2d 526 at 528 (1961). The argument is a curious variant on the renvoi theme: it does not so much consider the foreign conflicts rule as it stresses the fact that the foreign jurisdiction might, on occasion, resort to public policy. It is unlikely that Massachusetts would have done so in this case.
209 *Supra* note 205.
210 In *Trauth v. Northeast Airlines*, Civil No. 149–256, S.D. N.Y. [date unknown; cited by Currie (1963-1) p. 719 ff., and Cramton/Currie/Kay (1981) p. 116], an action arising from the same airplane crash in which Mr. Kilberg was killed, plaintiffs' deceased had his residence in New Jersey. Although the substantive law of New Jersey did not limit wrongful death recovery, a federal court sitting in New York saw fit to apply the Massachusetts limitation, "since New Jersey ... would apply the law of the place of injury." This motivation implies that a New Jersey court would not raise a public policy objection against the Massachusetts limitation, which absolves a New York court from performing a quality check.

sachusetts has a policy of encouraging enterprise by relieving it of the risk of unlimited liability for death; it has an interest in the application of that policy in *Kilberg* because the defendant is a Massachusetts enterprise ... New York has a policy of requiring the wrongdoer to provide full indemnity for the death, and has an interest in the application of its policy in *Kilberg* because the victim and his next of kin were residents of New York."[211] Even without an analysis of policies and interests, it could be argued on factual grounds that New York had a more significant relationship to the occurrence and the parties than Massachusetts. Since the defendant airline company, although incorporated in Massachusetts, was doing business in New York as well as in other states, its association with Massachusetts on account of its "domicile" in that state could be regarded as a less relevant factor than the domicile of an individual litigant would be.[212] A stronger contact could be indicated by the place where the defendant corporation solicited business from the deceased, or, generally, the place where the relationship between the parties was centered.[213] In combination with the New York domicile of Mr. Kilberg and his dependents[214] this relationship with New York could be said to outweigh Massachusetts' connection with the case, justifying application of New York law without the need to wield the magic wand of public policy.[215] Of course, in respect of a decision dating back to 1961 these choice of law alternatives are anachronistic, but they tend to suggest that the public policy argument in *Kilberg* was not directed towards the repellent contents of

---

211 Currie (1963-1) p. 704/705.
212 *Cf.* Korn (1983) p. 824.
213 *Cf.* Restatement Second § 145(2)(d).
214 Ironically, Mr. Kilberg did not have any dependents at the time of his death. His administrator had hoped to recover loss of accumulations of prospective earnings on a contract count, but this cause of action was rejected. In the event, plaintiff accepted a settlement for less than the $ 15,000 limitation, as wrongful death damages only covered pecuniary loss to dependents. "Thus the *Kilberg* decision was of no help to the plaintiff in the *Kilberg* case," observed Currie (1963-1) p. 695, note 21.
215 In *Semmelroth v. American Airlines*, 448 F.Supp. 730 (E.D. Ill. 1978), Illinois law was held to govern a wrongful death action brought by the administrator of an Illinois resident against a Delaware corporation with its principal place of business in New York. Applying the Illinois version of the most significant relationship test, the district court emphasized the domicile of the deceased and the place where the relationship between the parties centered.

Massachusetts law but rather the very applicability of that law as decreed by a too rigid conflicts rule.[216]

If it is true that the invocation of public policy in most tort decisions served to bend the strictness of the *lex loci* rule, it follows that a more flexible choice of law approach should greatly reduce the significance of the public policy principle and relegate it to its basic function of shielding the forum from intrinsically unjust foreign law. Very few conflicts of law between culturally compatible countries, and certainly between sister states,[217] would then impel the courts to take refuge in public policy, provided their conflicts rules are pliable enough to allow application of what the forum considers the "proper law". As the new choice of law approaches are characterized by creative flexibility – to the point of producing chaos and crisis, according to some critics – it might be feasible to subject this hypothesis to the test of modern judicial practice. This is easier said than done, however, because of the elusive meaning of the public policy concept. In a number of opinions, as a rule in the context of interest analysis, it appears as the equivalent of "policy" or "rationale", denoting the legislative objectives which are molded in a particular statutory rule of (forum) law.[218] It is here

---

216 *Gore v. Northeast Airlines, Inc.* 373 F.2d 717 (2d Cir. [N.Y.] 1967), was another wrongful death action arising from the "*Kilberg* crash", but it was decided a few years later. The district court had refused to invoke public policy against the Massachusetts limitation, in view of the fact that plaintiffs, the deceased's beneficiaries, had given up residence in New York following the accident. The Second Circuit reversed, not on the grounds of public policy, but because New York as the domiciliary state of the *passenger* was said to have an interest in the application of its law: New York's rule of unlimited recovery would "influence common carriers to exercise more care in transporting their passengers ..." Hence, the domicile of the passenger's *beneficiaries* was deemed irrelevant. *Ibid.* at 722.
217 Paulsen/Sovern (1956) p. 1016; Korn (1983) p. 939. Paulsen and Sovern, writing in 1956, used the expression "countries of the civilized world" (p. 1016). This circumscription might now be as objectionable as the way Savigny restricted the community of nations of his day to a league of countries united by their "*gemeinsame christliche Gesittung.*" Savigny (1849) p. 27. *Cf. supra* note 165 and accompanying text.
218 *Cf. Fox v. Morrison Motor Freight, Inc.* 25 Ohio St.2d 193, 267 N.E.2d 405 (1971): from the fact that the Ohio Constitution prohibited limitations on wrongful death damages, the Ohio Supreme Court inferred a "clearly-established public policy" *requiring* full compensation. The widow being the next of kin of an Ohio resident, Ohio was said to have a governmental interest in fair and adequate compensation. See also *supra* note 204 and accompanying text. →

that public policy assumes the different color of its positive function: it operates to promote actively the interests of the forum community[219] rather than check the quality of an eligible rule of foreign law. In effect, the difference between the two functions of public policy may be less clear-cut than it is in theory. The *Kilberg* holding on public policy could be taken to express either a negative judgment on the Massachusetts limitation or a positive appraisal of New York's interest in unlimited recovery. If the choice of law process is predicated on an evaluation of interests, reference to public policy is just another way of asserting that the jurisdiction concerned (usually the forum but sometimes even a foreign jurisdiction) has an interest in the application of its law.[220]

A conspicuous example of this approach is found in *Sweeney v. Sweeney*,[221] marking the equivocal attitude the Michigan Supreme Court

---

The opposite conclusion can be found in, *e.g.*, *Patch v. Stanley Works (Stanley Chemical Co. Div.* 448 F.2d 483 at 491 (2d Cir. [Conn.] 1971): the fact that Connecticut abolished its statutory ceiling on wrongful death damages "neither evidences a committed public policy against any limitation *qua* limitation nor evidences a recognition that while some limitations might be proper, the one involved here is not."

219 The District Court for the District of Columbia, however, pictured the process of interest analysis as one in which "the Court must consider whether the *public policy of a particular legislature* would be furthered, frustrated or irrelevant if applied in the case at bar and will displace the law of the forum only if the *policy* of the legislature of another forum has a stronger interest." *In re Air Crash Disaster near Saigon, Etc.* 476 F.Supp. 521 at 526 (1979); emphasis added. The phrase is quoted in *In re "Agent Orange" Product Liability Litigation* 580 F.Supp. 690 at 706 (E.D.N.Y. 1984).

220 *Cf. Bruck v. Eli Lilly & Co.* 523 F.Supp. 480 (S.D. Ohio, transf'd from Michigan, 1981): "We find no public policy strong enough to warrant application of Michigan law to this case. Michigan has no interest in this case; plaintiffs are citizens of Ohio, and the cause of action arose in Ohio, as did all events leading up to the deceased's illness and death."

In *Halstead v. United States* 535 F.Supp. 782 at 788 (D. Conn. 1982), a federal court in *Connecticut* juggled with the (affirmative?) "public policies" of several sister states at once: "For this court to apply the since rescinded, restrictive laws of *West Virginia* would be in obvious derogation of those public policies evidenced by the laws of *Colorado*. However, the court cannot ignore the public policies evidenced by the laws of West Virginia and must balance those with Colorado before reaching a decision." Emphasis added.

221 *Sweeney v. Sweeney* 402 Mich. 234, 262 N.W.2d 625 (1978).

displayed towards choice of law reform in torts.[222] The parties in this case were father and daughter, both Michigan residents. The daughter brought an action against her father for injuries she suffered in a car accident in Ohio. Following *Abendschein v. Farrell*,[223] a guest statute case in which the Supreme Court expressly refused to overrule the *lex loci* rule, the lower courts held Ohio law to apply to the issue of parental immunity and denied recovery. This time, the Supreme Court reversed. Taking "this opportunity to review the reasoning adhering to *lex loci delicti* in light of interim developments in Michigan law and public policy," and happy to find a way to "reach a proper result in this case without revamping Michigan's entire law of conflicts," the court set forth that "[t]he state of residence has a substantial interest in the parent-child legal relationship," and buttressed that argument by asserting that "Michigan's announced public policy is to permit a child to maintain a lawsuit ..."[224] In terms of the traditional doctrine, the latter phrase would refer to the positive function of public policy, which, of course, comes closer to the interest-evaluation of the present day than any of the other tenets of the neutral jurisdiction-selecting method. In my opinion, the expression "public policy" better be reserved for use in a traditional context, so as to indicate its distinct methodological premises. Still, its meaning in the *Sweeney* opinion seems clear enough[225] to support the conclusion that the Michigan Supreme Court was ready to embrace some form of interest analysis. However, its next argument in rejection of Ohio law throws new doubt upon the methodological stand it actually meant to take: "Automatic application of *lex loci delicti* in this daughter against father suit would frus-

---

222 Even when the court was finally ready to substitute a peculiar *lex fori* solution for the traditional *lex loci* regime, it did so without commitment: "We do not here adopt the law of dominant contacts or any other particular methodology, although any such reasoning may, of course, be argued where persuasive and appropriate." *Sexton v. Ryder Truck Rental, Inc.* and *Storie v. Southfield Leasing, Inc.* 413 Mich. 406, 320 N.W.2d 843 at 854 (1982), to be discussed in more detail *infra* chapter 7, text accompanying notes 29–35.
223 *Abendschein v. Farrell* 382 Mich. 510, 170 N.W.2d 137 (1969).
224 *Sweeney v. Sweeney* 402 Mich. 234, 262 N.W.2d 625 (1978) at 625, 627 and 628, respectively. It had been only six years before *Sweeney*, in 1972, that Michigan abandoned its own immunity rule!
225 It might be thought that the reference to the residence state's "substantial interest in the parent-child legal relationship" is nothing but an application of the relativity rule, another way of saying that Michigan is sufficiently involved to warrant public policy intervention. Even so, such "involvement" is measured in terms of interests rather than bare geographical affiliation.

trate an announced Michigan public policy."[226] On the face of it, this statement seems to deploy public policy in its negative function to shield Michigan from intolerable foreign law encroachments, leaving intact the principles of impartial jurisdiction-selection. This is apparently what the Michigan Court of Appeals inferred from the *Sweeney* decision when it interpreted its holding thus: "In choice of law cases, Michigan has traditionally followed the doctrine of *lex loci delicti* ... However, in *Sweeney v. Sweeney* ... the Court gave new life to a seldom applied exception to the rule of *lex loci delicti*, stating that 'the foreign law will not be recognized if contrary to the public policy of the forum'."[227] Obviously the Court of Appeals elected to support a traditional reading of the *Sweeney* opinion and to ignore the opening to an innovative approach.[228]

Could it be that decisions such as *Sweeney v. Sweeney* made use of the traditional public policy device to ease the transition from the jurisdiction-selecting method to a straightforward policy evaluation? Public policy and policy-oriented choice of law are linked by a common trait: they both rest on an evaluation of substantive law. It is true that public policy, in its customary defensive function, only gauges a preordained *foreign* law and supposedly measures its quality against fundamental values of the forum, whereas most modern approaches examine the contents of *all* relevant laws to ascertain their possible claim to ap-

---

226 *Sweeney v. Sweeney* 402 Mich. 234, 262 N.W.2d 625 at 628 (1978).
227 *Storie v. Southfield Leasing, Inc.* 90 Mich.App. 612, 282 N.W.2d 417 (1979), *aff'd*, 413 Mich. 406, 320 N.W.2d 843 (1982). See also: *Sexton v. Ryder Truck Rental, Inc.* 84 Mich.App. 69, 269 N.W.2d 308 (1978), *rev'd*, 413 Mich. 406, 320 N.W.2d 843 (1982). For a further discussion of these cases, see *infra* chapter 7, text accompanying notes 29–35.
228 In *Turner v. Ford Motor Co.* 81 Mich.App. 521, 265 N.W.2d 400 (1978), the Court of Appeals expressed its allegiance to the *Abendschein* ruling in the absence of "overwhelming evidence that the Supreme Court would overrule that decision today."
Only a few years before, in *Branyan v. Alpena Flying Service, Inc.* 236 N.W.2d 739 (Mich. App. 1975), the same court had displayed greater imagination. In this wrongful death action brought by Michigan plaintiffs against Michigan corporations, Presiding Judge Burns managed to ward off the wrongful death limitation of Virginia, the state where the accident occurred, by a combination of Michigan's public policy ("definitely fixed by statute"), interest analysis (Virginia having "relatively little interest", Michigan's interest being "great"), and an evaluation of "significant contacts." The *Abendschein* decision was distinguished on the grounds that the present action arose out of an airplane (rather than automobile) accident.

plication, not to check their relative quality vis-à-vis cherished forum values.[229] On the other hand, even though either way of appreciating the contents of substantive law may serve different purposes and produce different results, at their core is the aspiration to settle a conflict of laws in a way which is least offensive to any jurisdiction involved, yet conforms to established choice of law principles. Inevitably, the evolution of legal thought transforms settled rules and replaces jaded or untenable theory by inspiring new perceptions, which might in turn wear out or prove equally untenable. In modern American conflicts law, change came about rather suddenly and, as could be expected, the new theories were greeted with a fair amount of skepticism. It is not surprising, then, that the first faltering attempts to switch over to an unorthodox choice of law approach are marked by a certain methodological ambivalence. Understandably, the courts wanted to justify their departure from time-honored principles and long-standing precedent by enunciating any argument they could think of. In a number of cases, including *Babcock v. Jackson*, the outcome could be supported by any of the mutually corroborative components that made up the *ratio decidendi*, but the methodological principles they rely on are often incompatible. It is, therefore, not always easy to gather from a court's opinion whether it meant to depart from traditional choice of law at all – *vide* the *Sweeney* decision – or, in the event of unmistakable methodological change, to determine its particular brand – as evidenced by *Babcock*.[230] Confusion might be the price of progress. Conceivably, radical change loses some of its threat if it is wrapped in the soothingly familiar language of tradition. Predicated on the evaluation of substantive law the doctrine of public policy might help to achieve the transition from the conditional impartiality of the jurisdiction-selecting method to an unmitigated policy-oriented approach, their common terminology assuaging the impact of such a shift. This is not to say the resulting confusion should be dismissed as inevitable, but if it could be explained as a transient and possibly expedient by-product of a major choice of law development, academic scorn for

---

229 Evidently, the better law approach does focus on the quality of law. But it does not necessarily measure quality against forum standards nor does it operate on a basis of relativity, as public policy is supposed to do. See *infra* chapter 5, text accompanying notes 87–97.
230 See: Comments on Babcock v. Jackson, A Recent Development in Conflict of Laws, *63 Col. L.Rev.* 1212 (1963).

ambivalent choice of law decisions might be tempered with forbearance. A few examples may further such understanding.

In 1967 the Supreme Court of Florida attempted to steer a new course in torts choice of law when deciding a question on limitation of damages certified to the state court by the Court of Appeals for the Fifth Circuit.[231] It was held that Florida courts would refuse to apply the Illinois *lex loci delicti*, as its limit on wrongful death damages contravened Florida public policy. Having denounced the rationale of the place of wrong rule as "inapposite in the case of an unintentional tort – especially one where, as in the instant case, the 'place of wrong' was purely adventitious– mere 'happenstance'," the court felt inspired to supplement the public policy argument by adding: "Moreover, ... we can ... take the one small logical step forward and hold squarely ... that the strict *lex loci delicti* rule should be abandoned in favor of a more flexible rule which permits analysis of the policies and interests underlying the particular issue before the court."[232] As complementary arguments public policy and policy analysis also support the dissenting opinion in *Winters v. Maxey*, a guest statute decision of the Supreme Court of Tennessee. Both parties were Tennessee residents who had been involved in a car accident in Alabama. The court refused to abandon the *lex loci* principle, except for situations in which the foreign rule would be against "good morals or natural justice, or for some other reason its enforcement would be prejudicial to the general interests of our citizens."[233] The dissent argued that the

---

231 *Hopkins v. Lockheed Aircraft Corporation* 201 So.2d 743 (Fla. 1967).
232 *Ibid.* at 747. On rehearing, however, the majority reverted to its former position, so the federal court, having taken back the case, decided it on a traditional basis: *Hopkins v. Lockheed Aircraft Corp.* 394 F.2d 656 (5th Cir. [Fla.] 1968). The *lex loci* rule was not abolished in Florida until 1980 in *Bishop v. Florida Specialty Paint Co.* 389 So.2d 999 (Fla. 1980).
233 *Winters v. Maxey* 481 S.W.2d 755 at 756 (Tenn. 1972). The latter condition was met in *Trahan v. E.R. Squibb & Sons, Inc.* 567 F.Supp. 505 (M.D. Tenn. 1983), a products liability case turning on the long-term effects of diethylstilbestrol (DES), a medical drug taken by plaintiff's mother (in North Carolina) before plaintiff was born. Struggling with Tennessee's last event rule, the district court found no clear evidence of the place of (plaintiff's) injury. It took refuge in public policy: "There can be no more basic a public policy decision than one which allocates risk and social cost. This is the underlying concern and decision of § 402 A [of the Restatement Second of the Law of Torts]." The court applied the law of Tennessee, recognizing strict liability, since Tennessee was said to have strong public policy reasons to protect its citizens from dangerous drugs. →

Alabama guest statute was contrary to public policy "[a]nd this is particularly true since Alabama has no interest whatsoever in the enforcement of its regressive law in Tennessee."[234] Purists may scoff at such a mixed approach but it might help to sway the old school majority. When in *Wessling v. Paris* the Kentucky Court of Appeals re-examined the place of wrong rule and decided to replace it by its own brand of interest analysis, it felt compelled to denounce the Indiana guest statute at issue on the grounds of public policy, but this statement is preceded by an examination of the respective interests of Indiana and Kentucky and the conclusion that all interests involved were solely Kentucky interests.[235] Again, the invocation of public policy may be unnecessary and methodologically unsound, but it might have levered the transition: in later guest statute cases public policy is ignored.[236] Among the cases decided under one of the new approaches there are a few in which public policy is presented as a corrective factor.[237] In some of them such considerations result in the displacement of foreign law; in other instances the public policy plea is rejected. Yet, none of the opinions can be said to rely on the public policy argument alone, as

In another DES case, *Mizell v. Eli Lilly & Co.* 526 F.Supp. 589 (D. S.C. 1981), South Carolina choice of law dictated application of the California *lex loci delicti*. While under California law defendants had the burden of proving themselves innocent if they comprise a substantial share of the appropriate market ("market share liability"), South Carolina law placed the burden of proving negligence and proximate cause squarely on the plaintiff. The court bluntly stated that the California market share liability rule was in violation of South Carolina's public policy.

234 *Winters v. Maxey* 481 S.W.2d 755 at 759 (Tenn. 1972), diss. opinion *per* Humphreys, J. Again, this argument could be explained either as an example of interest analysis, or as an application of the relativity concept, another indication that public policy interlinks the two constructions; *cf.* supra text accompanying notes 219–220.

235 *Wessling v. Paris* 417 S.W.2d 259 at 260/261 (Ky. 1967). See also *infra* chapter 7, text following note 10.

236 In *Arnett v. Thompson* 433 S.W.2d 109 (Ky. 1968), attention focused on Ohio's interspousal immunity rule rather than its guest statute. A faint echo of the public policy doctrine may be heard, where the opinion reinforces the holding that Kentucky law should apply: "Particularly is this so since our court does not consider sound the claimed potential of family disunity that is the basis for the inter-spousal immunity doctrine, and since the policy of the law of this state is to allow recovery for injuries or death resulting from negligence." *Ibid.* at 113/114. In *Foster v. Leggett* 484 S.W.2d 827 (Ky. 1972) the Ohio guest statute was displaced on the strength of the new approach alone. See also *infra* chapter 7, text accompanying notes 17–23.

237 As opposed to those opinions in which the phrase "public policy" denotes the doctrine's positive function: *supra* text accompanying notes 219–220.

the outcome is always tenable on other, more compelling grounds. In these decisions public policy is never needed as a last resort. If its veto is enforced at all, it is apparently not because the disqualified foreign law was deemed intolerable *per se*, but because the foreign jurisdiction obviously had a lesser interest in the litigation or none at all. In short, public policy is still being used to achieve or to confirm appropriate choice of law results. For instance: in response to defendant's contention that punitive damages were contrary to Louisiana public policy, the Fifth Circuit merely said that Louisiana did not have a more significant relationship to the occurrence and the parties than Alabama, whose law allowed such damages.[238] Though a little less obvious, two decisions of the New York Court of Appeals, both written by Judge Fuld and both predicated on interest analysis, are likely to be in point as well. In *Oltarsh v. Aetna Insurance Company* the lower courts had held that direct actions, allowed by the applicable Puerto Rican law, were contrary to New York's public policy and as such not enforceable in New York courts. Having ascertained that, in addition to many factual contacts with this case, Puerto Rico had also "a legitimate interest in safeguarding the right of any persons injured within its borders," the Court of Appeals held that public policy was not violated and reversed.[239] While the defendant insurance company was not only doing business in Puerto Rico but in New York as well, it is not clear whether New York was regarded as a disinterested forum, or New York's possible interest considered subordinate to Puerto Rico's. In *Long v. Pan American World Airways, Inc.* the opinion removed any doubt on that score. The action was brought by the widow of a Pennsylvania resident who, on his way from Puerto Rico to his home, had died in an air crash over the border between Maryland and Pennsylvania. In respect of survival and wrongful death, these states had differing laws. In view of the policy of the Pennsylvania statute versus Maryland's "adventitious contact" with the case, Pennsylvania law was held to apply, New York being "disinterested in the possible conflict between the policies which underlie the statutes of Maryland and Pennsylvania." Even though the defendant airline company was

---

238 *Cooper v. American Express Company* 593 F.2d 612 (5th Cir. [La.] 1979). The tort at issue was invasion of privacy: an employee of a Louisiana collecting agency, hired by defendant, had made threatening telephone calls to an Alabama resident and her employer, an Alabama hospital, regarding debts incurred by her husband.

239 *Oltarsh v. Aetna Insurance Company* 15 N.Y.2d 111, 256 N.Y.S.2d 577, 204 N.E.2d 622 at 625 (1965).

incorporated in New York and had its principal place of business in the forum state, "that circumstance is insufficient ... to warrant either application of our substantive law or interposition of our public policy."[240] In both cases the public policy test could be explained as an independent check on the quality of foreign law, unrelated to choice of law observations. Yet, at this final stage New York contacts are not altogether ignored, so relativity may have come into play once more as a choice-influencing factor.

In the remaining cases public policy is used in corroboration of the promotion of forum interests supported by other choice of law principles. This is most obvious in *Schwartz v. Consolidated Freightways Corp. of Del.*, concerning contributory negligence on the part of a Minnesota truck driver. Proclaiming to follow "the Leflar methodology", the Minnesota Supreme Court had no doubts that Minnesota's comparative negligence rule should apply on the strength of the forum's "clear governmental interest in the outcome of plaintiff's case" as opposed to the minimal interest of Indiana, the state where the accident had occurred and where defendant's employee happened to have his domicile. In the light of Minnesota's overriding interest the court did not feel compelled to apply the better law test. But just in case the jury verdict would call for a judgment for the defendants under the law of Indiana. it declared it would be "within the ambit of this court's power to find such result contrary to basic state policy."[241] In a less hypothetical way, the New York Appellate Division circumvented the application of foreign law by resorting to public policy where straightforward interest analysis, or even contacts counting would have sufficed. In *Rakaric v. Croation Cultural Club*, the action arose from an accident in New Jersey where a New York minor was injured when handling a chain saw as a volunteer for defendant, the New Jersey branch of a charitable organization. Under New Jersey's charitable immunity rule defendant would not be liable, whereas in New York it had been decided, in a domestic case, that such a rule is "out of tune with the life about us, at variance with modern-day needs and with concepts of justice and fair dealing."[242] Citing *Neumeier v.*

---

240 *Long v. Pan American World Airways, Inc.* 16 N.Y.2d 337, 266 N.Y.S.2d 513, 213 N.E.2d 796 at 799 (1965).
241 *Schwartz v. Consolidated Freightways Corp. of Del.* 300 Minn. 487, 221 N.W.2d 665 at 669 (Minn. 1974).
242 *Bing v. Thunig* 2 N.Y.2d 656, 163 N.Y.S.2d 3, 143 N.E.2d 3 at 11 (1957).

Kuehner and *Cousins v. Instrument Flyers, Inc.*, the *Rakaric* court repeated that "the doctrine of *lex loci delicti* remains the general rule in tort cases to be displaced only in extraordinary circumstances."²⁴³ One of the circumstances warranting a departure from the general rule in the instant case is found in the objectionable nature of charitable immunity, a doctrine deemed contrary to New York public policy. The other grounds for the application of New York law belong to a different category: by way of a "center of gravity" test and a comparative evaluation of New York and New Jersey interests, much in the vein of *Babcock v. Jackson*, the court strove to support its contention that "extraordinary circumstances" made this case atypical. This curious blend of public policy and choice of law considerations demonstrates once more how elusive public policy's function can be. Why did the court refer to it at all? Was it because it wanted to underline the "New York State policy of assuring full recourse in its courts for injuries sustained by its domiciliaries,"²⁴⁴ thus using public policy not as a shield but as a weapon? If not, do we have here a specimen of public policy's mitigated effect under the relativity rule? Or was New Jersey's immunity rule thought to be intolerable, regardless of any New York involvement? If the *Rakaric* decision could be said to rely on interest evaluation, only the first explanation would be valid: as evidenced by the rejection of its own charitable immunity rule, New York's ("public") policy is such that indemnification of tort victims ranks higher than the protection of charitable assets, so when the victim is a New York domiciliary New York has an interest in his compensation. On the other hand, if the choice of law decision was predicated on a "grouping of contacts" approach, "[t]he prevalence of the greater number of contacts with New York" need not have to be "coupled with the alternative of having to apply a rejected and archaic principle

---

243 *Rakaric v. Croation Cultural Club* 76 A.D.2d 619, 430 N.Y.S.2d 829 at 835 (1980). The quotation is from *Cousins v. Instrument Flyers, Inc.*, 44 N.Y.2d 698, 405 N.Y.S.2d 441, 376 N.E.2d 914 at 915 (1978), which in turn relied on *Neumeier v. Kuehner* 31 N.Y.2d 121, 335 N.Y.S.2d 64, 286 N.E.2d 454 (1972). In the latter decision, however, Chief Judge Fuld was much more specific than the phrase "extraordinary circumstances" suggests: "The law to be applied is that of the jurisdiction where the accident happened *unless it appears that displacing the normally applicable rule will advance the relevant substantive law purposes of the jurisdictions involved.*" 286 N.E.2d at 458 (1972); emphasis added. More on New York's return to conflicts rules, *infra* chapter 6.

244 *Rakaric v. Croation Cultural Club* 76 A.D.2d 619, 430 N.Y.S.2d 829 at 839 (1980).

of charitable immunity."[245] As long as foreign law does not pose a real threat, there is no need for public policy's defensive force. I feel that most of the public policy puzzles in this case could have been avoided if the court had not followed the muddled choice of law approach it quoted. In *Rakaric v. Croation Cultural Club*, it appears, New York torts choice of law has come full circle to the *Mertz* and *Kilberg* era.

Although less ambivalent in its choice of law approach, the federal court deciding *Pancotto v. Sociedade de Safaris de Moçambique S.A.R.L.*[246] did confuse public policy with interest analysis. Plaintiff was an Illinois resident who went on a safari in Mozambique. While taking pictures of a hunting party she was hit by a swamp buggy driven by one of defendant's employees. One of the issues in this case pertained to the measure of damages: the law of Mozambique, unlike Illinois law, limited recovery for travel accidents to a maximum of $ 6,600 and did not allow damages for pain and suffering. The court acknowledged that Mozambique had a strong interest in the resolution of this issue, especially since defendant was not insured. However, Mozambique law was held to be contrary to Illinois public policy. In support of this pronouncement the court referred to the Illinois Constitution, providing that "every person should find a certain remedy in the law for injuries to his person." Apart from the fact that this provision does not necessarily require compensation according to *Illinois* standards, the public policy argument is not very convincing from a methodological point of view. It implies that choice of law reasoning compelled the court to turn to a foreign rule of decision. But even if the jurisdiction where the tort occurred may be thought to have a superior interest in *regulating conduct* within its borders, as to the *measure of damages* plaintiff's home state has as much an interest in his recovery as the other jurisdiction has in shielding its domiciliaries from liability. Why should such an "acute conflict"[247] be solved by way of a dubious evaluation of the foreign law's quality, when the court could have relied on the sensible choice of law principle that in a true conflict forum interests are given priority, or generally, that forum law applies unless there is a compelling reason for its displacement? Again, the reference to public policy could be taken as an awk-

---

245 *Ibid.*
246 *Pancotto v. Sociedade de Safaris de Moçambique S.A.R.L.* 422 F.Supp. 405 (N.D. Ill. 1976).
247 *Ibid.* at 408/409.

ward assessment of Illinois' interest in having its domiciliaries recover their losses. Whatever construction the court had in mind, in the *Pancotto* decision public policy is used once more as a choice-influencing factor, not as the ultimate quality test it is supposed to be.

What lessons can be learned from this aperçu of public policy case law? In my opinion, it is abundantly clear that in the area of torts choice of law, public policy is virtually dispensable. Featured by conflicts theory as a barrier to nefarious foreign law, it actually functions to cover deficiencies, real or imagined, of the forum's choice of law process. When public policy is invoked, it is either to circumvent the directions of an inflexible conflicts rule, or to corroborate the outcome of a more or less explicit evaluation of either contacts or interests. On the other hand, when foreign law is said to qualify for application, allowing public policy's services to be dispensed with, it is probably not the passable quality of the foreign law that inspires such magnanimity, but the absence of preponderant forum contacts or interests calling for the application of forum law, regardless of the quality of the foreign rule. I contend that at the root of all the decisions surveyed – especially the ones in which public policy did affect the choice of law result – there is an interest evaluation, not a quality judgment. Invocation of public policy seldom, if ever, gives vent to moral indignation at foreign law, but serves to protect forum interests. This perception is borne out by the generally accepted notion of relativity, which is hard to explain if public policy is viewed as a quality standard for substantive law. When evaluating foreign law, the forum either approves of its quality or it does not. Yet, public policy's sliding scale allows the same foreign rule to be applied in one case and rejected in another.[248] Since this phenomenon can hardly be put down to a judicial change of heart or selective indignation, there must be another reason why the forum is, or is not, indifferent to the applicability of such a rule. If indifference may be translated as "choice of law impartiality", its counterpart must be "forum bias", indicative of forum interests.[249]

248 *Cf.* the Dutch *Gold clause* decisions, *supra* note 163. See also note 206 for a comparable discrepancy between *Loucks* and *Kilberg*.
249 Verheul (1979) p. 112 ff., argues that one of public policy's functions is the protection of "state interests", where relativity "turn[s] out to be nothing but the connecting factor, a necessary element in any conflict rule" (p. 118). I fully agree with this observation, except that such a connecting factor is obviously inspired by forum (rather than "state") interests, not by a mere geographical connection as the term "connecting factor" might suggest.

The relativity doctrine calls for an assessment of the forum connection, not to be measured by mere geographical contacts but by the degree to which application of the foreign rule of law would affect the forum. In this way relativity mediates between the foreign jurisdiction whose law is held to apply and the forum state whose interest may be at stake, thus bringing together two seemingly opposite standards of choice of law. The objective aspect of the public policy criterion relates to the same geographical attachments the jurisdiction-selecting approach so dispassionately examines, but its other side represents the protective solicitude for forum interests which is characteristic of neo-statutist theory. Under the umbrella of interest analysis the two aspects are quite compatible, since governmental interests are not measured in the abstract but in relation to their factual connection to the case. In the framework of the allocation method, however, the policy aspect is incongruous. Yet, if it is assumed for a moment that the fundamental principle of the latter approach – whether its catchword be "Sitz," or "most significant relationship," or "proper law" – has not just geographical but also material connotations, the allocation rule with its "objective" connecting factor could be viewed as a formula of predetermined interest evaluation.[250] The most significant relationship, as expressed *a priori* by a single connecting factor or derived *ad hoc* from the joint geographical aspects of the case, could then be taken to refer to the jurisdiction most interested in the application of its law. In this perspective, public policy would be less a methodological anomaly than a heavy-handed instrument to tune up the traditional method's performance, especially if it relies on such abstract connecting factors as the *locus delicti*.

True, in the days of the vested rights theory and the rigid allocation method, the courts attempting to remedy unhappy choice of law results did not have much leeway. Blaming foreign law for the shortcomings of one's own conflicts law, however, is not the most elegant solution.[251] Obviously, the proper way to cure choice of law deficiencies is

---

250 *Cf.* Sauveplanne (1982) p. 80 ff.: "Although modern conflicts rules can still be formulated in a neutral way, by indicating allocation factors and allowing alternative choices or opening escapes on the basis of elements of spatial connection, the courts can, and do apply them according to criteria based on policies and contents."
251 Jessurun d'Oliveira (1975-3) p. 250, has noted that in judicial practice the invocation of public policy is experienced as "bad manners", which would explain a predilection for more subtle escape devices, such as characterization or manipulation of connecting factors. See also *supra* note 197.

not to camouflage them, but to improve on the rules that cause them. As the modern conflicts methodology represents a massive attempt at such improvement, the question remains whether its various approaches are capable of eliminating the necessity of choice of law correctives such as public policy.[252] In my opinion, the answer is simple. Any approach acknowledging the *prima facie* applicability of forum law requires a compelling reason for its displacement and has no need for public policy or other forms of quasi-justification to support the exclusion of foreign law. In respect of interest analysis, this is probably a valid premise.[253] Even if it were not, it will be clear that an approach advocating an undisguised assessment of policies and interests can do without the subterfuge of public policy to protect forum interests. It could even be said that this approach has institutionalized public policy's choice of law function, extending its reach to all jurisdictions involved instead of the forum alone.[254] In this light, the pretense of evaluating the quality of foreign law in order to safeguard forum interests, as demonstrated in the *Rakaric* and *Pancotto* decisions, is unnecessary and confusing. Unlike the blind jurisdiction-selecting method, I submit, interest analysis has no need for public policy –essentially a *defense* mechanism– as a means of asserting and gauging (forum) interests. In other words, while the relativity rule may owe its existence to the postulated neutrality of traditional choice of law, it has no place in a policy-oriented approach.

In the context of interest analysis, public policy should only be used to test the quality of the foreign rule of law. There are two possible answers to the question *when* this test should be performed. I have to admit that I never gave much thought to this question, assuming that a quality check, regardless of the choice of law technique, best be performed upon completion of the analysis. By that time, the court will have sorted out which of the involved jurisdictions have an interest in

---

252 *Cf.* Weintraub's criterion to measure "the desirability of any proposed method of conflict of laws analysis", *supra* note 1.
253 Currie (1963-1) p. 183; Strikwerda (1978) p. 156.
254 *Cf.* Justice Stafford's dissenting opinion in *Kammerer v. Western Gear Corp.* 635 P.2d 708 at 714, note 1 (Wash. 1981): "Few recent cases have employed a 'public policy' analysis to conflict of law decisions. This is not because public policy has become any *less* significant, however. Rather, many states ... use 'interest analysis' to determine choice of law, or use a 'better law' analysis. Both methods are based almost entirely on policy considerations, however."

the application of their laws. If one of them is the forum state itself, a court heeding Currie's injunction against interest-weighing will have no cause for public policy deliberations, as the applicable forum law is never subject to public policy's censure. In theory, then, only a disinterested forum might have a need for the residual function of the doctrine.[255] Furthermore, if it is established that the jurisdiction whose rule is at stake has no interest in its application, the court is saved from the trouble of explaining why it would have refused to apply the rule anyway. As applied in practice, however, interest analysis tends to induce a comparative evaluation of interests. In that process the courts are apt to deploy public policy as the same choice-influencing argument it used to be under the traditional method. Needless to say that censuring foreign law is not a proper approach to interest-weighing. To rule out any temptation in this respect, the quality of foreign law is best be measured at an earlier stage. It was Professor Strikwerda who suggested to me that there is no need to postpone the public policy test until all relevant interests are examined and identified.[256] Instead, the public policy test could be performed as soon as the issue has been formulated and the eligible rules of substantive rules have been traced. If the court were to find that the foreign rule does not pass muster, it should discard it right away, without assessing the possible interest of the jurisdiction concerned. If the rule in question proves unacceptable, such phasing may save the court from the toil of interest assessment, which is one possible advantage of Strikwerda's suggestion. More important, however, is the methodological validity of his proposition: if public policy is not to be used as choice of law factor, but only as a quality standard, the quality of the foreign rule should be measured without regard to any interest the foreign jurisdiction may

---

255 It could be argued that the forum state has an ultimate interest in upholding fundamental standards of justice as perceived by the forum community. This line of reasoning would imply that the forum cannot be disinterested when the selected rule of foreign law is intolerable *per se*. *Cf*. Leflar's ideas on the forum being "a repository of justice," to be discussed *infra* chapter 5, text accompanying notes 23–25.
256 In one of the theses appended to his dissertation, Strikwerda had already contended that the doctrine of relativity is premised on an incorrect demarcation of the stages of the choice of law process. Strikwerda (1978) proposition VII.

have in the application of its law. The best opportunity for an objective test, it would seem, comes just before the stage of interest identification.[257]

In Leflar's theory, public policy is altogether irrelevant. An approach calling for the "advancement of the forum's governmental interests," even in conjunction with "the maintenance of interstate and international order," is definitely forum-oriented and has no need for public policy as a corrective choice of law device. Furthermore, Leflar's better law consideration offers a final opportunity to review the material result, outshining public policy even in its residual function. Allowing a comparative evaluation of all eligible substantive law rules, the better law test does not necessarily measure their quality against fundamental forum values,[258] nor is the degree of *Inlandsbeziehung* a yardstick of quality control. In this respect, the better law consideration is not a complementary principle, as public policy is supposed to be, but

---

257 A decision hailing from the District of Columbia demonstrates the hazards of using public policy as a closing argument. In *Felch v. Air Florida, Inc.* 562 F.Supp. 383 at 385 (D. D.C. 1983), the plaintiffs had been passengers on board defendant's airplane when it crashed into the Potomac in Washington D.C. Although the man was not married at the time of the accident – he and his fiancée were living together in Virginia – he sought relief for damage "to his right to enjoy the love, services and affection of his wife." In Virginia, an independent suit for loss of consortium would not be allowed to the wife; under the law of the District of Columbia, both spouses could bring such a suit. At this point the district court could have decided that Virginia law was discriminatory and, therefore, contrary to the public policy of the District. Instead, it proceeded to identify the relevant interests. The District of Columbia was said to have "a strong interest in punishment and deterrence of wrongful conduct causing harm to the plaintiffs within its borders." On the other hand, Virginia would be "extremely interested in the welfare of its married residents. As between these two interests, the latter is of course most relevant to a loss of consortium claim." Anxious to reinforce this conclusion, the court managed to turn the public policy test upside down. Even under the law of the District, the court opined, plaintiff's claim would not be allowed, since the parties' quasi-married relationship violated Virginia's (!) public policy as expressed in a statute that intended to prohibit premarital cohabitation: "Such a relationship might well be in violation of the above-cited sections of the Virginia Code, provisions which, archaic though they might be, nonetheless represent the Virginia legislature's expression of that Commonwealth's public policy of encouraging and fostering marriage." *Ibid.* at 387.
258 Leflar (1977-1) p. 124.

a flexible means to achieve pragmatic justice. The Minnesota Supreme Court in *Schwartz*[259] could have done without public policy if it had followed the "Leflar methodology" all the way.

Maintaining a semblance of supranational neutrality, the most significant relationship approach might still have room for both of public policy's functions. If it is believed that the center of gravity is ascertained by disinterested contacts-counting, relativity might once more draw attention to forum interests that such an impartial approach tends to ignore. However, even without heeding the Restatement's injunction to take account of "relevant policies of the forum,"[260] the courts are apt to select contacts in an interest-conscious way, discounting those connections that imply the (undesired) displacement of forum law.[261] Thus, public policy's choice of law function is superseded by the flexibility of this jurisdiction-selecting approach. Even public policy's residual function could be by-passed by a result-selective manipulation of contacts. Since the most significant relationship approach, particularly in its Restatement Second variety, incorporates a mixture of subjective and objective choice of law criteria, judicial practice hardly needs public policy as a motive for the displacement of foreign law. Within the ambiguous context of the most significant relationship approach, its function will be mostly academic.

---

259 *Supra* note 241.
260 Restatement Second § 6(2)(b).
261 See *infra* chapter 3, note 42. In *Kammerer v. Western Gear Corp.* 635 P.2d 708 (Wash. 1981), one of the issues was whether the applicable California law, allowing punitive damages, should have been displaced by the law of Washington, the forum. The majority held that the most significant relationship centered in California, and that California had an interest in the application of its law. While agreeing that the "most significant contacts" approach would lead to California, the dissent argued that Washington had a strong public policy against general, unlimited punitive damages. Upon a meticulous examination of the various purposes of the doctrine, Justice Stafford concluded: "This state should not import such unsound, illogical, anachronistic, unfair laws when to do so would be to violate a long-standing public policy of our state and erode the heretofore firm foundation for excluding nonstatutorily authorized general, unlimited punitive damages." *Ibid.* at 720, diss. op. *per* Stafford, J.

Unless multistate torts are to be resolved by conflicts rules of the traditional, single-contact kind, I submit in conclusion, the role of public policy in this area of conflicts law is apt to be limited to minimal proportions. Its choice of law function should be redundant if the adopted conflicts method is flexible enough to support a preference for forum law when the forum state, on the grounds of its connection to the case, has an interest in the application of its law. Public policy's relativity is a complementary choice of law concept, discharging a function that should be left to choice of law itself. In its proper function, public policy assesses the quality of foreign law and, if necessary, it prevents incursions upon the moral beliefs of the forum community. Since tort litigation is generally meant to settle controversies of pecuniary import, it does not seem likely that the applicable law of torts will rightly be disqualified for being "pernicious or detestable." Yet, in this respect public policy cannot be completely discarded. Theoretically, any approach that allows for the application of foreign law may need public policy as an *ultimum remedium*. In practice, however, modern choice of law methodology should be result-selective enough to forestall effectively public policy's indelicate censure of foreign law.

4 Notice and proof of foreign law

The choice of law process much resembles a game of three-dimensional noughts and crosses. First, there is the linear dimension of substantive forum law, pointing to its own singular solution to the case at hand. Calling attention to the dispute's international aspects, conflicts law expands the purview of our legal orientation to a range of foreign systems, one of which will furnish the rule of decision. This is the second dimension. A third one is added by the conditions controlling the deployment of conflicts law itself. While substantive issues are determined according to substantive rules of decision, their appointment in turn being determined by the rules of choice of law, there is a third level of rules or principles which determine if, and to what extent, a multistate controversy is subjected to the operation of conflicts law and, possibly, foreign law. Premised on the instigation of civil proceedings, these rules belong to the ambit of procedural law. On the other hand, their scope is limited to multistate cases, and in that respect they are part of the law of conflicts. Operating at the interface of choice of law and civil procedure,[262] they demarcate the role of the court *vis-à-vis* the parties in respect of the choice and determination of foreign law. Basically, they either charge the court with the task of choosing and determining the applicable law, or they indicate application of forum law unless foreign law is pleaded and its content proved. The variants between these two extremes are manifold, but their common denominator is the distinction between matters of fact and matters of law.

In the Netherlands and many other European countries, it is well-settled now that neither choice of law nor the contents of foreign law need to be pleaded or proved. Regarded as matters of law, these questions are to be answered by the court *ex officio*.[263] If the parties in multistate litigation have refrained from asserting the relevance of foreign law, the court is bound to make the choice and, if necessary, to take judicial notice of a foreign rule of decision.[264] The doctrine of

262 Schlesinger (1973) p. 5, suggests that the academic classification of the problem largely depends on the demarcation between "fact" and "law" as determined by the prevailing choice of law theory; *infra* note 267. See also: Currie (1963-1) p. 11 ff. Inasmuch as Schlesinger focuses on the position of foreign law, this suggestion may have some merit, but the question if choice of law rules have the same procedural status as substantive rules must be settled at a higher level than that of conflicts law itself.
263 That the court is obliged to choose the applicable law without being prompted by either of the parties, can be inferred from two *Hoge Raad* decisions, one pertaining to the status of statutory conflicts rules, the other to that of judge-made rules. HR 5 June 1915, *W.* 9871, note E.M. Meijers; *NJ* 1915, 865 (*Ehlers & Loewenthal v. Van Leeuwen*); HR 8 April 1927, *W.* 11664; *NJ* 1927, 1110 note P. Scholten (*Benima v. Rohner*). See: Jessurun d'Oliveira (1971) p. 32 ff., p. 47 ff. Whether the *Hoge Raad* meant to imply that the determination of foreign law should be treated as a matter of law as well, is questionable. Judicial practice answers the question in the affirmative. *Cf.* De Boer (1979) p. 16 ff.
See also: article 15(1) of the Swiss Draft Statute on Private International Law: "The content of foreign law is to be established by the court on its own motion. For that purpose, the cooperation of the parties may be required."
264 In the Netherlands, France, Germany and other countries, foreign law has a special status in proceedings before the highest court. *Cf.* Jessurun d'Oliveira (1979-1); *id.* (1979-2) p. 39–58. At this level, a complaint on judicial error in the determination of foreign law will generally be dismissed. This peculiarity of cassation proceedings goes back to the nineteenth century, when it was the highest court's main function to safeguard a uniform interpretation of the newly codified law, not to redress occasional errors in the ascertainment of domestic or foreign law. *Cf.* Jessurun d'Oliveira (1979-2) p. 59. In Belgium, the highest court abandoned this view in →

party autonomy does not affect this responsibility, since the court, pursuant to the principles of its conflicts law, must still establish the validity of the parties' choice and, if foreign law was chosen, determine its content. However, in modern Dutch civil procedure, the borderline between the parties' responsibility for matters of fact and the court's control over points of law is fading. If the parties have refrained from briefing the choice of law question, the court may invite them to express their views in this respect, or persuade them to agree on the law to be applied, provided the matter in dispute does not preclude a (post-factum) parties' choice.[265] Similarly, the court may choose to consult with the parties on the contents of foreign law, especially if the applicable law is difficult to ascertain.[266] On principle, however, it is incumbent on the court to choose the applicable law and to determine its content on its own motion.

In the United States, the situation is different. Due to the purely adversary character of civil procedure in the tradition of the common law

    1980, when it held that a Belgian court should interpret foreign law as it is interpreted by the courts in the jurisdiction concerned: *Cour de Cassation* 9 October 1980, *Journal des Tribunaux* 1981, 70 (note Vander Elst). See: Erauw (1985) p. 108; Vander Elst (1983) p. 303.
265 Rb. Alkmaar 26 June 1980, no. 1022/1978, unpublished, discussed by J.W. Soek, *N.J.B.* 1980, p. 804; R. Kotting *N.J.B.* 1981, p. 103 (*Huyser v. Maud Frelin–Fredholm*): "Before the court will proceed to inquire into the Swedish statutory provisions for controversies such as the case at bar – an inquiry which is bound to cause a considerable delay in this litigation – the parties will be given the opportunity to express their views on the suggested proceeding or to notify the court that they have yet agreed on the applicability of substantive Dutch law to the contract in dispute."
266 See: HR 3 December 1982, *NJ* 1983, 354, *A.Ae* 1983, p. 385 (note Jessurun d'Oliveira), affirming Rb. Rotterdam 5 February 1979 (*Levi v. Turkiye Seker*); Rb. Arnhem 27 June 1985, *NIPR* 1985, no. 441 (*Hungarian Co-operative Foreign Trading Company v. Saray*). Decisions such as these reflect a trend towards a shared responsibility of court and parties for the ascertainment of foreign law. This development suggests a less strict observance of the "fact-law dichotomy" and lends credibility to Jessurun d'Oliveira's proposition that foreign law should be viewed as a *tertium genus* between matters of fact and points of law. Jessurun d'Oliveira (1971) p. 165; *id.* (1979-3) p. 104 ff. The trend is reinforced by the inclusion of five new articles in the Dutch Code of Civil Procedure, in connection with the ratification of the European Convention on Information on Foreign Law (London, 1968). The new provisions call for a consultation of the parties in respect of the court's decision to request information on foreign law *via* official agencies, pursuant to the Convention: articles 150, 151, 429 s, 429 t and 635 a of the Code of Civil Procedure. *Cf.* Jessurun d'Oliveira (1979-3) p. 99 ff.

–in which the court functions as a passive umpire overseeing the proceedings until it declares the "winner"– the parties are expected to identify the issues, including the choice and determination of foreign law. At common law, the court would remain responsible for the determination of domestic law, whereas foreign law was treated as a matter of fact: it had to be pleaded and proved by the party relying on it. Sometimes, a default in proof of foreign law was remedied by the presumption that the foreign law would be identical to forum law, but in other instances the court just dismissed the complaint or directed a verdict for the defendant.[267] This happened in *Walton v. Arabian American Oil Company*, a notorious decision in this respect, rendered by the Second Circuit in 1956. The plaintiff was a citizen of Arkansas who had been injured in an automobile accident in Saudi Arabia, due to the negligence of an employee of defendant, a Delaware corporation doing business in New York and Saudi Arabia. Although defendant would probably have been liable under both New York and Saudi-Arabian law, and although the court acknowledged that the defendant was in a far better position to obtain information on Saudi-Arabian law, it was the plaintiff who had the burden of proof and failed to discharge that burden. The Second Circuit affirmed the lower court's judgment against the plaintiff: the applicable *lex loci delicti* had not been proved, and the trial judge had been right in refusing to take judicial notice of a law as difficult to comprehend as Saudi-Arabian law.[268]

In the meantime, statutory enactments have mitigated the rigidity of the common law position. Generally, the determination of foreign law is now considered a question of law, which implies that the court may take judicial notice of its content, that it cannot be subjected to a jury verdict, and that, on appeal, the trial court's finding will be treated as a

---

267 *Cf.* Alexander (1975) p. 606. According to Schlesinger (1973) p. 4 ff., the result was largely dependent on the choice of law theory the court adhered to. Under the vested rights theory a foreign cause of action did not exist apart from the foreign law creating it. If foreign law is considered a "fact", failure to plead and prove the foreign law constitutes failure to prove a crucial "fact" and plaintiff must lose. Under the local law theory, forum law was the norm, and failure to prove foreign law would therefore not displace it.
268 *Walton v. Arabian American Oil Co.* 233 F.2d 541 (2d Cir. [N.Y.] 1956) *cert. denied*, 352 U.S. 872, 77 S.Ct. 97, 1 L.Ed.2d 77 (1956).

ruling on a point of law.[269] It should be noted that most statutes permit rather than compel the courts to take judicial notice: befitting the tradition of adversary procedure, the statutory authorization is usually discretionary.[270] Furthermore, it is generally restricted to sister state law, which implies that the law of a foreign country is still considered a question of fact and will not be noticed by the court.[271] In *Tolson v. Pan American World Airways, Inc.*, concerning a claim for punitive damages under the *lex loci delicti* of Panama, the court listed three courses of action in case of a party's failure to prove the law of a foreign country: (1) it could dismiss the action; (2) it could assume that the foreign law is identical to forum law; or (3) it could apply forum law as such.[272] A fourth, rather obvious option led the court in *Amdur v. Zim Israel Navigation Company* to determine Israeli law, by analogy, as it were, to the New York standards of judicial notice.[273] Mostly, however, lack of proof results in recourse to forum law. A clear statement to this effect can be found in *Stein v. Siegel*, decided by New

269 However, categorizing foreign law as a "question of law" does not remove all differences with domestic law. See Schlesinger (1973) p. 4, note 9: "If that had been the intention, the responsibility for ascertaining the foreign law would have been thrown wholly upon the court, and the court would have been instructed to ascertain the foreign law regardless of assistance offered by the parties ... Thus, it is crystal clear that foreign law is not treated like domestic law, which under all circumstances, and regardless of party presentation, must always be ascertained and determined by the court."
270 This might be one reason why the judicial notice solution is not particularly effective; *cf.* Alexander (1975) p. 614 ff., p. 617, claiming that "judicial notice has merely become another technique for avoiding the foreign law problem." Schlesinger (1973) p. 17, has pointed out that even a mandatory rule may have a permissive character, inasmuch as its conditions for mandatory judicial notice are subject to judicial interpretation.
271 In *Siegelman v. Cunard White Star* 221 F.2d 189 (2d Cir. [N.Y.] 1955), however, the Second Circuit did take notice of English law on its own motion. But when the plaintiff in *Walton, supra* note 268, invoked the *Siegelman* decision to persuade the court to take judicial notice of Saudi-Arabian law, the suggestion was rejected on the ground that "an American court can easily comprehend ... English decisions" but comprehension of Saudi-Arabian law was "to say the least, not easy." In *Frummer v. Hilton Hotels International, Inc.* 60 Misc.2d 840, 304 N.Y.S.2d 335 (1969), the court determined the English comparative negligence rule on its own initiative and ordered a new trial under English law. *Cf.* Weintraub (1980) p. 88, note 46.
272 *Tolson v. Pan American World Airways, Inc.* 399 F.Supp. 335 at 339 (S.D. Tex. 1975). The court opted for the third alternative, adding that "defendant agreed to the applicability of Texas law."
273 *Amdur v. Zim Israel Navigation Company* 310 F.Supp. 1033 at 1039 (1969), referring to Rule 4511 of the New York Civil Practice Law and Rules.

York's Appellate Division, in which the appellant had failed to prove the law of Austria: "Under the rules of evidence, a party must plead and prove the foreign law if he intends to establish from it a rule different from that of the forum ... Failure to meet this burden permits our courts to proceed under the assumption that the law of the foreign jurisdiction accords with the law of New York on the subject."[274] Less fortunate was the plaintiff in *Marcano v. Offshore Venezuela*, whose husband, defendant's employee, had been seriously injured in the course of his employment off the coast of Venezuela. After his death, the widow took up his claim for wrongful death damages as his personal representative. She relied on Venezuela law in support of her position that she had capacity to sue *in lieu* of the deceased, and on Louisiana law to establish that her claims were not extinguished. Refusing to resort to its own law, the Louisiana forum dismissed the action, since plaintiff's proof of Venezuela law was deemed insufficient to support her contention that she had capacity to sue.[275]

The question whether the operation of conflicts law, as such, should be triggered by (one of) the parties or by the court on its own motion, is hardly discussed in American conflicts literature. Even if the application of conflicts law is a "matter of law", this is no guarantee for

---

[274] *Stein v. Siegel* 50 A.D.2d 916, 377 N.Y.S.2d 580 (1975). More subtle was the decision of the Second Circuit in *Loebig v. Larucci* 572 F.2d 81 (2d Cir. [N.Y.] 1978), in which plaintiff had contended that the district court should have instructed the jury on the content of German law, as the accident that gave rise to his action had occurred in Germany. Distinguishing between "foreign common law" which was taken to be "the same as ours", and "foreign civil law", for which New York law would be substituted, the court elaborated: "Although New York law may be applicable in the absence of proof of German law, strict statutory refinements in New York law should not be held binding as the standard of care for operation of a vehicle in Germany." *Cf.* Currie (1963-1) p. 58 ff.

[275] *Marcano v. Offshore Venezuela* 497 F.Supp. 204 at 208 (E.D. La. 1980). The court probably expected some proof that plaintiff had been appointed by a surrogate court as the personal representative of the deceased. As Venezuela is likely to adhere to the doctrine of *saisine*, which precludes the judicial designation of a personal representative, it would have been very difficult for the plaintiff to prove her appointment as an administratrix. Application of forum law for want of a better solution was rejected on the grounds that "Louisiana's only interest in the present suit is that it happens to be the forum state. No interest of Louisiana would be served by applying its wrongful death statute to a foreign national concerning an accident which occurred abroad."

judicial activity, it seems.[276] In fact, the status of choice of law is usually assimilated to the position of foreign law. This suggests that, here too, the courts may exercise their discretion to call attention to the multistate aspects of the case if neither party has raised the choice of law issue. Various cases tend to substantiate this supposition. If the choice of law aspects of the litigation are controlled by the parties, it is reasonable to require that proper notice be given of a party's intent to invoke a foreign rule of law. It would be both unfair to the other litigant and contrary to procedural efficiency, if a party would be allowed to plead foreign law in one of the last stages of litigation, although it was assumed, thus far, that forum law applied. This was the issue in *Cousins v. Instrument Flyers*: after all the proof had been received and just before the jury was to be charged, the plaintiff suggested application of Pennsylvania law. Considering that "the parties and the court [had] proceeded, reasonably, in view of the many relevant factors, assuming that New York law would apply," the court decided that plaintiff was too late to change his choice of law strategy.[277] In *James v. Powell*, on the other hand, the New York Court of Appeals addressed the choice of law issue on its own motion, and surprised the parties by remanding the case and requiring proof of Puerto Rican law: "The parties have assumed that the substantive law of New York is completely dispositive of the appeal, and the courts below have in fact

---

276 But see Currie (1963-1) p. 74: "In this century the dominant philosophy has dictated the view that foreign law becomes material (as supplying the rule of decision, at least) merely because the choice-of-law rule refers to it, without more." Since the alternative proposition (foreign law must be "invoked by a party seeking advantage in its provisions") is thus ruled out, it would follow that the courts are obligated to apply choice of law rules on their own initiative. Whether they are so obligated or not, I submit, does not make much of a difference: if the choice of law initiative remains with the courts, while the foreign law they select must be proved by the parties, the status of choice of law still depends, basically, on the status of foreign law. In that perspective, Currie's suggestion that forum law be applied unless foreign law is invoked by the party relying on it, appears to be a sensible reaction to the ambiguity of the prevailing solution.

277 *Cousins v. Instrument Flyers* 376 N.E.2d 914, 44 N.Y.2d 698 at 700, 405 N.Y.S.2d 441 at 443 (1978). Thus, New York law was held to apply, "in the absence of compelling reason to apply belatedly another law, whether on the doctrine of *lex loci delicti* or otherwise." The court did find occasion to point out that "*lex loci delicti* remains the general rule in tort cases to be displaced in extraordinary circumstances," suggesting that such circumstances were present in the instant case. While this assumption would reinforce the court's decision to refuse application of the Pennsylvania *lex loci*, it is unclear what purpose this dictum was meant to serve. See *infra* chapter 6, text following note 52.

decided the case under such law. In so doing, they have overlooked the applicable choice of law principle which establishes that the legal consequences of the defendants' acts in this case must be determined under the law of Puerto Rico."[278] But in *Rolnick v. El Al Israel Airlines, Ltd.* New York law was applied "without resort to conflict of law principles," since the plaintiff had neither suggested that Israeli law applied nor had he supplied any information on its content.[279] In effect, this approach resembles the point of departure of California choice of law, repeated in a number of California decisions: "In short, generally speaking, the forum will apply its own rule of decision unless a party litigant timely invokes the law of a foreign state. In such event he must demonstrate that the latter rule of decision will further the interest of the foreign state and therefore that it is an appropriate one for the forum to apply to the case before it."[280] This statement underscores the dubious position of choice of law in American civil procedure: unless *foreign* law is invoked by one of the parties or suggested by the court as a matter of discretion, choice of law is likely to be ignored. This may tie in with the adversary character of Anglo-American procedure, which, even in its present-day mitigated form, tends to burden the parties with a heavier responsibility in forming the issues

278 *James v. Powell* 19 N.Y.2d 249, 225 N.E.2d 741, 279 N.Y.S.2d 10 at 15 (1967). The action was for interference with collection of judgment. In order to frustrate collection of a New York judgment, defendant had transferred real property he owned in Puerto Rico. The court held Puerto Rican law to apply as the law of the place where the property was located, considering that "the law of New York does not and cannot determine the extent to which property located outside the State is subject to execution by a judgment creditor. Therefore, whether or not the plaintiff was defrauded by the conveyance ... may not be resolved under our own rules." *Ibid.* p. 16.
See also: *Pelinski v. Goodyear Tire & Rubber Co.* 499 F.Supp. 1092 at 1093 (N.D. Ill. 1980), a personal injury action against the owner of the Nebraska premises where plaintiff had been injured. The parties "essentially assumed" that Nebraska law applied, but that did not stop the court from testing the soundness of their position: "Because this Court cannot indulge such an assumption, the choice of law question will be briefly addressed." It concluded that Nebraska law *did* apply.
279 *Rolnick v. El Al Israel Airlines, Ltd.* 551 F.Supp. 261 at 264, note 2 (E.D. N.Y. 1982). See *infra* note 282.
280 *Hurtado v. Superior Court of Sacramento County* 114 Cal.Rptr. 106, 522 P.2d 666 at 670 (1974), relying on *Reich v. Purcell* 67 Cal.2d 551, 63 Cal.Rptr. 31, 432 P.2d 727 (1967) and Currie's propositions on the *prima facie* applicability of forum law; *cf.* Currie (1963-1) p. 75, "rule" no. 3; p. 183. See also: *Beech Aircraft Corp. v. Superior Court* 132 Cal.Rptr. 541, 61 Cal.App.3d 501 at 522 (1976); *Gallagher v. Koppers Co., Inc.* 191 Cal.Rptr. 241 at 243 (Cal. App. 1983).

and informing the court than the one imposed by civil procedure in continental Europe.[281] It seems reasonable to conclude that an American court will generally leave it to the parties to give notice of the foreign law and to show its content: if they refrain from raising the choice of law issue, the court is likely to apply its own law.[282]

Viewed from a methodological angle, the "third dimension" of multistate litigation takes on a different color altogether. In practice, it should not make much of a difference whether the choice of law issue and the determination of foreign law is controlled by the court or by the parties. As long as courts and counsel are aware of their procedural responsibilities, the outcome of the case is likely to be the same. In view of the relatively poor amount of cases and materials on the subject, it would appear that the American legal profession has little difficulty in dealing with the choice of law aspects of civil litigation. However, if the mediation of conflicts law is controlled by the parties – whether directly or, by their control of the foreign law issue, indirectly – we are confronted with a methodological anomaly affecting both the allocation method and policy-oriented choice of law.

The former approach is premised on the selection of the jurisdiction supposed to be "most closely connected" to the instant case. Meant to locate the "center of gravity" of the legal relationship at issue, it ignores the contents of the eligible laws and its criteria may refer to any legal system in the world, regardless of the accessibility of its sources. The ultimate goal is (was?) uniformity of decision: if the "center of gravity" or "*Sitz*" is an unequivocal, objective criterion, predicated on unequivocal geographical factors, the action could be brought anywhere in the world and each forum would select the same law if it only adhered to this basic principle. These days, the neutrality of choice of

---

281 The general emphasis on statutory law and the mandatory character of the Codes of Civil Procedure in Europe tend to restrict the exercise of judicial discretion. As a rule, the parties are expected to supply the facts and to formulate the complaint or the defense, whereas the courts will formulate the issues and ascertain the rules of substantive law to be applied. This makes for a different and probably more precise delineation of the fact-law dichotomy than the one adhered to in the common law orbit.

282 If the choice of law issue is raised, the court is likely to take judicial notice of sister state law. See, however, Schlesinger (1973) p. 16: "In exercising this discretion, courts are naturally disinclined to engage in independent research concerning a strange legal system if they receive no help from counsel." See also: *ibid.* p. 20.

law is no longer defended on the ground of decisional harmony alone. The notion of "conflicts justice"[283] covers a whole range of choice of law objectives, most of which call for an unbiased, "supranational" attitude towards the eligible systems of substantive law. Whether the goal is uniformity of result or all-inclusive "conflicts justice", it will be readily understood that such lofty objectives cannot be achieved if the selection of the applicable law is made dependent on the procedural strategy, the financial resources, or the juridical skills of the parties and their counsel. The postulated neutrality of the allocation method presupposes a neutral attitude towards the choice of the applicable law. It is unlikely that such an attitude will be displayed by either of the parties.[284] If the objectives of the allocation method are to be taken seriously, the choice of the applicable law –and, by implication, its ascertainment– should be left, therefore, to the court.

Under a policy-oriented approach, burdening the parties with the responsibility for choice of law and foreign law is even more anomalous than it is in the context of jurisdiction-selection. Characteristic of the "neo-statutist" choice of law methodology is its premise that each substantive rule of law reflects a particular policy of the community in which the rule is in force. If that policy would be furthered by application of the rule to the actual dispute, the community in question (identified with the "state") is deemed to have an interest in the application of its law. Such an interest establishes the rule's "claim to application". In the theory of interest analysis, a "true" conflict of laws is, therefore, a conflict of state interests. In "false" conflict situations, the rules of substantive law of the jurisdictions involved may differ, but only one state asserts an actual interest in having its law applied: only one of the rules involved "claims application". Could it be argued, then, that such claims are non-existent until they have been discovered and proved by the parties? Are policies and interests mere figments of the juridical imagination, lying dormant in the recesses of civil procedure, until one of the parties decides to bring them to life and proves their existence? May governmental interests be ignored,

---

283 *Supra* note 3.
284 See: Kotting (1979) p. 79: "The litigants are not interested in conflicts law and foreign law; they want to be put in the right ... If only one of the parties possesses the knowledge [of foreign law], he must, as a matter of principle, be considered a false prophet; his procedural advantage does not lie in supplying objective information."

just because the parties ignore them? Considering that interest analysis has its roots in the philosophy of the sociological school, I suggest that the answer to these questions must be negative. If the law is viewed as an instrument of social control,[285] the decision whether or not its objectives require its application may not be left to the initiative of the individual litigant. A choice of law approach which takes the social function of law as its point of departure loses much of its credibility if the implementation of the social policies involved in multistate litigation is made dependent on party instigation. How serious should we take the judicial pronouncements on the "superior" or "paramount" interest of a foreign state in the application of its law, where such an interest is likely to be ignored if the parties choose to ignore the choice of law issue? What is the meaning of a solemn phrase on the admonitory or deterrent policy of the state where the tort occurred if its implementation depends in the first place on the plaintiff's readiness to invoke it? Why should we believe that the compensatory policy of the victim's home state should prevent that plaintiff becomes "a public charge" or "a ward of the state", if it is left to the plaintiff to invoke that policy?[286]

If the parties control the domain of foreign law, and if judicial notice is a matter of discretion, the operation of policy-oriented choice of law depends on the same conditions. While the allocation method would permit the courts to choose the applicable law on their own motion, without the slightest information on foreign law, any approach which is premised on an examination of the contents of possibly conflicting laws either requires proof by the parties or compels the court to take judicial notice of all the foreign laws involved before it can even begin to make a choice. This implies that, in effect, the principles of policy-oriented choice of law take on the same procedural status as the one attributed to rules of foreign law. Without information on the contents

---

285 Currie (1963-1) p. 64: "Law is an instrument of social control. Recognition of this fact, and emphasis on the economic and social policies expressed in laws, would lead to a fresh and constructive approach to conflict-of-laws problems."

286 Perhaps these questions are unfair. To the extent that the parties have ultimate control over the resolution of their dispute, which they have in most areas of private law, the advancement of state policies depends, first of all, on their decision to go to law. If a tort victim would rather be a "ward of the state" than bring an action against the tort-feasor, no rule of tort law can force him to change his mind, regardless of the policy it embodies. In this light, even the public law pretensions of a "rule of immediate application" –*supra* chapter 1, section 5– are relative.

of all the laws involved, a rule-selective approach to choice of law cannot function. Not even the better rule of law can be chosen until it is established that another rule is worse. At best, the court can establish whether or not the forum state has an interest in having its law applied.[287] But in order to find out whether another state also has an interest, possibly a more compelling one, its law must first be known.[288] Unless foreign law is treated on the same footing as domestic law and judicial notice becomes a mandatory procedure, I submit, policy-oriented choice of law can make no claim to methodological objectivity and stands to lose its credibility as a "rational" approach.[289]

There is one more point to consider, irrespective of method. It is true that in adversary proceedings both parties are given the opportunity to state their choice of law arguments and that, in case their positions differ, it is still the responsibility of the court to settle the issue. However, this line of reasoning is based on the assumption that, in terms of "arguing power", the parties in civil litigation are matched to each other. In reality, even if legal aid is available to indigent litigants, such equality is often fictitious, particularly in controversies between individuals and corporate enterprises. A case in point is *Sayers v. International Drilling Company N.V.*, a decision of the English Court of Appeal in a personal injury action. The plaintiff was an Englishman,

287 If the forum has no interest and the parties fail to establish the foreign law to the satisfaction of the court, even Currie sees no other solution than a decision on the merits: "No conflict of interest among states being apparent, justice between the parties becomes the sole consideration." Currie (1963-1) p. 65.
288 *Cf.* Weintraub (1968) p. 837/838 = (1980) p. 88/89: "Under a functional system of choice-of-law, however, no law could be chosen as the necessarily applicable law until the content of that law was known, its underlying policies determined, and a decision made as to whether or not these policies would be advanced by that law's application to the parties and the transaction before the court."
289 The futility of choosing in the blind is demonstrated in *McDermott v. Travellers Air Services, Inc.* 462 F.Supp. 1335 (M.D. Pa. 1979). This was an action for negligence and intentional infliction of emotional distress brought by an Arizona resident against a New York-based tour-operator and one of its tour leaders, a resident of Ireland. The contract relationship centered in Pennsylvania. One of the complaints was based on the unfriendly attitude taken by the Irish hostess when plaintiff slipped in the bathtub of her Irish hotel room and injured her wrist. The choice of law issue was resolved thus: "This Court has no idea what the law of Ireland relating to intentional infliction of emotional distress is but concludes that such a determination is not necessary in this case ... Arizona would appear to have the greatest interest in having its law applied so as to protect its citizens from the intentional infliction of emotional distress."

employed by the Dutch defendant, who had been injured in the course of his employment. The foreign law issue turned on the meaning of article 1638x of the Dutch Civil Code. With the assistance of a Dutch legal "expert", defendant was able to "prove" that Dutch law upheld the validity of an exemption clause in respect of the employer's liability for injuries caused by the victim's fellow-employees, provided such a clause was included in an "international contract." Since the plaintiff was unable to disprove the truth of defendant's "evidence", the court reluctantly found for defendant: "There was no explanation in the evidence of the Dutch lawyer as to what constitutes an international contract; nor any authority cited as to the effect of such a contract. However, there was no cross-examination and no evidence called on the part of the plaintiff on this issue. The judge accordingly had no alternative other than to accept as he did the evidence of the Dutch lawyer."[290] The proposition that the parties are equal to the task of choosing and ascertaining the applicable law –a task they are not required to fulfill in domestic cases– ignores the reality of civil procedure and tends to put the weaker party at an extra disadvantage. To me, that is the main reason to reject the Anglo-American position on notice and proof of foreign law.[291]

---

290 *Sayers v. International Drilling Company N.V.*, Court of Appeal 7 May 1971, 1 W.L.R. 1176 at 1182; 3 All.E.R. 163; 2 Lloyd's Rep. 105 (1971). In fact, article 1638x of the Dutch Civil Code has nothing to do with either the doctrine of *respondeat superior* or international contracts. It is a mandatory rule (voiding any agreement to the contrary) which holds the employer liable to his employees for his failure to enforce reasonable safety measures on the premises of his enterprise.

291 The same applies to the European propositions regarding the adoption of a *fakultatives Kollisionsrecht* or "optional choice of law". Advocated by Axel Flessner and other German authors, this doctrine attempts to circumvent the difficulties inherent in the application of foreign law by treating a multistate controversy as a domestic case unless one of the parties posits the applicability of foreign law. The difference with the Anglo-American approach is in the court's control of all points of law once foreign law has been invoked. See: Flessner (1970); Zweigert (1973) p. 435 ff.; Raape/Sturm (1977) p. 306 ff. *Contra:* Jessurun d'Oliveira (1976) p. 24; De Boer (1979) p. 31 ff.

Part Two

Beyond Lex Loci Delicti

Introduction

Is there a "crisis" in American conflicts law?

Since the early 1960's, European conflicts writers have been fascinated with the American "conflicts revolution." By now, the barrage of commentaries, explanations and critiques seems to have abated somewhat, but there is hardly a serious student of the conflict of laws today in Europe who is not acquainted to some degree with the teachings of Currie or the impact of *Babcock v. Jackson*. Most European scholars have been, and still are, critical of the fundamental departure from traditional conflicts thinking evinced by the American theories and judicial practice. Even if they reluctantly acknowledge the ingenuity of the revolution's protagonists they hasten to declare their disbelief in the viability of the new approaches if transplanted to Europe. In his rather pontifical general report to a colloquium on the influence of modern American conflicts theories in Europe,[1] Professor Vitta, while conceding that "there are some lessons to be learned from the American experience," warned against an indiscriminate acceptance of modern American choice of law methodology, pointing out that "these theories have evolved in a setting very different from ours and disregard the principle of certainty of the law to an extent considered unacceptable by a vast majority of European scholars."[2] These are recurrent themes in European comments. With the common law as a

---

1 The "Bologna Symposium" was held in June 1981. Papers by Vitta, Juenger, Reese, Lando, Siehr, Hanotiau, and Lowenfeld were published in 30 *Am.J.Comp.L.* 1–115 (1982).
2 Vitta (1982) p. 14.

mutual source, the substantive laws of the states of the Union, unlike those of European countries, would have developed along similar lines, supposedly facilitating the determination of their underlying policies.[3] On the other hand, it is argued, the common law tradition has allowed the courts to develop a judicial method which is thought to emphasize justice in the individual case rather than legal certainty. As a consequence, a technique of conflicts-solving not based on "rules" but on an "approach" may be acceptable to common law jurisdictions,[4] but not to legal systems in which judicial law-making is frowned upon.

Apart from being dismissed in Europe as impracticable, or even unjust[5] common law solutions, the new American approaches are criticized on principle as well.[6] The reliance on *lex fori*, whether occasioned by the flexibility of the most significant relationship test or by the structural preference it is given in Currie's governmental interest analysis or Ehrenzweig's *lex fori* approach, is vehemently condemned by those European scholars to whom conflicts law should retain its impartiality toward the contents and origin of interchangeable laws.[7]

3 *Cf.* Sauveplanne (1982) p. 76: "However, a system based on policy analysis presupposes a certain common background ... Such a common background exists in the United States. In the legal field this is formed by English law. In all but one of the American states the common law is still based on the English heritage and therefore a common legal core exists."
4 Hanotiau (1979) p. 335 ff., with references to Currie (1963-1) p.627, Cook (1942) p. 43, and Cavers (1933) p. 187/188.
On more than one occasion, a contemporary proponent of interest analysis, Professor Sedler, has set forth that "the courts should, in accordance with the common law tradition, apply judicial method to the resolution of conflicts problems, as they applied it to other areas of law." Sedler (1983-1) p. 1197. See also: Sedler (1967); *id.* (1970); *id.* (1973-1).
5 *Cf.* Hanotiau (1979) p. 334 ff. "The main vice of the change proposed by Currie, Cavers, Leflar and their disciples lies not so much in the logic of the system as in the virtually discretionary role it attributes to the courts, a source of uncertainty, and, therefore, of injustice ..."
6 It is often disregarded that "American" conflicts law does not exist as such, and that one jurisdiction's interpretation of a particular theory may vary from that of another. Expounding the vices of interest analysis by dint of cross-references to all jurisdictions where some variety is practiced may therefore be misleading. See, however, the opinion in *In re "Agent Orange" Product Liability Litigation* 580 F.Supp. 690 at 699 (E.D. N.Y. 1984), quoting Leflar (1977-1) p. 218: "The point to be emphasized is that the modern decisions, regardless of exact language, are substantially consistent with each other."
7 *Cf.* Hanotiau (1979) p. 335, p. 337 ff.

Furthermore, even if reserved to multistate conflicts within a federal setting, policy-oriented approaches are thought to be unworkable and no less conducive to manipulation than the traditional method with its result-selective escapes. It is said that policy analysis is irredeemably flawed by its implicit assumption that policies can be ascertained unambiguously.[8] First, this assumption would ignore the possibility that a rule of law may be meant to protect a number of disparate interests rather than express a single, well-defined policy. Furthermore, the critics say, it fails to acknowledge that different standards may apply to the construction of legislative or judicial intent and that the process of construction may either focus on actual intent or follow the normative beliefs of those engaged in it. Even if policies and interests were susceptible of unequivocal detection, it is further argued, only false conflicts can be disposed of, whereas true conflicts are still not amenable to rational resolution.[9] Currie, who has admitted to this inadequacy and suggested that the law of the forum be resorted to as long as the legislature[10] has not seen fit to furnish a solution to the essentially political question a true conflict represents, has been reproached for the parochialism and favoritism inherent in his approach and for the forum shopping it may encourage.[11] Other writers have come up with alternative solutions ranging from the application of the better law or a process of interest-weighing to a return to traditional, mechanical choice of law rules.

None of these attempts to reconcile justice in the individual case with the demand for certainty and predictability has met with solid approval in Europe. And even though an appreciable number of Amer-

---

8 Hanotiau (1979) p. 106 ff. In America, Brilmayer (1980) has raised the same point in a fierce attack on interest analysis. See also *infra* Part Three.
9 Even a staunch defender of interest analysis as Strikwerda (1978) p. 193, acknowledges this.
10 Currie probably meant the federal legislature, referring in several instances to Congress: a "competent legislative body" which has failed "to use its power to solve the problems." Currie (1963-1) p. 182/183, p. 602. *Cf.* Strikwerda (1978) p. 173/174. Even if this implies that Currie's perspective was narrowed to *interstate* conflicts law, it does not necessarily make his approach totally infeasible for international conflicts law, as some European authors have suggested.
11 The possibility of forum-shopping is inherent in any choice of law approach not premised on absolute neutrality. Since most European authors seem to look upon forum-shopping as a most repulsive phenomenon, they are likely to reject the new conflicts methodology out of hand, conveniently overlooking the fact that their "own" allocation method has long ceased to be as neutral as they claim it to be.

ican courts and writers seems to have been won over by the basic doctrine of interest analysis – whether in the vein of § 6 of the Restatement Second or in the more fundamental varieties – it can hardly be said that it is applied consistently, or that an explicit preference for one approach or another has emerged. In spite of the *Erie* doctrine and the corollary *Klaxon* rule, diversity cases display a tendency of the federal courts to turn a blind eye to the choice of law principles prevailing in the jurisdiction in which they sit.[12] In some state courts obvious splits of opinion manifest themselves, not only between the majority and the dissenters but, more ominously, between consecutive decisions of the same court.[13] It is undoubtedly true, moreover, that in some areas of conflicts law the new approaches have gained considerably more headway than in other ones, contracts and torts being the fields where most of their success was scored. This implies a methodological divergence which might induce the courts to waver between choice of law techniques, thus adding to the ambivalence and uncertainty already pervasive in modern conflicts law. In short, the fierce criticisms voiced by the champions of the traditional method would appear to be valid. To the European observer, the American conflicts revolution does seem to have fostered chaos and crisis, its theoretical foundation flawed by unsound presumptions, its practical development lacking even a minimum degree of consistency, and its outcome calling for a reappraisal of the traditional approach and, to close the circle, a fresh start.

On the other hand, it should be noted that there is a marked difference in legal style and thought between the continents. Most European critics, especially those steeped in the Romanist tradition, seem to be lacking a willingness to view the American developments from a different perspective than their own. They tend to favor logic, structure,

---

12 *Lester v. Aetna Life Insurance Company* 433 F.2d 884 (5th Cir. [La.] 1970) is the most blatant example, as the Fifth Circuit deemed the *Klaxon* principle inapplicable to situations in which "no conflict is present", including false conflict situations. In *Day & Zimmermann, Inc. v. Challoner* 423 U.S. 3, 96 S.Ct. 167, 46 L.Ed.2d 3 (1975), however, the U.S. Supreme Court denounced such departures from the *Klaxon* doctrine.

13 As demonstrated by the series of much-cited New York cases, such as *Dym v. Gordon* 16 N.Y.2d 120, 209 N.E.2d 792, 262 N.Y.S.2d 463 (1965); *Macey v. Rozbicki* 18 N.Y.2d 289, 221 N.E.2d 380, 274 N.Y.S.2d 591 (1966), and *Tooker v. Lopez* 24 N.Y.2d 569, 249 N.E.2d 394, 301 N.Y.S.2d 519 (1969), culminating in *Neumeier v. Kuehner* 31 N.Y.2d 121, 335 N.Y.S.2d 64, 286 N.E.2d 454 (1972) and its progeny.

codification of narrowly-defined rules of law, and shrink from flexibility, uncertainty and a dominant role of the courts in the development of law. As far as conflicts law is concerned, conceptualism has long prevailed in Europe. Even though the 'sixties did herald a grudging admission of its failures and the necessity to patch up some of its most obnoxious features, it has taken quite a while before this perception resulted in actual change. Opting for gradual adjustment instead of fundamental innovation, European conflicts theory and practice have generally remained within the bounds of tradition, an inclination which has helped to preserve the methodological structure of conflicts law. In view of continental Europe's legal heritage, this cautious attitude might be inevitable. Trained in deductive reasoning and doctrinal analysis, continental lawyers have a propensity to conceptual thinking.[14] Even if they are aware of the countervailing trends in contemporary jurisprudence, it is hard for them to get rid of this penchant for classification, dogma and abstract rules. Anglo-American law, on the other hand, with its emphasis on case-by-case adjudication, is much more suited to inductive reasoning, which might explain a greater willingness of the legal profession to accept methodological change. In this light, the European antagonism toward the American choice of law revolution may be rooted in rifts far below the technicalities of choice of law methodology. It is symptomatic, I feel, that the American efforts to adjust the new choice of law approaches to the antinomy of justice and consistency – a process for which the pervasive judicial method is most expedient – have generally met with misunderstanding, rebuke and derision this side of the Atlantic.

The prevalent criticism that the new approaches have sacrificed legal certainty to justice in the individual case reflects an unwarranted self-righteousness, hardly in tune with the realities of European conflicts law. In Europe, the traditional jurisdiction-selecting rules have given rise to the same dissatisfaction with their results and the same need for change as they did in pre-modern American conflicts law. Hence, the same manipulative devices, the same quasi-certainty and the same questionable results could be spotted. When change did come, it took

---

14 *Cf.* Audit (1979) p. 591: "Although Roman law could be described as a series of rules, and in its early days even a series of actions, Civil lawyers have long been trained to regroup the rules according to method and subject-matter. This process encourages definition of the main concepts as well as identification and assessment of the modes of reasoning prevailing in a particular branch of law."

other forms than it did in the United States, but it can hardly be denied that it reduced legal certainty just as much as the novel American approaches did, and for virtually the same cause. Thus, the rigid adherence to the nationality principle in family law was softened by the advent of alternative reference rules deferring to domicile. Open-ended choice of law rules alleviated the tyranny of *a priori* rules turning on a single connecting factor. The *favor* concept took on new meanings. The blurring distinction between public and private law gave rise to the phenomenon of "rules of immediate application," a doctrine which corresponds to interest analysis both in concept and in effect.[15] All these changes mitigated the rigidity of traditional European conflicts law and engendered the same result-selective adjudication the American approaches are reproved for. The price to be paid for this "softening process" is an inevitable reduction of legal certainty. Recognition of the "closest connection" as an expression of the allocation method's fundamental principle, for instance, implies its being used as a resourceful corrective in atypical situations, in which an abstract conflicts rule does not achieve its purpose of designating the law most closely connected to the issue in dispute. The Swiss and the Austrian statutes on conflicts law have adopted this construction, almost as a preamble.[16] Theoretically it could be maintained that the closest connection principle does not prejudice legal certainty, as it should be applied in an objective, *i.e.* merely geographical fashion. But this assertion does no more than pay lip-service to legal certainty, since the "proper law" may very well be determined in a result-selective and therefore subjective way, with implicit reference to policy considerations.[17] Nevertheless, just as blanket concepts (such as "good faith", "reasonable man" or "due care") have been gradually delineated by the courts, a concept like the closest connection could

---

15 The various ways in which traditional conflicts law is being modernized in Europe have been discussed in greater detail, *supra* chapter 1. The doctrine of the *lois d'application immédiate* is the subject of chapter 1, section 5, under the heading "priority rules."
16 Article 14 of the Swiss draft offers the courts more leeway to apply the "proper" law in atypical cases than does article 1 of the Austrian statute. The latter provision just serves to explain the statute's methodological point of departure; its *Grundsatz der stärksten Beziehung* is the underlying allocation principle from which the predetermined connecting factors of the subsequent conflicts rules are said to be derived. *Cf. supra* chapter 1, section 2, note 99 and accompanying text.
17 *Cf.* De Boer (1982) p. 14 ff. See also: *supra* chapter 1, section 2.

acquire a more specific meaning in due time, after the courts have had ample opportunity to establish its outline in relation to a large number of fact situations.[18] A "coagulation process" restores legal certainty, as firm rules emerge from a series of experiments with open-ended principles, but it is a process that takes time. The more room a new approach or doctrine leaves to interpretation, the more time is needed, it would seem. For that reason, it may still be too early to proclaim the definitive failure of the American conflicts revolution.

Since this book focuses on the methodology of *tort* choice of law, it may not be amiss to point out that legal certainty has a relative value in this field. Most torts are unintentional. They are marked by their accidental character. This implies that tortfeasors cannot usually be deemed to have acted in reliance on the applicability of a particular domestic law, and in that respect legal certainty, in the sense of predictability of result, is thought to be less relevant here than in *e.g.* the area of contracts or domestic relations.[19] Observing that "[t]he great majority of recent choice-of-law cases in the United States have involved suits brought to recover for personal injuries," Professor Reese offers several reasons why predictability has little value in this field.[20] Not only are tort cases in the United States frequently decided by juries and are the tort principles of the domestic law involved often vague and imprecise (as exemplified by the "mythical reasonable man"), but "[i]n addition, the field of personal injuries is one where persons rarely look before they leap and where they rarely contemplate the consequences

---

18 This is at least what happened when the Dutch courts in a series of decisions gave a more definite meaning to the "legal sphere" concept embodied in the torts provision of the Benelux Uniform Law on Private International Law: only in those cases in which both parties are domiciled in the same country is the *lex loci delicti* displaced by the law of the common domicile, thought to denote the "legal sphere" to which the legal consequences of the tort belong, or (to use the American terminology) the jurisdiction having the most significant relationship. *Supra* chapter 1, section 2, text following note 69.
19 It could be argued that, in view of the predominant role of liability insurance, legal certainty and predictability of result is still a cogent consideration in tort choice of law. From various sources of (mostly unwritten) information, I have gathered that the insurance industry has little understanding of, or interest in the choice of law process as such. Choice of law considerations do not seem to bear upon the actuarial process. More on this subject, *infra* chapter 8, section 1.
20 Reese (1982) p. 135.

of their conduct before engaging in it."[21] He also notes the emergence of "more precise rules of choice of law" in this area, based on the experience the New York Court of Appeals has had with the new approaches as applied to multistate torts. Such rules should not be seen, in my opinion, as an admission of failure, as one European commentator has implied.[22] Rather, they are the result of a string of experiments in which the relative certainty of traditional choice of law was suspended for a time so that new standards could be evolved from the freedom thus created and the experience gained. It is too facile to dismiss the labor of the American courts and writers as a waste of effort which did not produce a workable choice of law method and a set of fixed rules right away. Such an attitude is not devoid of a certain Old World arrogance, which is the more ungracious if the suggested alternatives suffer from the same, or worse, defects as the approaches one denounces. The conflicts revolution in the United States, at least in the field of torts, has a lot to show for, notably the substitution of the vested rights theory and its mechanical place of the wrong standard for a much more rational and subtle approach which might eventually yield a number of manageable rules.[23] Its radical solutions might not be fit to conquer Europe, but their considerable influence on the evolution of European conflicts law cannot be denied.[24]

21 *Ibid..* See also § 145 Restatement Second, comment b: "Likewise, the values of certainty, predictability and uniformity of result are of lesser importance in torts than in areas where the parties and their lawyers are likely to give thought to the problem of the applicable law in planning their transactions."
The same argument has been made in numerous cases, particularly those relying on Leflar's choice-influencing considerations, the first one stressing predictability of result. *Cf. infra* chapter 5, text accompanying note 83.
22 Hanotiau (1979) p. 225, applauding New York's reversion to conflicts rules in *Neumeier v. Kuehner* 31 N.Y.2d 121, 335 N.Y.S.2d 64, 286 N.E.2d 454 (1972): "On the one hand, [the decision] expresses the existence of a malaise among the proponents of interest analysis. On the other hand, it represents a retreat of the Court of Appeals in comparison with its previous decisions." *Cf.* Jayme (1974) p. 586.
23 See also Cavers (1965) p. 136/137, whose "principles of preference" are discussed *infra* chapter 4, section 4(c). Another experiment in formulating "policy-oriented rules" is described in chapter 6. See also *infra* note 103.
24 *Cf.* Sauveplanne (1982) p. 74: "Be that as it may, the European evolution, although it had an early start in European doctrine that was to some extent reflected in court decisions, in its later stage it became more or less strongly influenced by the American trends. Both authors, legislators and courts looked at the American examples and wondered whether or not they should follow them." I am skeptical of Sauveplanne's suggestion ("some interaction seems to take place") that Americans would have a similar interest in European developments.

However, if we are to assess the true state of affairs in American conflicts law, we must first take a closer look at the law in action. It is the judicial process, not legal theory, I suggest, that will most sharply reveal the virtues and vices of the new approaches, the inconsistencies and biases for which they are indicted, as well as the emerging patterns we try to detect. If there actually is a "crisis", we are bound to discover it by listening closely to the courts. Distressingly, the quantity of American cases dealing with multistate torts is so overwhelming that it defies an exhaustive and detailed examination. From a multitude of cases I have picked those that may be considered as clear samples of practical application of various policy-oriented choice of law theories, cases which display, when studied in context, a certain progress in the development of such practice, as well as cases presenting the same issue arising from opposite fact patterns. I will try to include without bias cases that either confirm or contradict the criticisms mentioned before. Again, the classification followed in this account is methodological rather than chronological or jurisdictional, although some special attention will be devoted to developments in those jurisdictions in which judicial reasoning is marked by its consistency or, as the case may be, by the lack of it. A strictly distinctive methodological approach, however, is not quite feasible since many courts have a propensity to strengthen their decisions by relying on several theories at once.[25] This is why some overlap is unavoidable. Since the following chapters are meant to show the practical side of policy-oriented choice of law, they will focus on actual case law, and little attention will be paid to the theoretical merits of each approach. This perspective is apt to screen from our observation several theoretical solutions which have not been endorsed by judicial practice, at least not explicitly. Hardly a case could be found in which any of Cavers' principles of preference was adopted, nor were there any decisions that could be said to rely specifically on the ideas or terminology of either Ehrenzweig, Weintraub, or Von Mehren and Trautman. To the extent that their theories have had a subliminal influence on the courts, they will be mentioned in an appropriate, but wider context.[26]

---

25 This trend has been canonized as "judicial eclecticism": Leflar(1977-1) p. 197 ff.; Reppy (1983). See also: Westbrook (1975).
26 Thus, Cavers' "territorial bias" will be discussed in the context of other territorial solutions to true conflicts (*infra* chapter 4, section 4(c), whereas Ehrenzweig's predilection for forum law fits in with the *lex fori* trend in Kentucky and Michigan (*infra* chapter 7).

Chapter 3
The Most Significant Relationship Approach

Prepared under the auspices of the American Law Institute, the *Restatements of the Law* reflect the judicial development of American law in most of its major areas. Summarizing the law in action in a number of detailed rules and providing comments and examples, the Restatements much resemble the annotated codes in use in European legal practice. However, since they lack the seal of legislative approval, their authority is persuasive at best, their status unofficial. The first Restatement of the law of conflicts, published in 1934, was conceived by Professor Joseph H. Beale, a proponent of the territorial theory of vested rights. Reflecting Beale's conceptualist conflicts philosophy, the Restatement First featured a system of jurisdiction-selecting rules, which precluded any consideration of either the particularities of the case at issue or the contents of the eligible laws. The target of vehement attacks by other scholars,[27] Beale's Restatement never achieved the ideal of uniform decisions its author envisioned. On the contrary, its rigid territoriality proved conducive to the judicial deployment of "escape devices", described in the previous chapter. By the time the American Law Institute decided to commission the Restatement Second, in the early 1950's, conflicts law was just on the verge of a transitional period. It took almost two decades before the final product was promulgated, the result "present[ing] a striking contrast to the first Restatement in which dogma was so thoroughly enshrined."[28] While Bealian dogma was rightly discarded, it is not very

---

27 Notably Ernest G. Lorenzen, who resigned from Beale's staff of advisors in the early drafting stages. Other early critics were Walter Wheeler Cook and David F. Cavers.
28 Herbert Wechsler, director of The American Law Institute, in his Introduction to the *Restatement of the Law Second, Conflict of Laws 2d*, St. Paul, Minn., 1971, p.vii.

clear by which choice of law philosophy the Restatement Second is supported instead. Since its leading principles were conceived, considered, and reconsidered while the American "conflicts revolution" was gaining momentum, it is not surprising that its methodological foundation consists of various incongruous elements which were borrowed from various new theories and forged into an oddly eclectic approach.[29] Opting for flexible jurisdiction-selecting rules combined with a checklist of choice of law policies, Professor Willis L.M. Reese, the Restatement Second's reporter, created a compromise between neutral allocation and policy evaluation.[30]

The key concept in the selection of the applicable law is the "most significant relationship". Referring to the law of the state which has the closest connection with the case, this open-ended criterion is usually embedded in a presumptive formula identifying the state or states most likely to have such a connection. In this respect, the allocation standard of the Restatement Second is similar to the one embodied in the "semi-open conflicts rule" that has emerged in European conflicts law.[31] On the other hand, the determination of the most significant relationship involves more than a bland assessment of the balance of factual contacts. Among the Restatement's general provisions is one cardinal section, § 6, in which the major "factors relevant to the

---

29 *Cf.* Korn (1983) p. 816: "The final product is a transitional document, reflecting the period's mood of flexibility and openness to new ideas, while refusing to abandon past learning entirely and remaining committed to the principle of decision according to rule to the extent that satisfactory rules exist or can be developed." According to Westbrook (1975) p. 439, "[e]clecticism is the most appropriate response to a field in which contradictions and change are inherent." See also: Reppy (1983) p. 655 ff.; Hay (1981) p. 1667.
30 In earlier publications, Professor Reese had already set forth several policies which "should guide the courts in deciding choice-of-law questions and in formulating rules for choice of law." Reese (1963) p. 682; Cheatham/Reese (1952). Of the ten policies listed in the 1963 article, eight have survived in the Restatement Second. One of these, pertaining to the forum's statutory directives on choice of law, was laid down in § 6(1). The two policies omitted in § 6(2) are: "(3) The court should apply its own local law unless there is good reason for not doing so," and "(10) The court should seek to attain justice in the individual case." Reese (1963) p. 682 and 690.
31 *Supra* chapter 1, section 2, text accompanying notes 52–110. *Cf.* Shapira (1970) p. 210; Vitta (1979) p. 166, p. 175 ff., p. 182.

choice of the applicable rule of law" are listed.[32] Superimposed on the most significant relationship criterion, this catalogue of choice of law policies is meant to guide the courts in choosing the appropriate rule of decision in those areas in which the accommodation of conflicting values has not yet found its expression in a specific conflicts rule: "In these areas, the courts must look in each case to the underlying factors themselves in order to arrive at a decision which will best accommodate them."[33] Ranging from "certainty, predictability and uniformity of result" to "the relevant policies of the forum," the choice of law principles of § 6 are neither exclusive nor compatible. Just as the "choice-influencing considerations" advocated by Professor Robert Leflar, their weight and interaction vary with the choice of law area involved.[34] Due to the inclusion of § 6, the choice of law ideology of the Restatement Second encompasses most of the modern approaches, from straightforward jurisdiction-selection to pure interest analysis. That is probably the reason why it is cited with approval in a great many decisions. As will be seen, judicial invocation of the Restatement's most significant relationship test conveys little information on the approach the court actually adopted.

Characteristic of the methodological ambivalence that pervades the Restatement Second is its central provision on torts, § 145:

"1. The rights and liabilities of the parties with respect to an issue in tort are determined by the local law of the state which, with respect to that issue, has the most significant relationship to the occurrence and the parties under the principles stated in § 6.

---

[32] They include: (a) the needs of the interstate and international systems; (b) the relevant policies of the forum; (c) the relevant policies of other interested states and the relative interests of those states in the determination of the particular issue; (d) the protection of justified expectations; (e) the basic policies underlying the particular field of law; (f) certainty, predictability and uniformity of result, and (g) ease in the determination and application of the law to be applied.

[33] Restatement Second, § 6, comment c on subsection (2), p. 13, referring to Wrongs and Contracts as examples of choice of law areas in which "the difficulties and complexities involved have as yet prevented the courts from formulating a precise rule, or series of rules, which provide satisfactory accommodation of the underlying factors in all of the situations which may arise."

[34] The "Leflar approach" will be further discussed in chapter 5. Leflar (1977-1) p. 219, noted that "[t]he seven 'factors' listed in § 6 cover the same ground as the first four of the choice-influencing considerations ... so that only the fifth of the considerations, preference for the better rule of law, is not covered." See also: Reppy (1983) p. 658; Leflar (1972-1) p. 473/474.

2. Contacts to be taken into account in applying the principles of § 6 to determine the law applicable to an issue include:
   (a) the place where the injury occurred,
   (b) the place where the conduct causing the injury occurred,
   (c) the domicil, residence, nationality, place of incorporation and place of business of the parties, and
   (d) the place where the relationship, if any, between the parties is centered.
   These contacts are to be evaluated according to their relative importance with respect to the particular issue."

This compromise between jurisdiction-selection and policy-weighing has provided the courts with a virtually unlimited license to motivate any choice of law result they prefer in the phraseology of the Restatement, which lends a semblance of legitimacy to even the most dubious decision. The most significant relationship formula accommodates geographical contacts-grouping as well as sophisticated interest analysis. Even straight application of the *lex loci delicti* can be justified by reference to the presumption that the "applicable law will usually be the local law of the state where the injury occurred" in a number of sections following § 145.[35] The key question the courts have to answer in their interpretation of such an adaptable standard pertains, of course, to the meaning of the term "significant". It is the same question that was answered *a priori* by Savigny and Beale when they formulated jurisdiction-selecting rules appointing the "seat" of a legal relationship, or, respectively, the place where the rights of the parties "vested", both of them being concerned with the closest connection between an (abstracted) legal relationship (or "rights and liabilities of the parties") and a particular jurisdiction. Abandoning the abstraction of *a priori* rules does not alter the question *how* the relative significance of the links between a given case and a number of jurisdictions should be determined, it only allows for different answers, according to the weight that is placed on one or another of the purposes conflicts law is deemed to further. Without reference to the "choice-influencing considerations" enumerated in § 6, the most significant relationship

---

[35] §§ 156(2), 157(2), 158(2), 159(2), 160(2), 162(2), 164(2), 165(2), 166(2), 172(2). Most of the black letter rules on torts, in fact, contain references to the local law of the state where the wrong occurred "unless ... some other state has a more significant relationship under the principles stated in § 6." *Cf.* the criticisms by Shapira (1970) p. 213 ff.; Leflar (1972-2) p. 269; Weintraub (1980) p. 277/278.

formula would indeed suffer from circularity, as Ehrenzweig has pointed out, "since the 'significance' of the relationship is the very question which the conflicts rule has to answer."[36] Yet, since the policy factors of § 6 are neither exhaustive nor hierarchical, and "vary somewhat in importance from field to field,"[37] the courts are still largely left to their own devices when called upon to perform a qualitative evaluation of contacts and their relative significance.

In torts, for example, the Restatement stresses "the needs of the interstate and international systems," "the policies of the forum and those of other interested states," and "ease in the determination and application of the chosen law" as overriding choice of law policies. Less important here are "the protection of justified expectations," "certainty, predictability and uniformity of result," and "the policies underlying the field of tort law."[38] However vague the most significant relationship test then still remains, it is clear that its "significance standard" should not be understood in a geographical way. It should not be construed as implying a mere contacts weighing process – as it generally is in the European interpretation of the "proper law" formula and its equivalents–, and certainly not as a quantitative technique of contacts counting. Instead, it should be taken to refer to the substantive laws possibly involved, as indicated by the contacts listed in § 145(2). An examination and comparison of the relevant substantive rules thus identified should shed light on their relative significance to

---

36 Ehrenzweig (1962) p. 351, 464; *id.* (1967-1) p. 138/139: "In all these formulas, what should be the result reached by a choice of law, namely, the ascertainment of 'a *center* of gravity,' of the '*most significant relationship*,' or of the '*proper* law', is offered to us as a premise for the choice." See also: Juenger (1969) p. 212: "Although it is printed in black letters, section 145 is not much of a rule since it fails to offer a definition of the central word 'significant.' Thus, the Restatement provisions on tort choice of law appear to be programmatic rather than normative."

37 Restatement Second, comment b to § 145, p. 415. *Cf.* the comment on § 6(2), *ibid.* p. 12. See also: Reese (1963) p. 692: "To reiterate, no one policy ... is of such paramount importance that it should always be given effect. Not only will the relative importance of these policies vary from one legal category to another, but each individual case is likely to present a different grouping of policies."

38 Comment b on § 145(1) at p. 415/416. Tortfeasors have "few, if any, justified expectations in the area of choice of law to protect." Certainty, predictability and uniformity of result "are of lesser importance in torts than in areas where the parties and their lawyers are likely to give thought to the problem of the applicable law in planning their transactions." Tort policies, such as deterrence or compensation, "are likely to point in different directions."

the matter in dispute. This construction emphasizes a policy-weighing approach to choice of law[39] in which the significance of the relationship of each concerned jurisdiction to the occurrence and the parties is measured by the relative import of its substantive laws rather than by a concentration of geographical contacts. Even though it might be conceded that, in many cases, each of these two standards will point to the same law, since the jurisdiction most closely connected to the case in a territorial way will often be the jurisdiction most "interested" in its outcome, it would be wrong to presuppose such a concurrence and refrain from the (more arduous) substantive test. Such an attitude would induce mechanical contacts counting which, apart from being liable to produce irrational results, is clearly not the solution the Restatement espouses. It cannot be denied, however, that the pervasive compromise between localization and policy analysis does call forth confusion as to the proper proceedings. The contacts enumerated in § 145(2) do suggest a localization approach based on contacts counting. On the other hand, if § 6 is controlling – as a closer examination of § 145 seems to confirm – the enumeration of contacts to be taken into account is nothing but a checklist, and a rather dispensable one at that, meant to aid the courts in identifying the jurisdictions most likely to have an interest in the matter in dispute. A discussion of these contacts might then be perceived as "a hindrance, an unhelpful ritual that ha[s] to be performed before the court could proceed to analyze the problem meaningfully in terms of interest and fairness."[40]

---

39 Leflar (1977-1) p. 184 note 10. In many cases, therefore, the most significant relationship is measured in terms of interests rather than contacts. See the examples discussed *infra*, text accompanying notes 64–72 and 90–100. Reppy (1983) p. 659 ff., contends that the Restatement Second approach, despite § 6 and its references to forum policy and foreign interests, is inconsistent with interest analysis theory: "Personally, I do not think Professor Reese intended section 6 to diminish in any way the focus on territorialism underlying his 'most significant relation' method. I consider section 6 a sop tossed in 1967 to the members of the American Law Institute who were unhappy with a purely territorial methodology." *Ibid.* p. 662.
40 Sedler (1972) p. 314. *Cf.* Weintraub (1980) p. 277: "Whether or not a particular contact with a state is significant for conflicts purposes cannot be known until one first knows exactly what domestic tort rules are in conflict and what the policies underlying those rules are ... The Restatement formulation, although probably consistent with an interest analysis, is likely to mislead courts and lawyers on this most basic element of that analysis."

In practice, most courts professing to adhere to the Restatement Second's precepts seem to be inclined to follow the interest-weighing approach and to play down the contacts evaluation prescribed in § 145(2). On the other hand, in a number of cases in which the most significant relationship test is adopted, often accompanied by references to the Restatement Second, not even an attempt at qualitative evaluation is made. Instead, these courts have contented themselves with the mere statement that their choice of the applicable law is based on the most significant relationship formula, without bothering to identify relevant contacts, or to consider them in the light of the principles stated in § 6. One example is *First National Bank in Fort Collins v. Rostek*, a Colorado landmark case in which the traditional place of wrong rule was abandoned. This wrongful death action arose from an airplane accident in South Dakota involving Colorado residents. Curiously, the Supreme Court mostly relied on the first two "Fuld principles" in justification of its refusal to apply South Dakota's guest statute,[41] announcing at the same time that "Colorado will adopt the general rule of applying the law of the state having the most 'significant relationship' with the occurrence and the parties, as presented and defined in Restatement (Second) Conflict of Laws, Vol. 1, sec. 145 (1969)." But nothing was said about the relevance of the choice of law factors of § 6.[42]

In other cases the most significant relationship formula is understood as a rather mechanical directive calling for an enumeration of relevant contacts. The four principal factors of § 145(2) are sometimes alluded to, whereas in other instances a token remark about the "interests"

---

41 For a discussion of the "Fuld principles", see *infra* chapter 6. According to Maryann Walsh, Case Note, 51 *Denver L.J.* 567 at 576 (1974), "[t]he Rostek decision specifically referred to rules, but the language indicated a strong bias toward the interest analysis." *Contra*: Case Note, 46 *U.Colo. L.Rev.* 107 at 109, 115 (1974), insisting that the court applied neither interest analysis nor the better law theory.

42 *First National Bank in Fort Collins v. Rostek* 182 Colo. 437, 514 P.2d 314 at 319 (Colo. 1973). See also: *Pust v. Union Supply Co.* 561 P.2d 355 (Colo. 1976); *Forward v. Cotton Petroleum Corp.* 540 F.Supp. 122 (D. Colo. 1982). Other examples are: *Bishop v. Florida Specialty Paint Co.* 389 So.2d 999 (Fla. 1980); *Hayden v. Krusling* 531 F.Supp. 468 (N.D. Fla. 1982); *Hanley v. Tribune Pub. Co.* 527 F.2d 68 (9th Cir. [Nev.] 1975); *Ducey v. United States* 713 F.2d 504 (9th Cir. [Nev.] 1983); *Santana, Inc. v. Levi Strauss and Co.* 674 F.2d 269 (4th Cir. [N.C.] 1982); *Michael v. Greene* 306 S.E.2d 144 (N.C. App. 1983); *Brickner v. Gooden* 525 P.2d 632 (Okla. 1974); *White v. White* 618 P.2d 921 (Okla. 1980);

involved is thrown in, but what actually follows is pure contacts counting. For instance, in *Hines v. Tenneco Chemicals, Inc.*,[43] a federal district court sitting in Texas obediently cited *Gutierrez v. Collins*, the decision in which the Texas Supreme Court had adopted the Restatement's most significant relationship test as its new approach to torts.[44] Having referred to both § 145 and § 6, the *Hines* court proceeded to count contacts: North Carolina was not only the place of conduct and injury in this products liability case, it was also the domicile of the plaintiffs, and the relationship between the parties, if any, centered in that state; defendant, on the other hand, was a Delaware corporation with its principal place of business in New Jersey and a major office in Texas. Without a word on any of the choice of law principles listed in § 6, the opinion concluded: "In view of not only the number of contacts North Carolina has with this case, but also their relative importance when compared to those contacts with Texas, this court will apply North Carolina law as the substantive law in the present action."[45]

This is not to say that the results thus reached are untenable under a less factual interpretation of the most significant relationship approach. Especially in cases in which the (fortuitous) place of the wrong is the only extraneous element of the case, a more careful evaluation of localizing factors in the light of the principles of § 6 may be redundant. For instance, the summary statement of the North Dakota Supreme Court in *Issendorf v. Olson* that North Dakota law applied on the basis of a "significant contacts approach" to a contributory negligence issue arising out of a car accident in Minnesota in which only

---

43 *Hines v. Tenneco Chemicals, Inc.* 546 F.Supp. 1229 (S.D. Tex. 1982).
44 *Gutierrez v. Collins* 583 S.W.2d 312 (Tex. 1979). The Supreme Court quoted both § 6 and § 145, holding that "in the future all conflicts cases sounding in tort will be governed by the 'most significant relationship' test as enunciated in Sections 6 and 145 of the Restatement (Second) of Conflicts. This methodology offers a rational yet flexible approach to conflicts problems. It offers the courts some guidelines without being too vague or too restrictive. It represents a collection of the best thinking on this subject and does indeed include 'most of the substance' of all the modern theories." *Ibid.* at 318.
45 *Hines v. Tenneco Chemicals, Inc.* 546 F.Supp. 1229 at 1232 (S.D. Tex. 1982). Other examples are: *Permagrain Products v. U.S. Mat & Rubber Co.* 489 F.Supp. 108 at 111 note 1 (E.D. Pa. 1980); *Evra Corp. v. Swiss Bank Corp.* 522 F.Supp. 820 (N.D. Ill. 1981); *Vicon, Inc. v. CMI Corp.* 657 F.2d 768 at 772 (5th Cir. [Miss.] 1981).

North Dakota residents were involved,[46] might be unconcerned with the needs of the interstate system, or with the relevant policies behind Minnesota's comparative negligence and North Dakota's contributory negligence rules, but the outcome of the case would probably not have been any different if these factors had been taken expressly into account. The court did venture to remark that it was "not particularly enamored with our rule of contributory negligence," but such mild criticism cannot rate as an inspired evaluation of policy factors.[47] The same can be said of the decision in *Mager v. Mager*, a subsequent North Dakota decision turning on immunity between Minnesota spouses involved in a car accident in Minnesota, the only link with North Dakota being the hospitalization of the plaintiff in that state.[48] Although North Dakota law had not known interspousal immunity for many years, whereas Minnesota had abolished it just five days after the accident occurred, the court nevertheless applied the immunity rule in force at the time of the accident, since Minnesota had "clearly" the most significant relationship.[49] Once again, these decisions would probably not have been different under a less factual interpretation of the most significant relationship test, but they scarcely reflect the policy-oriented tendencies inherent in the Restatement's reference to other factors besides mere localization.

46 *Issendorf v. Olson* 194 N.W.2d 750 (N.D. 1972). More explicit was a Florida Court of Appeal in *Harris v. Berkowitz* 433 So.2d 613 at 614/615 (Fla. App. 1983): "When the place of injury is fortuitous or bears little relation to the occurrence, the place of injury [in Maine] does not play a significant role in the selection of the applicable law ... All parties to this action are permanent residents of Florida. It is therefore impossible to ascertain any policy Maine might have in the application of its limitation of damages insofar as recovery by Florida residents for the death of decedent resulting from the negligence of another Florida decedent is concerned."
47 *Ibid.* p. 755. If anything, the remark had a "better law" flavor, which might have had Leflar's blessing but is not supported by any of the choice of law principles of § 6 Restatement Second. *Cf. supra* note 34.
48 *Mager v. Mager* 197 N.W.2d 626 (N.D. 1972).
49 *Ibid.* p. 628. See also: *Kalmich v. Bruno* 553 F.2d 549 (7th Cir. [Ill.] 1977) *cert. denied* 434 U.S. 940, 98 S.Ct. 432, 54 L.Ed.2d 300 (1977), in which plaintiff, a resident of Quebec, sought recovery for the confiscation of his property in Yugoslavia by the Nazis in 1941. Defendant, now a resident of Illinois being sued for conversion, had been appointed by the Nazis as a trustee of plaintiff's property. Referring to Illinois' version of the most significant relationship test, the 7th Circuit assumed "that the Illinois courts would choose to apply the substantive law of Yugoslavia to this case. Yugoslavia was the site of the tort and the injury, and we can think of no argument that would demonstrate that Illinois has a more significant relationship with this case than Yugoslavia." *Ibid.* at 552.

The risk involved in contacts counting is that it is too easily assumed, sometimes, that the state where the heaviest concentration of pertinent contacts is localized must also be the center of gravity in a nonphysical way, in other words: that that state would automatically have the greatest concern as well. This need not always be true, however. At least some doubt may be justified. In *Dashiell v. Keauhou-Kona Company*,[50] the Ninth Circuit had to apply Hawaii's choice of law principles to the issue whether a California plaintiff would be barred from recovery against a Hawaiian defendant on account of imputed contributory negligence. When on vacation in Hawaii, plaintiff had rented a golf cart from defendant and was injured in an accident on the cart path, due to the negligence of his wife. It was alleged that defendant had been negligent in the construction of the cart path and in not warning his clients of possible dangers. Defendant maintained that under the applicable California law, contributory negligence of a spouse would be imputed to the plaintiff, barring recovery. Unable to find any Hawaiian conflicts case in point, the court resorted to "the conflict of laws rules generally applied by the courts in this country" and held that in this case Hawaii had "the more significant relationship to the issue of imputed negligence," a finding it deemed in accordance with Restatement Second.[51] No attempt was made, however, to inquire into the function of imputed (contributory) negligence, which is usually said to deny to the negligent spouse the opportunity to profit, through the community property existing between them, from plaintiff's recovery.[52] In this respect the law of the matrimonial domicile might be controlling. It would not be amiss to consider this possibility if the Restatement's constant reference to § 6 is taken seriously.

In another federal case, *Rudin v. Dow Jones & Co., Inc.*, New York choice of law was said to dictate the application of "the law of the

---

50 *Dashiell v. Keauhou-Kona Company* 487 F.2d 957 (9th Cir. [Hawaii] 1973).
51 *Ibid.* p. 960. Section 166, concerning imputed negligence, suggests that § 145 be applied, which will "usually" lead to the law of the state where the injury occurred: § 166(2). In comment b on § 166, however, express reference is made to situations "where one spouse is injured ... through the negligence of the other spouse and of a third person." In that case, "it might be thought that the local law of the state of the spouses domicil should be applied to determine whether any recovery would be community property and thus would be shared by the negligent spouse (see § 258)."
52 *Cf.* Restatement Second, § 166, comment b and § 258; Weintraub (1980) p. 68, p. 275–276.

forum with the most significant contacts with the alleged tort," the tort in this case being libel.[53] Plaintiff, a California resident who happened to be Frank Sinatra's attorney, had written to the editor of defendant's business weekly regarding a previously published comment on certain stock transactions in which he was involved. Defendant's allegedly libelous statement consisted of a caption printed over plaintiff's letter to the editor, reading: "Sinatra's mouthpiece." The issue turned on proof of damages, as required by California law, against New York's strict liability rule for libel and defamation. Defendant pleaded application of California law, as plaintiff was a resident of California, and the publication was distributed there, which implied that plaintiff suffered his most significant injury in that state. The District Court quoted § 150(2) Restatement Second and conceded that "the state of most significant relationship will usually be the state where the person [who claims that he has been defamated] was domiciled at the time, if the matter complained of was published in that state." Yet, it did not hold California law to be applicable, but it asked for further proof as to the choice of law issue, offering a list of other localizing factors from which it might follow that "plaintiff has a significant relationship to a state other than the state of his domicile."[54] Oddly enough, the other factors to be considered had little to do with the plaintiff, as they included (apart from the place where the plaintiff suffered the greatest harm): the place where the principal activity to which the defamation related occurred; the domicile or place of incorporation of the publisher; his main publishing office; the state of principal circulation; the place of emanation; the place where the libel was first seen; and, finally, the forum. Such an approach suggests extensive contacts counting, not a willingness to go into the relative merits of New York's strict

---

53 *Rudin v. Dow Jones & Co., Inc.* 510 F.Supp. 210 at 216 (S.D. N.Y. 1981).
54 *Ibid.* p. 216. See also: *Grass v. News Group Publications, Inc.* 570 F.Supp. 178 at 185 (S.D. N.Y. 1983): "The usual presumption with regard to choice of law questions is that the plaintiff in a defamation or privacy action may invoke the law of the plaintiff's domicile. See Restatement (Second) of Conflict of Laws, § 150(2). Underlying this presumption is the view that the plaintiff's domicile is generally the place in which he enjoys the reputation allegedly besmirched, where he works and where he enjoys his privacy." In this case, however, the law of plaintiff's domicile was displaced by New York law on account of New York's more significant relationship.

liability rule or California's requirement that a cause of action for libel depends on proof of damages.[55]

A peculiar example of selective contacts counting should suffice to conclude this section on the quantitative variety of the most significant relationship approach. In *Western Energy, Inc. v. Georgia-Pacific Corp.*, most contacts seemed to converge in Oregon, the forum state, but it was decided that Louisiana law applied to the issue of negligent misrepresentation. Plaintiff and defendant both had their principal places of business in Oregon. The representations were received in Oregon and the damage was suffered there. The parties had entered into a contract in Louisiana, however, under whose law no cause of action for negligent misrepresentation is recognized between parties dealing with one another "at arm's length in a business setting." Oregon law would give the plaintiff a cause of action under these circumstances. Referring to the various contacts listed in § 148 Restatement Second, the Oregon Court of Appeals succinctly concluded, "Balancing these contacts, the trial court properly decided that the law of Louisiana applied."[56] The clue to the court's finding may be in a footnote: "The stipulation of the parties that the law of Louisiana applied with respect to the cause of action for breach of contract is further support for the conclusion that the significant 'contacts' were in Louisiana."[57] The place of contracting being the only physical contact with Louisiana, it does not seem likely to outweigh the preponderance of Oregon contacts. This is an unusual case in that the significance of the relationship between the tort issue and a particular state is neither related to the number of contacts nor to the principles of § 6, but primarily to the parties' stipulation that Louisiana law would apply to their contract. This finding resulted in the application of sister state law and the displacement of forum law in a case with a strong nexus to the forum. As such, the decision is an example of accessory choice of

---

55 See also: *Bio/Basics Intern. v. Ortho Pharmaceutical Corp.* 545 F.Supp. 1106 (S.D. N.Y. 1982), in which case the same court followed § 150 Restatement Second to the letter. For good measure, it threw in an unsupported statement about New York's interest being greater than that of Washington D.C., where the alleged defamation had occurred, but it kept silent on the interest of New Jersey, the state of defendant's place of business.
56 *Western Energy, Inc. v. Georgia-Pacific Corp.* 637 P.2d 223 at 229 (Or. App. 1981). More on the development of Oregon's version of the most significant relationship test, *infra* note 81.
57 *Ibid.* p. 229, note 8.

law[58] predicated on a rather eclectic construction of the most significant relationship approach.[59] Some speculation as to the real motives of the court to deny recovery is justified, it would seem.

Turning now to those cases in which the most significant relationship approach is perceived to rely on substantive law evaluation rather than contacts weighing, I will venture to select a few representative samples. To begin with, mention could be made of a landmark decision hailing from Illinois. The Illinois Supreme Court adopted the most significant relationship approach in 1970 in *Ingersoll v. Klein*, quoting Tentative Draft No. 9 of § 379 Restatement Second.[60] In a wrongful death action between Illinois parties it had to decide the issue whether the owner of a car –who had not been present at the

58 This phenomenon, which seems to be better known in Europe than it is in the United States, has the same effect as result-selective characterization. Under the principles of accessory choice of law, the issue is characterized as sounding in one category, whereas the conflicts rule pertaining to another choice of law area is applied. This approach is motivated by the notion that the relationship at issue is an offshoot of a primary relationship, usually between the same parties, without which it probably would not have come into existence. A common example is a delictual controversy between the parties to a contract. While the issue may sound in tort, the choice of law rule for contracts is applied on the strength of the contractual relationship. *Cf.* Kropholler (1969) p. 625 ff.; De Boer (1982) p. 29 ff.; *contra*: Binder (1955) p. 478–480.
59 It will be clear that accessory choice of law is a form of jurisdiction-selection and, therefore, not compatible with a policy-oriented approach. Under the Restatement's most significant relationship test, anything goes, apparently. In *El Cid, Ltd. v. New Jersey Zinc Co.* 575 F.Supp. 1513 (S.D. N.Y. 1983), concerning an alleged conspiracy to deprive the plaintiff of a concession of mining rights in Bolivia, the court not only totted up Bolivian contacts, but also referred to the *lex rei sitae* rule: "Although this action sounds in tort, and neither party seeks to have the [Bolivia property rights] determined here, we think that this well-established choice of law rule is ... at least important to our consideration." Another example is given *infra* note 83. See also: *Witherspoon v. Salm* 251 Ind. 575, 243 N.E.2d 876 (1969); *Hague v. Allstate Ins. Co.* 289 N.W.2d 43 (Minn. 1979), diss. op. *per* Otis, J. *Contra*: *Equilease Corp. v. Smith Intern. Inc.* 588 F.2d 919 (5th Cir. [La.] 1979), rejecting the suggestion that a contractual choice of law provision should govern the issue of fraud, allegedly committed by plaintiff's contract partners.
60 *Ingersoll v. Klein* 46 Ill.2d 42, 262 N.E.2d 593 (1970). The quoted section is the forerunner of § 145. It made no reference to general choice of law principles, only to the forum's duty to "consider the issues, the character of the tort, and the relevant purposes of the tort rules of the interested states." Curiously, Tentative Draft no. 9 of the chapter on Wrongs, dating from 1964, had been followed by the Proposed Official Drafts, Part I (introducing § 6) published in 1967, Part II (reformulating the torts provision) in 1968. The *Ingersoll* decision was rendered in 1970.

time the deceased drowned after the car in which he was riding as a passenger broke through the ice on the Mississippi river just within the territorial jurisdiction of Iowa – was liable for the damages caused by the driver, as he would be according to Iowa law. Discussing the advantages of the *lex loci* rule, being ease of application, predictability, symmetry of result in that the same law is applied to all actions arising out of one accident, and discouragement of forum shopping, the court concluded, "The fatal flaw of this so-called 'justification' for the place-of-injury rule is that you could enjoy each and every one of these vaunted advantages by agreeing to apply the law of New York (as our most populous State or as trust capital of the world or as the situs of the 1965 World's Fair) or the law of Alaska (as the law of our coldest State) to decide the infinitely various issues which might arise in interstate tort cases."[61] Consequently, the court abandoned the traditional rule: "Realization of unjust and anomalous results which may ensue from an application of *lex loci delicti* leads us to believe that a 'most significant contacts' rule best serves the interests of the State and the parties involved in a multi-State tort action,"[62] here resulting in the application of Illinois law. In spite of the reference to the "interests of the State and the parties involved," the court did not specify according to what standard the significance of contacts should be evaluated, but it did suggest a qualitative approach by remarking, " ... as applied to torts, the [vested rights] theory ignores the *interest* which jurisdictions

---

61 *Ibid.* p. 595. The suggestion to apply the law of Alaska had already been made by Currie (1963-1) p. 699/700, in his comment on *Kilberg v. Northeast Airlines* 9 N.Y.2d 34, 211 N.Y.S.2d 133, 172 N.E.2d 526 (1961): "Would it not be to the advantage of both the passenger and the airline to know in advance, before any crash occurs and, indeed, before any flight plan is filed, that all claims for injury and death will be governed by the law of Alaska? The text of that law could even be posted in airport waiting rooms, alongside the insurance vending-machines, as the laws on innkeeper's liability are posted inside the door of a hotel room."
I cannot resist the temptation to quote another passage in which Currie ridiculed his critics' adherence to "arbitrary and complex rules for choice of law". Addressing the situation in which, "[by] hypothesis, no policy of any state is involved," he wrote: "In all solemnity, I suggest that a nearly ideal choice-of-law rule for such cases would be that the governing law shall be that of the state first in alphabetical order," adding in a footnote: "This rule might impose undue hardship on the courts of states low in the alphabet, since they would be constantly burdened by the task of ascertaining foreign law, while states high on the list would have the advantage of frequently applying domestic law. This difficulty could be met by applying the rule of inverse alphabetical order for transactions occurring in odd-numbered years." *Ibid.* p. 609, text accompanying note 74.
62 *Ingersoll v. Klein* 46 Ill.2d 42, 262 N.E.2d 593 at 596 (1970).

other than that where the tort occurred may have in the resolution of particular issues."⁶³ It is not surprising, then, that subsequent Illinois decisions emphasized "the policies underlying conflicting rules of law" or the "predominant interest" of one of the states involved. In *Pancotto v. Sociedade de Safaris de Moçambique S.A.R.L.*, a federal court sitting in Illinois took *Ingersoll v. Klein* to mean: "The first step in the choice of law analysis is to isolate the substantive legal issues and determine whether the various states' tort rules conflict. If a potential conflict is discovered, the next step is to examine the contacts with the states, evaluating the importance of each contact in relation to the legal issue of the case."⁶⁴ The matter in dispute arose out of a safari accident in Mozambique: a swamp buggy driven by defendant's employee hit the plaintiff while she was taking pictures of the hunting party. Addressing the issue of negligent conduct, the court found that the standard of care of plaintiff's home state, Illinois, might be different from Mozambique's standard, the latter being derived from Portuguese law and requiring the degree of "diligence with which a law-abiding male head of a family would act."⁶⁵ After a careful evaluation of the interests Illinois had as the state of plaintiff's domicile, and Mozambique as the state where the conduct and injury had occurred, where the defendant had its place of business and where the parties' relationship centered, it was held that Mozambique, if the harmful conduct was unintentional, had only an attenuated interest in the application of its standards of conduct, while it might have a further interest in "insulating a domiciliary from liability." Illinois was thought to be interested in compensating "both the victim and her creditors" but in a true conflict such as this one, the *lex loci delicti* is

---

63 *Ibid.* p. 595; emphasis added. The opinion is couched in ambivalent language, however. Preceding the court's rejection of the traditional conflicts rule for torts, there is a general statement which has proved to support various interpretations, from a *lex loci* presumption to a preference for forum law, to be discussed *infra* text accompanying notes 85–100.
64 *Pancotto v. Sociedade de Safaris de Moçambique S.A.R.L.* 422 F.Supp. 405 (N.D. Ill. 1976); see also *supra* chapter 2, notes 246–247 and accompanying text. In *Mitchell v. United Asbestos Corporation* 100 Ill.App.3d 485, 55 Ill.Dec. 375, 426 N.E.2d 350 at 357 (1981), the Appellate Court cited several New York cases as authority for "a three-step process: ' ... first isolate the issue, next to identify the policies embraced in the laws in conflict, and finally to examine the contacts of the respective jurisdictions to ascertain which has a superior connection with the occurrence and thus would have a superior interest in having its policy or law applied.'"
65 Art. 487(2) of the Portuguese Civil Code, at the time in force in Mozambique.

only displaced if the tort's occurrence in the foreign state is fortuitous, which in this instance it was not. Thus, the Mozambique standards of conduct prevailed.[66]

In the same vein, a number of courts have perceived the Restatement's most significant relationship test as an approach that, to establish the significance of factual contacts, relies mainly on an evaluation of policies and interests. Applying Pennsylvania choice of law principles, a federal court referred to the Restatement and its four principal contacts as well as to "interests" involved, and proceeded to explain, "The law does not require us to apply the law of the state whose contacts are the most numerous, but rather demands sensitivity to the relative importance of each of the several contacts to the substantive policy of workmen's compensation," this being the issue in this case.[67] In *Wilcox v. Wilcox*, a decision which almost exclusively relied on interest analysis, the Wisconsin Supreme Court posited that " ... in order to determine the 'most significant relationship' consideration should be given to the policies and interests of the forum state, the tort state, and of other states that may have an interest by virtue of the domicile of the parties or other relevant factors."[68] In *Beaulieu v. Beaulieu*, the Supreme Judicial Court of Maine adopted "the new flexible approach of the Restatement (Second)" and construed it as a form of interest analysis: " ... we readily observe that Maine's contacts are quantitatively and qualitatively greater and that [our] governmental interest is of major significance, while Massachusetts contacts are merely fortuitous in that the accident happened there and its concerns, if any, are minimal."[69] In *Danner v. Staggs*, a case "reminiscent of a conflicts of law exam hypothetical," the Fifth Circuit made an

---

66 As to the measure of damages, the opposite result was reached: see *supra* chapter 2, notes 246–247 and accompanying text.
67 *Lewis v. Chemetron Corp.* 448 F. Supp. 211 at 213 (W.D. Pa. 1978). This approach was extended to contract actions in *Melville v. American Home Assur. Co.* 443 F.Supp. 1064 (E.D. Pa. 1977) *rev'd on other grounds* 584 F.2d 1306 (3d Cir. [Pa.] 1978).
68 *Wilcox v. Wilcox* 26 Wis.2d 617, 133 N.W.2d 408 (1965). See also: *Rungee v. Allied Van Lines, Inc.* 92 Idaho 718, 449 P.2d 378 (1968) in combination with *DeMeyer v. Maxwell* 103 Idaho 327, 647 P.2d 783 (Idaho App. 1982), confirming that in *Rungee*, the Supreme Court of Idaho adopted the Restatement Second approach with special emphasis on state interests.
69 *Beaulieu v. Beaulieu* 265 A.2d 610 at 616 (Me. 1970). *Accord: Adams v. Buffalo Forge Co.* 443 A.2d 932 (Me. 1982).

effort to understand Texas choice of law since *Gutierrez v. Collins*.[70] The action arose from a car accident in Texarkana, precisely on the stateline between Texas and Arkansas. The parties were girl friends, who had been on their way from a party in Texas to a bar in Texas when defendant took a fatal U-turn, causing her car to swerve from Texas into Arkansas. Plaintiff lived in the Arkansas part of the city, defendant in the Texas part. Both states had guest statutes, but since the Texas statute allowed recovery by non-relatives, plaintiff would prevail under Texas law. Having found that the four contacts listed in Restatement Second § 145(2) were in balance, the Fifth Circuit resorted to interest analysis. As defendant was a Texas resident, Arkansas had no interest in shielding her from liability for the injuries of an Arkansas guest. Texas, on the other hand, would want "the driver to be accountable to his or her passengers for negligence, unless the parties are related by blood or marriage."[71] An extra argument was found in § 6(2)(d), the protection of justified expectations. Living "three feet across the state line," and having a Texas driver's license, defendant "cannot use the law of Arkansas as a shield to avoid responsibility which Texas has determined that the driver of a car should have."[72]

Danner v. Staggs is one of the few tort cases in which more than a token reference is made to a choice of law principle listed in § 6, other than the two relating to state interests. Generally, judicial attention focuses on § 6(2)(b) and (2)(c), and nothing is said about any of the other factors that might bear upon tort choice of law.[73] In a few cases, such as *Danner*, the justified expectations of the parties were considered a relevant factor in tort choice of law, even though the comment

70 *Gutierrez v. Collins* 583 S.W.2d 312 (Tex. 1979), replacing *lex loci delicti* by the most significant relationship approach, a "rather nebulous test" according to the author of the opinion in *Danner v. Staggs* 680 F.2d 427 at 429 (5th Cir. [Tex.] 1982).
71 *Ibid.* p. 431. The court added, "Were the roles reversed, we might find that Arkansas had a relevant interest in the application of its law." In that case, there would have been a true conflict, it would seem. In terms of interest analysis, *Danner v. Staggs* was solved as a false conflict, but it could have been construed as an unprovided for case as well, depending on the purpose of Texas recovery rule. The false conflict construction suggests that the Fifth Circuit viewed the policy of the Texas statute as admonitory rather than compensatory.
72 *Ibid.* p. 432.
73 See, *e.g.*: *Griggs v. Riley* 489 S.W.2d 469 (Mo. App. 1972); *Johnson v. Spider Staging Corporation* 555 P.2d 997 (Wash. 1976); *Conlin v. Hutcheon* 560 F.Supp. 934 (D. Colo. 1983); *Guillory on Behalf of Guillory v. United States* 699 F.2d 781 (5th Cir. [La./Tex.] 1983).

on § 6(2)(d) Restatement Second expresses a different point of view: "There are occasions, particularly in the area of negligence, when the parties act without giving thought to the legal consequences of their conduct or to the law that may be applied. In such situations, the parties have no justified expectations to protect, and this factor can play no part in the decision of a choice-of-law question." In *Crim v. International Harvester Co.*, also decided by the Fifth Circuit pursuant to Texas choice of law, plaintiff had been awarded $ 55,000 in damages for defendant's failure to warn. Both parties had their places of business in Texas, plaintiff being a dealer of vehicles manufactured by defendant. Attending a demonstration of these vehicles in the Arizona desert, plaintiff caught a rare disease called "valley fever" caused by stirred-up spores near desert ground. He accused defendant of negligence for not warning him of the risk, in violation of the duty which Arizona law was said to impose on landowners and occupiers of land. The Fifth Circuit held that Arizona law applied and affirmed, not only because Arizona had an interest in defining the duty which Arizona landowners owe to their business invitees, but also because application of Arizona law would promote certainty and uniformity of result, as Arizona landowners should not be subjected to different legal duties depending on the invitee's domicile. "Finally," the court concluded, "application of Arizona's law protects the landowners' justified expectation that their obligations vis-à-vis their land are governed by the law of the land in which the land is situated."[74] One cannot help but wonder about the "justified expectation" of the plaintiff in this case.[75]

74 *Crim v. International Harvester Co.* 646 F.2d 161 at 163 (5th Cir. [Tex.] 1981).
75 In *Carver v. Schafer* 647 S.W.2d 570 at 577 (Mo. App. 1983), a wrongful death action brought against an Illinois tavern owner for the death of a Missouri police officer who had been struck and killed by an intoxicated patron, Missouri's plaintiff-favoring wrongful death statute was applied, instead of Illinois' Dram Shop Act which limited recovery to $ 20,000. The court conceded that the tavern owner may not have expected application of Missouri law, although he must have known that many of his patrons were Missouri residents. However, the plaintiffs would not have expected anything but Missouri law.
Defendant's expectations were emphasized in *Gallagher v. Koppers Co., Inc.* 191 Cal.Rptr. 241 (Cal. App. 1983), a products liability case, in which the court asserted that a manufacturer should be cognizant of the law of the place of injury if his product was distributed there. In *Baird v. Bell Helicopter Textron* 491 F.Supp. 1129 at 1146 (N.D. Tex. 1980), on the other hand, it was observed that "Bell manufactures aircraft which are sold worldwide. It cannot be said to have relied on the application of any particular jurisdiction's contribution statute."

The basic policies underlying the particular field of law, the choice of law principle expressed in § 6(2)(e), were emphasized by the Court of Appeals of Arizona in *Gordon v. Kramer*.[76] The parties in this guest statute controversy were both residents of Arizona, who had been making a trip through various states in defendant's car. In Utah, defendant had fallen asleep at the wheel, causing the accident in which plaintiff was seriously injured. Applying the most significant relationship test adopted in *Schwartz v. Schwartz*,[77] the court referred to §§ 145 and 146 of Restatement Second, and proceeded to examine the various principles of § 6. Ease of application was discarded as a relevant consideration, since it was easy enough to determine and apply Utah's guest statute. Predictability was also deemed of little importance, as the tort had not been preconceived. On the other hand, the court placed much weight upon the principle listed in § 6(2)(e): "The basic policy in the law of torts is to deter tortious conduct and provide compensation for the injured victim." Finding that "[a]pplication of the Utah law would defeat the basic tort policies of the State of Arizona and sanction wrongful conduct,"[78] without furthering any interest of Utah, the court held defendant liable under Arizona law, a conclusion which would have been supported just as well by straightforward interest analysis. The decision could serve as another illustration of Professor Reppy's harsh but valid criticism of § 6: "Examination of the five factors enumerated in section 6 in addition to the policy of the interested forum and the other interested states shows that many are almost silly and will never have any influence on the outcome of the choice of law process under the Restatement Second."[79]

The flexible formula of Restatement Second not only covers contacts counting or policy analysis, it also allows a number of mixed solutions

76 *Gordon v. Kramer* 124 Ariz. 442, 604 P.2d 1153 (Ariz. App. 1979).
77 *Schwartz v. Schwartz* 103 Ariz. 562, 447 P.2d 254 (1968).
78 *Gordon v. Kramer* 124 Ariz. 442, 604 P.2d 1153 at 1158 (Ariz. App. 1979).
79 Reppy (1983) p. 662 ff., explaining why the first, the sixth, and the seventh factors listed in § 6 are "silly." The needs of the interstate system are better served by the "flexible territorialism" on which Restatement Second was based before the insertion of § 6. Certainty, predictability and uniformity of result are endangered by "the vague section 6, with the uncertainty it creates concerning the role of state interests." Ease in the determination and application of the law to be applied is a silly consideration, since the determination would be easier "under a system sticking to territorial considerations unmixed with phantomlike state interests," whereas no court believing in the choice of law method it employs would "abandon it in a particular case because the law chosen ... raises some difficult problems."

borrowing from the various doctrines at once. As might be expected, some courts feeling insecure in adopting a single variety of the new approaches have chosen to reinforce their opinions by stacking several choice of law theories on top of one another. This happens, for instance, when the most significant relationship test is referred to as an alternative for the *lex loci delicti* rule, the court paying lip-service to one of the parties' plea to adopt a more flexible approach. Thus, the Wyoming Supreme Court, in *Brown v. Riner*, wanting to retain the *lex loci* rule in an action in which both plaintiff and defendant were Colorado residents, rejected plaintiff's argument that Colorado law should displace Wyoming's guest statute. It was said that adoption of the Restatement Second's solution "would be a repudiation of the position heretofore taken by this Court," but "even assuming arguendo that we should adopt such an approach, it would not produce a different result." This conclusion is questionable, since the only contact Wyoming had with this case was the fact that the car accident in which plaintiff was injured occurred in that state.[80] The Oregon Supreme Court, in *De Foor v. Lematta*, reached a more appropriate result. The action arose out of a helicopter crash in California, in which only Oregon parties were involved, and focused on the issue whether Oregon's wrongful death limitation or California's aviation guest statute should be applied. The court solved it by lumping all new choice of law theories together: "Under any choice-of-law theory except that which would apply the law of the place of injury without regard to any other considerations, the Oregon wrongful death law should apply to an action between Oregon domiciliaries in an Oregon court."[81] In

---

80 *Brown v. Riner* 500 P.2d 524 at 526 (Wyo. 1972). *Cf.* Restatement Second § 145, comment e.
81 *De Foor v. Lematta* 249 Or. 116, 437 P.2d 107 at 109 (1968). It should be noted that the court relied heavily on *Reich v. Purcell* 67 Cal.2d 551, 432 P.2d 727, 63 Cal.Rptr. 31 (1967), a California case decided by interest analysis, in support of this conclusion. The development of Oregon choice of law is described and criticized by Nafziger/Dixon (1981). The draft Restatement's most significant relationship test for torts was adopted in *Casey v. Manson Construction and Engineering Co.* 247 Or. 274, 428 P.2d 898 (1967), with emphasis on policies and interests. After *De Foor v. Lematta*, Oregon choice of law kept wavering between the Restatement's most significant relationship test and governmental interest analysis. In *Myers v. Cessna Aircraft* 275 Or. 501, 553 P.2d 355 (1976), the court resorted to the Restatement, § 175, to resolve a statute of limitations issue. In *Tower v. Schwabe* 284 Or. 105, 585 P.2d 662 (1978), on the other hand, the Restatement approach was spurned in favor of an interest evaluation.

Continental Oil Co. v. General American Transportation Corporation, a diversity suit brought in Texas at the time the courts of that state still retained the *lex loci delicti* rule, a federal court had to decide a strict liability issue arising out of the defective manufacture of railroad tanks. The tanks had been manufactured in Ohio, and were delivered in Texas, Pennsylvania and Ohio, pursuant to a contract governed by Oklahoma law. The court, faced with the difficulty that the place of injury could not be ascertained, expressed as its opinion that "a Texas court, confronted with the instant fact situation, would characterize the situs of the wrongful acts, Ohio, as the lex loci delicti in the absence of definite places of injury or damage," but added that the same result would be reached if Texas courts would employ the "most significant contacts test." It then proceeded to compare the interest of Ohio in controlling defendant's conduct to the "inferior interests" of Texas, Pennsylvania and Oklahoma, and concluded on a wistful note: "However, until such time as the Texas courts clearly adopt a functional test that encourages the rational selection of a single jurisdiction to govern the entire dispute, this Court must abide by the presently-existing maze of conflict rules which represent Texas law."[82] In this case, if we may believe the court, the traditional conflicts rule and the Restatement Second approach would happen to produce the same result. Yet, taken together, the opinions in *Brown v. Riner*, *De Foor v. Lematta* and *Continental* indicate that the persuasive value of stacking various conflicts approaches may be considered spurious.

In this context, the decision of a federal court sitting in Hawaii, in *DeRoburt v. Gannett Co., Inc.*, is a most curious example of Restatement eclecticism. Hammer DeRoburt was the president of Nauru, an independent island republic in the Pacific, who had sued defendant, a Delaware corporation having its principal place of business in New York, for a libelous article which had appeared in the "Pacific Daily News," a publication of one of defendant's subsidiaries in Guam. After the libel suit had been dismissed – on the act of state doctrine, no less– defendant wanted to recover attorneys' fees in the amount of $ 475,000. Again, the question which law applied was raised. The district court decided that, absent statutory provision, a "choice of law determination regarding a claim for attorneys' fees should be guided

---

82 *Continental Oil Co. v. General American Transportation Corporation* 409 F.Supp. 288 at 296/297 (S.D. Texas 1976).

by the applicable substantive law of the case."⁸³ Although Nauru law, despite Mr. DeRoburt's insistence, had not actually been applied to the libel suit, his claim having been denied under the act of state doctrine, the court did not think this really mattered. Observing that Hawaii had rejected the *lex loci delicti* doctrine and adopted a "modern approach emphasizing governmental interests, dominant contacts and policy factors," the court found that application of Nauru law to the claim for reimbursement of attorney's fees was "wholly consistent with the parties' justified expectations and a concern for predictability," particularly since the plaintiff had always insisted that Nauru law governed the libel suit. Furthermore, "Nauru's practice of awarding attorney's fees to the prevailing party is integrally connected with Nauru's overall scheme for tort compensation and therefore reflects an important foreign governmental interest."⁸⁴ The proposition that Nauru's policy of compensating tort victims gives it an interest in seeing an uncompensated Nauru plaintiff pay $ 475,000 for the legal expenses of his foreign opponents, must be rated as a most ingenious feat of result-selective choice of law.

That the place of the wrong rule maintains a prominent, if ambiguous, place under the most significant relationship test is demonstrated by a series of Illinois decisions relying on *Ingersoll v. Klein*, in which case the Illinois Supreme Court, adopting "the most significant contacts rule," had said: "In our opinion, the local law of the State where the injury occurred should determine the rights and liabilities of the parties, unless *Illinois* has a more significant relationship with the occurrence and with the parties, in which case the *law of Illinois* should

---

83 *DeRoburt v. Gannett Co., Inc.* 558 F.Supp. 1223 at 1226 (D. Hawaii 1983). This statement could be taken as another example of accessory choice of law (*supra* notes 58–59), if the matter of attorney's fees is viewed as an independent choice of law category, subjected to the law governing the libel issue. In terms of traditional choice of law, a procedural characterization would have been more plausible.

84 *Ibid.* p. 1226/1227. In *DeRoburt v. Gannett Co., Inc.* 83 F.R.D. 574 at 580 (D. Hawaii 1979), the same court had referred to *American forum* policy and to *defendant's* justified expectations, stating: " ... this Court believes that the public policy of the United States requires the application of the First Amendment to libel brought in the courts of this country; defendants in this case therefore justifiably expect constitutional protection of their free expression. Nevertheless, this does not necessarily foreclose the application of the law of Nauru insofar as it does not conflict with the First Amendment."

apply."[85] This forum-biased paraphrase of the Restatement's territorial approach to torts would imply that either *lex loci delicti* or *lex fori*, but no other law would qualify for application to tort issues in Illinois courts. Even so, the Illinois formula proved adaptable, as exemplified by several Illinois opinions.

In the first place, mention should be made of a type of decision featuring a colorless center of gravity approach in which the four contacts of § 145(2) Restatement Second are weighed *without* special emphasis on the place of injury. In *Semmelroth v. American Airlines*, for instance, plaintiff's deceased, a travel agent, had been invited by defendant for a fully paid trip to Mexico, where he was killed at the hands of unknown assailants. Plaintiff alleged that defendant had failed to warn the deceased that the particular Mexican state "was overrun by armed bands of guerillas and bandits." The court decided that Illinois law governed this issue, particularly because the deceased had been an Illinois resident and his relationship with defendant, a Delaware corporation with its principal place of business in New York, had centered in Illinois. The place of "injury" was not even mentioned as a relevant factor.[86]

Then there are the decisions in which the place of wrong is considered as a most significant contact. Consistent with both the *lex loci* presumption in *Ingersoll* and a policy-oriented choice of law approach, the opinion in *Jackson v. Miller-Davis Company and Ceco Corporation* emphasized the significance of the law of the place of injury in respect of issues of *conduct*, resulting in the application of the Indiana

---

85 *Ingersoll v. Klein* 262 N.E.2d 593 at 595 (1970); emphasis added. It should be noted that this statement preceded the rejection of the traditional *lex loci delicti* rule. See also, *supra* notes 60–63 and accompanying text.
86 *Semmelroth v. American Airlines* 448 F.Supp. 730 (E.D. Ill. 1978). Similarly, in *McIntosh v. Magna Systems, Inc.* 539 F.Supp. 1185 (N.D. Ill. 1982), the Illinois-centered relationship between the parties was deemed controlling, despite the fact that the place of injury was in North Carolina. In *Kramer v. McDonald's System, Inc.* 61 Ill.App.3d 947, 19 Ill.Dec. 21, 378 N.E.2d 522 (1978), on the other hand, Texas rather than forum law was held to apply as the law of the state having the most significant contacts with the dispute. Illinois was considered the state of the *locus delicti* in *MPL, Inc. v. Cook* 90 F.R.D. 570 (N.D. Ill. 1981), an action for unlawful appropriation of confidential information and trade secrets against Indiana machine buyers; the machines that were subject of the action had been designed, manufactured and purchased in Illinois.

"Dangerous Occupations Act."[87] Less subtle was the decision in *Pelinski v. Goodyear Tire & Rubber Co.*, a personal injury action in which Nebraska law was applied simply because "Nebraska was the place where the injury occurred and Illinois has no more significant relationship with the occurrence and with the parties."[88] What was called "the conventional *lex loci delicti* approach," was used in both *Hardly Able Coal Co., Inc. v. International Harvester Co.* and *DP Service, Inc. v. AM International* as an escape from situations in which the contacts and interests were found to be in equal balance.[89] This interpretation of the *Ingersoll* ruling turns the *lex loci* presumption into a subsidiary conflicts rule, to be applied as a solution to true conflicts, apparently.

In other cases, policies and interests dominate the choice of law considerations even more. Citing *Ingersoll* as representing "pre-eminent doctrine", the district court in *Pancotto v. Sociedade de Safaris de Moçambique S.A.R.L.*,[90] performed a full-fledged interest analysis before it resorted to the *lex loci* presumption to resolve the true conflict it had found to be present. Referring to both *Ingersoll v. Klein* and §§ 145 and 6 of the Restatement, the same court explained the significance standard in terms of interest analysis once more in *Forty-Eight Insulations v. Johns-Manville Products*: "Thus the contacts test is not an end in itself to be applied mechanically, but rather is a means reliably calculated to insure that the interests of the state with the most significant relationship to the occurrences will be protected,"[91] but no

---

[87] *Jackson v. Miller-Davis Company and Ceco Corporation* 3 Ill.Dec. 161, 44 Ill.App.3d 611, 358 N.W.2d 328 (1976). See also: *Leschkies v. Playboy Club of Lake Geneva, Inc.* 465 F.Supp. 80 (N.D. Ill. 1979): application of Wisconsin's "Safe Place Statute" which imposed a higher standard of care than the one prevailing in plaintiff's home state, Illinois.

[88] *Pelinski v. Goodyear Tire & Rubber Co.* 499 F.Supp. 1092 (N.D. Ill.). The opposite result was reached in *Harkcom v. East Texas Motor, Etc.* 104 Ill.App.3d 780, 60 Ill.Dec. 494, 433 N.E.2d 291 (1982), in which application of the Iowa *lex loci* to an action between Illinois parties was curtly rejected.

[89] *Hardly Able Coal Co., Inc. v. International Harvester Co.* 494 F.Supp. 249 at 250 (N.D. Ill. 1980); *DP Service, Inc. v. AM International* 508 F.Supp. 162 (N.D. Ill. 1981). See also: *R & L Grain Co. v. Chicago Eastern Corp.* 531 F.Supp. 201 (N.D. Ill. 1981), to be discussed *infra* chapter 4, section 4(c), text following note 334.

[90] *Pancotto v. Sociedade de Safaris de Moçambique S.A.R.L.* 422 F.Supp. 405 (N.D. Ill. 1976), discussed *supra* text accompanying notes 64–66.

[91] *Forty-Eight Insulations v. Johns-Manville Products* 472 F.Supp. 385 at 391 (N.D. Ill. 1979).

mention was made of the presumptive importance of the place of the wrong. In *Mitchell v. United Asbestos Corp.*, the *Pancotto* decision was cited as proof for the proposition that Illinois had "rejected the 'counting of contacts' approach in favor of the more sophisticated 'interest analysis' construction of the Restatement."[92]

As demonstrated by the opinion in *Pittway Corp. v. Lockheed Aircraft Corp.*, the Illinois *lex loci* presumption can be manipulated by substituting the place of conduct for the place of injury. The plaintiff, a Pennsylvania corporation doing business in Illinois, was owner of an aircraft manufactured by defendant, a California corporation with its principal places of business in Georgia and California. After cracks in the aircraft had been detected in Wisconsin, plaintiff sued the manufacturer for the costs of repairs and economic loss in the amount of $ 120,000. The law of Illinois, in this respect being identical to Georgia law, did not permit recovery of economic loss in this situation. While the District Court had applied Wisconsin law under the last event rule, the Seventh Circuit reversed and held the law of Illinois to be controlling. It arrived at this conclusion by relying on the Restatement's most significant relationship test as reformulated in *Ingersoll v. Klein*. Yet, Wisconsin law was rejected, first, because the actual place of injury was deemed indeterminate, as "[t]he harm that Pittway suffered ... was purely economic and as such was sustained in Illinois," and, second, because Wisconsin would not have an interest in the outcome of the case, Wisconsin's recovery rule being meant "to insure that Wisconsin residents and therefore indirectly Wisconsin itself are protected against such losses."[93] By contrast, it would be Georgia's policy "to protect the economic well-being of Georgia manufacturers and indirectly the State by limiting the scope of potential liability for product defects to that established contractually by the parties." For that reason, Georgia law should apply to this tort issue, but "[s]ince Georgia and Illinois law are the same, Illinois law is con-

---

92 *Mitchell v. United Asbestos Corp.* 100 Ill.App.3, 55 Ill.Dec. 375, 426 N.E.2d 350 at 356 (Ill. App. 1981), blending the consideration of the "basic policies underlying the particular field of law," listed in § 6(2)(e) Restatement Second, with outright interest analysis. See also: *Roman v. Delta Air Lines, Inc.* 441 F.Supp. 1160 at 1166 (N.D. Ill. 1977): "More recent cases point to an analysis of the interests or 'contacts' that a state has with an occurrence as the means of determining choice of law in tort cases."
93 *Pittway Corp. v. Lockheed Aircraft Corp.* 641 F.2d 524 at 528 (7th Cir. [Ill.] 1981).

trolling here."[94] It would seem that this curious mixture of contacts juggling, interest analysis, and "non-choice" is rather excessive just to circumvent the *Ingersoll* presumption that Wisconsin law would apply as *lex loci delicti* and to arrive at forum law.

My last example in this confusing series of Illinois decisions is *In re Air Crash Disaster near Chicago, Illinois on May 25, 1979*,[95] covering one hundred eighteen wrongful death actions, filed in various states and transferred to Illinois by the Judicial Panel on Multidistrict Litigation. Defendants were American Airlines, a Delaware corporation with its principal place of business in New York, later Texas, and its maintenance base in Oklahoma, and McDonnell Douglas Corporation, a Maryland corporation having its principal place of business in Missouri and a major establishment in California. The plaintiffs and their decedents were residents of fourteen different states or countries, claiming both compensatory and punitive damages. Addressing the question which law applied to the issue of punitive damages under Illinois choice of law,[96] the Seventh Circuit first determined which states had relevant contacts that should be taken into account, then examined the interests of these states in the application of their laws. Assuming that the states in which the plaintiffs were domiciled neither had an interest in disallowing them punitive damages, nor in imposing them on defendants, the court focused on the places of the alleged misconduct and the places of business of the two defendants, and found that the various state interests in imposing or denying punitive damages were evenly balanced: "This situation involves a total and genuine conflict: one jurisdiction allows punitive damages, the other does not. There does not seem to be any way to arrive at a 'moderate and restrained' interpretation of either policy so as to avoid a true

---

94 *Ibid.* More on this solution to "no-conflict" situations, *infra* chapter 4, section 1, text following note 29.
95 *In re Air Crash Disaster near Chicago, Illinois on May 25, 1979* 644 F.2d 594 (7th Cir. [Ill.] 1981). In this particular case, one of many arising from the Chicago air crash, defendants appealed from the district court's denial of their motions to strike the demands for punitive damages.
96 Pursuant to *Erie R. Co. v. Tompkins* 304 U.S. 64, 58 S.Ct. 817, 82 L.Ed. 1188 (1938) and *Van Dusen v. Barrack* 376 U.S. 612, 84 S.Ct. 805, 11 L.Ed.2d 945 (1965), the Circuit Court had to determine the applicable law under the choice of law principles of California, to be discussed *infra*, chapter 4, section 4(b), text accompanying notes 214–252, New York, Michigan, Puerto Rico and Hawaii.

conflict."⁹⁷ To solve this true conflict, the court reverted to the *lex loci* presumption. Although Illinois, whose law did not permit recovery of punitive damages in wrongful death actions, had not much of an interest in shielding non-resident defendants from excessive liability, it *did* have an interest, the court declared, in "not suffering air crash disasters and also in promoting air safety," an interest furthered by punitive damages. On the other hand, it had an interest in "encouraging air transportation corporations to do business in the state," an interest militating against punitive damages.⁹⁸ Even if Illinois was only the fortuitous place of injury, it could not be said that the interests of the other states involved, taken separately, were greater than those of Illinois, this being sufficient reason for the court to apply Illinois law and to strike the claims for punitive damages. As if this were not enough, the validity of the decision was checked against the choice of law principles of § 6. Not suprisingly, the justified expectations of the parties were not considered "helpful" in the resolution of the issue; the same was true in respect of the needs of the interstate system, or the basic policies underlying the field of punitive damages. On the other hand, application of Illinois law would comport with the factor certainty, predictability and uniformity of result, since Illinois' *lex loci* presumption "provides a principled means of decision which also creates certainty," whereas future defendants will now be "on notice that, under the 'most significant relationship' test, when there is a true conflict between the laws of states having equal interests in the issue of punitive damages, and when the place of injury has a strong interest in air safety and in protection of air transportation corporations, the law of the place of injury will apply."⁹⁹ Furthermore, the court concluded,

---

97 *In re Air Crash Disaster near Chicago, Illinois on May 25, 1979* 644 F.2d 594 at 615 (7th Cir. [Ill.] 1981). This is the terminology of Currie-style interest analysis, definitely not the language of Restatement Second.
98 *Ibid.*
99 *Ibid.* p. 616. The district court had referred to the certainty factor as well, reaching a different result. Having employed the "four contacts" test of § 145(2) Restatement Second, with regard to the purpose of the tort rule involved, the court applied the laws of the states in which defendants had their corporate headquarters at the time of the crash. Certainty, predictability and uniformity of result would best be achieved, the court opined, "by placing the responsibility for corporate conduct at the corporate headquarters where, as in the case of punitive damages, the purpose of the tort rule is to punish or to deter wrongful conduct, or to regulate the financial burdens on resident persons or corporations." *In re Air Crash Disaster near Chicago, Illinois on May 25, 1979* 500 F.Supp. 1044 at 1050 (N.D. Ill. 1980).

this rule is relatively simple and easy to apply. Covering more than ten pages packed with the latest choice of law wisdom, this exercise in Illinois tort choice of law ends on a Bealian note of territoriality, hardly in tune with the policy-inspired tone of the opinion.[100]

Even if the Illinois *lex loci* decisions should be understood as policy-oriented applications of the most significant relationship test, –the place of wrong reference being either a token reminder of the old days or a panacea for true conflicts– the Illinois decisions amply demonstrate the ambiguity of the Restatement Second's choice of law philosophy. Its flexibility supports anything from contacts counting to place of wrong manipulation, from interest evaluation to forum preference, as well as several combinations of these tactics, all under the aegis of the most significant relationship formula. At the root of this confusion is the Restatement Second's basic flaw: attempting to strike a balance between divergent choice of law considerations and territorial jurisdiction-selection, it combines contacts grouping on a factual basis with a policy evaluation of the substantive rules in conflict. While this compromise was meant to reconcile the demands of justice and legal certainty, the courts are left with the impossible task of straightening out the methodological contradictions inherent in the hybrid process of disinterested allocation and rule-selective policy-weighing. Having "one foot in the camp of *Restatement I* and the other foot in the camp of interest analysis,"[101] the Second Restatement is of little help in the adjudication of tort conflicts because of the question-begging character of the most significant relationship formula.[102] Re-

---

100 The author of the opinion, Circuit Judge Sprecher, was anxious to declare "that this result in no way signifies a return to the mechanical, wooden law of *lex loci delicti*. Rather, it emphasizes the fact that there must be some principled method of decision when the standard 'interest analysis' of conflicts law cannot settle the question." 644 F.2d 594 at 621 (7th Cir. 1981). This suggests that the Illinois *lex loci* presumption should be viewed as an *un*principled solution to true conflicts.
101 *Melville v. American Home Assurance Co.* 443 F.Supp. 1064 at 1084 (E.D. Pa. 1977), *rev'd* 584 F.2d 1306 (3d Cir. 1978).
102 Cavers (1965) p. 208, note 13, viewing the "question-begging character of 'most significant relationship' as a virtue in so far as it may induce courts to ask the right questions." See also: Shapira (1970) p. 212.

stating nothing but some incompatible points of departure, the Restatement's chapter on Wrongs tends to induce muddled reasoning and inconsistent results.[103]

---

[103] Thus far, the flexible most significant relationship formula seems to have been counterproductive to the construction of "new rules, relatively narrow in scope and large in number, which would take proper account of both the choice-of-law and local law values involved." Reese (1977) p. 40. In various other publications, the Reporter of Restatement Second suggested that an open-ended choice of law standard in those areas in which the courts have not yet been able to formulate more precise rules, is apt to further the rule-making process. See, *e.g.*: Reese (1972) *passim*; *id.* (1980) p. 732 ff.; *id.* (1983-1) p. 517 ff. If, in the area of tort choice of law, any "new rule" has emerged at all, it would be the hardly novel rule of *lex loci delicti*.

Chapter 4

Interest Analysis

In 1949, in a federal court in Massachusetts, Charles Gordon won an action for alienation of affections against Stanley Parker, who had been Mrs. Gordon's "paramour" while her husband was away in India. Massachusetts, where Mr. Parker had his home and where the alleged wrongful acts had been committed, gave the husband a right at common law to bring an action against the man who had deprived him of his wife's consortium. Pennsylvania, where the Gordons were domiciled, had abolished such causes of action. Finding no precedent for the central conflicts issue of this case, the Massachusetts district court was clearly not satisfied with the suggestion that Massachusetts law applied simply because the wrong had occurred in that state. Instead, it resorted to a comparison of the *purposes* of the laws in conflict and the *interests* of the states whose "social orders" were implicated. Pennsylvania, the state of the marital domicile, was said to be the state "that has the most sustained and profound interest in the marriage. If it does not give the husband a legal interest in protecting his wife's affections and consortium from strangers, no other state should." On the other hand, "Massachusetts also has an interest. She is concerned with conduct within her borders which in her view lowers the standards of the community where [the acts] occur. She also is concerned when her citizens intermeddle with other people's marriages." Having identified the concerns of each of the two states involved, the court proceeded to weigh their conflicting interests and found that the balance should be struck in favor of Massachusetts. For one thing, it considered that "regulating the social order and substituting legal process for self-help" is a fundamental policy of tort law, and that "the principal reason why [in the tort of alienation of affections] the state stamps conduct as wrongful is that so many people regard it as sinful, so many regard it as offensive to public morals, and so many are likely to take matters into their own hands if public tribunals are not available." Furthermore, the court doubted if the instant case involved an "implied policy" of the Pennsylvania statute: "Pennsylvania was concerned with not having Pennsylvania courts hear this sordid type of controversy and not having Pennsylvania citizens and visitors called upon to defend actions which have so often been motivated by spiteful or ulterior motives." Since the action was brought in Massachusetts, the "purification of Massachusetts courts" was no concern of Pennsylvania.[1]

Gordon v. Parker is not the only American conflicts case of the first half of this century in which mention is made of policies and interests. The U.S. Supreme Court used an interest analysis approach to constitutional choice of law cases as early as 1935.[2] Other courts, while faithful to traditional allocation, have occasionally examined the purposes of substantive rules and the pertinence of their application to the case at issue.[3] On the whole, however, judicial practice adhered to the principles of mechanical allocation, officially blind to the purposes of the rules at issue. Although David F. Cavers was probably the first American scholar to propose a result-selective process based on an appraisal of the contents of the conflicting laws in relation to the facts,[4] it was

---

1 *Gordon v. Parker* 83 F.Supp. 40 (D. Mass. 1949); all quotations at p. 42/43.
2 Inasmuch as these cases turn on the (extra)territorial reach of statutory law, the Supreme Court views the problem as one of statutory construction, which explains the consideration of state interests. See *e.g.*: *Alaska Packers Ass. v. Industrial Accident Commission of California* 294 U.S. 532 at 547/548, 55 S.Ct. 518, 79 L.Ed. 1044 (1935): " ... the conflict is to be resolved, not by giving automatic effect to the full faith and credit clause, compelling the courts of each state to subordinate its own statutes to those of the other, but by appraising the governmental interests of each jurisdiction, and turning the scale of decision according to their weight." See also: *Pacific Employers Ins. Co. v. Industrial Acc. Comm'n* 306 U.S. 493 (1939). *Cf.* Currie (1963-1) p. 203 ff.; p. 715 ff.
3 *Cf.* Cramton/Currie/Kay (1981) p. 241, citing *Emery v. Burbank* 163 Mass. 326, 39 N.E. 1026 (1895), *Lams v. F.H. Smith Co.* 36 Del. 477, 178 A. 651 (1935), and *Val Blatz Brewing Co. v. Industrial Comm'n* 201 Wis. 474, 230 N.W. 622 (1930) as examples.
4 Cavers (1933) p. 192 and *passim*. His "principles of preference," proposed in *The Choice of Law Process*, Ann Arbor, Mich. (1965), will be discussed *infra* section 4(c) of this chapter.

Brainerd Currie who, in the late 1950's, achieved a fundamental change in choice of law thinking through his brilliant essays on "governmental interest analysis."[5] Obviously, the time was ripe for a new jurisprudence of conflicts law.

The basic principles of interest analysis are well known. As exemplified by the considerations in *Gordon v. Parker*, it calls for an appraisal of the interest each of the jurisdictions involved would have in the application of its substantive rule to the case at bar. Since the analysis is a rule-selective process, each substantive issue must be defined separately so as to allow a careful match between the relevant facts and the rule of decision of each concerned jurisdiction.[6] To identify the respective interests, the court should then assess the policy embodied in each of the eligible rules of law, and determine whether application of the rule in question would actually advance that policy. In many cases, the court is bound to discover that only one of the jurisdictions involved has an actual interest in the implementation of its policy, the other state or states being "disinterested." Such "false conflicts" are easily disposed of by applying the rule of decision of the interested jurisdiction. Other cases are more difficult to solve, either because none of the states involved appears to be interested in the application of their laws, or because more than one jurisdiction proves to be interested. The first type of situation, the very existence of which is doubted by some authors, is generally referred to as "the unprovided-for case," whereas cases of the latter category have been labelled "true conflicts." Most of the doctrinal uproar following Currie's methodological propositions can be attributed to his suggestion that the resolution of true conflicts cannot be achieved by a judicial

---

5 The first of these appeared in 1958 and 1959 in various law reviews. A brief restatement of the fundamentals of Currie's interest analysis is found in his *Notes on Methods and Objectives in the Conflict of Laws*, Duke L.J. 171 (1959), reprinted in *Selected Essays on the Conflict of Laws*, Durham, N.C. (1963) p. 177–187.

6 Identification of the specific issue is known as *dépeçage* under the traditional approach. Splitting the various issues in a conflicts case allows the court to make a separate choice of law for each issue. This could result in "patchwork" decisions, in which the substantive rules of various jurisdictions are pieced together into a solution which would have been unavailable under any of the laws involved. "Such a result seems to resemble legislation more than choice among existing laws." Wilde (1968) p. 355. That is why *dépeçage* might be considered anomalous under a jurisdiction-selecting approach. In policy-oriented choice of law, on the other hand, it must be viewed as a basic principle. On the subject of "issue-splitting" and modern choice of law, see: Westen (1967) p. 114 ff.; Reese (1973-2); Weintraub (1980) p. 72 ff.

weighing of conflicting interests, which he deemed "a political function of a very high order,"[7] and that, in the absence of a preconceived choice by the legislature, the courts should generally apply their own law in such cases. This solution has earned interest analysis the reputation of being a parochial, forum-biased approach. Whatever the validity of this allegation, an increasing number of American courts have found interest analysis a preferable approach to choice of law, particularly in the fields of contracts and torts.

Stripped from their token reference to the Restatement Second and their inevitable contacts enumeration, many cases classified under the most significant relationship approach appear to be in reality examples of interest analysis. At least, interest analysis figures rather prominently among the aggregate choice of law techniques by which the "significance" of the relationship is determined. If these cases are added to the ones that can be properly said to rely on interest analysis alone, there is no doubt that this choice of law approach has been most widely followed by the American courts in the past two decades. In this chapter, I will discuss a number of illustrative cases, to show how interest analysis is used in practice and to point out some peculiar problems it entails. It will be seen that judicial practice does not bear out the accusation that interest analysis cultivates an unabashed preference for forum law. Currie's *lex fori* solution to true conflicts has not met with overt judicial approval, as attested by the oft-repeated statement that interest analysis purports to determine which state has the "greater interest,"[8] "a priority of interest,"[9] or "an overwhelming policy interest"[10] in the application of its law.

Many courts have tried to epitomize the essence of interest analysis, not always in the most felicitous terms. Citing *Mellk v. Sarahson*, in

---

7 Currie (1963-1) p. 182. More on true conflicts, *infra* section 4.
8 *Bankhaus Hermann Lampe K.G. v. Mercantile-Safe Dep.* 466 F.Supp. 1133 at 1146 (S.D. N.Y. 1979). See also: *Clark v. Celeb Publishing Inc.* 530 F.Supp. 979 at 982 (S.D. N.Y. 1981): "New York in tort cases, applies 'governmental interest analysis', which looks for the forum with the greatest interest in having its policies applied, and the most significant relationship with the facts and the parties."
9 *McSwain v. McSwain* 420 Pa. 86, 215 A.2d 677 at 682 (1966).
10 *In re Air Crash Disaster near Saigon* 476 F.Supp. 521 at 527 (D. D.C. 1979). See also: *Sharp v. Egler* 658 F.2d 480 at 484 (7th Cir. [Ind.] 1981): "Indiana's interests in this litigation are not only significant but are overwhelming in comparison to Kentucky's interests."

which case interest analysis had been adopted in New Jersey,[11] the Superior Court of New Jersey in *Wuerffel v. Westinghouse Corp.* expounded the "two-step analysis" this approach would require: "The court first determines the governmental policies evidenced by the laws of each related jurisdiction and determines which state has the paramount interest in having its law apply to the rights and liabilities of the parties. Secondly, the court must review the actual contacts of the parties with each related jurisdiction."[12] In Louisiana, interest analysis is also perceived as "a two step process," only the steps are different: "We must first determine whether a true or false conflict exists. If a false conflict exists, the law of the state that has the exclusive interest is applied."[13] The federal district court in the District of Columbia described interest analysis as a process in which "the Court must consider whether the public policy of a particular legislature would be furthered, frustrated or is irrelevant if applied in the case at bar and will displace the law of the forum only if the policy of the legislature of another forum has a stronger interest."[14] And the Supreme Court of Pennsylvania, citing its own landmark decision in *Griffith v. United Airlines*,[15] noted: "What should be sought is an analysis of the extent to which one state rather than another has demonstrated, by reason of its policies and their connection and relevance to the matter in dispute, a priority of interest in the application of its rule of law."[16] One

---

11 *Mellk v. Sarahson* 49 N.J. 226, 229 A.2d 625 (1967).
12 *Wuerffel v. Westinghouse Corp.* 148 N.J. Super. 327, 372 A.2d 659 at 662 (N.J. Super. 1977). A more accurate description was given in *Van Dyke v. Bolves* 107 N.J. Super. 338, 258 A.2d 372 at 374/375 (N.J. Super. 1969): "In sum, the appropriate procedure is to segregate the respective issues and then view each in light of the conflicting interests of the concerned states in resolving them under the local law."
13 *Bell v. State Farm Fire & Cas. Co.* 527 F.Supp. 300 at 302 (W.D. La. 1981), with reference to *Ardoyno v. Kyzar* 426 F.Supp. 78 (E.D. La. 1976).
American courts seem to have a penchant for describing choice of law as a "two-step process." See: *Proprietors Ins. Co. v. Valsecchi* 435 So.2d 290 at 294 (Fla. App. 1983): "Evaluation under the [Restatement Second] significant relationship test involves a two-pronged inquiry directed toward review of the factors in section 145 and section 6. Courts applying this two-pronged test locate the state with the most significant contacts in relation to the occurrence and to the parties with due regard for the policies underlying each of the competing states' pertinent laws."
14 *In re Air Crash Disaster near Saigon* 476 F.Supp. 521 at 526 (D. D.C. 1979). The same phrase was used in *In re "Agent Orange" Product Liability Litigation* 580 F.Supp. 690 at 706 (E.D. New York 1984).
15 *Griffith v. United Airlines* 416 Pa. 1, 203 A.2d 796 (1964).
16 *McSwain v. McSwain* 420 Pa. 86, 215 A.2d 677 at 682 (1966).

of the most succinct definitions of interest analysis was given by a federal court sitting in New York, in a contracts case: "the forum is to apply the law of the jurisdiction with the most interest in the problem and the most concern in the outcome of the litigation."[17] Although none of these statements adequately explains the nature or technique of interest analysis, they do convey an impression of judicial neutrality: the emphasis on interest weighing rather than analysis suggests that the forum is willing to consider foreign and forum interests alike from a supranational point of view, just as under the traditional allocation method it was deemed to treat all legal systems on an equal footing. This implication, presupposing criteria by which competing interests can be weighed at all, brings to mind Ehrenzweig's criticism that a choice of law rule calling for an evaluation of interests is "as wrong or circular as any theory based on legislative jurisdiction, vested rights or the 'significance' of contacts." Wrong, because the evaluation is to be "deduced from a nonexisting superlaw," circular "in so far as it must, in recognition of the nonexistence of such a superlaw, be based on rules of choice, a need for which it is designed to avoid."[18] The judicial descriptions of interest analysis further intimate that all jurisdictions involved would invariably have competing interests in the application of their respective laws. This suggestion ignores the notion of false conflicts (comprising situations in which the relevant rules of law are identical, as well as those in which only one jurisdiction has an interest in the application of its law), and denies the possible existence of the so-called "unprovided-for case", the situation in which "neither state cares what happens."[19] Before we jump to conclusions, let us take a closer look at case law, to see how the courts have actually dealt with false conflicts, true conflicts and the unprovided-for case. Perhaps the opinion writers are more adept in applying the principles of interest analysis than in describing them.

---

17 *Flammia v. Mite Corporation* 401 F.Supp. 1121 at 1126 (E.D. N.Y. 1975).
18 Ehrenzweig (1967-1) p. 63/64. The circularity of the Restatement's most significant relationship criterion has been mentioned *supra* chapter 3, text accompanying notes 35–36.
19 Currie (1963-1) p. 152/153.

1 False conflicts and no-conflicts

Before we can set out to study judicial performance, however, an explanation of the technical term "false conflict" is in order, since it is used in more than one sense and therefore tends to breed confusion. Dubbed the "abiding cornerstone of governmental interest analysis,"[20] the false conflict concept is properly linked to Currie's writings. In his essay on married women's contracts, an illuminating analysis of the problem in *Milliken v. Pratt*, he distinguished between conflicts cases that are "no real conflicts problems" and "problems that cannot be solved by any science or method of conflict-of-laws."[21] To Currie, a false problem of conflict of laws is essentially the situation in which application of one state's law will advance the interest of that state without impairing any interests of other states the case is associated with. Or, as the Fifth Circuit put it in its rebellious decision in *Lester v. Aetna Life Insurance Company*: "A 'false conflict' occurs when one of two states related to a case has a legitimate interest in the application of its law and policy and the other has none."[22] In these cases only one of several potentially applicable and conflicting laws has a claim to application, "wants to be applied,"[23] in spite of substantial contacts

---

20 Baade (1967) p. 144. *Cf.* Westen (1967) p. 76.
21 Currie (1963-1) p. 77 ff., at p. 107. "Familiar to the point of triteness," (Currie, *ibid.* p. 77), the celebrated conflicts case *Milliken v. Pratt* 125 Mass. 374 (1878) concerned the question which law applied to the validity of a contract made by a married woman whose domiciliary law limited her capacity to bind herself by contract, whereas the *lex loci contractus* held no such limitation.
22 *Lester v. Aetna Life Ins. Co.* 433 F.2d 884 at 890 (5th Cir. [La.] 1970) *cert. denied* 402 U.S. 909 (1971). In *Lester*, it was held that the *Klaxon* doctrine, requiring federal courts to apply the conflicts law of the state in which they sit, was inapplicable in cases in which "no conflict is present." This novel idea was followed in *Challoner v. Day & Zimmermann, Inc.* 512 F.2d 77 (5th Cir. [Tex.] 1975), but this time the U.S. Supreme Court intervened: *Day & Zimmermann, Inc. v. Challoner* 423 U.S. 3 at 4, 96 S.Ct. 167, 46 L.Ed.2d 3 at 5 (1975): "We believe that the Court of Appeals either misinterpreted our longstanding decision in Klaxon Co. v. Stentor Electric Mfg. Co... , or else determined for itself that it was no longer of controlling force in a case such as this. We are of the opinion that Klaxon is by its terms applicable here and should have been adhered to by the Court of Appeals."
23 Baade (1967) p. 145, quoting De Nova (1963) p. 818, 820, who used the phrase in his discussion of Rolando Quadri's unilateralist theory. The anthropomorphic notion that a rule of law "wants to be applied" is also used in explanations of the European doctrine of "priority rules" or *règles d'application immédiate*, discussed *supra* chapter 1, section 5.

other states may have with the facts. A real problem, then, is the situation "in which advancement of the interest of one state results in the subordination or impairment of the interest of the other,"[24] for which problem no choice of law theory can furnish a solution that is equally acceptable to both interested states.[25]

While Currie's distinction of true and false conflicts might suggest that the latter pose "no real conflicts problems," they can be neither identified nor disposed of without conflicts law intervention.[26] The expressions "true" and "false conflicts" denote at the same time a specific approach to be employed in solving choice of law problems and the result of its application, but not, as might be inferred from these terms, a foregone conclusion about the existence or non-existence of actual conflicts.[27] For if it did, any problem capable of being solved by a rational conflicts approach would be a false conflict.[28] Yet, the term "false conflict" is also used to indicate situations in which –even though the case is connected to more than one state– no conflict of laws arises. In such cases the potentially applicable laws are identical or have materially the same contents in respect of the point at issue.[29]

---

24 Currie (1963-1) p. 107.
25 This is how Baade (1967) p. 145, sums up Currie's basic position on true conflicts. Various scholars have aspired to formulate a choice of law theory that *does* furnish an acceptable solution to true conflicts. See *infra* sections 4(b) and 4(c).
26 Westen (1967) p. 78 ff. has blamed Currie for suggesting that false conflicts can exist independently from interest analysis, when he described interest analysis as "a workable means to identify them." Currie (1963-2) p. 756. Westen rightly points out that the idea of false conflicts cannot be separated from the method by which they are identified: "To the extent that a finding of false conflicts is a product of governmental-interest analysis, it is both improper and misleading to divorce that finding from the process which creates it." *Cf.* Ehrenzweig (1967-1) p. 87.
27 *Cf.* Leflar (1977-1) p. 187: "The trouble with ... the term [false conflict] was, and is, that it is easily misunderstood to mean that there is 'no conflict of laws' problem in the case." See also: Jessurun d'Oliveira (1971) p. 376.
28 Westen (1967) p. 78. *Cf.* Leflar (1977-1) p. 187: "A Bealian conservative could say that, since the law of the place of injury governs, any case in which the place of injury was known is a 'false conflict' case."
29 In *Rohm & Haas Co. v. Adco Chemical Co.* 689 F.2d 424 at 429 (3d Cir. [N.J.] 1982), for instance, the Third Circuit found that "the same result" would follow from application of either New Jersey or Pennsylvania law. "When such a 'false conflict' exists," the court continued, "New Jersey conflicts of law rules permit the resolution of the case without a choice between the laws of the two states." See also: Cavers (1965) p. 89: "The conflict may be found false in other cases because both laws are the same or would yield the same result." *Cf.* Leflar (1977-1) p. 188; Cramton/

Whichever choice the court prefers, it will not affect the outcome of the case, since the eligible laws do not conflict. Formally there may be a conflict of laws, to be resolved by choice of law principles, but for all practical purposes the case can be disposed of without their help.[30] No other choice of law principle is needed than that of "non-choice", or, as it was called by Professor Jessurun d'Oliveira, an "anti-choice rule,"[31] *viz.* a rule that allows the court to refrain from stating the applicable law in situations in which any choice would produce the same outcome of the case. Since the forum state, if only on the strength of jurisdiction, has an inevitable connection to the case at bar, forum law will usually serve as the touchstone by which identity of rules or compatibility of results can be measured. If the court is satisfied that there are no material differences between the various laws, it will either leave the choice of law issue undecided or refer to its own law.[32]

It will be clear that, used this way, the term "false conflict" does not denote a specific choice of law technique, as it does in its first sense, but relates to the conclusion that no choice is called for. Whichever choice of law approach or method is favored, whether rigid allocation

Currie/Kay (1981) p. 251; Morse (1978) p. 237/238. See also: Westen (1967) p. 79, describing false conflicts as "those cases where the laws of interested states do not conflict, either because only one state is found to be interested, or because the laws of several interested states are found to be compatible." Westen's reference to Currie (1963-1) p. 189, as his source of inspiration for this description must be mistaken, since Currie carefully distinguished between "related" states and "interested" states, and had nothing to say about situations in which the various laws are "compatible."

30 *Baird v. Bell Helicopter Textron* 491 F.Supp. 1129 at 1137 (N.D. Tex. 1980): "Before engaging in the [most significant relationship] analysis, this Court must determine the exact nature of the conflict or indeed, if a conflict even exists ... If no conflict exists, then the question of whose law should apply becomes moot." See also: *Beech Aircraft Corp. v. Superior Court* 132 Cal.Rptr 541, 61 Cal.App.3d 501 at 518 (1976).

31 *Cf.* the title of his dissertation: *De antikiesregel*, Jessurun d'Oliveira (1971). In the English summary of his book, the term was translated as "non-selection rule," but I feel that the phrase "anti-choice rule" captures the substance of the Dutch original slightly better. *Cf.* Jessurun d'Oliveira's own ruminations in this respect, *ibid.* p. 23.

32 There is a technical problem, however, in *e.g.* the Netherlands, where art. 99 of the Judicial Organization Act does not allow the highest court to review decisions on the contents of foreign law. It does make a difference, therefore, whether the forum applies its own law – subject to review – or foreign law – not subject to review. For a comparative survey on this subject, see: H.U. Jessurun d'Oliveira (1979-1). See also *infra* note 35.

or better law approach, the "anti-choice rule" suits any of them since it obviates the need for choice and therefore does not affect the standard of choice employed. To Currie, who defined the central problem of conflicts law as "that of determining the appropriate rule of decision when the interests of two or more states are in conflict – in other words, of determining which interest shall yield,"[33] the "no-conflict" situation is not really worth discussing, since it is without the scope of his perception of the choice of law problem and therefore outside the reach of conflicts law. At best it is a false conflict in the first sense, in that application of identical or compatible rules of law does not impair the interests of any of the related states, or, conversely, advances all relevant interests at once.[34] Still, the use of the same term for two distinct phenomena is confusing. So I will reserve the expression "false conflict" for the ambit of interest analysis. In that context it is meant to denote the situation in which there is no conflict of interests, as the application of one state's law, though differing from that of another, will not impair the other state's interest. For the situation in which the laws of the states connected to the case are identical or produce the same material result, I prefer the term "no-conflict" as it conveys the notion of non-conflicting laws and thus the absence of the necessity to choose between them.[35]

Conflicts law is never easy. Certain cases may present a false conflict and a no-conflict situation at the same time, as is demonstrated by the New Jersey case *Pfau v. Trent Aluminum Company*. This was an action by a guest-passenger for injuries sustained in a car accident in Iowa. The driver, a New Jersey resident, and the victim, a resident of

---

33 Currie (1963-1) p. 178. *Ibid.* p. 163: "The basic problem in conflict of laws is to reconcile or resolve the conflicting interests of different states."
34 See, however, Morse (1978) p. 237; Jessurun d'Oliveira (1971) p. 381; Westen (1967) p. 105–110, as well as Currie's writings on "restrained interpretation": this is also the way a true conflict could be construed away.
35 In countries in which (mis)application of foreign law will not be subject to final judicial review (*supra* note 32, and chapter 1, section 3, note 114), it does make a difference whether forum law or foreign law is applied to a no-conflict situation, not materially but procedurally. In that respect, a no-conflict situation still requires a choice between non-conflicting laws. In these cases, forum law may be chosen as the *prima facie* applicable law. *Cf. Fleury v. Harper & Row, Publishers, Inc.* 698 F.2d 1022 at 1025 (9th Cir. [Cal.] 1983): " ... inasmuch as the laws of the state of New York are identical with those of California, there is no reason to reject the law of the forum." See also: *infra* note 41.

Connecticut, were students in Iowa, on their way to Missouri on a weekend trip, when the accident occurred. The car was registered and insured in New Jersey in the name of a New Jersey corporation, owned by the driver's father. The Iowa guest statute was pleaded as a defense. The New Jersey Supreme Court first determined the policies underlying the Iowa guest statute and decided that these "would not appear to be relevant to the present matter," in other words: "Iowa has no interest in this suit."[36] But since New Jersey and Connecticut could still have an interest in the application of their respective laws, the case could not yet be disposed of as a false conflict. The court, establishing that the laws of Connecticut and New Jersey both allowed guest-passengers to be compensated by the host-driver in cases of ordinary negligence, took a shortcut, however, and concluded that "since Iowa has no interest in this litigation, and since the substantive laws of Connecticut and New Jersey are the same, this case presents a false conflict."[37] Put in less ambiguous terms this means that, as between the laws of Connecticut and New Jersey, there was a no-conflict situation, whereas the case presented a false conflict as between the interests of Iowa and those of New Jersey/Connecticut.[38]

With reference to the most significant relationship approach, a similar solution is recommended in the Restatement Second, where it says: "When certain contacts involving a tort are located in two or more states with identical local law rules on the issue in question, the case will be treated for choice-of-law purposes as if these contacts were

---

36 *Pfau v. Trent Aluminum Company* 55 N.J. 511, 263 A.2d 129 at 135 (1970).
37 *Ibid.* p. 136.
38 *Gordon v. Gordon* 387 A.2d 339 (N.H. 1978) was viewed as a combination of a no-conflict situation and a *true* conflict. The action arose from a car accident in New Hampshire. The parties were husband and wife, residing in Massachusetts at the time of the accident, and in Maine at the time of suit. The issue of interspousal immunity presented "no conflict" as between the laws of Massachusetts and New Hampshire, both allowing interspousal suits, but a "true conflict" as between Maine, disallowing the suit, and the other two jurisdictions. New Hampshire law was applied not only because it was considered the better law, but also because "the forum's interest in providing redress for one injured in New Hampshire, as well as the interests of Massachusetts in seeing its law applied, require us to hold that any interest of Maine, as domiciliary jurisdiction at the time of suit, in preventing this suit, must yield." *Ibid.* at 341.

grouped in a single state."³⁹ This "anti-choice rule" is designed to facilitate the determination of the most significant relationship. In effect, it reduces the number of states involved by the fiction that states having identical laws merge into a single legal territory where a single "uniform law" is in force.⁴⁰ In cases in which only two states are involved, this solution is clearly sensible and, as no choice between two identical laws is needed, it serves the simplification of the judicial task.⁴¹ But when the case is related to more than two states, with one of their laws being different, choice cannot be evaded. Under the most significant relationship test, which, apart from the considerations of § 6, is essentially a grouping-of-contacts approach, the courts can apply the Restatement's no-conflict rule to add up certain clusters of contacts and set them off to other clusters. In the context of the Restatement's territorialist philosophy, there is nothing against such arithmetic, as long as the contacts are "evaluated according to their relative importance with respect to the particular issue."⁴² But a court given to a quantitative interpretation of the most significant relationship approach might be tempted to use the "anti-choice rule" as a license to ignore the relative weight of certain contacts altogether. For instance, if the *lex loci delicti* and one party's home state law are materially the same, in contrast to the law of the other party's domicile, the Restatement's no-conflict solution might entice the court to put more emphasis on the place of the wrong than this contact would merit if all three laws were different. A fortuitous, and therefore irrelevant *locus delicti* could thus tip the scales, simply because it is added to one cluster of relevant contacts, previously in balance with the other cluster, on the

---

39 Restatement Second § 145, comment i, elucidated by the following illustration: "By conduct in state X, A injures B in state Y. X and Y have the same local law rules with respect to liability in tort for causing personal injuries. The case will be treated for the purposes of this Section as if conduct and injury had taken place in one state."
40 *Cf.* Jessurun d'Oliveira (1971) p. 377/378.
41 Jessurun d'Oliveira (1971) p. 385 ff. Simplification of the judicial task is the third of Leflar's choice-influencing considerations, *infra*: chapter 5. See also: Restatement Second § 6(2)(g), "ease in the determination and application of the law to be applied." *Cf. In re Air Crash Disaster at Washington, D.C. on January 13, 1982* 559 F.Supp. 333 (D. D.C. 1983): "When the laws of the various jurisdictions are not in conflict, for reasons of judicial efficiency the law of the forum may be applied." In this case, the District of Columbia forum was a transferee forum in multidistrict litigation, but this was no compelling reason for the court to "refer to several perhaps differently articulated but essentially identical theories of law."
42 Restatement Second, § 145(2).

strength of the material identity of the laws they refer to. In this situation, it would appear, the Restatement's no-conflict rule conjoins two discordant concepts in that it uses the identity of substantive laws as a tool of geographical allocation. As is demonstrated by the *Pfau* decision, such discordance cannot arise under the interest analysis approach, as it focuses on the contents of substantive laws rather than on the predominance of factual contacts.

2 False conflicts

The easiest cases to dispose of with the help of interest analysis, it would seem, are those in which parties from the same state are involved in an accident in a second state and the issue does not regard conduct. Whichever the forum state, these cases are usually identified as false conflicts, in the sense that only the parties' home state would have an interest in the application of its law.[43] The state where the wrong occurred can hardly be supposed to have an interest in the resolution of other issues than those affecting its standards of conduct or the compensation of its (third-party) domiciliaries. If for some reason the action is brought in a third state, the case may present a migratory[44]

---

43 "A state interest is present where application of the state rule to a dispute implements the underlying policy the state has adopted to promote the *welfare of its residents*. A state interest is lacking and therefore a state's rule should not be applied by the forum where the purpose of the rule would not be implemented by its application. Viewed another way, it can be said that a state rule should not be applied if it application protects a person not in the *class of persons* the rule was designed to protect." *Offshore Rental Co. v. Continental Oil Co.* 138 Cal.Rptr. 838 at 840 (Cal. App. 1977), paraphrasing Ratner (1974) p. 819, 820, p. 824; emphasis added.

44 As in *Gordon v. Gordon, supra* note 38. See also: *Perloff v. Symmes Hospital* 487 F.Supp. 426 (D. Mass. 1980). This was a medical malpractice suit brought by the mother of a minor on account of alleged negligence in a hospital in Massachusetts, the domiciliary state of mother and daughter. Having moved to California, the mother brought suit in that state, but the case was transferred to Massachusetts. The issue turned on the applicability of Massachusetts' charitable immunity rule. The district court, applying California's interest analysis, viewed the case as a false conflict, since all contacts at the time when the wrong occurred were located in Massachusetts.

4 – 239

or intertemporal complication,[45] which need not concern us here, but generally the forum state will then be disinterested altogether. It should be noted that in many jurisdictions the displacement of the *lex loci delicti* rule was occasioned by litigation arising from the simple law-fact pattern meant here.[46] To be sure, the courts in these landmark decisions did not espouse the same conflicts alternative, as they relied on doctrines varying from a characterization approach to the better law theory. But at the root of their dissatisfaction with the traditional rule must have been an unwillingness to apply the law of a state which "under no stretch of the imagination can be viewed as a concerned jurisdiction."[47] More complex cases, presenting true conflicts, were subsequently tackled, but the earliest departures from the traditional rule were prompted by cases in which the only foreign element was the place of the wrong.

Less well-known than *Grant v. McAuliffe*, *Haumschild v. Continental Casualty Company* or *Kilberg v. Northeast Airlines*,[48] another case tentatively paving the way for policy-oriented choice of law is *Emery v. Emery*. This California case is thought to be an instance of non-tort

---

45 In *Summers v. Interstate Tractor & Equipment Co.* 466 F.2d 42 at 49 (9th Cir. [Or.] 1972), a wrongful death action arising from an accident in Washington, the parties were Oregon residents. Nevertheless, the Ninth Circuit affirmed the lower court's decision that Oregon had no interest in the application of its wrongful death limitation: "The amendment repealing that law had passed the legislature and had been signed by the governor prior to the accident. Thus, although the limitation was still technically in effect, the policies and interests supporting the limitation had been officially rejected and abandoned in favor of the amended legislation which permits full compensation to the accident victim." In his dissenting opinion, Circuit Judge Trask rightly objected to this distortion of interest analysis: "It does not seem logical to suppose that when Washington removed its limitation of liability rule, it was doing so to favor Oregon residents." *Ibid.* p. 50.

46 E.g.: *Thompson v. Thompson* 105 N.H. 86, 96 A.L.R.2d 969, 193 A.2d 439 (1963); *Wilcox v. Wilcox* 26 Wis.2d 617, 133 N.W.2d 408 (1965); *Armstrong v. Armstrong* 441 P.2d 699 (Alaska 1968); *Schwartz v. Schwartz* 103 Ariz. 562, 447 P.2d 254 (1968); *Mitchell v. Craft* 211 So.2d 509 (Miss. 1968); *Wessling v. Paris* 417 S.W.2d 259 (Ky. 1967); *Beaulieu v. Beaulieu* 265 A.2d 610 (Me. 1970); *Jagers v. Royal Indemnity Company* 276 So.2d 309 (La. 1973); *First National Bank in Fort Collins v. Rostek* 182 Colo. 437, 514 P.2d 314 (1973).

47 *Kuchinic v. McCrory* 422 Pa. 620, 222 A.2d 897 at 899 (1966).

48 *Grant v. McAuliffe* 41 Cal.2d 859, 264 P.2d 944 (1953), *Haumschild v. Continental Casualty Company* 7 Wis.2d 130, 95 N.W.2d 814 (1959) and *Kilberg v. Northeast Airlines* 9 N.Y.2d 34, 211 N.Y.S.2d 133, 172 N.E.2d 526 (1961) were dubbed "the harbingers of interest analysis" by Weintraub (1980) p. 296 ff.

characterization.[49] Yet, decided in 1955, it seems to augur a policy-oriented approach, however veiled by the traditional reasoning of Justice Traynor's opinion. The action arose from a car accident in Idaho and involved a California family. The issue centered on intra-family immunity: could the plaintiffs (the minor daughters and their mother) maintain a suit against their father/husband who owned the car and their minor brother/son who had driven it with the father's consent although being an unskilled driver and not having had any sleep for more than 24 hours? Idaho law was held to be determinative to the question whether a cause of action accrued from the alleged facts. Since the defendants' conduct did not fall within the scope of the Idaho guest statute, the facts justifying wilful misconduct on the part of both father and son, this question was answered in the affirmative. As to the family immunity issue, it was held that this question was "more properly determined by reference to the law of the state of the family domicile,"[50] which might suggest a non-tort characterization. But the reason why both the *lex loci delicti* and the *lex fori* (as such) were rejected is not predicated on considerations of traditional allocation but directly derived from the interests of the state of the family domicile: "That state has the primary responsibility for establishing and regulating the incidents of the family relationship and it is the only state in which the parties can, by participation in the legislative processes, effect a change in those incidents."[51] By its reference to "state responsibility," this statement captures, in my opinion, the essence of the oft-misunderstood notion of "governmental interest." Rather than as a political abstraction having no interests beyond the administration of government proper, the state is viewed here as the reflection of the community whose collective and individual interests it coordinates and secures under the auspices of either public *or* private law. The state *qua* government may control public revenues or maintain law and order, but as an "organization of social life which exer-

---

49 See particularly: *Haumschild v. Continental Casualty Co.* 7 Wis.2d 130, 95 N.W.2d 814 (1959); the opinion by Justice Currie (!) suggests that the decision in *Emery v. Emery* turned on a classificatory choice between "a question of tort" and "one of capacity to sue." *Accord*: Leflar (1977-1) p. 272, note 7 and accompanying text.
50 *Emery v. Emery* 45 Cal.2d 421, 289 P.2d 218 at 223 (1955).
51 *Ibid.* See also: *Armstrong v. Armstrong* 441 P.2d 699 at 701 and 704 (Alaska 1968), holding that "the law of the litigants' matrimonial domicile should be given *priority* over the law of the place of the wrong in determination of interspousal liabilities and immunities in tort actions." Emphasis added.

cises sovereign power in behalf of the people"[52] it is concerned with all the ramifications of its social structure, including the domestic and transfrontier legal relationships in which its citizens engage. In *Emery*, it is clear that of the two states involved the community to whom the Emery family belonged, California, was the only one concerned with the resolution of the immunity issue, since it is hard to imagine why Idaho would have any "responsibility for establishing and regulating the incidents of the family relationship" between California-domiciled family members. In this respect, *Emery v. Emery* is a classic example of a false conflict.

Many guest statute cases have been identified as false conflicts, the state of the parties' common domicile having the sole interest in the application of its law. In most cases this finding may have been influenced by the fact that the parties were domiciled in the forum state, while the guest statute was part of the foreign law. *Babcock v. Jackson* is the model example of such a situation, although Judge Fuld's opinion with its mixture of contacts-grouping and interest-weighing did not explicitly term it a "false conflict." Verging on straightforward interest analysis the Missouri Supreme Court in *Kennedy v. Dixon* abandoned the "inflexible *lex loci delicti* rule in favor of the rule set forth in § 145 of the Proposed Official Draft of Restatement (Second)" and proceeded to determine Indiana's interest in having its guest statute apply to a host-guest relationship between Missouri parties, Indiana being the place of the wrong. The court conceded that "[t]he question of negligence ... should be determined by the law of the state where the tort occurred, because that is the state with the dominant interest concerning that issue." Indiana would only have a "real interest ... in requiring that Missouri residents comply with its standards of care for operation of motor vehicles on its highways," whereas "Missouri has a decided interest in having Missouri citizens who ride as passengers protected from negligent injury by Missouri hosts."[53] So, except as to the negligence issue, the only relevant interest in this case was Missouri's.

---

52 *Delaney v. Moraitis* 136 F.2d 129 at 130 (4th Cir. [Md.] 1943).
53 *Kennedy v. Dixon* 439 S.W.2d 173 at 185 (Mo. 1969). See also: *Clark v. Clark* 107 N.H. 351, 222 A.2d 205 (1966); *Kuchinic v. McCrory* 422 Pa. 620, 222 A.2d 897 (1966).

In *Wilcox v. Wilcox*, the case that marked Wisconsin's final break from tradition already heralded by the *Haumschild* decision, the most significant relationship approach was understood to require pure interest analysis. By determination of the policy underlying the guest statute of Nebraska, the state where Mrs. Wilcox had been injured in a car accident caused by her husband, it was concluded that the statute would only be "relevant" to a Nebraska host and his insurance company, whereas it was Wisconsin's policy to "provide compensation to a person when he has been negligently injured."[54] Since the parties were Wisconsin residents and Nebraska's only connection with the case was the happenstance that the accident had occurred in that state, there was no conflict of competing interests and Wisconsin law was applied. The same reasoning is found in *Mellk v. Sarahson*, a New Jersey decision reversing the trial court's holding that the guest statute of Ohio, the place of the wrong, was determinative in an action between New Jersey residents. The Supreme Court, adopting interest analysis, saw no reason why "Ohio has any real interest in having its guest statute apply to the present case to defeat recovery," while New Jersey did have a strong policy of "allowing an injured guest to sue his host for negligence."[55]

All cases so far identified as false conflicts have in common that the only state having an interest in the application of its law was both the state where the parties resided and the forum state. It might be surmised that if the parties have their common domicile in another jurisdiction than that of the forum, the courts would be ready to attribute to the parties' home state an exclusive interest in the application of that state's law. Such a hypothesis would stand to reason, since in these instances the only tie linking the forum to the matter in dispute is

---

54 *Wilcox v. Wilcox* 26 Wis.2d 617, 133 N.W.2d 408 at 415 (1965). The decision implies that, contrary to Nebraska, Wisconsin had an actual interest in the application of its law since all parties were Wisconsin domiciliaries. See, however, *Conklin v. Horner* 38 Wis.2d 468, 157 N.W.2d 579 (1968), to be discussed *infra* note 65 and accompanying text, in which case the court made it clear that it would apply Wisconsin law even if the parties were domiciliaries of another state.

55 *Mellk v. Sarahson* 49 N.J. 226, 229 A.2d 625 at 627 (1967). See also: *Beaulieu v. Beaulieu* 265 A.2d 610 (Me. 1970); *Freund v. Spencer* 46 Misc.2d 472, 260 N.Y.S.2d 149 (N.Y. Sup. Ct. 1965); *Kopp v. Rechtzigel* 273 Minn. 441, 141 N.W.2d 526 (1966); *Wessling v. Paris* 417 S.W.2d 259 at 260 (Ky. 1967); *Mullane v. Stavola* 101 N.J. Super. 184, 243 A.2d 842 (1968); *Tooker v. Lopez* 24 N.Y.2d 569, 249 N.E.2d 394, 301 N.Y.S.2d 519 (1969).

generally the place of the wrong and in the cases just discussed it was held that the state where the wrong occurred cannot be deemed to have a concern beyond issues of conduct. Yet, many courts have rejected the parties' domiciliary law and applied their own law coinciding with the law of the place of the wrong. Generally this resulted in the repudiation of a foreign rule of decision that may have been thought to be the "lesser" law, such as the limitation of liability by a guest statute or interspousal immunity. Presenting the converse fact situation of *Babcock v. Jackson*, the much-discussed case of *Kell v. Henderson* is illustrative. This was an action for personal injuries sustained in an automobile accident in New York. The parties were Ontario residents on a trip that was to begin and end in Ontario. The New York Appellate Division refused to allow the defendants to amend their answer to plead the Ontario guest statute as a defense, distinguishing the *Babcock v. Jackson* rationale on the ground that that case "was not intended to and did not change the established law of the State of New York that a guest has a cause of action for personal injuries against a host in an accident occurring within this state, whether those involved are residents or domiciliaries of this state or not."[56] In *Fosillo v. Matthews*,[57] a similar case but this time involving Massachusetts residents who on their way to a wedding celebration in New York had an accident in that state, the Massachusetts guest statute was rejected by a mere reference to *Kell v. Henderson*. Then came *Arbuthnot v. Allbright*,[58] again decided by the Appellate Division and presenting the same fact situation as *Kell*. Now the result was different, as the court relied on the principles that Judge Fuld in the meantime had laid down in his concurring opinion in *Tooker v. Lopez*,[59] the first one being applicable to the facts of this case: when the host-driver and the guest-passenger are domiciled in the same state and the car is registered there, then the law of that state should control and determine the standard of care which the host owes to his guest.

---

56 *Kell v. Henderson* 26 A.D.2d 595, 270 N.Y.S.2d 552 at 553 (1966).
57 *Fosillo v. Matthews* 30 A.D.2d 1049, 295 N.Y.S.2d 327, 248 N.E.2d 455 (1968).
58 *Arbuthnot v. Allbright* 35 A.D.2d 315, 316 N.Y.S.2d 391 (1970).
59 *Tooker v. Lopez* 24 N.Y.2d 569, 249 N.E.2d 394 (1969) at p. 404, to be repeated in his majority opinion in *Neumeier v. Kuehner* 31 N.Y.2d 121, 286 N.E.2d 454, 335 N.Y.S.2d 64 (1972). The "Fuld principles" will be discussed in detail *infra* chapter 6.

In terms of interest analysis none of these cases offers much guidance. But yet another New York decision, on all fours with *Kell, Fosillo* and *Arbuthnot*, restored a semblance of reasoning. In *Bray v. Cox*, the Appellate Division was again faced with the question whether the Ontario guest statute should apply to an action between Ontario residents arising out of a car accident in New York. The court firmly established the choice of law approach it wanted to follow: "Choice-of-law cases are resolved by an interest approach." New York was said to have "identifiable interests in applying New York law to an accident occurring within New York even though none of the parties is a New York resident."[60] These interests included: (1) highway safety to be promoted by the civil remedy of damages for negligent infliction of personal damages, (2) the economic protection of New York "vendors" furnishing medical and hospital care to injured parties, and (3) a public fiscal interest in assuring that indigent non-resident accident victims do not become public charges.[61] After establishing that Ontario by adopting a guest statute had meant to protect Ontario insurance companies, to maintain relatively low insurance rates, and to prevent collusive suits, the court concluded that not only New York's interests were at stake, but those of Ontario as well, considering that "defendant is insured by an Ontario insurer." Upon weighing the conflicting interests, the court found that in this case New York had a superior interest and consequently applied New York law, though "mindful of the contrary conclusion reached in *Arbuthnot v. Allbright*."[62] It might be true, then, that *Kell v. Henderson*, in spite of the laconic opinions of both the lower court and the Appellate Division, was in reality identified as a true conflict, as Professor Trautman suggests.[63]

60 *Bray v. Cox* 39 A.D. 299, 333 N.Y.S.2d 783 at 785 (1972).
61 *Ibid.* p. 786. *Cf. Milkovich v. Saari* 295 Minn. 155, 203 N.W.2d 408 (1973), also involving Ontario residents and turning on Ontario's guest statute: "We might also note that persons injured in automobile accidents occurring within our borders can reasonably be expected to require treatment in our medical facilities, both public and private ... with a consequent governmental interest that injured persons not be denied recovery on the basis of doctrines foreign to Minnesota." *Ibid.* p. 417.
62 *Bray v. Cox* 39 A.D. 299, 333 N.Y.S.2d 783 at 785/786 (1972).
63 Trautman (1967) p. 467. A less positive view is taken by Morse (1978) p. 243: " ... the different results achieved by the court in *Bray v. Cox* and *Arbuthnot v. Allbright*, suggest that interest analysis can become 'unprincipled' at least in cases involving guest statutes and parties with a common home who suffer injury in the forum state."

A similar true conflict construction is found in *Conklin v. Horner*, a Wisconsin case in which the defendant relied on the principles adopted in *Wilcox v. Wilcox*,⁶⁴ urging the court to apply the guest statute of his and the plaintiff's home state: both parties were residents of Illinois and they were travelling through Wisconsin in defendant's car when it crashed into a tree causing injuries to the plaintiff. The Wisconsin Supreme Court, however, found that in this converse fact situation Wisconsin had an interest, since it had a policy of compensating those who are injured by ordinary negligence, "whether they be residents of this state or whether they come from another jurisdiction."⁶⁵ As the Illinois guest statute was intended to shield defendants, there was a "serious conflict" in this case, which was solved with the help of Leflar's choice-influencing considerations, primarily the consideration of the advancement of the forum's interest in deterrence of reckless highway behavior. The same happened in *Gagne v. Berry*, a New Hampshire decision on the applicability of the Massachusetts guest statute. The parties were Massachusetts residents who on their way to a funeral in Maine had a collision with a third party in New Hampshire. As to the liability of the Massachusetts host-driver to his Massachusetts guest-passengers New Hampshire law was deemed controlling, since "the State of New Hampshire has an obvious interest in providing redress for injuries which occur on our highways," and even more so if the collision was with a car registered in New Hampshire. Apart from the fact that guest statutes were thought to be the "lesser law" and that a Massachusetts court, still adhering to the *lex loci delicti* rule, would have applied New Hampshire law to the case at bar, the New Hampshire Supreme Court refused to apply Massachusetts law because doing so "would defeat the deterrent effect of our negligence laws by allowing negligent conduct to go undeterred."⁶⁶

---

64 *Wilcox v. Wilcox* 26 Wis.2d 617, 133 N.W.2d 408 (1965), discussed *supra* text preceding note 54.
65 *Conklin v. Horner* 38 Wis.2d 468, 157 N.W.2d 579 at 583 (1968).
66 *Gagne v. Berry* 290 A.2d 624 at 626 (N.H. 1972). See also: *Griggs v. Riley* 489 S.W.2d 469 (Mo. App. 1972), involving a host-guest relationship between Illinois residents who had been involved in an automobile accident in the forum state, Missouri. An important consideration in this "true conflict" between the compensatory law of Missouri and Illinois' guest statute was the fact that the driver of the other car, a Missouri resident, was a third-party defendant: " ... and Missouri has an interest in protecting the rights of Missouri residents under [its contribution] statute. Application of the Illinois guest statute would obviate that right in this case." *Ibid.* p. 473.

It appears that, with the exception of *Arbuthnot v. Allbright*, the common denominator of all cases so far discussed is the forum's preference for its own law and the rejection of the foreign rule of decision shielding the defendant. If the parties are domiciled in the forum state, the *lex fori* is applied by way of a false conflict construction, the foreign state supposedly lacking an interest in the protection of a non-resident defendant. On the other hand, if the parties are not domiciled in the forum state and jurisdiction is based on the place of wrong connection, the forum state is said to have an interest competing with that of the domiciliary state, so a true conflict comes to light. Not surprisingly, the plaintiff usually prevails when the action is brought in a liability-imposing jurisdiction: the true conflict is solved in favor of forum law by a decidedly slanted interest-weighing process. What happens, then, in the converse situation, when instead of foreign law the law of the forum absolves the defendant from liability, the forum being either the *locus delicti* or the parties' home state? There are not many cases in which this question is addressed, obviously because the plaintiff, given a choice between litigation in a liability-imposing or a defendant-favoring jurisdiction, will opt for the former. If the plaintiff is aware of the profits to be gained from forum-shopping, he should have a fair chance to prevail, at least if his options include a liability-imposing jurisdiction where some form of interest analysis is practiced. Yet, in a few cases the action was brought before a court in a liability-restricting jurisdiction.

Fuerste v. Bemis is an Iowa case presenting the familiar fact situation of a host-guest relationship and an out-of-state automobile accident. This time the parties were Iowa residents who on their way from one point in Iowa to another travelled by way of Wisconsin. There, a collision occurred which resulted in the death of the guest passenger. The trial court held that Iowa's guest statute applied in view of Iowa's most significant relationship. The plaintiff appealed, claiming Wisconsin law should be controlling both as *lex loci delicti* and as the better law. The Supreme Court dismissed the case as a "false or spurious conflict," since Wisconsin did not have an interest, the standard of conduct of the parties while in Wisconsin not being at issue. The better law solution was said to be reserved for true conflict cases.[67]

[67] *Fuerste v. Bemis* 156 N.W.2d 831 (Iowa 1968). Plaintiff would probably have fared better had he brought his action before a Wisconsin court. In *Conklin v. Horner*, *supra* note 65, decided the same year, the Wisconsin Supreme Court had applied Wisconsin law in a host-guest controversy involving Illinois domiciliaries.

Less principled was the choice of law reasoning in a series of cases turning on interspousal immunity, a few of which were decided by courts of immunity states. Originally based on the common law doctrine of the unity of husband and wife, which required the husband to be joined in any suit involving the wife, interspousal immunity is justified by the proposition that suits between husband and wife tend to disrupt domestic felicity.[68] As already suggested in pre-modern decisions such as *Emery v. Emery* and *Haumschild v. Continental Casualty Co.*,[69] this implies that the only state apt to have an interest in the preservation of marital harmony will be the state of the matrimonial domicile. If the parties are domiciled in a non-immunity jurisdiction and the state of injury prohibits interspousal suits, the conflict must be deemed false, as the immunity state is not likely to have an interest in promoting the marital harmony between non-resident spouses.[70] A true conflict could only emerge, then, if the state where the wrong occurred has a policy of non-immunity and for some reason asserts an interest in the application of its recovery rule. If the action is brought in a recovery state, chances are that the plaintiff will prevail, either because the spouses are domiciled in the forum state, or because the case is construed as a true conflict.[71] Conversely, there is no guarantee that the forum of an immunity state, confronted with a tort action

---

68 *Purcell v. Kapelski* 444 F.2d 380 at 382 (3d Cir. [N.J.] 1971). *Cf. Huff v. LaSieur* 571 S.W.2d 654 at 655 (Mo. App. 1978), describing the purpose of Texas' interspousal immunity rule as one of "protecting and maintaining inviolable the marital relationship." See generally: Jayme (1967) p. 315 ff.; Felix (1968) p. 410 ff.
A second rationale is found in the prevention of collusion between the spouses against their insurer. *Zelinger v. State Sand and Gravel Co.* 38 Wis.2d 98, 156 N.W.2d 466 (1968): "The interspousal and parental immunities rest on the proposition that family peace is promoted thereby and perhaps as a by-product collusive suits are held to a minimum."
69 *Emery v. Emery* 45 Cal.2d 421, 289 P.2d 218 (1955), discussed *supra* text accompanying notes 48–52. *Haumschild v. Continental Casualty Co.* 7 Wis.2d 130, 95 N.W.2d 814 (1959). *Cf.* Jayme (1967) p. 325 ff.
70 *Cf.* Felix (1968) p. 419 ff. See *e.g.*: *Thompson v. Thompson* 105 N.H. 86, 96 A.L.R.2d 969, 193 A.2d 439 at 440 (1963): " ... suits between New Hampshire spouses are hardly a concern of Massachusetts." *Accord*: *Armstrong v. Armstrong* 441 P.2d 699 (Alaska 1968); *Schwartz v. Schwartz* 103 Ariz. 562, 447 P.2d 254 (1968); *Robertson v. McKnight* 609 S.W.2d 534 (Tex. 1980).
71 See, however, *Haynie v. Hanson* 16 Wis.2d 299, 114 N.W.2d 443 (1962), in which the Wisconsin court, still following *Haumschild*, refused to apply the plaintiff-favoring Wisconsin rule in an action between Illinois spouses.

between foreign spouses, will invariably treat the case as a false conflict and apply the foreign recovery rule.[72]

Apparently a false conflict, *Peters v. Peters*, decided by the Hawaii Supreme Court, is a lesson in versatile policy identification. Mr. and Mrs. Peters were domiciled in New York, whereas the tort had occurred in the forum state. While on vacation in Hawaii, the spouses had rented a car from a Hawaiian rental agency. Due to negligence of the driver, Mr. Peters, the car collided with a truck owned by a Hawaii corporation and plaintiff sustained personal injuries. By suing her husband, Mrs. Peters admitted in "a moment of candor," she intended to receive insurance proceeds from the lessor's insurer. In this situation, the court observed, family solidarity as one of the objectives of the Hawaii interspousal immunity rule was not threatened by a lawsuit. Assessing the interests involved, the court explained the absence of interspousal immunity in New York in mildly sarcastic terms: "Legislative wisdom in New York ... has concluded that the allowance of interspousal tort actions furthers the interests of the State and the welfare of its domiciliaries." Rather inconsequentially the court continued: " ... Hawaii's interest in promoting marital harmony pales in the light of New York's predominant interest in their marriage and welfare."[73] Nevertheless, due to another twist in the court's reasoning, Mrs. Peters lost her case. Despite Hawaii's lack of interest in the preservation of marital harmony between New York spouses, its interspousal immunity rule was held to apply, since the only party standing to lose if plaintiff prevailed would be the insurance company from whom the owner of the rented car had bought compulsory insurance: "And the insurance policies covering [the lessor's cars] undoubtedly are written with the laws of Hawaii in mind. To have New York law

---

72 In *Lyons v. Lyons* 2 Ohi St. 243, 208 N.E.2d 533 (1965), for instance, the Ohio court applied its interspousal immunity rule to an action between former Ohio residents, who after the occurrence had moved to Arizona, a non-immunity state. The opposite result was reached in *Huff v. LaSieur* 571 S.W.2d 654 (Mo. App. 1978), arising from an accident in Texas, an immunity state, in which Texas spouses were involved. Having moved to Missouri, a recovery state, the wife brought an action against her husband. Missouri law was applied, as the law of the marital domicile at the time of suit, since the marital relationship "is of concern to Texas only so long as the marriage has some continuing nexus with that State. Once that nexus has terminated it can be of little other than academic concern to Texas what happens to the marriage." *Ibid.* p. 655.
73 *Peters v. Peters* 634 P.2d 586 at 593 (Hawaii 1981).

govern a tort action arising from the operation of such a vehicle would, of course, contravene the expectations of both insurer and lessor." The court added that Hawaii's "booming tourism" precluded the adoption of a domiciliary approach to interspousal immunity, as it would result in increasing insurance premiums.[74] In other words: by suggesting that its interspousal immunity rule indirectly furthered Hawaii's precious tourist industry, the court managed to turn an apparent false conflict into a real one, which was quickly resolved by application of forum law.

In *Pevoski v. Pevoski*, the decision by which Massachusetts, at least in respect of certain tort issues, joined the jurisdictions that already had abolished the *lex loci delicti* rule, the court denied that its ruling would have any impact on insurance policies. The defendant husband invoked the Massachusetts immunity rule in an action arising out of a three-car collision in New York in which his wife, the plaintiff, had suffered personal injuries. All parties, including the operators of the other cars, were domiciled in Massachusetts. The court seemed to adopt a policy-oriented approach to the immunity issue, distinguishing "particular issues in which the interests of the lex loci delicti are not so strong." Ignoring *Kell v. Henderson* or *Bray v. Cox* and citing *Babcock v. Jackson* instead, the court proceeded to evaluate New York's interests: "New York has an undoubted interest in enforcing its traffic laws and in making its highways safe for travel but it has no legitimate interest in regulating the interspousal relationships of Massachusetts domiciliaries who chance to be injured within its borders."[75] Consequently, Massachusetts law applied, but in determining the content of that law the court found it had abrogated the common law rule of interspousal immunity in a case decided after the accident took place and held that the principle laid down in that case should apply here as well. Unimpressed by the possibility that the insurance industry would have relied thus far on Massachusetts' immunity rule, the court made it clear that its "decision will not in any serious way impair existing

---

74 *Ibid.* p. 594. This questionable argument will be discussed in greater detail, *infra* chapter 8, section 1, text accompanying notes 58–62.
75 *Pevoski v. Pevoski* 371 Mass. 358, 358 N.E.2d 416 at 417 (1976).

interests nor will any expectation be disappointed or any reliance defeated."[76]

If *Pevoski* was a false conflict decided as a no-conflict case, *Johnson v. Johnson* was characterized by the Supreme Court of New Hampshire as a true conflict but decided as if it were false. The spouses were Massachusetts citizens who had been involved in an automobile accident in New Hampshire. New Hampshire was a recovery state, while at the time of suit Massachusetts still maintained its immunity rule. Since it was the purpose of New Hampshire tort law "to give financial protection to persons injured on New Hampshire highways,"[77] the case presented a "true conflict" between the two laws. Nevertheless, the court decided that Massachusetts had the "more significant relationship," discounting its own asserted interest in highway safety by adding that application of the immunity rule was not likely to make Massachusetts' drivers less careful on New Hampshire highways. On the other hand, the court showed great concern for the presumed interests of defendant's insurer. Convinced that the risk of collusion in interspousal actions had influenced many states to retain the common law immunity rule, it speculated that "application of New Hampshire law would expose [defendant's] insurer to a greater risk than it might reasonably have expected to run, given the Massachusetts local law and the trend toward the choice of the domicile's interspousal law in interstate cases."[78]

In my opinion, the cases discussed so far are illuminating examples of the pliability of the false conflict concept, and perhaps of interest analysis as a whole. While some unexpected results may be attributed to

---

[76] *Ibid.* p. 418, citing *Bouchard v. DeGagne* 329 N.E.2d 114 at 116 (Mass. 1975). In his concurring opinion in *Pevoski*, Justice Quirico emphasized "that the existence of interspousal immunity, and the extent or limits thereof, should in no way be dependent on, or limited by, the existence of insurance covering the actions of the defendant spouse." *Ibid.*

[77] *Johnson v. Johnson* 107 N.H. 30, 216 A.2d 781 at 783 (1966).

[78] *Ibid.* Other true conflict constructions, decided in *favor* of the forum's recovery rule, can be found in *Zelinger v. State Sand And Gravel Co.* 38 Wis.2d 98, 156 N.W.2d 466 (1968) and *Purcell v. Kapelski* 444 F.2d 380 (3d Cir. [N.J.] 1971). See also: *Arnett v. Thompson* 433 S.W.2d 109 Ky. 1968). In *Gordon v. Gordon* 387 A.2d 339 at 341 (N.H. 1978), the New Hampshire Supreme Court found New Hamsphire's recovery rule to be the "better law," and refused to apply the immunity rule of Maine, the state of the marital domicile at the time of suit.

the nature of interest analysis, which I perceive as a principled *ad hoc* approach, the versatility of the courts in detecting and distinguishing various policies behind a single rule tends to diminish the method's persuasiveness. There is no telling what the courts will do next when confronted with relatively simple law-fact patterns such as host-guest cases or interspousal suits. There is some evidence that the courts in recovery states are apt to apply their own law, even if the foreign immunity state would seem to be the only interested jurisdiction. This is usually achieved by an ingenious construction of some forum interest, such as an interest in highway safety, the protection of the local medical profession, or the possible claims of (third-party) forum residents.[79] In some cases, however, the issue is decided as a false conflict, even if it entails application of a foreign guest statute or interspousal immunity rule. Cases decided in an immunity state are much fewer in number, unmistakably due to well-calculated forum-shopping, which precludes a systematic evaluation of their underlying choice of law reasoning. Yet, even in this small category some decisions seem to be mostly inspired by preconceived material results, for which a compelling policy or interest can always be provided. On the whole, I fear, judicial practice does not confirm my optimistic hypothesis that law-fact patterns of the type described – in which the parties are domiciled in one state, the wrong occurred in another, and the issue does not turn on conduct – are easily identified and resolved as false conflicts.

3 The unprovided-for case

Much has been written about a type of case which could be classified as the opposite of a true conflict. It was hinted at by Currie when he described a hypothetical variant of *Grant v. McAuliffe*[80] (in which the

---

79 All three of these interests were listed in *Purcell v. Kapelski* 444 F.2d 380 (3d Cir. [N.J.] 1971), as arguments for application of New Jersey law in an action between (former) Pennsylvania spouses. After the occurrence the parties were divorced, and defendant moved to California. See also: *Bray v. Cox* 39 A.D. 299, 333 N.Y.S.2d 783 at 786 (1972), discussed *supra* notes 60–61 and accompanying text.
80 *Grant v. McAuliffe* 41 Cal.2d 859, 264 P.2d 944 (1953). The action arose from a two-car collision in Arizona, and focused on the question whether tort claims did (California) or did not (Arizona) survive the death of the tort-feasor. All parties were Californians. Currie (1963-1) p. 128 ff. used sixteen variants on *Grant* to demonstrate the principles of interest analysis.

plaintiff would be a resident of Arizona rather than California), and it is usually referred to as the "unprovided-for case," in the sense that "neither state cares what happens."[81] The unprovided-for case belongs to the realm of interest analysis, as it denotes the situation in which neither of the states involved has an interest in the application of its law, their respective laws promoting contradictory policies but not actually conflicting. Currie surmised that "[t]raditionalists may stand aghast at this anomaly, and take it as proof of the unsoundness of the [interest] analysis."[82] At least one author proved him correct. Commenting on an actual unprovided-for case, *Neumeier v. Kuehner*,[83] Professor Twerski proclaimed that "[i]n this instance interest analysis had gone bankrupt," that it had "met its Waterloo," that "[t]he emperor indeed stands naked for all to see."[84]

To the proponents of interest analysis, the unprovided-for case is an embarrassing phenomenon indeed. Reminiscent of the problem of "negative conflicts" in a system of unilateral conflicts rules, it leaves the courts empty-handed in their quest for a rule of decision.[85] The obvious stopgap would be application of forum law, especially under an approach giving that law *prima facie* priority.[86] Yet, such a solution

---

81 Currie (1963-1) p. 152. At p. 168, he noted: "It does pose a very real problem of disposition. Whether it is to be regarded as a true problem of conflict of laws or not seems to be a formal and unimportant question, so long as we recognize what the problem is and what it is not."
82 *Ibid.* p. 152.
83 *Neumeier v. Kuehner* 31 N.Y.2d 121, 286 N.E.2d 454, 335 N.Y.S.2d 64 (1972), to be discussed *infra* text accompanying notes 95–100, and *infra* chapter 6, text following note 17 and *passim*.
84 Twerski (1973-1) p. 104, 107, 108 respectively.
85 The German expression *Normenmangel* ("lack of rules") is inapposite in this respect, since identification of the potentially applicable rules is one of the first steps required by interest analysis. In the process of identifying possible interests, however, the court will find that none of the rules claims application. Hence, *Interessenmangel* ("lack of interest") would be the more appropriate term.
86 *Cf.* Currie (1963-1) p. 156: " ... on the basis that this is the rational and convenient way to try a lawsuit when no good purpose is to be served by putting the parties to the expense and the court to the trouble of ascertaining the foreign law. No useful purpose will be served by ascertaining and applying [foreign law in an unprovided-for case], since the result is a matter of entire indifference in terms of the policies of both states." *Ibid.* p. 168, p. 189, note 3.

is not particularly convincing, as its justification is not derived from the principles of interest analysis itself, but premised on an axiomatic preference for forum law which, according to Currie, had been the normal source of decision until the "categorical imperative" of the Bealian choice of law rule compelled the courts "to apply the law of a designated foreign state, and no other."[87] By contrast, Professor Weintraub's suggestion that "no interest" tort cases should generally be resolved in favor of the plaintiff, questionable though it may be, is more in tune with the philosophy of interest analysis, as his solution is predicated on the notion that, in torts, there is a "broad common policy" supporting recovery and loss distribution.[88] Within the methodological context of interest analysis, this approach would appear more "principled" than Currie's *lex fori* presumption. In practice, it must be conceded, the plaintiff in an unprovided-for case will probably prevail either way. The *lex fori* presumption will have a plaintiff-favoring effect whenever the action is brought in a plaintiff-favoring jurisdiction, as is illustrated by the decision of the Oregon Supreme Court in *Erwin v. Thomas*. Plaintiff's husband had been injured in an accident in his home state Washington, due to the negligence of an Oregon truck driver employed by an Oregon corporation. Plaintiff brought an action against the driver for damages for loss of consortium, an action not recognized by Washington law. In Oregon, the forum state, the common law had been changed by statute, to the effect that married women were allowed to recover for negligently inflicted loss of consortium. Embarking on a precarious[89] analysis of policies and interests, the court first established that in respect of consortium, Washington had a policy of exempting Washington defen-

---

87 Currie (1963-1) p. 46: "There was a time when a court's application of foreign law was a phenomenon so remarkable that its explanation constituted the central problem of conflict-of-laws theory." Thus, Currie justified the *prima facie* applicability of forum law by presenting it as a time-honored principle, which "has the virtue of adaptation to the habits and inclinations of judges and lawyers, and is far less likely to lead to surprise, hardship and injustice than the contrary rule." *Ibid.* p. 47, p. 75.
88 Weintraub (1980) p. 345 ff., p. 270 ff. The "common policy" approach is also advocated by Professor Sedler. See *infra* text accompanying notes 120–130.
89 *Erwin v. Thomas* 264 Or. 454, 506 P.2d 494 at 495 (1973): "It is with some trepidation that a court enters into the maze of choice of law in torts cases. No two authorities agree."

dants from liability, whereas Oregon had elected to protect the wife's right to recovery. However, since defendant was an Oregon resident, the state of Washington had no interest in the application of its law. On the other hand, "it is stretching the imagination more than a trifle to conceive that the Oregon Legislature was concerned about the rights of all the nonresident married women in the nation whose husbands would be injured outside of the state of Oregon."[90] As neither state had an interest in the outcome of this litigation, the Oregon court did "what comes naturally" and applied Oregon law. Grumbling at this implicit invitation to forum shopping, the dissent considered the effect of this ruling: "Obviously the plaintiff could not bring this action in her state, Washington, but the majority opinion holds that by merely stepping over the state boundary into Oregon she is then bestowed with the right given wives who are residents of the state of Oregon, which includes the right of action for loss of consortium of her husband."[91] It is an uncomfortable thought, somehow, that in cases like this, the result depends more on the fortuity of the facts (triggering judicial jurisdiction) than on a well-reasoned choice of law evaluation.

On the other hand, the unprovided-for case is sometimes resolved by the *displacement* of forum law, to the (incidental?) advantage of forum residents. Such was the case in *Frummer v. Hilton Hotels International, Inc.*, involving a New York plaintiff, and in *Neumeier v. Kuehner*, involving a New York defendant.[92] Mr. Frummer had the misfortune of injuring himself severely when he took a shower in defendant's London hotel and slipped in the bath. Under New York's contributory negligence rule, plaintiff could not recover, whereas the English comparative negligence statute would allow compensation. Exploring the policies underlying the two rules, the court found that contributory negligence was "principally meant to be a device to limit the liability exposure of a defendant,"[93] which implied that New York had no interest in the application of its own rule as defendant was not a

---

90 *Ibid.* p. 496.
91 *Ibid.* p. 498.
92 *Frummer v. Hilton Hotels International, Inc.* 304 N.Y.S.2d 335 (1969). The real defendant in this case was the British Hilton corporation, subject to New York jurisdiction because the New York subsidiary of the Hilton conglomerate had been "doing business" in New York in behalf of the British subsidiary. *Cf.* Cramton/Currie/Kay (1981) p. 633. *Neumeier v. Kuehner* 31 N.Y.2d 121, 286 N.E.2d 454, 335 N.Y.S.2d 64 (1972).
93 *Frummer v. Hilton Hotels International, Inc.* 304 N.Y.S.2d 335 at 342 (1969).

New York resident. In view of the compensatory policy underlying the English statute, on the other hand, it could be said that England had little interest in the compensation of a New York resident, and "might prefer New York law, which would benefit its domiciliary in this case." Wondering if "this is a situation where no state has a compelling interest in having its law applied in order to vindicate some relevant policy," the court adopted the better law principle as "the honest and simple solution" and concluded that English law should apply, not only as the better law but also – rather surprisingly – because "application of New York law here would not serve any legitimate interest of New York, but would defeat a legitimate interest of England."[94]

New York law was also displaced, this time for the benefit of a New York *defendant*, in *Neumeier v. Kuehner*, a landmark decision in which the New York Court of Appeals reverted to choice of law rules in an ill-fated attempt to stem the tide of post-*Babcock* uncertainty.[95] It was again a car accident in Ontario which caused this transition in New York choice of law thinking. Unlike *Babcock*, however, the *Neumeier* litigation involved domiciliaries of different states. The (wrongful death) action was brought by the widow of an Ontario citizen. Her husband was a guest in the car of a New York resident, when it was struck by a train at a railroad crossing in Ontario. Both the New York host and the Ontario guest were instantly killed. The law-fact pattern of this case is comparable to that of *Erwin v. Thomas*, in that the law of defendant's home state, the forum, did allow recovery, whereas the law of the state where the plaintiff was domiciled, and where the accident occurred, did not. There the similarities end, however. Distinguishing *Tooker v. Lopez*,[96] in which case both host and guest were residents of the same jurisdiction, Chief Judge Fuld asserted that New York had no interest "in protecting the plaintiff guest domiciled [in a foreign jurisdiction] and injured there from legislation obviously addressed, at the very least, to a resident riding in a vehicle traveling

---

94 *Ibid.* p. 344. To the extent that the Court of Appeals considered foreign law preferable to its own, the *Frummer* decision is an exceptional example of the better law approach.
95 *Neumeier v. Kuehner* 31 N.Y.2d 121, 286 N.E.2d 454, 335 N.Y.S.2d 64 (1972). See *infra* chapter 6 for a description of the "Fuld principles", developed in *Tooker v. Lopez* 24 N.Y.2d 569, 301 N.Y.S.2d 519, 249 N.E.2d 394 (1969) and *Neumeier v. Kuehner*.
96 *Tooker v. Lopez* 24 N.Y.2d 569, 301 N.Y.S.2d 519, 249 N.E.2d 394 (1969).

within its borders."⁹⁷ At this point one would expect the conclusion that Ontario did not have an interest in the application of its law either. In *Babcock v. Jackson*, the court had assumed the sole purpose of the Ontario statute was to protect "Ontario defendants and their insurance carriers," so "[w]hether New York defendants are imposed upon or their insurers defrauded," could hardly be considered a valid legislative concern of Ontario.⁹⁸ Such reasoning would, indeed, have produced an unprovided-for case, but Chief Judge Fuld managed to steer clear of that dilemma by ascribing a different purpose to the Ontario guest statute, resurrecting the *lex loci delicti* rule at the same time. As the guest statute is now deemed to protect "owners and drivers against ungrateful guests," the opinion suggests that Ontario did have an interest in its application in disputes involving Ontario-domiciled passengers, an implication which would turn this case into a false conflict. In the final analysis, however, the choice of law decision in *Neumeier v. Kuehner* rests on the *prima facie* applicability of the place of wrong rule as prescribed by the third of the "Fuld principles".⁹⁹ In this respect, the decision does not shed much light on the solution of unprovided-for cases, but it does illustrate the hazards of policy assessment and the dubious demarcation of conflict types that interest analysis entails.¹⁰⁰

97 *Neumeier v. Kuehner* 31 N.Y.2d 121, 335 N.Y.S.2d 64, 286 N.E.2d 454 at 456 (1972).
98 *Babcock v. Jackson* 12 N.Y.2d 473 at 483, 240 N.Y.S.2d 743 at 750, 191 N.E.2d 279 at 284 (1963). On similar grounds *Tooker v. Lopez* 24 N.Y.2d 569, 301 N.Y.S.2d 519, 249 N.E.2d 394 (1969) had been decided as a false conflict, Michigan having no interest in protecting a New York defendant. *Cf.* Twerski (1973-1) p. 116: "Following *Tooker* reasoning and pure interest analysis, *Neumeier* must be recognized as an unprovided for case. If Michigan has no interest in applying its host-guest rule when the defendant is a New Yorker, why, pray, should Ontario have an interest in applying its host-guest rule when the defendant is a New Yorker?"
99 *Cf.* Sedler (1973-2) p. 128: "*Neumeier* was governed by the third principle. The law of Ontario, where the accident occurred, was presumptively applicable." See also: Jayme (1974) p. 585, p. 587.
100 See also: *Melville v. American Home Assur. Co.* 443 F.Supp. 1064 (E.D. Pa. 1977) *rev'd* 584 F.2d 1306 (3d Cir. 1978). This was an action sounding in contract, which was treated as an unprovided-for case by the district court, as a false conflict by the Third Circuit. The district court found guidance in the *Neumeier* decision: Chief Judge Fuld's territorial approach was understood as an explicit solution to the unprovided-for case dilemma, preferable to Currie's residual *lex fori* rule which tends to encourage forum-shopping. However, if the *Neumeier* court did not abandon interest analysis altogether – *cf.* Twerski (1973-1) p. 115; Sedler (1973-2) p. 132; Baade (1973) p. 163 – it probably regarded the law-fact pattern as a false conflict, not as an unprovided-for case: Twerski, *ibid.* p. 112; Shapira (1973) p. 175.

Another unprovided-for case that was solved by application of foreign law, this time to the *disadvantage* of a forum domiciliary, is *Bing v. Halstead*. Plaintiff brought an action for infliction of mental distress against her aunt, a resident of Arizona, who had written her a letter on an inheritance matter. This distressing letter had been sent from Arizona to New York and was forwarded from there to Costa Rica, where plaintiff had gone to live after breaking off all contacts with her family. Under Costa Rica law, plaintiff would not have a cause of action unless the aunt would have violated a criminal statute, which apparently was not the case. The choice of law reasoning in this case is convoluted, to say the least. First, it is announced that *lex loci delicti* prevails when interest analysis "does not point clearly to the law of any jurisdiction," a statement said to derive from *Neumeier v. Kuehner* and *Cousins v. Instrument Flyers*.[101] Since neither Arizona (the place of conduct), nor Costa Rica (place of injury and residence of the plaintiff), nor New York (domicile of the plaintiff)[102] was thought to have a compelling interest in the application of its law, it would follow that Costa Rica law was applied as the law of the place of injury, in accordance with the traditional construction of the place of the wrong rule. That conclusion was reached, however, after yet another attempt at interest analysis: "Where the issue is the standard of conduct, as it is here, rather than the extent of liability, it is appropriate to look to the place of the tort so as to give effect to that jurisdiction's interest in regulating conduct within its borders and it would be unthinkable to seek the applicable rule in the law of some other place."[103] One would think that in this case the jurisdiction most interested in regulating *conduct* would be Arizona, but the court did not see it that way. Citing a libel case in which the place of injury was one of the relevant contacts under a most significant relationship test,[104] it concluded: "Where tortious conduct occurs in one jurisdiction and injury in another, as is the

---

101 *Bing v. Halstead* 495 F.Supp. 517 at 520 (S.D. N.Y. 1980). *Cousins v. Instrument Flyers* 44 N.Y.2d 698, 405 N.Y.S.2d 441, 376 N.E.2d 914 (1978) will be discussed *infra* chapter 6, text following note 52.
102 Whether plaintiff kept her domicile in New York was a matter of debate. The court probably assumed she did, although it was acknowledged that she was a long-term resident elsewhere.
103 *Bing v. Halstead* 495 F.Supp. 517 at 520 (S.D. N.Y. 1980).
104 *Church of Scientology of California v. Green* 354 F.Supp. 800 (S.D. N.Y. 1973).

case here, the law of the place of injury applies." As a solution to the unprovided-for case, this decision is hardly commendable.[105]

A more consistent approach is found in *Hurtado v. Superior Court of Sacramento County*, although it could be doubted if this case really qualifies as an unprovided-for case. This was an action for wrongful death resulting from a car accident in California. Mr. Hurtado was a Californian, who had his cousin, visiting from Mexico, as a guest in his car when it collided with a truck. The guest died as a result of the collision. His widow, also a Mexican domiciliary, claimed damages for wrongful death. In separate proceedings, the trial court ruled that it intended to apply California law, rather than Mexican law which prescribed a limitation of damages for wrongful death. Hurtado then sought a writ of mandate directing the trial court to vacate its ruling, but the Supreme Court upheld the decision that California law applied. It was said that Mexico would not have an interest in having the limitation applied, since the purpose of such a rule is to protect defendants from excessive financial burdens or exaggerated claims, but in this case Mexico had no defendant residents to protect. Hurtado contended that California did not have an interest either, since a state's interest in a wrongful death action is "in determining the distribution of proceeds to the beneficiaries, and that interest extends only to local decedents and beneficiaries."[106] The court agreed that, as far as the Mexican plaintiffs were concerned, California had no interest in their having a statutory cause of action for wrongful death, but in respect of defendants "one of the primary purposes of a state in creating a cause of action in the heirs for the wrongful death of the decedent is to deter

---

105 *Cf.* Hay (1981) p. 1663, note 103: "The result is questionable. On interest analysis alone, it is not clear that the alleged intentional tort occurred in Costa Rica where the letter was read. It might instead be concluded that the alleged tort occurred in Arizona where the conduct occurred, thereby giving Arizona an 'interest' in the regulation of the conduct." Furthermore, Professor Hay contends that the first of the "Neumeier principles" would have supported application of either Arizona or New York law, not because the parties had a common domicile, but because "both of their domiciles recognized the alleged tort." *Ibid.* In other words: rather than as an unprovided-for case, *Bing* could be construed as a false conflict between Arizona/New York and Costa Rica.
106 This was a quotation from *Reich v. Purcell* 67 Cal.2d 551 at 556, 63 Cal.Rptr. 31 at 35, 432 P.2d 727 at 731 (1967), the landmark decision in which the California Supreme Court had adopted interest analysis. However, Hurtado's reading of *Reich* was said to be "inaccurate."

the kind of conduct within its borders which wrongfully takes life."[107] So, the case turned out to be a false conflict, and California law was applied.

As another example of ingenious policy assessment, the *Hurtado* decision appears to underscore the supposition, voiced by Professor Strikwerda, that unprovided-for cases do not exist. In his opinion, it is inconceivable that "an act or situation, which is generally considered as juridically relevant, fails to have an impact on any national community whatsoever." The effect of an occurrence upon a community implies that its interests are involved, which would normally rouse its normative sensibilities. From this premise Strikwerda infers the non-existence of a choice of law "vacuum": its presence must be attributed to a distorted interpretation of the policies underlying the relevant laws and their claims to application.[108] Attractive as this line of thought may be, in denying the existence of unprovided-for cases it adds to the problem of accurate policy assessment. This is demonstrated by another California case, *Hernandez v. Burger*, which again involved a California tortfeasor and a Mexican victim. This time, the car accident occurred in the Mexican territory of Baja California and resulted in personal injuries rather than death, but again the relevant Mexican rule of law limited the amount of recoverable damages while California law did not. The Court of Appeal distinguished *Hurtado* on the grounds that California had "no legitimate interest in the possible deterrent effect of its unlimited recovery rule on conduct in Mexico."[109] Since it had been decided in *Hurtado* that Mexico had "no

107 *Hurtado v. Superior Court of Sacramento County* 114 Cal. Rptr. 106, 522 P.2d 666 at 672 (1974). Weintraub (1980) p. 319, who doubts the validity of the deterrence rationale, "would prefer a more compelling argument to support the *Hurtado* result."
108 Strikwerda (1978) p. 156/157; *id.* (1986) p. 25, note 64.
109 *Hernandez v. Burger* 102 Cal.App.3d 795, 162 Cal.Rptr. 564 at 567 (Cal. App. 1980), citing *Reich v. Purcell* 67 Cal.2d 551, 63 Cal.Rptr. 31, 432 P.2d 727 (1967), which turned on the choice between Missouri's wrongful death limitation and Ohio's unlimited recovery rule, California being the disinterested forum: "In *Reich* the law of three states was potentially involved. The accident occurred in Missouri; the decedent and the plaintiffs resided in Ohio; and the defendant was a resident of California. Notwithstanding the fact that California was the forum and that the plaintiffs had become California residents after the accident, the court held that no legitimate interest of the State of California would be served by applying California's own domestic rule of damages." *Cf. infra* section 4(b), text accompanying notes 217–218.

interest in applying its limitation of damages" in a case in which "Mexico has no defendant residents to protect,"[110] it would follow that the *Hernandez* law-fact pattern presented an unmistakable unprovided-for case for once. Yet, *horror vacui* might have stirred the court's imagination when it conjured up a Mexican interest that turned the case into a false conflict: "Fostering tourism in Baja California is, of course, a legitimate interest of Mexico and the application of Mexico's limited damages law to nonresident motorists might well advance that interest."[111] In my opinion, the question whether an unprovided-for case does or does not exist is academic as long as the identification of policies and interests is such a capricious process that either argument can be upheld.

Professor Twerski has blamed interest analysis for placing too much emphasis on the interests of the domiciliary state in granting or denying recovery, and paying too little attention to the territorial dimensions of multistate fact patterns. The result might be an unprovided-for case: "Having defined the interests as domiciliary oriented, when you run out of domiciliaries to protect you run out of interests."[112] As an alternative, Twerski proffers the theory of "enlightened territorialism", an approach between the center of gravity test and interest analysis, apparently. Sharing the territorial bias of Cavers' principles of preference[113] and the Restatement Second, the territorialism Twerski advocates is "an attempt to view a juridical event in its total factual context to locate the vortex of that event."[114] It spurns the focus on isolated events pervading the First Restatement, as well as the return of territorial dogma in the Fuld principles. Instead, it calls for an

110 *Hurtado v. Superior Court of Sacramento County* 114 Cal.Rptr. 106, 522 P.2d 666 at 670 (1974).
111 *Hernandez v. Burger* 102 Cal.App.3d 795, 162 Cal.Rptr. 564 at 568 (Cal. App. 1980). A similar concern for local tourism, this time its own, was voiced by the Supreme Court of Hawaii in *Peters v. Peters* 634 P.2d 586 (Hawaii 1981), discussed *supra* text following note 72. In *Conklin v. Horner* 38 Wis.2d 468, 157 N.W.2d 579 at 586 (1968), discussed *supra* text accompanying note 65, the fact that Wisconsin was a "tourist state" was mentioned as an argument against application of the Illinois guest statute, as it would "substantially dilute the deterrent (as well as compensatory) effect of our negligence rule."
112 Twerski (1973-1) p. 108. *Ibid.* p. 107, p. 110.
113 Most emphatically in *Enlightened Territorialism and Professor Cavers – The Pennsylvania Method*: Twerski (1971).
114 Twerski (1973-2) p. 120 and 123. It should be noted that Twerski's territorial "view" is a normative concept, not an interpretation of judicial practice.

"overall" territorial view of the case, unless "the given policy at issue is so clear and unmistakable that the court feels comfortable with negating territorial considerations in favor of interests."[115] In Twerski's opinion, *Neumeier v. Kuehner* is an unprovided-for case that pure interest analysis is unable to solve adequately, as it ignores inescapable territorial considerations.[116] Attempting to reconcile the pull of a substantial territorial nexus with the dictates of interest analysis, "the courts began inventing interests to support the results they felt would be just." Thus, territorial considerations are wrapped in what Twerski calls *"ad hoc* interest analysis."[117] It must be conceded that the grounds of decision in *Neumeier v. Kuehner, Hurtado v. Superior Court of Sacramento County*, and *Hernandez v. Burger* tend to support this thesis. However, "enlightened territorialism" does not solve the problem of the unprovided-for case. In effect, this theory reduces interest analysis to a residual technique, to be used when the "center of a juridical event" cannot be established by territorial considerations alone. Since the unprovided-for situation can only be exposed by interest analysis –to be applied, according to Twerski, when territorial considerations are inconclusive–, it should be solved by non-territorial principles. As we have seen, one approach relies on the *prima facie* applicability of forum law,[118] another on a re-interpretation of policies,[119] both circumventing the perplexing conundrum of the unprovided-for case.

115 *Ibid.* p. 123. As far as interests are concerned, "a general territorial orientation ... would permit the courts to evaluate all the factual contacts and also assess the interests. Where the two reinforce each other it makes the outcome of the case all the easier to predict." *Ibid.* p. 123, note 46.
116 *Ibid.* p. 122, whereas "[t]he courts never have been willing to divest themselves of the anti-territorial thinking that was required by interest analysis." *Ibid.* p. 123: "By and large courts have felt uncomfortable with negating important territorial considerations."
117 *Ibid.* p. 122.
118 As in *Erwin v. Thomas* 264 Or. 454, 506 P.2d 494 (1973), discussed *supra* text accompanying notes 89–91. Of the four alternative solutions Currie suggested, this is the one he preferred. Currie (1963-1) p. 156. His other solutions either give priority to forum law on the assumption it is "the more enlightened and humane law," or withhold application of the forum's compensatory law if the plaintiff is a non-resident, or withhold its application only if the law of plaintiff's home state would deny compensation: *ibid.* p. 153 ff. The first of the latter solutions is rejected for being arbitrary, the other two for being discriminatory and, therefore, unconstitutional.
119 Implicit in Strikwerda's supposition that unprovided-for cases cannot exist: *supra* text accompanying note 108.

A less evasive approach was advocated by Professor Sedler who in a comment on *Neumeier v. Kuehner* endeavored to solve the unprovided-for case in terms of interest analysis.[120] The cornerstone of his solution is the premise that "all states have a common policy of allowing compensation to accident victims."[121] Imposition of liability, Sedler suggests, would further the compensatory policy underlying tort law. In the substantive law of some states, however, this policy may have been sacrificed in order to promote policies relating to other areas of law – Sedler calls them "anti-tort policies" – such as the protection of charitable immunities, insurance companies, family relationships, etcetera.[122] If in a given case it turns out that the involved state has no interest in the promotion of its non-tort policy, there is no need to sacrifice the common policy of compensation; consequently, a defense based on an anti-compensatory rule of law should be disallowed when application of that rule is irrelevant to the promotion of its underlying policy. In Sedler's opinion, *Neumeier* is an easy case if it is approached from this perspective. Application of the Ontario guest statute would further no interest of Ontario, whereas it would defeat the common policy of New York and Ontario allowing accident victims to recover from negligent drivers. The only state interested in shielding the host-driver and his insurer from liability would be the state where the defendant has his home, where the automobile is insured, and where the consequences of imposing liability will be felt. "If that state does not have a guest statute, this means that the only state interested in protecting the defendant and his insurer does not do so," which implies that the defense of guest statute immunity – an exception to the common policy of compensation – should be dis-

---

120 Sedler (1973-2) p. 137 ff. Since Sedler's choice of law philosophy is premised on both "the common law tradition of judicial method" and interest analysis, he deplores the development of narrow choice of law rules as those adopted in *Neumeier v. Kuehner*.
121 *Ibid.* p. 138. See also: Baade (1973) p. 166 ff., who does not attempt to specify the nature of a common policy in tort law. Weintraub (1980) p. 270 ff., who sees a "pervasive trend in tort law" toward loss distribution through liability insurance, suggests application of the law favorable to the plaintiff as a solution to true conflicts and unprovided-for cases in the area of torts. *Ibid.* p. 345 ff. *Cf. infra* note 129.
122 Sedler (1970) p. 52 ff.: " ... the policy behind the granting of immunity was not a tort policy, but a policy directly antithetical to the tort policies of compensation and deterrence. In this category I would put the cases involving the defenses of family immunity, charitable immunity and guest statutes, in other words, practically all of the leading 'false conflicts' cases."

allowed.[123] Going one step further, Sedler would even "generally hold the defendant liable if he is liable under the law of his home state, since such liability is consistent with the common policy of both states in providing compensation for accident victims."[124]

Sedler's "common policy" approach to unprovided-for tort cases, relies heavily on the premise that "[t]he trend of tort law is clearly in the direction of favoring compensation."[125] Much as I agree to this proposition, I am not persuaded by Sedler's solution. First of all, it does not make any difference for the decision of an unprovided-for case whether the common core of the law of torts is compensation, deterrence, or any other policy that holds the tortfeasor liable. If the exception to the general tort policy is not available as a defense –such as guest statutes, limitation of damages, charitable immunity and other "anti-tort" rules– plaintiff prevails, both in a domestic case and in multistate litigation, no matter the rationale of delictual liability. In other words, compensation is just one of several policies that could benefit the plaintiff; indemnification might well be a by-product of a policy of deterrence.[126] Second, and more important, the "common policy" theory ignores the fact that the jurisdictions involved espouse

---

123 Sedler (1973-2) p. 137/138. An experiment in "virgin adjudication", described by Professor Josephine King, proved that the majority of choice of law "nullifidians", a fresh class of second and third year law students at Hofstra University, did *not* see it that way: King (1973) p. 178 ff.
124 Sedler (1973-2) p. 139. *Cf.* the decision of the Rhode Island Supreme Court in *Labree v. Major* 306 A.2d 808 at 818 (1973), to be further discussed *infra* text accompanying notes 138–140. See also: Lopez (1980) p. 38 ff., proposing "The Law of the Domicile with Greater Compensation Rule." This rule calls for application of the plaintiff-favoring law unless the wrong occurred in defendant's home state and the law of that state allows less compensation.
125 Sedler (1973-2) p. 142, note 105, with reference to Weintraub (1971) p. 204 = Weintraub (1980) p. 270/271: "In [the] field of negligence or accident law, the trend has been markedly toward distribution rather than concentration of losses, through the device of liability insurance. The area of absolute liability is expanding in tort law. Even in tort areas still nominally based on the negligence-fault concept, cases that get to the jury usually result in plaintiffs' verdicts and the substantive rules have shown a continual development in favor of recovery."
126 *Cf.* Cavers (1965) p. 144: " ... the financial protection a state has prescribed, being part of its provision for the general security, is in part a sanction for wrongfully causing harm. As a consequence its purposes include elements of deterrence and retribution even though it may be couched in essentially compensatory terms."

divergent solutions for the very controversy the court has to decide.[127] In a domestic case, a guest statute defense is not likely to be rejected for the sole reason that there could not be collusion between host and guest, as the host was not insured. Even though the guest statute's policy is not furthered by its application, chances are that defendant will be exempted from liability, in the face of plaintiff's reliance on a basic policy of recovery.[128] Furthermore, even if there is agreement on a basic common policy of the law of torts, there are infinite divergences in respect of the *extent* of tort liability. This might be less of a problem in common law systems, in whose tradition remedies precede rights, yet it is difficult to understand why *e.g.* the *Neumeier* case, after rejection of the guest statute defense, should be treated as a domestic New York case rather than a domestic Ontario case. Finally, if there really is a *common* policy of recovery, it is difficult to perceive why it should not be heeded in true conflict situations as well as in the unprovided-for case,[129] or – if I may stretch the point – even in false conflicts. Basically, this theory supports a *favor* approach, for the benefit of the plaintiff, which could be used in any conflict that defies rational decision. In that respect, it is hardly less arbitrary than the "better law" approach.[130]

Obviously, the perception that, generally, the law of torts is based on a compensatory policy tends to induce the "domiciliary bias" for which Twerski reproved the proponents of interest analysis.[131] In the context of policy-oriented choice of law, it would seem, a rule of law embody-

---

127 *Cf.* Twerski (1973-1) p. 109. Even Weintraub (1972) p. 1259 ff., conceded that there are situations in which "there is substantial doubt as to whether we can realistically speak of a 'common policy'."
128 Baade (1973) p. 162 and 167: "Even an uninsured Ontario host-driver benefits from the Ontario guest statute ..."
129 Actually, the "choice of law rules for torts," proposed by Weintraub (1980) p. 346, are identical in respect of true conflict cases and "no interest" cases: " ... apply the law that will favor the plaintiff unless one or both of the following factors is present: (a) that law is anachronistic or aberrational; (b) the state with that law does not have sufficient contacts with the defendant or the defendant's actual or intended course of conduct to make application of that law reasonable."
130 To be discussed as one of Leflar's "choice-influencing considerations", *infra* chapter 5.
131 *Supra* note 112 and accompanying text. In a footnote, Sedler does allow for admonitory policies, as reflected, *e.g.*, in rules imposing strict liability on tavern keepers or manufacturers: Sedler (1973-2) p. 139, note 87. On the whole, however, he emphasizes the compensatory policy underlying tort law.

ing a policy of deterrence is primarily territorial in scope, whereas a compensatory policy implies protection of domiciliary interests. Yet, some unprovided-for cases highlight an unexpected blending of personal and territorial considerations. In these decisions, the absence of a limitation on liability in one of the states involved is seen as indicative of an admonitory policy of that state which not only extends to conduct within its territorial borders, but also to the out-of-state conduct of its citizens. Thus, by a change of perspective, the Gordian knot of the unprovided-for case is disentangled and need not be cut. Ordinarily, the policy of a recovery state would be construed as a concern for the compensation of its citizens in their capacity of victims.[132] Based on personalism, this interest is not at stake when the victim hails from another jurisdiction. Another aspect of the recovery policy could be qualified as territorial: unlimited liability might contribute to a higher standard of care to be observed by anyone, citizens and non-citizens alike, who acts within the territory of the recovery state.[133] By itself, this (territorial) concern is not affected when tortious conduct occurs elsewhere, even if the victim is a domiciliary of the recovery state. From yet another angle, a state's interest in unlimited liability could be seen as a concern for the standard of conduct it expects from its citizens, both at home and abroad.[134] Again, as an isolated aspect of a recovery policy, this (domiciliary) concern is immaterial when the tortfeasor has his home in another state. However, the legal process cannot be reduced to binary computation, and policy aspects cannot be separated from their context. Curiously, interest analysis is usually censured for being a pragmatic, hence unpredictable *ad hoc* approach. In my opinion, its greatest flaw is rather its classificatory tenor, inher-

---

132 Explicitly: *Fox v. Morrison Motor Freight, Inc.* 25 Ohio St.2d 193, 267 N.E.2d 405 at 408 (1971); *Jagers v. Royal Indemnity Company* 276 So.2d 309 at 313 (La. 1973); *Kasel v. Remington Arms Co.* 101 Cal.Rptr 314, 24 Cal.App.3d 711 at 734 (1972); *Kennedy v. Dixon* 439 S.W.2d 173 at 185 (Mo. 1969); *McSwain v. McSwain* 420 Pa. 86, 215 A.2d 677 at 682 (1966); *Turcotte v. Ford Motor Company* 494 F.2d 173 at 177 (1st Cir. [R.I.] 1974).
133 *Cf.*: *Conklin v. Horner* 38 Wis.2d 468, 157 N.W.2d 579 at 583, 586 (1968); *Hurtado v. Superior Court of Sacramento County* 114 Cal. Rptr. 106, 522 P.2d 666 at 672 (1974); *Jackson v. Koninklijke Luchtvaart Maatschappij, N.V.* 459 F.Supp. 953 at 955 (S.D. N.Y. 1978); *Kell v. Henderson* 47 Misc.2d 992, 263 N.Y.S.2d 647 at 650 (N.Y. Sup.Ct. 1965); *Oltarsh v. Aetna Insurance Company* 15 N.Y.2d 111, 256 N.Y.S.2d 577, 204 N.E.2d 622 at 625 (1965).
134 See the examples discussed below, notably *Labree v. Major* 306 A.2d 808 (R.I. 1973).

ent in the analytical, hence reductive "either/or" policy assessment it stands for.[135]

Now let us have a look at some opinions that circumvent the dilemma of the unprovided-for case by de-emphasizing the compensatory aspect of a recovery policy. The result must be a false conflict. In *Gravina v. Brunswick Corporation*, the plaintiff was a bowling prodigy whose name and photograph had been used without her consent in a nationwide advertising campaign of defendant. Rhode Island, plaintiff's home state, did not recognize a right of recovery for invasion of privacy, whereas she would have such a right under the law of Illinois, the state where defendant had its principal place of business. The federal district court observed that Rhode Island might have a slight, and in this case irrelevant, interest in "the promotion of a free and open business climate for visiting corporations."[136] On the other hand, Illinois was thought to have an interest in protecting its citizens against invasion of privacy. If this were viewed as a domiciliary interest based on a policy of compensating Illinois victims, or a territorial interest based on a policy of deterring conduct in Illinois that might harm Illinois citizens, one would think that the invasion of the privacy of a Rhode-Island citizen by defendant's advertising outside of Illinois could hardly be Illinois' concern. The district court was of a different opinion. Although Illinois law was held to apply primarily on the strength of a better law evaluation, the decision was reinforced by a false conflict construction. Skirting the looming "unprovided-for vacuum", the court subtly expanded the scope of Illinois' policy by reference to both personal and territorial aspects: "To the extent that Illinois public policy considers the invasion of privacy to be morally offensive, it is reasonable to perceive an Illinois interest in preventing *its corporations* from practicing such tortious conduct on non-residents as well as residents, especially when the conduct takes place partly in Illinois."[137]

A year later, this (extra)territorial point of view was confirmed by the Rhode Island Supreme Court in a case in which defendant's conduct occurred unequivocally outside the recovery state. *Labree v. Major* is

---

135 *Cf.* Twerski (1973-2) p. 399, asserting that "the highly structured, singleminded approach of interest analysis qualifies it as a rule of universal application." More on this subject, *infra* chapter 8, section 2, text following note 91, and chapter 9.
136 *Gravina v. Brunswick Corporation* 338 F.Supp. 1 at 6 (D. R.I. 1972).
137 *Ibid.* p. 4; emphasis added.

a straightforward guest statute case, in which Massachusetts was the place of the accident. The driver was a Rhode Island citizen, the guests were from Massachusetts. Since Massachusetts law protected host-drivers, whereas plaintiffs would be compensated under Rhode Island law, the law-fact pattern had the makings of a typical unprovided-for case. In effect, it was decided as a false conflict. Acknowledging that Massachusetts had no real interest in protecting a Rhode Island driver, the court addressed the issue of Rhode Island's interest: "Th[is] State has an interest in enforcing the standard of care of an automobile operator no matter where his guest resides."[138] This policy extends beyond Rhode Island's territorial limits, as Rhode Island drivers are expected to conform to this duty of care whether they are driving in Rhode Island or not. Not satisfied with an *ad hoc* decision, yet rejecting the third *Neumeier* principle, the Supreme Court held: "Thus, where a driver is from a state which allows a passenger to recover for ordinary negligence, the plaintiff should recover, no matter what the law of his residence or the place of the accident. We adopt this rule because the only state with an interest in protecting the driver and his insurer does not do so."[139] This sweeping rule is hardly in tune with interest analysis, as it attributes a fictitious extraterritorial scope to the recovery policy of the driver's home state even if that state's interest is limited to either the protection of its citizens or to the safety of its roads.

Equating the recovery policy of other states with its own, at least in guest statute cases, the Rhode Island Supreme Court found "nothing wrong in a state holding its citizens to a higher standard of care than that of the state to which they may travel, no matter who may be injured by their misconduct."[140] Conversely, the *Neumeier* court had refused to apply New York's more generous law, as it would "result in the exposure of this State's domiciliaries to a greater liability than that imposed upon resident users of Ontario's highways."[141] A marked contrast between the two positions is found in *Miller v. Gay*, an action brought in Pennsylvania by a Delaware guest against her Pennsylvania

138 *Labree v. Major* 306 A.2d 808 at 816 (R.I. 1973).
139 *Ibid.* p. 818. *Cf.* Sedler's proposition, dating from the same year: *supra* note 124 and accompanying text.
140 *Ibid.*
141 *Neumeier v. Kuehner* 31 N.Y.2d 121, 335 N.Y.S.2d 64, 286 N.E.2d 454 at 458 (1972).

host. Delaware, the state where the accident occurred, had a guest statute precluding recovery. Relying on *Griffith v. United Air Lines, Inc.* and *Cipolla v. Shaposka*,[142] the majority concluded that Delaware law applied, primarily because "inhabitants of a state (here Delaware) should not be accorded rights not given to them by their home states, just because a visitor from a state offering higher protection decides to visit there."[143] Not persuaded by this argument, the dissenting opinion urges application of Pennsylvania law, in view of Pennsylvania's "substantial" interest "in seeing that its licensed drivers are held to the standard of ordinary care in the operation of their motor vehicles," whether in Pennsylvania or elsewhere, obviously.[144]

The same "altruistic" reasoning is found in *Johnson v. Hertz Corporation*, a decision by a federal court in New York. Decided as a false conflict, this could just as well be another unprovided-for case, once more depending on the delineation of policies. Plaintiffs were residents of Massachusetts, who, on their way to Pennsylvania, had been injured in an automobile collision in New Jersey. The other car was registered in New York and owned by defendant. Under New York law, the owner of a car would be liable for negligence of the driver –who was said to have stolen, not rented, the car–, whereas the owner's liability would be limited under New Jersey law. In Massachusetts, ownership was regarded as *prima facie* evidence that the owner was also the driver. Although neither Massachusetts, plaintiffs' home state, nor New Jersey, the state where the accident occurred, would hold defendant liable under the circumstances, the district court emphasized that neither state had an interest in shielding him from liability, whereas New York's Vehicle and Traffic Law had "a policy aimed at protecting innocent victims of New York vehicle

---

142 *Griffith v. United Air Lines, Inc.* 416 Pa. 1, 203 A.2d 796 (1964). *Cipolla v. Shaposka* 439 Pa. 563, 267 A.2d 854 (1970).
143 *Miller v. Gay* 470 A.2d 1353 at 1356 (Pa. Super. 1983). This statement is consistent with *Cipolla v. Shaposka* 439 Pa. 563, 267 A.2d 854 at 856/857 (1970), the reverse law-fact pattern of *Miller* in that the host, not the plaintiff-guest, was domiciled in Delaware. Relying on Cavers' second principle of preference the *Cipolla* majority held: "[I]nhabitants of a state should not be put in jeopardy of liability exceeding that created by their state's laws just because a visitor from a state offering higher protection decides to visit there." More on Cavers' principles of preference, *infra* section 4(c).
144 *Ibid.* p. 1363.

registrants, whether injured or harmed in New York State or elsewhere ..."[145] Again, the recovery policy is credited with an extraterritorial reach not warranted by purely compensatory purposes, for it is hard to believe that New York would be truly *interested* in the compensation of any non-resident victim chancing to sue in its courts.[146]

These decisions reflect a "moralizing" interpretation of policies that are, or would seem to be, focused on compensation rather than deterrence. As admonitory policies, they might be thought to extend to out-of-state conduct of a state's citizens. If so, domiciliary rather than territorial interests are at stake, centering on resident *defendants*. On the other hand, since the scope of an admonitory policy is generally acknowledged as territorial[147] it could be asked if the reach of a recovery rule is not stretched beyond its purpose when it is said to follow the resident defendant wherever he goes. Whether this question can be answered conclusively depends on the feasibility of a realistic policy assessment. Unfortunately, the cases that give rise to the "unprovided-for" dilemma –virtually all of them solved as false con-

---

145 *Johnson v. Hertz Corporation* 315 F.Supp. 302 at 304 (S.D. N.Y. 1970). Since New York's car owner liability was tied to New York's compulsory insurance law (*cf.* § 388 and §§ 310 ff. N.Y. Vehicle and Traffic Law), it would follow that New York's interest was compensatory and did not extend to non-residents injured outside New York. *Cf.* the implicit criticism of the *Johnson* decision in *Kline v. Wheels by Kinney, Inc.* 464 F.2d 184 at 187, footnote 5 (4th Cir. [N.C.] 1972). See also: Sedler (1973-2) p. 140, note 94: "The policy represented by the requirement of compulsory insurance is clearly a compensatory one, and New York has no interest in applying that policy in favor of a non-resident injured elsewhere."

146 Similar skepticism was expressed in *Erwin v. Thomas* 264 Or. 454, 506 P.2d 494 at 496 (1973), *supra* text accompanying note 90. *Contra*: Shapira (1973) p. 172, who views a compensatory interest as an "interest, or rather principle, [which] emanates from community shaped and shared conventions of justice and expediency, from prevailing societal conceptions as to what constitutes fair compensatory practices. As such, this principle of justice expresses a 'general truth', in the sense of not being inherently restricted to domestic situations and local beneficiaries only." This notion seems to come too close to the Romanist concept of public policy to be useful in present-day interest analysis.

147 Out of many statements to this effect, a few are quite illustrative, as in: *Schulhof v. Northeast Cellulose, Inc.* 545 F.Supp. 1200 at 1205 (D. Mass. 1982); *Barr v. Interbay Citizens Bank of Tampa, Fla.* 635 P.2d 441 at 444 (Wash. 1981); *Jackson v. Miller-Davis Company* 3 Ill.Dec. 161, 358 N.E.2d 328 at 332 (Ill. App. 1976); *Continental Oil Co. v. General American Transportation Corporation* 409 F.Supp. 288 at 296 (S.D. Tex. 1976); *Gagne v. Berry* 290 A.2d 624 at 626 (N.H. 1972); and, as early as 1928, in *Levy v. Daniels' U-Drive Auto Renting Co.* 143 A. 163 at 164 (Conn. 1928).

flicts—[148] suggest a negative reply. In my opinion, the unprovided-for case is a logical possibility under an approach which is predicated on the idea that the spatial reach of a rule of law can be ascertained through a case-by-case analysis of its underlying policy. Addressing the "either/or" choice of law issue, such an approach must entail the reduction of complex, and often conjectural, legal objectives to a single rationale, decisive for the relevance of either jurisdiction's rule of law to the actual controversy. Those denying the existence of an unprovided-for case may have wanted to ignore the inevitability of such policy simplification, in an unconscious attempt, probably, to reconcile their rightful perception that legal objectives are multifarious and convoluted with their sincere appreciation of interest analysis. My unhappy conclusion is twofold: under the assumption that it is inconceivable that "neither state cares what happens," an unprovided-for case cannot exist. If so, the undeniable manifestation of this chimaera in the cases discussed above must be due to the discretionary nature of policy assessment. On the other hand, if we accept the "legal vacuum" as an actual possibility, brought to light by careful interest analysis, it defies a rational solution through interest analysis. In that respect the unprovided-for case equals its reverse: the true conflict.

4 True conflicts

For all its eloquent forcefulness, Professor Currie's theory of governmental interest analysis is less than convincing in its description and solution of the true conflict dilemma. Even if we accept the thesis that courts are incapable of assessing "the respective values of the competing legitimate interests of two sovereign states, in order to determine which is to prevail,"[149] even if we are willing to adopt Currie's "con-

---

148 Of the cases discussed above, *Erwin v. Thomas* 264 Or. 454, 506 P.2d 494 (1973), is the only decision in which the unprovided-for case was unequivocally acknowledged and treated as such.
149 Currie (1963-1) p. 182. See, however, Traynor M. (1961) p. 852 ff., 854/855: "State courts weigh competing interests in common-law and statutory interpretation cases every day ... In view of such pervasive interest weighing one may well ask what is so sacrosanct about conflicts cases that precludes courts from weighing the interests involved." See also: Horowitz (1974) p. 748.

structive give-it-up attitude" and apply forum law "when it appears that the task is impossible of accomplishment with the resources that are available,"[150] the theory fails in its definition of true conflict situations. In his earlier writings, Currie concentrated on the clear-cut dichotomy of true and false conflicts, a distinction that turns each case in which more than one jurisdiction has an interest, into a "problem that cannot be solved except by political action."[151] However, "to assert a conflict between the interests of the forum and the foreign state is a serious matter"[152] and should be a relatively rare occurrence, because "there is room for restraint and enlightenment in the determination of what state policy is and where state interests lie."[153] Carried by the notions of "moderate and restrained interpretation", "long-range enlightened self-interest" and "rational altruism", a third category of choice of law problems emerges in Currie's later work. This class of *avoidable conflicts* or *apparent true conflicts* is defined as "those [cases] in which it appears that each state would be constitutionally justified in asserting an interest, but on reflection conflict is avoided by a more moderate definition of the policy or interest of one state or the other."[154] The concept of moderate and restrained interpretation introduces an arbitrary factor into an otherwise rational and impartial analysis[155] for it invites the court to assess the policy of its own law and the forum's interest in its application in a relative way, by a confrontation of interests, hence by comparative evaluation. Not surprisingly, Currie's definition of avoidable conflicts has made his true conflict approach more vulnerable to the criticism his original "give-it-up" or *lex fori* solution already provoked. It was said that the process of moderate interpretation is essentially the same as that involved in weighing interests,[156] and that "rational altruism" does assign a significant politi-

150 Currie (1963-1) p. 121.
151 Currie (1963-2) p. 763, implying that Congress should perform the highly "political function" of determining the choice between competing state interests. *Cf.* Currie (1963-1) p. 272, p. 604.
152 Currie (1963-2) p. 757.
153 Currie (1963-1) p. 186; *cf.* Strikwerda (1978) p. 175 ff.
154 Currie (1963-2) p. 763.
155 Provided that courts are capable of assessing policies without prejudice. In her critique of interest analysis, Professor Brilmayer suggested that Currie's deduction of legislative intent may have been influenced "by his own normative beliefs about how far certain policies *ought* to reach." Brilmayer (1980) p. 400; emphasis in the original. See *infra* chapter 9.
156 Currie's own reformulation of this kind of criticism in his reply to Professor Hill: Currie (1963-1) p. 604. *Cf.* Hill (1960) p. 476 ff.; Shapira (1970) p. 182 ff.

cal function to the judiciary.[157] Calling the difference between defining and weighing interests "largely semantic" Currie is hardly able[158] to parry the implicit allegation that his hostility towards interest-weighing is selective, his true conflicts solution therefore inconsistent. It is clear that the definition of an avoidable conflict is fraught with uncertainty, since its identity must be discovered at the interface of interest determination and interest assertion. I am therefore inclined to ignore the frail and largely academic distinction between real and apparent conflicts.[159]

As a consequence, my "true conflicts" heading covers those cases in which the analysis displays (apparently) conflicting interests, irrespective of the manner in which they were judicially resolved. Although forum law was applied in many of these cases, it cannot be said that the courts have paid much heed to Currie's denunciation of interest-weighing. Instead, their decisions reflect a tendency to justify the choice of (forum) law, if only by dint of a none too cogent assessment of the "superior", "greater" or "paramount" interest. The better reasoned decisions display painstaking efforts to rationalize the process of interest-weighing. The normative approach chosen by these courts relies heavily on doctrinal sources, primarily on the "comparative impairment" theory, on Leflar's choice-influencing considerations, as well as on the "choice of law principles" in § 6 of the Restatement Second. Remarkably, there are virtually no decisions[160] in which the choice of law holding was predicated on "principles of preference", even though Cavers exemplified his theory by reference to multistate *torts*. To the extent that this approach purports to solve true conflicts in torts by a comparison of standards of conduct or of financial protection against injury, it has failed to make its mark in judicial practice. Still, Cavers' solution cannot be dismissed as just an academic contrivance. Abstracted from the various principles of preference, an overall "territorial bias" emerges which might have colored some of

---

157 Hill (1960) p. 477; Cavers (1963) p. 734, note 9; Cramton/Currie/Kay (1981) p. 271/272.
158 Currie (1963-1) p. 604 ff. *Cf.* Strikwerda (1978) p. 175/176 and *ibid.* note 3–142.
159 More on "moderation and restraint" as a tool to solve true conflicts, *infra* section 4(b), text following note 207.
160 With the notable exception of *Cipolla v. Shaposka* 439 Pa. 563, 267 A.2d 854 (1970), *infra* section 4(c), notes 306–326 and accompanying text.

the actual true conflict decisions, notably those relying on the place of wrong to tip the scales.

All in all, case law tends to display three major approaches to the solution of true conflicts. Apart from the *comparative impairment approach*, patented in California, either some form of *interest-weighing* or a *residuary lex loci solution* seems to have found favor with the courts, whereas the less demanding *lex fori* presumption is conspicuously absent.[161] Leflar's choice-influencing considerations, particularly his suggestion to apply the better law, are popular in various jurisdictions, not only used to motivate true conflict decisions but rather as an integral choice of law approach. For that reason I have made the "Leflar methodology" the subject of a separate chapter.[162]

a Weighing conflicting interests

"Can you weigh a bushel of horsefeathers against next Thursday?" is a curious rhetorical question which, translated to the true conflict dilemma, seems to receive a more affirmative answer from the courts than its learned authors meant to suggest.[163] In quite a number of cases interests are "balanced" or "weighed" against each other, with a semblance of impartiality, yet without a compelling rationale.[164] Some opinions contain a flat statement to the effect that one state has the

---

161 In some cases it was expressly rejected; see *e.g. Ardoyno v. Kyzar* 426 F.Supp. 78 at 80 (E.D. La. 1976) and *Girard Bank v. Mount Holly State Bank* 474 F.Supp. 1225 at 1238 (D. N.J. 1979). The supremacy of *lex fori* in Kentucky and Michigan is not limited to true conflicts, but pervades all decisions on tort choice of law. This phenomenon will be discussed separately, *infra* chapter 7.
162 *Infra* chapter 5.
163 Currie used it to preface his views on interest-weighing in *The Disinterested Third State*, (1963-2) p. 754, and traced its origin, *via* Justice Traynor and Dean Prosser, to an unidentified English judge.
164 In *Flammia v. Mite Corporation* 401 F.Supp. 1121 at 1126 (E.D. N.Y. 1975), a contracts case, a federal court in New York perceived New York's interest analysis approach as an *ad hoc* weighing-process: "That is, the forum is to apply the law of the jurisdiction with the most interest in the problem and the most concern in the outcome of the litigation." See also: *Glenway Industries, Inc. v. Wheelabrator-Frye, Inc.* 686 F.2d 415 at 417 (6th Cir. [Ohio] 1982): " ... Ohio requires the application of an interest analysis where the governmental interests of the states involved are weighed."

"greater"[165] or "superior"[166] or "strongest"[167] interest in having its law applied. When the courts do try to explain their motives, the reasoning is more persuasive, yet seldom convincing. These decisions may contain a token reference to the Restatement Second, both to § 145 ff. and to § 6, paving the way for contacts-counting or the promotion of forum interests. In other opinions one of the conflicting interests is belittled to the point of virtual non-existence, usually –but not always– to the effect that the interest of the forum state prevails. From a methodological point of view, these decisions can hardly be considered as examples of Currie's "moderate and restrained interpretation". In the first place, this concept was primarily meant to counteract a predilection for forum interests, which implies that the interest of the *forum* rather than that of a foreign jurisdiction should be reconsidered. Second, moderation and restraint were supposed to reduce the number of true conflicts, not to solve them. Thus, the cases to be discussed are premised on a real conflict of interests. An attempt to reduce the relevance of a foreign state's interest is usually nothing but an ill-disguised form of interest-weighing.

An example of this "reduction technique" is found in *Saalfrank v. O'Daniel*, a personal injury action arising from a car accident in Ohio. The plaintiff was a resident of Indiana, who sued both the driver, an Ohio resident, and the Indiana hospital in which he had been treated. Embracing Ohio's "balancing of interests approach", the federal court asserted that it was unclear what the law of Indiana would be in respect of the hospital's malpractice liability, making it "extremely difficult for this Court to speculate on the interests of Indiana." On the other hand, there was no doubt about Ohio's interests: "Obviously Ohio has an interest in not having its citizens who are claimed to be tortfeasors subjected to proportionally higher damage verdicts because of the subsequent malpractice of one who supplies medical services to the victim." Upon this feat of interest-weighing in the dark,

---

165 *Clark v. Celeb Publishing, Inc.* 530 F.Supp. 979 (S.D. N.Y. 1981).
166 *Bray v. Cox* 39 A.D.2d 299, 333 N.Y.S.2d 783 (1972).
167 *Engine Specialties, Inc. v. Bombardier, Ltd.* 605 F.2d 1 (1st Cir. [Mass.] 1979). See also: *supra* text accompanying notes 8–10.

Ohio law was held to apply.[168] Decided by a federal court in Massachusetts, *Schulhof v. Northeast Cellulose, Inc.* was an action arising from a midair collision between two small planes over Massachusetts. One of the issues involved the question of punitive damages, which were disallowed by the laws of New York (where the plaintiffs resided) and New Hampshire (the home state of all defendants but one), but allowed by the law of Massachusetts. Confronting the true conflict between Massachusetts' interest in deterring tortious conduct in its air space and New Hampshire's interest in protecting its local entrepreneurs against excessive liability, the court held the Massachusetts law of punitive damages to apply, since "New Hampshire cannot properly assert its policy of protecting local entrepreneurs in a manner which impinges upon the interest of another jurisdiction in regulating conduct within its own borders." In an attempt to justify this point of view, the court noted that New Hampshire, unlike other states, had no express prohibition against punitive damages, which left the strength of its policy "open to question."[169] The same type of argument was used in *Beasock v. Dioguardi Enterprises, Inc.*: plaintiff was a New York resident who brought a wrongful death action against defendants in Ohio and the District of Columbia for the death of her husband, caused by the explosion of a truck tire in New York. Addressing the issue of punitive damages, not allowed by New York law at the time of the accident, the Appellate Division found a true conflict between the interest of New York in protecting out of state as well as resident defendants from excessive liability (possibly arising "from a desire to promote commerce within the state"), and the interests of Ohio and the District of Columbia in enforcing a policy of deterrence and punishment.[170] Recalling that after the accident New York law had changed, now allowing punitive damages, the court deemed the interests of Ohio and the District of Columbia to be "superior": for

---

168 *Saalfrank v. O'Daniel* 390 F.Supp. 45 at 57 (N.D. Ohio 1975). The interests of the insurance industry provided an extra argument: " ... Ohio automobile liability insurance carriers can ascertain their underwriting risks and premiums best if their insured's rights to indemnification or contribution are governed by the law of Ohio rather than potentially diverse laws of several states."
169 *Schulhof v. Northeast Cellulose, Inc.* 545 F.Supp. 1200 at 1206/1207 (D. Mass. 1982).
170 *Beasock v. Dioguardi Enterprises, Inc.* 472 N.Y.S.2d 798 at 801 (A.D. N.Y. 1984).

New York could not be thought to have a strong policy against punitive damages by allowing them now.[171]

In some cases, interest-weighing amounts to little more than contacts-counting. Affirming the district court's choice of law ruling in a fraud case, in *Glenway Industries, Inc. v. Wheelabrator-Frye, Inc.*, the Sixth Circuit claimed adherance to Ohio's interest-weighing approach when it held the law of Pennsylvania to apply, taking into account that "defendant resides in Pennsylvania, and that the great majority of negotiations and contacts occurred at (defendant's) headquarters in Pittsburgh."[172] The same factual approach is found in *Blais v. Deyo*, in which case New York's Appellate Division reversed the lower court's decision that New York's more generous law applied to the measure of damages issue in a personal injury action brought by Canadian plaintiffs against New York defendants. Conceding that New York's unlimited recovery rule might express a New York interest in preventing New Yorkers from wrongdoing, the court nevertheless declared "that Quebec has a more substantial interest than New York in the compensation of the plaintiffs, residents of Quebec, when the accident occurred in Quebec."[173]

A more conscientious attempt at contacts-grouping in the *Babcock* tradition is found in the New Jersey decision *Mullane v. Stavola*.[174] The law-fact pattern of this guest statute case was on all fours with

---

171 *Ibid.* Because of the change in New York's law regarding punitive damages the case could be viewed as an intertemporal problem, presenting a true conflict at the time of the accident and a no-conflict situation at the time of suit. The opinion suggests that the time of the accident was considered decisive, hence the case was treated as a true conflict.
172 *Glenway Industries, Inc. v. Wheelabrator-Frye, Inc.* 686 F.2d 415 at 417 (6th Cir. [Ohio] 1982).
173 *Blais v. Deyo* 92 A.D.2d 998, 461 N.Y.S.2d 471 at 473 (1983). This statement was followed by an argument of a different order: " ... because plaintiffs could recover under the Quebec statute without proof of fault, Quebec's interest is greater." It is not clear whether plaintiffs were able to prove fault. If not, application of Quebec law, notwithstanding its limitation, was obviously more favorable to them than application of New York law. As in many judicial opinions, the real motive for the choice of law decision remains in the dark.
174 *Mullane v. Stavola* 101 N.J.Super. 184, 243 A.2d 842 (1968).

Dym v. Gordon and, in retrospect, *Tooker v. Lopez:*[175] the host and his passengers were domiciliaries of New Jersey, they were temporarily residing as students in Florida, the car belonged to defendant's mother and was registered in New Jersey, and the fatal accident occurred in Florida, a state with a guest statute. Setting out to assess the "paramount governmental interest" in this case, the *Mullane* court compared "Florida's policy goal in its guest statute against New Jersey's strong declared policy of compelling a host-driver to exercise ordinary care for the safety of his guest-passenger, and to compensate them for injuries caused by his negligence," and concluded that Florida's law must give way. Equating contacts with interests, the court held: "Even though Florida's 'contacts' may be quantitatively greater than New Jersey's they are qualitatively less significant. The salient consideration is that the parties at the time of the accident were domiciled in New Jersey. Their Florida residences were temporary."[176]

In effect, there is very little difference between interest-weighing and the qualitative approach to the most significant relationship test according to the precepts of the Restatement Second. As we have seen,[177] the interaction between § 145 ff. and § 6 should lead a conscientious court to make use of the Restatement's contacts test not as "an end in itself to be applied mechanically, but rather as a means reliably calculated to insure that the *interests of the state with the most significant relationship* to the occurrences will be protected."[178] In a number of decisions explicitly relying on the Restatement Second, the phrase "most significant contacts" was therefore interpreted in a non-physical sense, denoting the degree of interest a state was thought to assert in respect of the particular issue and its resolution. In *Continen-*

---

175 *Dym v. Gordon* 16 N.Y.2d 120, 262 N.Y.S.2d 463, 209 N.E.2d 792 (1965). The approach in *Dym* was expressly rejected in New Jersey; *Mullane v. Stavola* 101 N.J. Super. 184, 243 A.2d at 844 (1968): "I am convinced the majority of the court in *Dym* misapplied the rule in *Babcock* ..." *Tooker v. Lopez* 24 N.Y.2d 569, 301 N.Y.S.2d 519, 249 N.E.2d 394 (1969).
176 *Mullane v. Stavola* 101 N.J.Super. 184, 243 A.2d 842 at 845 (1968). See also: *Wendelken v. Superior Court in and for the County of Pima* 137 Ariz. 455, 671 P.2d 896 (1983); *Watts v. Pioneer Corn Company* 342 F.2d 617 (7th Cir. [Ind.] 1965); *Machleder v. Diaz* 538 F.Supp. 1364 (S.D. N.Y. 1982).
177 *Supra* chapter 3, text accompanying notes 60–79.
178 *Forty-Eight Insulations v. Johns-Manville Products* 472 F.Supp. 385 (N.D. Ill. 1979); emphasis added.

tal Oil Co. v. General American Transportation Corporation, for instance, a federal court in Texas interpreted the most significant *contacts* test as a most significant *interests* test when it compared the "greatest contact" of Ohio to the "inferior interests" of other jurisdictions.[179] Explaining Pennsylvania's choice of law principles in terms of the Restatement Second the federal court in *Lewis v. Chemetron Corp.* opined: "The law does not require us to apply the law of the state whose contacts are the most numerous, but rather demands sensitivity to the relative importance of each of the several contacts to the substantive policy of Workmen's compensation." Receipt of workmen's compensation benefits through the offices of a particular state would give that state "an overriding interest of controlling importance with respect to the choice of law question," the court held, thus equating a significant contact in § 184(a) of the Restatement Second with what amounts to a "superior interest".[180] The same equation, it may be recalled, was made implicitly by the Illinois Supreme Court in its landmark decision *Ingersoll v. Klein*: " ... a 'most significant contacts' rule best serves the interests of the State and the parties involved in a multi-State tort action."[181] With explicit reference to the four localizing factors of § 145(2) Restatement Second, a federal court sitting in Illinois rephrased the rule thus: " ... the next step is to examine the contacts with the states evaluating the importance of each contact in relation to the legal issues of the case."[182]

If these decisions suggest that a qualitative contacts approach is not much different from pure interest analysis, and that in the weighing process contacts and interests are interchangeable, the rationalization of true conflict solutions points up a curious crisscross approach when either contacts or interests are found to be in equal balance. Depen-

---

179 *Continental Oil Co. v. General American Transportation Corporation* 409 F.Supp. 288 at 296 (S.D. Tex. 1976).
180 *Lewis v. Chemetron Corp.* 448 F.Supp. 211 at 213 (W.D. Pa. 1978).
181 *Ingersoll v. Klein* 46 Ill.2d 42, 262 N.E.2d 593 at 596 (1970); *supra* chapter 3, notes 60–63 and accompanying text.
182 *Pancotto v. Sociedade de Safaris de Moçambique S.A.R.L.* 422 F.Supp. 405 at 407 (N.D. Ill. 1976). In *Hardly Able Coal Co., Inc. v. International Harvester Co.*, 494 F.Supp. 249 at 250 (N.D. Ill. 1980), the same court repeated its allegiance to the "four factors test" of § 145 and continued: "If the weighting of the several factors is equal, the conventional *lex loci delicti* approach that was once uniformly applied in torts cases prevails." Resorting to the *lex loci* presumption "now that all interests are in balance," the court equated "factors" with "interests".

dent on their point of departure, these decisions attempt to sway a balance of contacts through interest-weighing, or a balance of interests through contacts-weighing. In *Johnson v. Spider Staging Corporation*, the Supreme Court of Washington envisaged a situation in which application of the most significant relationship rule would produce an equal balance of contacts. Referring to § 6, the court suggested that in such cases the solution should be found in "consideration of the interests and public policies of potentially concerned states and a regard as to the manner and extent of such policies as they relate to the transaction in issue."[183] On the other hand, interest analysis may be supplemented by contacts-weighing when a true conflict is discovered. Two cases, one decided by the First Circuit, the other by a district court in Louisiana, are illustrative for this position. In *Mason v. Southern New England Conf. Ass'n, Etc.*, a conscientious attempt was made to reach a decision by reference to the Restatement, particularly to § 6. It was found that Maine, the forum state, and Massachusetts, the state where plaintiff had been injured, both had an interest in the application of their respective laws. Before yielding to the *lex loci* presumption of § 146, the First Circuit tried another approach: "These policies therefore at best furnish no principle for choosing which law to apply; if the dominance of Massachusetts *contacts* makes that state's interests more weighty, the balance may tip against the plaintiff's wishes."[184] In the second case, *Karavorikos v. Indiana Bus Co.*, the district court viewed the Louisiana variety of interest analysis as a two-step process. First, the court asserted, it should be decided whether the case presents a false or a true conflict. If a true conflict is found, the second step would imply an application of the most significant relationship test according to the four factors of § 145(2).[185]

---

[183] *Johnson v. Spider Staging Corporation* 555 P.2d 997 at 1001 (1976). In this case, interest analysis revealed a false conflict.
[184] *Mason v. Southern New England Conf. Ass'n, Etc.* 696 F.2d 135 at 138 (1st Cir. [Me.] 1982); emphasis added.
[185] *Karavorikos v. Indiana Bus Co.* 524 F.Supp. 385 (E.D. La. 1981). Curiously, another district court sitting in Louisiana explained the second step to entail an application of § 6: "The 'most significant relationship' test promulgated in the Restatement, Conflict of Laws (Second) is slightly more precise than interest analysis, though the two operate almost identically, to call for a comparison of governmental interests." *Bell v. State Farm Fire & Cas. Co.* 527 F.Supp. 300 at 303 (W.D. La. 1981).

In practice, interest-weighing as a solution to true conflicts amounts to little more, I find, than application of an embellished center-of-gravity test. Not surprisingly, most of the decisions discussed above are dominated by the influence of the Restatement Second. As a means to "intelligently 'evaluate' rather than mechanically count the contacts"[186] interest analysis is used as a component of the most significant relationship approach, not as an autonomous choice of law method. Interest analysis, no doubt, is of great assistance in the process of weighing contacts under a qualitative center-of-gravity approach. If such an evaluation displays a balance of interests, the contacts must be deemed to be in balance as well, for the weight of each contact is assessed by reference to interests. When the interests or contacts are found to be poised, the weighing process is over. It has revealed a true conflict or, depending on the court's point of departure, a balance of contacts, but at this point it has served its purpose and loses its decisive potential.[187] The solution of a true conflict should therefore be sought beyond interests or contacts: at this stage another evaluation of their relative weight must be considered specious. On the presumption that true conflicts can be solved at all, a better approach may be the one that uses normative criteria, such as William Baxter's comparative impairment analysis.

---

186 Weintraub (1980) p. 277, describing the antithesis between the "method of conflicts analysis" envisioned in the last sentence of § 145 and the four contacts listed in that section: "Whether or not a particular contact with a state is significant for conflicts purposes cannot be known until one first knows exactly what domestic tort rules are in conflict and what the policies underlying those rules are."

187 Under an interest analysis approach, contacts become irrelevant once the respective interests have been assessed and they are of no avail in the solution of true conflicts. Conversely, an approach that relies on contacts to establish the most significant relationship could make use of interest analysis when the contacts are in balance. Yet, if the analysis then reveals a true conflict, one cannot turn back to contacts-weighing to break the tie. In this perspective, the reasoning in both *Mason v. Southern New England Conf. Ass'n, Etc.* 696 F.2d 135 (1st Cir. [Me.] 1982), *supra* note 184, and *Karavorikos v. Indiana Bus Co.* 524 F.Supp. 385 (E.D. La. 1981), *supra* note 185, must be deemed unsound. If factual contacts are allowed to tip the scale in a true conflict situation, interest analysis is turned upside down and might as well be skipped in favor of a straightforward contacts-grouping approach.

b Comparative impairment analysis: the California answer

The most positive rebuttal of Currie's thesis that true conflicts cannot be solved by normative criteria came from California and was voiced by Professor William F. Baxter in an article on *Choice of Law and the Federal System*, published in 1963.[188] His response to Currie's "give-it-up philosophy" is positive in the sense that it goes beyond an implacable refutation of the *lex fori* formula. Accepting the basic premises of interest analysis, Baxter made a valiant attempt to propose a rational alternative for the stopgap solution to true conflicts. Known as "comparative impairment analysis", his theory did not attract much academic or judicial attention until 1974, when it was integrated in a "restatement" of California choice of law principles by Professor Harold W. Horowitz.[189] A virtual California specialty,[190] comparative impairment analysis came into its own when the California Supreme Court, citing both Baxter and Horowitz, explicitly adopted it in *Bernhard v. Harrah's Club*.[191] Essentially a balancing process, the comparative impairment approach defies Currie's prohibition against interest-

---

188 Baxter (1963) p. 1 ff.
189 Horowitz (1974) p. 719 ff.; *cf.* Kay (1980) p. 581. Horowitz has been criticized by both Ehrenzweig (1974) p. 783 ff., and Kay *ibid.* for his suggestive interpretation of the California decisions from which he constructed his "restatement". With the dubious support of a 19th century decision on slavery – *Ex Parte Archy* 9 Cal. 147 (1858); *cf.* Horowitz 17 *U.C.L.A. L.Rev.* 587 (1970)– Horowitz implied that the comparative impairment principle, and other principles of interest analysis, had been part of California's conflicts law all along.
190 The major publications on this subject were written by California professors of law and published in California law reviews.
In *Johnson v. Johnson* 107 N.H. 30, 216 A.2d 781 (1966), the Supreme Court of New Hampshire applied Massachusetts' interspousal immunity rule rather than the New Hampshire *lex loci delicti* that would have allowed the action between Massachusetts spouses. The court did not think that the purposes of New Hampshire law would be "seriously impaired" by application of the spouses' domiciliary law. *Ibid.* p. 783. Although the case was said to present a true conflict, it was decided by the adoption of a jurisdiction-selecting rule hinging on the spouses' domicile as the controlling contact. For that reason, I submit, the use of a phrase reminiscent of Baxter's theory was of no consequence. The treatment of this case in Cramton/Currie/Kay (1981) p. 293, suggests differently, however.
191 *Bernhard v. Harrah's Club* 16 Cal.3d 313, 546 P.2d 719, 128 Cal. Rptr. 215, *cert. denied*, 429 U.S. 859 (1976); *infra* text accompanying notes 233–240. The opinion by Justice Sullivan assumes that the comparative impairment principle had already been applied in 1957 in *People v. One 1953 Ford Victoria* 48 Cal.2d 595, 311 P.2d 480 (1957). *Contra*: Kay (1980) p. 581, note 37. →

weighing.[192] Unconvinced by Currie's contention that the courts are neither in the position nor equipped to compare conflicting interests, Baxter was unwilling to accept the residuary *lex fori* rule as a suitable solution. Conceding that his principle might be vulnerable to attack for being "vacuous in content and uncertain in application," he accused Currie of sacrificing the goal of predictability to a much greater extent by advocating a solution that turns upon the fortuitous circumstance of forum selection by the plaintiff.[193] The mainstay of his theory is the proposition that "the process of resolving choice cases is necessarily one of allocating spheres of legal control among states."[194] In true conflict cases, this process would entail a search for the "pertinence" of each of the conflicting rules, *i.e.* "[t]he extent to which the purpose underlying a rule will be *furthered* by application or *impaired* by nonapplication."[195] In other words, the question whether a state has an interest in the application of its law should be answered in a relative way, not by an absolute "yes" or "no". In Baxter's opinion, the respective claims to application of the conflicting rules are capa-

At this point, I should like to draw attention to a historical oddity. In the Netherlands, as early as 1947, Professor L.I. de Winter appears to have advocated comparative impairment analysis *avant la lettre*. In a visionary article on the "social functions of substantive law as a criterion for the solution of choice of law problems," he used Pillet's distinction between *lois de garantie sociale* and *lois de protection individuelle* as a stepping-stone to his own "functional choice of law method". This approach calls for an analysis of the "social interests" that each of the involved jurisdictions may have in the application of its law. The next step is that of "assessing if, and to what extent these interests will be impaired when the law of another concerned jurisdiction rather than forum law is applied to the matter at issue. This way, it is established which state would be most impaired by the application of some other state's law, and a final test should then reveal whether application of the law of the former state will also be acceptable to the other states involved." De Winter, (1947) p. 153, reprinted in: *Naar een sociaal I.P.R., Een keus uit het werk van L.I. de Winter,* Deventer, 1979, p. 3 ff; p. 42. In the course of his academic career, De Winter gradually drifted away from a policy-oriented approach to choice of law, in preference to the traditional jurisdiction-selecting method, and did no longer pursue the theme of comparative impairment.

192 *Cf.* Posnak (1983) p. 781, note 252.
193 Baxter (1963) p. 20 ff. Baxter made a distinction between "primary predictability" (the parties' ability to predict, prior to any litigation, the legal consequences of their conduct), "secondary predictability" (the parties' ability to predict the outcome of the litigation once it had started in an identified forum), and "doctrinal uniformity" (consensus among the potential forums on the outcome of litigation). In this context, Baxter referred to "primary predictability."
194 Baxter (1963) p. 22 and *passim*.
195 *Ibid.* p. 9; emphasis added.

ble of being measured by "comparative pertinence".[196] His yardstick is the degree to which the "objectives"[197] of each rule will be impaired by non-application. As an example, Baxter offers a hypothetical in the area of products liability in which the ordinary negligence rule of State X is contrasted with the strict liability rule of State Y. If it is assumed that State X has a policy of protecting manufacturers who can be identified with X, whereas State Y wants to protect consumers identified with Y, orthodox interest analysis would reveal a true conflict in a case involving an X manufacturer and a Y consumer. Yet, "[t]he prima facie pertinence of Y law will be diminished if the consumer, though residing in Y, is domiciled in X (or in any other state which follows the X rule) or if he has died and a wrongful death or survival action is being maintained for the benefit of relatives identified with X (or any other state which follows the X internal rule)."[198] Conversely, X's interest in protecting the manufacturer might be less "pertinent" if the manufacturer, though incorporated in X, has its principal place of business in Y. Performed in this detached, objective way, Baxter maintains, the comparative impairment test is based on "the normative criterion of implementing state policies,"[199] and should therefore be preferred to "disputable super-value judgments."

On the other hand, even if the comparative impairment test should be understood as a judicial assessment of the relative strength of competing state policies, not as an evaluation of their "relative worthiness", it still requires interest-weighing.[200] Baxter himself acknowledged that

196 *Ibid.* p. 11, note 23.
197 Baxter distinguished between "internal" and "external governmental objectives": *ibid.* p. 17. The former are "those underlying each state's resolution of conflicting private interests," even in wholly domestic cases. External objectives are peculiar to choice of law situations: "They are the objectives of each state to make effective, *in all situations involving persons as to whom it has responsibility for legal ordering,* that resolution of contending private interests the state has made for local purposes." (*ibid.*); emphasis added. Strikwerda (1978) p. 179, clarified this cryptic distinction by substituting "policy" for "internal objective", and "interest" for "external objective". *Cf.* Kay (1980) p. 580: "[Baxter's] notion was that interested states had not merely internal policy objectives as Currie had said, but also external objectives – the desire to have other states respect the value judgments embodied in the state's internal policy where the focal point of that policy was directly at issue in an interstate case."
198 Baxter (1963) p. 11.
199 *Ibid.* p. 20.
200 *Cf.* Note, Comparative Impairment Reformed: Rethinking State Interests in the Conflict of Laws, 95 *Harv. L.Rev.* 1079, 1083, note 19; p. 1095 (1982).

state courts, being "active participants in the formulation and implementation of local policies," might display a certain forum bias in deciding which of the competing policies should yield.[201] For that reason, he urged that the comparative impairment balancing process should be controlled by federal law, to be developed and monitored by federal courts.[202] While this proposition emphasizes the limitation of Baxter's approach to interstate (rather than international) conflicts, it could be asked whether it was meant to be used as an autonomous principle of state law without foundation in federal law, as it is now in California.[203] At any rate, in the light of his federalist attitude, Baxter's response to the objections against interest-weighing might have been more in accord with Currie's point of view than the proponents of either approach have wanted to acknowledge: Currie himself suggested that, in time, a solution for true conflicts might be found on an interstate or international level.[204] Ignoring Baxter's conviction that "[r]esponsibility for allocating spheres of legal control among member states of a federal system cannot sensibly be placed elsewhere than with the federal government,"[205] Horowitz encouraged a balancing process by state courts, in which they should use comparative impairment as one of the criteria.[206] Not surprisingly, the California state courts have used comparative impairment analysis as a versatile tool in those cases in which California was one of the interested jurisdictions. As a result, judicial invocation of Baxter's theory seems to cover various choice of law techniques, ranging from jurisdiction-selection to interest-weighing. To the extent that the latter approach

---

201 Baxter (1963) p. 23. Placing the responsibility for such a decision in the hands of state courts would be the same as transferring the responsibilities of a baseball umpire to "the first team member who managed to rule on a disputed event."
202 *Ibid.* p. 23 ff., p. 41/42; *cf.* Kay (1980) p. 580 ff. Baxter concluded that *Klaxon Cc v. Stentor Elec. Mfg. Co.* 313 U.S. 487 (1941), requiring federal courts to apply the choice of law principles of the state in which they sit, should be overruled, and that "the comparative impairment principle should be adopted as the standard for applying both the Rules of Decision Act and the full-faith-and-credit-to-laws mandate."
203 Kay (1980) p. 581; p. 584, note 53.
204 Currie (1963-1) p. 121. *Cf.* Kay (1980) p. 579/580.
205 Baxter (1963) p. 23.
206 Horowitz (1974) p. 747 ff. The other elements in resolving true conflicts would be: consideration of multistate policies (p. 758 ff.) and consideration of relevant interests of the parties (p. 776 ff.).

entails an evaluation of the "better" or "worthier" state policy, it has produced precisely the "super-value judgments" its author rejected.[207]

Baxter defined true conflicts as "cases in which each state has some interest in the application of its law"[208] and was probably not aware of the concept of "moderate and restrained interpretation", Currie's final refinement of his theory. Nor did Horowitz make a distinction between "apparent true conflicts" and "true conflicts". Yet, in *Bernhard v. Harrah's Club*,[209] Justice Sullivan announced that a reconsideration of the forum's interest could be approached under the comparative impairment principle, thus linking Currie's idea of "conflict avoidance" to Baxter's technique of interest evaluation and inviting stern dogmatic criticism from Professor Kay. In her opinion, the comparative impairment approach should be reserved, if at all, for the solution of unavoidable conflicts. Merging the two techniques "has made the courts overly hasty to identify true conflicts," entailing a regrettable lack of patience and precision in the examination of the content of local policy, as well as a tendency to parochialism that places an unnecessary strain on interstate harmony.[210] On the other hand, Strikwerda has pointed out that −unlike Leflar's better law concept, Currie's ultimate forum preference, or Cavers' plaintiff-protective bias− comparative impairment is really more useful as an objective standard to test the relative strength of the respective conflicting interests than as a norm for the final choice between competing rules in an unavoidable conflict. In other words, comparative impairment would enable the court to calibrate the nuances between avoidable and true conflicts to such a degree that the final choice can be evaded in most cases.[211] I agree with Strikwerda that the stages of interest

---

207 Baxter (1963) p. 18. *Cf.* Reppy (1983) p. 677, discussing several California decisions; Kay (1980) p. 609: "It is ironic indeed that California, whose judges had adhered mostly to Currie's teachings, should have succumbed to the temptation to make just the sort of normative judgments about the relative 'values' of competing state policies and interests that he and Baxter both deplored."
208 Baxter (1963) p. 8.
209 *Bernhard v. Harrah's Club* 16 Cal.3d 313, 546 P.2d 719, 128 Cal.Rptr. 215, *cert. denied* 429 U.S. 859 (1976).
210 Kay (1980) 604 ff.
211 Strikwerda (1978) p. 190. I believe that this is the same position as the one taken by Horowitz, who seems to use comparative impairment analysis as a means of relative interest identification. Horowitz (1974) p. 753, viewing "accommodation of

identification and interest-weighing are interrelated and therefore incapable of precise demarcation.[212] For that reason, I fail to perceive the practical value of Professor Kay's dogmatic distinction between conflict-avoidance by moderate and restrained interpretation and conflict-solution by comparative impairment analysis.[213] In my view, both approaches are basically weighing-techniques, each lacking a precise or "normative" weighing-standard. Both are therefore conducive to manipulation, as various commentators of *Bernhard* and *Offshore* have proved implicitly by advancing alternative solutions under either approach.

California was one of the first states to experiment with choice of law methodology. In *Grant v. McAuliffe*, decided in 1953, the California Supreme Court circumvented the *lex loci delicti* standard in a survival action between California parties, by characterizing the survival issue

> state policies as a problem of *allocating domains of law-making power* in multistate contexts – limitations on the *reach* of state policies – as distinguished from evaluating the wisdom of those policies." Emphasis added. *Cf.* Kay (1980) p. 584, criticizing Justice Sullivan's opinion in *Bernhard v. Harrah's Club*: "[Horowitz] would ... bring Baxter's principle into play at the stage at which Currie would have employed moderate and restrained interpretation. In his heroic effort to reconcile the Horowitz 'Restatement' with Currie's method, Sullivan used Currie's terminology, but functionally applied only Horowitz's theory."

212 *Ibid.* p. 175/176; *supra* text accompanying notes 156–159. In this context, "interest-weighing" should be understood as the relative evaluation of competing interests.

213 The two Supreme Court decisions Professor Kay criticizes for merging the two concepts tend to support the view that the outcome need not be different under either approach. In both cases, the decision turned on the interpretation of forum policy. Such an interpretation is both the first step to conflict avoidance by "restraint and moderation", and to an evaluation of the degree to which a forum interest would be impaired by application of the competing rule. Thus, in *Bernhard v. Harrah's Club* 16 Cal.3d 313, 546 P.2d 719, 128 Cal.Rptr. 215, *cert. denied*, 429 U.S. 859 (1976), *infra* notes 233–240 and accompanying text, the conflict could have been avoided by a less "expansive" interpretation of California's common law, or by the concession that Nevada's policy would be more impaired than California's.

In *Offshore Rental Co. v. Continental Oil Co.* 22 Cal.3d 157, 583 P.2d 721, 148 Cal.Rptr. 867 (1978), *infra* notes 245–252 and accompanying text, the outcome would have been different as well, if the court had held to its "assumption" that California had a policy of protecting the employer of key employees, or if it had asserted that California's policy of protecting employers would be more impaired than Louisiana's policy of limiting recovery to non-corporate employers and shielding corporate defendants.

as procedural.[214] In *Emery v. Emery* the law of the family domicile was applied in an intrafamily suit between California family members involved in an accident in Idaho.[215] Subsequent decisions gradually tended towards interest analysis,[216] until this approach was explicitly embraced for multistate torts in *Reich v. Purcell*, decided in 1967.[217] It should be noted that in all of these cases the majority opinion was written by (Chief) Justice Roger J. Traynor. *Reich v. Purcell* is California's answer to *Babcock v. Jackson*. The decision stirred a lot of excitement[218] since it did away with the vestiges of *lex loci delicti*, but in reality the case presented a fairly ordinary false conflict, with a little intertemporal twist. Plaintiffs were residents of Ohio, but when the car accident that gave rise to the action occurred, they were on their way to California where they contemplated settling permanently; the defendant happened to be a Californian. Missouri, the state where the two cars collided, limited recovery in wrongful death actions, while neither Ohio nor California had such a limitation. It was held that Ohio law applied, since California was thought to be a disinterested forum, whereas Missouri could only be interested in the regulation of conduct, not in the compensation of non-resident beneficiaries at the expense of a non-resident defendant. In essence, *Reich v. Purcell* presented a no-conflict situation between California and Ohio, and a false conflict as far as Missouri was concerned.

This line of reasoning was quickly adopted by the California Court of Appeal, not always to the satisfaction of California's Supreme Court. In *Ryan v. Clark Equipment Company*,[219] plaintiff's decedent had been killed in an accident in Oregon in the course of his employment by an Oregon corporation. His widow, an Oregon resident, brought an action in California against the manufacturer of the allegedly defec-

---

214 *Grant v. McAuliffe* 41 Cal.2d 859, 264 P.2d 944 (1953); an alternative characterization made the issue one of administration of decedents' estates.
215 *Emery v. Emery* 45 Cal.2d 421, 289 P.2d 218 (1955), discussed *supra* section 2, text accompanying notes 49–52.
216 *People v. One 1953 Ford Victoria* 48 Cal.2d 595, 311 P.2d 480 (1957): forfeiture of chattel mortgagee's interest; *Bernkrant v. Fowler* 55 Cal.2d 588, 12 Cal.Rptr 266, 360 P.2d 906 (1961): validity of an oral agreement to make a will.
217 *Reich v. Purcell* 67 Cal.2d 551, 432 P.2d 727, 63 Cal.Rptr. 31 (1967).
218 See *e.g.* the Comments on *Reich v. Purcell* by Cavers, Cheatham, David Currie, Ehrenzweig, Gorman, Horowitz, Kay, Leflar, Rosenberg, Scoles, Trautman, and Weintraub in 15 *U.C.L.A. L.Rev.* 556–647 (1968).
219 *Ryan v. Clark Equipment Company* 268 Cal.App.2d 679, 74 Cal.Rptr. 329 (1969).

tive vehicle her husband had been operating. The defendant was a Michigan corporation doing business in Oregon and California. Oregon law limited recovery for wrongful death, while Michigan law did not. Oregon's limitation was applied on the grounds that Oregon, both the state where the accident occurred and where the decedent's family resided, was the only state having a "real" interest in the compensation of the decedent's survivors. By construing away Michigan's possible interest in the regulation of manufacturers' activities, the court was able to decide *Ryan* as a false conflict. However, the California Supreme Court would have reversed the decision, had it been asked to do so. Rejecting *Ryan* as supportive of defendant's position in *Hurtado v. Superior Court of Sacramento County*, the court took the opportunity to criticize the Court of Appeal for failing to see that *Ryan* had presented a true conflict, as both Oregon and Michigan had a legitimate interest in the measure of damages. Michigan had an interest in subjecting a Michigan corporation to unlimited liability for committing a tortious act in Michigan, in order to deter such conduct. Oregon's policy of limiting damages, on the other hand, gave that state an interest, not (as the Court of Appeal had deduced from *Reich*) in the compensation of survivors, but in the protection of resident defendants from excessive liability. In *Ryan*, "[t]he defendant manufacturing corporation, while not incorporated in Oregon, was lawfully doing business there and Oregon had an interest extending to such a resident business entity in applying that state's limitation of damages in order to protect such defendant's financial security."[220] Unfortunately, the *Hurtado* opinion did not reveal how this true conflict in a disinterested third state[221] should have been solved.

---

220 *Hurtado v. Superior Court of Sacramento County* 11 Cal.3d 574, 114 Cal.Rptr. 106, 522 P.2d 666 at 673 (1974), discussed *supra*, section 3, text following note 105. "To the extent that any language in Ryan v. Clark Equipment Co. is inconsistent with this opinion it is disapproved." *Ibid.* p. 674.
221 Reppy (1983) p. 669/670, has characterized *Ryan* as an unprovided-for case ("a zero-interest or true-disinterested conflict"), on the assumption that such cases arise when "the law of the plaintiff's domicile favors defendant, and vice versa." *Ibid.* p. 648. However, in the opinion of the Supreme Court, Michigan had an interest in deterrence, Oregon in the protection of defendants doing business in Oregon. Whether or not Reppy's definition ignores the possibility of territorial interests (I think it does), it proves to be narrower than judicial practice will have it. *Cf.* Horowitz (1974) p. 745. →

Another dubious decision by the California Court of Appeal is *Kasel v. Remington Arms Co.* The action arose out of a hunting accident in Mexico in which a California citizen was injured. In Mexico, he had bought defective ammunition, manufactured in Mexico by a Mexican corporation, affiliated to defendant. One of the shells caused plaintiff's gun to explode, injuring his hand. California law allowed the plaintiff to sue the manufacturer's American parent company under a strict product liability theory, whereas Mexican law limited both the standard of liability and the measure of damages. The Court of Appeal dismissed as insignificant any interest Mexico might have in protecting Mexican manufacturers from excessive liability since no Mexican citizen was involved in the litigation.[222] That left California's interest in the compensation of injured Californians, or, more generally, the interest of the victim's home state: in respect of the compensation of its domiciliaries, that state would have "the greatest interest."[223] By belittling Mexico's interest to the point of irrelevance, the court unnecessarily turned a true conflict[224] into a false one. If the court had acknowledged that absolving the American parent company

> Since Clark Equipment Co. was not only doing business in Oregon but in California as well – probably the basis of California jurisdiction – it is remarkable that neither the Court of Appeal in *Ryan* nor the Supreme Court in *Hurtado* found it necessary to discuss the possible interests of the forum state.
> Duintjer Tebbens (1979) p. 253 viewed the *Ryan* case as "a classic example of (unsuccessful) forum shopping." In his opinion, "the real ratio decidendi of the case is that forum shopping should not be rewarded." However, since the *Hurtado* court viewed *Ryan* as a true conflict, forum shopping in California could prove to be quite advantageous to plaintiffs from defendant-favoring states suing manufacturers from consumer-protecting states, California belonging to the latter category. *Cf. infra* text accompanying note 228.

222 The court saw no need to consider the laws of Delaware, the state of incorporation, or Connecticut, the state where Remington had its headquarters, since neither party had pleaded applicability of these laws. This is another illustration of the disparity between interest analysis and a restrictive approach to notice and proof of foreign law, discussed *supra* chapter 2, section 4.
223 *Kasel v. Remington Arms Co.* 101 Cal.Rptr. 314, 24 Cal.App.3d 711 at 734 (1972). The *Kasel* decision has been criticized by Duintjer Tebbens (1979) p. 255, for its circular reasoning: the fact that the defendant was an American company eclipsed any interest of Mexico, but Remington could only be *made* a defendant if California's strict product liability rule applied.
224 *Cf.* Horowitz (1974) p. 751: A proper "analysis of Mexican policy would identify a true conflict in *Kasel*. Remington so argued, in effect, by contending that application of California law would result in Remington's shifting the cost of compensating the plaintiff to the Mexican-based enterprise – a consequence which would be contrary to Mexican policy."

from liability would actually advance the Mexican policy of protecting commercial enterprises, it would still have had several options to solve the resulting true conflict in favor of California law.[225]

On closer examination, the policy-oriented California decisions display a remarkable judicial adroitness in turning true conflicts and unprovided-for cases into false conflicts, obviating the need to apply some sophisticated "break device".[226] Apart from *Ryan* and *Kasel*, we have already seen two other examples in *Hurtado v. Superior Court of Sacramento County* and *Hernandez v. Burger*,[227] both cases qualifying, in my opinion, as unprovided-for situations but for the creative construction of an interest on the part of the *locus delicti* state. This tendency to avoid true conflicts might be inherent in the premises of California-style interest analysis, as explained in several opinions: the substantive law of California is *prima facie* applicable and will not be displaced unless one of the parties timely invokes the law of a foreign state and demonstrates that a real interest of that state will be furthered by application of its law without impairing California interests.[228] As a means to conflict avoidance, the false conflict construction may be based on "moderate and restrained interpretation"[229] or interest-weighing.[230] Apparently, the latter approach was followed in *Kasel*

---

225 It could have followed Currie's *lex fori* presumption, or Baxter's comparative impairment principle. Horowitz (1974) p. 751, claims that the court did apply the Baxter test. No visible trace of it is found in the opinion, however.
226 I owe the phrase to Reppy (1983) p. 646 and *passim*.
227 *Hurtado v. Superior Court of Sacramento County* 11 Cal.3d 574, 522 P.2d 666, 114 Cal.Rptr. 106 (1974), *supra*, section 3, text following note 105; *Hernandez v. Burger* 102 Cal.App.3d 795, 162 Cal.Rptr. 564 (1980), *supra* section 3, text following note 108.
228 E.g.: *Beech Aircraft Corp. v. Superior Court* 132 Cal.Rptr. 541, 61 Cal.App.3d 501 at 522 (1976); *Camp v. Forwarders Transport, Inc.* 537 F.Supp. 636 at 638 (C.D. Cal. 1982); *Fleury v. Harper & Row, Publishers, Inc.* 698 F.2d 1022 at 1025 (9th Cir. [Cal.] 1983). See, however, *Cable v. Sahara Tahoe Corp.* 93 Cal.App.3d 384, 155 Cal.Rptr. 770 at 776 (1979): "Earlier notions that the law of the forum was controlling in the absence of a 'compelling reason' for displacing it ... have no place in the comparative impairment equation."
229 This approach was announced but not followed in *James v. Bell Helicopter Co.* 715 F.2d 166 at 169 (5th Cir. [Tex./Cal.] 1983).
230 *Strassberg v. New England Mut. Life Ins. Co.* 575 F.2d 1262 at 1264 (9th Cir. [Cal.] 1978): "Therefore, if application of a foreign decisional rule will not *significantly* advance the interests of the foreign state, a California court will conclude that the conflict is 'false' and apply its own law." Emphasis added.

and *Ryan*.[231] Consequently, comparative impairment was mentioned in many opinions as the California solution to true conflicts[232] but the courts rarely put it to the test of practice.

The first opportunity for the California Supreme Court to demonstrate the workings of Baxter's theory came in *Bernhard v. Harrah's Club*,[233] a true conflict between the interests of California and Nevada. The defendant was a Nevada corporation that owned and operated a gambling casino in Nevada for which it advertised in other states, including California. It became a party to this litigation through the intoxication of one of its patrons, a Californian who had been served too many alcoholic beverages in the course of a night's entertainment at the casino. While still in an intoxicated state he drove back to California and collided there head-on with a motorcycle operated by the plaintiff, also a California resident. Plaintiff alleged that Harrah's Club had been negligent in furnishing alcoholic beverages to someone already intoxicated and that such negligence was the proximate cause of his injury. Nevada law did not impose liability for plaintiff's injuries on the tavern keeper,[234] whereas he would be liable under a fairly

---

231 *Kasel v. Remington Arms Co.* 24 Cal.App.3d 711, 101 Cal.Rptr. 314 at 330 (1972): California's interest in the compensation of its residents "*outweighs* any interest Mexico may have in regulation of its own manufacturers." *Ryan v. Clark Equipment Company* 268 Cal.App.2d 679, 74 Cal.Rptr. 329 at 331 (1969): "Oregon's interest in the compensation of her residents for wrongful death *overrides* any possible concern of Michigan in the regulation of the activities of manufacturers." Emphasis added.
232 In *Gallagher v. Koppers Co., Inc.* 191 Cal.Rptr. 241 (Cal. App. 1983), a product liability action, the Court of Appeal was obviously confused. Referring to § 146 and § 6 of the Restatement Second, the opinion stated that "[g]enerally speaking in tort actions" the law of the place of injury would be applied unless some other state had a more significant relationship. Governmental interest analysis was viewed as "another consideration" advanced by the Restatement, yet "required only when there is a true 'conflict' in that two or more states have a legitimate interest in having their laws applied." In such cases, the court went on, comparative impairment should be the decisive criterion. *Ibid.* p. 244.
233 *Bernhard v. Harrah's Club* 16 Cal.3d 313, 546 P.2d 719, 128 Cal.Rptr. 215, *cert. denied* 429 U.S. 859 (1976).
234 In *Hamm v. Carson City Nuggett, Inc.* 85 Nev. 99, 450 P.2d 358 (1969), the Nevada Supreme Court had held that violation of a criminal statute, prohibiting the sale of liquor to intoxicated persons or habitual drunkards, did not constitute negligence *per se*. Absent legislative action, the court was unwilling to extend civil liability to the tavern owner.

recent California judge-made rule.[235] Since Nevada had an obvious interest in shielding the defendant, and California in protecting the plaintiff, the court quickly discovered that "in the instant case for the first time since applying governmental interest analysis as a choice of law doctrine in *Reich*, we are confronted with a 'true' conflicts case."[236] Merging Currie's moderate and restrained interpretation with Baxter's comparative impairment analysis,[237] the court then proceeded to "re-examine" the policy underlying California's dramshop law, and found that the imposition of liability on tavern keepers was meant to "prevent tavern keepers from selling alcoholic beverages to obviously intoxicated persons *who are likely to act in California* in the intoxicated state."[238] Since defendant had advertised in California and had solicited the business of Californians, it had "put itself at the heart of California's regulatory interest."[239] On the premise that Nevada already subjected tavern owners to criminal penalties under a statute prohibiting the sale of liquor to intoxicated persons, whether from Nevada or from California,[240] the court concluded that Nevada's policy of shielding tavern owners from civil liability would not be significantly impaired by application of California law, as (civil) liability would only be imposed on Nevada tavern owners actively soliciting California patronage: their increased economic exposure should be considered as a foreseeable and insurable business risk.

---

235 *Veseley v. Sager* 5 Cal.3d 153, 485 P.2d 151, 95 Cal.Rptr. 623 (1971). Under this rule, civil liability would result from violation of a California criminal statute (section 25602 of the Business and Professions Code). The defendant in *Bernhard* argued that application of California law to the issue in this case would give the California criminal statute an extraterritorial effect. However, the Supreme Court extended the scope of the *Veseley* decision by imposing civil liability "on the basis of negligence apart from statute." *Bernhard v. Harrah's Club* 546 P.2d 719 at 727 (1976). Legislative repeal abolished the entire doctrine of liability of tavern owners and social hosts: *cf. Cable v. Sahara Tahoe Corp.* 93 Cal.App.3d 384, 155 Cal.Rptr. 770 (1979); Kay (1980) p. 585, note 43; *infra* text accompanying notes 241–244.
236 *Bernhard v. Harrah's Club* 16 Cal.3d 313, 128 Cal.Rptr. 215, 546 P.2d 719 at 722 (1976).
237 Much to the distress of Professor Kay (1980) p. 583 ff.
238 *Bernhard v. Harrah's Club* 546 P.2d 719 at 725 (1976); emphasis added.
239 *Ibid.*
240 However, Nevada's criminal statute was repealed in 1973, two years after the accident that gave rise to *Bernhard* occurred: Odwald (1976) p. 114. This might indicate a regressing Nevada policy in respect of the regulation of tavern owners: *cf.* Case Note, Bernhard v. Harrah's Club etc., 1976 *Brigham Young U. L.Rev.* 953 at 969 (1976); Weintraub (1980) p. 323.

The opposite result was reached in *Cable v. Sahara Tahoe Corp.*, again involving a California-domiciled plaintiff and a Nevada tavern owner.[241] This time, however, plaintiff suffered injuries as a result of a car accident in *Nevada*, where she temporarily resided. A second difference with *Bernhard* was the fact that, in the meantime, the California legislature had abrogated the decisions extending the liability of commercial and noncommercial suppliers of alcoholic beverages: by amending the relevant statutory provisions it reinstated the rule that the furnishing of alcoholic beverages is not the proximate cause of injuries resulting from intoxication.[242] On the assumption that application of (former) California law would still impose liability on defendant, the Court of Appeal had to decide the case as a true conflict, to be solved under the comparative impairment approach. It distinguished *Bernhard* by defining the scope of California's policy as limited to "Nevada conduct causing injury in *California*,"[243] and by determining that, contrary to *Bernhard*, there was no logical connection between defendant's advertising campaigns in California and plaintiff's injuries, since they had been inflicted upon her by an intoxicated Nevada resident. In the court's final analysis, the only forum interest in this case rested on plaintiff's status as a California domiciliary who would probably become a public charge. That did not suffice to indicate a serious impairment of California policy by application of Nevada law. The controlling factor in this case, however, seems to be the "lack of currency" of California's regulatory policy since its repudiation: " ... it is obvious that the impairment of such a repudiated policy has a minimal effect upon California's governmental interest."[244]

Better law overtones seem to have directed the result of the comparative impairment analysis in *Offshore Rental Co. v. Continental Oil*

---

241 *Cable v. Sahara Tahoe Corp.* 93 Cal.App.3d 384, 155 Cal.Rptr. 770 (1979).
242 The amendments dated from 1978, whereas Miss Cable's accident occurred in 1975, but an amendment does not necessarily nullify an existing cause of action: *Cable v. Sahara Tahoe Corp.* 93 Cal.App.3d 384 at 398, 155 Cal.Rptr. 770 at 779 (1979).
243 Rather than injury to *Californians*. 93 Cal.App.3d 396, 155 Cal.Rptr. 778; emphasis added.
244 *Cable v. Sahara Tahoe Corp.* 93 Cal.App.3d 384 at 398, 155 Cal.Rptr. 770 at 779 (1979).

Co.²⁴⁵ The plaintiff in this case was a California corporation with its principal place of business in California but also doing extensive business in Louisiana. One of its vice-presidents, at the time of the accident a resident of Texas, flew from Houston to Louisiana for a business meeting with defendant's representatives. While waiting to be taken to an offshore drilling site he was injured on the Louisiana premises of defendant's enterprise. Continental Oil was a Delaware corporation with headquarters in New York doing business in California and Louisiana. Although the victim was compensated by Continental Oil, the corporation he worked for brought an action to recover no less than five million dollars in damages for loss of services of a "key employee". Louisiana law barred such an action if, as in this case, the employer was a corporate entity and the employee qualified as a "free servant".²⁴⁶ In California, on the other hand, no such distinction had ever been made in respect of the "relatively obscure section of the California Civil Code"²⁴⁷ that permitted recovery for loss of services. Expressly rejecting the *lex fori* solution to true conflicts, the Supreme Court referred to the theories of Baxter and Horowitz to support its intention to apply the comparative impairment principle. It described this approach as an attempt "to determine the relative commitments of the respective states involved" with the help of "the history and current status of the states' laws; the function and purpose of those laws."²⁴⁸ Since the court had already determined that both California and Louisiana, in view of the policies underlying their respective laws, had an interest in the outcome of this case,²⁴⁹ little more was said about the "function and

---

245 *Offshore Rental Co. v. Continental Oil Co.* 22 Cal.3d 157, 583 P.2d 721, 148 Cal.Rptr. 867 (1978).
246 *Offshore Rental Co. v. Continental Oil Co.* 583 P.2d 721, 22 Cal.3d 157 at 162, 148 Cal.Rptr. 867 at 870 (1978); *cf.* Kay (1980) p. 587. The Louisiana Civil Code (article 174), allowing the master to bring "an action against any man for beating or maiming his servant," had been thus interpreted in a domestic case: *Bonfanti Industries, Inc. v. Teke, Inc.* 224 So.2d 15 (La. App. 1969), *aff'd* 226 So.2d 770 (La. 1969).
247 Kay (1980) p. 586; Cal. Civ. Code § 49(c).
248 *Offshore Rental Co. v. Continental Oil Co.* 583 P.2d 721, 22 Cal.3d 157 at 166, 148 Cal.Rptr. 867 at 873 (1978).
249 Louisiana was said to have a policy of "protect[ing] negligent resident tort-feasors acting within Louisiana's borders from the financial hardships caused by the assessment of excessive legal liability or exaggerated claims resulting from the loss of services of a key employee." Defendant was "clearly" a member of the class which Louisiana law sought to protect. California, on the other hand, had an "interest in protecting California employers from economic harm because of negligent injury →

purpose" of the conflicting laws, except for a cryptic remark on the relevance of the place of the wrong: "At the heart of Louisiana's denial of liability lies the vital interest in promoting freedom of investment and enterprise *within Louisiana's borders*, among investors incorporated both in Louisiana and elsewhere."[250] The key to the *Offshore* decision is in the court's emphasis on the history and current status of the conflicting laws. Recovery for loss of an employee's services is viewed as "obsolete", "hoary", "antique", "archaic", "isolated", "unusual" and "outmoded", whereas the Louisiana courts were said to have joined the "main stream of American jurisdictions" by shaping its statutory provision into the "prevalent", "progressive", "compelling", "stronger", "more current" rule it is now.[251] The conclusion is hardly surprising: application of the California statute is denied since it "has historically been of minimal importance in the fabric of California law" and because "Louisiana's interests would be the more impaired if its law were not applied."[252]

The federal courts that, pursuant to the *Klaxon* doctrine, have been obliged to apply California conflicts law, have struggled with comparative impairment analysis as well.[253] In *Camp v. Forwarders Transport, Inc.*, the district court dutifully applied the principles of governmental interest analysis, emphasizing the need to identify the "actual

---

to a key employee inflicted by a third party." Its policy of protection would not be limited to occurrences within California, "since California's economy and tax revenues are affected regardless of the situs of physical injury." *Ibid.* 22 Cal.3d 157 at 164, 148 Cal.Rptr. 867 at 871.

250 *Ibid.* 22 Cal.3d 157 at 168, 148 Cal.Rptr. 867 at 874; emphasis in the original. It could be asked how this consideration would have affected the outcome if Offshore had sued Continental for loss of services of a key employee injured *outside* Louisiana.

251 *Ibid.* 22 Cal.3d 157 at 166 ff., 148 Cal.Rptr. 867 at 872 ff. (*passim*). The court borrowed some of these phrases from Freund (1946) p. 1216, 1224. "The strength with which a state's policy is held" (22 Cal.3d 165, 148 Cal.Rptr. 872) is a factor derived from the functional approach advocated by Von Mehren and Trautman (1965) p. 377; *cf.* Kay (1980) p. 588.

252 *Ibid.* 22 Cal.3d 157 at 169, 148 Cal.Rptr. 867 at 875.

253 *In re Paris Air Crash of March 3, 1974* 399 F.Supp. 732 (C.D. Cal. 1975) was an action arising from the crash of a Turkish Air Lines plane in France. It was decided before *Bernhard v. Harrah's Club* and no mention was made of comparative impairment. It was held that the interests of "both California and the United States" outweighed any interest of any other state or nation in the determination of the measure of damages. →

stake, as opposed to the hypothetical interest, that the potentially concerned states have in the litigation."[254] The action, which arose out of a fatal automobile accident in Oklahoma, involved plaintiffs from California and a corporate defendant having its principal place of business in New Jersey. The most difficult issue in this case, to be solved with the help of comparative impairment, turned out to be plaintiffs' standing to sue for wrongful death. New Jersey law limited the class of persons having standing to sue in wrongful death actions to those entitled to take intestate property of the decedent, whereas California allowed all members of the decedent's immediate family to bring the action. Since California's wrongful death statute manifested a policy to protect the decedent's family members and dependents, whether they were his heirs or not, and since the plaintiffs were California residents who might have to seek public assistance if they were denied recovery, it was clear that California had an interest in having its law applied. New Jersey, on the other hand, would have "an interest in the protection of its resident corporations from excessive damage awards in wrongful death cases."[255] The court then proceeded to apply the comparative impairment test. First, it noted, application of New Jersey law would leave the plaintiffs totally empty-handed, since it did not merely reduce the amount of damages but barred the plaintiffs from any remedy.[256] Second, the New Jersey defendant carried liability insurance and could pass on the costs of insurance or a damage award to its customers through the operation of the market mecha-

---

In *Browne v. McDonnell Douglas Corp.* 504 F.Supp. 514 (N.D. Cal. 1980), a products liability action brought by plaintiffs from several countries against the California-based manufacturer of an airplane that had crashed in Yugoslavia, the court used comparative impairment analysis to discover a false conflict. This might have been an instance of "moderate and restrained interpretation" by a fusion of governmental interest analysis with comparative impairment, along the lines of Horowitz's theory; see: *supra* note 211.

254 *Camp v. Forwarders Transport, Inc.* 537 F.Supp. 636 at 638 (C.D. Cal. 1982), citing *Strassberg v. New England Mutual Life Ins. Co.* 575 F.2d 1262 (9th Cir. [Cal.] 1979), in which case the Ninth Circuit referred in turn to *Hurtado*. See also: *Bernhard v. Harrah's Club* 16 Cal.3d 313, 128 Cal.Rptr. 215, 546 P.2d 719 at 723 (1976): "This process of reexamination requires identification of a 'real interest as opposed to a hypothetical interest on the part of the forum." Here, the reference was to Sedler (1971-2) p. 224.

255 *Camp v. Forwarders Transport, Inc.* 537 F.Supp. 636 at 641 (C.D. Cal. 1982).

256 *Ibid.* p. 642.

nism.[257] Third, New Jersey should not be allowed to profit from its decision to "attract industry by creating a relatively lax wrongful death statute at the cost of depriving some of the state's residents of damages attributable to defendant's negligence."[258] For these reasons, California's interests would be "gravely impaired" if New Jersey law was applied. Again, the result seems to be carried by a better law consideration.

A different approach, illustrative of the versatility of comparative impairment analysis, was chosen by the Seventh Circuit when it had to apply California choice of law principles in *In re Air Crash Disaster near Chicago, Illinois on May 25, 1979*.[259] The central issue in this case focused on the question whether punitive damages should be paid by the manufacturer and the owner of a plane that had crashed in Illinois, allegedly due to "egregious" manufacture and maintenance. Whereas the plaintiffs were domiciled in various states and countries, the manufacturer was a Maryland corporation doing business in Missouri; the airplane had been designed and built in California. The defendant airline company was a Delaware corporation doing business in New York; its maintenance base was in Oklahoma. Under certain circumstances punitive damages would be allowed by the laws of Missouri and Oklahoma, not by the laws of California and New York. The district court had held that California's interest in shielding the defendant manufacturer from excessive liability was limited, as compared to Missouri's interest in deterring tortious conduct by its resident corporations. In respect of the airline company, Oklahoma's policy would not be severely impaired by application of New York law. In effect, comparative impairment analysis resulted in application of the

---

257 "In contrast, if dependent California residents are deprived of a cause of action and are forced to seek public assistance, the taxpayers of California will bear the burden." *Ibid.*
258 *Ibid.* The court anthropomorphized the State of New Jersey as a "free rider" that "cannot reasonably expect" to "get all the benefit of increased business activity while other states would share the burden created by a lax wrongful death statute."
259 *In re Air Crash Disaster near Chicago, Illinois on May 25, 1979* 644 F.2d 594 (7th Cir. [Cal./Ill.] 1981), *cert. denied sub nom. Lin v. American Airlines, Inc.* 454 U.S. 878 (1981). The various cases arising from the airplane crash were transferred to Illinois by order of the Judicial Panel on Multidistrict Litigation. Under *Erie R. Co. v. Tompkins* 304 U.S. 64, 58 S.Ct. 817, 82 L.Ed. 1188 (1938) and *Van Dusen v. Barrack* 376 U.S. 612 (1964), the transferee court must apply the choice of law rules of the states where the actions were originally filed.

law of principal place of business of each defendant.[260] The circuit court of appeals, however, decided that, in respect of either defendant, both the state of the principal place of business and the state of misconduct had "strong commitments to their respective policies."[261] In a situation in which "the states with the most relevant interests were also determined to have equal interests," the Seventh Circuit resorted to the Illinois *lex loci delicti*, disallowing punitive damages, on the imaginative theory that "Illinois was severely affected by this major disaster and Illinois also has strong interests in the protection of airplane-related industries."[262] Once more we have come full circle to the original conflicts rule.

It is a fair guess that application of comparative impairment analysis by a Nevada court in *Bernhard*, a New Jersey court in *Camp*, or a court sitting in Missouri or Oklahoma in *In re Air Crash Disaster near Chicago* would have produced the opposite result in each case.[263] This would suggest that comparative impairment is not the objective standard that Baxter meant it to be, and that state courts are not in a position to solve true conflicts by "normative criteria".[264] In my opinion, judicial application of the theory is arbitrary and manipulative. The California experience reveals that comparative impairment analysis is used as a cloak for eclecticism covering a number of distinct

260 *In re Air Crash Disaster near Chicago, Illinois on May 25, 1979* 500 F.Supp. 1044 (N.D. Ill. 1980).
261 *In re Air Crash Disaster near Chicago, Illinois on May 25, 1979* 644 F.2d 594 at 625 (7th Cir. [Cal./Ill.] 1981).
262 *Ibid.* p. 625/626; see also: *supra* chapter 3, text accompanying notes 95–100. The Ninth Circuit also applied California choice of law in *In re Pago Pago Aircrash of January 30, 1974* 692 F.2d 764 (9th Cir. [Cal.] 1982) and held that the law of the principal place of business of the defendant airplane manufacturer (Washington) applied, freeing the manufacturer of liability, rather than the *lex loci delicti* of American Samoa. *Cf.* Case Note: What Law Applies? In re Pago Pago Aircrash etc., 1982 *Tr. Law. Guide* 1079–1100.
263 In respect of the *Bernhard* decision, several commentators have expressed this view: Note, Choice of Law for True Conflicts, 65 *Calif. L.Rev.* 290, p. 303 (1977); Leflar (1977-2) p. 22; Kay (1980) p. 606/607; Weintraub (1980) p. 324.
264 Nor federal courts, for that matter, as long as they have to be faithful to the choice of law principles of the jurisdiction in which they sit. In *Day & Zimmermann, Inc. v. Challoner* 423 U.S. 3, 96 S.Ct. 167, 46 L.Ed.2d 3 (1975), the U.S. Supreme Court made it clear that federal courts are still bound to the *Klaxon* doctrine. *Cf. supra* section 1, note 22. Having traced the history of the full faith and credit clause, Baxter (1963) p. 41/42, came to the conclusion that "*Klaxon* should be overturned." *Cf. supra* note 202.

policy-oriented approaches as well as ordinary jurisdiction-selection. Wrapped in sophisticated language, the California decisions display a methodological inconsistency that does not speak well for the viability of Baxter's theory. Barely concealed by the "comparative pertinence" phraseology, the *ratio decidendi* in *Offshore* and *Camp* is essentially the better law consideration.[265] *Offshore* could double as an example of a no-conflict solution, since it was likely that a modern interpretation of California's "obscure" substantive law would have absolved the corporate tortfeasor from liability for the loss of services of plaintiff's key employee. In *Bernhard*, I feel, the court did "what comes naturally" and applied its own law to resolve a dispute in which Nevada's interest was certainly no less than California's.[266] In effect, it followed Currie's recommendation to apply *lex fori* whenever there is no good reason for doing otherwise.[267] The reasoning in *Cable* could be explained as an instance of moderate and restrained interpretation: California had at best an interest in the compensation of a California plaintiff (not – as in *Bernhard* – in the deterrence of wrongful conduct in California) but Miss Cable's ties with her home state were tenuous, since she was living and working in Nevada when the accident occurred.[268]

265 *Offshore Rental Co. v. Continental Oil Co.* 22 Cal.3d 157, 583 P.2d 721, 148 Cal.Rptr. 867 (1978); *Camp v. Forwarders Transport, Inc.* 537 F.Supp. 636 (C.D. Cal. 1982). As to *Offshore* see: McDougal (1984) p. 483, note 2, p. 507; Reppy (1983) p. 674; Hay (1981) p. 1660, note 95; Kay (1980) p. 589, note 82; Juenger (1980) p. 421/422; Kanowitz (1978) p. 297 ff.
266 *Bernhard v. Harrah's Club* 16 Cal.3d 313, 546 P.2d 719, 128 Cal.Rptr. 215 (1976), *cert. denied* 419 U.S. 859 (1976). According to Reppy (1983) p. 671, comparative impairment analysis was misapplied in *Bernhard*: application of California law defeated Nevada's interest in the protection of resident tavern keepers "one hundred percent", while "California's interest in seeing a California tort victim receive compensation would not have been wholly sacrificed by the application of Nevada law, since the victim had already had a cause of action against the drunk tortfeasor or could recover against his own insurer if the drunk had no liability insurance."
267 Currie (1963-1) p. 119: "The sensible and clearly constitutional thing for any court to do, confronted with a true conflict of interests, is to apply its own law. In this way it can be sure at least that it is consistently advancing the policy of its own state. It should apply its own law ... simply because a court should never apply any other law except when there is a good reason for doing so." See also: *supra*, section 3, notes 86–87 and accompanying text.
268 *Cable v. Sahara Tahoe Corp.* 93 Cal.App.3d 384, 155 Cal.Rptr. 770 (1979). *Cf.* Kay (1980) p. 595 ff., p. 593: "I submit that the analysis performed in *Cable*, while cast in the language of comparative impairment, is an example of moderate and restrained reinterpretation of the forum's policy." See also: *Browne v. McDonnell Douglas Corp.* 504 F.Supp. 514 (N.D. Cal. 1980), *supra* note 253. →

A return to jurisdiction-selection seems to have decided the airplane disaster cases. The district court in *In re Air Crash Disaster near Chicago* identified the state whose interest would be most severely impaired with defendant's place of principal business, not on the basis of careful interest evaluation but as an abstract and general rule.[269] Territorial considerations, on the other hand, governed the result the Seventh Circuit reached in that case, and might have influenced the court in *Offshore*.[270] In neither case the interests of the *locus delicti* state supported the emphasis on the place of the wrong in the courts' opinions. I submit that the comparative impairment approach, contrary to its author's intentions, primarily functions as a cover-up device for result-selective *ad hoc* decisions. Even if the analysis is performed in a conscientious manner, the opinions are unconvincing and give the impression that the same results could have been reached in a less roundabout way, without the courts wrapping them in quasi-normative reasoning.

As a tool of policy-oriented choice of law comparative impairment analysis has limited possibilities. Designed to solve only true conflicts, it offers no guidance in the process of assessing policies and interests in order to classify the case as a true, false, or unprovided-for conflict.[271]

To the extent that the recent legislative action on tavern owners' liability (see text accompanying note 242) could be viewed as an attempt to improve California's substantive law, the *Cable* decision could also be explained in terms of the better law approach. However, there was an obvious split of opinion between California's legislature and judiciary on the question what constituted the "better" law.

269 *In re Air Crash Disaster near Chicago, Illinois on May 25, 1979* 500 F.Supp. 1044 (N.D. Ill. 1980): "As we stated previously, where the law of the principal place of business conflicts with the place where the particular conduct occurred, *generally* the former should prevail." Emphasis added. See also *In re Pago Pago Aircrash of January 30, 1974* 692 F.2d 764 (9th Cir. [Cal.] 1982), *supra* note 262.

270 *In re Air Crash Disaster near Chicago, Illinois on May 25, 1979* 644 F.2d 594 (7th Cir. [Cal./Ill.] 1981).

271 Theoretically, comparative impairment analysis could be used as a "more or less objective standard to determine the relative weight of conflicting governmental interests, or, to use Currie's phrase, as an instrument 'to construe away the conflict'." Strikwerda (1978) p. 190; *cf. supra* text accompanying notes 211–213. In that sense, it would serve conflict avoidance through "moderate and restrained interpretation" rather than the solution of real conflicts. In judicial practice, however, comparative impairment is invoked to support any form of intuitive interest-weighing, which would neither be acceptable to Currie nor to Baxter. *Cf.* Kay (1980) p. 580, p. 583 ff., p. 604 ff.

It is incapable of solving unprovided-for cases since it is impossible to calculate to which degree a non-existent interest will be impaired by application of the other state's law.[272] As to true conflicts, comparative impairment is hardly a viable criterion, even in theory, since it can only be used as a "break device" in the few cases in which application of one state's law will not completely defeat the other state's interest. In the usual true conflict situation, "the states with the most relevant interests are also determined to have equal interests."[273] All in all, I am not convinced of the merits of Baxter's theory. Considering the questionable use the courts have made of it, I think that the comparative impairment approach has failed to provide the normative solution to true conflicts Baxter promised. As applied in practice, it is no worse than other solutions to this dilemma, but it is hardly any better.

c Territorial solutions

The last type of solution I should like to discuss covers two normative approaches which have in common that they both feature the place of wrong as a prominent and ultimately decisive factor. Despite their methodological contrasts, the "principles of preference" devised by Professor David F. Cavers and the black letter rules of the Restatement Second tend to lead to the same result when it comes to breaking a tie in tort choice of law. As applied to the true conflict dilemma, the territorial bias inherent in Cavers' "principles" corresponds to the *lex loci* presumption pervading the Restatement's chapter on torts, inasmuch as they both rest on a "principled preference" for a territorial break device. For that reason, and well aware of methodological objections, I have ventured to bring the two together under one territorial heading.

---

272 *Cf.* Reppy (1983) p. 671, note 127: "It should be observed that comparative impairment cannot be used as a device to break true-disinterested or zero-interest conflicts ... In this situation neither state has an interest to be impaired."

273 *In re Air Crash Disaster near Chicago, Illinois on May 25, 1979* 644 F.2d 594 at 625 (7th Cir. [Cal./Ill.] 1981). See also *supra* text accompanying note 256. *Cf.* Reppy (1983) p. 671, note 130: "[A]pplication of either law arguably results in a 100 % wipe-out of the other state's interest." Besides, if comparative impairment would be a self-sufficient "break device", the California courts would not have felt the need to complement this criterion with additional principles, as "restated" by Horowitz (1974) p. 747 ff. *Supra* notes 206–207 and accompanying text.

Throughout his academic career, Professor Cavers has been searching for a choice of law method that would promote justice in the individual case as well as certainty and predictability. In a seminal article, published in 1933, he criticized the blindfold jurisdiction-selecting method for ignoring the substance of the relevant rules of law, and put forward an "academic proposal" for a process of comparative analysis and evaluation of the competing laws.[274] Against the objection that such an *ad hoc* approach would preclude the attainment of certainty or uniformity, Cavers suggested that *stare decisis* would exert a stabilizing influence, at least in those cases "wherein the patterns of fact and of substantive domestic laws are constantly reduplicated in experience."[275] Gradually, the courts would develop standards for the evaluation of multistate law-fact patterns until, eventually, a new body of rules would emerge, capable of achieving "just decisions." We know now that it has taken several decades before the American courts came to accept the basic proposition of the approach Cavers advocated: choice of law issues should be decided by an evaluation of competing rules of substantive law in relation to the facts. We also know, however, that judicial practice has not succeeded in stabilizing the policy-oriented choice of law process by the development of reliable and consistent guides for decision. Attempting to demonstrate the feasibility of such affirmative principles, Cavers used his classroom experience to formulate "reasonable grounds for preferring one state's law to another's in situations where their conflict could not be held false or readily avoided."[276] These efforts resulted in seven "principles of preference" meant to provide a "rational basis" for the solution of true conflicts.[277] It should be noted, once again, that Cavers considered his proposals as

---

274 Cavers (1933) p. 192 ff. In his "critique" of the territorial view and the vested rights theory, Cavers joined earlier critics in their attack on "deductive methodology", notably Cook (1924) and Lorenzen (1924), at the same time disagreeing with them about the proper alternative; *cf.* Cavers (1965) p. 7 ff.
275 Cavers (1933) p. 196. On several occasions, Cavers has emphasized that he never meant to advocate a "free law" approach and that his concept of "justice in the individual case" was quite compatible with choice of law rules, as long as those rules "were formulated with a view to producing results consistent with fairness to the parties and with concern for the policies underlying the competing laws." Cavers (1972) p. 169 = Cavers (1976) p. 654. See also: Cavers (1965) p. 75 ff.
276 Cavers (1965) p. 133.
277 They were published in 1965 in *The Choice-of-Law Process*. Principles 1–5 cover multistate torts (p. 139 ff.), but the fifth principle (p. 177) is included for the sake of argument and subsequently rejected; see *infra* note 285. Principles 6 and 7 (p. 181 ff.) deal with contracts and conveyances.

"academic ideas" that were addressed "to the law schools rather than to the courts, just as in 1933."[278] This explains why the principles "do not form a system," why they cover just a few legal categories, and why their terms are broad enough to allow conversion of the principles into sets of specific rules for distinct situations.[279] Nevertheless, it was Cavers' hope "that principles of the sort I have been advancing here may ultimately become part of the judicial process for choice of law."[280]

The principles of preference are structured as conflicts rules, "painfully reminiscent of the *Restatement* black letter."[281] Indeed, their composition and wording would not preclude their application out of the policy-oriented context in which they were created. They are premised on the assumption that the choice of law process is neutral and unbiased, in the sense that any legal rule, whether foreign or domestic, is eligible for application on the premise of equality, provided the requirements of a particular principle of preference are met.[282] However, since Cavers conceived his principles as generalized solutions to *true conflicts* only,[283] they should be considered as rules containing pre-determined criteria for interest-weighing, not for impartial geographical allocation. A common trait of all seven principles is the implicit requirement that the conflicting rules of law are comparatively evaluated, mostly for the purpose of contrasting higher and lower standards of protection. The first principle, for instance, requires a comparison of the tort law of the state of injury to that of the state where the tort-feasor acted or had his home: "Where the liability laws of the state of injury set a *higher* standard of conduct or of finan-

---

278 *Ibid.* p. 204. *Id.* (1933) p. 204: "In the law schools alone can ideas of this sort take root; once having rooted there, the process of transplanting them to less sheltered fields may be gradual, but it is sure." See also: Baade (1967) p. 143, p. 145 ff.
279 Cavers (1965) p. 136/137.
280 *Ibid.* p. 205. In his 1970 lectures before the Hague Academy of International Law, Cavers emphasized once more that the specific rules he had suggested were less important to him than the approach he advocated: "I feel greater confidence in the concept of principles of preference than I do in the particular principles I have proposed." Cavers (1970) p. 158.
281 Cavers (1965) p. 136.
282 *Cf.* Strikwerda (1978) p. 187, note 3-259, affirming that such eligibility may be subject to the intervention of public policy. Furthermore, forum law might have priority if its application is indicated by statutory directives: Cavers (1965) p. 163, note 32; p. 204, p. 215; *id.* (1970) p. 153.
283 Cavers (1965) p. 137, p. 151; but see *infra* text accompanying notes 301-304.

cial protection against injury than do the laws of the state where the person causing the injury has acted or had his home, the laws of the state of injury should determine the standard and the protection applicable to the case, at least where the person injured was not so related to the person causing the injury that the question should be relegated to the law governing their relationship."[284] When the places of conduct and injury coincide, application of the *lex loci delicti* is also required by the second principle, covering cases in which that law sets a *lower* standard of conduct or of financial protection than the law of the victim's domicile. In cases in which defendant's conduct caused foreseeable injury, the third principle accords the out-of-state plaintiff the benefit of special standards of conduct or liability prevailing in the state where defendant acted, even if such special controls or sanctions do not exist in the state of injury. Contrary to the first three principles, the fourth is "antiterritorialist" in the sense that it gives priority to the law that the parties have in common: if the law of the state in which their relationship has its "seat" sets higher standards of conduct or of financial protection than the law of the state of injury, the former law should be given priority, generally for the benefit of the plaintiff.

From this survey of the four tort principles[285] it becomes apparent that, in essence, the "preferences" are quite similar to the choice of law principles in § 6 of the Restatement Second, or from Leflar's choice-influencing considerations.[286] There are, of course, two important differences. Unlike the other two sets of policy factors, the principles of preference are limited in scope: they only address true conflict situations. Second, their policy values are cloaked in rules which allow a fairly straightforward subsumption of law-fact patterns and do not re-

---

284 *Ibid.* p. 139; emphasis in the original.
285 The fifth principle also hinges upon the seat of a relationship, but it is the converse of the fourth proposition: if the standards of the state where the parties' relationship has its seat are *lower* than those imposed by the state of injury, the former law should be applied, generally for the benefit of the defendant. Cavers disapproved of this principle, envisaging interspousal immunity and guest statute cases in which application of the higher standards of *lex loci delicti* might yield a more appropriate solution: "Probably, therefore, this principle would not achieve general acceptance. Certain states would give effect to the exception it poses to the first principle for certain relationships and not for others. Some states would reject it out of hand." For that reason, Cavers had little confidence in the merits of the fifth principle. Cavers (1965) p. 180; *id.* (1970) p. 158.
286 To be discussed in the next chapter.

quire the rating of choice-influencing factors in each individual case, a necessity under the Leflar approach or under § 6. Apart from the values of certainty and uniformity promoted by a "rules approach", and the regard for governmental interests on which the Cavers approach is founded, two distinct "choice-influencing considerations" are worked into the principles for torts.[287] The first one is the "territorialist bias" to which Cavers frankly admits, at the same time acknowledging that "[t]oday the tendency is to lean in the opposite direction."[288] Under the first three principles, true conflicts are solved by a preference for *lex loci delicti*,[289] while the domiciliary law of plaintiff and/or defendant is elected only – under principles 4 and 5 – if it happens to coincide with the law of the state where their relationship arose. It should be remembered that the law of the parties' common domicile will displace *lex loci delicti* in many false conflict cases; in this respect, the territorialist bias mainly affects the solutions to true conflicts. Cavers has explained his territorial preference by pointing out that "states and nations are territorially organized," which would imply that their laws are meant "to safeguard the health and safety of people and property within their bounds."[290] Such a system, which might either benefit the endangered public or the people whose activities may cause harm, would be impaired if its law is displaced by the domiciliary law of either plaintiff or defendant. For that reason, a foreign defendant should not be allowed to invoke the lower standards of his home state against the local victim. Conversely, a foreign plaintiff should not have the benefit of his home state law against a local defendant: by entering a state or nation, a visitor exposes himself "to the risks of the territory and should not expect to subject persons living there to a

---

287 *Cf.* Strikwerda (1978) p. 188 ff. The same considerations might have influenced the formulation of the other principles, not here discussed.
288 Cavers (1965) p. 134; p. 139. *Cf.* Reilly (1974) p. 1029 ff.
289 Under the first principle (liability laws of state of injury set higher standard of conduct or of financial protection than those set by law of place of conduct or domiciliary law of defendant), the law of the state of injury is decisive. Under the second principle (liability laws of state in which defendant acted and caused injury set lower standard than those set by law of victim's domicile), the *lex loci delicti* should be applied. Under the third principle (state in which defendant acted has established special controls over conduct causing foreseeable harm) the law of the place of conduct controls.
290 Cavers (1965) p. 140.

financial hazard that their law had not created."²⁹¹ Furthermore, the interest of the state of injury in providing "general security" extends beyond compensation: "its purposes include elements of deterrence and retribution even though it may be couched in essentially compensatory terms."²⁹² In short, the territorialist bias is justified by the traditional considerations supporting the place of wrong rule: the notion that tort law would contribute to the *prevention* of wrongful conduct and, on the other hand, the assumption that citizens and visitors of the state where the wrong occurred have certain *expectations* concerning the extent of their rights and liabilities in tort.²⁹³

The second choice of law policy the principles of preference support comes close to Leflar's better law consideration, at least in its ordinary plaintiff-protective interpretation.²⁹⁴ With the exception of the second rule, the tort principles offer the victim the benefit of the "higher" or "special" standards of conduct or financial protection.²⁹⁵ Having conceived the principles as rules "which would either reflect multistate policies or provide the basis for a reasonable accommodation of the laws' conflicting purposes,"²⁹⁶ Cavers apparently believed that such accommodation would best be achieved by a preference for the plaintiff-protective law. Since all states experience the "need to maintain physical or financial protection against injury-causing conduct," a preference for more demanding standards of conduct and for better financial protection is "most likely to achieve mutual acceptance."²⁹⁷ Although this pro-compensation bias, at least in effect, is reminiscent of the judicial interpretation of Leflar's better law consideration, the two approaches are structurally different. Cavers has rejected a conflicts solution based on an abstract appraisal of the respective merits of conflicting rules of substantive law, as it "neutralizes" the circumstances of the case by allowing the court "simply to express a prefer-

---

291 *Ibid.* p. 147. In interstate cases, Cavers suggests, a solution based on a "personal law of torts" might violate the principle of equal protection, under the Equal Protection Clause or the Privileges and Immunities Clause of the U.S. Constitution. *Ibid.* p. 135, p. 144.
292 *Ibid.* p. 144. See also: Cavers (1970) p. 155/156.
293 *Cf.* Dubbink (1947) p. 49 ff.; Strikwerda (1978) p. 188.
294 *Infra* chapter 5, text accompanying notes 79–81.
295 *Cf.* Strikwerda (1978) p. 189; Baade (1967) p. 162; Reilly (1974) p. 1030. It will be remembered that Cavers retracted the fifth principle: *supra* note 285.
296 Cavers (1965) p. 64.
297 *Ibid.* p. 140/141, p. 160.

ence between the two rules on the score of 'justice and convenience'."[298] Instead, the principles of preference call for a neutral comparison of conflicting rules of law and provide pre-determined solutions for specific law-fact patterns. As such, they do not allow an evaluation of substantive law quality without regard to the facts, as encouraged by the better law approach. While the plaintiff-protective effects of the better law test depend on the forum's appreciation of its own tort law, the pro-recovery bias of most of the principles of preference is rooted in the universal notions[299] Cavers needed as a base for "rational solutions".

In this light, the principles are more than "guides for decision" in true conflict cases. Both the territorialist bias and the preference for the higher standard of conduct and protection suggest that the function of the law of torts is mainly admonitory. This perception is not only relevant to the solution of true conflicts, but it is also apt to play an important part at an earlier stage in the process of interest analysis, when it is ascertained if a state has an interest at all.[300] In fact, Cavers later amended his original proposition that the principles were only meant to solve true conflicts, absent legislative directives: "On reflection, I would revise that limitation: I believe that the principles may on occasion be useful in ascertaining whether and how a legislature has spoken on a question of choice and whether the conflict is false or may readily be avoided."[301] Yet, the two examples Cavers used to explain

---

298 It is not the intrinsic superiority of one rule of law to another, but the actual result that counts: "It is therefore the circumstances of the case that one must look for the problem." *Ibid.* p. 86; p. 122/123. *Cf.* Baade (1967) p. 153 ff. But see Cavers (1983) p. 479, in a letter to Currie: "Although I agree with you thoroughly that a choice between competing laws on the strength of their relative virtues should not be the mainspring of any choice-of-law system, I do think you are unduly puritanical about the possibility that a court might give the laws' relative merits some weight."
299 *Cf.* Ehrenzweig (1971) p. 237. Apart from the idea that choice of law decisions should reflect parties' expectations and the assumption that tort law generally purports to deter wrongful conduct, another supranational notion underlying Cavers' propositions is "conflicts justice", a concept he owed to Kegel (1964) p. 184/185: "What is considered the best law according to its content, that is, *substantively*, might be far from the best spatially ... One must be ready, therefore, to accept the concept of a specific *justice of conflict of laws*, as distinguished from the justice of substantive law." See: Cavers (1970) p. 148, p. 158; *id.* (1971-2) p. 360; *id.* (1972) p. 168 = *id.* (1976) p. 653.
300 *Cf.* Strikwerda (1978) p. 188 ff.; Von Mehren (1975) p. 959.
301 Cavers (1970) p. 153; p. 191; *id.* (1971-1) p. 221; Traynor, R. (1971) p. 239.

his new position are not very enlightening. Both *Gaither v. Myers*[302] and *Schmidt v. Driscoll Hotel, Inc.*[303] presented false conflicts, as Cavers acknowledged, in which application of the law of the state where defendant acted and had his home would further the admonitory policy of that state without frustrating the defendant-protective policy of the state of injury. Both cases were decided to the benefit of the plaintiff, by application of the "special controls" established in the state in which defendant acted. In this respect, application of the third principle of preference would have brought the same result. But it is hard to see how resort to this principle would aid the court "to determine whether apparently conflicting laws produced a true or a false conflict," as Cavers wanted us to believe.[304] If the owner of the stolen car in *Gaither* had been a resident of Maryland, leaving his key in the lock of his car after parking it in the District of Columbia, the conflict would be true: the interest of the District in deterrence would have to be measured against Maryland's interest in shielding resident car owners from liability. The third principle would still entitle the plaintiff to recovery, but in what way does it facilitate interest analysis?

Although there is hardly a case in which the court let itself be guided by any of the principles of preference Cavers proposed, there are several phenomena in judicial choice of law practice which correspond with his basic theory. Emulating Cavers, the New York Court of Appeal made a bold but probably misguided attempt to distill hard and fast rules from its policy-oriented experience in tort choice of law. Considering the confusion that followed the introduction of Judge Fuld's "Neumeier principles", one is inclined to prefer the more sophisticated alternatives proffered by Cavers.[305] Furthermore, in a

---

302 *Gaither v. Myers* 404 F.2d 216 (D.C. Cir. 1968): Maryland resident sustained injuries in a hit and run car accident in Maryland; the negligent owner of the stolen car, a resident of the District of Columbia, would be liable under a District of Columbia statute, not under the law of Maryland.
303 *Schmidt v. Driscoll Hotel, Inc.* 249 Minn. 376, 82 N.W.2d 365 (1957): this was a dramshop action brought by a Minnesota resident, injured in Wisconsin, against a Minnesota tavern owner; under Wisconsin law, the tavern owner would not be liable for wrongful conduct of intoxicated patrons, while Minnesota had a dramshop law.
304 Cavers (1970) p. 191.
305 The "Fuld principles" or "Neumeier rules", or vice versa, were adopted by the New York Court of Appeals in *Neumeier v. Kuehner* 31 N.Y.2d 121, 286 N.E.2d 454, 335 N.Y.S.2d 64 (1972); they will be discussed *infra* chapter 6.

number of jurisdictions given to policy-oriented approaches, tort choice of law is marked by a distinct territorialist bias, and although this trend cannot be ascribed directly to Cavers, it does accord with a major premise of his approach. In these jurisdictions, tort choice of law is often predicated on a *lex loci* presumption which derives from an implicit recognition of the regulatory or admonitory policy of the state where the tort occurred. This approach defers to *lex loci delicti* in cases in which the conflicting interests are in balance.

The one case I found in which the court actually relied on one of Cavers' principles of preference is *Cipolla v. Shaposka*, decided by the Supreme Court of Pennsylvania.[306] At issue was the choice between the liability-imposing law of Pennsylvania, the state where the plaintiff was domiciled, and the guest statute of Delaware, defendant's home state. The parties were schoolmates in Delaware and the accident occurred in that state while the plaintiff, having been offered a ride to his home in Pennsylvania, was a guest in defendant's car. Realizing that the case presented a true conflict, the court set out to measure the contacts each state had with the accident, "on a qualitative rather than quantitative scale." Apart from plaintiff's domicile, there were no other contacts linking Pennsylvania to the occurrence. On the other hand, the fact that the automobile involved in the accident was registered and garaged in Delaware was said to give that state another relevant contact besides the domicile of the defendant, for "it appears that insurance rates will depend on the state in which the automobile is housed rather than the domicile of the owner or driver."[307] For that reason, the court concluded that Delaware's contacts were "qualitatively greater" than Pennsylvania's, but it did not rest its decision to apply the Delaware guest statute on this rationale alone. Relying on Cavers' second principle of preference, the majority reinforced its decision to apply the law of Delaware by stating: "Inhabitants of a state should not be put in jeopardy of liability exceeding that created by their state's laws just because a visitor from a state offering higher protection decides to visit there."[308] It was acknowledged that this view was highly territorial, but "as a general approach [to true con-

306 *Cipolla v. Shaposka* 439 Pa. 563, 267 A.2d 854 (1970).
307 *Ibid.* p. 856. The court did not think that the *locus delicti* was a relevant contact, since the Delaware guest statute did not set out a rule of the road. *Ibid.* p. 856, note 2. *Cf.* the comment by Felix, *infra* note 322.
308 *Ibid.* p. 856/857. Cavers (1965) p. 146 ff.

flicts] a territorial view seems preferable to a personal view."[309] In his dissenting opinion, Justice Roberts first rejected the majority's assertion that the place where an automobile is housed is a relevant contact. As the Delaware guest statute did not purport to lower the insurance rates of Delaware car owners, but was meant "to protect one who generously without accruing benefit, has transported another in his motor vehicle,"[310] Delaware and Pennsylvania would have but one relevant contact each: the domicile of the host and guest respectively. Justice Roberts further believed that the emphasis on territoriality was misplaced. Since the guest statute was not enacted to regulate conduct, "defendant was not in any sense relying on Delaware law when he was driving."[311] With the contacts and interests of both involved jurisdictions evenly balanced, Justice Roberts concluded, the better law criterion should be applied as the appropriate solution to true conflicts, in this case resulting in a preference for the "emerging policy" and "sounder view" represented by Pennsylvania's liability-imposing law.

As might be expected, the commentators of *Cipolla v. Shaposka* were divided on both its method and result, despite Professor Peterson's optimistic suggestion that the outcome would be supported by almost any choice of law approach, including the Restatement Second, Ehrenzweig's *lex loci stabuli* criterion, Currie's "moderate and restrained interpretation" of forum law, the "functional analysis" advocated by Von Mehren and Trautman, and even Leflar's choice-influencing considerations.[312] Cavers himself found the majority's contacts evaluation "a needlessly tortuous way" to justify application of Dela-

---

309 *Cipolla v. Shaposka* 439 Pa. 563, 267 A.2d 854 at 857 (1970).
310 *Cipolla v. Shaposka* 439 Pa. 563, 267 A.2d 854 at 858 (1970), citing several Delaware cases.
311 *Ibid.* p. 859. The same would apply, Justice Roberts continued, to defendant's father, the owner of the car: "Nor do I believe that the defendant's father was relying on Delaware law when he paid his premiums. It seems doubtful to me that the insured ever took into account the possibility that a Pennsylvania guest could not recover against him for a Delaware accident, but could for one in Pennsylvania or New Jersey." *Ibid.*
312 Peterson (1971) p. 437. For further comments, see: *Symposium on Cipolla v. Shaposka – An Application of "Interest Analysis"*, with contributions by Cavers, Twerski, Sedler, Felix, Seidelson, Peterson, Pelaez, and Ehrenzweig: 9 *Duquesne L.Rev.* 347–465 (1971); *infra* note 322.

ware law,³¹³ but he was understandably pleased with the second line of reasoning the *Cipolla* court adopted. Professor Twerski, the advocate of "enlightened territorialism"³¹⁴ and Cavers' most ardent supporter, rhapsodized over the court's "judicial instincts" and "common sense",³¹⁵ but wished it had adopted an even stronger territorial view, one that would take into account the "time and space elements" Twerski deems "an important facet of the human experience."³¹⁶ Addressing the "locus of the relationship" problem the *Cipolla* court ignored, he surmised that Cavers would have opted for application of Pennsylvania law if a "nominal Pennsylvania relationship between Cipolla and Shaposka could have been established." Twerski's "enlightened territorialism", however, hardly allows such exceptions: "I am unwilling to support the application of anything but Delaware law when a Delaware driver is driving in his home state unless the Pennsylvania relationship between the plaintiff and defendant has true depth and dimension to it."³¹⁷ Similar existential considerations led Professor Sedler to an opposite conclusion. If Twerski found himself "pushed to an even stronger territorial bias than Cavers,"³¹⁸ Sedler's analysis of *Cipolla* forced him to become a "pure anti-territorialist" advocating "a personal law of torts in automobile accident cases."³¹⁹ To Sedler, one "existential-legal component" of cases like *Cipolla* is the fact that "the decision to cross a state line will not usually depend on legal considerations." Due to American geographical conditions, he contends, people identify with the area in which they live rather than a state: " ... in functional, socio-economic and mobility terms, ... [the Pennsylvania/Delaware state line] is not real insofar as the day-to-

---

313 Cavers (1971-2) p. 362, note 8.
314 *Supra* section 3, text accompanying notes 112–115.
315 "*Cipolla v. Shaposka* is a good case. It is strong not because it adopted a Cavers' principle of preference or because it indulged in a rigorous interest analysis. The strength of Cipolla lies in the willingness of the court to trust its judicial instincts of fairness and justice to the parties over the overly sophisticated attempts of the scholars to intellectualize legal concepts to the point of absurdity. Having attempted to support with argumentation that the territorial bias is based on some rather common sense notions about law and its functions in our complex world, I revel in the court's decision. Evenhanded justice had a good day in Pennsylvania." Twerski (1971) p. 393.
316 *Ibid.* p. 382.
317 *Ibid.* p. 390.
318 *Ibid.*
319 Sedler (1971-1) p. 398, p. 409.

day life of the people living in the area is concerned."[320] Observing that Pennsylvania law would have been applied (possibly on the strength of Cavers' first principle of preference) if Michael Cipolla had been injured in his home state rather than in Delaware, Sedler argues that "the result in an interstate automobile accident case should not depend on which side of the state line it occurred."[321] Thus, application of Pennsylvania law would not produce fundamental unfairness or defeat the legitimate expectations of the Delaware defendant (or, more realistically, his insurance company which happened to be a Pennsylvania corporation). Since plaintiff's domicile gave Pennsylvania an interest, the Pennsylvania Supreme Court would have been justified in applying its own law, according to Sedler.

These antithetical comments[322] illustrate the two major practical objections against Cavers' tort principles. The first one concerns the subsidiary "seat of the relationship" criterion in principles 1, 2 and 4. In *Cipolla*, the parties were schoolmates in Delaware, but the accident occurred when the parties were on their way to plaintiff's home in Pennsylvania in order to pick up some tools that plaintiff had borrowed from defendant; process was served upon defendant when he was playing golf with the plaintiff in Pennsylvania. Since the host-guest relationship "was the focal point of *Cipolla*,"[323] the court should

---

320 *Ibid.* p. 399.
321 *Ibid.* p. 404.
322 I will refrain from discussing the other contributions to the *Cipolla* symposium, *supra* note 312, since they are less poignant in respect of the territoriality issue. Ehrenzweig (p. 459 ff., p. 464/465) rejected virtually all aspects of the decision, including the suggestion that the court had deferred to his *lex loci stabuli* solution. Pelaez (p. 446 ff., p. 451) advocated an "interested *lex fori* test," compelling the forum to apply its own law "whenever it has a legitimate, somewhat more than minimal, interest in the cause." Peterson (p. 437 ff., p. 440) emphasized the difficulties of interest-weighing in the light of his contention, derived from Currie, that "a court is and should remain a mere handmaiden to the legislature, implementing as best it can the legislative will." Seidelson (p. 423 ff.) discussed some constitutional aspects and evaluated the dissent's better law approach, concluding that the renvoi doctrine would have supported the application of Delaware law. Felix (p. 413 ff.) contrasted the dissent's better law approach to the twofold reasoning of the majority opinion, noticing in the latter a curious discrepancy between the rejection of the place of wrong as a relevant factor in the contacts evaluation, and the emphasis on territoriality in the discussion of justified expectations.
323 Twerski (1971) p. 388.

have attempted to determine its seat, if it seriously meant to adopt Cavers' propositions. It will be clear that in this respect, the principles of preference lend themselves to manipulation, especially in cases in which the relationship stretches across state lines. If it could be argued that the relationship between Cipolla and Shaposka centered in Pennsylvania rather than Delaware, the fourth principle should have been applied, giving plaintiff the benefit of the higher Pennsylvania standards. Because of this ambiguity, Twerski refused to support Cavers' seat-of-the-relationship exception in case of "synthetic relationships which have no 'time and space' dimensions,"[324] but such a condition raises the question when a relationship does qualify for the exception, and therefore fosters the same ambiguity.[325] The second objection concerns the unhappy consequences of the territorial bias. As several commentators, including Cavers, pointed out, Cipolla could have recovered if the accident had occurred on the Pennsylvania side of the state line. Since he happened to be injured in Delaware, however, he was barred from recovery. "Thus, the *human* result would depend on whether the accident occurred on the Delaware or Pennsylvania side of the line, a difference of a few miles," Sedler observed.[326] This is hardly the "rational solution" to true conflicts that Cavers envisaged. In this respect, the *Cipolla* decision demonstrates once more that true conflicts present a deadlock which cannot be broken by reasoned solutions. The proposed principles of preference, I submit, are no more "rational" than other suggestions meant to break the true conflict tie. Since they rest on axiomatic premises, such as the regulatory purpose of tort law or the relevance of party expectations, I am not convinced that their territorial bias is preferable to any of the other biases encountered in policy-oriented choice of law.

After *Cipolla*, the Pennsylvania courts have made no further attempts to apply or develop principles of preference. If they cite the decision at all, it is generally to support a finding that one of the concerned juris-

---

324 *Ibid.* p. 390.
325 *Cf.* Cramton/Currie/Kay (1981) p. 356/357.
326 Sedler (1971-1) p. 411; *cf.* the dissenting opinion by Justice Roberts, *supra* notes 310–311 and accompanying text.

dictions has the "greatest interest" in the application of its law.[327] In *Krick v. Carter*, it was vaguely described as a decision "that withdrew somewhat from *Griffith* abandonment of the lex loci approach," but the court distinguished *Cipolla* on the grounds that its holding did not concern interspousal immunity, at issue in *Krick*.[328] In *Orawsky v. Jersey Cent. Power and Light Co.*, there are still some territorial overtones which could be associated with the second principle of preference, since the court attributed "primary significance" to the place of wrong now that defendant resided in the state where the tort occurred. Plaintiff was a Pennsylvania resident who had been injured on defendant's property in New Jersey when he dove from a bulkhead into shallow water. Under New Jersey law, a land owner did not have a duty to keep his premises safe for use by others. Following the *Cipolla* rationale, the court held New Jersey law to apply, for "[a] landowner should be able to rely on the law of the state where the land is situated in determining what duty is owed to people using the land and what measures should be taken to fulfill that duty."[329] Since the issue focused on conduct, the decision is not particularly revealing in respect of Pennsylvania's territorial bias. A more interesting case is *Miller v. Gay*, presenting the reverse of the *Cipolla* law-fact pattern in that the plaintiff-guest was domiciled in Delaware and the defendant-

---

327 *E.g McDermott v. Travellers Air Services, Inc.* 462 F.Supp. 1335 (M.D. Pa. 1979). In *Kiehn v. Elkem-Spigerverket A/S Kemi-Metal* 585 F.Supp. 413 (M.D. Pa. 1984), the same district court observed that Pennsylvania's "interest analysis is 'territorial based' only to reflect basic principles of fairness, as outlined in *Cipolla.*" See also: *Hager v. Etting* 268 Pa.Super. 416, 408 A.2d 856 (1979). According to the district court for Pennsylvania's Western District, however, Pennsylvania tort choice of law conforms to § 145 Restatement Second: *Lewis v. Chemetron Corp.* 448 F.Supp. 211 (W.D. Pa. 1978); *Conservation Council of Western Australia, Inc. v. Aluminum Co. of America (ALCOA)* 518 F.Supp. 270 (W.D. Pa. 1981). See also: *Permagrain Products v. U.S. Mat & Rubber Co.* 489 F.Supp. 108 at 111, note 1 (E.D. Pa. 1980): " ... under Pennsylvania law, in a tort action the law which has the most significant relationship with the parties governs," followed by contacts counting.
In *Griffith v. United Air Lines, Inc.* 416 Pa. 1, 203 A.2d 796 at 806 (1964), the Supreme Court of Pennsylvania replaced the traditional place of wrong rule by "a more flexible rule" requiring qualitative evaluation of "the *policies* underlying the significant relationships to the controversy." Emphasis added. The references to *Babcock v. Jackson* may have persuaded some courts that Pennsylvania had adopted a contacts-grouping approach rather than interest analysis.
328 *Krick v. Carter* 477 F.Supp. 152 at 155 (N.D. Pa. 1979).
329 *Orawsky v. Jersey Cent. Power and Light Co.* 472 F.Supp. 881 at 883 (E.D. Pa. 1977).

host in Pennsylvania. As in *Cipolla*, the accident that gave rise to the action occurred in Delaware, but here, of course, we are dealing with an unprovided-for case, since neither state had an interest in the application of its law. The Superior Court applied the Delaware *lex loci delicti*, relying heavily on § 6 of the Restatement Second, with emphasis on certainty, predictability and uniformity of result. An additional argument, however, was found in *Cipolla*. If domiciliaries of the *locus* state should not be held to the higher standard of liability of plaintiff's home state, just because a foreign plaintiff decided to visit, the court reasoned, then an analogous argument could be made in the reverse situation: "Analogously, we conclude that inhabitants of a state (here Delaware) should not be *accorded rights not given them by their home states*, just because a visitor from a state offering higher protection decides to visit there."[330] It should be noted that none of Cavers' tort principles would cover the instant case, in which the state where the wrong occurred, having the *lower* liability standard, was also plaintiff's home state. The second principle is based on the assumption that the victim hails from a state where the standards are higher than those of the *lex loci delicti*. The fourth principle assumes that the standards of the state where the seat of the relationship is located are higher than those of the place of wrong, but in this case the lower court had decided that the parties' relationship centered in Delaware. Even the fifth principle would not be applicable, as it assumes the standards of the state where the relationship has its seat to be lower than those of the state of injury.

Leaving these half-hearted experiments with "principled preferences", I now turn to those cases in which the territorial bias stems from a different methodological source. Here, it is the Restatement Second that seems to have induced the courts to solve true conflicts in favor of *lex loci delicti*. Their position is clearly stated in *Hardly Able Coal Co., Inc. v. International Harvester Co.*, decided by a federal court in Illinois: "If the weighting of the several factors is equal, the

---

330 *Miller v. Gay* 470 A.2d 1353 at 1356 (Pa. Super. 1983); emphasis added. In his dissenting opinion, Judge Spaeth rejected this analogy: "Here, appellant, by driving his automobile into Delaware, did not put himself in jeopardy of incurring greater liability than that to which he was already subject in Pennsylvania, his home state. Instead, although a non-resident of Delaware, he seeks to use the Delaware Guest Statute as a shield, which is very different from the situation in *Cipolla*, where a Delaware resident invoked the statute." *Ibid.* p. 1360.

conventional *lex loci delicti* approach that was once uniformly adopted in torts cases prevails."[331] It will be remembered that, in *Ingersoll v. Klein*, the Illinois Supreme Court had adopted a "most significant contacts" rule which is usually understood as a policy-oriented version of the Restatement's most significant relationship test.[332] Thus, the district court in *Hardly Able*, a product liability action, compared Illinois' interest in imposing liability on Illinois manufacturers with Kentucky's interest in according limited recovery, found them in equal balance,[333] and applied Kentucky law as the law of the place of injury.[334] If it could be doubted whether *Hardly Able* presented a true conflict, in *R & L Grain Co. v. Chicago Eastern Corp.*, another product liability action, the conflict between the laws and interests of Wisconsin and Illinois concerning the issue of economic loss was true enough. Plaintiff, a Wisconsin corporation, had bought a grain storage bin manufactured by the Illinois defendant. It was alleged that certain defects in the bin's design made it unsuitable for storing grain in the harsh Wisconsin winter. At any rate, its roof had collapsed causing property damages and economic loss. Under the circumstances,

331 *Hardly Able Coal Co., Inc. v. International Harvester Co.* 494 F.Supp. 249 at 250 (N.D. Ill. 1980).
332 *Ingersoll v. Klein* 46 Ill.2d 42, 262 N.E.2d 593 (1970); *supra* chapter 3, text accompanying notes 60–63. The *Ingersoll* opinion contains too many references to "state interests" to warrant a more factual test. The federal courts sitting in Illinois have generally established the most significant relationship by interest evaluation. See however: *DP Service, Inc. v. AM International* 508 F.Supp. 162 (N.D. Ill. 1981), in which case the most significant relationship test was applied as a contacts-grouping approach, revealing an "even balance" of *contacts*.
333 Kentucky law did not allow recovery of damages for economic loss, while under the circumstances, Illinois law apparently did. Since the plaintiff was a Kentucky corporation having its principal place of business in Illinois and defendant had manufactured the defective bulldozer in Illinois, it would seem that the case presented a false conflict. I fail to see what interest Kentucky – as the state where the wrong occurred and where the plaintiff was incorporated– could have in refusing the *plaintiff* to recover damages for economic loss.
334 The Seventh Circuit, in *Pittway Corp. v. Lockheed Aircraft Corp.* 641 F.2d 524 (7th Cir. [Ill.] 1981), followed a more subtle approach when it addressed the issue of damages for economic loss. Plaintiff was a Pennsylvania corporation doing business in Illinois; it sued Lockheed, a California corporation with principal place of business in Georgia, for the costs of repairs on an allegedly defective airplane and for economic loss. The defects had been discovered in Wisconsin. The district's court decision to apply Wisconsin law under the last event rule was reversed for several reasons, one of them relating to the ambiguous place of wrong criterion: "The harm that Pittway suffered ... was purely economic and as such was sustained in Illinois." *Ibid.* p. 528. *Cf. supra* chapter 3, text accompanying notes 93–94.

Illinois law disallowed recovery of economic loss, while Wisconsin law permitted such recovery. The district court acknowledged that in this case both states had an interest in having their respective laws applied, and decided: "In sum, the factors favoring the application of Wisconsin law are of equal significance as those favoring the application of Illinois law. Therefore, the latter do not overcome the presumption in favor of application of the law of the place of injury, Wisconsin."[335] The same *lex loci* presumption must have compelled the court in *Pancotto v. Sociedade de Safaris de Moçambique S.A.R.L.* to resort to the doctrine of public policy in order to escape application of Mozambique's limitation of damages in an action brought by an Illinois plaintiff against a Mozambique tour operator. Having established that Mozambique had a strong interest in the protection of its corporations against excessive liability, while Illinois had an equally strong interest in full compensation for its citizens, the court could only avert application of *lex loci delicti* by the invocation of public policy.[336]

Louisiana is another jurisdiction whose courts have turned to the Restatement Second for guidance, at least for the solution of true conflicts. In *Jagers v. Royal Indemnity Company*,[337] the Louisiana Supreme Court had adopted an interest-oriented approach to torts, declaring without much ado that this intra-family immunity case presented a false conflict. It thereby abruptly overruled *Johnson v. St. Paul Mercury Insurance Company*[338] in which it had indignantly reversed the intermediate court's decision to abandon *lex loci delicti*. When the Fifth Circuit, in *Brinkley & West, Inc. v. Foremost Insurance Company*, had to divine how Louisiana courts would solve *true* conflict cases, it decided to remand and have the lower court establish the interests of all 18 states where defendant had tortiously interfered with contractual relationships.[339] The district court in *Ardoyno v.*

---

335 *R & L Grain Co. v. Chicago Eastern Corp.* 531 F.Supp. 201 at 206 (N.D. Ill. 1981).
336 *Pancotto v. Sociedade de Safaris de Moçambique S.A.R.L.* 422 F.Supp. 405 (N.D. Ill. 1976); *supra* chapter 3, text accompanying notes 64–66. The public policy argument was not very convincing, as it was based on a provision in the Illinois Constitution entitling "every person ... to a certain remedy in the law for injuries to his person." *Supra* chapter 2, section 3, text accompanying notes 246–247.
337 *Jagers v. Royal Indemnity Company* 276 So.2d 309 (La. 1973).
338 *Johnson v. St. Paul Mercury Insurance Company* 256 La. 289, 236 So.2d 216 (1970).
339 *Brinkley & West, Inc. v. Foremost Insurance Company* 499 F.2d 928 (5th Cir. [La.] 1974).

Kyzar took this decision to mean that true conflicts should be solved along the lines of the Restatement Second, more specifically the provisions predicated on a *lex loci* presumption. In this case, plaintiffs were attorneys who practiced in Louisiana, mainly in behalf of Mississippi clients. Defendant, a Mississippi attorney, was sued for making slanderous remarks about plaintiffs to one of their prospective clients in Mississippi, a tort for which Mississippi law –in contrast to Louisiana law– would allow punitive damages. Since Louisiana was said to have an interest "in protecting the integrity of its judicial system ... from what it might consider inherently speculative awards"[340] while Mississippi had an interest in preventing intentional torts committed within its boundaries, the case presented a true conflict. Citing § 149 and § 6 of the Restatement Second, the court applied Mississippi law. Not only had the defamatory remarks been made in that state, but this solution would also further some of the choice of law policies listed in § 6, notably the advancement of the interstate system and the protection of justified expectations. A similar combination of Restatement provisions was relied on in *Karavorikos v. Indiana Motor Bus Co.*, another action for punitive damages, this time brought by an Ohio resident who was injured in Louisiana when he was struck by a bus owned by the Indiana defendant. Upholding Louisiana's interest in avoiding speculative jury awards of punitive damages, allowed in both Ohio and Indiana, the court had little to say about the interests of these states and proceeded to decide the case as a true conflict. Since the action was for personal injuries, the solution was found in the *lex loci* presumption of § 146 and plaintiff's claim was rejected.[341]

To conclude these observations on the role of the place of wrong in the determination of true conflicts, I should like to mention two more cases, one from Maine and one from Missouri, in support of the proposition that the *lex loci* presumption is as arbitrary as any of the other

---

340 *Ardoyno v. Kyzar* 426 F.Supp. 78 at 83 (E.D. La. 1976).
341 *Karavorikos v. Indiana Motor Bus Co.* 524 F.Supp. 385 (E.D. La. 1981). It is interesting to note that the court did not think that Louisiana was a fortuitous *locus*: "Plaintiff was in Louisiana as part of a work crew on a construction job in the state. Defendant's bus was operated in Louisiana as part of a chartered tour. Thus, Louisiana has more than a fortuitous interest in both parties." *Ibid.* p. 389.
  For a Louisiana case in which the true conflict dilemma was solved by a conscientious weighing of the policy factors listed in § 6 Restatement Second without recourse to § 145 ff., see: *Bell v. State Farm Fire & Cas. Co.* 527 F.Supp. 300 (W.D. La. 1981).

true conflict solutions described before. In *Mason v. Southern New England Conf. Ass'n, Etc.*, a Maine resident claimed damages for personal injuries she sustained when she was hit by a motion picture screen that fell down during a party at defendant's school in Massachusetts. Defendant was a charitable, non-profit organization incorporated under Massachusetts law, which law entitled it to charitable immunity. Facing the immunity issue, the First Circuit took its cue from Maine's Supreme Judicial Court in *Adams v. Buffalo Forge Co.*[342] and set out to "determine whether the presumptive applicability of the law of the state of injury (Massachusetts) was overcome by policy considerations or by an imbalance of contacts."[343] The court then checked the § 6 considerations. Those relating to the needs of the interstate system, parties' expectations, and certainty and predictability were discarded as factors more relevant to consensual relationships than to torts, while those relating to the policies of the forum and other interested states were found to be in equal balance. In other words, a true conflict presented itself. The court solved it by applying Massachusetts law, with the surprising motivation that ease of application, one of the principles of § 6,[344] justified application of § 146. Obviously, if this principle would pertain to conflicts law itself, ease of application could justify any "simple" choice of law decision, particularly the application of forum law.

The last case to be discussed in this context is *Carver v. Schafer*, a wrongful death action brought in Missouri against an Illinois tavern owner by the widow and children of a Missouri police officer.[345] Their deceased had been struck and killed in Missouri by a car operated by an intoxicated patron of defendant. Illinois' Dram Shop Act limited recovery for wrongful death against the tavern owner to $ 20,000, whereas Missouri did not limit recovery under its wrongful death statute. Although Illinois and Missouri had some policies in common,

---

342 *Adams v. Buffalo Forge Co.* 443 A.2d 932 (Me. 1982). The *Adams* decision confirmed Maine's endorsement of the Restatement Second approach in *Beaulieu v. Beaulieu* 265 A.2d 610 (Me. 1970).
343 *Mason v. Southern New England Conf. Ass'n, Etc.* 696 F.2d 135 at 137 (1st Cir. [Me.] 1982).
344 Restatement Second, comment j on § 6(2): "Ideally, choice-of-law rules should be simple and easy to apply. This policy should not be overemphasized, since it is obviously of greater importance that choice-of-law rules lead to desirable results. The policy does, however, provide a goal for which to strive."
345 *Carver v. Schafer* 647 S.W.2d 570 (Mo. App. 1983).

particularly deterrence and compensation, a true conflict was found between Missouri's interest in unlimited compensation of its residents and Illinois' interest in protecting its dramshop owners from excessive liability. Unlike the First Circuit in *Mason*, the Missouri Court of Appeals did place some weight on the predictability factor in § 6. Since defendant's establishment was not too far from the Missouri state line, it was to be expected that some of its patrons would be Missouri residents. Furthermore, the plaintiffs would not expect anything but application of Missouri law. Yet, this factor was not considered decisive, for the court proceeded to cite several cases in which the *lex loci* presumption prevailed, in this case warranting application of Missouri law as the law of the place of injury.[346] I have no quarrel with the result in *Carver* but I wonder why, from a methodological point of view, the *lex loci* presumption provides a more convincing solution than the one embodied in the *prima facie* applicability of forum law or *ad hoc* interest-weighing. As I see it, Missouri's presumptive interest stemmed from the fact that plaintiffs and their deceased were Missouri domiciliaries; by itself, the occurrence of the accident in Missouri did not give that state an interest in compensating the victims.[347] The predictability factor, on the other hand, would seem to be considerably more compelling in *Mason*, in which it was rejected, than in *Carver*, where the court needed an argument to reinforce the *lex loci iniuriae* presumption. In tort choice of law generally, certainty and predictability are dubious considerations. In *Carver*, their support is spurious.

---

346 The court even went so far as to examine the constitutionality of its choice of law, which is a nice touch considering that Missouri law was applied as *lex loci*, not as *lex fori*. Inspiration was found in *Allstate Ins. Co. v. Hague* 449 U.S. 302, 101 S.Ct. 633, 66 L.Ed.2d 521 (1981), to be discussed *infra* chapter 7, text accompanying notes 50–51, in which the U.S. Supreme Court endorsed application of forum law on the sole ground that the forum has "a significant contact" with the case.

347 The court listed three policies behind unlimited recovery: "One policy is to provide for the economic well-being of the decedent's dependents so that they will not become wards of the state. A second policy is to provide funds with which to pay creditors of the decedent. A third policy furthered by allowing unrestricted judgments for wrongful death is to promote the admonitory effect such judgments would have on potentially negligent defendants." *Carver v. Schafer* 647 S.W.2d 570 at 577 (Mo. App. 1983). While the first two policies were deemed relevant, the third one was not, since application of Missouri law would have "minimal deterrent effect on persons and entities [such as defendants] who reside and conduct their business affairs outside this state." *Ibid.*

The territorial solutions in Illinois, Louisiana and other jurisdictions mostly draw on Restatement Second authority.[348] Accordingly, they display the same methodological ambivalence that characterizes the Restatement as a whole. The *lex loci* presumption suggests that the state where the wrong occurred will usually have the "greater interest in the determination of the particular issue."[349] In that respect, it incorporates the two choice of law principles of § 6 that require a relative evaluation of the policies of the forum and other interested states. On the other hand, it is meant to further "the choice-of-law values of certainty, predictability and uniformity of result and ... of ease in the determination and application of the applicable law."[350] In my opinion, it is a matter of speculation whether, in true conflict situations, the *locus* state will generally have the greater interest. Furthermore, the choice-influencing factors tied into the Restatement's *lex loci* presumption are hardly compatible, since they derive from disparate choice of law ideologies. For that reason, I consider the territorial solution of true conflicts an unhappy compromise between traditional jurisdiction-selection and predetermined interest-weighing. Certainty, predictability, and uniformity of result are no more warranted by a (*lex loci*) presumption than by an ad hoc weighing process or a *lex fori* solution, while the territorial factor is not necessarily indicative of a state's interest, let alone a state's *greater* interest, in the determination of other issues than that of conduct. In short, the arguments advanced in favor of the *lex loci* presumption for the solution of true conflicts are no more valid than those supporting any other way to break the tie.

---

348 In Massachusetts, for example, a federal court construed the decision of the Massachusetts Supreme Judicial Court in *Pevoski v. Pevoski* 371 Mass. 358, 358 N.E.2d 416 (1976), "as an endorsement of the tort approach of the Restatement (Second)," and translated it into a *lex loci* presumption: *Schulhof v. Northeast Cellulose, Inc.* 545 F.Supp. 1200 (D. Mass. 1982). In fact, the *Pevoski* opinion relied heavily on *Babcock v. Jackson* and did not even mention the Restatement. Its emphasis on *lex loci* concerned the interest of the *locus* state in the standard of conduct issue and is more in tune with straightforward interest analysis than with the Restatement's approach. *Cf. Engine Specialties, Inc. v. Bombardier, Ltd.* 605 F.2d 1 (1st Cir. [Mass.] 1979).
349 Restatement Second, § 146 and 147, comment c.
350 *Ibid.*, with reference to § 6.

Chapter 5

Leflar's Choice-influencing Considerations

Of all the celebrities in the Hall of Fame of American conflicts law no one has enjoyed more explicit endorsement from the judiciary than Professor Robert A. Leflar. Unquestionably, the teachings of Professors Currie, Cavers, Ehrenzweig, and Reese have changed the course of conflicts law in the United States and their influence has pervaded conflicts theory in other parts of the world. Yet, in American case law their authority may have been confirmed by the adoption of their methods, but not by the use of their names. Leflar's name, on the other hand, graces the majority opinion in numerous decisions. The "Leflar methodology",[1] consisting of five "choice-influencing considerations", has become a source of inspiration for the courts of New Hampshire, Minnesota, Wisconsin and Rhode Island[2] whereas the

1 *Schwartz v. Consolidated Freightways Corp. of Del.* 221 N.W.2d 665 (Minn. 1974); Todd (1980) p. 438; Felix (1980) p. 427.
2 I do not find the Rhode Island decisions relying on the Leflar approach particularly instructive, as most of them turn on interest analysis and contain at best a token remark on other choice-influencing considerations. *Cf.* Mühl (1982) p. 84 ff. In *Woodward v. Stewart* 104 R.I. 290, 243 A.2d 917 (1968), the Rhode Island Supreme Court abandoned the traditional *lex loci delicti* rule in favor of an interest-weighing approach, supported by choice-influencing considerations, but the case was basically treated as the false conflict it presented. The decision in *Turcotte v. Ford Motor Company* 494 F.2d 173 at 177 (1st Cir. [R.I.] 1974) is based on pure interest analysis. Except for an opening statement on Rhode Island's choice of law principles in which the Leflar approach is mentioned, and a footnote on the better law, the opinion does not refer to specific choice-influencing considerations. Only in *Gravina v. Brunswick Corporation* 338 F.Supp. 1 (D. R.I. 1972), discussed *supra* chapter 4, section 3, text accompanying notes 136–137, did the federal district court rely mostly on the better law consideration. Finding none of the competing interests (as between Rhode Island, plaintiff's home state, and Illinois, defendant's principal place of business) compelling, the court resorted to the better law criterion and decided for the plaintiff under Illinois law.

the "better law" approach has found support in even more jurisdictions. Leflar would be the first to agree, I surmise, that his contribution to the methodology of conflicts law is less than a full-fledged conflicts theory, or even a systematic body of choice of law principles.[3] Presenting his considerations as "a practical working basis for choice-of-law decisions,"[4] he emphasized that his "is not a new program for choice-of-law adjudication in any other sense. Rather it is a somewhat idealized description of the present system of choice-of-law decision designed to accept substantially what happens now, together with current trends, and to give the real reasons (which on the whole are good reasons) for the law as it currently operates."[5] Identifying "choice of law policies" is a continuous process, he submits, to which all authorities on the law of conflicts are contributing. For Beale the primary consideration would be mechanical simplicity of the choice of law rule; Yntema has stressed "security" and "comparative justice"; while Cavers has tried to formulate his evaluation of choice of law policies in "principles of preference". It is Leflar's modest position that his contribution "can make no claim to originality nor much to new insight. It merely undertakes to restate the considerations that have, expressly or impliedly, always underlain common-law choice-of-law decisions, as others from time to time identified them."[6] A recurrent theme in Leflar's writings is the "judicial eclecticism" he finds characteristic of modern American choice of law: the courts are apt to follow a "multi-faceted approach" combining several of the new theories to support the outcome.[7] Not surprisingly, the author of an approach that borrows from several theories to support practically any sensible choice of law decision is quite content with this unmistakable, but disputable[8] trend. In that respect, Leflar is not an adherent of any particular

---

3 *Cf.* his personal letter to Margarete Mühl (1982) p. 182.
4 Leflar (1977-1) p. 193.
5 Leflar (1966-1) p. 327; *cf.* Reppy (1983) p. 690, note 208. See also *infra* note 82.
6 Leflar (1966-1) p. 282.
7 Leflar (1972-1) *passim*; Leflar (1977-1) p. 197, p. 219 ff., p. 284 ff.; Leflar (1977-2) *passim*. See generally: Westbrook (1975).
8 See: Reppy (1983) p. 646 "With this article I join the ranks of those who are critical. Indeed, I find most examples of eclecticism deplorable. The technique usually deprives choice of law of any certainty; it becomes incomprehensible to lawyers and lower court judges who cannot deal with a choice of law problem in ignorance of the choice of law method employed by the forum."

school of thought in contemporary conflicts law, and his propositions should not be understood as just another variety of interest analysis,[9] let alone as a solution to true conflicts only.[10] However, an analysis of Leflar-inspired case law will reveal how easy it is to turn a false conflict into a true one by the artificial construction of forum interests, paving the way for a *lex fori* solution, a better law approach, or both. Like the "choice of law principles" in § 6 of the Restatement Second, Leflar's choice-influencing considerations are adaptable to all kinds of methodological reasoning. For that reason, I feel, a separate treatment of the "Leflar methodology" is warranted.

The reason why this approach has met with such remarkable judicial approval might lie in its author's pragmatic points of view. Meant to be used "as a practical (though not mechanical) test of the rightness of choice of law rules and decisions,"[11] the choice-influencing considerations do not control but rather explain and justify choice of law motivation. Since they "have been present and operative all along, and have been motivating reasons behind every choice-of-law rule that was ever formulated and every case that was ever decided," they should be considered as guides to "realistic reasoning", obviating the need for fictions and cover-up devices.[12] There is no priority among the considerations, some of them might be irrelevant to certain issues, and the possibility of conflict between them must be accepted as a matter of course. Without the encumbrance of dogma or abstruse the-

---

9 See his criticism of governmental interest analysis: Leflar (1977-1) p. 210 ff.
10 According to Mühl (1982) p. 62, the choice-influencing considerations are specifically meant to solve true conflicts. She explains, however, that Leflar attributes a wider scope to this concept than other conflicts scholars would: in his terminology a true conflict would be any choice of law situation in which the concerned jurisdictions have different rules of substantive law, producing conflicting results. Weintraub (1980) p. 328 ff., on the other hand, would reserve the use of the better law criterion to true conflicts in the usual sense, *viz.* situations in which two states "each have a policy underlying its different domestic law that would be significantly and legitimately, not hypothetically and officiously, advanced by application of its domestic law."
11 Leflar (1966-1) p. 281.
12 *Ibid.* p. 324/325. *Cf.* Leflar (1977-3) p. 974. See also his letter to Ms. Mühl, *supra* note 3, in which he explains the background of his better law consideration: "I felt that real reasons for decision should be openly stated, not covered up, and I tried to frame an objective summation of that real reason, not in terms of preferred results ('better parties') but in terms of a choice between the competing rules of law, on their own merits."

ory, the Leflar approach is extremely flexible and therefore probably more suited to common law adjudication than to the rule-oriented judicial process in Europe.[13]

Taking the catalogues of policy factors listed by Cheatham/Reese and Yntema[14] as a point of departure, Leflar lists five considerations that should help to "produce some improvement in the results of adjudication along with a substantial improvement in understanding the results."[15] The first one is "predictability of results": this two-fold ideal comprises the thought that parties to a consensual transaction should be able to anticipate its legal consequences, and the time-honored notion that any forum should reach the same choice of law decision on a given set of facts. In other words, this consideration supports party autonomy and should produce decisional harmony.[16] The second consideration is "maintenance of interstate and international order", which is much the same as the old concept of *comitas*, both between the states of a federal system and internationally. It covers both "an orderliness that will make our federal system work with reasonable efficiency in the choice-of-law field" and a deference to the state that is "in the best position to insist upon ultimate enforcement of its rule."[17] In the third place there is the consideration of "simplification of the judicial task", to be understood as a compromise between the efficiency of the judicial process and the notion that the law exists for the convenience of society and its members. This consideration supports the application of *lex fori* in procedural matters, unless the procedural rule is outcome-determinative and not too difficult to apply. Simplicity and ease of application would also be furthered by simple choice of law rules, but the virtue of mechanical conflicts rules might

---

13 *Cf.* Strikwerda (1978) p. 186; Ehrenzweig (1967-1) p. 98; De Nova (1966) p. 594 ff. See also: Mühl (1982) part III (p. 140 ff.), dealing with the contrasting ways in which the methodological problem of assessing the better or more favorable law is solved in American and German conflicts law respectively. *Cf. supra* chapter 1.
14 Cheatham/Reese (1952); Yntema, (1957).
15 Leflar (1966-1) p. 327.
16 Leflar (1977-1) p. 205: " ... so that forum-shopping will benefit neither party." It would seem that this latter aspect of predictability sets a highly ambiguous standard: it suggests that a court should conform to foreign choice of law principles if it finds its own conflicts rule to be different from that of other concerned jurisdictions. If the foreign jurisdiction would do likewise, decisional harmony would be frustrated anyway. *Cf.* the discussion of renvoi, *supra* chapter 2, section 2.
17 Leflar (1977-1) p. 207/208.

be outweighed by other considerations.[18] In this respect, the third consideration, no less than the former two, is more a directive for lawmakers than a guideline on adjudication.[19] The fourth and fifth considerations, on the other hand, could be useful in selecting (rather than formulating) the appropriate choice of law criteria. "Advancement of the forum's governmental interest" is reminiscent of Currie's brand of interest analysis. However, Leflar's warning against "an unreasoning fall-back on forum preference" and his criticism of what he terms an "artificial search for governmental interests"[20] seem to set him apart from Currie on this score. Furthermore, the consideration concerning the maintenance of interstate and international orderliness counterbalances the suggestion that *lex fori* should prevail in close cases. In this respect Leflar's position is somehow equivocal: his considerations would support both interest-weighing and a preference for forum law as valid solutions to true conflicts. This ambivalence ties in with the extended scope he attributes to the concept of governmental interests. Interest analysis should be more than a concern for a narrowly defined and rigidly confined function of a particular rule of law: a governmental interest "must include all the relevant concerns that the particular government, not only as a sovereign entity but as a repository of justice, may have in a set of facts or an issue."[21] Finally, the fifth consideration calls for the "application of the better rule of law", a most controversial precept since it is premised on the acceptability of

---

18 In this context, Leflar originally (1966-1, p. 288) advocated the "[m]inimization of conflicts problems by weeding out 'false conflicts'," by which he obviously meant no-conflict situations: " ... if the laws of both states, relevant to the set of facts, are the same, or would produce the same decision in the lawsuit, then there is no real conflict at all, and the case ought to be decided under the law that is common to both states." *Cf. Hunker v. Royal Indemnity Co.* 57 Wis.2d 588, 204 N.W.2d 897 at 901/ 902 (1973), on the use of the term "true conflict".
I fail to see how a no-conflict situation could simplify the judicial task. In his textbook, in which he liberally quoted from his earlier articles, Leflar omitted this passage, and explained the difference between "false conflicts" and "no-conflicts" more precisely: Leflar (1977-1) p. 187 ff.; see also: Leflar (1980) p. 465 ff.
19 *Cf.* Strikwerda (1978) p. 185.
20 Leflar (1966-1) p 291: "Since some reasons, usually a variety of them, can be called up in support of almost any rule of law that is on the books anywhere, it is nearly always possible for a good lawyer to conjure up governmental interest in just about any state that has any connection with a set of facts." The truth of this statement is demonstrated by some of the Wisconsin and Minnesota decisions to be discussed *infra* text accompanying notes 47–64 and 70–78.
21 Leflar (1977-1) p. 210/211, p. 186.

"super-value judgments".[22] If it does not serve to explain judicial practice in retrospect, the better law consideration should be understood as an invitation to the courts to do justice in the individual case. Leflar emphasizes that comparative justice should be achieved by means of a choice between substantive rules of law, not by a preference for one of the parties or for a specific result. This implies a fairly abstract, and therefore possibly more objective comparison of competing rules of law than the phrase "better law" suggests. Still, Leflar's own examples clearly demonstrate the inevitability of prejudice inherent in this approach. Discussing a series of tort choice of law decisions, he consistently praises those in which the plaintiff prevailed, and spurns those in which the court found for the defendant.[23] Leflar's view of a state's legal system as a "repository of justice for residents and non-residents alike"[24] obviously implies that a "justice-dispensing court" should displace defendant-protective rules (such as limitations of damages, guest statutes, or immunities), not because the plaintiff should be protected, but because the plaintiff-protective rule should be considered as the better law *per se*.[25]

Comparing Leflar's choice-influencing considerations with the "choice-of-law principles" listed in § 6 of the Restatement Second, we recognize "maintenance of interstate and international order" in "the needs of the interstate and international systems",[26] "simplification of the judicial task" in "ease in the determination and application of the

---

22 *Cf.* Strikwerda (1978) p. 186; Westbrook (1975) p. 461. See also: Strikwerda (1986) p. 19, contrasting the better law consideration with European *favor* concepts, discussed *supra* chapter 1, section 4.
23 Leflar (1972-1) p. 460 ff., calling the decision in *Dym v. Gordon* an "aberration"; Leflar (1977-2) p. 20 ff.; Leflar (1980) p.457 ff. However, in his discussion of *Allstate v. Hague* 449 U.S. 302, 101 S.Ct. 633, 66 L.Ed.2d 521 (1981), to be discussed *infra* chapter 7, text following note 47, Leflar pointed out that even if a plaintiff-protective rule (as in this case the Minnesota "stacking rule") could be deemed to be the "better law", the other four choice-influencing considerations could dictate a decision for the defendant, as he would have expected in *Hague*: Leflar (1981) p. 1086, note 32 and p. 1089, note 48. A different correlation of considerations might also explain his criticism of *Rosenthal v. Warren*, 475 F.2d 438 (2d Cir. [N.Y.] 1973), to be discussed *infra* chapter 6, text accompanying notes 51–52, even though the Second Circuit did apply New York's plaintiff-protective, and, therefore, probably "better" rule.
24 Leflar (1977-2) p. 21; *cf.* Leflar (1977-1) p. 212; Leflar (1980) p. 458, note 6.
25 *Cf.* Reppy (1983) p. 659, p. 690 ff.
26 § 6(2)(a).

law to be applied",[27] whereas "advancement of the forum's governmental interests" is echoed in "the relevant policies of the forum".[28] The Restatement's concern for "the relevant policies of other interested states and the relative interests of those states in the determination of the particular issue", in § 6(2)(c), is partly covered by Leflar's broad definition of governmental interests,[29] and partly by the consideration concerning interstate and international orderliness. "Predictability of results" is probably not much different from the Restatement's "protection of justified expectations" in combination with "certainty, predictability and uniformity of result".[30] "The basic policies underlying the particular field of law",[31] finally, is a concern that Leflar claims to have included under the heading of "predictability of results", as it "may well, for multistate cases, be one favoring predictability of socio-economic consequences by sustaining transactions entered into by parties acting in good faith."[32] Conspicuously absent from the Restatement's list of policy factors is the better law consideration.[33] It can hardly be denied, however, that this consideration, more than any of the other ones, has influenced the tort decisions based on the "Leflar approach", while it might even be true that it was a motivating factor, as Leflar suggests, in many other cases in which it was not explicitly referred to.[34]

The better law approach has stirred considerable controversy among academic writers. Ehrenzweig has pointed out that application of the better rule of law, at least if it is the forum's own law, is "an ancient

---

27 § 6(2)(g).
28 § 6(2)(b).
29 The ideal of a state's legal system as a repository of justice "should inhere in the governmental interests of any state." Leflar (1977-2) p. 21; *cf. supra* not 21 and accompanying text.
30 § 6(2)(d) and (f) respectively
31 § 6(2)(e).
32 Leflar (1966-1) p. 284. Comment h on § 6(2), concerning "Basic policies underlying the particular field of law," supports this elusive idea: "This factor explains in large part why the courts seek to apply a law that will sustain the validity of a contract against the charge of commercial usury or the validity of a trust of movables against the charge that it violates the Rule Against Perpetuities."
33 *Cf.* Leflar (1972-2) p. 271; Leflar (1977-1) p. 219.
34 *Cf.* Leflar (1972-1) p. 467, endorsing the "Kentucky approach" (to be discussed *infra*, chapter 7, text following note 7), despite the "primitive reasoning" on which it is founded, for being "a simple and outright preference for the forum state's own 'better law'." See also: Leflar (1977-1) p. 219; Reppy (1983) p. 652.

tradition which apparently succumbed only to the nineteenth century's internationalist conceptualism."[35] Juenger has praised the better law approach as an explicit recognition of the result-selective approach he supports.[36] Weintraub commends the use of the better law criterion in torts cases, provided that two conditions are met: it should only be resorted to in true conflict situations,[37] and the standards by which the better law is to be selected should be objective, i.e. based on "the objective evidence of case law and statute that, over a period of time, many jurisdictions that had the rule in question have abandoned it and adopted what the forum regards as the 'better' rule."[38] To Weintraub, the "better" substantive law is primarily the rule "that is in step with general modern trends in the area," as opposed to "anachronistic or aberrational" rules.[39] Posnak advocates the adoption of a "well-Curried Leflar approach" based on Currie's interest analysis in combination with Leflar's choice-influencing factors for the solution of both true conflicts and unprovided-for situations.[40] On the other hand, Cavers has recognized the better law criterion as "an inevitable psychological reaction in marginal cases, a tendency not to be encouraged but to be taken into account in explaining decisions."[41] Endorsing this point of view, Westbrook has objected that "[u]se of the better

---

35 Ehrenzweig (1967-1) p. 97. This tradition would range from the priority given by the early statutists to the forum's *statuta favorabilia* (as against foreign *statuta odiosa*) to the application of the forum's better law, either overtly or by resort to gimmicks. Ehrenzweig's position on the better law approach is ambiguous. He has applauded the better law consideration as a "promise in multistate tort law," viewing it mostly as a proper explanation of forum preference; Ehrenzweig (1967-2) p. 853 ff; Ehrenzweig (1967-1) p. 100 ff. On the other hand, as he spurned "superlaw" considerations and "super-value judgments", Ehrenzweig can hardly be thought to have favored the (supposedly bilateral) better law criterion as decisive for the selection of the applicable rule of law. *Cf.* his contribution to a symposium on "The Value of Principled Preferences": Ehrenzweig (1971) p. 236 ff., especially note 10: "Happily [the court in *International Planning Ltd. v. Daystrom Inc.*] at least spared us the 'better rule' approach which Cavers so convincingly refutes."
36 Juenger (1969) p. 230 ff.; *cf.* Westbrook (1975) p. 431.
37 See *supra* note 10; Weintraub (1980) p. 274, p. 328 ff.
38 Weintraub (1971) p. 245.
39 Weintraub (1980) p. 273 ff.
40 Posnak (1983) p. 732 ff. In his opinion, choice of law is premised on "the application of forum law to all issues unless some objection is seasonably made," in which case foreign law should be applied if a foreign jurisdiction is the only one having a specific interest in an issue (false conflict).
41 Cavers (1971-1) p. 215; see also: Cavers (1972) p. 169 = Cavers (1976) p. 654. See also: *supra* chapter 4, section 4(c), note 298.

rule in deciding which law should apply misconceives the nature of the task confronting the court," as it assumes either the role of a "super appellate court" or that of the state's legislature when it endeavors to weigh the merits of conflicting rules of substantive law against each other.[42] In Von Mehren's opinion, the choice-influencing considerations have little to contribute to the solution of the choice of law problem, whereas the better law approach "probably complicates the problem even further, unless general agreement were to exist on the standards by which superiority was to be judged."[43] This criticism is borne out by the observations of several authors who have noted that, as a rule, an overt judicial invocation of the better law principle is a prelude to the application of forum law.[44]

New Hampshire was one of the first jurisdictions in which the Leflar approach was explicitly adopted as the approved rationale in torts choice of law. In terms of interest analysis *Clark v. Clark* presented a false conflict, as the issue focused on the application of a foreign guest statute (that of Vermont) in an action for damages between New Hampshire spouses.[45] Setting a trend for the resolution of multistate tort cases by choice-influencing considerations, Chief Justice Kenison discarded as largely irrelevant the considerations of predictability, maintenance of interstate order, and simplification of the court's task. In the absence of any interest of Vermont, advancement of forum interests dictated application of New Hampshire's ordinary negligence rule, which was thought to be "preferable" to Vermont's guest statute anyway. Other New Hampshire cases reveal a more questionable use of the "forum interest" consideration in combination with the better law criterion. In *Gagne v. Berry* the law-fact pattern was the reverse of *Clark v. Clark*: the accident had occurred in New Hampshire, the forum state, whereas the parties were domiciled in Massachusetts, the state having the guest statute. Consistent with *Clark*, application of the guest statute was rejected on the grounds that the New Hampshire law of ordinary negligence was considered the "sounder or better law" as opposed to the "lesser law" of Massachusetts, but the decision also relied on the notion that New

---

42 Westbrook (1975) p. 461. *Cf.* Hanotiau (1979) p. 153; Strikwerda (1986) p. 19/20.
43 Von Mehren (1975) p. 952/953; *cf.* Lorenz (1977) p. 81; Hohloch (1984) p. 234.
44 Cramton/Currie/Kay (1981) p. 338 ff.; Sedler (1977-2) p. 1007 ff., p. 1029 ff.; Mühl (1982) p. 66 ff.
45 *Clark v. Clark* 107 N.H. 351, 222 A.2d 205 (1966).

Hampshire had an interest in the regulation of conduct of motorists within its territory: "Adoption of the Massachusetts law in this case would defeat the deterrent effect of our negligence laws by allowing negligent conduct to go undeterred."[46] This line of reasoning turns a false conflict into a real one, on the strength of a dubious interest of the forum state. The following Wisconsin and Minnesota cases are illustrative of this kind of manipulation.

In Wisconsin, another jurisdiction in which the Leflar approach is firmly established, a forum interest is easily construed by the assertion that Wisconsin has an interest in regulating conduct within its territory. The decision in *Heath v. Zellmer* hinged on Wisconsin's policy of "penalizing" unsafe conduct on its highways.[47] As far as the action concerned the host-guest relationship between Indiana and Ohio domiciliaries who had been involved in a car accident in Wisconsin,[48] the issue was whether the Ohio-Indiana guest statutes or Wisconsin's ordinary negligence rule applied. Analyzing the policy of the Indiana guest statute as one of protecting the host, his insurer, and possibly other parties to the accident,[49] the Wisconsin Supreme Court held it to

46 *Gagne v. Berry* 290 A.2d 624 at 626 (N.H. 1972). The same argument is used in *Gordon v. Gordon* 387 A.2d 339 at 341 (N.H. 1978), in which case the interspousal immunity rule of Maine, the state of the parties' domicile at the time of suit, was rejected as "antiquated", "archaic and in disrepute", and contrary to the "forum's interest in providing redress for one injured in New Hampshire." This decision would appear to overrule *Johnson v. Johnson* 107 N.H. 30, 216 A.2d 781 at 783 (1966), in which it was said that "[r]ecognition of the Massachusetts immunity rule will not render Massachusetts drivers less careful on our highways since their own and their wives' safety will still be jeopardized by carelessness on their part." The court then adopted "a single rule" that would "render the spouses' domicile the controlling contact for choice-of-law purposes, regardless whether it grants or denies [interspousal] immunity." It should be noted that *Johnson* was decided in 1966, shortly before the choice-influencing considerations were adopted in *Clark v. Clark*.
47 *Heath v. Zellmer* 35 Wis.2d 578, 151 N.W.2d 664 (1967).
48 The host was a resident of Ohio, who had borrowed the car from her father, an Indiana resident. The plaintiff-guest was also domiciled in Indiana. The driver of the other car was a resident of Wisconsin.
49 The Indiana guest statute "evinces a desire to (a) prevent collusive suits between hosts and guests; (b) prevent the ingratitude of the guest who sues his kindly host (bites the hand that feeds him); (c) protect the host from being obligated far more than he bargained for (a judgment when he only offered a ride); (d) keep intact a fund (the host's assets) so it can be reached by other parties to the accident whose claims are assumed to have a vague moral priority over the claims of the gratuitous guest. It is clear that the policy of the Indiana statute is to shield the host, and therefore his insurer, from some liability." *Ibid.* p. 669.

be in conflict with the purposes of Wisconsin law, said to be "compensatory, admonitory and deterrent." Emphasizing the deterrent effect of Wisconsin's law of negligence, the court relied on the choice-influencing consideration of forum interests when it claimed that "the choice of Wisconsin law would further this state's interest in regulating conduct on Wisconsin highways and penalizing that conduct when it is negligent." The opinion concluded with the better law consideration: forum law was deemed to be the "sounder" law, whereas Indiana law was thought to be an "anachronism". In my opinion, the construction of a Wisconsin interest in this case is highly artificial: between the Indiana and Ohio parties the case should (and could) have been decided either for the defendants as a false conflict, or for the plaintiff on the strength of the better law consideration alone.[50]

In *Conklin v. Horner*, another guest statute case, there were even less contacts with the forum state than in *Heath*. On a trip in Wisconsin as a guest of defendant, plaintiff suffered injuries when they crashed into a tree. Both parties were domiciled in Illinois, the state having the guest statute. Referring to choice-influencing considerations the court construed a "serious conflict" between Illinois' interest in shielding an Illinois host and his insurer, and Wisconsin's interest in deterring negligent conduct on its highways. Being a tourist state that attracts large numbers of vehicles from other states, including immunity jurisdictions, Wisconsin was said to have a policy of protecting not only the injured party but also Wisconsin medical creditors and the Wisconsin taxpayers, who would have to foot the bill if the foreign plaintiff would not be allowed to recover. Application of the Illinois guest statute, deemed to be "anachronistic", would therefore "substantially dilute the deterrent (as well as compensatory) effect of our negligence law."[51] Considering that there was no evidence of any Wisconsin claims for compensation, I find the construction of a forum interest in

---

50 See also: *Zelinger v. State Sand and Gravel Co.* 38 Wis.2d 98, 156 N.W.2d 466 at 472 (1968): Wisconsin law applied in an action arising out of a collision in Wisconsin, involving plaintiffs domiciled in Illinois and a Wisconsin defendant. It was said that Wisconsin's interest in the non-existence of guest statutes, interspousal and parental immunities was "to promote the spreading of the risk and fasten liability in torts on a moral basis of fault."
51 *Conklin v. Horner* 38 Wis.2d 468, 157 N.W.2d 579 at 586 (1968). For a critical analysis of the *Conklin* opinion, see: Weintraub (1980) p. 329.

this case highly factitious, and, in view of the better law consideration, unnecessarily parochial.[52]

The same can be said of *Decker v. Fox River Tractor Co.*, a federal decision under Wisconsin choice of law, concerning contributory negligence. One of the plaintiffs, Pennsylvania farm owners, had been injured when operating a forage harvester which was bought in Pennsylvania, but manufactured in Wisconsin by defendant. Under Pennsylvania law contributory negligence was a complete bar to recovery, whereas Wisconsin had a comparative negligence rule. The first three choice-influencing considerations were deemed insignificant for the choice of law decision in this case. Although Wisconsin law was said to be the better law, the district court hesitated to decide the case on this argument alone: "It is perhaps too easy to let the 'better rule of law' factor dominate the other four and be solely determinative of the choice of law."[53] The construction of a Wisconsin governmental interest provided the court with another reason to apply Wisconsin law. Stressing that Wisconsin's comparative negligence rule was already forty years old, and that it contained a legislative decision that negligent plaintiffs should not go uncompensated, the court assumed that application of any other rule would damage Wisconsin's interest. This rationale is not very convincing, as it focuses on a policy of compensation rather than deterrence, thus suggesting that Wisconsin has an interest in the compensation of any tort victim, regardless of his domicile or the place of injury. If Wisconsin's comparative negligence rule would be meant to protect the plaintiff, this case could be thought to present an unprovided-for situation:[54] it could be argued that Pennsylvania would not have an interest in protecting out-of-state tortfeasors, whereas Wisconsin would not be interested in the compensation of out-of-state victims. However that may be, in view of the

---

52 I am not convinced by the proposition that, since a guest statute defense is usually defeated by proof of gross negligence, or willful or wanton conduct, the real issue in guest statute cases would involve standards of conduct (*cf. Hunker v. Royal Indemnity Co.* 57 Wis.2d 588, 204 N.W.2d 897 at 904) which would give a state a stronger interest in the regulation of conduct on its highways. I cannot believe that the juridical distinction between standards of conduct has any bearing on the host-driver's actual conduct on the road. In that respect, the interest of the *locus* state is fictitious. More on this subject, *infra* chapter 8.
53 *Decker v. Fox River Tractor Co.* 324 F.Supp. 1089 at 1091 (E.D. Wis. 1971).
54 Sedler (1977-2) p. 1030.

forced assertion of a Wisconsin interest, it would seem that in reality the *Decker* decision is based on a pure better law consideration.

Although the previously discussed decisions would seem to compel a different conclusion, the Wisconsin brand of the Leflar approach does not always call for the application of forum law. In *Hunker v. Royal Indemnity Co.*, Ohio law was applied to the question whether an Ohio resident could sue his co-employee, also an Ohio resident, and the co-employee's insurer for damages arising out of a car accident in Wisconsin.[55] An Ohio statute did not allow suits against co-employees if the plaintiff had collected workmen's compensation, whereas Wisconsin law permitted such a suit. Again, the case was viewed as a true conflict:[56] Wisconsin was deemed to be an interested jurisdiction, not only because it was concerned with the safety on its highways and the rights of Wisconsin creditors possibly involved, but also because Wisconsin is a "justice-seeking jurisdiction" whose "courts are concerned that justice be done irrespective of the origins of the party litigants."[57] Ohio, on the other hand, had an interest in industrial safety and industrial peace, protected by its workmen's compensation law. The decision relies mostly on the consideration of predictability of results, in this case the expectation of the employees and the insurer that the legal consequences of an industrial accident would be governed by Ohio law. Wisconsin's policy of compensating those who are injured by negligent acts was sufficiently satisfied by the workmen's compensation award plaintiff had received under Ohio law. The better law consideration did not exclude Ohio law, since its application

---

55 *Hunker v. Royal Indemnity Co.* 57 Wis.2d 588, 204 N.W.2d 897 (1973).
56 Possibly influenced by Leflar's broad definition of *false* conflicts, the Wisconsin Supreme Court occasionally uses the term "true conflict" to denote any situation in which "the choice of one law as compared to another [will] determine the outcome": *Decker v. Fox River Tractor Co.* 324 F.Supp. 1089 (E.D. Wis. 1971); *Lichter v. Fritsch* 77 Wis.2d 178, 252 N.W.2d 360 (1977); *Tillett v. J.I. Case Co.* 580 F.Supp. 1276 (E.D. Wis. 1984). In this sense, a true conflict is the opposite of a no-conflict situation rather than a product of interest analysis. However, the cases here discussed may be called true conflicts in either sense: in all of them, choice of law was "outcome-determinative", and all of them were said to present a conflict of interests between Wisconsin and the foreign jurisdiction involved.
57 *Hunker v. Royal Indemnity Co.* 57 Wis.2d 588, 204 N.W.2d 897 at 900 (1973). *Cf. Milkovich v. Saari* 295 Minn. 155, 203 N.W.2d 408 (1973), to be discussed *infra* text accompanying notes 70–74.

could not be characterized as a "drag on the coattails of civilization."[58] The court implied, however, it deemed its own law to be superior, and that it would have applied it as the better law if a Wisconsin victim had been involved.[59] This suggests the same relativity in evaluating the quality of law that we encountered in the analysis of public policy decisions, and it should be rejected for the same reasons.[60]

Another Wisconsin decision in which foreign law was applied despite the professed high quality of Wisconsin law is *Lichter v. Fritsch*. The defendant was a mental patient in a hospital in Illinois who stole an Illinois-registered car and caused an accident in Wisconsin, injuring plaintiff. Under Illinois law, the owner who leaves his car unattended would have to disprove negligence; Wisconsin law would absolve him from liability. To support the application of Illinois' plaintiff-protective law, the court relied on the consideration of predictability of results: the car owner would have expected *prima facie* liability as the legal consequence of this unintended contingency. Surprisingly, even though Wisconsin law would have protected the car owner in this situation, application of Illinois law was thought to be "consistent with the policy and theory of Wisconsin law to compensate the victim."[61] Thus, both Illinois' interest in "protection of life, limb and property by prevention of recognized hazards" and Wisconsin's general interest in compensation were satisfied. The court was reluctant, however, to evaluate the quality of either law. Instead, it hinted that Illinois might not have the better rule of law, since it was a minority rule, in force in few jurisdictions. Nevertheless, the Wisconsin plaintiff prevailed.

58 *Ibid.* p. 907; the phrase was coined by Chief Justice Kenison in *Clark v. Clark* 107 N.H. 351 at 355; 222 A.2d 205 at 209 (1966).
59 *Hunker v. Royal Indemnity Co.* 57 Wis.2d 588, 204 N.W.2d 897 at 907 (1973). Nine years later, the Supreme Court of New Hampshire was of a different opinion: in *LaBounty v. American Ins. Co.*, 451 A.2d 161 (N.H. 1982) the co-employees were residents of New Hampshire, worked for a Massachusetts corporation, and had an accident in Maine. Workmen's compensation had been awarded under Massachusetts law. New Hampshire law did not bar a suit between fellow-employees, whereas the laws of Massachusetts and Maine did. Application of New Hampshire's plaintiff-protective rule was rejected, since New Hampshire did not have a relevant interest on the strength of domicile alone, whereas the better law consideration pointed to the law of Massachusetts or Maine: "The trend in the last decade has been to bar such suits," *viz.* between fellow-employees.
60 See *supra* chapter 2, section 3, text accompanying notes 169–171; *ibid.* text following note 249.
61 *Lichter v. Fritsch* 77 Wis.2d 178, 252 N.W.2d 360 at 363 (1977).

Wisconsin's tort choice of law displays an unmistakable trend towards plaintiff-favoring decisions.[62] The outcome is usually predicated on the consideration of Wisconsin interests and Wisconsin's better law. The *Hunker* decision is an exception: first, because it relied on predictability of results rather than forum interest or better law as an overriding consideration, and, second, because the court found for defendant. In terms of interest analysis the decision is easily explained as a false conflict, and this might have been the court's real motive to deny full compensation.[63] The *Lichter* case is only exceptional in that the opinion emphasizes the consideration of predictability, whereas it could have relied on the better law consideration which tends to support a pro-plaintiff decision.[64] The other cases are basically "better law decisions", in my opinion. I am not convinced by the contention –implicit in *Heath*, *Conklin* and *Decker*– that a Wisconsin interest would be affected in virtually any case involving tortious conduct in Wisconsin. To me, the consideration of forum interests in these cases is therefore dubious and far-fetched.

In his analysis of a series of Minnesota decisions, all of them relying on choice-influencing considerations, Professor Reppy has contended that the "Minnesota Supreme Court could make the method simpler to apply if it would announce to the bench and bar what is clear from an analysis of the opinions: there is only one choice-influencing consideration, not five."[65] In Minnesota the overriding consideration of the better law invariably supports application of Minnesota law, culminating in a choice of law ruling that even Leflar himself admits to be "marginal".[66] Having experimented with interest analysis in

---

62 Reppy (1983) p. 698.
63 *Hunker v. Royal Indemnity Co.* 57 Wis.2d 588, 204 N.W.2d 897 at 906 (1973): " ... it is doubtful that Wisconsin has any identifiable or serious governmental interest in having an Ohio resident recover more than the expressed policy of that state permits."
64 *Cf.* Reppy (1983) p. 696, note 234: "Surprisingly unwilling to declare the out-of-state law better, which it obviously was to a believer in Leflar's method, the Wisconsin Supreme Court relied on considerations number (1) and (2) to reach the result the 'better law' approach compelled."
65 *Ibid.* p. 695.
66 Leflar (1981) p. 1089, on *Hague v. Allstate Ins. Co.* 289 N.W.2d 43 (Minn. 1979) aff'd *sub nom. Allstate v. Hague* 449 U.S. 302, 101 S.Ct. 633, 66 L.Ed.2d 521 (1981), to be discussed *infra* chapter 7, text following note 47.

Schmidt v. Driscoll Hotel,[67] *Balts v. Balts*,[68] and *Kopp v. Rechtzigel*,[69] the Minnesota Supreme Court converted to the "Leflar methodology" in *Milkovich v. Saari*.[70] Both the law-fact pattern and the opinion in this case are remarkably similar to those in *Conklin v. Horner*.[71] The parties were domiciliaries of a jurisdiction with a guest statute, Ontario, and the car accident that gave rise to this action occurred in the forum state, Minnesota. Again, two considerations supported the choice of Minnesota's common law rule of liability: advancement of forum interests and application of the better law. The main governmental interest of Minnesota was said to be that of a "justice-administering state", unwilling to apply "rules which, however accepted they may be in other states, are inconsistent with our own concept of fairness and equity." The deterrent effect of common law liability and the fear of unpaid (Minnesota) hospital bills were mentioned as factors giving rise to additional, but less compelling, forum interests. In conclusion, the court declared its own law to be "superior", and discarded the Ontario guest statute as lacking a persuasive rationale. This particular consideration occasioned a dissenting opinion by Justice Peterson, objecting that the law of an American forum might not be the better law for Canadian citizens who may be assumed to "have

---

67 *Schmidt v. Driscoll Hotel* 249 Minn. 376, 82 N.W.2d 365 (1957): discussion of the interests of Wisconsin (the state where the plaintiff had been injured in a car accident) and Minnesota (where all parties were domiciled) in an action for damages under Minnesota's dram-shop act.
68 *Balts v. Balts* 273 Minn. 419, 142 N.W.2d 66 (1966): Wisconsin had no interest in the application of its parental immunity law in an action between mother and son, both residents of Minnesota.
69 *Kopp v. Rechtzigel* 273 Minn. 441, 141 N.W.2d 526 (1966): the guest statute of South Dakota, the state where the accident occurred, did not apply in an action between Minnesota residents, since Minnesota had an "overriding concern" in the relationship of the parties and the adjudication of their rights.
70 *Milkovich v. Saari* 295 Minn. 155, 203 N.W.2d 408 (1973). The first reference to choice-influencing considerations, as applied in *Clark v. Clark*, had already been made in *Schneider v. Nichols* 280 Minn. 139, 158 N.W.2d 254 (1968), to be followed by *Bolgrean v. Stich* 293 Minn. 8, 196 N.W.2d 442 (1972). In both cases, however, the center of gravity approach predominates. In *Bolgrean*, the better law consideration "reinforces" the decision.
71 *Conklin v. Horner* 38 Wis.2d 468, 157 N.W.2d 579 (1968); *supra* text following note 50.

concurred in the rule of law of their own government as just."[72] My main objection to the *Milkovich* decision, however, regards the artificial construction of a Minnesota forum interest. Calling the administration of justice a concern of the forum's legal system creates a governmental interest of the forum state in *any* litigation before its courts.[73] In that interpretation, the "advancement of forum interests" consideration is essentially a paraphrase of the better law criterion, and might as well be left out. Since Leflar's first three considerations are generally considered irrelevant in interstate torts,[74] the better law standard would appear to be the sole choice of law criterion for Minnesota torts choice of law.

However, two Minnesota cases would seem to contradict this hypothesis. *Schwartz v. Consolidated Freightways Corp. of Del.*, which was an action for damages arising out of a truck accident in Indiana, involved a Minnesota plaintiff and a Delaware corporation doing business in Delaware and Ohio. Indiana had a contributory negligence rule, which, if applied, would bar plaintiff from any recovery; under Minnesota's comparative negligence rule plaintiff would be awarded 90 % of the damages. The opinion relied almost exclusively on the governmental interest consideration: since the economic impact of plaintiff's injuries would be felt by Minnesota residents, Minnesota was said to have "a clear governmental interest in the outcome of

---

72 *Milkovich v. Saari* 295 Minn. 155, 203 N.W.2d 408 (1973), diss. opinion *per* Peterson J., who further pointed out that plaintiff had first initiated proceedings in the courts of Ontario, but later brought her action in Minnesota, which proved to be an instance of fruitful forum shopping. See also: Case Note, Conflict of Laws: Minnesota Rejects the 'Significant Contacts' Doctrine in Favor of the 'Better Law' Test, 58 *Minn. L.Rev.* 199–210 (1973), criticizing the decision for ignoring Ontario's interest, and the better law approach for compelling the judiciary to "perform the function of deciding which law embodies the better social policy."
73 But see: *Bigelow v. Halloran* 313 N.W.2d 10 (Minn. 1981): application of the law of plaintiff's home state Iowa in an action against the estate of a Minnesota decedent. Iowa law allowed survival of the cause of action, Minnesota law did not. Advancement of forum interests, understood as an interest in the service of justice, induced the court to apply the "better" Iowa law. The decision disproves the presumption that Minnesota choice of law would invariably result in the application of forum law.
74 *Myers v. Government Employees Insurance Company* 225 N.W.2d 238 (Minn. 1974), to be discussed *infra* text accompanying notes 76–77. Even if one of them (predictability in particular) would be taken into account, the forum interest and better law considerations would still operate jointly in favor of Minnesota law: Reppy (1983) p. 692/693.

plaintiff's case," while Indiana's interest would be minimal.[75] The court then rejected the better law test as redundant in a case in which Minnesota had an "overriding" governmental interest. The same happened in *Myers v. Government Employees Insurance Company*, in which case a Minnesota plaintiff brought a direct action against the insurer of a Louisiana resident. The insurer was a Washington D.C. corporation doing business in both Louisiana and Minnesota. Although Minnesota law did not allow direct actions, permissible under Louisiana law,[76] the Minnesota Supreme Court managed to find for the plaintiff without relying on Louisiana's plaintiff-protective (and therefore arguably "better") rule, but instead by discovering an interest of Minnesota. How application of defendant-protective forum law could result in a finding for the plaintiff, is best explained by quoting from the opinion: "Here, the vested rights of plaintiffs granted by Louisiana statute are enforceable under the Minnesota statute and Minnesota's governmental interest dictates that we should permit such enforcement. Therefore, we need not consider or make any choice of better law under the facts of this case."[77]

In my opinion, both cases present false conflicts. In *Schwartz*, Indiana (the state where the accident occurred) could hardly be thought to have an interest in barring the plaintiff from recovery pursuant to its contributory negligence rule; if we ignore the possible interests of Ohio or Delaware, which were not discussed, only Minnesota as plaintiff's home state had a valid claim to application of its law. In all probability, the better law test would have brought the same result.[78] The

---

75 *Schwartz v. Consolidated Freightways Corp. of Del.* 221 N.W.2d 665 at 668 (Minn. 1974). The possible interests of Ohio or Delaware were not considered.
76 More precisely: Minnesota would uphold a provision in an insurance policy denying a tort victim any rights against the insurer, until he would have won his case against the tortfeasor. Louisiana law invalidated such contractual provisions. *Cf.* Reppy (1983) p. 694, note 226.
77 *Myers v. Government Employees Insurance Company* 225 N.W.2d 238 at 244 (Minn. 1974).
78 For persuasive authority the court could have turned to *Frummer v. Hilton Hotels International Inc.* 304 N.Y.S.2d 335 at 344 (1969), involving the choice between England's comparative and New York's contributory negligence rule: " ... resort to the 'better law' principle might be the honest and simple solution, which would also lead to the adoption of England's rule as the controlling law here." In *Mitchell v. Craft* 211 So.2d 509 (Miss. 1968), Mississippi's comparative negligence statute was held to be the better rule of law as opposed to Louisiana's contributory negligence rule. See also: *Tillett v. J.I. Case Co.* 580 F.Supp. 1276 (E.D. Wis. 1984).

Myers court could have decided the case as a false conflict by simply admitting that Louisiana, not Minnesota, had the "substantial governmental interest": since the Louisiana rule permitting direct actions was said to be predicated on a policy of protecting the general public, *including non-residents*, rather than the insurer, it was obviously meant to elevate the standards of the insurance business. Its application would therefore be apposite in any direct action against an insurance company doing business in Louisiana. The strange choice of law twist by which the Minnesota Supreme Court achieved the "enforcement" of Louisiana's plaintiff-protective rule, despite the emphasis on Minnesota's substantial interest, suggests that in reality the *Myers* decision was inspired by a better law consideration, not by a concern for forum interests. If so, both *Schwartz* and *Myers* would still support the thesis that "better law" is the one and only choice of law standard in Minnesota.

If anything is clear from the foregoing discussion, it is the judicial tendency to use the Leflar approach, particularly the better law consideration, as a motive for plaintiff-protecting decisions. Whether the considerations dictate application of forum law or foreign law, whether the decision is predicated on predictability of results, on the advancement of forum interests, or on the better law, the outcome is generally a finding for the plaintiff. The two exceptions I found were both decisions in suits between fellow-employees in which the plaintiff had already received workmen's compensation.[79] All other cases

---

[79] *Cf. Hunker v. Royal Indemnity Co.* 57 Wis.2d 588, 204 N.W.2d 897 (1973), *supra* notes 55–60 and accompanying text. *LaBounty v. American Ins. Co.* 451 A.2d 161 (N.H. 1982), *supra* note 59. In both cases the expectations of the parties as to the legal consequences of the occurrence were emphasized, whereas the consideration of predictability of results is generally said to be irrelevant in tort actions. The *LaBounty* opinion suggested that the better rule of law might be the one that, contrary to New Hampshire's own rule, bars suits between fellow-employees. In *Hunker*, the court felt that its own law, permitting these suits, was better than that of Ohio, but since the plaintiff was an Ohio resident, it did not press the point.
By contrast, there was no question that foreign law was better than New Hampshire forum law in *Maguire v. Exeter & Hampton Electric Company* 114 N.H. 589, 325 A.2d 778 at 780 (1974), an earlier New Hampshire case, in which the unlimited recovery rule of Maine, plaintiff's home state, was deemed to be superior to New Hampshire's wrongful death limitation. Plaintiff's deceased had been killed in New Hampshire in the course of his employment in that state. In this true conflict, New Hampshire law was applied, benefiting the New Hampshire defendant, since the fact that decedent had been a resident of Maine was "not enough, standing alone, to →

were decided in favor of the tort victim, and in most of them the primary considerations were advancement of governmental interests and/or application of the better law. Not surprisingly, forum law applied in most cases: the Leflar approach seems to prevail in those jurisdictions that can self-righteously claim to have the better law, generally benefiting the plaintiff.[80] In a few cases, the law of a foreign jurisdiction was applied. While it was seldom deemed to be superior, it generally favored plaintiffs who had their domicile in the forum state.[81]

These observations on the application of Leflar's theory[82] lead me to a negative conclusion. In multistate tort law, the first three considerations are of little value. Predictability of results is usually overlooked since the parties to a tort action are not likely to have planned the tortious occurrence; if they had thought about its legal consequences at all, they would probably expect the law of their respective home

---

warrant the application of Maine law to the issue of damages." *Cf.* Hay (1981) p. 1645, note 4; Weintraub (1980) p. 326/327.

80 In this respect, the courts seem to be motivated by the same plaintiff-protective trend that inspired Weintraub's "presumption in favor of recovery" in true conflicts and unprovided-for cases. Weintraub (1980) p. 271; *supra* chapter 4, section 3, note 129 and accompanying text. Generally perceived as "better", modern tort law is characterized by a recovery-favoring tenor, whereas older, "anachronistic" laws are still based on defendant-protective notions, such as the "negligence-fault concept" or immunities. Weintraub, *ibid.*

81 *Bigelow v. Halloran* 313 N.W.2d 10 (Minn. 1981), *supra* note 73, is the only exception in this respect: under the applicable Iowa law the Iowa plaintiff prevailed against a Minnesota defendant. *Zelinger v. State Sand and Gravel Co.* 38 Wis.2d 98, 156 N.W.2d 466 (1968), *supra* note 50, and *Decker v. Fox River Tractor Co.* 324 F.Supp. 1089 (E.D. Wis. 1971), 324 F.Supp. 1089 (E.D. Wis. 1971), *supra* text following note 52, were the only cases in which foreign plaintiffs prevailed against forum-based defendants.

82 It will be clear, I trust, that my comments are not concerned with Leflar's descriptive explanation of judicial performance, but with the normative effect of his writings. At first, his investigations into the courts' real reasons for decision resulted in a descriptive account of five major choice of law motives. Later, when some courts started to refer to his analysis as if it were a new choice of law theory, the choice-influencing considerations gradually acquired a normative status, both in judicial practice and in the law reviews. In this curious cross-fertilizing process, Leflar's observing comments were metamorphosed into the "Leflar approach" now in use as a set of normative principles.

states to apply.[83] Maintenance of interstate and international order is generally explained as a minimum standard of involvement of the state whose law is applied: "no more is required than that a court not apply the law of a state which does not have a substantial connection with the total facts and the particular issue being litigated."[84] It is hard to imagine a decision in which the court would not be able to satisfy this requirement. Simplification of the judicial task is seldom mentioned as a choice-influencing factor; if it is, this consideration is said to pose no problem "since the courts are fully capable of administering the law of another forum if called upon to do so."[85] That leaves us with the controlling considerations of advancement of forum interests and application of the better law. As applied by the courts, the first test usually leads to a comparative assessment of interests, no different from straightforward interest analysis. In that respect, the Leflar approach has little to add to conflicts methodology. In those cases in which a forum interest was established by a mere reference to the forum state's policy of "dispensing justice",[86] or by the construction of an admonitory policy, the true motive for the decision, I submit, was the better law consideration.

Apart from his explanation of judicial practice, Leflar's main contribution to the solution of choice of law problems in torts is, in my opinion, his canonization of the better law principle.[87] On the assumption that the service of justice is any court's prime concern and that justice is best served by the application of the superior rule of law, the

83 *Clark v. Clark* 107 N.H. 351, 222 A.2d 205 (1966); *Gordon v. Gordon* 387 A.2d 339 (N.H. 1978); *Milkovich v. Saari* 295 Minn. 155, 203 N.W.2d 408 (1973); see, however: *Lichter v. Fritsch* 77 Wis.2d 178, 252 N.W.2d 360 (1977); *LaBounty v. American Ins. Co.* 451 A.2d 161 (N.H. 1982).
84 *Milkovich v. Saari* 295 Minn. 155, 203 N.W.2d 408 (1973); *LaBounty v. American Ins. Co.* 451 A.2d 161 (N.H. 1982).
85 *Milkovich v. Saari* 295 Minn. 155, 203 N.W.2d 408 (1973). If the eligible foreign law is more exotic than it is in interstate cases, this consideration might have a different impact.
86 In *Wallis v. Mrs. Smith's Pie Co.* 261 Ark. 622, 550 S.W.2d 453 (1977), the Arkansas Supreme Court purported to adopt the Leflar approach. The opinion relied mostly on the most significant relationship test, however, except for the statement (at p. 458) that " ... probably the truest governmental interest the forum has is 'in the fair and efficient administration of justice', and in our opinion application of our [comparative negligence] statute better achieves that result." *Cf.* the criticism by Hogue (1978) p. 713 ff.
87 *Cf.* Juenger (1980) p. 418 ff.

better law consideration would seem to be a reasonable criterion for the decision of any legal issue, including choice of law problems. I am willing to believe that the better law consideration is therefore an important motive for numerous choice of law decisions that are not readily explained by the prevailing principles of conflicts law. However, if the better law test is in effect the only choice of law standard, little is left of the "logical and legal bases of the conflict of laws." A choice between two rules based on a preference for what is supposed to be the "better" law is ultimately a matter of taste,[88] hence to be measured by no other yardstick but judicial intuition. The central choice of law problem is thus reduced to an *ad hoc* evaluation of the relative quality of conflicting laws, with a fair chance that forum law will be deemed superior. For that reason, I would reserve the better law consideration, if at all, for cases defying rational solution, generally true conflicts and unprovided-for cases.[89] If each jurisdiction involved can be said to have a valid claim to application of its law, whether on account of a significant relationship or on the strength of its governmental interest, the choice is arbitrary anyway.[90] The opposite is true in two-state situations in which one jurisdiction is only marginally involved. There is nothing arbitrary or irrational, I find, in applying the law of both parties' home state rather than the law of the state where the tort happened to occur. I fail to see why such a case should be treated differently from a purely domestic case, for no better reason than that the place of wrong happened to be abroad. The decision in *Fuerste v. Bemis* may illustrate this point of view. The case presented a classic false conflict: driving through Wisconsin on their way from one point in Iowa to another, an Iowa host and an Iowa guest had an accident in which the guest was killed. If the accident had occurred in Iowa, no one would have doubted that the Iowa guest statute should be applied. Why, then, should the Iowa Supreme Court be obliged to reject its own guest statute in favor of the "better" Wisconsin law, now that the state of Wisconsin had a marginal connection with the occurrence?

---

88 A federal court in New York was unable to apply the better law test to the issue of joint liability, since "the respective jurisdictions generally have not yet made determinative judgments as to what their law is on this substantive issue." *Chance v. E.I. DuPont De Nemours & Company, Inc.* 371 F.Supp. 439 at 448 (E.D. N.Y. 1974). Surely, the court could have expressed a preference for what, in its own view, the better law *should* be.
89 *Cf.* Posnak (1983) p. 732 ff.; Weintraub (1980) p. 274, p. 328 ff.
90 Strikwerda (1978) p. 193.

Refuting plaintiff's argument to that effect, the court stated that the better rule of law could only be applied in true conflict situations, and it added: "It is not for us to consider which is the better law when the policy making body of the state has spoken."[91]

Even as a means to solve insoluble conflicts the value of the better law principle can be disputed. As we have seen, most opinions relying on choice-influencing considerations ended up with a preference for forum law. In some of them it was suggested that the quality of conflicting rules of law can be measured by objective or universal standards: modern rules are said to be better than "antiquated" ones, or a law in force in a majority of jurisdictions is supposed to be superior to a minority rule.[92] In theory, the better law consideration is neutral and impervious to forum preference. Yet, it is unlikely that a court will admit to the inferior quality of its own law, unless it is willing to change it. The Supreme Court of Oregon, rejecting the better law principle, put it this way: "It is obvious that such a criterion for choice of law would result in the application of the law of the forum in each case

---

91 *Fuerste v. Bemis* 156 N.W.2d 831 at 834 (Iowa 1968). As in *Fuerste*, the decisions in which the better law consideration was expressly rejected generally resulted in a finding for the defendant:
Byrn v. American Universal Ins. Co. 548 S.W.2d 186 at 190, note 22 (Mo.App. 1977): Iowa's guest statute applied in an action arising out of an accident in Iowa, in which a Missouri guest and her Iowa host were killed; the better law approach, advocated by the plaintiff, was rejected as "an extreme theory adopted by the State of Wisconsin ... criticized for its obvious imprecise method of application."
Mager v. Mager 197 N.W.2d 626 (N.D. 1972): better law test denied in a North Dakota decision on interspousal immunity under Minnesota law between Minnesota spouses.
Issendorf v. Olson 194 N.W.2d 750 (N.D. 1972): North Dakota's contributory negligence rather than Minnesota's comparative negligence rule applied in an action between North Dakota residents involved in a car accident in Minnesota; the North Dakota Supreme Court was "not particularly enamored" with its own defendant-protective rule, refusing to call it "better" than the law of Minnesota. Nevertheless, forum law was applied on account of North Dakota's significant contacts.
Tower v. Schwabe 284 Or. 105, 585 P.2d 662 (1978): Oregon's guest statute applied in an action between an Oregon guest, injured in British Columbia, and an Iowa host. See also *infra* text accompanying note 93.
92 The latter standard would appear to support rejection of a progressive rule, in favor of one that the other jurisdiction might consider "anachronistic"; *LaBounty v. American Ins. Co., supra* note 59.

because every forum thinks it has created the best rule of law; otherwise it would not have established the rule."[93]

A preference for foreign law on account of its higher quality should be regarded as an implicit criticism of forum law. If the court is in a position to improve on its own judge-made law, a proper function of a state supreme court, it should do so on the very occasion that gave rise to dissatisfaction with forum law. Otherwise, it would evade "its responsibility to overrule or modify outdated or clearly erroneous judicial rules."[94] If the court chooses the foreign law in preference to a forum *statute*, it is "assuming powers which should be left to its own state legislature."[95] I submit that a court that ultimately chooses foreign law because it is thought to be better than forum law, discriminates against the parties in domestic cases in which application of the "lesser" domestic law is inevitable.[96] On the other hand, criticizing a foreign rule by rejecting it in favor of the "better" forum law might be less objectionable, for it does not create disparity between multistate and domestic decisions, nor does it touch on the forum's own judicial or legislative responsibilities. Yet, such criticism could be deemed "presumptuous and inappropriate"[97] as it defies the other state's prerogative to determine what its law should be. Moreover, if the better law approach should not be used to justify the choice of foreign law, it loses its function as a comparative superiority test, and therefore its

93 *Tower v. Schwabe* 284 Or. 105, 585 P.2d 662 at 664 (1978).
94 Westbrook (1975) p. 461.
95 *Ibid.*
96 This is precisely what the Dutch *Hoge Raad* did in a decision on the marital property regime between an American husband and a French wife living (mostly) in the Netherlands. Having formulated a new set of alternative reference rules for this type of issue, the court denied that Dutch law would apply in this particular case, although the new rules made that conclusion inevitable. It was suggested that well-to-do spouses would rather not be bound by the Dutch statutory regime of community property: had the parties been Dutch, they would have stipulated separation of property. In other words: under the circumstances, the court deemed Dutch law to be the lesser law. HR 10 December 1976, *NJ* 1977, 275, note J.C. Schultsz, (*Chelouche v. Van Leer*). In a domestic case, however, the Dutch community property regime would have been enforced absent a marriage contract to the contrary, and the financial position or the implied intentions of the spouses would have been deemed irrelevant. On the *Chelouche* decision, see: H.U. Jessurun d'Oliveira/I.S. Joppe/A.G. Lubbers/P.W. van der Ploeg/J.C. Schultsz, *Veto over de lex fori en andere interessante kanten aan HR 10 december 1976*, Deventer, 1977. See also: H.U. Jessurun d'Oliveira, Case Note, *A.Ae.* 1977, p. 195 ff., p. 202/203.
97 Westbrook (1975) p. 461.

5 – 346

raison d'être. Without the better law principle, the forum would still be in a position to ward off unwelcome foreign law by resorting to the doctrine of public policy, provided that the foreign law is truly perceived as repulsive and therefore unacceptable. In close cases, such as true conflicts, the premise of *prima facie* applicability of forum law is a less obtrusive argument for forum preference than the better law consideration. For these reasons, I fail to see the value of the Leflar approach for the law of multistate torts.

Chapter 6

The Comeback of Lex Loci Delicti: The New York Experience

Dating back to Huber and Story, the territorial approach to choice of law was based on the premise that a state's lawmaking power is demarcated by its territorial boundaries and therefore limited to the regulation of persons or things within its own territory.[1] Consequently, the law to be applied in multistate situations should be the law of the state having legislative jurisdiction over the persons, property or acts involved. In American conflicts law this notion developed into the maxim that "events are to be governed by the law of the state in which they occur,"[2] which became the principal tenet of Professor Beale's Restatement and the vested rights theory he advocated.[3] In respect to torts, the territorial view brought the transition from *lex fori* to *lex loci*

---

1 Ulricus Huber, *Praelectiones Juris Romani et Hodierni*, Pars II, lib. I, tit. III, no. 2, Franeker, 1689, maxim 1 and 2; Joseph Story, *Commentaries on the Conflict of Laws*, 2d ed., Boston, 1841, § 18 ff.
2 Shaman (1980) p. 228.
3 A typical example of this approach is found in *Gray v. Gray* 87 N.H. 82, 174 A. 508 at 511 (1934): "Generally speaking, the law is territorial, conceived of spatially as governing within the jurisdiction, and creating there rights and obligations which will be respected and enforced elsewhere." An echo of the territorial sovereignty principle is still heard in *Parets v. Eaton Corp.* 479 F.Supp. 512 (E.D. Mich. 1979): plaintiff was a Michigan resident working in South America for an Ohio corporation. Allegedly due to his Hispanic origin, he was discharged from his job, which would be a violation of the Michigan Fair Employment Practices Act and the Michigan Constitution. His claim of employment discrimination was rejected, however, since "no constitution or statute can have effect beyond the limits of the sovereignty by which it is adopted or enacted." *Ibid.* p. 515.

delicti,[4] with the "last event" rule as the Restatement's finishing touch for situations in which the wrong and the injury occurred in different states.[5] In the meantime, the *lex loci delicti* rule has been abandoned in most of the United States,[6] to be replaced by a variety of solutions, generally premised on some form of substantive law evaluation. Yet, the territorial approach has survived in a number of jurisdictions in which the courts are either waiting for the state legislature to change the traditional rule,[7] or for the time when the dust of transitional turmoil will have settled and "a satisfactory substitute for the lex loci delicti rule will be developed."[8] Even in these jurisdictions *lex loci delicti* is not as unassailable as it once was. In some cases, the court tried to appease the party that urged rejection of the traditional rule by assuming "arguendo" that a different approach would not produce a different result.[9] Other courts, while maintaining that *lex loci delicti* is still the prevailing conflicts rule for torts, are willing to make an exception in the particular case before them. For instance: in North Carolina, torts choice of law is dominated by the place of wrong rule, but in an action involving unfair and deceptive trade practices, the North Carolina Court of Appeals substituted the most significant rela-

---

4 The place of wrong rule is not as old as may be believed. *Cf.* Ehrenzweig (1967-1) p. 71: "Treatment of tort law as quasi-criminal since Bartolus, or as remedial since Story, pointed to the law of the forum without resort to conflicts rules." In the 19th century, American courts generally applied *lex fori* to multistate torts. See *e.g.*: *Anderson v. The Milwaukee & St. Paul Railway Co.* 37 Wis. 321 (1875), which was not overruled until 1904 in *Bain v. Northern Pac. Ry. Co.* 120 Wis. 412, 98 N.W. 241 (1904).
5 *Restatement, Conflict of Laws* (1934) § 377.
6 *Cf.* the surveys by Hohloch (1984) p. 169 ff., note 247 and p. 167 ff., note 245; Kay (1983) p. 582 ff., p. 591 ff.; Sedler (1983-2) p. 593, note 4; Weintraub (1980) p. 305, note 47. See also: *Sexton v. Ryder Truck Rental, Inc.* 413 Mich. 406, 320 N.W.2d 843 at 849, note 10 (1982). According to a dubious and unspecified count by the 6th Circuit in *Bailey v. Chattem, Inc.* 684 F.2d 386 at 393, note 5 (6th Cir. [Tenn.] 1982), " ... Tennessee is one of only four states which still follow the [*lex loci delicti*] rule."
7 *Friday v. Smoot* 211 A.2d 594 (Del. 1965); *White v. King* 244 Md. 348, 223 A.2d 763 (1966).
8 *Heidemann v. Rohl* 86 S.D. 250, 194 N.W.2d 164 at 169 (1972); *McMillan v. McMillan* 253 S.E.2d 662 (Va. 1979). See also: *Rhoades v. Wright* 622 P.2d 343 at 351 (Utah 1980) *cert. denied*, 454 U.S. 897 (1981): adoption of interest analysis will be "saved for another day."
9 *Brown v. Riner* 500 P.2d 524 at 526 (Wyo. 1972), discussed *supra* chapter 3, text accompanying note 80. See also: *Crossley v. Pacific Employers Ins. Co.* 198 Neb. 26, 251 N.W.2d 383 (1977); *Young v. Mitchell* 437 F.Supp. 348 (S.D. Fla. 1977); *Johnston Associates, Inc. v. Rohm & Haas Co.* 560 F.Supp. 916 (D. Del. 1983).

tionship standard for the traditional approach.[10] The Fourth Circuit went even further by deciding that North Carolina courts, while adhering "unequivocally" to the *lex loci* principle, would limit its application to wrongful death and personal injury actions, using a more flexible approach, presumably the most significant relationship test, in all other types of multistate torts.[11] Similar arguments were used in several workmen's compensation decisions, in which the court managed to skirt traditional jurisdiction-selection on the theory that the issue whether the victim could sue his fellow-employee should be characterized as a conflicts category *sui generis*, for which interest analysis provided an appropriate solution.[12] Another ingenious way of sidestepping *lex loci delicti* is demonstrated in *Saloomey v. Jeppesen & Co.*, in which the Second Circuit used its position as a federal diversity court to persuade the Connecticut state courts to replace the traditional rule by the Restatement (Second) approach. Admitting that under *Klaxon* it had a duty to ascertain what conflicts rule a Connecticut court would follow, the *Saloomey* court ventured to suggest that the rule of *lex loci delicti*, that clearly prevailed in Connecticut in *automobile* tort cases, would not govern wrongful death actions arising from *aviation* accidents. Thus, "the district court should not be faulted in predicting, on the facts here, that a Connecticut court would choose the 'most significant relationship' test embodied in Restatement (Second) of Conflict of Laws § 145 (1971)."[13] Apart from these inventive endeavors to circumvent the traditional rule, the courts have, of course, used the more obvious pretexts for its displacement as well.[14]

10 *Andrew Jackson Sales v. Bi-Lo Stores* 314 S.E.2d 797 (N.C. App. 1984).
11 *Santana, Inc. v. Levi Strauss & Co.* 674 F.2d 269 (4th Cir. [N.C.] 1982).
12 See *e.g.*: *Simaitis v. Flood* 182 Conn. 24, 437 A.2d 828 (1980) and *Hauch v. Connor* 295 Md. 120, 453 A.2d 1207 (Md. 1983), both decisions relying on policies and interests; *cf.* the Case Note on *Hauch*, 43 *Md. L.Rev.* 204–223 (1984). The district court in *O'Brien v. Tri-State Oil Tool Industries, Inc.* 566 F.Supp. 1119 (S.D. W.Va. 1983), on the other hand, was not persuaded by this line of reasoning and stuck to West Virginia's "venerable conflicts rule."
13 *Saloomey v. Jeppesen & Co.* 707 F.2d 671 at 674 (2d Cir. [Conn.] 1983). The decision by the District Court was published as *Halstead v. United States* 525 F.Supp. 782 (D. Conn. 1982). The dissent in *Saloomey* refused to believe that there was any "real uncertainty as to what choice-of-law rule Connecticut's Supreme Court would apply in this case" and rejected the "strained distinction now relied upon." *Ibid.* p. 679.
14 *E.g.*: *Smith v. Cessna Aircraft Co., Inc.* 571 F.Supp. 433 (M.D. N.C. 1983) and *Loughan v. Firestone Tire & Rubber Co.* 624 F.2d 726 (5th Cir. [Ohio transf. to Fla.] 1980): procedural characterization of statute of limitations. Dissenting opinion in *Winters v. Maxey* 481 S.W.2d 755 at 759 (Tenn. 1972): Alabama guest statute

While the jurisdictions still adhering to the territorial approach have not quite succeeded in staying aloof from the policy notions of modern choice of law, some of the courts that first rejected the rigid territoriality of the vested rights theory and proudly proclaimed their allegiance to policy-oriented conflicts law seem to have reverted to their original belief in the importance of the *locus delicti*. This disturbing phenomenon can be observed in several jurisdictions, but nowhere has it had a more disorienting effect than in New York. Ironically, this development might be attributed to one of the pioneers of judicial choice of law innovation, Chief Judge Fuld. Having explored the frontiers of choice of law methodology in *Babcock v. Jackson*,[15] he first unfolded a "set of basic principles" for the solution of guest statute cases in his concurring opinion in *Tooker v. Lopez*,[16] which

---

thought to be contrary to public policy. *Mizell v. Eli Lilly & Co.* 526 F.Supp. 589 (D.C. S.C. 1981): substance/procedure dichotomy and public policy (either the court's Latin or the printer's accuracy could be improved: "all matters relating to the right of action are governed by the *lex loci delecti* rather than the *lex forti*." Ibid. p. 594).

15 *Babcock v. Jackson* 12 N.Y.2d 473, 191 N.E.2d 279 (1963). In *Dym v. Gordon* 16 N.Y.2d 120, 209 N.E.2d 792 (1965) Judge Fuld contributed a dissenting opinion that subsequently may have swayed the majority in *Macey v. Rozbicki* 18 N.Y.2d 289, 221 N.E.2d 380 (1966), in which he concurred; cf. the concurring opinion by Judge Keating in *Macey, ibid.* p. 385.

16 *Tooker v. Lopez* 24 N.Y.2d 569, 249 N.E.2d 394 at 404 (1969), concurr. opinion *per* Fuld, Ch.J. They are:

"1. When the guest-passenger and the host-driver are domiciled in the same state, and the car is there registered, the law of that state should control and determine the standard of care which the host owes to his guest.

2. When the driver's conduct occurred in the state of his domicile and that state does not cast him in liability for that conduct, he should not be held liable by reason of the fact that liability would be imposed upon him under the tort law of the state of the victim's domicile. Conversely, when the guest was injured in the state of his own domicile and its law permits recovery, the driver who has come into that state should not – in the absence of special circumstances – be permitted to interpose the law of his state as a defense.

3. In other situations, when the passenger and the driver are domiciled in different states, the rule is necessarily less categorical. Normally, the applicable rule of decision will be that of the state where the accident occurred but not if it can be shown that displacing that normally applicable rule will advance the relevant substantive law purposes without impairing the smooth working of the multi-state system or producing great uncertainty for litigants. (Cf. Restatement, 2d, Conflict of Laws, P.O.D., pt. II, §§ 146, 159 [later adopted and promulgated May 23, 1969].)"

were adopted by the majority in *Neumeier v. Kuehner*.[17] The "Fuld principles", as I would like to call them,[18] are basically jurisdiction-selecting rules predicated on a coincidence of connecting factors and a residuary *lex loci* standard. To determine the standard of care which the host owes to his guest, the first principle calls for application of the law of the state where both parties are domiciled and the host's car is registered. The second principle absolves the driver from liability if his conduct occurred in the state of his domicile and if that state has a guest statute, whereas such a defense will not be allowed, absent special circumstances, in case the guest was injured in his own home state and the law of that state permits recovery. The third principle is meant to cover the remaining situations in which the passenger and the driver are domiciled in different states, but it contains a "mumbo-jumbo escape clause"[19] which at least has the virtue of reminding us that the principles stem from a policy-oriented background.

If the Fuld principles may be considered as an attempt to translate the judicial experience of *ad hoc* interest analysis into a set of comprehensive conflicts rules for guest statute cases, the first principle would cover false conflict situations, on the assumption that the state where the accident occurred has no interest in having its law applied, whether that law imposes liability on the host or frees him from liability.[20] The other two principles would cover true conflicts and unprovided-for cases, all of which are ultimately solved by the territorial factor of the place of wrong. The second principle implies that the wrong occurred in either the driver's or the passenger's home state,

---

17 *Neumeier v. Kuehner* 31 N.Y.2d 121, 286 N.E.2d 454, 335 N.Y.S.2d 64 (1972), discussed *supra* chapter 4, section 3, text accompanying notes 95–100.
18 Since they were first divulged in *Tooker v. Lopez* and some lower courts did not wait until *Neumeier v. Kuehner* to apply them, I find the more common reference to "the *Neumeier* rules" – Korn (1983) p. 873 ff.; Weintraub (1980) p. 314 ff.; Hay (1981) *passim* – somewhat confusing.
19 Reppy (1983) p. 681, note 164.
20 In several cases, however, the *locus* state was said to have an interest in the application of its liability-imposing law, because one of its purposes would be the regulation of conduct. See *e.g.*: *Bray v. Cox* 39 A.D.2d 299, 333 N.Y.S.2d 783 (1972); *Gagne v. Berry* 290 A.2d 624 (N.H. 1972); *Conklin v. Horner* 38 Wis.2d 468; 157 N.W.2d 579 (1968). See also: *Hotaling v. Smith* 63 A.D.2d 219, 406 N.Y.S.2d 627 (1978); *Bing v. Halstead* 495 F.Supp. 517 (S.D. N.Y. 1980).

which would give that state an interest in the protection of its domiciliary. The "other situations", covered by the third principle, must be those in which the law of the driver's home state does *not* shield him from liability, whereas the passenger's home state has a guest statute.[21] If host and guest are domiciled in different states and the accident occurred in a third state, the latter principle would apply as well, but if the laws of the domiciliary states are the same, it would stand to reason that the "normally applicable rule" of *lex loci delicti* will be displaced, since this situation could be analyzed as a false conflict between the law of the *locus* state and the two non-conflicting domiciliary laws.[22] Apart from such special circumstances, however, the three Fuld principles could be reduced to two, since "normally" either the law of the parties' common domicile (principle 1) or the law of the state where the accident occurred prevails (principle 2 or 3). In other words, the law to be applied is generally *lex loci delicti* unless both parties are domiciled in the same state, not being the state where the accident occurred.[23]

From a methodological point of view, the Fuld principles can be faulted for their lack of a sound theoretical basis. Since they were said to derive from the Court of Appeals' experience in accommodating competing interests in guest statute cases,[24] one would think that the three rules would summarize the principles of interest analysis. Measured by their emphasis on the place of wrong, however, they are more in tune with the detached territorialism of conventional choice of law. In the opinion of Professor Twerski, the advocate of "enlightened ter-

---

21 This is, of course, the law-fact pattern of *Neumeier v. Kuehner* itself: "Since the passenger was domiciled in Ontario and the driver in New York, the present case is covered by the third stated principle." *Neumeier v. Kuehner* 31 N.Y.2d 121, 335 N.Y.S.2d 64, 286 N.E.2d 454 at 458 (1972).
22 *Cf.* Reppy (1983) p. 680, note 164. See also: *Pryor v. Swarner* 445 F.2d 1272 (2d Cir. [N.Y.] 1971), to be discussed *infra* text following note 41.
23 *Cf.* Sedler (1973-2) p. 136.
24 *Cf.* Fuld's concurring opinion in *Tooker v. Lopez* 24 N.Y.2d 569, 301 N.Y.S.2d 519, 249 N.E.2d 394 at 403 (1969). However, this experience was rather limited, since the guest statute cases that had been before the Court of Appeals all involved domiciliaries of the same state, the situation addressed by the first principle. *Cf.* Korn (1983) p. 880: " ... the second and third rules not only lack a foundation in any of the court's post-*Babcock* decisions but are in fact inconsistent with much of the reasoning in them."

ritorialism", the first Fuld principle "is consistent only with pure interest analysis of the Currie variety," in its implicit assumption that the state where the wrong occurred will rarely assert an interest when the parties are domiciled elsewhere.[25] Several New York decisions indicate that the *locus* state does have an interest in the application of its law as long as it allows the plaintiff to recover, not if it has a guest statute.[26] This would imply that the first principle reflects New York's pre-*Neumeier* choice of law only in those cases in which the accident occurred in an immunity state and the parties were domiciled in a recovery state, but not in the reverse situation.[27] Another methodological flaw in the first principle is the inclusion of the place of registration. Several critics have submitted that this last factor, probably meant to protect the insurer or insurance rates in the state of registration, should have been omitted.[28] It will usually prove to be redundant, since most vehicles are registered in the state of defendant's domicile. If not, neither of the other two principles adequately serves the interests of the insurance company; in that respect, the place where the policy was issued would be a better criterion.[29] Furthermore, the combination of common domicile and place of registration creates a lacuna in those cases in which the two factors point to different states: none of the Fuld principles covers the situation in which

---

25 Twerski (1973-2) p. 118. His objection to Currie and his followers concerns the "tremendous emphasis on the *interest of the domicile state of the parties in granting or denying recovery.*" *Ibid.* p. 107; emphasis in the original. On "enlightened territorialism", see *supra* chapter 4, section 3, text accompanying notes 112–117.

26 *Kell v. Henderson* 26 A.D.2d 595, 270 N.Y.S.2d 552 (1966); *Fosillo v. Matthews* 30 A.D.2d 1049, 295 N.Y.S.2d 327, 248 N.E.2d 455 (1968), *supra* chapter 4, section 2, text accompanying notes 56–57; *Rye v. Kolter* 39 A.D.2d 821, 333 N.Y.S.2d 96 (1972), *infra* note 41. A prominent exception is *Dym v. Gordon* 16 N.Y.2d 120, 209 N.E.2d 792, 262 N.Y.S.2d 463 (1965), in which Colorado, the state where the accident occurred, was said to have a threefold interest in the application of its guest statute. However, after *Tooker v. Lopez* 24 N.Y.2d 569, 249 N.E.2d 394, 301 N.Y.S.2d 519 (1969), *Dym* is generally regarded as dubious precedent. In his concurring opinion in *Tooker*, 249 N.E.2d 394 at 407, Judge Burke concluded that "it is apparent that our decision in *Dym* is overruled."

27 *Cf.* Sedler (1973-2) p. 133 ff.; Reilly (1974) p. 1016 ff.

28 Korn (1983) p. 881 ff.; Reppy (1983) p. 680, note 164; Weintraub (1980) p. 314/315.

29 Besides, a guest statute is not necessarily intended to protect the insurer. *Cf.* Reppy (1983) p. 680, note 164. The majority in *Tooker v. Lopez* 249 N.E.2d 394 at 399, note 1 (1969), deciding whether or not the Michigan guest statute should apply, noted: "The Michigan courts have suggested that the purpose of their guest statute is to protect the owner of the vehicle." More on the purposes of guest statutes: *infra* chapter 8, section 1.

the parties are domiciled in the same state and the car in which they had their accident was registered elsewhere.[30]

The second and third principles, on the other hand, are dominated by an isolated territorial factor which will usually preclude an appraisal of interests. Since the place of wrong criterion cannot be considered as a formalized expression of interest analysis in the abstract, it is either incompatible with interest analysis altogether, or it should be seen as a give-it-up formula by which true conflicts or unprovided-for cases can be solved. As we shall see, the New York courts have applied the third Fuld principle to cases in which the parties were domiciled in different states with identical laws, in contrast to the law of the *locus* state. Such cases cannot be solved by application of the first principle, as it is premised on common domicile. Yet, under a policy-oriented approach, the *lex loci* presumption of the third principle is untenable in this type of case, for the state where the wrong occurred is probably least interested in the application of its law. In other words, the territorial standard of the third principle is at best an expedient means to solve unprovided-for cases,[31] but it is an inappropriate criterion for the solution of false conflicts outside the scope of the first principle. All in

---

30 *Cf.* Korn (1983) p. 883: "In light of the major roles of automobile rental agencies and industrially owned fleets in modern American life, this hiatus cannot be lightly dismissed." See *e.g. Pahmer v. Hertz Corporation* 32 N.Y.2d 119, 296 N.E.2d 243, 343 N.Y.S.2d 341 (1973). Driver and passenger were New York domiciliaries who had rented a car in California. Chief Judge Fuld, who wrote the opinion, did not need to amend his three principles, since California's guest statute had just been declared unconstitutional in *Brown v. Merlo* 8 Cal.3d 855, 506 P.2d 212, 106 Cal.Rptr. 388 (1973). For that reason it could not be asserted as a defense. *Cf.* Seidelson (1981) p. 223.
31 Professor Sedler has noted that the *lex loci* presumption of the third principle gives rise to an irrational discrepancy between the case in which an Ontario plaintiff is injured by a New York defendant in New York (plaintiff prevails) and that in which he is injured by the same New York defendant in Ontario (defendant prevails). The difference could be explained by the assumption that New York has a territorial interest in the protection of non-residents injured in New York. However, since the first Fuld principle leaves an Ontario plaintiff empty-handed if he were injured in New York by another Ontario resident, "[t]he distinction effected by the third rule then cannot rationally be explained with reference to any New York interest." Sedler (1973-2) p. 136. See also: Korn (1983) p. 880 ff.

all, Fuld's creation turns out to be a quaint assemblage of territorialism, pre-determined center of gravity, and random policy notions.[32]

It could be argued that these methodological shortcomings will be mitigated by the qualifying clauses in the second and third principles, which would allow for interest-oriented exceptions. Yet, the courts that felt bound to *Neumeier* have largely ignored them. Although several arguments would support the displacement of the "normally applicable rule" in *Neumeier v. Kuehner*,[33] the Court of Appeals saw no need to deviate from the *lex loci* principle in the very case in which it was adopted. In fact, Fuld's majority opinion states a number of reasons why displacement of the Ontario guest statute would impair the "smooth working of the multi-state system," without furthering New York's interest.[34] The judicial reluctance to depart from the basic principles may be rooted in the unsettling disparities in their formulation and the availability of an escape. The first principle is not subjected to any proviso at all. The second principle allows for "special circumstances" only in situations in which the guest was injured in the state of his domicile, not if the injury occurred in the home state of the host. The third principle envisages the displacement of *lex loci delicti* "if it can be shown that displacing that normally applicable rule will advance the relevant substantive law purposes without impairing the smooth working of the multi-state system or producing great uncertainty for litigants." While it is clear that this lengthy exception has the flavor of interest analysis, there is no indication whether or not the laconic reference to "special circumstances" in the second principle should be explained in the same vein. In addition to these uncertainties there is the question if and why the Fuld principles should be

32 *Cf.* Baade (1973) p. 163: " ... Chief Judge Fuld's curious amalgam of interest analysis, rule-positivism, and self-congratulation." The third ingredient of this mixture is found in Fuld's *Neumeier* opinion, in which he quotes at length from a laudatory article by Reese (1971), entitled *Chief Judge Fuld and Choice of Law*.
33 Kay (1983) p. 534, note 79 and accompanying text; Von Mehren (1977) p. 34 ff.; Hancock (1975) p. 785 ff.; Baade (1973) p. 161 ff.; Sedler (1973-2) p. 138; Shapira (1973) p. 175 ff.
34 By stating that application of New York law "at the expense of a New Yorker" would result "in the exposure of this State's domiciliaries to a greater liability than that imposed upon resident users of Ontario's highways," Fuld invited the charge of unfair discrimination against a non-resident plaintiff in favor of a local defendant. *Neumeier v. Kuehner* (1972) 31 N.Y.2d 121, 335 N.Y.S.2d 64, 286 N.E.2d 454 at 460/461, diss. opinion *per* Bergan J. *Cf.* Korn (1983) p. 889 ff., p. 898 ff.; Weintraub (1980) p. 316; Leflar (1977-3) p. 20; Shapira (1973) p. 172.

reserved for the resolution of guest statute cases, as their author suggested in both *Tooker* and *Neumeier*. Whether the choice of law problem is defined in terms of interest analysis (revealing no-conflicts, false conflicts, true conflicts and unprovided-for cases) or in terms of jurisdiction-selection (depending on spatial affiliation), if a set of *rules* is created to streamline *ad hoc* adjudication it is hard to perceive why their scope should be limited to the issue of guest statute immunity. Structurally, that issue does not differ from other multistate tort problems, such as interspousal, parental, or charitable immunity, vicarious liability, wrongful death limitations, or survival.[35] It will be seen that this question has troubled the New York courts as well, adding to their disorientation and disunity. Chief Judge Fuld's premature attempt "to assure a greater degree of predictability and uniformity"[36] has fostered so much confusion that the author of the opinion in *Himes v. Stalker*, seven years after *Neumeier*, had good reason to write in despair: "While the legal academicians continue to enjoy a Bacchanalian revelry of law review delights and the Appellate Courts attempt to soothsay whether the majority, or the concurring, or the dissenting opinions of the last Court of Appeals determination should be followed, and the trial courts wallow in the legal quagmire and seek to divine an initial decision that hopefully will pass muster with its respective Appellate Division and if not, will merit approval of the Court of Appeals, the unfortunate litigant involved in the tort conflict problem pays for appeal upon appeal."[37]

There are relatively few cases in which the Fuld principles have been adopted explicitly, but their inherent territorialism seems to be pervasive, even outside New York. A first endorsement came in *Arbuthnot v. Allbright*, a case that fell within the scope of the first principle: both parties were residents of Ontario, the car in which they were driving was garaged and insured in Ontario, while the accident occurred in

---

35 In *Farber v. Smolack* 20 N.Y.2d 198, 229 N.E.2d 36, 282 N.Y.S.2d 248 (1967), in which vicarious liability of a car owner was at issue, the Court of Appeals had stated that "there is no logical basis to distinguish the application to out-of-state accidents of the New York law of liability to gratuitous guests and the New York law of liability arising from permissive use of a vehicle." 282 N.Y.S.2d 252. *Cf.* Korn (1983) p. 951/952.
36 *Neumeier v. Kuehner* 31 N.Y.2d 121, 335 N.Y.S.2d 64, 286 N.E.2d 454 at 457 (1972).
37 *Himes v. Stalker* 99 Misc.2d 610, 416 N.Y.S.2d 986 at 991 (N.Y. Sup.Ct. 1979), *per* Horey, J.

New York.[38] Quoting from Fuld's concurring opinion in *Tooker v. Lopez*, the Appellate Division's Third Department relied on the first principle when it chose to apply Ontario's guest statute, thus reaching a result that was the opposite of its decision in *Kell v. Henderson*.[39] However, in *Bray v. Cox*, an identical case that was decided two years later by the Appellate Division's *Fourth* Department, the Fuld principles were completely ignored.[40] "Mindful of the contrary conclusion reached in *Arbuthnot v. Allbright*," the court applied New York law after a careful evaluation of New York and Ontario interests.[41]

In the meantime, between *Tooker* and *Neumeier*, the Second Circuit had alluded to the Fuld principles in *Pryor v. Swarner*, a case arising from a car collision in Ohio in which a New York guest and a Florida host were involved. Emphasizing that "Judge Fuld did not write the majority opinion in *Tooker*," the court turned to "basic doctrines" and embarked upon an analysis of New York, Florida and Ohio interests. Nevertheless, it did arrive at a result compatible with an unqualified application of the third principle by upholding the "common policy of the *lex loci* and the state where the defendants reside and obtained

---

38 *Arbuthnot v. Allbright* 35 A.D.2d 315, 316 N.Y.S.2d 391 (1970); *supra* chapter 4, section 2, text accompanying notes 58–63.
39 *Kell v. Henderson* 26 A.D.2d 595, 270 N.Y.S.2d 552 (1966); *supra* chapter 4, section 2, text accompanying notes 56–63. *Arbuthnot* and *Kell* had the same law-fact patterns and were both decided by the Third Department. *Kell* was distinguished "into oblivion" – Reese (1971) p. 564 – on procedural grounds, since that case turned upon the question whether defendant's motion to amend his pleading to assert the Ontario guest statute was timely filed. *Cf.* Reilly (1974) p. 1012. According to Leflar (1977-1) p. 280, note 2, *Kell* was overruled by *Arbuthnot*.
40 *Bray v. Cox* 39 A.D.2d 299, 333 N.Y.S.2d 783 (1972); *supra* chapter 4, section 2, text accompanying notes 60–63. It should be noted that the Court of Appeals handed down its decision in *Neumeier v. Kuehner*, canonizing the Fuld principles, just eight days after the *Bray* decision. See: *Himes v. Stalker* 99 Misc.2d 610, 416 N.Y.S.2d 986 at 990 (N.Y. Sup. Ct. 1979).
41 *Bray v. Cox* 39 A.D.2d 299, 333 N.Y.S.2d 783 at 786 (1972). With the exception of *Arbuthnot v. Allbright*, the Appellate Division has been quite consistent in its disposal of New York/Ontario guest statute cases. In *Rye v. Kolter* 39 A.D.2d 821, 333 N.Y.S.2d 96 (1972), the Fourth Department's decision was less elaborate than it was in *Bray*, but the result was the same. Relying on *Fosillo v. Matthews* 30 A.D.2d 1049, 295 N.Y.S.2d 327, 248 N.E.2d 455 (1968), which in turn relied on *Kell v. Henderson* 26 A.D.2d 595, 270 N.Y.S.2d 552 (1966), the court held that Ontario's guest statute did not apply to an accident in New York giving rise to an action between Ontario residents.

insurance" and refusing to apply New York's more generous law.[42] In a way, the decision is also compatible with the second principle. Since both the law of defendant's domicile and the *lex loci delicti* had a guest statute, they could be equated as non-conflicting laws, both shielding the host-driver. A similar equation was used by another federal court sitting in New York when it seized upon the qualifying clause of the third Fuld principle to displace the *lex loci delicti* and reject the guest statute defense. In this case, *Chila v. Owens*, the host-guest relationship between the New Jersey plaintiff and the New York defendant centered in Ohio, where they were both college students and where the accident occurred. Since neither of the domiciliary states had a guest statute, the district court reverted to the first principle of common domicile, since "logic and fairness suggest that New York would equate the New Jersey claimant's position to that of its own domiciliary."[43] On the other hand, there are several New York decisions displaying a less flexible interpretation of the Fuld approach. In *Towley v. King Arthur Rings, Inc.*,[44] the Court of Appeals, citing *Neumeier v. Kuehner*, abruptly decided that Colorado's guest statute applied as *lex loci delicti* to an accident involving an Iowa guest and a New York host. Since the court did not even inquire whether Iowa had a guest statute,[45] it may be asked under what circumstances the exception to the third principle is ever to apply.

If *Neumeier* and *Towley* were instrumental in reinstating *lex loci delicti* as the general rule for guest statute cases, the Court of Appeals' decision in *Cousins v. Instrument Flyers, Inc.* contributed to the expansion

---

42 *Pryor v. Swarner* 445 F.2d 1272 at 1276/1277 (2d Cir. [N.Y.] 1971). The "common policy" argument is reminiscent of the propositions by Sedler and Weintraub on the solution of unprovided-for cases and/or true conflicts, discussed *supra* chapter 4, section 3, text accompanying notes 120–130, and note 88 respectively.
43 *Chila v. Owens* 348 F.Supp. 1207 at 1210 (S.D. N.Y. 1972). *Cf.* a similar suggestion made by Hay (1981) p. 1663/1664, note 103, in his analysis of *Bing v. Halstead*, discussed *supra* chapter 4, section 3, text accompanying notes 101–105.
44 *Towley v. King Arthur Rings, Inc.* 40 N.Y.2d 129, 351 N.E.2d 728, 386 N.Y.S.2d 80 (1976).
45 It also failed to note that the Colorado guest statute had been repealed in the meantime: Weintraub (1980) p. 317. Iowa did have a guest statute – see Kay (1983) p. 534, note 85 – but it appears that defendant's driving qualified as wanton conduct or gross negligence, so that recovery could be granted anyway; *cf.* Herzog (1983) p. 140, note 178. That would mean that *Towley* ultimately presented a no-conflict situation.

of the territorial view to other areas of tort choice of law.[46] Federal and lower courts had already ventured to apply the Fuld principles to other issues than guest statute immunity, and even if they did not mention them expressly, the opinions reflect a resurgent territorial spirit. One of the more explicit examples is *Rogers v. U-Haul Co.*, turning on vicarious liability. Plaintiff's deceased, a resident of Alabama, had been killed in a car accident in Pennsylvania while on a trip from New York to Alabama. The driver was a New York resident who had rented the car from defendant in New York. Under Pennsylvania law, the negligence of the driver would not be imputed to the owner of the vehicle, whereas New York law would hold the owner vicariously liable. Citing the third Fuld principle in *Neumeier*, the Appellate Division declared that "this case calls for the application of the normal rule, i.e., the rule of the state where the accident occurred, Pennsylvania."[47] It was acknowledged that the state most interested in the application of its law would be Alabama, the state of the victim's domicile, but considering that the parties had limited the choice of law issue to the question whether Pennsylvania or New York law applied, the court saw no reason to displace the "normal rule", for New York's compensatory interest was not at stake. Instead, it applied the law of the jurisdiction that could hardly be thought to have an interest in the outcome of this case.[48] In *Belisario v. Manhattan Motor Rental, Inc.*, another action on the vicarious liability issue, the Appellate Division supported its decision to apply the New Jersey *lex loci delicti* with a variety of reasons, ranging from the "ancient" origin of the traditional rule to the absence of a New York interest, but it kept silent about the Fuld principle it had applied in *Rogers*.[49] Other courts have managed to avoid the dictates of the Fuld formula altogether by assuming that the principles would only apply to the issue of guest statute immunity. This happened, for instance, in *Chance v. E.I. DuPont De Nemours & Company, Inc.* a diversity action turning on the issue of joint liability, where it was said that "the specific resolution of conflicts problems by the New York courts in guest statute cases, while helpful in suggesting

---

46 *Cousins v. Instrument Flyers, Inc.* 44 N.Y.2d 698, 376 N.E.2d 914, 405 N.Y.S.2d 441 (1978).
47 *Rogers v. U-Haul Co.* 41 A.D.2d 834, 342 N.Y.S.2d 158 (1973).
48 *Cf.* Sedler (1977-1) p. 213/214.
49 *Belisario v. Manhattan Motor Rental, Inc.* 48 A.D.2d 477, 370 N.Y.S.2d 574 (1975). It should be noted that *Rogers* had been decided by the Appellate Division's Second Department, while *Belisario* was before the First Department.

a general approach, provides little assistance in resolving the choice-of-law issues raised in the present case."[50] In *Rosenthal v. Warren*, a malpractice suit by a New York citizen to recover against a Massachusetts hospital and the surgeon who had operated on her husband, both the district court and the Second Circuit applied New York law, mainly on the theory that New York had "a very strong policy against wrongful death limitations in connection with its citizens and next of kin."[51] Although this case would have presented a fine opportunity to apply the second rule in *Neumeier* – Dr. Warren would have been protected by Massachusetts law, which was both the law of his domicile and the *lex loci delicti* – the Fuld principles were virtually ignored in both instances. In the opinion of the Second Circuit, the *Neumeier* decision was obviously irrelevant: "In no way ... did the court retreat from the position it had staked out in *Kilberg* and *Miller*, refusing to apply other states' wrongful death limitations in the case of the death of a New York domiciliary."[52]

At first sight, *Cousins v. Instrument Flyers* is hardly a landmark choice of law decision. Plaintiff was a New York resident who had suffered personal injuries resulting from the crash of a rented airplane in Pennsylvania. Although the parties and the trial court had proceeded on the assumption that New York law would apply to the issues of products liability and contributory negligence, plaintiff's "highly experienced" counsel suddenly changed his strategy and suggested that Pennsylvania law be applied. By that time, defendants had succeeded in proving plaintiff's contributory negligence, which barred him from recovery under New York law, but not under the law of Pennsylvania. The procedural issue before the Court of Appeals was whether plaintiff could change his choice of law tactics after all the evidence had been received and just before the jury was to be charged. It was held that he could not and that he was therefore not entitled to a new trial.

50 *Chance v. E.I. DuPont De Nemours & Company, Inc.* 371 F.Supp. 439 at 445 (E.D. N.Y. 1973).
51 *Rosenthal v. Warren* 342 F.Supp. 246 (S.D. N.Y. 1972), *aff'd*, 475 F.2d 438 at 446 (2d Cir. [N.Y.] 1973), *cert. denied*, 414 U.S. 856, 94 S.Ct. 159, 38 L.Ed.2d 106. The Second Circuit's public policy argument stemmed from *Kilberg v. Northeast Airlines, Inc.* 9 N.Y.2d 34, 172 N.E.2d 526, 211 N.Y.S.2d 133 (1961), discussed *supra* chapter 2, section 3, text accompanying notes 200–216, and *Miller v. Miller* 22 N.Y.2d 12, 237 N.E.2d 877, 290 N.Y.S.2d 734 (1968). The *Miller* case was decided as a false conflict, however, not by a crude public policy argument.
52 *Rosenthal v. Warren* 475 F.2d 438 at 442 (2d Cir. [N.Y.] 1973).

The more arresting part of *Cousins*, however, is the court's dictum: "It is true that *lex loci delicti* remains the general rule in tort cases to be displaced only in extraordinary circumstances."[53] It was hinted that an exception to the rule is permissible if the place of wrong is fortuitous, as it most often is in airplane crash cases, but the policy-oriented proviso of the third Fuld principle was not mentioned. On the other hand, the citation of *Neumeier v. Kuehner* suggests that the court was willing to expand the scope of the principles to other issues than the one involved in guest statute cases, for *Cousins* was based on strict liability and involved the issue of contributory negligence. However that may be, the *Cousins* formula confirmed that New York had reverted to territorialism and that interest analysis was no longer the preferred approach to multistate torts, probably not even in cases in which the place of wrong standard is clearly inappropriate. For the present,[54] the decision appears to be the Court of Appeals' final contribution to the development of New York's tort choice of law,[55] leaving the federal and lower state courts to their own devices. Some of them obediently quoted the *lex loci delicti* formula from *Cousins*, "nebulous and ephemeral" as they found it to be[56] and tried to decide how "extraordinary" the circumstances would have to be to justify an exception to the rule.[57] Other courts felt free to pursue different courses, probably on the assumption that the rule in *Cousins* was only dictum and that the New York approach to multistate torts was still dominated by

---

53 *Cousins v. Instruments Flyers, Inc.* 44 N.Y.2d 698, 376 N.E.2d 914, 405 N.Y.S.2d 441 at 442 (1978).
54 I concluded my research in New York case law in november 1984. Unless I overlooked a major decision, the New York Court of Appeals had little to say on tort choice of law in the six years following *Cousins*.
55 *Cf.* Korn (1983) p. 946. A brief memorandum opinion in *Croft v. National Car Rental* 56 N.Y.2d 989, 453, N.Y.S.2d 631, 439 N.E.2d 346 (1982), adds little to our information. There is a reference to *Neumeier* and a statement to the effect that the (British) plaintiff had not succeeded in identifying either a significant New York "interest" or sufficient "contacts" with New York to justify the displacement of the (Vermont) *lex loci delicti*. *Cf.* Herzog (1983) p. 186.
56 *Himes v. Stalker* 99 Misc.2d 610, 416 N.Y.S.2d 986 at 992 (N.Y. Sup. Ct. 1979).
57 *Rakaric v. Croation Cultural Club* 76 A.D.2d 619, 430 N.Y.S.2d 829 (1980), discussed *supra* chapter 2, section 3, text accompanying notes 243–245. *Fosen v. United Technologies Corp.* 484 F.Supp. 490 (S.D. N.Y. 1980); *Patton v. Carnrike* 510 F.Supp. 625 (N.D. N.Y. 1981); *Accusystems, Inc. v. Honeywell Information Systems* 580 F.Supp. 474 (S.D. N.Y. 1984); *O'Rourke v. Eastern Air Lines, Inc.* 730 F.2d 842 (2d Cir. [N.Y.] 1984).

Babcock and its notions of "contacts-grouping" and "center of gravity", whatever they meant. The results of all these contrarieties are baffling.

Charting the New York choice of law chaos in torts after *Cousins* is hardly worth the effort, since it can only lead to the conclusion that "no two authorities agree."[58] The courts' opinions prove that widely divergent choice of law theories will serve to support any outcome. There are discrepancies between trial courts and appellate courts, between state and federal courts, and there are discrepancies on every level. A few examples may suffice to support this contention. *Himes v. Stalker* was said to present a true conflict between New York's interest in compensating the victim of a car accident that had occurred in New York, and Pennsylvania's interest in shielding the Pennsylvania car owner from vicarious liability.[59] Although all parties involved were Pennsylvania residents, New York law was applied, mainly because the court was "convinced that the principle of *lex loci delicti* should apply generally to tort conflict problems" and because New York's substantive law purposes would be more advanced than those of Pennsylvania.[60] The Appellate Division zigzagged between *lex loci delicti*,[61]

---

58 The phrase was used by Justice Holman in *Erwin v. Thomas* 264 Or. 454, 506 P.2d 494 at 495 (1973), describing why "[i]t is with some trepidation that a court enters the maze of choice of law in tort cases."
For a survey and critique of "the twenty year civil war in choice of law" with special emphasis on New York developments, see: Korn (1983); the martial simile is found at p. 957. Professor Korn takes a dim view of the current state of New York choice of law: "I cannot think of any field of law that has in modern times become as hopelessly jumbled as the present New York law of conflicts." *Ibid.* p. 956. See also: Reppy (1983) p. 678 ff.; Kay (1983) p. 525 ff.
59 *Himes v. Stalker* 99 Misc.2d 610, 416 N.Y.S.2d 986 (N.Y. Sup. Ct. 1979). *Cf. Rogers v. U-Haul Co.* 41 A.D.2d 834, 342 N.Y.S.2d 158 (1973), discussed *supra* text accompanying notes 47–48.
60 *Cf. McClaney v. Utility Equipment Leasing Corp.* 560 F.Supp. 1270 (N.D. N.Y. 1983), also involving vicarious liability. The court cited *Himes v. Stalker*, *Neumeier v. Kuehner*, *Babcock v. Jackson* and § 174 Restatement Second as authority for its decision to apply New York law to an accident in New York injuring a New York plaintiff.
61 *Camporese v. Port Authority of N.Y. and N.J.* 63 A.D.2d 771, 415 N.Y.S.2d 28 at 29 (1979) *aff'd* 49 N.Y.2d 814, 403 N.E.2d 961, 426 N.Y.S.2d 977 (1980): "The accident occurred in New Jersey and by agreement of the parties, the law of that state was applied to the substantive issues."

interest weighing,[62] contacts counting,[63] back to *Babcock*-style interest weighing,[64] and on to a policy-oriented version of the Restatement's significant relationship approach.[65]

As far as the federal courts are concerned, the confusion is even more pronounced – literally so: "Unfortunately," the district court for the Southern District of New York declared, "it is far from easy to deduce how a New York court would resolve the present conflict. There appears to be a slight discrepancy between the views of the New York Court of Appeals and the Second Circuit on the forum's conflicts standards ... The Second Circuit has taken note of New York's apparent trend back to *lex loci*, but has not accepted it."[66] That was putting it mildly. The Second Circuit, first in *Rosenthal v. Warren* then in *O'Connor v. Lee-Hy Paving Corp.*,[67] had refused to apply *lex loci*

---

62 *Knieriemen v. Bache Halsey Stuart Shields* 74 A.D.2d 290, 427 N.Y.S.2d 10 (1980), *infra* text following note 78; *cf.* Reppy (1983) p. 679, note 162.
63 *Grancaris v. J.I. Hass Co.* 79 A.D.2d 551, 434 N.Y.S.2d 19 (1980): the place of wrong rule and the rule that looks for "the greatest cluster of contacts" both pointed to Maryland. See also: *Rakaric v. Croation Cultural Club* 76 A.D.2d 619, 430 N.Y.S.2d 829 (1980), in which the "extraordinary circumstances" exception was used as an opportunity for grouping factual contacts; *cf.* Korn (1983) p. 954 ff., p. 957.
64 *Blais v. Deyo* 92 A.D.2d 998, 461 N.Y.S.2d 471 at 473 (1983): "The approach used in resolving choice-of-law issues in tort cases is the 'grouping of contacts' or 'center of gravity' approach," followed by pure interest analysis; see also *supra* chapter 4, section 4(a), note 173 and accompanying text.
65 *Beasock v. Dioguardi Enterprises, Inc.* 472 N.Y.S.2d 798, at 800 (A.D. 1984): "Effect is now given to the law of the jurisdiction where the injury occurs, unless, with respect to the particular issue, another state has a more significant relationship." This statement was followed by interest analysis, which resulted in a finding that other jurisdictions than New York had "superior interests." *Cf. In re Air Crash Disaster near Chicago, Illinois on May 25, 1979* 644 F.2d 594, at 629 (7th Cir. [N.Y./Ill.] 1981): " ... the New York test is the functional equivalent of the Restatement (Second) test ..." *Cf.* Reppy (1983) p. 684, note 173, describing this statement as "untenable" in light of *Tooker v. Lopez*: " ... [it] illustrates how desperately guidance from the New York Court of Appeals on the present choice of law methodology is needed."
66 *Cooperman v. Sunmark Industries Div. of Sun Oil* 529 F.Supp. 365 at 368 (S.D. N.Y. 1981).
67 *Rosenthal v. Warren* 475 F.2d 438 (2d Cir. [N.Y.] 1973) *cert. denied*, 414 U.S. 856, 94 S.Ct. 159, 38 L.Ed.2d 106; *O'Connor v. Lee-Hy Paving Corp* 579 F.2d 194 (2d Cir. [N.Y.] 1978) *cert. denied sub nom. Lee-Hy Paving Corp. v. O'Connor*, 439 U.S. 1034, 99 S.Ct. 639, 58 L.Ed.2d 696, *reh. denied* 99 S.Ct. 2023, 441 U.S. 918, 60 L.Ed.2d 391.

delicti if that law would hurt a New York plaintiff. The *O'Connor* case, like *Rosenthal v. Warren*, presented a law-fact pattern that fell within the scope of the second Fuld principle, allowing the defendant to interpose the law of his domicile coinciding with the place of injury as a defense. The action was brought by the widow of a New York domiciliary who had been killed in an industrial accident in Virginia, allegedly due to the negligence of defendant's employee. Lee-Hy Paving Corp. was a Virginia construction company that did not do any business in New York, whereas its employee was a Virginia resident. Under Virginia law, the widow would be barred from further recovery, having received death benefits under (New York's) Workmen's Compensation Law, while New York law would allow her to sue the tortfeasor and his employer for more. This choice of law issue was resolved in accordance with *Rosenthal v. Warren*, but hardly in agreement with *Neumeier v. Kuehner*: "Although we do not pretend to full understanding of *Babcock v. Jackson* ... and the many decisions of the Court of Appeals in its wake and might think that, in the light of fifteen years of experience under *Babcock*, the departure from the certainty of the *lex loci delictus* rule was not such a famous victory as it first appeared to be, ... we see no indication that the highest court of New York has wavered in its determination to afford New York tort plaintiffs the benefit of New York law more favorable than the law of *lex loci delictus* whenever there is a fair basis for doing so."[68] Thus, the Second Circuit ignored the Fuld principles once more, preferring to resolve this true conflict, as in *Rosenthal*,[69] by an implicit better law consideration. However, in *O'Rourke v. Eastern Air Lines, Inc.*,[70] the latest statement of the Second Circuit's viewpoint I found, territorial considerations seem to prevail. The action was brought on behalf of the estate of a Greek citizen who had been killed in an airplane crash in New York. Defendants were the United States, under the Federal Tort Claims Act, and the airline company. The district court had held that a New York court would apply New York law either as *lex loci delicti* or as the law of the state with the greater governmental interest. On appeal, application of New York law was challenged, apparently because Greek law, at least in plaintiff's opinion, would grant even

---

68 *O'Connor v. Lee-Hy Paving Corp* 579 F.2d 194 at 205 (2d Cir. [N.Y.] 1978).
69 *Cf.* Leflar (1977-1) p. 281.
70 *O'Rourke v. Eastern Air Lines, Inc.* 730 F.2d 842 (2d Cir. [N.Y.] 1984).

more generous damages than those awarded under New York law.[71] Criticizing the New York Court of Appeals for creating "an inconsistent body of precedent with seemingly similar cases decided differently," the Second Circuit discussed both *Neumeier v. Kuehner* and *Cousins v. Instrument Flyers, Inc.* and came to the conclusion that *lex loci delicti* was New York's general rule in tort cases. It saw no reason to resort to the "extraordinary circumstances" exception in *Cousins*, despite the Court of Appeals' suggestion that such an escape would be acceptable in airplane crash cases, in which "the place of the wrong, if it can even be ascertained, is most often fortuitous."[72] Instead, the decision to stick to *lex loci* was reinforced with an interest analysis argument: even if the case was treated as a (true) conflict between the laws of Greece and New York, plaintiff had failed to demonstrate that Greece had "an interest significant enough" to displace either New York's interest in the application of its law or the normal rule of *lex loci delicti*.[73] Thus, the Second Circuit killed two birds with one stone: in a curious blend of interest-weighing and jurisdiction-selection it rejected the "extraordinary circumstances" exception to the general *lex loci* rule, intimating at the same time that New York's interest was superior.

This was not the first time that a federal court in New York tried to reconcile the territorial approach with interest analysis. In *Bing v. Halstead*, the district court for the Southern District of New York turned the *Cousins* dictum upside down and added a touch of Currie, stating: "When the interest analysis does not point clearly to the law of any jurisdiction, the law of the place where the tort occurred pre-

---

71 In wrongful death actions, New York law would allow recovery of pecuniary damages only, while Greek law was said to recognize an award for intangible losses. The district court had awarded the estate $ 982,100 against the United States, mainly for loss of past and future support, and $ 75,000 against Eastern Air Lines under the Warsaw Convention. The Second Circuit reduced the first amount by an average of 21 %, finding in particular that an award of $ 150,000 for loss of parental guidance and $ 44,000 for loss of marital services was "so excessive as to shock the Court's conscience," now that the deceased had been a Greek seaman and was away at sea ten months a year.
72 *Cousins v. Instrument Flyers, Inc.* 44 N.Y.2d 698, 376 N.E.2d 914, 405 N.Y.S.2d 441 at 442 (1978).
73 *O'Rourke v. Eastern Air Lines, Inc.* 730 F.2d 842 at 850 and note 13 (2d Cir. [N.Y.] 1984).

vails."[74] Compared with the Second Circuit's eclectic approach in *O'Rourke*, this statement – if it means that true conflicts should ultimately be resolved by resort to the territorial factor of the place of wrong – is at least methodologically consistent. But in *Masera v. Trans World Airlines, Inc.*, a wrongful death action arising from an airplane crash over the Ionean sea, no policies or interests were mentioned and the "prevailing" center of gravity test was used as an excuse for totting up factual contacts. Application of Italian law shielded the defendant airline company, a Delaware corporation having its principal place of business in New York, from the claims brought by Italian plaintiffs.[75]

Surveying the New York cases discussed above, one would be inclined to think that a New York forum is generally inspired by a "home team bias",[76] which dictates choice of law decisions in favor of New York domiciliaries, whether plaintiff or defendant. Although the results in *Neumeier v. Kuehner, Rosenthal v. Warren, O'Connor v. Lee-Hy Paving Corp., O'Rourke v. Eastern Air Lines, Inc.* and *Rakaric v. Croation Cultural Club* tend to substantiate this suspicion, it is contradicted by a number of other decisions, notably *Pryor v. Swarner, Bing v. Halstead, Belisario v. Manhattan Motor Rental, Inc.* and *Patton v. Carnrike*, in which the New York plaintiff or defendant did *not* prevail. In *Beasock v. Dioguardi Enterprises, Inc.*, the Appellate Division noted that "[i]t is not New York's policy to enhance the recovery of its residents by the application of a more favorable foreign rule."[77] Yet, the New York plaintiff, seeking punitive damages that were not allowed in New York (the state of his domicile, the place of injury and the forum), prevailed against defendants in Ohio and the District of

---

74 *Bing v. Halstead* 495 F.Supp. 517 (S.D. N.Y. 1980). The year before, the same court and the same district judge had professed that "[p]ursuant to *Babcock v. Jackson* ... and its progeny, choice of law for tort actions is determined by governmental interest analysis, i.e. which forum has the most significant contacts with the facts and the parties; which forum has a greater interest in having its policies, as reflected in the relevant law, applied?" *Bankhaus Hermann Lampe K.G. v. Mercantile-Safe Dep.* 466 F.Supp. 1133 at 1146 (S.D. N.Y. 1979) *per* Broderick, D.J.
75 *Masera v. Trans World Airlines, Inc.* 492 F.Supp. 950 (S.D. N.Y. 1980).
76 Korn (1983) p. 898 ff.
77 *Beasock v. Dioguardi Enterprises, Inc.* 472 N.Y.S.2d 798 at 801 (A.D. N.Y. 1984). The court quoted from the opinion in *Gordon v. Eastern Air Lines, Inc.* 391 F.Supp. 31 at 34 (S.D. N.Y. 1975), to be discussed *infra* text accompanying notes 85–87. See also: *Cooperman v. Sunmark Industries Div. of Sun Oil* 529 F.Supp. 365 at 369 (S.D. N.Y. 1981).

Columbia, because it was found that these jurisdictions had "superior interests" compared with New York's interest in protecting "out of state as well as resident defendants from excessive liability."[78] In *Knieriemen v. Bache Halsey Stuart Shields*, however, the opposite result was reached. The plaintiff was a Louisiana resident seeking punitive damages for alleged breach of contract, fraud and negligence on the part of the Louisiana office of the New York defendant. In this situation, New York law would allow punitive damages whereas Louisiana was said to have a "strong policy against them." This time, the Appellate Division saw fit to deny the action, on the theory that Louisiana had an interest in seeing that its domiciliary would receive "only such damages as will fairly compensate him," while there would be no point in providing a "wholesome example" by punishing defendant, since it was not the New York headquarters but its Louisiana agent that had engaged in "morally culpable conduct."[79] New York's defendant-protective law was also applied in *Walkes v. Walkes*. This wrongful death action arose from a tragic family visit of an elderly couple, living in Florida, to their son and daughter-in-law in New York. While in the young couple's home, plaintiff's wife tripped and fell from a flight of stairs, allegedly due to the negligence of her son, the defendant. According to the district court, New York had the greatest concern in the damages issue, since New York was both the domicile of defendant and the situs of the accident and "clearly ha[d] a strong interest in having its law applied to protect defendant."[80] The court distinguished *Rosenthal v. Warren* on the grounds that New York's law, "while potentially affording somewhat less recovery than available under Florida law, will adequately ensure that Florida's interest in the compensation for its domiciliary will be satisfied." New York law could therefore not be considered as "archaic or unjust."

---

78 *Beasock v. Dioguardi Enterprises, Inc.* 472 N.Y.S.2d 798 at 801 (A.D. N.Y. 1984).
79 *Knieriemen v. Bache Halsey Stuart Shields* 74 A.D.2d 290, 427 N.Y.S.2d 10 at 13 (1980).
80 *Walkes v. Walkes* 465 F.Supp. 638 at 641 (S.D. N.Y. 1979). Plaintiff had claimed damages for grief, mental anguish and loss of companionship under Florida law, while New York law would only award damages for pecuniary loss in case of wrongful death.

The recurrent notion that "unfair and anachronistic" rules should not be applied to the detriment of New Yorkers is reminiscent of the better law approach, particularly the Weintraub variant.[81] In New York, the phrase goes back to *Kilberg v. Northeast Airlines, Inc.*, where it was said that New York courts should protect "our own State's people against unfair and anachronistic treatment."[82] Judge Fuld, in *Babcock v. Jackson*, quoted another passage from *Kilberg* in which it was deemed "unjust and anomalous" to subject traveling New Yorkers to varying laws.[83] In *Neumeier v. Kuehner*, Fuld quoted *Kilberg* again: " ... New York has a deep interest in protecting its own residents, injured in a foreign state, against unfair or anachronistic statutes of that state ..."[84] These phrases are echoed in more recent decisions, such as *Rosenthal v. Warren* and *Gordon v. Eastern Air Lines, Inc.*, ostensibly to justify the preferred treatment of New York plaintiffs.[85] The *Gordon* case arose from an airplane crash in Florida in which plaintiff's husband, a New York resident, was killed. The defendant was a Delaware corporation with its principal place of business in Florida. At issue was the measure of damages, particularly the question if plaintiff was entitled to damages for loss of consortium: New York law did not allow such damages, but Florida law did. The opinion is a blend of interest analysis, some *Neumeier* notions, and the better law approach in reverse. As the district court saw it, Florida "could have no interest whatsoever in how much money a New York jury would award a New York resident in a New York court." In that respect, the case presen-

---

81 Weintraub (1980) p. 270 ff., p. 345 ff. "Very often a true conflict will occur between a rule that is in step with general modern trends in the area, and a rule that is clearly an anachronistic lag in the development of the law of its jurisdiction. In such circumstances resolution should be in favor of the rule that is more representative of current developments." *Ibid.* p. 273. It should be noted that Weintraub did not mean to suggest that this solution be used in "pseudo-conflicts" for the sole purpose of avoiding a "poor local rule when in fact there is no true conflict."
82 *Kilberg v. Northeast Airlines, Inc.* 9 N.Y.2d 34, 211 N.Y.S.2d 133, 172 N.E.2d 526 at 527/528 (1961).
83 *Babcock v. Jackson* 12 N.Y.2d 473, 240 N.Y.S.2d 743, 191 N.E.2d 279 at 282 (1963); *Kilberg v. Northeast Airlines, Inc.* 9 N.Y.2d 34, 211 N.Y.S.2d 133, 172 N.E.2d 526 at 527 (1961).
84 *Neumeier v. Kuehner* 31 N.Y.2d 121, 335 N.Y.S.2d 64, 286 N.E.2d 454 at 456 (1972).
85 *Rosenthal v. Warren* 475 F.2d 438 at 446 (2d Cir. [N.Y.] 1973); *Gordon v. Eastern Air Lines, Inc.* 391 F.Supp. 31 at 34 (S.D. N.Y. 1975). *Cf.* Korn (1983) p. 908 ff.

ted a false conflict.[86] Echoing the condition for the displacement of *lex loci delicti* in the third *Neumeier* principle, the court gave a muddled interpretation of the rule: " ... failure to apply New York law in this case would impair the smooth working of the multi-state system and produce great uncertainty for litigants by sanctioning forum shopping." Since the *lex loci delicti* was the law of Florida, it could not possibly follow from the third Fuld principle that New York's law should either be applied, or that it should be displaced. Finally, it was found that New York had an interest in the protection of "its own residents ... against the unfairness, if any, of 'anachronistic' foreign laws and from the denial of recovery under such laws."[87] In this case, however, the foreign law turned out to be more favorable to the (New York) plaintiff than the forum's own law. It could therefore hardly be considered "unfair" or "anachronistic". The reasoning in *Gordon* proves that the references to "unjust", "anomalous", "absurd" or "archaic" laws have more to do with the traditional public policy exception than with the better law criterion. The Leflar approach advocates the displacement of *any* substandard rule of law, regardless of its origin or the domicile of the plaintiff.[88] In New York, on the other hand, the emphasis is on the injustice of a *foreign* law and the protection of *forum* residents. The "absurdity test" might have been appropriate in *Rosenthal v. Warren* or *O'Connor v. Lee-Hy Paving Corp.*, but in *Gordon v. Eastern Air Lines, Inc.* and in *Walkes v. Walkes* it served no purpose whatsoever.

Even if the decisions discussed so far do not prove that New York courts are biased towards the interests of New York domiciliaries or corporations, one thing is abundantly clear: in New York tort choice of law anything is possible. There is not a single criterion that the courts have even *tried* to use consistently. *Lex loci delicti* may remain the general rule in tort cases, as the Court of Appeals had it in *Cousins*, but too many contradictory decisions rob this statement of any

---

86 *Contra*: Reppy (1983) p. 682, note 168, qualifying the case as a "true-true conflict." Since Professor Reppy refers to "New York's unlimited damages law," his perception of the issue might be different from mine. See, however, Leflar (1977-1) p. 281, referring to the "more liberal damages rule that prevailed in Florida" as opposed to "New York's restrictive rule."
87 *Gordon v. Eastern Air Lines, Inc.* 391 F.Supp. 31 at 34 (S.D. N.Y. 1975).
88 *Cf. supra* chapter 5, text accompanying notes 22–25.

meaning. Few cases were resolved by reference to the *locus delicti* alone.[89] In most, the place of wrong just reinforced a domiciliary factor, but there is no way of knowing in which situations it will be combined with the domicile of the plaintiff,[90] the domicile of the defendant,[91] or when *lex loci* will be displaced by the law of plaintiff's domicile,[92] the law of defendant's domicile,[93] or by the law of the parties' common

---

89 For instance: *Himes v. Stalker* 99 Misc.2d 610, 416 N.Y.S. 986 (N.Y. Sup.Ct. 1979), *supra* note 56: Pennsylvania plaintiff, Pennsylvania defendant, New York *locus*, plaintiff prevails; *Bing v. Halstead* 495 F.Supp. 517 (S.D. N.Y. 1980), *supra* note 74: Costa Rica law applied as the law of the place of injury in an action between a New York plaintiff, who was also a long-time resident of Costa Rica, and an Arizona defendant; defendant prevailed. To the extent that *O'Rourke v. Eastern Air Lines, Inc.* 730 F.2d 842 (2d Cir. [N.Y.] 1984), *supra* note 70, was an action against the United States under the Federal Tort Claims Act, New York law was applied as *lex loci delicti*, not as the domiciliary law of the U.S. government; defendant prevailed.
90 As it was in *Neumeier v. Kuehner* (1972) 31 N.Y.2d 121, 286 N.E.2d 454, 335 N.Y.S.2d 64: Ontario plaintiff, New York defendant, Ontario *locus*, defendant prevails; *Knieriemen v. Bache Halsey Stuart Shields* 74 A.D.2d 290, 427 N.Y.S.2d 10 (1980), *supra* note 79: Louisiana plaintiff, New York defendant, Louisiana *locus*, defendant prevails.
91 As in *Belisario v. Manhattan Motor Rental, Inc.* 48 A.D.2d 477, 370 N.Y.S.2d 574 (1975), *supra* note 49: New York plaintiff, New Jersey defendant, New Jersey *locus*, defendant prevails; *Walkes v. Walkes*, 465 F.Supp. 638 (1979), *supra* note 80: Louisiana plaintiff, New York defendant, New York *locus*, defendant prevails; *Patton v. Carnrike* 510 F.Supp. 625 (1981): Pennsylvania plaintiff, New York defendant, New York *locus*, plaintiff prevails; and to a certain extent in *Pryor v. Swarner* 445 F.2d 1272 (2d Cir. [N.Y.] 1971), *supra* note 42: New York plaintiff, Florida defendant, Ohio *locus*, defendant prevails; Ohio and Florida laws both shield defendant.
92 This happened in *Rosenthal v. Warren* 475 F.2d 438 (2d Cir. [N.Y.] 1973), *supra* note 51: New York plaintiff, Massachusetts defendant, Massachusetts *locus*, plaintiff prevails; *O'Connor v. Lee-Hy Paving Corp.* 579 F.2d 194 (2d Cir. [N.Y.] 1978), *supra* notes 67–68: New York plaintiff, Virginia defendant, Virginia *locus*, plaintiff prevails; *Rakaric v. Croation Cultural Club* 76 A.D.2d 619, 430 N.Y.S.2d 829 (1980), *supra* chapter 2, section 3, notes 243–245: New York plaintiff, New Jersey defendant, New Jersey *locus*, plaintiff prevails; and *Masera v. Trans World Airlines, Inc.* 492 F.Supp. 950 (S.D. N.Y. 1980), *supra* note 75: Italian plaintiff, New York defendant, *locus sine lege*, Italian law applied, defendant prevails; *Gordon v. Eastern Air Lines, Inc.* 391 F.Supp. 31 (1975), *supra* note 85: New York plaintiff, Florida defendant, Florida *locus*, defendant prevails.
93 *Beasock v. Dioguardi Enterprises, Inc.* 472 N.Y.S.2d 798 (A.D. 1984), *supra* note 77: New York plaintiff, Ohio and District of Columbia defendants, New York *locus*, plaintiff prevails.

domicile.[94] As far as the Fuld principles are concerned, it is quite clear that the New York courts, including the Court of Appeals, have not wanted to pursue the "rules approach" Fuld had laid down. At most, some vague notion of territoriality has taken hold of New York choice of law, a notion which has effectively crushed the innovative drive that once distinguished New York from other jurisdictions. What is left, I fear, are the ruins of a choice of law revolution gone wrong, leaving the New York courts with less than they started with: a vaguely conditional *lex loci* rule without theoretical foundation, without appreciable judicial support, and hence without authority of law.

---

94 This is, of course, the well-known false conflict situation resolved in *Babcock v. Jackson* "and its progeny", but even in these cases there was not always consensus: cf. *Arbuthnot v. Allbright* 35 A.D.2d 315, 316 N.Y.S.2d 391 (1970), *supra* note 38: Ontario parties, New York *locus*, Ontario law applied, defendant prevails; *Bray v. Cox* 39 A.D.2d 299, 333 N.Y.S.2d 783 (1972), *supra* note 40: Ontario parties, New York *locus*, New York law applied, plaintiff prevails; *Himes v. Stalker* 99 Misc.2d 610, 416 N.Y.S.2d 986 (N.Y. Sup.Ct. 1979), *supra* note 59: Pennsylvania parties, New York *locus*, New York law applied, plaintiff prevails.

Chapter 7
Beyond Interest Analysis: The Supremacy of Lex Fori

Whatever its methodological foundation, choice of law is premised on the forum's willingness to accept a foreign rule of decision as a potential substitute for its own. Without this principle, no choice of law system can exist. Characteristic of the traditional jurisdiction-selecting method is its postulated neutrality: all legal systems being equal and interchangeable, the choice between them must be made without bias, hence without regard to their (foreign) provenance. This implies, at least in theory, that forum law as such has no privileged status. Whether or not it will be chosen as the applicable law, depends solely on the match between the conflicts rule's localizing criterion and one or more of the actual facts. Nevertheless, even under the neutral allocation method an unmistakable "homeward trend" has manifested itself in practice. Suffice it to mention just a few of its probable causes. In systems in which the content of foreign law should be determined *ex officio*, the courts' predilection for forum law may stem from their uneasiness with unfamiliar foreign law.[1] In the second place, judicial dissatisfaction with the results of mechanical allocation has led to the use of various "escape devices" by which application of inappropriate or disagreeable foreign law could be circumvented in favor of *lex fori*.[2]

---

1 *Cf.* Kegel (1985) p. 81; De Boer (1979) p. 13 ff.; Kotting (1979) p. 72. See, generally, *supra* chapter 2, section 4.
2 *Supra* chapter 2. In modern European conflicts law, the need for escape devices has been mitigated by the development of "rational" conflicts rules. Ideally, these rules, discussed *supra* chapter 1, sections 2–4, refer to the jurisdiction deemed to be most concerned, or to the law deemed most suitable for application to the actual controversy. Since they are either open-ended, or based on a presumption, or turn on alternative connecting factors, forum law is usually eligible and it is often selected. →

Thirdly, when the principles of jurisdiction-selection fail to provide an answer, forum law is likely to be applied for want of a better solution.³

While the pervasive preference for forum law cannot be squared with the premises of neutral allocation, the reality of a "homeward trend" is acknowledged, in one way or another, in the theories of policy-oriented choice of law. Inasmuch as the Restatement Second features an impartial "most significant relationship" approach, it certainly does not encourage forum-biased solutions. On the other hand, at least two of the choice of law principles listed in § 6 tend to support the precedence of forum law despite the presumptive applicability of foreign law. Consideration of the "relevant policies of the forum" has provided many courts with a welcome excuse to apply their own law, even if the relevant policies of other interested states would have warranted a more neutral choice, particularly one along the lines of the Restatement's presumptions. "Ease in the determination and application of the law to be applied" is another consideration that might influence the courts to resort to their own law, but in practice this factor is seldom mentioned. Of the five choice-influencing considerations in Leflar's catalogue, the better law test is apt to justify the choice of forum law. As we have seen, most courts motivating their choice by a better law consideration express a firm preference for their own law. To Currie, who posited the *prima facie* applicability of forum law, the forum would be justified in giving precedence to its own law whenever the forum state asserts an interest in its application, regardless of the possible interests of foreign states. A foreign rule of decision would not be entitled to application unless there is a false conflict in which the

---

This is especially true in those areas in which the forum's social values are apt to influence the choice of law process. For that reason, it has been suggested by Kotting (1985) p. 1346, and Strikwerda (1986) p. 26, that choice of law's point of departure should be application of forum law, subject to carefully defined exceptions for situations in which the values and objectives underlying forum law are not at stake.

3 In Dutch conflicts law, this used to be the solution to choice of law problems arising from collisions at sea: *supra* chapter 1, section 2, text preceding note 76. As a residuary solution, *lex fori* is also applied in Dutch divorce choice of law in case the parties have different nationalities and are domiciled in different countries; see, however, *supra* chapter 1, section 4, note 149 and accompanying text.

forum has no interest.[4] Although the courts have not heeded Currie's injunction against interest-weighing, they still tend to prefer forum law in most true conflicts and unprovided-for cases. In sum, the choice of law approaches that take account of the contents of substantive law are generally less adverse to the "trend to stay at home"[5] than the allocation method. However, none of them endorses a principled forum preference. Even in Currie's theory, the *prima facie* applicable forum law will be displaced by foreign law if the forum state has no interest at stake.[6]

In this light, an openly professed forum bias is a curious phenomenon, even in modern American choice of law. Yet, its existence can no longer be denied. The first symptoms of a *lex fori* trend can be noticed

4 In true conflicts and unprovided-for cases, Currie would apply forum law: *supra* chapter 4, sections 3 and 4. A problem for which Currie had no convincing answer is the situation in which two or more foreign jurisdictions have an interest in the application of their respective laws and the forum has none, the problem of the disinterested third (forum) state. Although Currie denounced the better law solution for true conflicts, he did suggest that a disinterested forum *could* apply "the more enlightened and humane [rule]" to break the true conflict between foreign laws. Currie (1963-2) p. 778. All in all, however, he seemed to prefer application of forum law, provided it coincides with the law of at least one of the interested states. *Ibid.* p. 780.
5 Ehrenzweig (1967-1) p. 104, preferring this phrase to Nussbaum's "homeward trend", since "this metaphor is based on the statutist assumption of a foreign governing law from which we must 'return'."
6 It will be recalled that Currie's *lex fori* solution to true conflicts rests on his conviction that the courts are not in a position to assess the relative values of competing interests, this being "a political function of a very high order." Hence, the choice of forum law for true conflicts is justified by "the failure of Congress to use its power to solve the problems." Currie (1963-1) p. 182. It follows that Currie's forum preference is not dictated by principles of conflicts law but rests on his perception of the constitutional delimitation of powers.
In Ehrenzweig's writings, the supremacy of forum law is more pronounced. Contending that all choice of law theories, including interest analysis, deduce their criteria from a "non-existing superlaw", Ehrenzweig argued for "application of the domestic rule as the basic or residuary one" in all cases in which no "true rule of choice" can be found. Ehrenzweig (1965) p. 344/345. Whether it may be displaced by a foreign rule of decision, depends on the "all-decisive" policy of forum law itself: even if domestic law is found to be inapplicable to foreign facts, an examination of the foreign rule in the light of forum policy may still call for application of forum law. *Ibid.* p. 348/349; *id.* (1967-1) p. 94 ff. On Ehrenzweig's *lex fori* theory, see generally: Siehr (1986) p. 49 ff. In the Netherlands, the writings of Huib Drion, *supra* chapter 1, note 26, reflect a similar preference for forum law, provided it is applied by a "natural forum." Drion (1949); *id.* (1964).

in a series of Kentucky decisions which, in my opinion, are much less in tune with the principles of "judicial method and the policy-centered approach to choice of law" than at least one commentator wanted us to believe.[7] What came to be dubbed the "Kentucky approach" at a symposium on one of its offshoots,[8] is both an ambiguous and eclectic solution, which seems to warrant application of forum law "whenever possible."[9] A less captivating, yet more descriptive sobriquet would be: "sufficient enough contacts approach", as it denotes the key to the new choice of law standard adopted by Kentucky's highest court. In view of the few cases available, a separate treatment of Kentucky's new choice of law might be considered an effort of trifling value. Furthermore, a solution predicated on a normative preference for forum law can hardly be aligned with the policy-oriented approaches on which we have concentrated so far. That is why I have hesitated to bring up the Kentucky approach at all. However, some of the opinions do have a policy-oriented drift, which lends support to the view that "contacts" should be equated to "interests" and that the Kentucky alternative is still rooted in the methodology of policy-oriented choice of law. If so, the Kentucky decisions may have heralded the demise of interest analysis and the advent of a new style of choice of law reasoning in which the relevance of interests is reduced to marginal proportions. Not only did the "sufficient enough reason" test receive the blessing of the U.S. Supreme Court, but it also persuaded the Michigan Supreme Court to abandon its long-time adherence to impartial allocation and proclaim its belief in the supremacy of forum law. For these reasons, the emerging *lex fori* approach in Kentucky and Michigan does merit a closer look.

The three relevant Kentucky cases turn on more or less the same issue: can a foreign statute shield defendant from liability while Kentucky law would allow the plaintiff to recover? In *Wessling v. Paris*, the Court of Appeals came to grips with traditional method for the first time. As most of the landmark cases in which the *lex loci delicti* rule

---

7 Sedler (1973-1) p. 389 ff. Weintraub (1973) p. 422, is equally positive in his suggestion that the Kentucky decisions are supported by a policy-oriented approach, much in conformity with Weintraub's own propositions on tort choice of law.
8 *Foster v. Leggett* 484 S.W.2d 827 (Ky. 1972). Participants in the symposium were Reese, Sedler, Twerski and Weintraub; their comments were published in 61 *Ky. L.J.* 368 ff. (1973).
9 *Harris Corp. v. Comair, Inc.* 712 F.2d 1069 at 1071 (6th Cir. [Ky.] 1983).

was renounced, *Wessling* presented a clear-cut false conflict: the parties were residents of Kentucky, they had been involved in a car accident just over the Kentucky border in Indiana, and defendant invoked the guest statute of that state. Re-examining the *lex loci* rule that had so far prevailed in Kentucky conflicts law, the court observed: "It would be strange if under Kentucky law the respective rights of the parties should undergo some metamorphosis at a point on the bridge just before reaching the Indiana shore."[10] Another tack is chosen – interest analysis, it would seem – leading Chief Judge Williams to the conclusion that "the State of Indiana has no interest whatsoever in this Kentucky lawsuit." Indiana might have an interest in protecting host/drivers from claims by passengers, but "surely this must extend no further than an interest in protecting Indiana residents or those who sue in Indiana courts."[11] Thus, the *lex loci delicti* was displaced in favor of Kentucky law and plaintiff prevailed.

Wessling v. Paris did reject the traditional rule, but it was unclear what specific variety of the policy-oriented choice of law it embraced instead. That question was addressed the next year in *Arnett v. Thompson*. Here the law-fact pattern was just the opposite from that in *Wessling*: the parties, husband and wife, were residents of Ohio and had a car accident in Kentucky. Ohio law would not permit recovery in this case, the defendant being protected by both a guest statute and an interspousal immunity rule. First turning to the methodological issue, the court observed that in *Wessling v. Paris* the *lex loci delicti* rule was not replaced by the most significant relationship approach of Restatement Second, adding cryptically that the application of that theory should be limited to "very clear cases." Instead, the suggestion that some form of interest analysis had been adopted was reinforced by a statement that seems to be in complete agreement with Currie's views on true conflicts: "Upon further study and reflection the court has decided that the conflicts question should not be determined on the basis of a *weighing* of interests ..." although it is as yet unclear why the present case would pose a true conflict. The solution the court prefers to interest-weighing is the "rule of sufficient enough contacts," which

---

10 *Wessling v. Paris* 417 S.W.2d 259 at 260 (Ky. 1967). The stateline between Kentucky and Indiana coincides with the Ohio river.
11 *Ibid.* p. 260. It is difficult to perceive how anyone *suing* in an Indiana court could be *protected* by the Indiana guest statute.

means that the conflicts question should be determined "simply on the basis of whether Kentucky has *enough* contacts to justify applying Kentucky law."[12] The court specified two situations in which this condition would be met: (a) if the accident occurred in Kentucky, and (b) if the parties were residents of Kentucky and the accident occurred elsewhere. Obviously, interest analysis was forsaken at this point, not only because the court reverted to jurisdiction-selecting rules,[13] but mainly because the relation between the issue in the particular case and the policies behind conflicting rules addressing that issue was discarded as a relevant choice of law factor. Even if we take a more charitable view and assume that the court meant to limit its ruling to immunity cases such as *Wessling v. Paris* and the case at bar, its line of reasoning is still hard to explain in terms of interest analysis. What interest could Kentucky possibly have in the application of its compensatory rule on the strength of the *locus* connection alone? The mere statement that "the policy of the law of this state is to allow recovery for injuries or death resulting from negligence"[14] is not a sufficient explanation, as it answers only one of the preliminary questions posed by an interest analysis approach. The next question should focus on the spatial reach of the compensatory rule, to be inferred from its underlying policy, so as to prepare the answer to the final question in this policy-oriented process: does the forum have an interest in applying its law to the issue in the *instant* case? It follows that it was definitely not interest analysis the Kentucky Court of Appeals was practicing in *Arnett v. Thompson*.

At a symposium on the "Kentucky approach", two of the learned commentators tried to justify *Arnett* by suggesting that Kentucky did have an interest in this particular case. Conceding that generally "the state of injury has no real interest in applying its [compensatory] law" to an immunity issue between parties from a non-recovery state, Professor Sedler advanced the rather psychological argument that the Arnetts, although technically domiciled in Ohio, were "Kentuckians at heart," which might have been "the principal reason for the Court's

---

12 *Arnett v. Thompson* 433 S.W.2d 109 at 112 (Ky. 1968); emphasis in the original.
13 In Europe, this would be called a unilateral conflicts rule: *lex fori* applies if the tort occurred in the forum state or if the parties are residents of the forum.
14 *Ibid.* p. 113; see also: *infra* text accompanying note 40.

decision."¹⁵ Professor Weintraub was even more explicit: "Because the Arnetts had such close ties with Kentucky at the time of the accident and because of the great likelihood that they would, as they have, soon resume their Kentucky residence, there is substantial doubt as to the relevance of the Ohio host-protection and marital-harmony policies."¹⁶ If Sedler merely hinted at the possibility of a true conflict between Ohio and Kentucky law, Weintraub seemed to infer that *Arnett* presented a false conflict, Kentucky rather than Ohio being the concerned jurisdiction.

The real test came with *Foster v. Leggett*.¹⁷ Again, the Ohio guest statute was at issue, but this time the parties did not reside in the same state: the deceased guest/passenger had her home in Kentucky, whereas the host/driver was a resident of Ohio, the state where the accident occurred. The balance of this straightforward fact pattern shifts somewhat toward Kentucky by the circumstance that the parties, who had been dating for a year, were working for the same Kentucky employer, whereas the defendant, while a citizen of Ohio, often stayed at a Kentucky YMCA, where he rented a room by the week. To the champion of the most significant relationship test, Professor Reese, *Foster v. Leggett* is therefore "a close case where much can be said for the application of Kentucky law."¹⁸ Yet, it was not the Restatement Second the Kentucky Court of Appeals relied on when applying Kentucky law. Having denounced once more the "unfair,"

---

15 Sedler (1973-1) p. 383. From Mrs. Arnett's attorney, Sedler obtained the information that the Arnetts came from Kentucky, returned there most weekends to visit relatives, and hoped to return there as soon as employment conditions would improve; it appears that the Arnetts never returned to Ohio after the accident and remained in Kentucky: *ibid.* p. 384, text accompanying note 36. Professor Reese seems to have missed this information, or else he did not consider it relevant. In his comment on *Arnett*, he just suggested that the decision may have been inspired by a consideration of "the basic policies underlying the particular field of law that is involved," which is, of course, one of the Restatement's choice of law principles: § 6(2)(e). Reese (1973-1) p. 372.
16 Weintraub (1973) p. 424, referring to the information supplied to Professor Sedler by Mrs. Arnett's attorney.
17 *Foster v. Leggett* 484 S.W.2d 827 (Ky. 1972).
18 Reese (1973-1) p. 369. And: "It is difficult to imagine a case where the contacts were more equally divided or where the interests of the states involved were in greater equipois." *Ibid.* p. 373. It would seem that this observation emphasizes one of the Restatement Second's inherent weaknesses: the lack of a compelling criterion to decide close cases such as this one.

"unjust," "antiquated," and "controversial" *lex loci* rule, the court proclaimed its new conflicts theorem: "When the court has jurisdiction of the parties its primary responsibility is to follow its own substantive law. The basic law is the law of the forum, which should not be displaced without valid reasons." Neither policy analysis nor the most significant relationship test were deemed proper approaches to test that validity, as the displacement of Kentucky law is rejected "if there are significant contacts – not necessarily the most significant contacts – with Kentucky."[19]

Whereas this last statement in the majority opinion confirmed the dismissal of the Restatement's approach, the dissent asserted that policy analysis was rejected as well: "The decision of the majority ... opens Kentucky as a forum which will instantly apply its own law upon any excuse whatever, regardless of policy considerations of sister states to the contrary."[20] Yet, the latter approach could have produced the same result. If account would be taken of the conflicting interests of Ohio (protection of Ohio host-drivers and their insurers, for short) and Kentucky (compensation due to Kentucky victims), an interested forum could easily justify the application of forum law to the resulting true conflict.[21] Although the Restatement's Reporter would have preferred application of Ohio law to the present case, he did acknowledge that "[u]nder the circumstances, one could hardly criticize application of either Kentucky or Ohio law."[22] *Foster v. Leggett* might even be explained as a fine example of the most significant relationship approach, in that the court – by grouping all relevant contacts with both Kentucky and Ohio – seemed to be most concerned to establish in which state the case had its center of gravity, an effort it could have spared itself if the "enough contacts" test were the decisive standard.

If *Wessling v. Paris* could be taken to announce the adoption of interest analysis, *Foster v. Leggett* seems to indicate the court's adherence to the quantitative variety of the most significant relationship theory. However, the three cases taken together betray a radical departure

---

19 *Foster v. Leggett* 484 S.W.2d 827 at 829 (Ky. 1972).
20 Diss. opinion *per* Reed, J., *ibid.* p. 831.
21 *Cf.* Sedler (1973-1) p. 385: "In terms of interest analysis [*Foster*] differed from both [*Wessling* and *Arnett*] in that here a true conflict was clearly presented, since the plaintiff was from a recovery state and the defendant was from an immunity state."
22 Reese (1973-1) p. 373.

from either choice of law approach.[23] Interest analysis is virtually ignored in both *Arnett* and *Foster*, whereas the Restatement's approach is negated not only by the basic *lex fori* presumption advanced in *Foster*, but also by the emphasis on "enough" or "sufficient" contacts in both *Arnett* and *Foster*. From a methodological point of view, therefore, the "Kentucky approach" is in a class by itself.

This interpretation is confirmed by two decisions in which the Sixth Circuit viewed Kentucky's new choice of law as distinctly forum-oriented. In *Grant v. Bill Walker Pontiac-GMC, Inc.*, turning on the vicarious liability of a truck owner, the defendants were domiciled in North Carolina and Georgia, whereas plaintiff's deceased had been a resident of Kentucky, which was also the *locus* state. Without any reference to either state's interests, the Sixth Circuit affirmed that Kentucky law governed the vicarious liability issue: "While Kentucky purports at least to follow the significant contacts rule in determining which law to apply, ... we think it clear that the district judge was correct in concluding that 'Kentucky strongly favors the application of its own law when it is the forum whenever it can be justified'."[24] In support of the choice of forum law, the court just mentioned the Kentucky domicile of the deceased, the place of the accident, and the forum. Whether these contacts represented any Kentucky interest, was obviously irrelevant. Even more explicit is Kentucky's forum bias

---

23 Sedler (1973-1) p. 384/385, would not agree. In his interpretation, the Kentucky cases did reject the most significant relationship test of the Restatement Second, but as far as interest analysis is concerned he only admits to the rejection of "any weighing of the conflicting interests of the concerned states." In his view "[t]he sufficient contacts test could be interpreted as a shorthand way of saying that Kentucky will apply its own law whenever it has an interest in doing so and the application of its law is not unfair to either party or his insurer." *Ibid.* p. 391. Kentucky's "real interest" would lie in allowing resident plaintiffs as well as non-resident plaintiffs injured in Kentucky to recover. Apart from the tenuous argument that Kentucky would have an interest in the compensation of non-resident plaintiffs, the line of reasoning and the wording of *Arnett* and *Foster* do not seem to lend much credibility to this interpretation. Twerski (1973-2) p. 418, is not sure whether "contacts mean interests" but seems to be inclined to read some form of interest analysis into the Kentucky opinions.

24 *Grant v. Bill Walker Pontiac-GMC, Inc.* 523 F.2d 1301 at 1304 (6th Cir. [Ky.] 1975. Whether the Georgia or the North Carolina defendant was the owner of the truck, was another issue, possibly governed by North Carolina law. However, "the question of vicarious liability for the torts of another would, nevertheless, be governed by the law of Kentucky," which would shield the owner from liability anyway. *Ibid.*

in *Harris Corp. v. Comair, Inc.*, in which the only Kentucky contact was the occurrence of an airplane crash in that state. The plaintiff was a Texas corporation claiming damages for the loss of services of deceased, one of its employees in Ohio. Noting that "Kentucky courts have apparently applied Kentucky substantive law *whenever possible*," the Sixth Circuit held that "[t]he occurrence of an accident in Kentucky is, by itself, sufficient to justify application of Kentucky law."[25] Added support for this interpretation was found in a recent contracts decision by the highest Kentucky state court, holding that "Kentucky law will apply to a contract issue if there are sufficient contacts and no overwhelming interests to the contrary, even if the parties have voluntarily agreed to apply the law of a different state."[26] This led the Sixth Circuit to the conclusion "that Kentucky applies its own law unless there are overwhelming interests to the contrary."[27]

In Michigan, the Supreme Court took a long time before it was finally ready to denounce the battered regime of *lex loci*. In *Sweeney v. Sweeney*, decided in 1978, it was still able to reach an acceptable result "without revamping Michigan's entire law of conflicts" by resorting to public policy.[28] The Court of Appeals obediently cited this decision in *Sexton v. Ryder Truck Rental, Inc.* and *Storie v. Southfield Leasing, Inc.*, both cases turning on vicarious liability and demonstrating the

---

25 *Harris Corp. v. Comair, Inc.* 712 F.2d 1069 at 1071 (6th Cir. [Ky.] 1983); emphasis in the original.
26 *Ibid.*, citing *Breeding v. Massachusetts Indemnity and Life Ins. Co.* 633 S.W.2d 717 (Ky. 1982).
27 *Harris Corp. v. Comair, Inc.* 712 F.2d 1069 at 1071 (6th Cir. [Ky.] 1983). A second issue in this case, indemnification for benefits paid by plaintiff under Ohio's workmen's compensation, was treated as a contractual problem. Since the employment relationship centered in Ohio, the law of that state was held to apply. Curiously, the court relied heavily on the authority of "LeFlar" and seemed to have suddenly forgotten the Kentucky precedent from which it had just quoted.
28 *Sweeney v. Sweeney* 402 Mich. 234, 262 N.W.2d 625 at 627 (1978), discussed *supra* chapter 2, section 3, text accompanying notes 221–222. A few years before, in 1975, the Michigan Court of Appeals had ventured to adopt the "better view" represented by policy-oriented decisions hailing from California (*Reich v. Purcell*), Illinois (*Ingersoll v. Klein*), Iowa (*Fabricius v. Horgen*), Pennsylvania (*Griffith v. United Airlines*) and the District of Columbia (*Tramontana v. VARIG*). This wealth of methodological alternatives must have flustered the court, as it managed to blend interest analysis, contacts-counting and public policy into one very confused opinion: *Branyan v. Alpena Flying Service, Inc.* 236 N.W.2d 739 (Mich. App. 1975); see also: *supra* chapter 2, section 3, note 228.

arbitrary nature of the public policy argument. In *Sexton*, the plaintiff was a Michigan resident who suffered serious injuries when the rented truck in which he rode overturned in Virginia; defendant was a Florida corporation, doing business in many states (including Michigan), from whom plaintiff's Michigan employer had rented the truck. Contrary to Michigan law, the Virginia *lex loci delicti* did not provide for owner's liability. The Court of Appeals held that Virginia law applied, considering that its owner-protecting rule did not contravene Michigan's public policy.[29] In *Storie v. Southfield Leasing, Inc.*, plaintiff's deceased, a Michigan resident, had been a passenger in an airplane leased from defendant, a Michigan corporation. He was killed when the plane crashed in Ohio in the course of what should have been a round-trip business journey from Michigan to Ohio. The Ohio *lex loci delicti* did not provide for aircraft ownership liability, but Michigan law did. In this case, the Court of Appeals decided to deploy public policy to avoid application of Ohio law.[30] Leave for appeal was granted in both cases, and in 1982 the Michigan Supreme Court ruled on the two of them together. After a survey of the pros and cons of *lex loci delicti* and the methodological alternatives to jurisdiction-selection, Justice Williams, writing for the majority, came to the conclusion that "in the real world the argument of certainty, the chief argument in favor of *lex loci delicti*, no longer is tenable," whereas avoidance of forum shopping, the other argument supporting the traditional rule, was "not a strong argument as against citizens of the forum state who presumably have every reason of convenience and economy to be entitled to service in their own state." Seeing no real reason to retain the rule of *lex loci delicti*, and, on the other hand, "a good reason and practical pressure in Michigan for the forum state to apply its own law," the court held: " ... where Michigan residents or corporations doing business in Michigan are involved in accidents in another state and appear as plaintiffs and defendants in Michigan courts, the courts will apply the *lex fori*, not the *lex loci delicti*, and we do so without reference to any particular state policy."[31]

While this last phrase suggested the rejection of a policy-oriented approach, Professor Sedler was convinced, once again, that Michigan

---

29 *Sexton v. Ryder Truck Rental, Inc.* 84 Mich.App. 69, 269 N.W.2d 308 (1978).
30 *Storie v. Southfield Leasing, Inc.* 90 Mich.App. 612, 282 N.W.2d 417 (1979).
31 *Sexton v. Ryder Truck Rental, Inc.* and *Storie v. Southfield Leasing, Inc.* 413 Mich. 406, 320 N.W.2d 843 at 854 (1982) *per* Williams, J.

had converted to his cherished "judicial method and the policy-centered conflict of laws." Conceding that the *Sexton-Storie* court did not adopt any choice of law approach in particular, he submitted that it did not need to do so anyway: " ... experience indicates that whenever a court adopts judicial method and the policy-centered conflict of laws as the basis of the choice of law process, the interest analysis approach will play a very important part in the court's resolution of choice of law issues."[32] It must be granted that Justice Williams did mention interests, but he did so when rebutting the forum-shopping argument, which would seem to give his "interest analysis" a jurisdictional color: " ... the forum state generally has an interest in seeing that its injured citizens are *well-served* and that its citizen defendants are afforded every protection that such citizens would have in their own state. Additionally, where both the plaintiff and the defendant are citizens of the forum state, the state where the wrong took place will normally have no interest in the *litigation*."[33] Nevertheless, the seed of confusion was sown. In his concurring opinion, Justice Levin paraphrased the majority's holding as a rule requiring application of forum law whenever there would be "insufficient reason for applying the law of another state," this being the case when both litigants are Michigan parties. Both he and Justice Kavanagh would have preferred to "go the distance and declare that Michigan law will apply in all personal injury and property damage actions without regard to whether the plaintiffs and defendants are all Michigan persons unless there is compelling reason for applying the law of some other jurisdiction."[34] Unfortunately, we are left in the dark as to the nature of the "compelling reason" to displace forum law, but to Sedler it was obvious that it meant a reflection on the presence or absence of "interests" of the involved states in having their laws applied.[35]

---

32 Sedler (1983-1) p. 1208 ff.; p. 1211.
33 *Sexton v. Ryder Truck Rental, Inc.* and *Storie v. Southfield Leasing, Inc.* 413 Mich. 406, 320 N.W.2d 843 at 854 (1982); emphasis added.
34 *Ibid.* p. 858, *per* Levin, J., positing that this was also the thrust of the concurring opinion by Justice Kavanagh. There is only one statement to this effect in the latter's opinion and, in my opinion, it is hardly conclusive: "We no longer consider the [foreign place of wrong] controlling or even of great significance." *Ibid.* p. 857.
35 Sedler (1983-1) p. 1211: "The rationale for the holding in *Sexton-Storie*, as contained in both the Williams and Kavanagh-Levin opinions, illustrates judicial reliance on interest analysis to resolve choice of law questions." See also: *ibid.* p. 1216, p. 1218.

This interpretation comes close to the one espoused by the Michigan Court of Appeals in *Smith v. Pierpont*, a malpractice suit brought by a Michigan couple against a Michigan physician following an unsuccessful vasectomy. The only extraneous factor in this case was the place of the wrong, the Wisconsin office of defendant where the operation had been performed. Contrary to Wisconsin law, Michigan law did not require that medical malpractice claims first be submitted to mediation before they could be heard in court. Deciding that Michigan law applied to this issue, the court held that "in a tort action commenced in this state, the law of this state is to be applied unless the court determines that a *superior foreign state interest* exists which calls for the application of the foreign law in order to reach a just resolution of the controversy. We think the presumption of *lex fori* is a logical and reasonable approach in that the fact that a Michigan court can obtain jurisdiction over the parties involved generally corresponds with a substantial level of state interest in the outcome of the litigation."[36] One troubling aspect of this holding is its suggestion that Michigan is bound to have an interest whenever it is the forum. Even more disturbing is the absence of any attempt to establish which policies were at stake, or to point out why Michigan did and Wisconsin did not have an interest in the application of its law. True, the opinion contains a few references to "the interests" of the forum, bolstered by the proposition that "the economic consequences of the tort will be felt most strongly in the forum state." But if such gratuitous statements should be taken to mean that choice of law in Michigan has now become a "policy-centered process", a mere mention of "forum interests" will lend methodological credibility to *any* decision in which forum law is applied. To me, the token references to unspecified interests in both *Sexton-Storie* and *Smith v. Pierpont* are no more "policy-oriented" than the consideration of "overwhelming interests to the contrary" in Kentucky's *lex fori* presumption.[37] Both in Kentucky and in Michigan,

---

36 *Smith v. Pierpont* 333 N.W.2d 165 at 167/168 (Mich. App. 1983); emphasis added. In an earlier case, *Severine v. Ford Aerospace & Communications* 118 Mich.App. 769, 325 N.W.2d 572 (1982), the Court of Appeals had refused to apply the new learning to a tort action turning on wrongful discharge and employment discrimination. Pennsylvania law was applied as the law of the place where the harmful effect occurred, since the *Sexton-Storie* doctrine only applied to personal injury and property damages actions; other torts would still be governed by *lex loci*.

37 *Cf. supra* text accompanying notes 26–27: *Harris Corp. v. Comair, Inc.* 712 F.2d 1069 at 1071 (6th Cir. [Ky.] 1983); *Breeding v. Massachusetts Indemnity and Life Ins. Co.* 633 S.W.2d 717 (Ky. 1982).

I submit, choice of law has reached a stage beyond interest analysis. To apply forum law "whenever possible" appears to be its only methodological tenet. Since the highest courts in both states, probably in the best tradition of "judicial method", have conveniently refrained from pointing out a possible "good reason" for the displacement of forum law, the *lex fori* presumption may prove to be one of the most accommodating standards in contemporary American conflicts law.

In further evaluation of the Kentucky/Michigan approach, two major objections can be raised. The most obvious one is of a practical nature. As is demonstrated by at least two of the Kentucky decisions, *Arnett v. Thompson* and *Harris Corp. v. Comair, Inc.*, the *lex fori* presumption is conducive to forum-shopping, to say the least. If transient connections with the forum are discounted in the assessment of in personam jurisdiction, as many agree they should,[38] the only relevant contact with Kentucky in *Arnett* and *Harris* was the circumstance that the accident occurred there. Even though a single territorial contact, by itself, may be deemed sufficient to establish long-arm *jurisdiction*, as a *choice of law* factor it derives its significance mainly from the forum law presumption. It might be asked, then, in which situation the jurisdictional relevance of forum contacts will fail to support the presumption that forum law applies. If the plaintiff succeeds in persuading the court that the case is sufficiently connected to the forum state to uphold its jurisdiction, he will stand a fair chance that the "sufficient reason" test warrants the application of *lex fori in foro proprio*. Whether such coupling of jurisdiction and choice of law is appropriate or not, depends largely on the operative jurisdictional standards. Without the aid of a rather strict *forum conveniens* doctrine, defendants in Kentucky or Michigan courts might find themselves at a disadvantage.[39] In his comment on Michigan's new choice of law, Profes-

---

38 *Cf.* Leflar (1977-1) p. 48, and note 6 for further references. Weintraub (1980) p. 118, on the other hand, observes that the changes in the area of in personam jurisdiction of state courts "have usually been in the direction of expanding state court jurisdiction."

39 It should be noted that the *lex fori* approach advocated by Ehrenzweig does impose different standards on the assertion of jurisdiction if forum-shopping is to be discouraged: Ehrenzweig (1965) p. 350 ff.; *id.* (1967-1) p. 107 ff. As far as Currie's *lex fori* presumption might encourage forum-shopping, it should not be overlooked that, under his approach, the test whether forum law should be displaced turns on the absence of a forum *interest*, not on the absence of sufficient forum *contacts*. In *Arnett* this would have resulted, no doubt, in the application of the law of the parties' →

sor Sedler discussed the familiar situation in which residents of Ontario, a guest statute jurisdiction, are involved in an automobile accident in Michigan. If the action were brought in Michigan, he would apply Ontario law: "The only real interest here lies with the parties' home state, Ontario, and its law should be applied to deny recovery." Yet, Sedler also acknowledges the possibility that, for more than one reason, Michigan might assert an interest in the application of its plaintiff-protecting law. Since the assertion of such an interest is likely to reflect the forum's preference for its own better law, Sedler would "strongly disagree" with the view that a state's compensatory policy extends to all persons injured within its borders.[40] I am afraid that Michigan and Kentucky courts will not even go into an assessment of policies, the bare fact that the accident occurred in the forum state being "sufficient reason" to apply forum law. If so, the likelihood of forum shopping in these states can hardly be discounted.[41]

The second objection affects the rationale of the *lex fori* approach. The "enough contacts" or "sufficient reason" test turns on the presumption that forum law applies unless the forum connection is "insufficient", whatever that word may mean in terms of conflicts methodology. It could be argued that judicial method will supply the answer to that question in due time, after the Kentucky and Michigan courts have had the opportunity to deal with multifarious cases presenting the same issue at the center of all sorts of fact patterns.[42] But such

domicile Ohio, the only interested state. *Cf.* Weintraub (1973) p. 423/424, who would have applied Ohio law but for the fact that "the Arnetts' close ties with Kentucky made it extremely likely that denial of compensation to the wife would have a significant impact within Kentucky."
40 Sedler (1983-1) p. 1215.
41 According to Shapira (1970) p. 45/46, "the case against forum shopping seems overstated and logically tied to the traditional, blind pursuit of the goal of uniformity of result." While I do not oppose the proposition that forum law should be applied "where the choice-of-law methodology adhered to by the forum ultimately fails to offer a rational solution for a given conflicts controversy" (*ibid.* p. 55), I do have reservations in respect of an approach that canonizes application of forum law as a "rational solution" *per se*, thereby increasing the opportunities for successful forum shopping in such a way that it puts the defendant at an unreasonable disadvantage. On forum shopping, generally, see Siehr (1984).
42 *Cf.* Sedler (1973-1) p. 379/380: " ... in time a body of decisional law will emerge providing guidelines for the resolution of future cases." In conclusion, p. 392, Professor Sedler expressed the hope "that the Kentucky Court will define 'sufficient contacts' as 'interest and fairness' and will abandon territorialism once and for all." *Cf.* Weintraub (1973) p. 419, p. 428.

confidence in the judicial process tends to overlook the uncomfortable truth that, thus far, the Kentucky and Michigan courts have left us without a clue as to the theoretical structure on which their approach is founded. The *Foster v. Leggett* commentators, except Reese, were agreed that the Kentucky Court of Appeals did not follow the guidelines of the Restatement Second. It is also obvious that neither the "Fuld principles" nor Leflar's choice-influencing considerations, nor Baxter's comparative impairment approach have inspired the "home-team bias" of the Kentucky and Michigan courts. Not surprisingly, Sedler and Weintraub assumed that the decisions on which they gave their comments were rooted in the interest analysis doctrine they both champion. Although their opponent Twerski was less categorical and did not rule out the possibility of a different interpretation,[43] he accepted the policy-oriented rationale, so he could launch another attack on the evils of interest analysis. However, apart from *Wessling v. Paris*, the Kentucky cases hardly support this assumption. The only observation on policies is found in *Arnett*, where it was said that "the policy of this state is to allow recovery for injuries or death resulting from negligence."[44] But since the court refrained from determining the spatial claim to application of the rule or rules supporting this policy in relation to the facts, this remark – which was included as an afterthought in answer to the interspousal immunity doctrine the court deemed "unsound" – amounts to little more than a gratuitous statement on the contents of the better law of Kentucky. In that respect it might even be maintained that *Arnett* is a demonstration of Leflar's better law solution. Professor Reese, observing that "the opinion gives no indication of what interest, if any, of Kentucky was served by the application of its law," surmised that "perhaps the principal motivating factors behind the decision were the Court's desire to give recovery to the wife and its dislike for the Ohio interspousal immunity rule and the Ohio guest-passenger statute."[45] Even so, the Court of Appeals should have explicitly stated the reasons supporting its conclusions so as to provide guidance to the courts in the decision of future cases. If the principle or rationale employed by a court in an opinion is not "expressed with sufficient precision to make reasonably clear the proper boundaries of its application," Professor Reese warn-

---

43 Twerski (1973-2) p. 412, note 55, referring to Professor Reese's reading of the Kentucky cases: *infra* text preceding note 45.
44 *Arnett v. Thompson* 433 S.W.2d at 114 (Ky. 1968).
45 Reese (1973-1) p. 370.

ed, there will be a serious danger that "it will be applied in situations which involve different values but which do fall within its literal terms."[46] The "enough contacts" test, as employed in *Arnett* and *Foster*, not only lacks the stipulated precision, but as a choice of law approach it is also flawed by the absence of a rational justification for the application of forum law. To a slightly lesser extent, the same holds true for the Michigan decisions. In *Sexton-Storie*, the fact that the parties were Michigan residents or corporations doing business in Michigan was deemed "sufficient reason" to apply forum law. If this holding could still be interpreted as a ruling on a false conflict, therefore still in tune with interest-oriented choice of law, the opinion in *Smith v. Pierpont* paved the way for a radical *lex fori* approach by coupling choice of law to jurisdiction, subject to a perfunctory inquiry into the possible existence of a "superior foreign interest."[47] The unexplained assumption that judicial jurisdiction generally corresponds with a "substantial level of state interest" does not do much to reinforce the theoretical foundation of this approach.

In this context, mention should be made of a recent U.S. Supreme Court decision which marks the methodological autonomy of state courts in adjudicating choice of law issues and gives countenance to the unprincipled forum bias in Kentucky and Michigan. It differs from the cases just discussed in that it originated from Minnesota and, more important, that the Minnesota Supreme Court had arrived at its choice of forum law by an approach couched in fairly orthodox policy-oriented language. Its main import, however, lies in the U.S. Supreme Court's implicit endorsement of the emerging *lex fori* approach. In *Hague v. Allstate Ins. Co.*, the Minnesota forum was faced with the peculiar issue of "stacking" insurance coverage. Plaintiff's husband, a resident of Wisconsin, had died in an accident in his home state when his son's motorcycle on which he was a passenger was struck from behind by an automobile driven by another Wisconsin resident. The operators of the two vehicles were not insured, but the deceased did have insurance for each of the three automobiles he owned. The policies included an "uninsured motorist clause" covering injuries the

---

46 *Ibid.* p. 368/369.
47 *Cf. Breeding v. Massachusetts Indemnity and Life Ins. Co.* 633 S.W.2d 717 (Ky. 1982) and *Harris Corp. v. Comair, Inc.* 712 F.2d 1069 (6th Cir. [Ky.] 1983), *supra* text accompanying note 27: forum law applies " ... unless there are overwhelming interests to the contrary."

insured might suffer through the negligence of uninsured motorists, whether or not his own car was involved in the accident. The maximum coverage was $ 15,000 per car. Under Wisconsin law, the insurance company would only be liable for $ 15,000, but Minnesota law would permit the insured to "stack" the amount covered, *i.e.* to multiply the uninsured motorist coverage by the number of cars insured. The "Minnesota connection" may come as a surprise, but it is explained by the circumstance that Mrs. Hague had moved to that state after the accident. The Supreme Court of Minnesota affirmed the lower court's choice of Minnesota law, permitting recovery in the amount of $ 45,000, on the ground that Minnesota had an interest in "compensating injured plaintiffs to the maximum extent of their injuries," as well as in the administration of Minnesota estates. Devoted to Leflar's analysis of choice-influencing considerations since *Milkovich v. Saari*,[48] the court relied heavily on the better law factor, admitting that the Minnesota contacts might not be "in themselves, sufficient to mandate application of Minnesota law."[49] In this respect the decision is reminiscent of the Kentucky and Michigan cases, from which it differs, however, in that it is predicated on an established choice of law approach and clearly states the reasons why the Minnesota stacking rule should not be displaced by Wisconsin law.

The issue before the U.S. Supreme Court went to the question whether, in the light of federal constitutional standards, Minnesota had "a significant contact or significant aggregation of contacts, creating state interests such that application of its law was neither arbitrary nor fundamentally unfair."[50] Writing for a majority of only four,[51] Jus-

---

48 *Milkovich v. Saari* 295 Minn. 155, 203 N.W.2d 408 (1973), discussed *supra* chapter 5, text accompanying notes 70–72.
49 *Hague v. Allstate Ins. Co.* 289 N.W.2d 43 at 49 (Minn. 1979).
50 *Allstate Ins. Co. v. Hague* 449 U.S. 302 at 312, 101 S.Ct. 633, 66 L.Ed.2d 521 at 530 (1981). The test that is formulated here is derived from *Home Ins. Co. v. Dick* 281 U.S. 397, 50 S.Ct. 338, 74 L.Ed. 926, 74 A.L.R. 701 (1930); *John Hancock Mutual Life Ins. Co. v. Yates* 299 U.S. 178, 57 S.Ct. 129, 81 L.Ed. 106, (1936), both finding insufficient forum contacts, and from *Alaska Packers Assn. v. Industrial Accident Commission of California* 294 U.S. 532, 55 S.Ct. 518, 79 L.Ed. 1044 (1935); *Cardillo v. Liberty Mutual Ins. Co.* 330 U.S. 469, 67 S.Ct. 801 (1947); *Clay v. Sun Insurance Office, Ltd.* 377 U.S. 179, 84 S.Ct. 1197, 12 L.Ed.2d 229 (1964), finding adequate forum contacts to sustain the choice of forum law.
51 One Justice took no part in the consideration and decision of the case; there was one concurring opinion, whereas three Justices dissented.

tice Brennan upheld the Minnesota decision, as he found three contacts with Minnesota which, in the aggregate, permitted selection of Minnesota forum law: (1) the deceased had been employed in Minnesota; (2) the appellant company was present in Minnesota and was doing business in that state; and, (3) Mrs. Hague moved to Minnesota after the accident and became a resident of that state. Each of these three contacts was said to account for a Minnesota interest in this litigation. They can be paraphrased thus: (1) Minnesota had an interest in the safety and well-being of its work force; (2) it also had an interest in the regulation of an insurance company's obligations insofar as they affected Minnesota residents (Mrs. Hague) or longstanding members of Minnesota's workforce (Mr. Hague); and (3) it had an interest in full compensation for Minnesota residents or personal representatives appointed in Minnesota. The marginal test of choice of law quality was thereby satisfied: the aggregation of Minnesota's contacts with the parties and the occurrence, creating state interests, was sufficient to justify application of Minnesota law.

At a symposium on *Allstate*,[52] Professor Kozyris gave a pessimistic summary of the Supreme Court's stance on the constitutionality of choice of law decisions: " ... *Allstate* signals the Supreme Court's further retreat from the choice-of-law field; and it suggests that even 'plainly unsound'[53] conflicts rules will be constitutional so long as they are not totally irrational."[54] By its terms alone, the "sufficiently significant contacts" test leaves the courts considerable latitude to apply forum law, but its application in *Allstate* implies that practically any pretext will be considered valid reason for doing so. In his dissenting opinion, Justice Powell criticized the majority for "giv[ing] substance to the tenuous contacts between Minnesota and this litigation," which he considered "either trivial or irrelevant for the furthering of any public policy of Minnesota": (1) no interest of the forum state relating to employment was furthered by permitting stacking of insurance

---

52 Symposium on *Allstate Ins. Co. v. Hague*, 14 *U.C.Davis L.Rev.* 889–906 (1981), Professors Lowenfeld, Silberman, Peterson, Kozyris and Juenger participating.
53 This was Justice Stevens' characterization of the Minnesota Supreme Court's decision to apply its own law in *Allstate*: 449 U.S. 302 at 324, 66 L.Ed.2d 521 at 537 (1981), conc. opinion *per* Stevens, J.
54 Kozyris (1981) p. 905. Expressing doubts on "the Supreme Court's ability to improve American conflicts law," Professor Juenger praised *Allstate* for leaving state courts "ample leeway in multistate cases," and for upholding the "supremely sensible decision" of the Minnesota Supreme Court. Juenger (1981) p. 907, p. 915–917.

coverage; (2) the forum state had no interest in regulating the insurer's conduct unless it were related to property, persons, or contracts executed within the forum state; and (3) the post-accident change of residence of the plaintiff/widow was unrelated to the substantive legal issues presented by the litigation.[55] These cogent arguments highlight the forum-selecting opportunities implicit in the Supreme Court's constitutionality test. Given the minimal contacts the forum must have with multistate litigation so as to assert jurisdiction,[56] it is hard to imagine under what circumstances choice of forum law will not pass the Court's "sufficiently significant contacts" test. An imaginative forum will doubtlessly be able to list enough contacts which, in the aggregate at least, constitutionally support the choice of its own law. If this inference from *Allstate Ins. Co. v. Hague* is correct, it follows that the choice of law process has come to depend largely on jurisdictional rather than autonomous standards,[57] and that "the Supreme Court should ... strengthen the due process requirement of a definite nexus between the claim and the forum to justify the exercise of judicial jurisdiction."[58]

Returning now to the cases discussed before, there can hardly be any doubt that Kentucky's "enough contacts" approach and Michigan's "sufficient reason" test are well within the constitutional limits of *Allstate*. No more is required than that the contacts linking the respective law-fact patterns to the forum can be considered indicative of forum interests. This may be doubtful in cases such as *Arnett v. Thompson*, and *Harris Corp. v. Comair, Inc.*, in which the place of wrong constituted the only forum contact, but then, as the dissenting opinion of Justice Powell pointed out, it was doubtful in *Allstate*. The main difference between Kentucky's "enough contacts" test and the Supreme

---

55 *Allstate Ins. Co. v. Hague* 449 U.S. 302 at 337–339, 101 S.Ct. 633, 66 L.Ed.2d 521 at 546/547 (1981) diss. opinion *per* Powell, J. *Accord*: Silberman (1981) p. 861; Kozyris (1981) p. 898 ff.
56 *Cf.* Peterson (1981) p. 872; Kozyris (1981) p. 892 ff., p. 895: "And recent decisions have routinely upheld jurisdiction absent specific, claim-related forum contacts by the defendant." Kozyris specifically referred to "doing business" in the forum state as a tenuous, yet prevailing jurisdictional basis. See also: Weintraub (1980) p. 118, *supra* note 38.
57 The emphasis on jurisdiction in the *Allstate* comments tends to bear out this observation. *Cf.* Peterson (1981) p. 872: " ... decisions about judicial jurisdiction often and perhaps even normally control choice of law."
58 Kozyris (1981) p. 895.

Court's choice of law standard is in the determination of "state interests", as the *Allstate* test calls for "a significant contact or significant aggregation of contacts, *creating state interests.*"[59] This requirement suggests that interest analysis has been canonized, and that "the test would not be satisfied simply by identification of a contact recognized as the 'connecting factor' in a traditional choice rule, but would require in addition the identification of the interest created by that contact in the state to which the rule leads."[60] In that respect both the Kentucky and the Michigan decisions are lacking: no identification of interests can be found in any of them. On the other hand, the way the U.S. Supreme Court managed to inflate Minnesota's interests in the *Allstate* case – on the strength of little more than the Minnesota Supreme Court's preference for its own stacking rule– suggests that the interest requirement will be easily satisfied by a token allusion to forum contacts and the interests they *might* represent: the *Allstate* test supports rather than discourages the forum bias exemplified in the Kentucky and Michigan decisions. " ... *Allstate* allows state courts to premise their choice of law decisions on any rationale, including the preference for the forum rule as the one best suited to do justice," Juenger concluded.[61] In my opinion, doctrinal acquiescence to this development is to be deplored if it is not countervailed by a serious reconsideration of the limits to judicial jurisdiction. Greater latitude in jurisdiction necessitates closer scrutiny of the choice of law issue. Conversely, if a natural preference for forum law is taken for granted, the validity of the grounds for jurisdiction should be tested carefully, lest conflicts law loses its *raison d'être* altogether.

---

59 *Allstate v. Hague* 449 U.S. 302 at 313, 101 S.Ct. 633, 66 L.Ed.2d 521 at 531 (1981); emphasis added.
60 Peterson (1981) p. 882.
61 Juenger (1981) p. 915. The courts in Kentucky and Michigan will readily find a "rationale" in the concurring opinion of Justice Stevens in *Allstate*: "I question whether a judge's decision to apply the law of his own State could ever be described as wholly irrational. For judges are presumably familiar with their own state law and may find it difficult and time consuming to discover and apply correctly the law of another State. The forum State's *interest in the fair and efficient administration of justice* is therefore sufficient, in my judgment to attach a presumption of validity to a forum State's decision to apply its own law to a dispute over which it has jurisdiction." *Allstate Ins. Co. v. Hague* 449 U.S. 302 at 326, 101 S.Ct. 633, 66 L.Ed.2d 521 at 539 (1981), conc. opinion *per* Stevens, J.; emphasis added.

Part Three

The Viability of Policy-oriented Choice of Law

Introduction

Almost a quarter of a century has passed since the New York Court of Appeals first broke away from traditional choice of law in torts.[1] Since 1963, American courts in a steadily increasing number of jurisdictions have been experimenting with the various methods of policy-oriented conflicts law. Applying the new approaches in hundreds of cases,[2] they have gained a vast experience in assessing policies, weighing contacts and evaluating interests, especially in tort choice of law. In that area, there is now a wealth of material from which conclusions can be drawn

---

1 *Babcock v. Jackson* 12 N.Y.2d 473, 240 N.Y.S.2d 743, 191 N.E.2d 279 (1963). According to the Appellate Court of Indiana, in *Horvath v. Davidson* 148 Ind.App. 203, 264 N.E.2d 328 (1970), it was the Indiana Supreme Court that heralded the new era in American conflicts law. As early as 1945, it would have adopted a "Babcock approach" *–avant la lettre*, it would seem– in a contract case: *W.H. Barber Co. v. Hughes* 223 Ind. 570, 63 N.E.2d 417 (1945). To be sure, the opinion does have a modern ring: "The court will consider all acts of the parties touching the transaction in relation to the several states involved and will apply as the law governing the transaction the law of that state with which the facts are *in most intimate contact.*" *Ibid.* 63 N.W.2d 423; emphasis added. The main difference with *Babcock*, of course, is the absence of any reference to the *interests* of the states involved. See also: *supra* chapter 4, note 2.

2 According to McDougal (1984) p. 495, "[American] cases in which choice of law issues are raised must be in excess of 1,000 per year." Professor McDougal's estimate was based on a computer search for the year 1982, revealing 544 *reported* cases, 200 of which were state *appellate* cases. The total number may therefore be much larger. In the course of my own (non-electronic) research, I collected over 600 cases, mostly decided by higher state courts and federal courts, in which the *modern approaches* in conflicts law were either applied to *tort* issues or discussed in the context of *tort* choice of law.

that were once premature.³ By now, the evolution of American conflicts law has produced many more cases to be studied, compared and analyzed than those in the celebrated chain of New York guest statute decisions.⁴ If we are to appraise the merits of policy-oriented choice of law, the reservoir of relevant case law can hardly be large enough. The more cases available, the more accurately the methodological quality can be ascertained.

Having surveyed the major branches of the policy-oriented choice of law methodology in the light of a few hundred illustrative cases, I think the time has come to reap the fruits of these investigations. In the following chapters, I intend to discuss the pros and cons of interest analysis and to evaluate its viability as a method of choice of law. Since I consider interest analysis as the prototype from which most variants of policy-oriented choice law depart,⁵ the emphasis will be on the advantages and drawbacks of this particular approach. The main question I intend to address in the next chapters is not if interest analysis is a theoretically sound approach to choice of law, but, to put it bluntly, if it "works" in practice. I am convinced that, on a theoretical level, any legal theory can be faulted in some respect. Interest analysis is

---

3 Notably those reflected in the title of Kegel's Hague lectures in 1964. His fierce criticism of interest analysis is largely academic, in the sense that his attack on Currie's theory is not buttressed by arguments derived from the law in action. The only relevant cases Kegel mentions are those which Currie adapted to demonstrate his approach – e.g. *Milliken v. Pratt* 125 Mass. 374, 28 Am.Rep. 241 (1878), and *Grant v. McAuliffe* 41 Cal.2d 859, 264 P.2d 944, 42 A.L.R.2d 1162 (1953) – and *Babcock v. Jackson* 12 N.Y.2d 473, 191 N.E.2d 279, 240 N.Y.S.2d 743 (1963), decided just one year before Kegel delivered his lectures.
4 *Babcock v. Jackson* 12 N.Y.2d 473, 240 N.Y.S.2d 743, 191 N.E.2d 279 (1963); *Dym v. Gordon* 16 N.Y.2d 120, 209 N.E.2d 792, 262 N.Y.S.2d 463 (1965); *Macey v. Rozbicki* 18 N.Y.2d 289, 221 N.E.2d 380, 274 N.Y.S.2d 591 (1966); *Tooker v. Lopez* 24 N.Y.2d 569, 249 N.E.2d 394, 301 N.Y.S.2d 519 (1969); *Neumeier v. Kuehner* 31 N.Y. 2d 121, 286 N.E.2d 454, 335 N.Y.S.2d 64 (1972).
5 This is true, obviously, for all approaches that mainly purport to solve the true conflict dilemma, such as the comparative impairment approach or Cavers' principles of preference. Also included are Leflar's choice-influencing considerations, the Restatement Second approach, and even the Fuld principles, to the extent that they require an *ad hoc* evaluation of policies and interests, or embody a predetermined interest analysis. Arguably, neither a factual center of gravity test ("contacts-counting") nor the *lex fori* approach prevailing in Kentucky and Michigan qualifies as an expression of policy-oriented choice of law. Yet, the decisions in which these solutions were adopted do not escape the influence of policy considerations completely.

surely no exception.[6] However, on the assumption that the theory of interest analysis, though not impregnable, compares favorably with other doctrinal alternatives, putting the theory into practice might reveal drawbacks that cannot be obviated by any scholarly discourse. On the other hand, practice may either confirm or contradict a theoretical objection more clearly and convincingly than a host of academic arguments. Since there is a wealth of literature on the theory of policy-oriented choice of law, whereas systematic studies on its operative quality are relatively scarce, I am opting for a practical evaluation.

To some scholars, my reflections on the actual practice of policy-oriented choice of law may appear unrealistic or naive, in that I presume to judge a method by the quality of judicial performance. They might object that an unprincipled, result-selective decision is nothing but an incidental deviation, an unhappy slip without any bearing upon the validity of the misused choice of law approach as such. Or they might say that the courts are still experimenting with policy-oriented choice of law and that it takes time before their decisions will display the degree of consistency I seem to expect. Some might even maintain that the decisions described are eminently sensible and completely in tune with the method employed, which means that my evaluation rather than the decision should be faulted. Others, of course, will denounce any policy-based decision, since they were never convinced by its underlying theory in the first place. In sum, it could be argued that the way a choice of law approach is applied in practice does not necessarily prove that it is a workable or unworkable method. Still, I maintain that a conclusion on the methodological merits of policy-oriented choice of law can be based on the aggregated case law described in this book. When I set out to investigate the actual results of the transformation in American choice of law thinking, I saw the theory of policy-oriented choice of law, Currie's interest analysis in particular, as a very sensible, rational approach which agreed much more with my view of the social function of law than did the philosophy underlying the neutral allocation method. As a matter of fact, I still think that, in theory, interest analysis is the best reasoned approach to choice of law

---

6 One of the first critics of the theory was Professor Hill (1960), who published his article before interest analysis had been adopted by any court. Kegel's critical analysis has already been mentioned: *supra* note 3. See also: Brilmayer (1980).

that was ever conceived.[7] It was, therefore, in a positive frame of mind that I collected the material that was to give me the answer to the central question of this book: does policy-oriented choice of law achieve practical results which are not only consistent with the theory on which they rest, but also valid in terms of fairness, efficiency and reliability? The only way to find out, I submit, is by examining as many policy-oriented choice of law decisions as possible. The bigger their number, the less an occasional misconstruction of the theory will matter, and the more clearly pervasive inconsistencies stand out. The longer the period of judicial experience, the more reliable the aggregated information becomes, while the risk of misinterpreting the courts' overall performance gradually diminishes. It is my belief that, in the area of torts, I have gathered sufficient data, covering a sufficiently extended period of time, to let me draw some plausible conclusions on the viability of policy-oriented choice of law.

The criteria I have been using and will continue to use in evaluation of the practical application of policy-oriented choice of law reflect my ideas on the goals of law in general. To describe my standard of methodological viability, I can think of no better formulation than the one given by Amos Shapira in his study on the "interest approach" to choice of law: "A system for handling choice-of-law questions, or for that matter any kind of legal questions, must of necessity be workable as well as rational and fair. It must provide courts with adequate guiding procedures and working tools so as to make it pragmatically operative. Otherwise it might rightly be condemned as unworkable or conducive to chaos."[8] On the other hand, the much-criticized allocation method may serve as a kind of minimum standard. Assuming that policy-oriented theory offers a more rational, an "intellectually sounder" solution to the choice of law problem than the one based on the methods of Savigny or Beale, we are bound to check its performance against the results of traditional jurisdiction-selection. Despite its pretended neutrality, the latter approach has proved to be quite

---

7 *Cf.* Drion (1964) p. 235: "Intellectually it is perhaps the soundest approach to choice of law questions in the field of torts – which makes it so attractive for the university professor – but as a practical legal tool it is as fit for the day to day handling of legal problems as is a scalpel for cutting meat." It should be noted that Drion was a university professor when he wrote this, a few years before his appointment to the Dutch *Hoge Raad*.
8 Shapira (1970) p. 155/156, with reference to Currie (1963-1) p. 110.

adaptable to the predisposition of the courts to choose whatever law they deem "proper". Due to a host of exceptions, reservations and escapes, traditional choice of law practice is hardly a model of methodological consistency. In this respect, policy-oriented choice of law ought to be more convincing: as a rational approach, premised on the investigation of actual claims to application, it should have no need for result-selective manipulation. If it only serves to camouflage an unreasoned judicial preference, it loses much of its presumed advantage over the allocation method. Hence, the consistency of policy-oriented reasoning, both in single decisions and in accumulated case law, is a pervasive criterion in my evaluation of the modern American choice of law methodology.

The subject of the following discussion will be American case law in which the choice of law decision is based on, or at least inspired by, interest analysis. In the previous chapters, this approach has been examined on a "horizontal level", *i.e.* without much regard for the particular issue or other aspects of the case that might distinguish one policy-oriented decision from another. For a proper evaluation of interest analysis, it will not do to compare a wrongful death action with, let us say, a libel suit, even if either of the two can be identified as a false conflict or an unprovided-for case. That is why I propose to explore a number of cases in a "vertical" way, by concentrating on decisions that have more in common than their methodological underpinnings. In the category of guest statute decisions, there is abundant material for such an analysis. Not only is the issue in these cases usually quite clearcut – will defendant be allowed to plead the guest statute as a defense? – and therefore readily comparable, but in this field there are also fewer problems apt to cloud the choice of law motivation, such as the possible complications pertaining to the place of wrong, the "domicile" of a corporate entity, or the substance/procedure characterization. Although I agree with Juenger that the guest statute problem is a "vanishing issue", written about "ad nauseam" by conflicts authors, while other, more important issues are unduly neglected,[9] I feel justified in rehashing the guest statute case law because its volume supports the most scrupulous evaluation of interest analysis as a methodological alternative and allows the most accurate compari-

---

9 Juenger (1982) p. 132, mentioning in particular the conflicts problems posed by no-fault insurance and corporate transactions.

sons between judicial points of view. I intend to focus on the two problems which are generally considered as the major stumblingblocks of interest analysis: the feasibility of policy assessment and the hazards of relative interest evaluation. If it can be shown that the American courts have learned to surmount the difficulties posed by these cornerstones of interest analysis, the most cogent arguments against policy-oriented choice of law will prove to be invalid. If they cannot be disproved, however, there is no point in further evaluation, for a method premised on impracticable procedures must be impracticable altogether.

Chapter 8

The Guest Statute Problem

What is commonly known as a "guest statute" is a rule of law[10] which, subject to certain conditions, frees the negligent driver from liability to the injured passenger. While the common law would shift the burden of loss from the injured guest to the negligent host, the guest laws deprive the non-paying passenger of a cause of action by limiting or abrogating the host's duty of care. A typical example of a guest statute is the one that used to be in force in Oregon: "No person transported by the owner or operator of a motor vehicle, an aircraft, a watercraft, or other means of conveyance, as his guest without payment for such transportation, shall have a cause of action for damages against the owner or operator for injury, death or loss, in case of accident, unless the accident was intentional on the part of the owner or operator or caused by his gross negligence or intoxication."[11] Most guest statutes are concerned with highway accidents, but in a number of states, as in Oregon, their scope extends to other means of transportation as well.[12] Virtually all guest statutes are predicated on the condition

---

10 As the name implies, the rule is usually enacted in a statute. In Massachusetts, Georgia and Wisconsin, however, the doctrine was developed by the courts. *Cf.* Widger (1974) p. 659, note 1. See also: McDougal (1979) p. 741, note 38; Cavers (1965) p. 297, note 11.

11 Oregon Rev.Stat. 30.115, repealed in 1979 (Oregon Laws 1979, chapter 866); *cf. Fisher v. Huck* 50 Or.App. 635, 624 P.2d 177, note 1 (1981).

12 *Cf.* Widger (1974) p. 660, note 7, on the Delaware guest statute as amended in 1949: 47 Del.Laws 91, chapter 49, 1. In *Bishop v. Florida Specialty Paint Co.* 389 So.2d 999 (Fla. 1980), the aviation guest statute of South Carolina was at issue, that of South Dakota in *First National Bank in Fort Collins v. Rostek* 182 Colo. 437, 514 P2d. 314 (1973). Both California's aviation and automobile guest statutes were mentioned in *De Foor v. Lematta* 249 Or. 116, 437 P.2d 107 (1968), while Georgia's common law guest "statute" was referred to in *Kuchinic v. McCrory* 422 Pa. 620, 222 A.2d 897 (1966), an airplane accident case.

that the owner or operator of the vehicle not be paid for his services to the passenger. The Ontario guest statute, for instance, would not be applicable to cases in which "a vehicle [is] operated in the business of carrying passengers for compensation,"[13] an exception which, according to Professor Trautman's information, the Canadian courts have been willing to extend to expense-sharing passengers in non-commercial transportation arrangements.[14] Another condition typical of most guest statutes concerns the host's conduct: generally, a guest statute absolves the host from liability in case of ordinary negligence, but if it can be established that the host was guilty of "wilful or wanton misconduct", "gross negligence", or "reckless disregard of the rights of others", or if the accident was due to his deliberate recklessness or intoxication,[15] full responsibility will be imposed. In effect, this proviso increases the burden of proof on the part of the plaintiff-guest,[16] who is required to show aggravated rather than ordinary negligence.

The first guest statutes date from an era when road traffic was not as massive and hazardous as it is nowadays.[17] Inevitably, an increasing number of automobile accidents gave rise to litigation on the standard

---

13 Ontario Highway Traffic Act, Ont. Rev.Stat. (1960), chapter 172, § 105(2), amended by Ont. Stat. 1966, chapter 64, § 20(2), Ont. Rev.Stat. 1970, chapter 202, § 132(3). Until this amendment, the Ontario guest statute would not even allow recovery for gross negligence and wilful misconduct.
14 Trautman (1967) p. 469. The status of the guest is one of the "many knotty little problems involving petty and otherwise entirely inconsequential points of law" on which the courts of appeal had to rule in this area: Prosser (1984) p. 216. In *Kruzie v, Sanders* 23 Cal.2d 237, 143 P.2d 704 (1943), for instance, it had to be decided if helping the defendant to select Christmas presents placed the plaintiff outside the category of gratuitous guests. According to the California Supreme Court, it did.
15 According to Baron Rolfe in *Wilson v. Brett* 11 M.&W. 113 at 116, 152 Eng.Rep. 737 (1843), these forms of harmful conduct could be described as ordinary negligence "with the addition of a vituperative epithet." The phrase "aggravated negligence" expresses the various degrees of carelessness beyond ordinary negligence: Prosser (1984) p. 208 ff.; McDougal (1979) p. 740.
16 *Tooker v. Lopez* 24 N.Y.2d 569, 301 N.Y.S.2d 519, 249 N.E.2d 394 at 396 (1969); *Mentry v. Smith* 18 Wash.App. 668, 571 P.2d 589 (1978).
17 *West v. Poor* 196 Mass. 183, 81 N.E. 960 (1907), involving the driver of a milk wagon as the host and a child as his uninvited guest, seems to be the source of the American development of the doctrine. Cavers (1965) p. 297, note 11; Widger (1974) p. 661, note 15. Prosser (1984) p. 215, note 70, cites an Australian case decided as early as 1869.

of care a host-driver owes to the guest-passenger. At first, some courts, willing to shield the host, groped for analogies in more familiar areas, such as the licensor-licensee relationship,[18] gratuitous bailment,[19] or assumption of risk.[20] Later, when automobile traffic grew heavier and host-guest litigation started to burden the courts, state legislatures stepped in to settle the issue. Between 1927 and 1939, guest statutes of the type described were enacted in twenty-six of the United States.[21] In the meantime, the constitutional validity of the Connecticut guest statute, the first of these enactments, had been upheld by the U.S. Supreme Court: meant to rid the courts of "vexatious litigation" arising from automobile guest cases ("a permissible legislative object"), Connecticut's statutory abrogation of common law rights did not violate the equal protection clause of the Constitution.[22] Nevertheless, for as long as they exist, guest statutes have been criticized by courts and scholars alike. Instead of discouraging "vexatious litigation", they gave rise to an infinite variety of legal technicalities to be settled in court. Instead of protecting the friendly driver from ungrateful passengers, they shielded the insurance companies and left the injured guest empty-handed. Their underlying policies were found wanting and their constitutionality remained dubious. Furthermore, it became clear that, since the days of the first guest statute enactments, the problems of automobile accident law had changed considerably. Compulsory liability insurance had become a universal phenomenon, and in an increasing number of states some form of no-fault legislation was introduced, a compensation scheme which provides reparation of

---

18 This doctrine limits the liability of a land owner to a "licensee", *i.e.* one who, with the owner's consent, comes upon the land for his own purposes, and is therefore neither an "invitee" nor a trespasser. Prosser (1984) p. 415 ff.
19 *Massaletti v. Fitzroy* 228 Mass. 487, 118 N.E. 168 at 176/177 (1917): "The measure of liability of one who undertakes to carry *gratis* is the same as that of one who undertakes to keep *gratis*."
20 *O'Shea v. Lavoy* 175 Wis. 456, 185 N.W. 525 (1921), overruled in *McConville v. State Farm Mutual Automobile Insurance Co.* 15 Wis.2d 374, 113 N.W.2d 14 (1962). In the majority of American jurisdictions, however, the issue would still be subject to the common law rule imposing liability on the host in case of ordinary negligence. The rise of the guest laws did not come about until the 1930's. *Cf.* Widger (1974) p. 663.
21 Widger (1974) p. 665; Prosser (1984) p. 215.
22 *Silver v. Silver* 50 S.Ct. 57, 74 L.Ed. 221, 280 U.S. 117 at 122 (1929). Widger (1974) p. 666; Prosser (1984) p. 216, note 82; McDougal (1979) p. 747/748. However, eight years later, in 1937, the Connecticut legislature decided to repeal its guest statute: *cf.* Prosser *ibid.*; Widger (1974) p. 669, note 71.

personal injury losses without regard to individual fault, based on compulsory insurance.[23] Before long, legislators became aware of the anomalous coexistence of a guest statute barring recovery for ordinary negligence and a no-fault insurance plan allowing recovery up to a statutory maximum. The 1970's marked the decline of the guest laws. In 1969, the Vermont statute was repealed, an example that was followed in Massachusetts in 1971 and in Florida in 1972. In 1973, the Supreme Court of California struck down its statute as unconstitutional.[24] Since then, repeals, amendments and judicial nullifications have eliminated the guest laws in most states.[25]

It goes without saying that guest statutes are controversial rules of law, even in domestic cases. From the moment they were created, they have been criticized for infringing constitutional standards, or for just being unfair. After their hey-day had passed, they were said to "contradict the spirit of the times,"[26] and to give rise to "discriminatory treatment of auto guests."[27] In choice of law cases, therefore, one would expect frequent invocation of the doctrine of public policy, provided the forum state itself never had a guest statute, or had abolished it in the meantime. Whether the forum is devoted to interests analysis or prefers the traditional conflicts rule, public policy could ultimately ward off the threat of a foreign guest statute claiming application, or applicable as a rule of *lex loci delicti*. Considering that the vast majority of multistate guest cases was decided in favor of recovery, it is remarkable that the public policy device was never deployed. In *Winters v. Maxey*, the Supreme Court of Tennessee noted that it would only displace *lex loci delicti* if a foreign rule would be "against good morals or natural justice, or [if] for some other reason, its enforcement would be prejudicial to the general interests of our citizens."[28] Since both host and guest were domiciled in Tennessee, one would expect that the applicable Alabama guest statute would be neu-

---

23 See, generally, Kozyris (1972) and (1973); Prosser (1984) p. 606 ff. One of the most influential proposals on no-fault insurance was the Keeton-O'Connell Plan, introduced by Professors Robert E. Keeton and Jeffrey O'Connell: *Basic Protection for the traffic Victim: A Blueprint for Reforming Automobile Insurance*, 1965.
24 *Brown v. Merlo* 8 Cal.3d 855, 106 Cal.Rptr. 388, 506 P.2d 212 (1973).
25 Prosser (1984) p. 216; Widger (1974) p. 676 ff. They remain in only a handful of states and abolition might be imminent there as well: Prosser (1984) p. 217.
26 *Clark v. Clark* 107 N.H. 351, 222 A.2d 205 at 210 (1966).
27 *Brown v. Merlo* 8 Cal.3d 855, 106 Cal.Rptr. 388, 506 P.2d 212 at 224 (1973).
28 *Winters v. Maxey* 481 S.W.2d 755 at 756 (Tenn. 1972).

tralized by invocation of the public policy exception. Although this is precisely what the dissent urged the court to do, the majority saw no reason to depart from the "uniform rule of lex loci delicti" and denied recovery. Another case in which the majority refused to be persuaded by the dissent's public policy argument is *Dym v. Gordon*, one of the prominent New York guest statute cases. In the opinion of Judge Burke, writing for the majority, Colorado not only had a threefold interest in the application of its guest statute, it was also the state having the most significant contacts with the controversy. Although New York, the state where both parties were domiciled, would have an interest in the compensation of the guest, the domiciliary factor was deemed less important than the fact that the parties' relationship centered in Colorado. As to public policy intervention, the court's opinion of the fairness of the Colorado statute was obviously not low enough to warrant its displacement: "The principles justifying our refusal to apply foreign law on the ground of public policy are well defined, and a mere difference between the foreign rule and our own will not warrant such refusal."[29] One of the dissenters, Chief Judge Desmond, cited both *Kilberg v. Northeast Airlines* and *Babcock v. Jackson* to support his contention that "public policy calls for a reversal" of the Appellate Division's holding that Colorado law must apply,[30] but even though many commentators decried the reasoning and the result in *Dym*, they did not endorse this particular argument.

In this respect, Leflar's better law consideration has found considerably more support. Landmark decisions, such as *Clark v. Clark*, *Heath v. Zellmer* and *Milkovich v. Saari*, all involved a foreign guest statute

---

29 *Dym v. Gordon* 16 N.Y.2d 120, 262 N.Y.S.2d 463, 209 N.E.2d 792 at 796 (1965). Judge Burke then quoted the well-known public policy standard laid down by Cardozo in *Loucks v. Standard Oil Co.* 224 N.Y. 99, 120 N.E. 198 at 202 (1918); *supra* chapter 2, section 3, text accompanying note 190.

30 *Dym v. Gordon* 16 N.Y.2d 120, 262 N.Y.S.2d 463, 209 N.E.2d 792 at 801 (1965). *Cf.* Cavers (1965) p. 305 ff., commenting on the dissent's public policy argument. It should be noted that, despite Chief Judge Desmond's ambiguous language, the public policy argument in *Kilberg* differs from *Babcock*'s "public policy" approach. In *Kilberg v. Northeast Airlines, Inc.* 9 N.Y.2d 34, 211 N.Y.S.2d 133, 172 N.E.2d 526 at 528 (1961), the New York Court of Appeals refused to apply the Massachusetts wrongful death limitation, as it was deemed to be "completely contrary to our public policy." The references to "public policy" in *Babcock* had nothing to do with the "negative" function of the doctrine, but were meant to denote the forum's interests in the application of its own law.

which the court refused to apply because it deemed its own law to be "preferable",[31] "sounder"[32] or "superior."[33] Although there are marked differences between the public policy doctrine and the better law theory,[34] as applied in practice they seem to have a common denominator: an unreasoned preference for what the forum views as "sound" or "fair" or "just", qualities most courts complacently attribute to their own law. The same forum bias might well have influenced the many guest statute decisions in which the court managed to find for the plaintiff on the grounds of a seemingly detached and rational analysis of policies and interests. In too many cases, especially those in which both parties were domiciliaries of the same state, the result comes as a surprise to the student of conflicts methodology, regardless of his stand on the "soundness" of guest statutes.[35] This would suggest that policy-oriented approaches lend themselves as conveniently to judicial manipulation as the conflicts doctrines discussed in chapter 2. After a closer inspection of the policies underlying guest statutes, I will come back to this supposition.

1 Guest statute policies

In retrospect, it is not difficult to perceive that guest statutes have served a number of distinct purposes. Before the advent of the automobile and the rise of liability insurance, the common law rule that required a host to exercise ordinary care when transporting a passenger prevailed in most states. Obviously, the few jurisdictions that did limit the host's liability for injuries to his guest had not adopted such a rule to discourage "vexatious" host-guest litigation, or to shield the insurance business, or to keep insurance premiums low. More

---

31 *Clark v. Clark* 107 N.H. 351, 222 A.2d 205 at 210 (1966).
32 *Heath v. Zellmer* 35 Wis.2d 578, 151 N.W.2d 664 at 675 (1967).
33 *Milkovich v. Saari* 295 Minn. 155, 203 N.W.2d 408 at 417 (1973).
34 *Supra* chapter 2, section 3, text following note 257.
35 Those in favor of the guest's recovery must have been baffled by *Dym v. Gordon*, while those in favor of a host's limited liability must have been appalled by *Conklin v. Horner*, discussed *supra* chapter 4, text accompanying notes 64–65, chapter 5, text accompanying notes 51–52. Those who pretend to study conflicts law from a "supranational" height and without bias must have been perplexed by either decision.

likely, these early judge-made guest laws expressed social disapproval of the ungrateful guest suing the kindly host. "Don't bite the hand that feeds you," was the adage justifying the bar to the guest's recovery.[36] The early analogies with the licensor-licensee relationship and assumption of risk doctrine indicate that the protection of the host rested primarily upon the notion that one may not look a gift horse in the mouth,[37] or that the guest who knows the risk involved in riding with the host has a free choice to assume or avoid it, and should not be allowed to shift the burden of loss to the host. In many cases, the host is seen as the "good Samaritan" who is kind enough to help others without benefit to himself, a benefactor who certainly does not deserve to be sued by the one he succored. Along these altruistic lines, the Iowa Supreme Court in *Rainsbarger v. Shepherd* described the policy of the Iowa guest statute as one purporting "to cut down litigation arising from the commendable unselfish practice of sharing with others transportation in one's vehicle and protect the Good Samaritan from claims based on negligence by those invited to ride as a courtesy."[38] To my mind, there is a ring of morality in this kind of rationale. It suggests that the host-guest relationship is predicated on the correlative precepts of unselfishness and gratitude. Accordingly, in this pre-insurance era, guest statutes were expected to encourage hospitality as socially desirable behavior. Protected by guest statutes, drivers willing to offer a ride would not be deterred "by the fear that through some misfortune they would be charged with gross negligence and be compelled to defend suits for exorbitant sums."[39] The hospi-

---

36 *Crawford v. Foster* 110 Cal. App. 81, 293 P. 841 at 843 (1930); *Clark v. Clark* 107 N.H. 351, 222 A.2d 205 at 209 (1966).
37 *Cf.* Prosser (1984) p. 412; p. 489.
38 *Rainsbarger v. Shepherd* 254 Iowa 486, 118 N.W.2d 41 at 44 (1962). See also: *Byrn v. American Universal Ins. Co.* 548 S.W.2d 186 (Mo. App. 1977) on the policy of the Iowa guest statute; *Chila v. Owens* 348 F.Supp. 1207 (S.D. N.Y. 1972) on the policy of the Ohio guest statute.
39 *Shea v. Olson* 185 Wash. 143, 53 P.2d 615 (1936). Prosser (1984) p. 215, note 76, cites an Arkansas decision in which "the related goal of encouraging car pooling" was mentioned: *Davis v. Cox* 268 Ark. 78, 593 S.W.2d 180 (1980). See: Cavers (1965) p. 298; McDougal (1979) p. 743, p. 752. See also: Widger (1974) p. 664, quoting from a Note –18 *Cal. L.Rev.* 184 (1930)– by a guest statute advocate: "[S]uch suits should be discouraged, inasmuch as they are unsportsmanlike and an abuse of hospitality; they saddle the owner or driver of the car with an unreasonable burden and thereby discourage invitations to guests, thus preventing those who cannot afford to own automobiles from obtaining the health and pleasure derived from their use."

tality rationale seems to have gained considerable legislative support during the years of the Depression, when, of necessity, many came to depend on hitch-hiking for transportation.[40] These were also the years when most guest statutes came into being. Apart from the lack of statistical evidence substantiating the professed fear of hitch-hiker suits, the hitch-hiker argument – and the hospitality rationale in general – lost most of its force with the rise of automobile liability insurance. It was expressly refuted in a number of decisions, most extensively in a 1973 California decision: *Brown v. Merlo*. Attacking the notion that guest statutes would encourage hospitality by discouraging ingratitude, the California Supreme Court pointed out that a guest's suit for damages can hardly be viewed as an act of ingratitude towards the host if the real defendant in host-guest litigation is not the host, but his insurer. Even if guest statutes were originally based on the social values of hospitality and gratitude, at the time providing a valid rationale, the advent of widespread liability insurance has undermined its validity, the court concluded.[41] The same thought had already been put into words by Ehrenzweig in 1960: "This [hospitality v. ingratitude] rationale would fail completely in the vast majority of cases where the host carries liability insurance, and will become totally meaningless with the achievement of the goal of general or near-general insurance which, with or without compulsion, is sought by both the public and the insurance industry."[42]

---

40 Widger (1974) p. 664; Leflar (1966-2) p. 1595; Prosser (1984) p. 216, note 77. Rumor has it that the Ontario guest statute was supported by the Premier of Ontario, because he had been sued personally by a pair of ungrateful hitch-hikers. *Cf.* Trautman (1967) p. 470; Baade (1973) p. 154. In fact, none of the reported guest statute cases does involve hitch-hikers. *Cf.* Sedler (1973-1) p. 389: "the fictitious 'ungrateful hitchhiker' has yet to make his appearance in an actual case." In the fourth edition of his monumental textbook, Dean Prosser noted (1971, p. 187, note 8): "In legislative hearings there is frequent mention of the hitch-hiker, who gets little sympathy. The writer once found a hitch-hiker case, but has mislaid it. He has been unable to find another."
41 *Brown v. Merlo* 8 Cal.3d 855, 106 Cal.Rptr. 388, 506 P.2d 212 at 215, 221 (1973). See: Diane Smith Coscarelli, Comments: The California "Owner-Passenger" Statute: Remnants of an Unconstitutional Guest Law, 11 *U. San Francisco L.Rev.* 345–378 (1977).
42 Ehrenzweig (1960-1) p. 599. See also: *Clark v. Clark* 107 N.H. 351, 222 A.2d 205 at 210 (1966); *Labree v. Major* 306 A.2d 808 at 815 (R.I. 1973): " ... compulsory automobile liability insurance clouds the rationale of the policy that a gross-negligence standard was necessary to protect against ungrateful guests."

Paradoxically, the growing popularity of liability insurance and the budding perception that "[i]n the overwhelming majority of cases the real party in interest will be the insurance company, not the host-driver,"[43] destroyed the original guest statute rationale and generated a cluster of new functions. Gradually, the protection of the uninsured, unselfish host was reduced to a secondary policy of guest statute legislation, as the focus of attention shifted to the interests of the insurance industry and its clients, and to the increasing burden of automobile accident litigation. The latter concern, which is mentioned in some cases as a justification of guest statutes, stemmed from the steadily increasing use of automobiles as a means of transportation and the concomitant rise of the automobile accident rate. In *Silver v. Silver*, the U.S. Supreme Court recognized the possibility of "vexatious litigation" arising from automobile guest cases as a valid legislative concern and a suitable matter of state regulation.[44] In several other cases, the need "to cut down litigation" between automobile hosts and guests was mentioned as a distinct guest statute policy.[45] The theory is, of course, that guest statutes generally bar the guest's recovery in case of ordinary negligence on the part of the host, thus discouraging the guest from asserting his claim in court. In practice, however, the guest statutes seem to have had the opposite effect: the pliable terminology of guest statutes ("gross negligence", "guest", "gratuitous", "riding in a vehicle") invited a barrage of questions on statutory construction and gave rise to a flood of litigation.[46] In this respect, too, the develop-

---

43. McDougal (1979) p. 752. Sedler (1973-1) p. 389: " ... a guest-host suit, as most personal injury actions, is in reality not a suit between the victim and the nominal defendant, but, as everyone knows, between the victim and the defendant's insurer." See also: Judge Keating's concurring opinion in *Macey v. Rozbicki* 18 N.Y.2d 289, 274 N.Y.S.2d 591, 221 N.E.2d 380 at 385 (1966): " ... the real party in interest, the insurer, ... who has calculated the premium and issued the policy in accordance with New York law."
44. *Silver v. Silver* 50 S.Ct. 57, 74 L.Ed. 221, 280 U.S. 117 at 123 (1929).
45. For instance: in *Rainsbarger v. Shepherd* 254 Iowa 486, 118 N.W.2d 41 at 44 (1962), it was given as the rationale of the Iowa guest statute; see also: *Pfau v. Trent Aluminum Company* 55 N.J. 511, 263 A.2d 129 at 131/132 (1970). In *Conlin v. Hutcheon* 560 F.Supp. 934 at 937 (D. Colo.), decided in 1983, "reduc[ing] the amount of litigation" was still mentioned as one of the policies of the Nebraska guest statute.
46. Widger (1974) p. 671. According to McDougal (1979) p. 750, note 77, "guest statutes increase, rather than decrease, the amount of litigation." In a study by Lascher – "Hard Laws Make Bad Cases – Lots of Them (The California Guest Statute)," 9 *Santa Clara Law.* 1, 24 (1968) – quoted by McDougal, the number of domestic guest statute cases decided by the courts of first instance in California is estimated to be "some 25,000 to date" (*i.e.* 1968, the date of publication of Lascher's article).

ment of guest statute policies is paradoxical. While guest statutes were once meant to prevent congestion in the courts, the necessity of improving judicial efficiency is now used as an argument for their repeal.[47]

A more current reason for guest statute legislation, in fact the rationale most often relied on in case law and comments, was advanced by the insurance industry. With the general acceptance of liability insurance as a necessary financial protection from the hazards of automobile traffic, a problem emerged that made the insurance companies worry over their profits, or –if that does not amount to the same thing– over the rates they were charging. The root of all evil, it appears, was the assumption that automobile accidents causing injuries to non-paying guest passengers were conducive to fraud and collusion. Allegedly, host and guest were in an eminent position to defraud the liability insurer of the host-driver by agreeing to twist or fabricate the facts in court. The Washington Supreme Court, in *Shea v. Olson*, summarized the problem thus: "It is a matter of common knowledge ... that because of a friendly regard for the guest, and knowing that he himself will not have to pay the bill anyway, the host is willing to admit, and often testify to, a state of facts other than it actually is and thus deprive the insurance company of the benefit of a good defense."[48] Most commentators agree that the rise of guest statute legislation in the 1930's was largely due to "persistent and effective lobby-

---

47 Prosser (1984) p. 217, note 88; Widger (1974) p. 678. Of course, it is difficult to prove that guest statute litigation does or does not add substantially to the judicial work load. Other factors might be much more important, in the first place the rising number of traffic accidents. In a study instigated by the Institute for Civil Justice, a research unit within the Rand Corporation, it was found that the percentage of personal injury actions in the Los Angeles Superior Court, most of them involving automobile accidents, rose from 20 % of the civil docket in 1930 to 60 % in 1980, the total number of civil filings having increased from 466 in 1880 to more than 70,000 in 1980. *Cf.* The Institute for Civil Justice, *An Overview of the First Five Program Years, April 1980 – March 1985*, p. 19, referring to Molly Selvin and Patricia A. Ebener, *Managing the Unmanageable: A History of Civil Delay in the Los Angeles Superior Court*, R-3165-ICJ, 1984. From the same source, I gathered that no-fault insurance and the existence of a "tort threshold" (defining the minimum amount for which the victim can sue) are probably the most effective means to reduce automobile accident litigation, whereas changing from contributory negligence to some form of comparative negligence appears to have only a modest effect. *Ibid.* p. 48. The repeal of host-guest legislation was not mentioned as a relevant factor.
48 *Shea v. Olson* 185 Wash. 143, 53 P.2d 615 (1836).

ing on the part of liability insurance companies."[49] There is hardly any doubt that the insurance industry played a dominant part in persuading state legislatures that guest statutes were necessary to curb the increasing number of collusive suits. The success of the insurance lobby can be measured by the host of critical comments following the introduction of this particular brand of special interest legislation.[50]

The critics have attacked the collusion rationale on various grounds. Depriving the automobile guest from a cause of action for fear of collusion was viewed as a particularly nasty example of "throwing out the baby simply because the bath water gets dirty once in a while."[51] In this respect, the guest statutes were thought to be "overinclusive", since they are premised on the suspicion that hosts and guests are generally inclined to defraud the insurance company by collusion and perjury. At the same time their scope is "underinclusive", in that they focus on just one minor category of tort victims, non-paying guests, while fraud and collusion might occur in numerous other situations in which a (social, contractual, or family) relationship between the tortfeasor and the victim exists.[52] Furthermore, the "wholesale elimination" of one particular class of tort victims on the grounds of possible collusion seems an extreme measure in the light of alternative remedies for fraud and perjury, particularly and more appropriately the sanctions of criminal law.[53] In response to a collusion defense in an intrafamily immunity suit, the Washington Supreme Court opined: " ... the fact that there may be greater opportunity for fraud or collusion in one class of cases than another does not warrant courts of law in closing the door to all cases of that class. Courts must depend upon the efficacy of

---

49 Prosser (1984) p. 215. See also: Widger (1974) p. 664. Baade (1973) p. 152, quoting from various documents on the legislative history of the Ontario guest statute, found a statement in the *Newspaper Hansard* of March 30, 1935 explaining that the bill to amend Ontario's Highway Traffic Act " ... is the answer of the department to the insurance companies' plans to double the passenger liability insurance rates in the Toronto area on April 1."
50 *Cf.* Prosser (1984) p. 215, note 75; p. 216, note 83; Widger (1974) p. 667 ff.; Baade (1973) p. 152, note 18, 19. One title is particularly revealing: Allen, 61 *Am. L.Rev.* 77 (1927), "Why Do Courts Coddle Insurance Companies?"
51 *Henry v. Bauder* 213 Kan. 751, 518 P.2d 362 at 370/371 (1974).
52 *Brown v. Merlo* 8 Cal.3d 855, 106 Cal.Rptr. 388, 506 P.2d 212 at 215 and 226 (1973). McDougal (1979) p. 751/752, note 81. Widger (1974) p. 682.
53 *Cf.* Widger (1974) p. 668 and 675. A higher standard of proof, *e.g.* evidence by witnesses or expert opinion rather than personal evidence, would be another possibility.

the judicial processes to ferret out the meritorious from the fraudulent in particular cases."[54] My own objections to the collusion rationale are mainly practical. In the first place, I have never quite understood the danger of collusion as such. Assuming that host and guest are willing to defraud the host's liability insurer, I can see[55] three possibilities for collusion: (1) there was no accident at all, or (2) if there was one, the guest's injuries were not due to the negligence of the host, but to lack of care on his own part, or that of a third party, or (3) the damages the guest actually suffered were less than those claimed. No collusion is needed in the first situation, since the insured could claim the fictitious damages all by himself if he could somehow substantiate them, a bit of a problem to anyone trying such a scheme. In the second situation, collusion would pay if the guest or third party were uninsured, and if – in the case of the third-party tortfeasor – all parties involved would be willing to cooperate. In hit-and-run accidents, the insurer could be defrauded by a host taking the blame for the benefit of the guest's recovery. The third possibility must be a familiar hazard to the insurance business, but not one that warrants legislative action in respect to automobile host-guest relationships only. Besides, if insurance companies are bent on neutralizing the effects of collusion, they would have the option, it would seem, either to increase their rates, or to provide in their policies that there be no coverage in case of accidents involving a guest.[56] However that may be, I fail to see how guest legislation can provide the answer to collusion. As guest statutes generally

---

54 *Borst v. Borst* 41 Wash.2d 642, 251 P.2d 149 at 155 (1952). See also: *Rozell v. Rozell* 281 N.Y. 106, 22 N.E.2d 254, 123 A.L.R. 1015 (1939).
55 I had just arrived at this point in my writing when, by some quirk of fate, I happened to be involved as a Dutch guest-passenger in an automobile accident in Belgium. The driver was a domiciliary of the Netherlands, where the car was also insured and garaged. Having sustained minor injuries, I had some occasion to ponder over this opportunity to defraud the driver's liability insurer. Any lucrative collusion scheme I could think of, however, would be shattered by the evidence of the doctor who gave me first aid, or the mechanic who towed the car to a nearby dump-yard. On the other hand, the accident confirmed my belief that the place of wrong has no relevance whatsoever, least of all in this type of situation, to the determination of the law governing the rights and liabilities between hosts and guests.
56 *Cf. Signs v. Signs* 156 Ohio St. 566, 103 N.E.2d 743 (1952), in which case the latter argument was used in the context of parental immunity. As a means to safeguard insurance funds, the insurance contract offers better possibilities, I would think, than those expected from guest legislation. To counteract the danger of collusion, the insurance company could agree to cover the insured's liability to (certain classes of) guests for a higher premium.

do not apply to paying guests or to situations in which the host is guilty of aggravated misconduct, it should not be too difficult for those willing to collude against the insurance company to spin a plausible tale on the passenger's payment for the ride or on the driver's recklessness.[57] Purporting to make lying unprofitable, the guest statutes can be easily circumvented, I am afraid, by a slightly different lie.

Complementing the collusion rationale is the policy of reducing the cost of insurance, which is sometimes advanced as a separate argument in favor of guest laws. It was the main reason for the majority in *Cipolla v. Shaposka* to apply the guest statute of Delaware, the state where defendant's car was garaged, "for it appears that insurance rates will depend on the state in which the automobile is housed rather than the domicile of the owner or driver."[58] Taken at its face-value, this motive for limiting the host's liability does seem to have some merit. It stands to reason that the cost of liability insurance will decrease the more the insured are absolved from liability. Arguably, the actuarial calculus should reflect the extent to which the law frees automobile owners and drivers from liability, resulting in lower premiums in guest statute states. In a much-quoted article, however, Professor G. Robert Morris exposed this "zone of risk" approach as fallacious, as it misconstrues the concept of risk and overlooks actuarial realities.[59] It is Morris' thesis that, while the "entrepreneur" tries to esti-

---

57 *Cf.* McDougal (1979) p. 751; Ehrenzweig (1960-1) p. 599.
58 *Cipolla v. Shaposka* 439 Pa. 563, 267 A.2d 854 at 856 (1970). In his dissenting opinion, Chief Justice Bell rejected this argument on several grounds: *ibid.* at 858. See also: McDougal (1979) p. 743; Couch (1970) p. 108. The validity of the "insurance premium rationale" is accepted, at least implicitly, in *Kopp v. Rechtzigel* 273 Minn. 441, 141 N.W.2d 526 at 527 (1966); *Bolgrean v. Stich* 293 Minn. 8, 196 N.W.2d 442 at 444 (1972); *Bray v. Cox* 39 A.D.2d 299, 333 N.Y.S.2d 783 at 786 (1972); *Chila v. Owens* 348 F.Supp. 1207 at 1211 (1972), and *Foster v. Leggett* 484 S.W.2d 827 at 831 (Ky. 1972), to cite just a few cases.
59 Morris G. (1961). The "zone of risk" theory, espoused by Dean Young B. Smith in "Frolic and Detour", 23 *Col. L.Rev.* 444 (1923), was thus summarized by Morris (p. 556): " ... the entrepreneur [*i.e.* a business corporation or a household] can only be expected to insure those risks which he can foresee are incident to his enterprise. Therefore, enterprise liability should be limited to that zone of risk which the entrepreneur can anticipate. Fairness dictates that losses occurring beyond the boundaries of that zone should not be attributed to the entrepreneur." The theory has influenced many authors, including Professor Ehrenzweig who, in connection with tort choice of law, expanded it to a "zone of foreseeable laws concept" (Morris, p. 559). *Cf.* his views on "enterprise liability under foreseeable and insurable laws": Ehrenzweig (1960-1), (1960-2) and (1960-3).

mate his *personal* risk in the light of his foresight, the actuary's estimate of the total cost of enterprise liability –risk *in general*– is based on hindsight. The latter calculus draws on the aggregate experience of past losses and comprises numerous factors the individual entrepreneur would not take into account. Whether or not the law of a particular state holds the host-driver liable for the injuries to his guest has very little impact on the quantum of risk which determines the cost of insurance: a diminished risk of guest claims could be increased, or vice versa, by other factors, such as traffic congestion, highway design, or population density. What counts in reality is the aggregate loss covered by automobile liability insurance in a particular "rating territory", of which only a very small portion can be attributed to guest claims. Professor Hancock put it this way: "In fixing premiums, insurance companies do not and cannot take into account such uncertain and minuscule factors as the potential application of particular rules of domestic law. To make statistically reliable forecasts of future losses, they must necessarily use a vast body of highway accident loss experience, including hundreds of claims that did not involve antiguest statutes at all."[60] Although the cost of automobile liability insurance does vary from state to state, the different rates do not reflect the existence or nonexistence of guest statutes, which implies that other factors dominate.[61] Ironically, one of those factors could be the increased cost of guest statute litigation concerning the "many knotty little problems" this type of legislation has produced, to the extent that the insurance industry bears the expense. In any event, the notion that guest statutes would help to keep insurance premiums down is not confirmed by actuarial practice. It is noteworthy that, when state legislatures started to repeal their guest laws in the late 1960's and early 1970's, the insurance industry made no objection.[62]

Another guest statute policy, one that was uncovered in *Dym v. Gordon*, is said to assure "priority of injured parties in other cars in the assets of the negligent defendant."[63] If the guest is excluded from the class of persons to whom the host-driver is liable, other claimants will

---

60 Hancock (1975) p. 780, note 24.
61 Widger (1974) p. 675/676, cites a survey by Tipton –11 *U.Fla. L.Rev.* 287 (1958)– who compared the liability insurance rates in guest statute and non-guest statute jurisdictions and found no differences pertaining to the extent of the host's liability.
62 Widger (1974) p. 676–678; Prosser (1984) p. 215, note 75.
63 *Dym v. Gordon* 16 N.Y.2d 120, 262 N.Y.S.2d 463, 209 N.E.2d 792 at 794 (1965).

have better prospects of full recovery. It is doubtful whether any state legislature adopting a guest statute has been motivated by such an objective. In his dissenting opinion in *Dym*, Judge Fuld pointed out that the domestic cases discussing the Colorado guest statute at issue did not mention this policy. Nor had it been proposed in scholarly writing on the subject of guest statutes in general.[64] On the other hand, Cavers supported the "injured non-guest rationale" as a valid legislative concern, for "the problem with which it is concerned is not fanciful," but he also pointed out that "the driver's insurance policy – if he had one – would ordinarily provide greater coverage for an accident in which there was more than one claimant."[65] Fanciful or not, the new rationale gained some status in several judicial opinions since *Dym*. In *Heath v. Zellmer*, for instance, the Supreme Court of Wisconsin listed as one of the policies evinced by the Indiana guest statute "a desire ... to keep intact a fund (the host's assets) so it can be reached by other parties to the accident whose claims are assumed to have a vague moral priority over the claims of the gratuitous guest."[66] In New York, however, the *Dym* construction was soon abandoned. Writing for the majority in *Tooker v. Lopez*, Judge Keating called it a "teleological argument" contradicted by statutory history. If guest statutes were meant to give priority to other injured parties than the guest, the host's liability to his guest should have been ruled out altogether, even in case of gross negligence: " ... we fail to perceive any rational basis for predicating th[e] protection [of injured non-guests] on the degree of negligence a guest is able to establish."[67] I should like to add that I find the "injured non-guest rationale" highly speculative. If it comes

---

[64] Weintraub (1980) p. 268, note 4.
[65] Cavers (1965) p. 298, note 12 and accompanying text. Cavers' comments on *Dym v. Gordon* appeared in an appendix to his book; they were written before the *Dym* decision was printed.
[66] *Heath v. Zellmer* 35 Wis.2d 578, 151 N.W.2d 664 at 669 (1967). See also: *Cipolla v. Shaposka* 439 Pa. 563, 267 A.2d 854 (1970) at 857/858 (Roberts, J. dissenting); *Chila v. Owens* 348 F.Supp. 1207 (S.D. N.Y. 1972).
[67] *Tooker v. Lopez* 24 N.Y.2d 569, 301 N.Y.S. 519, 249 N.E.2d 394 at 397 (1969). Other courts have rejected the "injured non-guest rationale" more bluntly: *Pryor v. Swarner* 445 F.2d 1272 at 1275 (2d Cir. [N.Y.] 1971): " ... we conclude that the residence of the passengers in the second car, or even the fact that there was a second car, is irrelevant to the choice of laws which the New York courts would make in this case." *Mentry v. Smith* 18 Wash.App. 668, 571 P.2d 589 at 590 (1978): the fact that the driver of the other car was from Oregon (the state where the accident occurred and where a guest statute was in force) was irrelevant as "she is not a party to this action."

to sharing the funds of the defendant host or the proceeds of his insurance policy, there may be other claimants than guests or injured non-guests. In *Bray v. Cox*, New York's Appellate Division emphasized the validity of New York's pro-guest policy which purportedly assures compensation to those who furnish medical and hospital care to injured parties. Furthermore, the court recognized the state's "public fiscal interest in assuring that indigent non-resident accident victims do not become public charges and that, if they do, [the state] can recoup its welfare expenses from the victim's recovery."[68] Constituting the counterpart of the "injured non-guest rationale", these policies are equally spurious.[69] If the host's assets must be shared, they are obviously not sufficient to cover the aggregate loss of all parties involved. If the guest is barred from recovery, he might become a public charge and his medical creditors might go unpaid, to the advantage of injured non-guests and those who gave them medical assistance. If the guest is allowed to recover, along with all other parties involved, there might not be enough for any of them. Theoretically, the host could become a public charge in either case.

Now that we have touched the question on what grounds lawmakers have *refused* to limit the host's liability, it might be useful to examine the negative policy some courts have attributed to guest statutes. In *Wilcox v. Wilcox*, for instance, the Supreme Court of Wisconsin described the policy of Nebraska's guest statute as "a negative one," as it was the statute's objective "not to penalize misconduct that amounts to ordinary negligence."[70] Hence, the court inferred, a guest statute can hardly be said to further highway safety, a governmental concern which is subordinated to the purposes of guest legislation. In other words, a guest statute jurisdiction would have sacrificed its interest in

68 *Bray v. Cox* 39 A.D.2d 299, 333 N.Y.S.2d 783 at 785/786 (1972). A similar argument was advanced by the Supreme Court of Michigan in *Milkovich v. Saari* 295 Minn. 155, 203 N.W.2d 408 at 417 (1973): "We might also note that persons injured in automobile accidents occurring within our borders can reasonably be expected to require treatment in our medical facilities, both public and private ... with a consequent governmental interest that injured persons not be denied recovery on the basis of doctrines foreign to Minnesota."
69 *Cf.* McDougal (1979) p. 744: "Since there is no assurance that such [medical] creditors will be paid from the funds received by the injured party, it is extremely doubtful that the payment of doctors and hospitals is a factor taken into consideration by decisionmakers in promulgating compensatory policies like ordinary negligence."
70 *Wilcox v. Wilcox* 26 Wis.2d 617, 133 N.W.2d 408 at 416 (1965).

deterring hazardous conduct to the private interests of the host and his insurer. Conversely, the absence of a guest statute would indicate a policy of furthering safe driving. In choice of law cases, this is a popular argument for the rejection of a foreign guest statute, as, for instance, in *Heath v. Zellmer*, another well-known Wisconsin decision: "To employ the Indiana law in this instance would remove the deterrent effect of our law of negligence, while the choice of Wisconsin law would further this state's interest in regulating conduct on Wisconsin highways and penalizing that conduct when it is negligent. It would promote safe driving on Wisconsin highways."[71] On the other hand, some opinions insist that the issue of host-guest liability has nothing to do with conduct or the standard of care. In *Fuerste v. Bemis*, for instance, the Iowa Supreme Court decided that the liability of the Iowa host to his Iowa guest would be governed by the Iowa guest statute; Wisconsin, the state where the accident had occurred, was said to have no interest in any issue in this case: "The standard of conduct of the parties while in Wisconsin was not an issue here ..."[72] The same argument was used in *Woodward v. Stewart*, a Rhode Island case involving Rhode Island parties: although the accident had occurred in Massachusetts, a state having a guest statute, the court rejected the suggestion that Massachusetts would be an interested jurisdiction, for the driver's conduct was not at issue.[73] In my opinion, the latter decisions make more sense than those in which it is suggested that guest statutes would have some bearing upon highway safety. Even though an examination of the host's conduct might be required in guest statute cases turning on alleged gross negligence,[74] the real issue is generally the

71 *Heath v. Zellmer* 35 Wis.2d 578, 151 N.W.2d 664 at 675 (1967). See also: *Conklin v. Horner* 38 Wis.2d 468, 157 N.W.2d 579 at 586 (1968); *Gagne v. Berry* 290 A.2d 624 at 626 (N.H. 1972); *Labree v. Major* 306 A.2d 808 at 816 (R.I. 1973); *Gordon v. Kramer* 124 Ariz. 442, 604 P.2d 1153 at 1156 (Ariz.App. 1979).
72 *Fuerste v. Bemis* 156 N.W.2d 831 (Iowa 1968).
73 *Woodward v. Stewart* 104 R.I. 290, 243 A.2d 917 (1968). A similar argument is found in *Cipolla v. Shaposka* 439 Pa. 563, 267 A.2d 854 at 856, note 2 (1970): " ... the fact that the accident occurred in Delaware is not a relevant contact because the Delaware [guest] statute does not set out a rule of the road." See also: *Milkovich v. Saari* 295 Minn. 155, 203 N.W.2d 408 at 414 (1973): " ... the rule in question, unlike rules of the road and definitions of negligence, does not bear upon vehicle operation as such."
74 One of the issues in *Emery v. Emery*, 45 Cal.2d 421, 289 P.2d 218 (1955), concerned the meaning of "reckless disregard of the rights of others" for which the host would be liable under the guest statute of Idaho, as opposed to "wilful misconduct", the exception laid down in California's guest statute.

extent of the host's liability. In *Kennedy v. Dixon* the Supreme Court of Missouri had to decide whether the Indiana guest statute applied to a suit between Missouri parties who had been involved in an accident in Indiana. The court rightly observed that "Indiana's only real interest is in requiring that Missouri residents comply with its standards of care for operation of motor vehicles on its highways." Missouri, on the other hand, was the only state that could have an interest in determining the extent of host-guest liability between Missouri domiciliaries.[75]

Defining policies in the negative, by establishing which objectives the law is *not* meant to achieve, is a hazardous enterprise, especially if the contrast between positive and negative policies is used to assert a forum policy, as happened in *Wilcox*. Contrasting its own pro-recovery rule with Nebraska's guest statute, the Wisconsin Supreme Court appeared to deduce a positive Wisconsin policy of deterrence from Nebraska's negative policy of not penalizing ordinary negligence. The syllogism underlying such reasoning is equally false, I submit, as one which would use the absence of a guest statute as indicative of a policy supporting collusion and ingratitude. A guest statute is no more meant to invite negligent driving than its absence expresses a policy of furthering highway safety. For that reason, the Supreme Court of Oregon, in *Tower v. Schwabe*, rejected plaintiff's contention that the legislature of British Columbia had decided to repeal its guest statute to induce a higher standard of care on British Columbia highways, an assertion that would have helped to establish a British Columbia interest in plaintiff's recovery. The court was not convinced that the repeal had been inspired by a legislative concern with conduct. If it had, the court doubted its effect: "It is unlikely that a driver's actions will be influenced by a reduction in the standard of care he or she owes to one small portion of the class of potential plaintiffs."[76] Most writers agree that there is no relation between highway safety and the standard of care prevailing in either pro-recovery states or guest statute states. "The motorist who has invited a guest, should not and will not drive

75 *Kennedy v. Dixon* 439 S.W.2d 173 at 184/185 (Mo. 1969). In *Sharp v. Egler* 658 F.2d 480 at 484 (7th Cir. [Ind.] 1981), the Seventh Circuit applied Indiana's guest statute in an action between a Kentucky guest and an Indiana host who had been involved in an Indiana accident. Examining Indiana's interests in this litigation, the court listed the protection of Indiana host-drivers, the protection of Indiana insurers from collusive suits, and, surprisingly, the operation of motor vehicles on Indiana roads.
76 *Tower v. Schwabe* 284 Or. 105, 585 P.2d 662 (1978).

more or less carefully according to whether he, or his liability insurer, will be held liable merely for his gross negligence or for whatever the jury may find to have been negligence, with or without moral fault," noted Ehrenzweig with characteristic conviction.[77] To Professor McDougal, who considers loss distribution the primary goal of pro-recovery rules, it is "less than clear" whether the ordinary negligence doctrine expresses an interest in deterring negligent conduct; at best, deterrence would be a secondary objective.[78] And Professor Ratner, who is willing to acknowledge deterrence as one of the purposes of "some" tort recovery rules, does not believe that the absence or presence of a guest statute has any bearing on the driver's conduct, even assuming he is aware of any difference in rules: "Automobile drivers are primarily deterred by concern for their own safety and for the safety of family members or friends who may be with them. That overwhelming consideration (plus the threat of a traffic citation) engulfs other concerns."[79] In short: if multistate host-guest litigation focuses on the issue whether or not a guest statute should be applied to shield the host from liability for ordinary negligence, the matter in dispute is not the host's conduct but his liability. The standard of care argument is therefore irrelevant and sheds no light on the actual policy of a guest statute; the enacting state may have had many motives for its host-protecting rule, but the promotion of unsafe driving was surely not one of them. Conversely, if the absence of a guest statute should tempt the court to invent a legislative concern for safe highway conduct, the argument would almost certainly be spurious, as it is based upon considerations that may or may not have motivated the legislature *not* to change the common law.[80]

---

77 Ehrenzweig (1960-1) p. 599. See also: *Witherspoon v. Salm* 142 Ind.App. 655, 237 N.E.2d 116 at 123 (1968), *rev'd on other grounds*, 251 Ind. 575, 243 N.E.2d 876 (1969), in which case the Appellate Court of Indiana expressed the same sentiment: "It is nonsense to consider the possibility that a host who proposes to transport a guest from one state to another would first sit down and analyze the substantive law in each state through which he might have to travel and so plan his journey as not to drive through the states which impose a higher standard of care upon a host."
78 McDougal (1979) p. 744.
79 Ratner (1974) p. 830/831.
80 This might be different if a state legislature would have contemplated adoption of a guest statute, refusing to pass it for the specific reason that limited liability would encourage unsafe driving. I have not been able to find any evidence of such a motive.

Reviewing the various rationales attributed to guest statutes, one is inclined to reject them all for the poor and sometimes speculative arguments on which they rest. Even if the particular objective a guest statute was meant to achieve was valid at the time of enactment, changing conditions could soon render it obsolete and irrelevant. Some of them were probably no more than teleological inventions of an imaginative court, without any foundation in legislative reality. Other goals, however real they may have been to the advocates of guest legislation, were never accomplished. All in all, the history of the guest statute is not particularly uplifting. Nevertheless, we did encounter a number of policies that were actually attributed, right or wrong, to guest laws. The foregoing critique was not meant as an indictment of these controversial rules of law, but should serve as a means to the evaluation of interest analysis as a practicable choice of law method. In that respect, it supports the interim conclusion that an accurate policy assessment is more complicated than some authors would hope, and its results less unequivocal than some courts pretend. In the case of guest statutes, policy inspection reveals traces of Christian morality, special-interest protection, and actuarial speculation. The ingredients of a guest statute, or most other rules of law for that matter, are diverse and their blend is not likely to serve a single purpose. In time, the rule may have acquired new functions, obscuring its original design and raising questions of actual legislative intent versus normative beliefs.[81] The resulting composite is fraught with ambiguity.

In choice of law, chances are that a court in a pro-recovery jurisdiction paints a distorted picture of the policies underlying a foreign guest statute, not always out of prejudice but because of insufficient information. A case in point is Judge Fuld's analysis of the Ontario guest statute in *Babcock v. Jackson*. His only source of information was a note in a Canadian law review in which the author cited no authority for the statement –quoted in *Babcock*– that the Ontario statute was meant to "prevent the fraudulent assertion of claims by passengers, in

---

[81] *Cf.* Brilmayer (1980) p. 400 and *passim*. *Id*. (1984) p. 562: "Interest analysts inject their own normative preferences into choice of law discussions, but attempt to evade detection by masquerading these preferences as 'legislative policy'."

collusion with the drivers, against insurance companies."[82] In a comment on *Kell v. Henderson*, Professor Trautman came up with a quite different explanation. Based upon research into the pertinent Canadian case law, his findings pointed to a legislative concern for the owner of the car rather than for the insurer. As Trautman has it, the Ontario rule was meant to mitigate the owner's vicarious liability to the driver's guest, reflecting "a view that it was unfair to impose this imputed liability to a gratuitous passenger."[83] He acknowledged that this conclusion did not follow from a textual interpretation of the statute, as it shields not only the owner but the driver as well. Instead, Trautman based it –*a contrario*, it would seem– on two decisions in which the court refused to relieve the owner of vicarious liability to his injured *employee*. In his Fuld eulogy, Professor Reese slightly misinterpreted Trautman's analysis by emphasizing the ingratitude rationale: "Further research ... has revealed the distinct possibility that one purpose, and perhaps the only purpose, of the statute was to protect owners and drivers against suits by ungrateful guests."[84] Professor Baade, apparently, was not convinced. Concentrating on the legislative history of the Ontario statute, in a comment on *Neumeier v. Kuehner*, he concluded that "the sole apparent legislative purpose of the Ontario guest statute as enacted in 1935 and as amended in 1966 is to protect insurance companies against claims which would necessitate an increase of motor vehicle insurance rates in Ontario."[85] These discussions have not proved particularly enlightening to the courts when they had to rule on yet another Ontario guest statute case. In *Macey v. Rozbicki*, the majority ignored the purposes of the statute altogether, but to

---

82 *Babcock v. Jackson* 12 N.Y.2d 473, 240 N.Y.S.2d 743, 191 N.E.2d 279 at 284. The note had appeared in 1936: Survey of Canadian Legislation, 1 *U. Toronto L.J.* 358, p. 366. Reese (1971) p. 554, note 22 and p. 558, in a rather derogatory way, called it a "student note", but according to Baade (1973) p. 153, note 19, "[t]he author of that comment, J.J. Robinette, was at that time the editor of the Ontario Law Reports, a member of the Faculty of Law of Osgoode Hall, in practice in Toronto. He is presently one of the leaders of the Ontario bar."
83 Trautman (1967) p. 468/469.
84 Reese (1971) p. 558, citing Trautman as the initiator of this research.
85 Baade (1973) p. 156. In a footnote –*ibid.* p. 163, note 59– Baade quoted Reese's reference to Trautman's "further research." He then invited the reader to make up his own mind as to the quality of such further research, adding: "He may also ponder the spectacle of one American citing a second American who refers to a third American's views as to the purpose of a Canadian statute." Since Baade himself refrained from discussing these American sources, we are left in the dark as to Baade's views on Reese's views on Trautman's views.

Judge Keating, in his concurring opinion, there was "no doubt" that the Ontario legislature had wanted to prevent fraud and collusion against the insurer, but no authority was cited to substantiate this assertion.[86] When it was Judge Fuld's turn again, in *Neumeier v. Kuehner*, he obligingly quoted Reese paraphrasing Trautman, and acknowledged the possibility that the Ontario guest statute was primarily inspired by a desire to protect the owner and driver against the guest's ingratitude.[87] On the other hand, when the Minnesota Supreme Court was faced with the Ontario guest statute in *Milkovich v. Saari*, it took its cue from Leflar. Whether Ontario had wanted to prevent collusive suits, or to give vent to "a vague disapproval of a guest 'biting the hand that feeds him'," the court did not even want to know: "Neither rationale is persuasive."[88]

As an exercise in comparative law, policy assessment is an arduous, time-consuming and risky undertaking for which few lawyers are properly equipped. If it comes to foreign law, most judges[89] and attor-

---

86 *Macey v. Rozbicki* 18 N.Y.2d 289, 274 N.Y.S.2d 591, 221 N.E.2d 380 at 385, note 1 (1966). Writing for the majority in *Tooker v. Lopez* 24 N.Y.2d 569, 301 N.Y.S.2d 519, 249 N.E.2d 394 (1969), however, Judge Keating had occasion to repeat his statement, this time citing the same Canadian note from which Judge Fuld had quoted in *Babcock*. It will be remembered that the "injured non-guest rationale", introduced in *Dym v. Gordon*, *supra* text accompanying note 63, was retracted in *Tooker*. This juggling with the policies of Colorado, Michigan and Ontario confirms that guests laws are generally perceived as interchangeable rules serving identical purposes.
87 *Neumeier v. Kuehner* 31 N.Y.2d 121, 335 N.Y.S.2d 64, 286 N.E.2d 454 at 455 (1972). In the meantime, the Appellate Division had struggled with a true conflict between the laws of New York and Ontario in *Bray v. Cox* 39 A.D.2d 299, 333 N.Y.S.2d 783 (1972). "Protection of Ontario insurers", "maintenance of relatively low Ontario insurance rates", and "prevention of collusive suits" were listed as distinct policies.
88 *Milkovich v. Saari* 295 Minn. 155, 203 N.W.2d 408 (1973). Leflar's prompt did not contain any specific information on the purposes of the Ontario guest statute, but disqualified all guest statutes for being "unfair" and "undesirable": Leflar (1966-2) p. 1595.
89 In countries, such as the Netherlands, where questions of foreign law are generally considered as questions of law rather than fact, requiring the court to determine foreign law *ex officio*, bench and bar are faced with the same problems. In the U.S.A., there is no uniform approach to the issue of judicial notice: as a rule, a question of sister-state law is treated as a question of law, to be determined by the court, but judicial notice is generally understood as a discretionary rather than mandatory proceeding when the law of a foreign country is involved. See, generally,

neys are helpless amateurs, who need to call in an expert on the particular law, or to telex a confrère abroad, or to do their own laborious research – with dubious results. Even if the language of the foreign law is not a problem, there may be doubts as to the present validity of the rule, its pertinence to the case at issue, its construction and interpretation, its rank in the hierarchy of law sources, etcetera. True, the perils of comparative research are considerably less serious when its object is sister-state law, or a legal system belonging to the same law family as forum law. And, true, the difficulties in determining foreign law should not be exaggerated in certain areas, such as the guest statute cases, where accumulated experience stored in voluminous case law should bolster the student's assurance. However, the problem we are dealing with is not the determination of the plain *content* of foreign law, nor its interpretation or current validity. Our research is concerned with *policies*, and therefore with subliminal influences and contradictory interests that helped shape the legal formula in which they are sealed. In this respect, there are several differences between policy-oriented choice of law and traditional jurisdiction-selection. Both methods are premised on an accurate assessment of the contents of foreign law. Under the traditional approach, such an assessment is not required if the conflicts rule points to forum law, whereas interest analysis calls for an investigation of each legal system involved, if only to determine whether there is a conflict at all. Furthermore, traditional conflicts law is not concerned with the rationale of either domestic or foreign law, but merely appoints the rule of decision, preparatory to ordinary subsumption. On the other hand, to determine whether or not a rule was *meant* to apply to the case at issue, interest analysis depends on a preparatory assessment of both the contents *and* the purposes of the relevant rules of law. Next, it should be established whether the purpose of each rule is actually served by its application. After that, the case can be classified as a true or a false conflict, or as an unprovided-for case, subject to the pertinent approach or approaches. The whole process is considerably more complicated than that of allocation and application of the selected foreign or domestic law, and presupposes commensurate skills in comparative law. For that reason,

---

Cramton/Currie/Kay (1981) p. 56 ff.; Leflar (1977-3) p. 259 ff.; Weintraub (1980) p. 86 ff. In case the burden of proving foreign law falls upon the party invoking its application, the court is spared both the effort and possible blunders incident to investigations into some unfamiliar legal system. See, generally, *supra* chapter 2, section 4.

I feel doubtful about the first and principal premise of interest analysis, which assumes the feasibility of policy assessment. In theory, the required investigation, though not impossible, is even more difficult than the determination of foreign substantive law under the jurisdiction-selecting approach, for it does not stop at establishing the law's content, but needs to unearth the policies and purposes that created it. In practice, as we have seen in our examination of the relatively simple guest rules, policy assessment is anything but foolproof. Although the contents of guest laws are clear enough to allow straightforward subsumption, it is hard to find out which objectives they were actually meant to achieve. Even if the various purposes of a guest statute can be identified severally, their joint expression is bound to be equivocal, as it covers disparate objectives. As a preliminary step in the choice of law process, I submit, the analysis of guest statute policies is inconclusive and therefore open to manipulation.

2 The spatial reach of a guest statute

Undaunted by the skepticism the last paragraph may have evoked, we will now set out to examine the relation between the policy of a guest statute and its spatial reach. In my opinion, this is an intermediate step between policy assessment and the subsequent process of determining a state's interest in the light of its contacts with the individual case. When discussing the workings of interest analysis, most authors tend to ignore this particular question,[90] implying that the spatial reach of a rule is automatically revealed by either policy assessment or *ad hoc*

---

[90] *Cf.* Weintraub (1980) p. 267; Leflar (1977-1) p. 185, p. 210; Strikwerda (1978) p. 163 ff.; Ratner (1974) p. 819. Currie mentioned it only in passing, as in his discussion of a North Carolina statute on purchase-money mortgages: "On the assumption that states, like individuals, act primarily for the furtherance of their own interests and the interests of their people, we may reasonably state that the purchasers protected were: (a) resident citizens of North Carolina; (b) perhaps also nonresident citizens of North Carolina; and (c) such other persons as may be entitled under the Constitution, or on the basis of considerations of decency and far-sighted self-interest, to equal treatment with local citizens." Currie (1963-1) p. 417.

interest determination.[91] By itself, however, policy assessment sheds no light on the territorial reach of the rule in question, while *ad hoc* interest determination is nothing but a subsumptive technique dependent on a correct assessment of the rule's spatial scope in the abstract. While interest analysis has been criticized for being an unpredictable, *ad hoc* approach to choice of law, I contend that it is a method premised to a large extent on *a priori* reasoning. Once it is established that two or more states are involved, the content, policy and spatial reach of their respective rules of decision can be determined without recourse to the facts of the individual case. The specific fact pattern is only relevant to the question whether it answers the spatial description inferred from the preceding policy analysis. This last step – requiring no more than tentative subsumption – must be repeated as many times as there are differing rules of decision, and will lead to the categorization of the case as a false, unprovided-for or true conflict. In other words, to the extent that interest analysis is predicated on an evaluation of the possible claims to application embodied in the laws of the jurisdictions involved, such claims must first be verified on a normative level –*i.e.* in the abstract, without regard to the specific case– to allow an *ad hoc* verification of a state's actual interest in application of its law to the case at issue.

Since there are no scope rules expressing the legislature's views on the reach of a guest statute in multistate situations, a plausible demarcation must be deduced from each of the various policies advanced. It will be clear that such reasoning, however plausible, cannot be entirely free from speculation. Furthermore, since we have found a number of relevant policies, it should be anticipated that the territorial scope of a guest statute cannot be determined unambiguously. Such disparate objectives as the promotion of hospitality, or the prevention of vexatious litigation, or safeguarding the stability of insurance rates are likely to produce incompatible spatial indicia. This is a problem

---

91 The tendency to disregard deductive logic and to eschew dogmatic reasoning may be inherent in the common law tradition with its emphasis on precedent and case law, and in the way American legal scholars are used to propound their theories. In legal education, the prevailing case method encourages an inductive way of thinking in which a concrete fact situation, not a particular rule of law, is the point of departure. This might help to explain why American academicians are generally less bent on strictly logical, deductive, or systematic constructions than most of their colleagues in continental Europe.

that will have to be discussed at a later stage, when we can appreciate its full extent. At this point, several assumptions must be accepted. First and foremost, there is Currie's premise that "[r]ules of law exist not because, in the nature of things, they must, but because there is a policy to be effectuated."[92] In this respect, Currie was clearly influenced by the realist or sociological movement in American jurisprudence. One of the most poignant statements inspired by this school of thought is the thesis that "[t]he law is both a result of social forces and an instrument of social control."[93] In this perspective, a rule of law should be applied if the social policy it is meant to further is actually served by its application, both in domestic and multistate situations.[94] The choice of law problem can thus be perceived as a potential conflict between the policies pursued in differing social systems in regard to the matter in dispute. However, one need not be an adherent of sociological jurisprudence to appreciate the merits of Currie's paradigm. To accept the first premise of interest analysis, one should at least acknowledge that the law is more than a set of senseless rules. Operating in a community, it is apt to embody social values and to perform social functions. The cornerstone of policy-oriented choice of law is the notion that all rules of law are meant to further specific purposes and that these purposes, revealed by ordinary construction and interpretation,[95] determine the rule's relevance to multistate situations.

The second assumption posits a general limitation of a rule's spatial reach: since states and nations are territorially organized and each of them has its own legal order,[96] it must be taken for granted that the extraterritorial reach of a state's law is not unlimited. Lawmakers generally do not pretend to be God, and the precepts they create are not meant to be universal. In fact, they seldom think about the spatial dimensions of the domestic rules they lay down. There are several

92 Currie (1956) p. 266, cited by Strikwerda (1978) p. 164.
93 Friedmann (1967) p. 296 ff., discussing the American realist movement and Roscoe Pound's "theory of social interests" or "social engineering". *Ibid.* p. 336 ff. Pound and his successors "pursue[d] a line of thought originated by Ihering and Bentham, that is the approach to law as a means to a social end and as an instrument in social development." *Ibid.* p. 339. *Cf.* Currie (1963-1) p. 64, p. 183, p. 631; Shapira (1970) p. 51; Strikwerda (1978) p. 161.
94 *Cf.* Ratner (1974) p. 824; Strikwerda (1978) p. 164.
95 Currie (1963-1) p. 367, p. 377, and *passim*.
96 *Cf.* Cavers (1965) p. 135.

reasons why a rule of law is not supposed to have a universal reach. Some of these are dogmatic, such as those predicated on public international law,[97] while other ones are based on more practical considerations, particularly the likelihood that an overextensive domestic rule will not be observed abroad, or that a judgment in which it was applied will not be recognized elsewhere. However, in the absence of explicit statements on the spatial reach of a rule, we need not concern ourselves with the doctrine of legislative jurisdiction, for it will be assumed that lawmakers, had they considered the matter, would neither want to exceed their authority, nor promulgate overextensive, and therefore ineffective laws. At the same time, this assumption suggests a normative approach to the problem of spatial delimitation: since there is no point in asking what the spatial reach of a rule *is*, the question is what it *should* be.

From these presuppositions follows a third one: the outer limits of a rule's spatial scope are determined by the motives that can be reasonably imputed to the authority creating the rule.[98] Since it is not likely that lawmakers are concerned with the welfare of any community or individual but their own, we may safely assume that laws are generally meant to further domestic interests, which should be understood as the individual or collective interests of all those belonging to a particular legal community –whether citizens, domiciliaries, or residents– including its members abroad. It can hardly be believed that the Ontario legislature, when enacting its guest statute, intended to rule out the liability of, let us say, Japanese hosts transporting Japanese guests on Japanese territory in Japanese cars insured by Japanese insurers. Instead, it must be assumed that it was motivated by a concern for any host-guest relationship somehow affecting Ontario. In general, then, lawmaking authorities will be concerned with individuals affiliated

---

97 See, generally, Akehurst, 46 *British Year Book of International Law* 145, at 170 ff. (1972/1973).
98 *Cf.* Currie (1963-1) p. 377, referring to *legislative* purposes and intentions. Since legislation is not the only source of law that can be subjected to policy analysis, I use the word "authority" or "lawmakers" to include the authors of judge-made law, regulations, etcetera.
For the sake of clarity, policy changes through the dynamics of social development and their consequences for a rule's spatial reach are deliberately ignored in this chapter. The "myth of legislative intent" (Brilmayer 1980), as well as the complications inherent in policy assessment in general, will be examined later, *infra* chapter 9.

with their territory by reason of their citizenship, domicile or residence,[99] and with acts and occurrences affecting their community as a whole. Conversely, a rule of law in force in a particular community is not meant to govern fact situations that neither touch that community as such, nor involve any of its members.[100] The distinction between individual and collective involvement hints at the dichotomy of personalism and territorialism which plays such an important part in neo-statutist theory. On completion of the guest statute discourse, this subject will be further discussed.

Bearing in mind these general premises of spatial delimitation, we will now focus on the scope of the guest statute in the light of its various rationales. It will be remembered that the original guest statute policy, the one that prevailed in the pre-automobile era, had an air of morality to it. Denying the free passenger a cause of action for negligence of the driver, the rule expressed disapproval of what was obviously perceived as unacceptable social behavior on the part of a *guest*. The other side of the coin shows a policy of encouraging hospitality, a rationale pertaining to the proper conduct of a *host*. Thirdly, in the "good Samaritan" perspective, the guest laws could also be viewed as legislative or judicial expressions of a desire to shield the kindly host from his guest's ingratitude. The differences are slight, but they are relevant to the rule's spatial reach. Clearly, to the extent that the "good Samaritan" rationale focuses on the host driver in need of protection from ungrateful guests, the scope of the guest statute, as any rule purporting to shield an individual, must be thought of as personal. In this respect, the guest statute expresses the community's concern with the plight of host-drivers established there; it is unlikely that it was intended to shield the foreign host who happened to pass by.[101] If,

99 This observation includes corporate entities which have their place of incorporation, headquarters or place of business in the state concerned.
100 *Cf.* Strikwerda (1978) p. 161 ff. I use the word "community" as a neutral substitute for "state" or "nation". For some reason, several critics of Currie's theory have refused to understand that the term "governmental interest" or "state interest" stands for the interest of a legal community represented by executive authority. Let it be stressed again that, in the context of interest analysis, the word "state" is used – metaphorically, for all I care – to denote the collectivity of an autonomous social system.
101 *Cf. Miller v. Gay* 470 A.2d 1353 at 1361 (Pa. Super. 1983): " ... while one purpose of the [Delaware] statute is to protect Delaware hosts from the ingratitude of their guests, the scope of that protection is limited. ... [Delaware's] interest in protecting out-of-state hosts must therefore be still more limited."

however, the guest law primarily serves the purpose of educating passengers to show gratitude for services rendered –the "don't bite the hand that feeds you" ethic– its policy is admonitory and it may be surmised that its scope includes every passenger being picked up or being transported in the jurisdiction where the rule is in force. As a behavioral exhortation, the guest statute urges *all* passengers in the state, domiciliaries and visitors alike, to be grateful guests.[102] The same applies to the hospitality rationale. It wants *all* drivers in the state, whether they belong there or not, to be kindly hosts, willing to offer free rides to anyone in need of transportation. While it might somewhat stretch our imagination, it could be argued that a rule of law which stimulates car-pooling and encourages motorists to pick up hitch-hikers serves several public interests, such as lowering the cost of highway maintenance and traffic regulation, or alleviating the need for public transport services. In this respect, both citizens and visitors are expected to contribute to the welfare of the community whenever they make use of its highway system. Similarly, to the extent that a guest statute is meant to elevate the driver or the passenger to higher planes of social behavior, its spatial reach must be thought of as territorial; everyone within the territory of a community, including visitors, is supposed to observe the standards of conduct the community maintains. The admonition "When in Rome, do as the Romans do," tells the visitor to comport himself in a Roman fashion, to the benefit of both the Romans and the guest. Ultimately, standards of conduct are the means by which any society pursues harmony within its domain. It follows that their scope includes visitors, who could be seen as temporary members of the social order that created the rule. A model example of this type of standard is the rule of the road, which must be observed by all travellers within the territory where it applies, and nowhere else. On the other hand, it could be argued that certain standards of conduct have an extraterritorial dimension inasmuch as they are meant to induce exemplary behavior on the part of the indigenous

---

102 *Cf.* Couch (1970) p. 108, discussing the Arkansas guest statute in the context of *Johnson v. St. Paul Mercury Ins. Co.* 256 La. 289, 236 So.2d 216 (1970), in which all relevant contacts –except the *locus*– pointed to Louisiana: " ... as a result of the accident occurring within its borders, Arkansas had an interest in preventing an ungrateful attitude, though expressed by an out-of-stater."

members of a community wherever they go.[103] In *Labree v. Major*, the Supreme Court of Rhode Island suggested as much: "We find nothing wrong in a state holding its citizens to a higher standard of care than that of the state to which they may travel, no matter who may be injured by their misconduct."[104] While I do not hold with this *"noblesse oblige"* type of argument, we have seen that some courts did use it to establish an interest of the state whose law they wanted to apply anyway.[105] Since the hospitality and ingratitude rationales are both imbued with morality, it is very difficult to repudiate the contention that a guest statute has a territorial and a personal reach at the same time, requiring citizens of a guest statute state, whether at home or abroad, to be grateful guests and hospitable hosts. In fairness to the American judiciary, I must admit I have not found a decision in which a guest statute was applied on the grounds of its admonitory policy.[106] Still, in the absence of judicial authority, my theoretical construction may seem tenuous, but it is not, I submit, untenable in the light of other imaginative arguments the courts have advanced in the process of spatial delimitation.[107]

---

103 In this respect, the maxim "Once an Englishman, always an Englishman" comes to mind. In *Fisher v. Huck* 50 Or.App. 635, 624 P.2d 177 at 180 (1981), this proud phrase was used to illustrate the extraterritorial reach of a (British Columbia) rule *protecting* the (British Columbia) guest in Oregon, but it is only fair to assume that universal rights entail universal duties.
104 *Labree v. Major* 306 A.2d 808 at 818 (R.I. 1973).
105 *Supra* chapter 4, section 3, text accompanying notes 140–146.
106 Usually, it is the other way around. In *Labree*, the court held the *host* – a Rhode Island citizen– liable to his Massachusetts guests, on the ground that the forum's higher standard of conduct followed him abroad. Logically, however, the same argument could be reversed: the court could have held the *guests* to the Massachusetts guest statute, reasoning that it was meant to induce gratitude on the part of Massachusetts citizens, even outside their home state. *Labree* would then have presented a true conflict. In effect, the case was decided as a false conflict: *supra* chapter 4, section 3, text accompanying notes 138–140. By the same token, it could be argued that it was an unprovided-for case. All depends on the court's assessment of "relevant" policies and the spatial dimensions attributed to each of them.
107 As, for instance, the argument that a policy of "fostering tourism" requires application of *lex loci delicti*. In *Hernandez v. Burger* 102 Cal.App.3d 795, 162 Cal.Rptr. 564 (1980), *supra* chapter 4, section 3, text accompanying notes 109–111, the beneficiary of this construction was the tourist *driver*, a Californian on holiday in Mexico; in *Conklin v. Horner* 38 Wis.2d 468, 157 N.W.2d 579 (1968), *supra* chapter 5, text accompanying notes 51–52, the court found for the tourist *passenger*, a visitor from Illinois travelling in the "tourist state" Wisconsin.

Next on our list of guest statute policies is the desire to further judicial efficiency by preventing "vexatious litigation." Although it is doubtful whether any guest statute was ever written for the exclusive purpose of relieving the courts of an excessive load of automobile accident cases, it is not difficult to perceive that the only jurisdiction which could possibly have an interest in the application of the guest statute on these grounds is the forum. As a protective measure for the benefit of a state's judicial system, the guest statute must have been conceived as a rule with a strictly territorial reach: the rule should be applied in any host-guest litigation taking place in the state where it is in force, while it is wholly irrelevant to litigation conducted elsewhere. In this respect, a guest statute could be viewed as a rule of procedural law – comparable, for instance, to a rule that disallows appellate review of certain orders– which, under the traditional regime of *lex fori* governing matters of procedure, can only be invoked within the forum state. It is highly questionable whether the guest statutes have actually helped to reduce the volume of automobile accident litigation,[108] but even if they did not, that is no reason to discount either the policy as such, or the spatial description derived from it.

The most common explanation of guest statutes, as we have seen, is the collusion rationale. Being the result of effective lobbying, the rule purportedly shields the insurance industry from the fraudulent assertion of claims by colluding hosts and guests. Again, it is immaterial whether or not the policy is justified by actual practice or by the actual results of its implementation. What counts is the legislative intent, misguided as it may seem, and the spatial dimensions that can be deduced from it. Looking at the protective aspect of the collusion policy, we may safely assume that its advocates envisioned their "own" insurance companies as the principal beneficiaries. This poses no problem when the insurer is a small business operating in only one state, but the reach of the guest statute is much less obvious if the insurance company in question is called "Allstate", "Federal" or "Continental" and carries on business "Nationwide".[109] Equally dubious is the question whether the rule was designed to protect the insurance company whose only connection with the guest statute state is its place of incor-

---

108 See: *supra* section 1, note 47.
109 *Cf. Cipolla v. Shaposka* 439 Pa. 563, 267 A.2d 854 at 858, note 5 (1970), diss. opinion *per* Roberts, J.

poration. In view of the probability that most host-drivers will procure liability insurance from a local office in their home state, the insurer's actual place of business would seem to be a more realistic criterion for the spatial delimitation of the collusion rationale than the place of incorporation or the place where the company's main office is situated. Yet, the possibility that a state enacted a guest statute to shield every insurance company incorporated or maintaining headquarters in that state cannot totally be discounted.[110] Another facet of the collusion rationale is, again, admonitory: it expresses a certain moral indignation regarding fraud and seeks to counteract the temptation of dishonest gain. In this respect, the spatial limits of a guest statute are difficult to define. Again, the argument could be made that its reach is territorial as well as extraterritorial. It warns citizens and visitors alike that no collusion will be tolerated within the jurisdiction that adopted the rule.[111] At the same time, the statute "follows" the indigenous community members wherever they go, as a warning that collusion never pays, not even abroad. In sum: the collusion rationale could be relevant (1) to all claims arising from accidents within the guest statute state, regardless of the parties' domicile; (2) to all claims arising from guest-host relationships involving at least one member of the guest statute jurisdiction, regardless of the place where the accident occurred; and (3) to all claims that, but for the guest statute, would be covered by insurance companies incorporated, maintaining headquarters, or doing business in the guest statute state, regardless of other circumstances.

Less conducive to speculation on the guest statute's spatial reach is the "insurance premium rationale", holding that elimination of host-guest liability would keep the cost of liability insurance at a minimum. As an economic argument for guest statute enactment, this rationale pertains to the public interest of the community in a state-wide "rating

---

110 Widger (1974) p. 664/665, note 37, noted that the first state to enact (*and* repeal) a guest statute was the "insurance capital" Connecticut.
111 This territorial definition obviously presumes that collusion can be "located" in the guest statute state. In practice, it might be difficult to pinpoint the fraudulent collaboration between host and guest to a specific territory. The place where the accident occurred would seem to be irrelevant in this respect.

territory".[112] Yet, this community interest cannot be translated into a territorial criterion which would make the guest statute applicable to all claims arising from accidents within the rating territory. Rather, claims are allocated to the territory of the insured "even if the accident giving rise to the claim was outside the territory, the claimant resided outside the territory, or suit was brought in a remote jurisdiction."[113] It follows, then, that an effective use of the guest statute, at least in the light of the "insurance premium rationale", requires its application whenever the defendant-host belongs to the group whose collective risk determines the average insurance premium. This will generally be the case if the host is a resident or domiciliary of the guest statute state, at least if his car is registered and garaged in that state as well. In this respect, the spatial reach of a guest statute is personal rather than territorial, for it is linked to the indigenous car owner.[114]

The last of the guest statute policies we found is the one envisioned by the New York Court of Appeals in *Dym v. Gordon*: the protection of the injured third party. As the majority in *Dym* saw it, a guest statute would keep the host's assets intact for other victims than the injured guest, particularly "the persons in the car of the blameless driver."[115] Fictitious as this rationale may be, it has gained some academic and judicial support[116] and therefore deserves its own spatial demarcation.

112 Morris G. (1961) p. 560 ff., p. 567 ff. In reality, a state is divided into several "rating territories", demarcated by "functional lines, to separate urban from rural conditions, mountains from plains, etc. In practice, many territories are bounded by city limits and county lines." *Ibid.* p. 564.
113 Morris G. (1961) p. 565. However, in *Conklin v. Horner* 38 Wis.2d 468, 157 N.W.2d 579 at 584 (1969), the Wisconsin Supreme Court suggested that an insurance company doing business nationwide would not rely solely upon local laws for setting its rates. Justice Roberts, in his dissenting opinion in *Cipolla v. Shaposka* 439 Pa. 563, 267 A.2d 854 at 858 (1970), wondered if the benefits of the "insurance premium rationale" attributed to Delaware's guest statute "would inure to Delaware residents or merely aid insurance companies doing business in Delaware."
114 As a rule, the defendant-host is also the owner of the car, or at least the one who pays the insurance premium. If not, the spatial reach of a guest statute should be associated with the domicile or residence of the insured owner. To avoid ambiguity on this score, it might be better to define the spatial criterion derived from the "insurance premium rationale" as "the place where the insured automobile is registered and housed": *Cipolla v. Shaposka* 439 Pa. 563, 267 A.2d 854 at 856 (1970); Morris G. (1961) p. 574; Ehrenzweig (1960-1) p. 603. However, this concept has a less "personal" connotation than a reference to indigenous car owners.
115 *Dym v. Gordon* 16 N.Y.2d 120, 209 N.E.2d 792 at 794 (1965).
116 *Supra* section 1, text accompanying notes 63–69.

Trying to perceive what could have moved a fictitious legislature to give priority to the claim of an injured third party over the claim of the guest, one can only speculate that the beneficiaries of such priority would be the victims for whom, ultimately, the state takes responsibility: its own domiciliaries or residents. There might be a moral reason why the non-guests should prevail in a contest over the host's assets,[117] but I do not think that this is sufficient to extend the implicit protection of the "injured third party rationale" to foreign victims. In theory, then, a guest statute could claim application on these grounds whenever the injured third party is a member of the community where the rule is in force, regardless of the place of the accident and regardless of the ties the community may or may not have with either host or guest. In this respect, the spatial reach of the statute is difficult to classify. Since it is meant to protect the injured third party at home and abroad, it is not territorial. Yet, it is only personal in a roundabout way. Its criterion is not the personal link between either host or guest and the guest statute state, even though it is *their* controversy the statute addresses. The only relevant factor here is the link with the third party victim, whose potential recovery is at best indirectly determined by the statute. As far as the "injured third party rationale" is concerned, the scope of the rule is therefore based on personalism, but only by implication.[118]

I do not think that any sensible conclusion on the spatial reach of a guest statute can be inferred from its *negative* policies, for instance the one intending "not to penalize the host's ordinary negligence."[119] Since the principal beneficiary of this objective is obviously the host-driver, it could be thought that its purview is limited to hosts belonging

---

117 This was suggested by the Supreme Court of Wisconsin in *Heath v. Zellmer* 35 Wis.2d 578, 151 N.W.2d 664 at 669 (1967), *supra* section 1, text accompanying note 66.
118 To a certain extent, the same could be said in regard to the collusion rationale, as it narrows the spatial reach of a guest statute to situations in which the *insurer*, not the host or the guest, belongs to the guest statute community. Yet, since the insurer "substitutes" for the host, who will usually be a member of the same community, the personal aspect of the collusion rationale is stronger.
119 *Wilcox v. Wilcox* 26 Wis.2d 617, 133 N.W.2d 408 at 416 (1965); *supra* section 1, text accompanying notes 70–80. "Not to penalize" is not the equivalent, in my opinion, of "to reward". In other words, an affirmative construction of a negative policy interpretation tends to distort its message even further and, consequently, does not give us a better grasp of its spatial reach.

to the guest statute community. On the other hand, the positive counterpart of this policy is the one that seeks to deter negligent conduct, an admonitory policy which is generally defined as territorial. Logically, I would say, its negative equivalent deserves the same territorial reach and should extend to all traffic within the guest statute state regardless of the parties' domicile or residence: if the guest statute is viewed as a rule of conduct, its scope should not be limited to indigenous hosts. Conversely, if the absence of a guest statute is construed as indicative of a state's conduct-improving policy, it follows that all drivers, including foreign host-drivers, should be "penalized" for disobeying the local standard of conduct. But if that state allows the guest a cause of action mainly because recovery would safeguard local "vendors", medical creditors and the state itself against the guest's destitution (the converse of the "injured third party rationale"), its recovery policy is premised on personalism, positing a substantial connection between the vendors or creditors and the recovery state. As far as public resources are concerned, the only relevant link I can think of is the one between the guest and the state whose public charge he may become in case of non-recovery, his home state.

After these attempts at spatial definition, we are still left with the question if, in multistate situations, the various guest statute policies are compatible. Although it should be taken for granted that no legislature has actually contemplated pursuing all of the assorted policies at once and that some of the objectives described were judicial fabrications, it is far from clear which particular purpose or purposes should be attributed to any one guest statute. In *Pfau v. Trent Aluminum Company*, turning on the applicability of the Iowa guest statute, the Supreme Court of New Jersey conscientiously listed (and haphazardly delimited) the five major policies it had construed from Iowa case law: (1) cutting down litigation in Iowa courts; (2) preventing (Iowa?) hitch-hikers from suing the host; (3) protecting Iowa insurers from collusion; (4) protecting "good Samaritan" Iowa host-drivers; and (5) preventing (Iowa?) guests from displaying ingratitude.[120] Although the parties were students at a college in Iowa and the accident occurred there, the Iowa statute was said to be irrelevant, since it would only be meant to "apply to Iowa domiciliaries, defendants in-

---

120 *Pfau v. Trent Aluminum Company* 55 N.J. 511, 263 A.2d 129 at 131 (1970).

suring motor vehicles there, and persons suing in its courts."¹²¹ In *Dym v. Gordon*, the New York Court of Appeals attributed three distinct purposes to the Colorado guest statute: "the protection of Colorado drivers and their insurance carriers against fraudulent claims, the prevention of suits by 'ungrateful guests', and the priority of injured parties in other cars in the assets of the negligent defendant."¹²² There is no point in citing other cases in which a guest statute was found to serve more than one purpose, because they prove no more than that the courts are quite adept at selecting and emphasizing "relevant" purposes. Little can be learned from these decisions about the scope of the rule in general, and nothing at all about the interaction of its purposes in relation to its reach. As I see it, the spatial dimensions of a guest statute are as varied as its policies. In the abstract, they are incompatible *per se*, although it is possible that some of the criteria for the rule's spatial delimitation happen to coincide. The domicile of the host, for instance, is relevant to both the admonitory "hospitality rationale" and the policy of protecting "good Samaritans". In the individual case, incompatible spatial criteria may or may not influence the outcome. In *Pfau*, they all happened to militate against application of the Iowa guest statute, but in *Dym* they pointed in different directions. Although the criteria pertaining to the protection of the driver and his insurance carrier were not met (the driver being a New Yorker, insured in New York), the spatial connection derived from the "injured third party rationale" established a Colorado interest all the same (the actual third party obviously thought to be a Coloradan).¹²³

---

121 *Ibid.* p. 132. More or less the same catalogue of policies is recited in *Conlin v. Hutcheon* 560 F.Supp. 934 at 937 (D. Colo. 1983), holding that Nebraska's guest statute should not bar plaintiff's recovery, since none of Nebraska's policies "concerning hitchhikers, good samaritans, insurance rates, collision [!] suits by its citizens or the amount of litigation in its courts" would be furthered.
122 *Dym v. Gordon* 16 N.Y.2d 120, 209 N.E.2d 792 at 794 (1965). As rephrased by Judge Burke, it should be noted, the first policy not only protects the insurer but the host as well. With whom could the guest possibly collude to defraud the *host*? The injured third party perhaps?
123 In fact, he was from Kansas; see *infra* section 3, note 134 and accompanying text. It is unclear which spatial delimitation the court attributed to the "ingratitude rationale." If its scope would extend to all guests being given a free ride *in Colorado*, the guest statute could have claimed application on the strength of this policy as well. If it were limited to "Colorado guests" – as its first rationale was limited to "Colorado drivers and their insurance carriers" – it could be asked whether Colorado *domiciliaries* or Colorado *residents* were meant. In *Dym*, "[b]oth plaintiff and

Should it be concluded, then, that a guest statute can claim application if none but one of its various policies would be furthered in the individual case? Or should the court try to divine the relative import, present value, and plausibility of each policy before selecting a preponderant one?[124] I do not think that any convincing answer can be given to these questions. Whatever solution one prefers, the whole process of spatial delimitation is arbitrary if, at the court's discretion, more than one policy can be brought into play.

If these reflections on the spatial reach of a guest statute have provoked impatience or exasperation, I hope it is not the caliber of my arguments that caused the reader's annoyance, but the whimsical inferences they allow. Studying the vagaries of policy assessment and spatial delimitation, one becomes increasingly suspicious of the premises of interest analysis. As far as the guest statute is concerned, none of the propositions regarding its policies and spatial reach, I submit, can be proved (or *disproved*) with absolute certainty. An imaginative mind will have little difficulty in selecting and emphasizing the one guest statute rationale that justifies either application or displacement of the rule. As we have seen, an interest of the guest statute state could be asserted on the grounds of territorial and/or personal criteria, requiring that one of the following factors points to the jurisdiction where the rule is in force: (1) the place where the accident occurred; (2) the citizenship, domicile or residence of the host; (3) the citizenship, domicile or residence of the guest; (4) the forum; (5) the place of incorporation, main office, or place of business of the host's insurer; (6) the place where the host was insured and paid the premiums, usually coinciding with his domicile and the place where his car is registered and garaged; and (7) the citizenship, domicile or residence of (injured) third parties. Given the fact that the guest statute state is somehow associated with the actual dispute – otherwise there would have been no need to examine its law – it is hard to imagine a case in which none of these factors is present. In other words, if the controversy must be decided in favor of the host, it should not be too difficult to justify an interest of the guest statute state in the application of its

---

defendant, domiciled in New York, were *temporarily residing* in Colorado." *Dym v. Gordon* 209 N.E.2d 792 at 793; emphasis added.

124 This was implied in *Dym*: Colorado's interest in securing a fund for injured third parties was viewed as an interest "over and above the usual interest which Colorado may bring to bear on all conduct occurring within its boundaries." *Dym v. Gordon* 209 N.E.2d 792 at 794.

law. On the other hand, it is just as easy to discount any criterion that could establish such an interest, particularly if the host is domiciled in a recovery state. All that is needed in that case is some emphasis on the collusion rationale and the inference that the guest statute protection neither extends to insurers doing business in defendant's home state nor affects the insurance premiums fixed for defendant's "rating territory". If an interest of the guest statute state cannot be denied, the result is bound to be a true conflict, since the recovery rule on which the plaintiff relies can surely boast as many fancy reasons for application as the guest statute. The resolution of a true conflict opens up new avenues to the material result desired; this next stage in the process of interest analysis is even more capricious and arbitrary than the one we are examining now. At this point, I submit that policy assessment and spatial delimitation are open to manipulation, which implies that interests can be asserted at will and that the outcome of the case is really determined by other factors than the argumentation required by interest analysis. Put another way, it is my contention that the precepts of interest analysis, no less than those of traditional conflicts law, can be molded to fit a preconceived material result. Instead of chaining a number of plausible arguments leading up to an inescapable conclusion, interest analysis enables the courts to wrap a predetermined outcome in unprovable teleological statements on isolated policies and "home-made" interests. If this sounds harsh, I propose to review a few of the guest statute cases decided with the help of interest analysis, so as to test the credibility of my contention.

3 A systematic survey of policy-oriented guest statute decisions

In this section, I intend to survey a series of current law-fact patterns in guest statute litigation, using the policy-oriented case law discussed in the two previous sections of this chapter. Even if we limit the number of choice of law variables to four (the respective domiciliary laws of plaintiff and defendant, *lex loci delicti* and forum law), and even if we assume that these laws either allow or do not allow the guest to recover, without complications as to the required degree of negligence, there is still a large number of possible permutations between the wholly domestic situation, in which all variables coincide, and the ultimate choice of law situation, in which each variable is different.[125] However, an exhaustive examination of all these hypothetical law-fact patterns is neither feasible nor helpful. I suggest that a survey of the five most common patterns will suffice to give us a valid impression of the choice of law reasoning in multistate guest statute adjudication. A regrouping of the cases according to their law-fact patterns should enable us to concentrate on the policy-oriented argumentation without being distracted by factual peculiarities. Statistically, I am sure, this survey of guest statute case law is definitely inconclusive. But then, it was not my intention to measure the law in action against the laws of probability. Actually, most cases were decided in favor of the guest, which might have something to do with the fact that most actions were brought in plaintiff-favoring jurisdictions. In the few cases in which the host prevailed, the action was generally, but not always, brought in the state having the guest statute. Generalities aside, it appears impossible to predict the outcome of any single guest statute case, whatever the composition of its law-fact pattern.

The fact pattern most frequently encountered in guest statute litigation involves a host-driver and a guest-passenger who are domiciled in the same state and had an automobile accident in another state. The reason why this type of situation is so common is obvious: in most cases, the parties are friends or relatives living in the same state, often in the same town, who were on their way to a planned destination, sometimes within their own home state,[126] when they got involved in an out-of-state accident. More often than not, the place where the accident occurred can be described as "fortuitous", in the sense that neither of the parties had any ties with that state, their trip had not begun there, and it was not meant to end there either. Another feature of the typical guest statute case is the circumstance that the action is brought in the jurisdiction whose domestic rule allows the guest to recover. As a rule, this is either the parties' home state, or the state where the accident occurred, but, evidently, the adjudicatory jurisdic-

---

125 It should be noted that, in the abstract, even a domestic case gives rise to two law-fact patterns: one in which the domestic law allows recovery, and one in which it does not.
126 In *Fuerste v. Bemis* 156 N.W.2d 831 (Iowa 1968), for instance, the parties were both Iowa residents, travelling from one point in Iowa to another by way of Wisconsin, where they collided with another car.

tion of the recovery state could be based on other grounds as well. The high percentage of guest statute cases decided by courts in recovery states suggests that forum shopping is a rewarding strategy.

Pattern 1: both parties domiciled in recovery state, also the forum

If the parties are both living in the recovery state and the action is brought there as well,[127] the case is apt to be classified as a false conflict. Plaintiff's home state may be thought to have an interest in the compensation of one of its domiciliaries, whereas the *locus* state is unlikely to have an interest in the protection of the non-resident host or his insurer. This line of reasoning was indeed followed in most cases of this category. Prime examples are, of course, *Babcock v. Jackson*, *Wilcox v. Wilcox*, *Wessling v. Paris*, *Mellk v. Sarahson* and other landmark cases in which the regime of *lex loci delicti* was abandoned in favor of a policy-oriented approach.[128] In few of these decisions an explicit reference to guest statute policies can be found, whereas even less attention is paid to their spatial delimitation. A typical case is *Kennedy v. Dixon*, in which the Missouri Supreme Court merely pointed out that Indiana could only have a "real interest" in the negligence issue, not in the determination of the host-guest relationship between Missouri parties.[129] A relatively clear statement as to the policy and spatial reach of the Ontario guest statute was made in *Babcock*

---

127. For the assessment of the possibly conflicting policies, it should not make any difference where the action is brought: at this stage, interest analysis is supposed to be a neutral approach. However, the present survey does not seem to bear out this proposition.
128. *Babcock v. Jackson* 12 N.Y.2d 473, 240 N.Y.S.2d 743, 191 N.E.2d 279 (1963); *Wilcox v. Wilcox* 26 Wis.2d 617, 133 N.W.2d 408 (1965); *Wessling v. Paris* 417 S.W.2d 259 (Ky. 1967); *Mellk v. Sarahson* 49 N.J. 226, 229 A.2d 625 (1967).
129. *Kennedy v. Dixon* 439 S.W.2d 173 (Mo. 1969). Other courts just decided that the guest statute state had "no interest" or that the case presented a "false conflict": *Clark v. Clark* 107 N.H. 351, 222 A.2d 205 at 209 (1966): Vermont has no relevant interest; *Mellk v. Sarahson* 49 N.J. 226, 229 A.2d 625 at 627 (1967): Ohio has not any real interest; *Woodward v. Stewart* 104 R.I. 290, 243 A.2d 917 at 922 (1968): Massachusetts has no interest; *Kuchinic v. McCrory* 422 Pa. 620, 222 A.2d 897 (1966): false conflict between Pennsylvania's recovery rule and Georgia's guest statute. In *DeMeyer v. Maxwell* 103 Idaho 327, 647 P.2d 783 at 786 (Idaho App. 1982), the court surmised that Oregon had not a strong policy in favor of guest statutes anymore, while Idaho followed the "basic policy of negligence law to allow a person to recover."

v. Jackson. Considering that the statute was meant to prevent fraudulent claims against insurance companies, Judge Fuld deduced that the Ontario legislature had envisaged claims asserted against *Ontario* defendants and their (Ontario?) insurance carriers.[130] In other cases, more emphasis is placed on the protection of the kindly host, provided he is a domiciliary of the guest statute state.[131] A most extensive description of the guest statute rationale was given in *Wilcox v. Wilcox.* Apart from a *negative* policy ascribed to the Nebraska guest law, the court mentioned several other guest statute purposes in general: "The general purpose of a guest statute of the Nebraska type is said to be for the purpose of preventing the ingratitude of a gratuitous guest who sues his kindly host or for the purpose of limiting the opportunity for collusive host-guest-suits, and, in addition with considerable authority, the purpose is said to be the protection of the host and his insurer from judgments."[132] The Wisconsin Supreme Court paid little attention to the spatial implications of these policies. It merely asserted that the Nebraska statute could only be relevant to a Nebraska host and his insurance company, concluding that the "fortuitous" place of wrong "should not now inure as a windfall to any of the defendants."

In all decisions mentioned thus far, the scope of the foreign guest statute was obviously perceived as personal, therefore neither ap-

---

130 *Babcock v. Jackson* 12 N.Y.2d 473, 240 N.Y.S.2d 743, 191 N.E.2d 279 at 284 (1963). A similar observation can be found in *Kopp v. Rechtzigel* 273 Minn. 441, 141 N.W.2d 526 at 527 (Minn. 1966), in addition to the "insurance premium rationale". See also: *Mentry v. Smith* 18 Wash.App. 668, 571 P.2d 589 at 591 (1978): the purpose of preventing fraudulent claims by increasing the guest's burden of proof cannot be vindicated if the insurer is an insurance carrier in another jurisdiction.
131 See: *Wessling v. Paris* 417 S.W.2d 259 at 260 (1967): "While it might be said that Indiana has a policy of protecting drivers on their highways from claims by passengers, surely this must extend no further than an interest in protecting *Indiana* residents or those who sue in Indiana courts." Emphasis added. See: *supra* chapter 7, note 11. See also: *Mullane v. Stavola* 101 N.J. Super. 184, 243 A.2d 842 (1968): "Florida, however, has little or no interest in denying a remedy for injuries suffered in Florida involving New Jersey domiciliaries. Florida's concern operates to avoid imposition of excessive financial burdens on [Florida?] host-drivers ..." *Gordon v. Kramer* 124 Ariz. 442, 604 P.2d 1153 at 1158 (Ariz. App. 1979): "Utah has no interest in protecting Arizona residents from suits brought in Arizona courts."
132 *Wilcox v. Wilcox* 26 Wis.2d 617, 133 N.W.2d 408 at 416 (1965), with reference to Weintraub (1963) p. 220. The "negative" policy was discussed, *supra,* section 1, text accompanying note 70; section 2, text accompanying note 119.

plicable to a non-resident guest nor to a non-resident host or his insurer. For that reason, the plaintiffs prevailed in all cases. If both parties are domiciled in a recovery state, the foreign guest statute could only claim application, one would think, on the grounds of its admonitory policy, requiring every visitor to heed the foreign community's standards in respect of hospitality and gratitude, or possibly because a domiciliary of the guest statute state was involved in the accident as a third party. Since the recovery state must have at least an interest in the compensation of its domiciliaries, the result of this interpretation is bound to be a true conflict. If the court would follow a *lex fori* solution to this type of conflict, the plaintiff would still prevail. But, as we have seen, few courts have followed Currie's precepts in this respect. In *Dow v. Larrabee*, decided by the New Hampshire Supreme Court, it was held that the Massachusetts guest statute applied to an action between New Hampshire residents, apparently because the guest statute was viewed as a rule pertaining to *conduct*: "It cannot be denied that Massachusetts has an interest in regulating the standards of behavior of persons traveling upon its highways, and the liability which shall result for injuries suffered there in consequence of such behavior. This interest appears to us more significantly related to this accident than any interest which this state may have had because the parties who were traveling on Massachusetts highways and entered into a host-guest relationship there were residents of this state."[133] In other words, if New Hampshire had an interest at all, it was sacrificed to Massachusetts' presumed interest in what would seem to be the regulation of conduct within its borders. Another example, of course, is *Dym v. Gordon*, in which Colorado's interest in the application of its guest law was based mainly on the statute's hypothetical "injured third party rationale". If this were a correct assessment of Colorado policy, the guest statute's spatial reach would be limited to situations in which a Coloradan third party is actually involved in the accident. In

---

133 *Dow v. Larrabee* 107 N.H. 70, 217 A.2d 506 at 508 (1966). The case was decided shortly before *Clark v. Clark* 107 N.H. 351, 222 A.2d 205 (1966), presenting a similar law-fact pattern. This time, New Hampshire was said to "have an interest in applying [the New Hampshire negligence rule] to New Hampshire residents." Furthermore, the forum rule was deemed "preferable" to Vermont's guest statute. *Ibid.* p. 209/210. Curiously, the court suggested that it had followed the traditional conflicts rule in *Dow v. Larrabee*: " ... we have used the place of wrong rule for want of a better one even though our dissatisfaction with its application was evident, Dow v. Larrabee, 107 N.H. 70, 217 A.2d 506." *Ibid.* p. 207.

fact, the other car in *Dym* was driven by a resident from Kansas and was registered there as well, apparently.[134] Plaintiff's contention that New York had a "dominant governmental interest" in the compensation of its domiciliary was rejected as insufficient grounds for the application of New York law, in light of the "most significant contacts" and the "dominant interest" of Colorado. To the extent that *Dym* was based on interest analysis, New York's actual interest was sacrificed to a hypothetical interest of Colorado. In *Tooker v. Lopez*, the New York Court of Appeals retracted this argument and reverted to the *Babcock* line of reasoning.[135]

Pattern 2: both parties domiciled in guest statute state, also the forum

Very few cases present this law-fact pattern, obviously because the plaintiff-guest is apt to bring his action in the recovery state, even if that state has no other connection to the case than the fact that the accident occurred there.[136] In the abstract, cases fitting this pattern would be false conflicts, unless the scope of the forum's guest law is viewed as territorial, or conversely, the compensatory rule of the *locus* state would be given an extraterritorial reach. In the three cases I found, little was said about the purposes of either law, even less about their scope, but it was clear that the forum state asserted an interest in the application of its guest statute. *Fuerste v. Bemis* was decided as a false conflict: since "[t]he standard of conduct of the parties while in

---

134 *Dym v. Gordon* 16 N.Y.2d 120, 209 N.E.2d 792 at 799 (1965), diss. opinion *per* Judge Fuld, who, for that reason, asserted that "[t]he majority's emphasis on the involvement of another vehicle in the accident ... [was] misplaced."

135 Thus, the purpose of the Colorado guest statute was deemed to be "prevention of fraudulent claims against *local* insurers or the protection of *local* automobile owners." *Tooker v. Lopez* 24 N.Y.2d 569, 301 N.Y.S.2d 519, 249 N.E.2d 394 at 397 (1969); emphasis added. As to the policy of the Michigan guest statute actually at issue in *Tooker*, see *ibid.* p. 399, note 1: "The Michigan courts have suggested that the purpose of their guest statute is to protect the owner of the vehicle."

136 See *infra*: pattern 5. Of course, there would be no call for the plaintiff to shop around for another forum if his home state were still devoted to the traditional conflicts rule and the accident had occurred in a recovery state. See: *Friday v. Smoot* 211 A.2d 594 (Del. 1965): action between Delaware parties arising from an accident in New Jersey; New Jersey's recovery rule applied as *lex loci delicti*. Since both Maryland and Michigan adhered to *lex loci delicti*, forum shopping would not have helped the plaintiff in *White v. King* 244 Md. 348, 233 A.2d 763 (1966): Michigan's guest statute applied as *lex loci delicti* to an action between Maryland residents.

Wisconsin [was] not an issue here," the only rule claiming application was Iowa's guest statute.[137] The Appellate Court of Indiana, in *Witherspoon v. Salm*, said little more about the purpose of the Indiana guest law than that it favored the host. Kentucky's interest, on the other hand, was said to be "in the application of its law for the protection of *Kentucky* domiciliaries, *as well as non-residents*, from the misconduct of drivers operating on *Kentucky* highways." Nevertheless, the Indiana plaintiff who had been injured on a Kentucky highway was not entitled to protection: " ... Kentucky's interest in the protection of an Indiana guest in a suit to recover from an Indiana host is minimal."[138] The purpose of Oregon's guest statute was defined in terms of hospitality and gratitude in *Tower v. Schwabe*, the Oregon residence of the parties obviously being sufficient to establish an Oregon interest by implication.[139] Since the interest of the *locus* state in the application of its recovery rule was consistently denied, each case in this category was treated as a false conflict, the forum state being the only interested jurisdiction. Consequently, the host-defendant prevailed each time.

Pattern 3: plaintiff domiciled in recovery state, also the forum

This pattern covers situations in which either two or three states are involved, depending on defendant's domicile in either the *locus* state or in a third state. A "two-state situation" is likely to give rise to a true conflict, since plaintiff's home state will probably have an interest in his compensation, whereas the guest statute of defendant's home state will claim application under practically any definition of its spatial reach. If the accident occurred in a third state which is also a recovery state, there might still be a true conflict between the laws of the domiciliary states, the *locus* state being disinterested unless its recovery rule is thought to express a policy of deterrence. On the other hand, if the third state has a guest statute and the host is a domiciliary of a recovery state, the conflict is likely to be false. A third possibility

---

137 *Fuerste v. Bemis* 156 N.W.2d 831 (Iowa 1968). The Iowa Supreme Court refused to apply Wisconsin's recovery rule as the better law, the quality of the respective laws said to be relevant to the solution of true conflicts only.
138 *Witherspoon v. Salm* 142 Ind.App. 655, 237 N.E.2d 116 at 124/125 (1968) *rev'd on other grounds*, 251 Ind. 575, 243 N.E.2d 876 (1969). The Supreme Court characterized plaintiff's claim to compensation as a contractual right, governed by the provisions of Indiana's Workmen's Compensation Act.
139 *Tower v. Schwabe* 284 Or. 105, 585 P.2d 662 (1978).

was presented by *Pryor v. Swarner*, a case in which both defendant's home state (Florida) and the *locus* state (Ohio) had guest statutes, while the law of the forum (New York) permitted recovery. Having decided that the "Fuld principles" did not cover the instant case, the Second Circuit turned to "basic doctrines" and conscientiously described all policies involved. New York was said to have a policy "allowing its *resident* plaintiff-guests to recover against their hosts on the basis of mere negligence at least where the defendant-host carries mandatory motor-vehicle insurance whose premiums are calculated with this potential risk taken into account."[140] A major purpose of Florida's guest statute would be "the protection of the insurers against collusive suits" implying that the Florida defendant paid insurance premiums which "were calculated with Florida's guest statute in mind." Ohio's policy, finally, was deemed to rest "not merely on protecting its insurers but on a theory that it is 'ungrateful' for a guest to seek recovery for mere negligence."[141] Whether this policy gave Ohio an actual interest in this case, remained an open question. Since the Ohio and Florida guest statutes "coincided", the only question the court intended to answer was whether New York would have an interest in having its law applied. It concluded that New York courts would not apply New York law "to allow recovery by the plaintiff against the common policy of *lex loci* and the state where the defendants reside and obtained insurance." The decision suggests some form of interest-weighing, although the ambiguous description of New York's recovery policy does not rule out the possibility that the court solved the case as a false conflict.

The other cases in this category are all "two-state conflicts", the defendant being domiciled in the *locus* state. While the decision in *Foster v.*

140 *Pryor v. Swarner* 445 F.2d 1272 at 1276/1277 (2d Cir. [N.Y.] 1971); emphasis added. This statement suggests that the reach of New York's recovery rule is determined by the "insurance premium rationale", a dubious assertion in the light of New York decisions such as *Kell v. Henderson* 26 A.D.2d 595, 270 N.Y.S.2d 552 (1966) or *Fosillo v. Matthews* 30 A.D.2d 1049, 295 N.Y.S.2d 327, 248 N.E.2d 455 (1968), in which recovery was granted in actions involving domiciliaries of a guest statute state.
141 *Ibid.* p. 1277. The "injured third party rationale" was rejected, not only because the occupants of the other car, residents of Tennessee, were probably not injured but mostly because the presence of third-party "non-guests" had been deemed irrelevant in *Tooker v. Lopez* 24 N.Y.2d 569, 301 N.Y.S.2d 519, 249 N.E.2d 394 (1969).

Leggett turned on Kentucky's "sufficient enough contacts approach", which led to application of forum law without an examination of the reach of Ohio's guest statute, the dissent did mention it as a rule intended to protect the Ohio defendant: "Surely it was meant to protect him while he drove on Ohio highways."[142] A clear example of a true conflict solution is the decision in *Cipolla v. Shaposka*, in which the court balanced Pennsylvania's interest in the recovery of its residents against Delaware's interest in low insurance rates in respect of Delaware-based automobiles.[143] *Byrn v. American Universal Ins. Co.* is another example of an "altruistic" choice of law. Decided by the Missouri Court of Appeals, the case turned on the applicability of Iowa's guest statute. Since the Iowa rule was meant "to protect the good Samaritan from liability to free-riding passengers," the court inferred that Iowa had an interest in the protection of the Iowa host, but since Missouri had an interest in protecting the Missouri plaintiff-guest, the case presented a true conflict, which was solved in favor of Iowa law.[144] It is curious, in my opinion, that forum law was displaced in each case in which the court made a serious attempt at interest analysis, particularly when it recognized the law-fact pattern as a true conflict, as it did in *Cipolla* and *Byrn*, and possibly in *Pryor* as well.

Pattern 4: defendant domiciled in recovery state, also the forum

Here, too, a distinction could be made between "two-state" and "three-state situations", depending on the coincidence of plaintiff's domicile and the place of wrong. If there is such a coincidence, the case is apt to qualify as an unprovided-for situation: the foreign guest statute was probably no more meant to protect non-resident hosts than the forum's recovery rule was meant to protect non-resident

---

142 *Foster v. Leggett* 484 S.W.2d 827 at 831 (1972), diss. opinion *per* Reed, J. See also: *Schneider v. Nichols* 280 Minn. 139, 158 N.W.2d 254 (Minn. 1968), in which case Minnesota law was applied in favor of a Minnesota guest who had been injured in defendant's home state North Dakota. The opinion is not particularly instructive, as it has little to say on the policies and interests involved.
143 *Cipolla v. Shaposka* 439 Pa. 563, 267 A.2d 854 (1970), discussed *supra* chapter 4, section 4(c), text accompanying notes 306–321. Different views on the policies underlying Delaware's guest statute were expressed in Justice Roberts' dissenting opinion: *ibid.* at 857; see also: *supra* section 2, text accompanying notes 109–114.
144 *Byrn v. American Universal Ins. Co.* 548 S.W.2d 186 (Mo. App. 1977), with reference to both § 145(2) Restatement Second and *Cipolla v. Shaposka*. The better law test was rejected as "an extreme theory."

guests. This is different, of course, if the recovery rule is deemed to influence the standard of care of forum residents wherever they go, or if a purely territorial reach is attributed to the guest statute. In "three-state situations" both plaintiff's home state and the *locus* state may have a guest statute, a pattern still likely to present an unprovided-for case.[145] If the plaintiff is domiciled in a recovery state, the conflict is probably false, but if the accident occurred in a recovery state and plaintiff's home state is the only state having the guest statute, we are likely to find an unprovided-for case again. A "two-state situation" was present in *Labree v. Major*, in which the Supreme Court of Rhode Island discounted Massachusetts' interest in the protection of a Rhode Island host against an ungrateful Massachusetts guest. Although one would surmise that, conversely, Rhode Island would have no interest in the protection of the Massachusetts plaintiff, the court turned the case into a false conflict by asserting that Rhode Island had "an interest in enforcing the standard of care of an automobile owner no matter where his guest resides."[146] Since the accident occurred in Massachusetts, this admonitory policy extended to Rhode Island citizens driving beyond the Rhode Island state line, obviously. The opposite result was reached in *Neumeier v. Kuehner*, but since this case was ultimately decided by the third of Judge Fuld's neo-conflicts-rules it hardly counts as a valid example of interest-inspired guest statute adjudication.[147] The Superior Court of Pennsylvania seemed to acknowledge it was trying to solve an unprovided-for case in *Miller v. Gay*, involving a Pennsylvania host and a Delaware guest injured in her home state: where Pennsylvania protected the host and Delaware the

---

145 Yet, in *Bolgrean v. Stich* 293 Minn. 8, 196 N.W.2d 442 (1972), the Minnesota Supreme Court had little trouble to assert Minnesota's "greater interest" in the application of its recovery rule. The plaintiff was domiciled in North Dakota, the accident occurred in South Dakota, and both states had guest statutes. The North Dakota guest statute had a scope rule, limiting its spatial reach to occurrences "on the highways of North Dakota." The court further considered the insurer of a Minnesota vehicle would charge rates applicable to Minnesota risks.
146 *Labree v. Major* 306 A.2d 808 (R.I. 1973). A similar argument is found in *Danner v. Staggs* 680 F.2d 427 at 431 (5th Cir. [Tex.] 1982): the accident occurred in defendant's home state, Texas, and involved a resident of Arkansas, a guest statute state. Plaintiff prevailed, since Arkansas had no interest in the protection of a Texas host, while Texas wanted "the driver to be accountable to his or her passengers for negligence."
147 *Neumeier v. Kuehner* 31 N.Y.2d 121, 335 N.Y.S.2d 64, 286 N.E.2d 454 (1972), discussed *supra* chapter 6, text accompanying notes 17–19 and *passim*.

guest, " ... neither state seems to have a significant relationship as to the issue of guest v. host protection." Despite the dissent's assertion that Pennsylvania did have a "substantial interest in having its law apply to this case," the court fell back on considerations of certainty and predictability and applied Delaware law as *lex loci delicti*.[148]

The situation in which host and guest are domiciled in different recovery states, whereas the accident occurred in the guest statute state, is structurally identical to the first law-fact pattern I described, in which both parties live in the same plaintiff-favoring forum state. Here, too, it is difficult to perceive why either forum law or the law of plaintiff's home state should yield to the foreign guest statute. In *Chila v. Owens*, plaintiff was a New Jersey domiciliary, defendant a New Yorker, both of them students in Ohio at the time of the accident. The district court refused to apply Ohio's guest statute, equating New York's interest with that of New Jersey, and comparing it to that of Ohio. In fact, the case was treated as a false conflict, in which forum law substituted for the identical law of the only interested state, New Jersey.[149] In the same vein, a federal court in Colorado, in *Conlin v. Hutcheon*, decided that Nebraska had no interest in the application of its guest statute to an action between an Illinois guest and a Colorado host, driving a car owned by an Iowa resident. Since the litigation would "not affect Nebraska policies concerning hitchhikers, good samaritans, insurance rates, collusion suits by its citizens or the amount of litigation in its courts," application of Nebraska law was not warranted, whereas Colorado's interest "in applying its law and policies to

---

148 *Miller v. Gay* 470 A.2d 1353 (Pa. Super. 1983). The dissenting opinion by Judge Spaeth does not reveal on what grounds Pennsylvania's compensatory policy would extend to an out-of-state victim injured in his own home state.
149 *Chila v. Owens* 348 F.Supp. 1207 (S.D. N.Y. 1972). See: *supra* chapter 6, text accompanying note 43. See also: *Gross v. McDonald* 354 F.Supp. 378 at 381 (E.D. Pa.): the guest was a student in Kentucky who was injured in Indiana while riding as a passenger in the car of an Irish citizen at that time employed in Kentucky, but later taking up residence in New Jersey. Defendant was served in Pennsylvania where he was temporarily residing, before moving on to Singapore. Concentrating on the interests of Indiana and Kentucky, the district court just noted that "Indiana has no interest in this suit at all and Kentucky has a strong nexus; hence displacement of Indiana's guest rule will advance relative substantive law purposes without impairment of the working of the multi-state system." In respect of the guest statute issue, Pennsylvania was apparently considered to be a disinterested forum.

those who seek relief in its courts is paramount."[150] Similarly, in *Pfau v. Trent Aluminum Company*, the Supreme Court of New Jersey applied its own law to a host-guest controversy arising from an accident in Iowa and involving a Connecticut plaintiff and a New Jersey defendant. Since Iowa's connection to the case did "not relate to any interest or policy behind Iowa's guest statute," the court concluded that the case presented a false conflict and decided to "afford the Connecticut plaintiff the same protection a New Jersey plaintiff would be given."[151] It appears, then, that all cases in this fourth category of law-fact patterns, with the exception of *Neumeier v. Kuehner*, were decided in favor of the guest.[152]

Pattern 5: accident occurred in recovery state, also the forum

Generally, the guest can bring an action in the state where the accident occurred on the basis of a so-called "long-arm statute". As far as torts are concerned, these enactments confer jurisdiction over defendants who allegedly committed a tortious act within the forum state.[153] In

---

150 *Conlin v. Hutcheon* 560 F.Supp. 934 at 937 (D. Colo. 1983). The court did mention the interests of Iowa ("minimal") and, more interesting, Illinois, the plaintiff's home state: "Illinois has some interest in the conduct of the plaintiff and the possible use of its facilities and resources in the care of the plaintiff." While I think I understand the latter consideration, I am mystified by Illinois' presumed interest in the "conduct" of the plaintiff.
151 *Pfau v. Trent Aluminum Company* 55 N.J. 511, 263 A.2d 129 at 137 (1970). As to the meaning of the term "false conflict" in this context, see *supra* chapter 4, section 1, text accompanying notes 36–38.
152 Another, even less elucidating exception than *Neumeier* is *Towley v. King Arthur Rings Inc.* 40 N.Y.2d 129, 386 N.Y.S.2d 80, 351 N.E.2d 728 (1976), discussed *supra* chapter 6, text accompanying note 44. In this case, the New York Court of Appeals decided to apply Colorado's guest statute in an action between an Iowa plaintiff and a New York defendant who had met while on vacation in Colorado. However, the decision was motivated by a blunt reference to the third "Fuld principle", calling for application of *lex loci* when host and guest are domiciled in different states. In this respect, the case hardly qualifies as a policy-oriented decision. Furthermore, the court was oblivious to the fact that Colorado had repealed its guest statute, while Iowa still had one; *supra* chapter 6, note 45.
153 *Cf.* Weintraub (1980) p. 153 ff.; Leflar (1977-1) p. 61 ff., p. 71 ff. Included are acts and omissions within the forum state, as well as extraneous acts and omissions which caused harmful consequences in the forum state. In Europe, the EEC Convention on Jurisdiction and Recognition of Foreign Judgments generally achieves the same result by conferring tort jurisdiction on the *forum loci delicti*: article 5(3). The European Court of Justice gave an extensive interpretation to this provision by →

quite a few cases, the plaintiff-guest must have seized upon this jurisdictional ground to sue the defendant-host in a recovery state, even though both parties lived in the same guest statute state. If the forum's recovery rule would express a concern for the compensation of injured residents only, all of these cases would present false conflicts, the domiciliary state of the parties being the only state likely to have an interest in the application of its (guest) law. Obviously, this was not the view taken by the courts, since the plaintiff prevailed in all cases I examined but one. First, there is the curious chain of New York decisions, beginning with *Kell v. Henderson*, in which New York law was applied to permit an Ontario guest to recover against an Ontario host. In *Kell*, the Ontario guest statute was not even discussed. The Appellate Division just held that it was the "established law of New York that a guest has a cause of action for personal injuries against a host in an accident occurring within this state whether those involved are residents or domiciliaries of this state or not."[154] Presenting exactly the same law-fact pattern, *Arbuthnot v. Allbright* was resolved in favor of the defendant-host, mostly on the strength of the first of the principles Judge Fuld had recently laid down in his concurring opinion in *Tooker v. Lopez*.[155] The third "Fuld principle" was applied in *Saleem v. Tamm*, involving an English guest, an Ontario host and a New York third party defendant. The court's argument in support of its decision to apply New York law has a policy-oriented ring, but has little to do with the actual policies and interests at issue: since the liability of the third-party defendants would have to be determined by New York law, application of any other law to the liability of the host "cannot be considered advancing the relevant substantive law purposes without impairing the smooth working of the multi-state system or producing great uncertainty for litigants."[156] Interest analysis was back again in

> deciding that the plaintiff could opt to bring his action either in the state where the act had been committed or in the state where the injury occurred: European Court of Justice 30 November 1976, 21/76, *NJ* 1977, 494, note J.C. Schultsz (*French Potassium Mines*).

154 *Kell v. Henderson* 26 A.D.2d 595, 270 N.Y.S.2d 552 at 553 (1966). In *Fosillo v. Matthews* 30 A.D.2d 1049, 295 N.Y.S.2d 327, 248 N.E.2d 455 (1968), a mere reference to *Kell* sufficed to motivate the court's decision to apply New York law to an action between Massachusetts parties who had been involved in a New York accident.

155 *Arbuthnot v. Allbright* 35 A.D.2d 315, 316 N.Y.S.2d 391 (1970). *Tooker v. Lopez* 24 N.Y.2d 569, 301 N.Y.S.2d 519, 249 N.E.2d 394 at 403 (1969). See *supra* chapter 6, text accompanying notes 38–41.

156 *Saleem v. Tamm* 67 Misc.2d 335, 323 N.Y.S.2d 764 at 766 (N.Y. Sup. Ct. 1971).

Bray v. Cox, presenting an identical law-fact pattern to the one in *Kell* and *Arbuthnot*. Having listed three "identifiable interests" of New York, *viz.* "highway safety, economic protection of New York vendors, and State public fiscal interests," and at least two "pertinent interests" of Ontario, *viz.* "protection of Ontario insurers and maintenance of relatively low Ontario insurance rates" as well as "prevention of collusive suits," the Appellate Division resorted to interest-weighing to resolve the resulting true conflict. It was concluded that New York had a "superior interest" in having its law applied.[157]

Similar true conflict constructions were used in other recovery states to hold the out-of-state host liable to the out-of-state guest. In some of these cases, the interest of the forum state in the compensation of nonresidents was founded on the admonitory policy of the recovery rule, which would be frustrated by application of a foreign guest statute. In *Conklin v. Horner*, for instance, the Supreme Court of Wisconsin held that Wisconsin's compensatory policy extended to all injured passengers, "whether they be residents of this state or whether they come from another jurisdiction," as application of a defendant-favoring rule would "substantially dilute the deterrent (as well as compensatory) effect of our negligence law."[158] In other decisions the facts permitted the courts to advance a different argument to establish the presence of some forum interest. In *Griggs v. Riley*, the driver of the other car involved in the accident, who was joined as a third party defendant, was a Missouri resident. Discussing the policies of Missouri and Illinois, the state in which host and guest were domiciled, the Missouri Court of Appeals first discarded the Illinois guest statute. Although it was the policy of Illinois "to protect gratuitous hosts from ungrateful guests," Illinois would have no interest in this litigation since an Illi-

---

157 *Bray v. Cox* 39 A.D.2d 299, 333 N.Y.S.2d 783 (1972). In *Rye v. Kolter* 39 A.D.2d 821, 333 N.Y.S.2d 96 (1972), a perfunctory reference to *Fosillo v. Matthews* 30 A.D.2d 1049, 295 N.Y.S.2d 327, 248 N.E.2d 455 (1968), *supra* note 140 and chapter 6, note 41, sufficed to deny application of the Ontario guest statute.
158 *Conklin v. Horner* 38 Wis.2d 468, 157 N.W.2d 579 at 586 (1968). See also: *Gagne v. Berry* 112 N.H. 125, 290 A.2d 624 at 626 (1972): "Adoption of the Massachusetts law in this case would defeat the deterrent effect of our negligence laws by allowing negligent conduct to go undeterred." In this case, the parties were Massachusetts domiciliaries who had been on their way to a funeral in Maine when, in New Hampshire, they had a collision with another car, driven by another Massachusetts domiciliary.

nois court would have applied Missouri law as *lex loci delicti*: Illinois' interest in protecting the host would, therefore, extend no further than its borders.[159] On the other hand, since Missouri was said to have an interest in protecting the rights of Missouri residents under its contribution statute, which rights would be obviated by application of the Illinois guest statute, Missouri law was held to apply.[160] Still another forum interest was identified by the Minnesota Supreme Court in *Milkovich v. Saari*. The case arose from an accident in Minnesota and involved Ontario domiciliaries. Focusing more on the policy of its own recovery rule than on the purposes of Ontario's guest statute, the court rejected the idea that rules pertaining to host-guest liability, "unlike rules of the road and definitions on negligence," had any bearing upon a state's interest in the safety of its highways. Instead, Minnesota's interest was the interest of a "justice-administering state." Furthermore, it was noted, " ... persons injured in automobile accidents occurring within our borders can reasonably be expected to require treatment in our medical facilities, both public and private." The fact that there was no evidence that the plaintiff-guest had been treated in a Minnesota hospital was obviously irrelevant: " ... we are loath to place weight on the individual case for fear it might offer even minor incentives to 'hospital shop' or to create litigation-directed pressures on the payment of debts to medical facilities." Since the court disapproved of Ontario's guest statute anyway, it is not surprising that it found neither of its rationales persuasive, and that it held Minnesota law to apply.[161]

If one thing is clear from the foregoing overview, it is the inconsistency of the policy-oriented motivation in guest statute decisions. True, few

159 See also: *supra* chapter 2, section 2, text accompanying notes 141–146.
160 *Griggs v. Riley* 489 S.W.2d 469 (Mo. App. 1972). An argument of a different order was used by the Supreme Court of Ohio in *Schiltz v. Meyer* 29 Ohio St.2d 169, 280 N.E.2d 925 (1972), arising from an accident in Ohio in which the host and guest were Kentucky residents. The law-fact pattern in this case is different from that of the other cases discussed so far, in that Ohio, the forum state, had a guest statute, whereas Kentucky was a recovery state. Considering that the plaintiffs had elected to sue in Ohio, the court reasoned: "In so doing, they have increased our governmental interest beyond that of merely being the state in which the accident occurred. We now have the additional interest of advancing, in our courts, those policies which our General Assembly has seen fit to maintain in this area of tort law."
161 *Milkovich v. Saari* 295 Minn. 155, 203 N.W.2d 408 (1973), discussed *supra* chapter 5, text accompanying notes 70–74.

of them are based on straightforward interest analysis; in most of them the courts relied on a mixture of policy-oriented approaches, ranging from the most significant relationship approach to the better law consideration. Nevertheless, in virtually all of these cases some attempt at interest identification was made, and in that respect alone the results are baffling. As could be expected, the most compelling *ratio decidendi* is found in the easiest type of case, the one in which both parties are domiciled in the forum state, and even in that category the results are not always consistent. The other law-fact patterns described are more complicated, but that seems insufficient justification for the far-fetched constructions some courts devised to escape a more obvious outcome. In guest statute adjudication everything seems possible, not only in terms of justice in the individual case but also, and particularly, in respect of choice of law motivation. The purposes of a recovery rule appear to be at least as varied as those of a guest statute, and equally adaptable to the actual circumstances. In a recovery state, the courts pay more attention to their own law than to the foreign guest statute. If they do try to identify the policy behind a foreign guest statute, it is done in a most perfunctory way, and hardly any thought is given to its spatial implications. Mostly, the emphasis is on forum policy, which leaves little room for an assessment of potential foreign interests. This pervasive forum bias could be explained by a general acceptance of Currie's *lex fori* solution to true conflicts. However, in the few cases in which the court identified the case as a true conflict, the assertion of a forum interest seems tenuous, not to say fictitious or fabricated. On the whole, the reasoning is haphazard, superficial, and sometimes spurious.

Many opinions give the impression that the choice of law motivation was tailored to a preconceived outcome. That may well be the only explanation of the erratic results in policy-oriented guest statute adjudication. Increasingly, guest statutes are considered anachronistic rules of law, no longer in tune with the conditions of present-day transportation. In a recovery state, the courts are apt to disapprove of a rule which, in effect, shields not so much the host as his insurer, thus preventing a more adequate distribution of loss. Although I sympathize with the underlying notion that the injured guest should not go uncompensated for the benefit of the insurance industry, I object to the distorted choice of law reasoning by which the courts achieve their goal. If the consequences of guest statute application are unacceptable, it should be displaced for being offensive to the forum's sense of justice, and not because of some pseudo forum interest in highway safety or the protection of imaginary medical creditors or injured third parties. On the other hand, if the guest statute is not deemed sufficiently "pernicious and detestable" to warrant deployment of the public policy doctrine, it might be asked if it should be displaced at all, absent a genuine interest of the recovery state. A vague dissatisfaction with the quality of foreign law is not enough, in my opinion, to deny its application. However, if an unsatisfactory foreign rule must be evaded, I would even prefer a blunt better law decision to the quasi-objective drivel about policies and interests I found in most guest statute cases. In that respect, I appreciate the relative candor of the Wisconsin Supreme Court in *Heath v. Zellmer*, explaining why it refused to apply the Indiana guest statute in an action involving an Indiana guest and an Ohio host driving a car registered and insured in Indiana. Having construed a true conflict out of Wisconsin's interest in deterring unsafe driving and Indiana's interest in protecting the car owner and his insurer, the court acknowledged it just did not like guest statutes: "If the forum state is concerned, it will not favor the application of a rule of law repugnant to its own policies."[162] According to Shapira's definition,[163] a viable choice of law technique must be "workable, rational and fair." Measured by the quality of policy-oriented guest statute adjudication, interest analysis does not pass that test. As the courts use it primarily to camouflage their disapproval of "repugnant" foreign law, it hardly functions as a "rational" approach. In this light, interest analysis appears to be an unnecessarily cumbersome method to achieve the same "fair" results that can be reached, with considerably less effort, by way of a straight better law approach. If it is "workable" at all, its practical efficiency is minimal.

---

162 *Heath v. Zellmer* 35 Wis.2d 578, 151 N.W.2d 664 (1967). Apparently, this argument was not enough. Guided by Leflar's choice-influencing considerations, the court once more emphasized the importance of Wisconsin's deterrent policy and its interest in penalizing negligent conduct on Wisconsin highways. It further asserted that Wisconsin had the better law, and dismissed the Indiana guest statute as an "anachronism." *Ibid.* p. 675 ff.

163 *Supra* text accompanying note 8.

Chapter 9

The Ambiguities of Policy-oriented Choice of Law

Is it reasonable to ask the impossible? Is it fair to insist on a rational approach to choice of law, achieving justice in the individual case and legal certainty at the same time? To me, the answer to such questions is positive. Of course, I am well aware that my expectations are unrealistic and that the philosopher's stone is an illusion. When it comes to improving the human condition, the law will always be an imperfect instrument. Knowing our limitations, however, should not stop us from reaching beyond present-day possibilities. There is no point in sitting back and taking flaws for granted without trying to detect their causes and think of a cure. My criticism of choice of law practice is not meant, therefore, as a reproach to the inventors of theories or the authors of judicial opinions, but as a probe into the validity of the methodological tenets on which they rely. It is meant to expose ambiguities disguised as arguments, to show up false reasoning and inner inconsistency, to determine the weak spots of a theory applied in practice. By dissecting the results of the policy-oriented methodology, we may acquire an insight into the real motives behind choice of law adjudication, and that could be the next point of departure in our never-ending quest for perfection.

Looking back on the conclusions of the previous chapters, I must confess to a growing disenchantment with policy-oriented choice of law. Although I still think that interest analysis, the common denominator of most variants, is a sensible, well-reasoned approach to the choice of law problem, it can hardly be denied that, in practice, it performs less convincingly than its theory would suggest. To the extent that the courts use interest analysis as (part of) their choice of law motivation, many of the decisions I described give the impression of being geared to a "just result" irrespective of the policies and interests involved. Yet, if justice in the individual case were the only choice of law objective worth striving for, the better law consideration would probably be the most compelling rationale. In a few cases, some sort of policy analysis is thrown in to buttress the choice of the "better" (forum) law, but in most decisions a magical mix of contacts, interests and forum preference is concocted to convince us of the "paramount interest" of the forum state. If the choice of foreign law should remain an exception, the *lex fori* approach, as espoused in Kentucky and Michigan, would seem to be a plausible alternative to convoluted interest analysis. Nevertheless, in the majority of American jurisdictions multistate tort cases are decided with at least some help of policy-oriented choice of law. It is the thesis of this chapter that, due to the ambiguities of its method, the process of evaluating policies and interests is no less conducive to result-selective manipulation than the traditional allocation method ever was. Since there are more links in the chain of policy-oriented arguments than there are in the traditional choice of law process – each extra step offering additional opportunity for unrestrained result-selective reasoning – the new approaches afford the courts even more leeway in adjusting their choice of law motivation to a predetermined result. In this chapter I intend to examine just how much leeway there is for such manipulation in the various stages of policy-oriented choice of law, and for what reasons the courts would make use of it.

It is my conviction that a viable choice of law approach should be flexible enough to promote justice in the individual case, but at the same time dependable enough to achieve certainty and efficiency.[1] Policy-oriented choice of law is a reaction to the rigidity of traditional jurisdiction-selection and its questionable aspiration for "conflicts justice". No longer based on "rules" but on an "approach", the new choice of law methodology features a mode of conflicts resolution which requires the court to perform a series of *ad hoc* appraisals with no other guidelines than the mainstays of the theory's methodological framework. Such an approach is wide open to result-selective considerations, which are apt to carry just results, but tend to frustrate meth-

---

1 *Cf.* Shapira's description of a "workable" method of choice of law, *supra* chapter 8, text accompanying note 8.

odological reliability. It follows that the drawbacks of policy-oriented choice of law do not lie in its capacity to achieve justice in the individual case, but in the excessive flexibility of its operation. The more room the law leaves for judicial interpretation, the greater the danger of *Kadi-Justiz*. Considering the American experience in the area of multistate torts, I submit that the greatest flaw of the policy-based choice of law methodology is its unreliability. To substantiate this allegation, I suggest a closer look at the possible causes.

In the process of policy-oriented choice of law, the first step entails identification of the substantive issue. In common law systems, in which the forms of action used to be restricted to the number of available writs, the parties still control the framing of the issue, including the issue in law.[2] American courts will have little difficulty, therefore, in determining the extent of the controversy in terms of substantive law. In civil law jurisdictions, this might be different: with or without the assistance of the parties, the issues are generally formed by the court in reliance on the facts and the *petitum*, plaintiff's claim or complaint. Actually, identification of the issue is a necessary step under both policy-oriented choice of law and traditional jurisdiction-selection. The latter approach needs it as a preliminary step in the process of characterization, facilitating the decision whether the controversy should be labelled a "family relationship-something", a "contract-something", a "tort-something", etcetera.[3] Under policy-oriented choice of law, it is a preliminary step towards the selection of the various rules which may claim application. While the characterization process, as such, represents a choice which may be influenced by result-selective considerations, the formulation of the substantive issue need not be affected by such teleology. Translation of the guest statute issue into the question whether or not the negligent host is liable to his injured guest, does not compel the court to characterize it as a delictual issue under the allocation method, nor does it predetermine the outcome of the policy-oriented choice of law process. This implies that, at this level, the result-selective opportunities are relatively slim under either approach. It will be clear that identification of the issue is not meant to lever a methodological switch from interest analysis to

---

[2] Schlesinger (1973) p. 25, making an exception for foreign law issues: "With respect to the procedural treatment of foreign law, we have largely abandoned the common-law tradition."

[3] Sedler (1970) p. 48; *supra* chapter 2, section 1, text accompanying note 12.

jurisdiction-selection. This happened in several cases turning on issues which were labelled procedural.[4] Whether an action is timely brought or not, for instance, is a question which could be characterized as substantive or procedural, but under a policy-oriented approach such classifications do not, or, at any rate, should not matter. What counts is the actual interest each of the involved jurisdictions may have in the application of its statute of limitations. Characterization of the issue should only be needed in the context of allocation.

At the next stage of policy-oriented choice of law, information must be gathered on the substantive laws involved. This step requires an examination of the multistate aspects of the case, as each of them points to a jurisdiction whose law may claim application. It is here that the first problems emerge. To a large extent, they are related to one of conflicts law's pervasive problems: the demarcation of the procedural responsibilities of the court *vis-à-vis* the parties.[5] On the assumption that matters of fact are controlled by the parties, the court is bound by their statements of fact and, unless it is disputed by the other party, this information is the basis of any subsequent determination. It is theoretically conceivable, therefore, that the court, unaware of the multistate caliber of the controversy, will decide it as a domestic case. In practice, this is an improbable supposition, since the pleadings and other documents submitted are likely to give sufficient indication of extraneous aspects to call attention to possible choice of law problems.[6] On the other hand, if the parties have supplied all information available, the court will have to weed out those details that are clearly irrelevant to the choice of law issue, just as it weeds out irrelevant information in a domestic fact pattern.

---

4 *Supra* chapter 2, section 1, text accompanying notes 61–69.
5 *Supra* chapter 2, section 4.
6 Apart from the rules of evidence, there might be a rule of civil procedure enabling the court, as a matter of discretion, to ask the parties for additional factual information. Of course, if the facts are insufficient to support the cause of action, the case will be dismissed, but in multistate litigation, especially in proceedings upon default, failure to supply relevant choice of law information may go unnoticed by the court and need not result in dismissal. In other words, the parties generally control the range of eligible laws by their control over matters of fact. To the extent that the court is obliged to take judicial notice of certain facts, as it may be in determining adjudicatory jurisdiction, it is likely to use that knowledge in subsequent stages of the proceedings.

The juridification of the factual dispute, *i.e.* the selection of legally pertinent facts, is one of many discretionary moments in the adjudicatory process, and the choice of law stage is no exception. Suppose that the parties in a guest statute case are both New York domiciliaries, one of them being an Italian, the other an American; they meet in California, and decide to drive home together in the American's car, registered in New Jersey; on their way from California to New York *via* Nebraska, they decide to make a detour to Minnesota to see the driver's grandmother, a Swedish national; from there, they drive through Wisconsin into Illinois, where they have an accident; let us assume that Illinois has a guest statute. Are the contacts with California, Minnesota, and Wisconsin –not to mention Nebraska– relevant to the guest statute issue? Could Sweden be a concerned jurisdiction? Or Italy? New Jersey perhaps? This example may illustrate the theoretical difficulties inherent in the juridification of the dispute, as well as the actual likelihood that irrelevant facts will not be pleaded. If they are, the court will probably ignore them. The Swedish citizenship of defendant's grandmother would seem to have little bearing on the host-guest relationship at issue. The same is true in respect of the contacts with Nebraska, Minnesota, Wisconsin and other states the parties passed through on their way to New York. The California contact may be relevant, since the trip was arranged in that state, and the fact that defendant's automobile was registered in New Jersey might be a significant factor as well, particularly in light of some of the policies underlying guest statute legislation.[7] To test the legal pertinence of multistate aspects, the court should appraise the outer limits of a state's possible concern and ask itself if it is at all conceivable that the

---

7 At this stage, we do not "know" anything yet about guest statute policies. Without such knowledge, particularly about the possible relation between guests statutes and the insurance factor, the place where the automobile is registered, insured and garaged may well be deemed totally irrelevant. In reality, I presume, the courts do not follow the consecutive stages of policy-oriented adjudication as they are here described. More likely, they shape their decisions by switching back and forth between stages. *Cf.* Crombag/De Wijkerslooth/Cohen (1973) p. 8 ff., characterizing the adjudicatory process as "regressive reasoning." See also: Schoordijk (1972) p. 9: "It is in relation to the facts that a rule of law acquires such content and nuance that it can do *justice* to the facts." In both texts, reference is made to Josef Esser's *Vorverständnis und Methodenwahl in der Rechtsfindung*, Frankfurt, 1970.

state involved could assert an interest in the application of its law.[8] At this stage, preceding the investigation of the contents of the laws involved, such a test is bound to be somewhat speculative. Yet, unless the circle of involvement is drawn wide enough to include those states whose possible interests may be doubtful as yet, the subsequent calculus of interests could be distorted, and then the whole analysis would be pointless.

Having ascertained which jurisdictions have a potential interest in the resolution of the controversy, the court will have to obtain information on the contents of the various rules of law involved. As we have seen,[9] the American approach to the problem of notice and proof of foreign law tends to frustrate the methodical consistency of policy-oriented choice of law, inasmuch as its operation comes to depend on the parties' willingness and ability to demonstrate the true contents of the laws involved, or on the discretion of the court to make its own investigations. If the necessary information on a foreign state's law is lacking, the actuality of its concern cannot be assessed and this implies a distortion of any subsequent evaluation, particularly if only one foreign state is involved and the forum state is disinterested. Under the allocation method, the problem of notice and proof of foreign law is technically the same: if the parties fail to prove the designated foreign law, the court may either dismiss the action or apply forum law for want of a better solution. As a choice of law technique, however, it is not dependent on the consideration of foreign law: premised on an examination of relevant facts rather than relevant laws, it can function without any need for information on the contents of the laws involved. Furthermore, since it only requires information on one rather than all of the laws involved, the danger of distortion due to misinterpretation of foreign law is considerably less than it is under an approach for which correct information on all pertinent rules of law is a *conditio sine*

---

8 *Cf.* Strikwerda (1978) p. 162/163, who would use the "general function" of any rule of law – which is "the protection and advancement of the well-being of the community and its members" – as an indication for its potential claim to application: " ... a state's substantive law cannot be deemed to claim application if the interests involved in the determination of a multistate issue in no way affect the interests of the state – the social system – in which the rule is in force." Strikwerda refers to a similar criterion formulated by Von Mehren/Trautman (1965) p. 104: "Is there an element in the transaction that makes it relevant to ask what a particular jurisdiction thinks about the transaction?"

9 *Supra* chapter 2, section 4.

qua non. In this respect, the problem of notice and proof of foreign law has much more of an impact on policy-oriented choice of law than it has on blind jurisdiction-selection.

Let us proceed on the dubious assumption that the content of each of the eligible laws has been correctly determined, either by the court or by the parties, and that there is no doubt whatsoever on the actual outcome of the case under the law of each jurisdiction involved. At this point, some important decisions should be made. In the first place, the case may be found to present a no-conflict situation: having identical contents or achieving the same material result in respect of the point at issue, the eligible rules of law are apparently not in conflict, obviating the need for a choice between them.[10] In the second place, this may be the moment for a quality check on the contents of all foreign substantive rules. As I have suggested before,[11] deployment of the doctrine of public policy at this stage accords best with its function. Before the stage of interest identification, the court has no choice but to measure the quality of foreign law without regard to any interest the foreign jurisdiction may have in the application of its law. This procedure precludes the possible abuse of public policy as a choice-influencing factor at the stage of interest evaluation.[12] Thus, public policy would perform the same function under either choice of law approach: for the rejection of a foreign rule on account of its substandard quality, it should make no difference whether the court relies on interest analysis or on traditional allocation.

The next step in the process of policy-oriented choice of law is crucial. Having ascertained the extent of the potential conflict of laws, the court must now determine whether the eligible rules of law do or do not claim application to the actual controversy. To that end, it will be necessary to identify the *interests* at stake, which implies an assess-

---

10 *Supra* chapter 4, section 1. Although no choice may be needed for the resolution of the controversy as such, there may be compelling reasons for choosing anyway: *ibid.* note 32.
11 *Supra* chapter 2, section 3, text accompanying notes 255–257.
12 This implies that Leflar's better law consideration, *supra* chapter 5, text accompanying notes 22–25, 35–44, 87–97, should be saved for a later stage. If the court were to decide at this point which of the eligible rules of law it deems to be the "better" one, other *choice-influencing* considerations, notably those relating to interests, would never come into play.

ment of the *policy* behind each rule, and an appraisal of its *spatial reach* in relation to the facts.[13] In my opinion, this stage represents the Achilles heel of interest analysis. Here, each determination is open to question, each assertion debatable, each conclusion dubious. When Currie posited that policies should be ascertained by "the familiar process of construction and interpretation,"[14] he oversimplified the problem considerably. As Currie had it, statutory construction and interpretation "involves an attempt to ascertain what the legislature meant, in part by reference to definitions that have been established in other contexts for terms employed in the statute, and in part by resort to such 'legislative history' as may be available; beyond this, it involves an attempt to ascertain the legislative purpose, and to impute to the legislature an 'intention' to include the marginal situation or not, according to whether analysis indicates that inclusion would serve, or disserve, or be irrelevant to that purpose."[15]

However, policy assessment can hardly be identified with the "ordinary" process of statutory construction. Normally, in "applying" a rule of law, the court must match the facts against the legal concepts embodied in the rule. Such tentative subsumption requires a continuous interpretation of both law and facts. The court should ask, for instance, if a passenger who was injured while helping the negligent driver with his Christmas shopping, qualifies as a "guest" within the meaning of the forum's guest law. One of the relevant factors in these deliberations *may* be the guest statute's policy, but other considerations are likely to carry more weight. In other words: policy assessment is just one facet of statutory construction, and hardly a matter of routine at that.[16] Yet, interest analysis focuses exclusively on the pol-

---

13 *Supra* chapter 4, text following note 6. See also: *supra* chapter 8, sections 1 and 2, on the policies and spatial delimitation of guest statutes.
14 Currie (1963-1) p. 183/184, and *passim*.
15 *Ibid.* p. 377.
16 By referring to the "ordinary" or "familiar" process of statutory construction, Currie suggested that clarifying statutory ambiguities and filling legislative lacunae is any court's daily business. Most cases decided by trial judges, however, are pretty straightforward, their outcome usually depending on the sufficiency of evidence or on the court's appreciation of the facts. The "marginal situations" in Currie's description of statutory construction are exceptions not only by definition. Statutory provisions are generally clear enough to be applied without the need for construction in the majority of cases. An investigation of underlying policies is seldom needed. See also *infra* note 19.

icy of the rule: the crucial aspect of Currie's brand of statutory construction is legislative intent. The difficulties encountered in this kind of interpretation should not be underestimated, not even when the court is dealing with its own law. Even the purpose of forum law may be elusive, particularly if the rule in question delegates extensive powers to the court to decide the issue at its discretion. An open-ended rule on the amount of damages, for instance, may be based on a plaintiff-protective policy, but if the forum steadfastly disallows damages for pain and suffering or other immaterial loss, the purpose of such rulings could be protection of the tort-feasor.[17] What is the "policy" behind the doctrine of proximate cause? How to determine the purpose of assumption of risk? The rationale of contributory negligence? The objective of vicarious liability? Even in the forum's own law, I submit, very few rules can be explained in specific policy terms alone. If legal policies can be ascertained at all,[18] their definition is bound to be over-inclusive, saying little more than that the rule in question appears to be predicated on "a policy of deterrence" or that it might be meant to "protect the tort victim" or "shield the defendant."[19]

---

17 The measure of damages is one of the topics in tort law that defies policy analysis. In a defamation action against the National Enquirer, brought in California, the well-known comedienne Carol Burnett won an award of more than one million dollar for damages she allegedly sustained as a result of defendant's report that she had been seen in a restaurant in Washington D.C. in the company of Henry Kissinger, talking loudly, spilling her wine, and probably drunk. In fact, Ms. Burnett claimed, she was a teetotaller. If she had brought her action in a Dutch court, she would have received nominal damages at best. Is the policy behind the California law on damages different from the one underlying Dutch law? Could it be maintained that the Netherlands and California have a common policy of compensation? If so, why the disparity in its implementation?
18 *Cf.* Atiyah (1983) p. 73: "But in many circumstances it is very difficult to say what are the purposes of the law. A particular section or paragraph of an Act of Parliament may be extremely obscure, and its purposes may be as enigmatic as its effect. Further, the common law, or even statute law, once encrusted with interpretative case-law, is not the work of a single mind, or even of a small number of minds. Much of the common law is the work of generation after generation of judges, layer upon layer of juristic interpretation and commentary and classification. To discern general purposes in the laws thus made is often quite impossible."
19 Most courts are satisfied with this kind of broad definition. It is a rare case, usually adjudicated at the highest level, in which the court is more specific on the policies behind a particular rule of substantive tort law.

Statutory interpretation is difficult enough in respect of forum policy, but when it comes to grasping the purposes of foreign law the court faces a host of additional problems, ranging from the inaccessibility of foreign materials to the question whether it should adopt the other jurisdiction's views on interpretation, or adhere to its own.[20] Begging the reader's indulgence, I will resort once more to the guest statute example to paint a clearer picture of the problems involved in interest identification by way of statutory construction. Let us take the familiar New York-Ontario guest statute cases. It will be assumed that the text of Ontario's guest statute is beyond doubt: in essence, it frees the host-driver from liability for the consequences of ordinary negligence.[21] To distill the legislative policy (or policies) from such a rule, the New York forum must first have some idea of its interpretative options. First, it could choose to investigate the original purpose of the statute: if policies are to be revealed by legislative intent, it might be appropriate to rely on legislative history.[22] Chances are that the Ontario legislators who created and enacted the statute were inspired by divergent yet compatible motives, leading to a final product supporting various policies. This would explain the contradictory conclusions of Professors Trautman and Baade on the original purpose of the Ontario guest statute.[23] On the other hand, even without an amendment, the character of the Ontario statute might have changed over the years. Its

---

20 Under the allocation method, the problem of statutory construction is less acute. Having selected the applicable law, the court must discover the content of the rule of decision and find out how it would be interpreted by the courts in the jurisdiction where it is in force. There is no need, however, to determine the underlying policy or spatial reach of the applicable rule, a process demanding much greater interpretative skills. On the other hand, the allocation method may give rise to different, but equally complicated problems, such as those occasioned by secondary characterization (*supra* chapter 2, section 1, text following note 34) or renvoi (*supra* chapter 2, section 2).

21 *Cf.* Baade (1973) p. 150, note 4, quoting § 132(3) of the Ontario Highway Traffic Act, as amended in 1966: "Notwithstanding subsection 1, the owner or driver of a motor vehicle, other than a vehicle operated in the business of carrying passengers for compensation, is not liable for any loss or damage resulting from bodily injury to, or the death of any person being carried in, or upon, or entering, or getting on to, or alighting from the motor vehicle, except where such loss or damage was caused or contributed to by the gross negligence of the driver of the motor vehicle."

22 Actually, this strategy might not always be feasible. *Cf.* Brilmayer (1980) p. 399: "Many states do not even publish legislative histories, and those that do rarely document the legislators' views on territorial reach."

23 *Supra* chapter 8, section 1, text accompanying notes 83–85.

original purposes may have faded into the background, while the dynamics of social developments could have given new life to an otherwise obsolete rule. One of the oldest objectives of guest statute legislation was the enforcement of moral convictions pertaining to a driver's hospitality and a passenger's gratitude.[24] Widespread liability insurance made this policy obsolete, but the rule survived and acquired the new function of protecting the insurer, hence the premium-paying public collectively.[25] It could be asked, therefore, if a historical approach to statutory construction is a meaningful way of identifying policies, which, after all, is one of the preliminaries to interest determination.[26]

Confronted with a domestic case, the court will usually interpret its own statutory law according to the prevailing adjudicatory standards in the forum state, including its theory on statutory construction, its conception of *stare decisis*, the relevance or irrelevance of doctrinal opinion, and so on. There is little doubt that the court will also observe these standards when applying forum law to a multistate controversy. But choice of law is premised on the notion that, on occasion, application of foreign law is warranted. By accepting this premise, the forum is bound to recognize the potential authority of the foreign rule of decision whenever its conflicts law calls for its application. In my opinion, this surrender of normative authority implies the acceptance of foreign law *as interpreted and applied* by the courts of the foreign jurisdiction concerned. Thus, a New York court should interpret the Ontario guest statute as if it were an Ontario court trying to divine the purpose of its own substantive law. If it does not, it is likely to give a distorted interpretation of Ontario law. A comparative survey of guest statute legislation in Colorado, Michigan, and Ontario[27] is meaningless, it would seem, if an Ontario court would base its interpretation on legislative history only. Likewise, references to text-

---

24 *Ibid.* text accompanying notes 36–42.
25 In chapter 1, section 5, note 212, I mentioned a similar functional metamorphosis in the history of article 6 of the Dutch *Buitengewoon Besluit Arbeidsverhoudingen* ("Special Decree on Labor Relations").
26 In my opinion, a rule of foreign law, no less than domestic law, should be explained in terms of its actual, present-day function, which implies that historical investigations tend to lose their import as the rule in question dates further back in history.
27 As demonstrated in respect of the Michigan guest statute in *Tooker v. Lopez* 24 N.Y.2d 569, 301 N.Y.S.2d 519, 249 N.E.2d 394 (1969), *supra* chapter 8, section 1, note 86.

books, treatises and law review articles are inapposite if the foreign jurisdiction confers no authority on doctrinal sources. The same applies to the forum's reliance on constructive intent, *i.e.* the imputed rather than the actual purpose of a rule, if such interpretation would be invalid in the jurisdiction concerned. Teleological interpretation might be an especially attractive technique in policy-oriented choice of law, as it furnishes accommodating substitutes for an obscure or unidentified policy, but it will be clear that a teleological construction of foreign law is apt to distort the policy of the rule as perceived by the community in which it is in force.[28] Teleological is, for instance, the interpretation by which the forum pretends that the foreign jurisdiction would not pursue a certain policy unless it would actually be furthered by application of the rule in which it is embodied. If it is assumed that the Ontario guest statute is meant to protect the insurance industry, this line of reasoning would preclude its application in case the host is uninsured.[29] Needless to say that, in a domestic case, an Ontario court would have no choice but to apply the rule if the case fits its terms.[30] Similar teleological speculation may be occasioned by intertemporal complications. These and other problems of policy interpretation are much less simple than the proponents of interest analysis suggest when referring to the "familiar process of statutory construction."

---

28 Such judicial self-delusion resulted in application of the Colorado guest statute in *Dym v. Gordon* 16 N.Y.2d 120, 262 N.Y.S.2d 463, 209 N.E.2d 792 (1965), *supra* chapter 8, section , text accompanying notes 63–64, and in rejection of the Massachusetts guest statute in *Gagne v. Berry* 290 A.2d 624 (N.H. 1972), *supra* chapter 4, section 2, text preceding note 66.
29 *Cf.* Baade (1973) p. 162, considering the *Neumeier v. Kuehner* situation from the perspective of an Ontario court: "Even an uninsured Ontario host-driver benefits from the Ontario guest statute; and it seems somewhat grasping, if not chauvinistic, to treat the insured foreigner worse than the uninsured Ontarian – especially since the law strongly disapproves of the latter. Such a disposition of the case by an Ontario court would evoke the image of the hick probate judge who highhandedly pretermits a Soviet heir because, according to his limited lights, there is no such thing as private property in the Soviet Union."
30 Yet, Currie (1963-1) p. 160, suggested that Arizona's policy of freeing the heirs of the tort-feasor from liability (*actio personalis moritur cum persona*) would be irrelevant in case the tort-feasor is fully insured: "In that event, any interest of Arizona in the matter evaporates completely ..." *Contra:* Brilmayer (1980) p. 412/413: "This is surely nothing like ordinary statutory construction. In purely domestic cases, the Arizona courts would not look to the presence of insurance to determine whether the Arizona abatement law should apply."

If the assessment of legislative intent is difficult enough in respect of substantive policies as such, the interpretation of the rule's purpose in terms of spatial delimitation may well be impossible. Accusing the "interest analysts" of substituting their own normative beliefs for actual legislative intent, Professor Lea Brilmayer has made out a strong case against one of the principal tenets of Currie's theory. "[I]n the vast majority of cases," she contends, "legislatures *have* no actual intent on territorial reach."[31] If they do, they seem to be motivated more by traditional "system values", such as decisional harmony or judicial efficiency, than by the very policy the substantive rule is meant to further. This would explain why many scope rules limit the spatial reach of a statute by a territorial rather than personal criterion,[32] even though the latter standard would be more appropriate in light of the protective policy expressed in the substantive rules.[33] Apart from the merits of this argument,[34] it cannot be denied that the relation between policy-oriented choice of law and scope rules is extremely complicated. In the first place, it may be asked whether legislative delimitation of the substantive rule's spatial reach has any bearing on the determination of its policy. Since the spatial criteria of the scope rule

---

31 Brilmayer (1980) p. 330; emphasis in the original. *Id.* (1984) p. 562.
32 See also: Martin (1984) p. 586, note 25: "One could argue, for example, that those areas that have received legislative attention are most likely to be those where certainty is at a premium, and in these areas, territorial rules, rather than the more uncertain approach of Currie, offer more certainty."
33 In *Bolgrean v. Stich* 293 Minn. 8, 196 N.W.2d 442 (1972), for instance, one of the reasons to reject application of the guest statute of North Dakota was found in its scope rule, limiting the statute's spatial reach to situations in which the guest was injured "on the highways of North Dakota." If the North Dakota legislature intended its guest statute to protect North Dakota hosts and their insurers, one is inclined to think, it should have given the rule a different scope. Conversely, it could be argued that the substantive policy of the North Dakota guest statute must be derived from its scope rule. If so, it would stand for a policy of deterrence, affecting any host or guest driving together through North Dakota.
34 Brilmayer (1980) p. 424 ff.: "Existing choice-of-law statutes demonstrate that simplicity, predictability and multistate harmony motivate state legislatures just as they have motivated all conflicts theorists except the interest analysts ... We find statutes that make the rule of lex loci govern the permissible interest on loans, statutes that make forum law apply to all torts or crimes committed in airplanes over forum territory, and statutes that make the law of the place of execution or performance govern interpretation of wills. None of these statutes is phrased in terms of benefiting forum residents, although many serve protective or compensatory purposes. The effect on forum residents is never mentioned as either a sole or an alternative basis for applying forum law."

may be predicated on disparate legislative motives, they must be deemed inconclusive in respect of the enactment's substantive policy as such. This suggests that a scope rule has no bearing on the purpose of the rule and may be ignored at the stage of policy assessment.

On the other hand, it could be argued that a scope rule precludes the need for policy identification, as it determines the statute's spatial reach *per se*, regardless of its policy. This argument poses the troubling question whether the spatial reach of a substantive rule should be derived from its policy as such, or from its scope rule. Suppose that the Ontario guest statute would have been accompanied by a scope rule, restricting its application to situations in which *the host-driver is a citizen of Ontario*. Is it a valid assumption, then, that Ontario qualifies as an interested jurisdiction whenever the defendant-host is an Ontarian? If so, it does not seem to matter what purpose the statute was meant to achieve, whether protection of the host, his insurer, injured third-parties, or the level of insurance rates. Now suppose that the New York legislature has enacted a statute which allows victims of *traffic accidents occurring in New York* to recover against negligent drivers.[35] In a domestic case, a New York host would be liable for the injuries of his New York guest, whereas in Ontario the claim of an Ontario guest against an Ontario host would be defeated. But if the accident occurs in Ontario, and the victim is the New York guest of an Ontario host, interest identification according to the respective scope

---

35 According to § 388 of the New York Vehicle and Traffic Law, "every owner of a vehicle used or operated in this state shall be liable and responsible for death or injuries." *Rye v. Kolter* 39 A.D.2d 821, 333 N.Y.S.2d 96 (1972). This provision was "designed to insure that innocent victims ... may be recompensed for the injury and financial loss inflicted upon them." *Shafarman v. Ryder Truck Rental, Inc.* 100 F.R.D. 454 (S.D. N.Y. 1984). More specifically, however, it purports to impute the negligence of the driver to the absent owner, not to establish a choice of law rule for any automobile accident occurring in New York: *Fosillo v. Matthews* 30 A.D.2d 1049, 295 N.Y.S.2d 327, 248 N.E.2d 455 (1968); *McClaney v. Utility Equipment Leasing Corp.* 560 F.Supp. 1270 (N.D. N.Y. 1983). Nevertheless, it was cited in *Kell v. Henderson* 47 Misc.2d 992, 263 N.Y.S.2d 647 at 650 (Sup. Ct. 1965) to support the decision that the Ontario guest statute did not apply to an action for personal injuries between Ontario residents who had been involved in an accident in New York. Although the issue did not turn on vicarious liability, the court did use § 388 to reinforce its ruling: "This section of the law is not limited to New York State residents, and, consequently, out of state owners or operators who elect to use the highways of our State subject themselves to this statute." The Appellate Division ignored this argument: *Kell v. Henderson* 26 A.D.2d 595, 270 N.Y.S. 552 (1966).

rules would compel either forum to treat the case as a false conflict resulting in the application of the Ontario guest statute. In the formal sense of its statute's scope rule, New York would only have an interest in the compensation of its domiciliary if the accident occurred in New York. Without the scope rule, however, New York's compensatory policy would probably be interpreted as extending to New York victims, whether injured in New York or abroad, and that would turn our hypothetical into a true conflict between the laws of New York and Ontario. Conversely, an accident in New York involving Ontario parties would probably give rise to a false conflict construction if New York's compensatory policy is taken at face value, but if its territorial scope rule must be heeded, the conflict would be true.[36]

The scope rule problem highlights the inherent difficulty of interest identification. Here, the court is confronted with an explicit legislative expression of the substantive rule's spatial reach. Yet, if such evidence of actual legislative intent does not accord with the forum's appreciation of the substantive policy in relation to the facts, it might be unwilling to accept it. In other words, the scope rule may dictate a result which does not agree with the court's perception of the substantive rule's spatial reach in light of its presumed policy. If it had the chance, it might want to amend the scope rule so as to include or exclude, as

---

36 Strikwerda (1978) p. 154 ff., discusses a Dutch case to illustrate the discrepancy between legislative definition of a rule's spatial reach and actual interests: HR 23 June 1972, *NJ* 1973, 36 (note A.R. Bloembergen). The issue turned on the availability of an *action directe* against the liability insurer of the tort-feasor. Both jurisdictions involved, the Netherlands and Germany, allowed such an action. However, the Dutch rule was premised on the condition that the accident had occurred in one of the Benelux countries, whereas German law required that the defendant insurance company had its place of business in Germany. Since the accident had occurred in Germany and the insurer was established in the Netherlands, neither condition was met. If this law-fact pattern would have been subjected to interest analysis, the respective scope rules would have turned it into an unprovided-for case, neither jurisdiction claiming application of its law. If we ignore the scope rules, the case would present a no-conflict situation, since there was no conflict between the substantive laws involved. If, nevertheless, a choice must be made, the case should be treated as a false conflict: Dutch substantive law should be applied as the law of the only jurisdiction having an interest in the protection of Dutch victims against Dutch insolvent tort-feasors, Germany being merely the *locus* state. Actually, the case was decided under the allocation method, resulting in application of Dutch law, including its scope rule, hence in dismissal of the direct action. *Cf.* Strikwerda (1978) p. 72 ff.

the case may be, the controversy at issue. Whether the courts are *allowed* to substitute their own normative beliefs for the possibly unhappy expressions of legislative intent, is questionable to say the least. In this respect, much depends on the adjudicatory philosophy to which the forum is supposed to adhere. Since the accepted measure of judicial freedom is not universal, choice of law adds an extra dimension to this question as well: if the forum state supports creative judicial interpretation, allowing the courts to bend a statutory rule to fit their sense of justice, it may be asked if they enjoy the same freedom in interpreting the law of a jurisdiction in which the judicial function is perceived as merely declaratory.[37] Even if it is assumed that scope rules are no more than tentative indications of a substantive rule's spatial reach, and that the court's *ad hoc* interpretation of substantive policy may warrant a different delimitation, it is difficult to believe that such an appraisal can be performed without preconceived notions on the result to be achieved.[38] Constructive intent is a deceptive means of identifying actual interests, particularly those of a foreign jurisdiction. Still, it seems to be the one and only interpretative technique that fits the process of interest identification. If the courts are free to substitute their own ideas on spatial delimitation for the predetermined criteria of a scope rule, actual legislative intent is likely to be subordinated to the forum's normative imputations whenever the former construction is at variance with the result desired. When evidence of actual legislative intent is dubious or absent altogether, as it is in most cases, the fiction of constructive intent is the only tool available.

---

37 Strikwerda (1978) p. 155/156, has argued that scope rules need not be taken into account if they would lead to "unacceptable" choice of law decisions. Since "foreign scope rules are not binding on the forum," the court is free to ignore them. In respect of an unacceptable scope rule of the forum state itself, he would deploy "the usual (interpretative) techniques" the courts generally use to escape application of inadequate or obsolete statutory law and its undesirable results. Acknowledging that such an escape is not always available, Strikwerda would still want the court to be guided by proper results rather than the letter of the law. In my opinion, these suggestions avoid the question whether a scope rule should or should not be viewed as indicative of (predetermined) state interests under a policy-oriented approach.

38 I am well aware, of course, that such notions always influence judicial activity. I have no quarrel with the proposition that the adjudicatory process often – not always – entails retrograde legal reasoning on the basis of a preconceived material result. See also *supra* note 7. My objections are against the method of rationalizing choice of law results, which, if applied correctly, seems too arduous to be workable and too arbitrary to convince.

That brings us to the question by which criteria the spatial reach of substantive law could be gauged in the absence of an explicit delimitation by the legislature. Are there any standards to guide us through the maze of policies, interests and presumed intent? To answer this question, it might be helpful to classify substantive policies into the three categories Professor Brilmayer detected in Currie's writings: "These policies can be categorized as protective, compensatory and regulatory, for in drawing multistate implications from statutes, Currie relied upon their protective, compensatory, and regulatory aspects."[39] If we confine ourselves to multistate torts, the focus of this book, it is not implausible to argue that substantive tort rules are either compensatory (allowing recovery to the tort victim), protective (shielding the tortfeasor from liability) or regulatory (influencing conduct). If this were a valid classification scheme, the spatial dimensions of the compensatory and protective policies could be delineated by a domiciliary factor, and those of a regulatory policy by a territorial criterion.[40]

However, there are at least two flaws in this line of reasoning. The first one stems from the assumption that a substantive rule would fit only one category. In fact, the rule may serve more than one purpose. A guest statute may be defendant-protective, but as we have seen,[41] it is not too difficult to ascribe a regulatory policy to such rules as well. Similarly, a recovery rule may be plaintiff-protective, but, at the same time, it may have a deterrent effect, and in that respect its underlying policy is both compensatory and regulatory. While a regulatory policy is not incompatible with either the compensatory or the protective nature of the rule in question, the spatial dimensions attributed to these policies differ. By itself, this divergence does not affect the feasibility of interest analysis. If New York's recovery rule is based on a policy of compensating New York victims *and* a policy of promoting

---

39 Brilmayer (1980) p. 394, referring to Currie's analysis of married women's contract cases as an example of his approach to a protective policy, his treatment of survival actions as a demonstration of the nature of a compensatory policy, and his discussion of rules of the road or Sunday blue laws as an illustration of the spatial implications of a regulatory policy.
40 As Professor Brilmayer, *ibid.* p. 395 ff., points out, this is the basis of Currie's interest calculus: a protective policy is designed to benefit resident defendants (Currie [1963-1] p. 86, p. 724), a compensatory policy favors resident plaintiffs (Currie [1963-1] p. 144/145, p. 732), and a regulatory policy is meant to promote certain conduct within the state (Currie [1963-1] p. 58, p. 59).
41 *Supra* chapter 8, section 1.

highway safety in New York, New York has an interest if the plaintiff is a New Yorker injured at home or abroad, or a non-resident injured in New York. The real problem that comes to light here is the probability that most multistate tort cases are actually true conflicts.[42] If an interest in the implementation of compensatory and protective policies is triggered by the domiciliary factor, chances are that there is either a true conflict or an unprovided-for case whenever the parties live in different states and the laws of those states differ. Even if they are domiciled in the same state, a regulatory policy of the *locus* state could turn an apparent false conflict into a true one. If the elimination of false conflicts is "the great virtue of Currie's analysis,"[43] its value, in tort choice of law at least, would appear to be negligible. Maybe Professor Twerski was right, after all, when he called attention to the emperor's clothes.[44]

The second flaw inherent in a classificatory approach to interest identification concerns the spatial dimensions attributed to each category. While it is true that the proponents of interest analysis tend to rely mostly on the domiciliary factor when it comes to determining the spatial dimensions of compensatory or protective policies, it is questionable whether such a restrictive interpretation of legislative intent

---

42 *Cf.* Brilmayer (1980) p. 398/399: "This splintering of policies increases the likelihood that the [forum] state will have an interest and predisposes the method toward forum law. Furthermore, it creates a bias toward recovery because pro-recovery statutes are the most likely to serve several different policies, namely compensatory and regulatory ones. The plaintiff's power to choose the forum contributes further to the pro-recovery bias; interest analysis permits different courts to reach different results by honoring their respective states' interests, and the plaintiff naturally selects the most favorable forum." See also: Ely (1981) p. 176 ff.
43 Traynor M. (1961) p. 847. *Cf.* Currie (1963-2) p. 756: "The clearest contribution of governmental-interest analysis to conflict-of-laws method is that it establishes the existence of such false conflicts and provides a workable means of identifying them." See also: Baade (1967) p. 145, characterizing the false conflict case as "the abiding cornerstone of governmental-interest analysis."
44 Twerski, *Neumeier v. Kuehner: Where Are the Emperor's Clothes?* (1973) p. 108: "Having defined the interests as domiciliary oriented, when you run out of domiciliaries to protect you run out of interests. The emperor indeed stands naked for all to see."

is warranted.[45] Professor Ely has argued that it is based on the erroneous assumption "that a state can be interested only in *helping* its own by applying its rules so as to assure that they will win their lawsuits, that consequently it can have no interest in causing a local to *lose* his or her case."[46] In his opinion, an interest in having defendant pay the damages is the "flipside" of an interest in compensating the plaintiff, which implies that the plaintiff-protecting jurisdiction not only has an interest in the compensation of a local victim, but in sanctioning the local tort-feasor as well. A compensatory policy, Ely implies, expresses both a concern for the victim and moral disapproval of wrongful behavior. One could object that the latter concern is based on a regulatory policy, discouraging harmful conduct. Although this might be a valid classification of the policy, it destroys the assumption that the spatial reach of a regulatory policy is always territorial. The scope of a rule representing a moral standard may well be universal. At any rate, such a rule may have a personal reach, admonishing residents to comport themselves according to their home state standards wherever they go.[47] Conversely, it could be argued that the "flipside" of a protective policy, shielding the defendant, is a policy of influencing plaintiff's behavior, as it is in the "gratitude rationale" of a guest statute. But even the protective policy itself could be complemented by an admonitory policy, such as the one expressed in the "good Samaritan" argument of guest statute case law.[48] Furthermore, the protective policy might be an expression of moral beliefs which tend to reach beyond state limits and may even give rise to a forum interest *per se*, regardless

---

45 The domiciliary criterion might be less self-evident in countries in which nationality rather than domicile or residence is considered the most relevant personal connection, even outside the sphere of family law. This would imply, *ex hypothesi*, that the protection of an Italian living in New York does not only affect New York: it might be Italy's concern as well. Saying that Italy *ought* to be disinterested, may eclipse the Italian interest but that does not make it any less real.
46 Ely (1981) p. 196; emphasis in the original.
47 In *Labree v. Major* 306 A.2d 808 (R.I. 1973), the Rhode Island Supreme Court relied on precisely this kind of "moral" consideration when it held a Rhode Island citizen to the Rhode Island standard of care, although the wrongful conduct had occurred in Massachusetts. *Supra* chapter 8, section 1, text following note 103. See also: *supra* chapter 4 section 3, text accompanying notes 140–146.
48 *Supra* chapter 8, section 1, text accompanying notes 36–42. Similarly, it is conceivable that an admonitory purpose is attributed to a charitable immunity rule: shielding charities from liability might encourage philanthropists to create charitable funds. Etcetera. If actual legislative intent cannot be verified, any argument of this kind can be maintained.

of the place of wrong or the domicile of the parties.[49] Apart from these policy conglomerations, there may be other values underlying a rule of law, which defy classification and add to the ambiguity of the rule's spatial reach. As demonstrated by the guest statute decisions, the operation of law affects other interests than those of the parties alone. The protective policy of a guest statute does not just benefit the host. Indirectly, it benefits his insurer and, ultimately, the premium-paying public. Indirectly, it may also benefit the victim's medical creditors, "local vendors", or injured non-guests. Could such a policy still be called protective, or is it protective in respect of the host and compensatory in respect of third parties? Is a policy against "vexatious litigation" protective or regulatory or both? Even if these questions can be answered unequivocally, and even if the spatial dimensions of each policy aspect can be gauged exactly, it is hard to escape the impression that most multistate controversies actually present true conflicts.[50] If so, interest analysis is little more than a complicated way of demonstrating that we have been dealing with a choice of law problem.

It would seem that we are back at the "myth of legislative intent." I do not believe that classification of policies facilitates the process of interest identification in any way. First, a rule of law usually embodies various objectives, which implies that its overall policy is apt to fit several categories at once. Second, the assumption that the spatial reach of the rule can be inferred from the type of policy it embodies is questionable. There is no compelling reason why the reach of a regulatory policy cannot be extraterritorial, or why the scope of a compensatory policy must always be personal. If there were such reasons, con-

---

49 *Cf.* Martin (1984) p. 589, suggesting that "the forum always has a moral judgment on the dispute, but the strength of its desire to impose that judgment on the parties varies both with the number and the nature of the connections between the forum and the dispute and with the intensity of the moral judgment of the forum." Professor Martin then draws a parallel with the public policy doctrine, which he obviously views as a sliding choice of law corrective. On public policy and relativity, see *supra* chapter 2, section 3, text accompanying notes 158–159 and 168–171, and text following note 249.

50 *Cf.* Martin (1984) p. 585/586: "[T]his wider conception of state interests makes most cases into true conflicts unless they concern plaintiffs and defendants with a common domicile. Clearly Currie and his supporters thought that his approach had solved many more problems than the common-domicile cases." Not even those, I am afraid. The compensatory or protective policy of the domiciliary state could still conflict with a regulatory policy of the other state.

flicts law would still be predicated on the tenets of classic statutism. Third, and methodologically of crucial importance, policy-oriented choice of law was not meant to be a classificatory approach: it proceeds "directly, without the benefit of choice of law rules, to a consideration of the competing domestic laws in order to make a choice between them."[51] It has been acclaimed and excoriated for being an *ad hoc* approach to conflicts resolution, offering little more than a few methodical principles and the framework of judicial method for guidance. Classification is a conceptual tool, too blunt for a dissection of the tangled policies and interests in the individual case. Thus, in the absence of rules and analytical concepts, the whole process of interest identification comes to depend on free-style interpretation. Since evidence of legislative intent is likely to be scarce or lacking altogether, the courts have little to go on but their own normative sensibilities, the actual controversy to be decided, and, quite likely, the substantive result they want to reach. Can there be any doubt, then, that judicial imputations of obscure legislative intent are necessarily colored by the court's normative appreciation of a policy and its spatial reach, by its awareness of the other variables presented by the law-fact pattern, and by its preference for a certain outcome? Is it at all possible, in the process of interest identification, to separate *is* from *ought*, and to ignore the question "how far certain policies *ought* to reach?"[52] Is there much difference between reasonable imputation and teleological interpretation when policies and interests must be construed from the contents of the rules in conflict? Considering the case law discussed in the previous chapters, I am convinced that the answer to these questions is no.

If "teleological interpretation is ultimately the only relevant, decisive method of statutory construction,"[53] the conclusion that interest identification is a teleological process is hardly revealing. However, while teleological argumentation may be warranted in domestic cases, it is doubtful whether it is an appropriate form of legal reasoning in the

---

51 Hancock (1961) p. 367, distinguishing between the classificatory, the functional and the result-selective approach to the choice of law problem.
52 Brilmayer (1980) p. 400.
53 Schoordijk (1972) p. 13, note 3: "Indeed: the result, and nothing but the result must count. From various interpretative techniques, the jurist chooses the one that leads to a socially desirable result ... The choice is determined by the goal the interpreter wishes to achieve."

informative stages of policy-oriented choice of law, particularly when the focus of investigation is on foreign law. Interest identification is a preliminary step in the process of conflicts resolution, to be repeated as many times as there are possibly concerned jurisdictions. It is meant to reduce the circle of involved states to those which can claim an *actual* interest in the application of their laws. In that respect, its function is informative rather than decisive. The value of information depends on its reliability: the more it is distorted or falsified, the less informative value it has. It follows that the preliminary steps in policy-oriented choice of law should be performed as objectively as possible, without preconceived ideas on the result of the instant investigation, or on the final outcome of the case. Teleological interpretation colors the plain meaning of the rule in question, it distorts its underlying policy, and it alters the policy's spatial dimensions. The only purpose it serves is judicial self-delusion. When result-selective considerations enter into the search for actual legislative intent, the process of interest identification is likely to be dominated by fictions: it is not the actual policy or the actual interest that counts, but the constructive policy and the constructive interest. Actual policies and interests are unknown and therefore irrelevant; relevant is what the court decides to be relevant, the policy or interest that conforms to the court's perception of what *ought* to be a relevant policy or an actual interest. There is nothing wrong with constructive interest identification, except that it robs interest analysis, hence policy-oriented choice of law in general, from its vaunted methodological integrity. In its claim to provide a rational framework for the choice of law process lies the greatest ambiguity of this approach. Due to the lack of objective criteria for interest identification, I submit, interest analysis can never be the "rational" choice of law method it aspires to be.

There is hardly any point in discussing the last stage of policy-oriented choice of law, the resolution of the conflict that was not found to be false. True conflicts must be a residuary category of cases in which the courts have not been able to reduce the competing interests to less than two. In the unprovided-for case, on the other hand, the reduction must have gone too far: the conclusion that none of the jurisdictions involved has an actual interest in the application of its law, we know now, depends on a (too?) narrow interpretation of their policies, which only underscores the ambiguity of interest determination.[54] In

---

54 *Supra* chapter 4, section 3, text accompanying notes 108–111.

either case, the solution is problematic. A true conflict is a Gordian knot, almost by definition.[55] As we have seen, it could be cut in various ways. Currie would apply forum law for want of a higher decisional standard than the one preferred at state level. Others would resort to territorial criteria, such as the place of wrong for true conflicts in torts. Another solution, particularly for the unprovided-for case, turns to the common or basic policies of the relevant field of law, which would compel a plaintiff-favoring decision in tort cases. Whatever the theoretical merits of these propositions, they are clearcut and easy to apply in practice. Ambiguous, on the other hand, is any process that requires a comparison of competing interests or conflicting rules of law. Interest-weighing belongs to this category, as well as comparative impairment analysis, its more structured equivalent; so does the better law approach. Here, result-selective arguments are bound to predominate, but since the rule-selecting process is now beyond its informative stages, in fact beyond the stages of interest analysis as such, there is less reason to object to the ambiguity inherent in this ultimate choice. Verification of foreign policies and interests presupposes evenhandedness and detachment, but once the forum has ascertained that more than one jurisdiction lays claim to application of its law, the stage of investigation is over and normative considerations come into play. The case must now be decided, so the tie must be broken. Since interest analysis does not furnish a normative approach to the true conflict conundrum, a result-selective solution would seem to be as valid as any predetermined "break device."

True conflict solutions reveal various biases which have no place in orthodox interest analysis. Yet, it is more than likely that they have influenced the previous stages of policy-oriented choice of law all the same. One of them is the ubiquitous forum bias, the court's "natural" predilection for its own law. Although Currie favored application of forum law as a solution to true conflicts, he did not condone forum bias at the stage of policy assessment and interest identification. On the contrary, his concept of moderate and restrained interpretation was a direct answer to the possibility that "in the short run, without considering how other states or higher authority might react, the state would

---

55 Strikwerda (1978) p. 193: "I incline to the view that, on principle, true conflicts are irresolvable, that they are not amenable to a normative solution."

... be doing all it could to maximize its own interests."[56] Nevertheless, judicial practice betrays a distinct "homeward trend" under any of the approaches discussed in Part Two of this book, culminating in an undisguised forum preference in Kentucky and Michigan. Interest analysis is no exception: what should be an objective verification of a rule's possible claim to application is bound to be colored by the same forum bias that affects true conflict resolution. Many of the decisions in which a potential true conflict or unprovided-for case was "construed away" were probably motivated more by a desire to apply forum law than by conscientious interest evaluation. In this perspective, the better law factor appears to be just a different aspect of forum bias rather than an autonomous choice-influencing consideration. While it is used occasionally to support application of foreign law, in which case it might camouflage a bias of a different kind, it is generally invoked to justify the choice of *lex fori*. Where the better law argument is mentioned explicitly, it is used as a normative factor, but in Leflar's catalogue of choice-influencing considerations it serves to explain the fact that the courts "will normally prefer the law that makes good sense when applied to the facts."[57] If Leflar is right, such better law notions must influence the courts not just when they are about to resolve true conflicts, but, subliminally perhaps, at every stage of the choice of law process, regardless of the method applied.

Other questionable but unmistakable choice-influencing factors, at least in the case law involving multistate torts, are the "pro-recovery" and the "pro-resident" biases. A general plaintiff-protective sentiment seems to have inspired the motivation of many policy-oriented decisions in the area of torts. Not surprisingly, this particular bias usually coincides with forum policy, but the exceptions suggest that the forum's *favor laesi* cannot just be assimilated with the homeward trend. The same applies to the "pro-resident" bias which may induce

---

56 Currie (1963-1) p. 89; p. 616 ff. See also: *id.* (1963-2) p. 757. On moderate and restrained interpretation, see *supra* chapter 4, section 4, text accompanying notes 152–159, 211–213 and note 271.
57 Leflar (1977-1) p. 214. In this respect, the better law consideration promotes judicial honesty: "Our experience tells us that it was better for the courts to reach the results they have reached, choosing the better law by means of the manipulative devices they employ, than for them to disregard superiority in rules of law altogether. It would be worse for them to make mere mechanical choices of governing law, or to follow any other system that disregards proper choice-influencing considerations. But honesty is the best policy, even in judicial opinions." *Ibid.* p. 215.

the court to choose whatever law is favorable to forum residents, whether plaintiff or defendant.[58] In view of the opportunities for forum-shopping, a resident plaintiff will probably benefit from all three biases at once. On the other hand, a resident defendant has a fair chance to prevail against a foreign plaintiff: a pro-resident bias, possibly in combination with forum preference, easily outweighs the interests of all other jurisdictions concerned.

The theory of policy-oriented choice of law has no room for such biases. Forum preference may determine the solution of insoluble conflicts, but it is not acknowledged as a normative factor in the process of interest identification. The pro-recovery and pro-resident biases may be implicit in a calculus of interests in which policies are viewed as domiciliary-oriented,[59] but in view of the theory's *ad hoc* character, such generalizations have no normative value. At any rate, the proponents of interest analysis have never advocated a return to statutist classification. Their theory rejects both *a priori* principles and slanted choice-influencing considerations such as a preference for forum residents, a sympathy for tort victims or a predilection for the better (forum) law. On principle, interest analysis is an objective, unbiased approach to a potential conflict of interests. In practice, however, it proves to be a highly result-selective technique, providing excellent camouflage for all kinds of biases. The friction between the theory's aspiration for realistic policy assessment and the result-selective tendencies inherent in the adjudicatory process engenders a quasi-objective style of reasoning which is no less deceptive than that of the much-criticized decisions of Bealian description.

Due to its discretionary character, policy-oriented choice of law affords ample opportunity for the courts to motivate any result they

58 *Cf.* chapter 4, section 3, text accompanying notes 92–100.
59 *Cf.* Brilmayer (1980) p. 398, asserting that interest analysis implies all three biases, including forum bias, at once: "The pro-resident bias results from the assumption that protective and compensatory policies of the forum can be invoked only by forum residents. Residents thus have the best of two worlds: they can claim the benefits of these policies in multistate cases without incurring the corresponding costs. The pro-recovery and pro-forum biases stem from the assumption that when a statute embodies several policies, any one of them may trigger the finding of an 'interest.' Thus, a forum statute that embodies regulatory and compensatory policies gives rise to a governmental interest if the plaintiff is a resident of the forum or if the offensive conduct occurred there."

deem appropriate in the circumstances of each individual case. No rule compels them to explain why an exception is justified. No principle restrains their predisposition to forum standards. No doctrine confirms or denies the soundness of their judicial intuition. Instead, they are supposed to divine legislative intent, to estimate policies, and to speculate about interests, which is difficult enough in respect of forum law but next to impossible when the content of an unfamiliar foreign rule is the only information to go on. Given so much latitude and so little normative guidance, the courts are bound to resort to the balancing process of discretionary adjudication. It is not surprising, therefore, that the policy-oriented reasoning in judicial opinions is almost invariably colored by the result. Result-selective motives, I submit, explain most of the inconsistencies, ambiguities, and incomprehensibilities encountered in the policy-oriented case law I described in the previous chapters. Virtually any decision in which the choice of law argumentation is dubious, obscure, or specious can be interpreted as a result of a weighing process in which many other factors than just governmental interests are balanced. Apart from the various biases mentioned before, all sorts of imponderables may influence the court's "subconscious" motivation. They could range from dedication to justice to a concern for certainty and predictability, from the recognition of justified expectations to a sense of judicial efficiency. If all these factors, and more, have an impact on the adjudication of domestic cases, surely they will have some impact on the choice of law process as well. To a large extent, these values are the same as Yntema's "choice of law objectives", the "policy factors" of Cheatham and Reese, Leflar's "choice-influencing considerations" and the "choice of law principles" listed in § 6 of the Restatement Second. While these catalogues give adequate descriptions of the major choice-influencing factors, which may give us an insight into the process of choice of law adjudication, they do not provide normative criteria for conflicts resolution. Rather, they summarize the points of departure of a viable system of choice of law rules and principles.

The interest-oriented approach to choice of law offers a methodical framework which does not support normative criteria. Its guidelines are nothing but methodical instructions. Meant to describe the objectives and procedures of the method as such, they determine the object of inquiry and delineate the various stages of investigation, but they provide no standards by which the courts can gauge their actual findings. The theory of interest analysis has nothing to offer when it comes to appraising policies and verifying interests in the individual case. With its emphasis on *ad hoc* adjudication, it relies on judicial discretion and does not foster the conception of normative principles. Premised on an extremely narrow concept of the choice of law problem, it reduces a conflict of laws to a potential conflict of interests. The presence or absence of a state's interest in the application of its law in view of the circumstances of the individual case is the only choice-influencing factor it recognizes. In combination, this inherent disregard for system values and the lack of normative criteria preclude the development of rules or principles in which all values that affect the choice of law process, not just interests, can be harbored and coordinated. Although the interest-based approach to choice of law discounts most of these values, its methodical latitude enables the courts to couch any choice-influencing consideration in the required language of policies and interests. Such adaptability might help the method to survive, but, at the same time, it demonstrates the irremediable flaws of the policy-oriented choice of law.

Conclusion

"... until someone comes along with a better idea."[60]

There is no happy end to this book. When I set out to explore the results of policy-oriented choice of law adjudication, I did expect to discover some discrepancies between theory and practice. Since no method can be perfect, there were bound to be drawbacks, occasional weak spots, and incidental snags in its operation. I was anxious to find them, analyze them and, hopefully, come up with suggestions for curing them. To me, interest analysis presented an attractive and convincing choice of law theory which deserved to be promoted as a valid alternative to the obsolete allocation method, since it accommodated contemporary views on the function of law and did away with the factitious approach to the choice of law problem that characterized both Beale's Restatement and Europe's Savignian conflicts law. In the course of my research, I gradually realized that the weaknesses of policy-oriented choice of law are incurable *per se*. Since its basic approach is premised on the assumption that a substantive rule's spatial reach can be inferred from its policy, which implies that legislative intent can be ascertained unequivocally, the method loses its *raison d'être* if such assumptions prove to be invalid. Any conceivable remedy for this inherent flaw strikes right at the heart of the method's underlying philosophy. Any predetermined criterion by which the process of interest identification could be structured would defeat the characteristic flexibility of this *ad hoc* approach. Since normative adaptations would distort the policy-oriented approach to choice of law beyond recognition, they must be considered unacceptable.

---

60 Currie (1963-3) p. 1242, referring to the problem of the disinterested forum. Obviously, any improvement of the choice of law process depends on someone's "better idea."

Unfortunately, I am well aware that I am not that "someone with a better idea" to whom Currie would defer. I can neither think of a plausible way to improve the operation of interest-oriented choice of law, nor can I come up with a feasible alternative. However, I feel compelled to offset the negative conclusions of this book by making a few positive suggestions. They are inspired by a reappraisal of the methodological options we have. On the one hand, there are the variants of policy-oriented choice of law, ranging from interest analysis to the "Leflar approach", and from the compromise of Restatement Second to the *lex fori* presumption in Kentucky and Michigan. On the other hand, there is the common core of traditional jurisdiction-selection, still prevalent in Europe, but shifting towards a less internationalistic, more result-oriented conception of the objectives of conflicts law. The adoption of (semi-)open conflicts rules, the formulation of functional allocation criteria, and the cautious acceptance of the doctrine of priority rules have achieved a transition in European conflicts law from blind jurisdiction-selection to a more subtle form of choice of law. There is room for other considerations than those pertaining to predictability and uniformity of result, and the need for escape devices is gradually disappearing. Surprisingly, contemporary European conflicts law seems to be less conducive to manipulation than its modern American counterpart, which suffers from a discrepancy between its single-minded concentration on policies and the excessive flexibility it allows in the actual process of policy identification. I do not doubt that, under either approach, the choice can generally be justified in terms of result. In the majority of cases, I submit, the forum's application of a policy-oriented approach would lead to results which will generally correspond with those produced by way of the "refurbished" allocation method. If it is the substantive result that counts, I am reasonably sure that the courts will be able to find a way to achieve it, regardless of the dictates of the choice of law approach they employ. However, it was not the actual outcome of a case I was interested in when testing the quality of policy-oriented choice of law adjudication, but the methodological consistency of the court's argumentation. On that score I am left unconvinced and disappointed.

To the extent that interest analysis is the quintessence of the new American approaches, none of them escapes the charge of being ambiguous and therefore open to manipulation, with the possible exception of the *lex fori* approach. Stripped from its reference to the policies and interests of § 6, the Restatement Second has little more to offer than a series of semi-open conflicts rules and a few rather vague choice-influencing considerations. In that respect, the most significant relationship approach comes close to the modern European ideas on allocation, allowing for atypical circumstances and no longer totally blind to the substantive law factor. The "Leflar approach" is likely to be reduced to the choice of the better law when governmental interests are eliminated from the list of choice-influencing considerations, the other ones generally being treated by the courts as auxiliary factors, if not completely ignored. I have rejected the better law consideration for being an unprincipled means of conflicts resolution, even in true conflict situations. If it were to be used as an overriding choice of law criterion, it would become a license for undisguised *Kadi-Justiz*, and that is why it should be rejected out of hand. The *lex fori* presumption, supported by the highest courts in Kentucky and Michigan and implicitly endorsed by the U.S. Supreme Court in *Allstate v. Hague*, is hardly based on policy-oriented notions, unless one of the "sufficient reasons" for displacing forum law would be the absence of a forum interest *vis-à-vis* another state's obvious interest in the application of its law. Since it is as yet unclear under what circumstances Kentucky or Michigan courts would be willing to relinquish their forum preference, the relevance of policies and interests is dubious. Taken at face value, the "sufficient enough (forum) contacts" approach in Kentucky and the "sufficient reason" standard in Michigan suffer from a different kind of ambiguity than the one for which I have blamed the other branches of modern American choice of law methodology. Here, it is not the method which is open to question – in fact, there *is* no method, let alone theoretical justification for this approach – but the normative pretensions of the solution itself. I object against the arbitrariness of a choice of law criterion by which the relevance of foreign law is measured against an indeterminate "sufficiency" factor. There may be several good reasons to postulate the *prima facie* applicability of forum law, particularly as a solution to true conflicts, but an inarticulate forum bias is not good enough for me.

To someone who firmly believed in the methodological validity of "neo-statutism" and considered its approach to choice of law intellectually superior to mechanical jurisdiction-selection, it is hard to admit that, in practice, the two alternatives are equally objectionable. Although the hard-fought battle of the American conflicts revolution has been won by the proponents of the new methodology, their victory has brought a new kind of conceptualism which is no less "metaphysical" than that of nineteenth century conflicts law.[61] As a methodological point of departure, the myth of legislative intent matches the myth of the seat of the legal relationship in conceptual deceptiveness. The seat of a legal relationship is a metaphor which is capable of expressing the main principle of any allocation philosophy, whether it supports a mechanical, functional or result-selective approach to jurisdiction-selection. It says nothing about the criteria to be used in the allocation process, which implies that the seat of the legal relationship can be determined according to the choice of law objectives presently prevailing in the forum state. The tenet of legislative intent could also be seen as a symbol, expressing the notion that the process of rule-selection is governed by unspecified normative values which the courts should try to couch in policy-oriented criteria. Such a development would gradually enable the courts to identify policies and interests by predetermined standards, along the lines of Cavers' principles of preference, or by way of a classification of substantive rules according to their function. Thus, the concept of "legislative intent" could be explained as the point of departure of policy-oriented choice of law: it would be no more than an abstract methodological principle from which all of the actual rule-selecting criteria are to be derived. Obviously, such abstractions would totally transform the characteristic pragmatism of the approach. They would bring back the very conceptualism against which the champions of the new approaches revolted. The net result of all their fervor would be the emergence of an "enlightened" allocation method, not unlike the one that has emerged, without much strife, in contemporary European conflicts law.

Looking back on the developments in American and European conflicts law during the last twenty-five years, I am inclined to put more faith in the future of the allocation method than in that of policy-oriented choice of law. To be sure, many objections can be raised against the principle of jurisdiction-selection; I have raised them myself often enough. The allocation method is not nearly the ideal solu-

---

61 Brilmayer (1980) p. 392: "Interest analysis merely substitutes one set of metaphysical premises for another, leaving the body of conflicts law with a remedy every bit as distressing as the disease it was designed to cure." *Ibid.* p. 430.

tion to the choice of law dilemma. But then, neither is interest analysis, or any of the other interest-based approaches practiced in America. Even those who firmly believe in the viability of policy-oriented choice of law will have to admit that the caliber of its actual performance is a far cry from the cogency of its theory. If I have learned anything from my surveys of American case law, regardless of the choice of law technique, it is not to expect methodological consistency or strict argumentation. On the other hand, I was never very impressed with the potency of European conflicts reasoning, inasmuch as it relied on an arsenal of result-selective escape devices. While my dissatisfaction with either approach may suggest a censorious attitude, I have actually resigned myself to the inadequacy of any choice of law method, realizing that a conflicts problem is not amenable to a normative solution which does justice to all of the domestic and foreign interests involved. In that perspective, any choice of law decision is likely to be a compromise between conflicting values, effected according to the guidelines of the forum's conflicts law. To facilitate the framing of such a compromise, conflicts theory should not only blueprint a plausible *modus operandi*, but it should also provide the courts with workable standards. Clearly, when it comes to practical guidelines, the allocation theory has much more to offer than just a few methodological pointers or a list of choice-influencing considerations. In that respect, it is attuned to the conceptualistic legal tradition of continental Europe, just as the nature of policy-oriented choice of law process suits the tradition of Anglo-American jurisprudence.

Much as I have thought about it, I cannot come up with any "better idea" than the suggestion that, on both sides of the Atlantic, we stick to our own inadequate methods and try to make them perform as adequately as possible. As far as European conflicts law is concerned the blind allocation method has been transformed over the past decades into a serviceable approach to choice of law. Based on a theoretical framework which is much more ambivalent and eclectic than that of the American methodology, its rules and doctrines have been changed, molded and adapted to fit the needs of the mobile community of today's world. The result is a patchwork of methodological odds and ends, which may lack the theoretical credibility of a brand-new conception, but has the advantage of being a tried and true working method. As we have seen in chapter 1, the "refurbished" allocation method no longer relies exclusively on the hard and fast conflicts rules which used to preclude an appropriate choice in exceptional cases. The heyday of blind jurisdiction-selection and its quasi-dogmatic trickery seems definitely over. The problem of *characterization* hardly arouses academic interest anymore, since there is a reasonable consensus on the doctrine's points of departure and most of the actual problems have been settled by precedent. Occasionally, a new kind of issue may give rise to the question of its classification, but, on the whole, the doctrine appears to be beyond controversy. The *renvoi* problem is another subject to which little attention is paid in modern conflicts literature. Since contemporary European conflicts theory is shifting towards the view that international uniformity of result is not the only objective of the choice of law process, the doctrine of renvoi has lost much of its theoretical value and conceptual attraction. *Public policy*, finally, is still a fixture of European choice of law theory, but its practical import seems to be lessening. In the Netherlands, at least, it is a rare case in which it is mentioned at all, let alone deployed as a shield against obnoxious foreign law.

Not much is left, at present, of the dubious function these doctrines performed as choice of law correctives. The advent of a more flexible approach to allocation has largely obviated the need for such escape devices. Modern European conflicts law not only supports the formulation of sensible conflicts rules, but it also leaves the courts sufficient leeway to achieve sensible choice of law results by allowing departures from the norm in atypical cases. The difference between the traditional escape devices and the new kinds of expedients is the straightforwardness of the latter. Specifically conceived to prevent or redress the inappropriate results of abstract allocation, they promote a forthright line of reasoning and clarity of argumentation, doing away with the need for doctrinal camouflage of result-selective allocation. By themselves and in combination, the new features of the allocation method have helped to improve its performance considerably, enhancing its credibility and the justification of its results. The *semi-open conflicts rule*, which evolved from the proposition that allocation should be based on an *ad hoc* center of gravity test, is a compromise between the flexibility of the "proper law" theory and the *a priori* character of a "rules approach". Providing an escape from the rigidity of abstract allocation whenever the actual circumstances indicate a closer connection with another jurisdiction, such a rule may tempt the courts to weigh contacts according to other criteria than that of their factual relevance. In that respect, semi-open conflicts rules can be used in a result-selective way, which tends to reduce their normative value. On the other hand, they also express a presumption of the closest connection which cannot simply be ignored. Therefore, any rejection of the presumptive *lex causae* in favor of another jurisdiction's law will have to be justified, and that will surely compel the courts to reconsider their motives. In my opinion, the semi-open conflicts rule is an improvement on the abstract formula that dominated conflicts law in the first half of this century. Depending on the quality of its predetermined connecting factor, it could be an efficient means of choosing the law most suitable to govern the individual case.

Favor concepts and the doctrine of priority rules have little in common except their result-selective orientation. A *favor*-based conflicts rule is designed to bring about a predetermined material result, whether the validation of a transaction, the dissolution of a marriage, or the recognition of an illegitimate child. While such rules technically conform to the allocation principle, they usually embody some substantive policy of the forum state,[62] and in that respect they are of a quite different caliber than that of "ordinary" conflicts rules. *Favor*-inspired allocation could be particularly useful in those areas in which the forum's social values carry sufficient weight to take precedence over other choice of law considerations. However, this form of jurisdiction-selection might be subject to an objection similar to the one against the better law consideration in American conflicts practice. It is based on an evaluation of the quality of the eligible law according to standards prevailing in the forum state. In effect, *favor*-based allocation supports a predetermined forum bias, just as the better law consideration sanctions an *ad hoc* preference for forum law. In "*favor*-susceptible" areas, an undisguised *lex fori* approach would generally achieve the same objectives in a more direct and therefore more efficient way.[63] The *doctrine of priority rules* is premised on the same methodological principles as the ones underlying policy-oriented choice of law, and is geared, basically, to the same objectives. Its bilateral variant comes close to interest analysis, in that it presupposes the feasibility of un-

---

62 *Favor* concepts which owe their existence to the "need to reconcile the ideal of international harmony with the reality of discordant legal systems," *supra* chapter 1, section 3, text accompanying notes 141–144, are of a different order, as they have their origin in the policies of conflicts law itself, not in those of substantive law.
63 *Cf.* Strikwerda (1986) p. 26; Kotting (1985) p. 1346.

equivocal policy identification, regardless of the origin of the rule at issue. In that respect, the doctrine of priority rules suffers from the same ambiguities that taint its American counterpart. In modern European conflicts practice, the doctrine has a very limited effect. It is generally reserved for situations turning on the applicability of the forum's (semi-)public law, whereas foreign law and most rules of private law remain subject to the ordinary allocation process. Thus, a methodological dichotomy is introduced into the choice of law process, which has given rise to the question whether a substantive rule does or does not qualify as a potential priority rule. This new type of characterization problem, which adds to the inherent ambiguity of the doctrine, could largely be evaded by restricting its ambit to the realm of (semi-)public law. The exclusion of private law would facilitate the choice of method, thereby furthering the clarity of conflicts adjudication.

To some extent, *functional allocation* could be viewed as an abstract form of policy-oriented choice of law. It could be argued that a functional conflicts rule is based on an *a priori* calculus of interests. In that perspective, its connecting factor stands for the presumption that the jurisdiction to which it refers has a claim to application of its law. The conflicts rule for maintenance obligations, for instance, turning on the domicile of the creditor, could thus be explained as a short-hand expression of predetermined interest evaluation: the creditor's home state is presumed to be concerned with the maintenance of its domiciliaries; even if another state would have a competing interest – in protecting the debtor, for instance – that interest must yield. I am the first to admit that this translation of functional allocation in terms of interest analysis is questionable. I do believe that, in the turmoil of interest-based *ad hoc* decisions, some "policy-oriented conflicts rules" might crystallize.[64] However, such rules, contrary to those used in

---

[64] The Dutch decisions pertaining to the *Buitengewoon Besluit Arbeidsverhoudingen*, *supra* chapter 1, section 5, text accompanying notes 212–214, may serve as an example. For years now, the Dutch courts have resolved these cases according to the interest-oriented doctrine of priority rules, ascertaining in each individual case whether the Netherlands had an interest in the application of its law. From this body of case law, the following unilateral conflicts rule could be derived: the question whether an employee may be dismissed without an official license is governed by the *B.B.A.* whenever the employee is likely to fall back on the Dutch job market, which is generally the case when he is domiciled in the Netherlands. *Cf.* Van Maanen (1981) p. 796, p. 813.

functional allocation, are bound to be unilateral, because they are based on forum policy and geared to that policy's spatial reach. Furthermore, functional allocation is a variant of jurisdiction-selection, therefore hardly on a par with the rule-selecting process of interest analysis. Its predetermined criteria preclude an *ad hoc* interest evaluation and may refer to a foreign law which, because of its contrary policy, does not claim application at all. Nevertheless, a functional conflicts rule does express an allocation philosophy which has come a long way from the fact-oriented "closest connection" approach. Its connecting factor could be seen as the key to a normative interest identification and evaluation: it determines which state *ought* to have an interest in the matter, and, at the same time, ignores all other possibly interested jurisdictions because the designated state's interest *ought* to be superior. Thus viewed, functional allocation is a form of policy-oriented jurisdiction-selection. It performs best in situations in which the substantive policies of the involved jurisdictions are basically the same, but their statutory expressions differ. It is doomed to fail, obviously, whenever it points to the law of a jurisdiction whose policy is radically different from the one on which the functional conflicts rule is premised. In my opinion, functional allocation is both a sensible and a practicable approach to the choice of law problem in those areas in which there is a certain degree of international, interstate, or interregional consensus on the basic policy underlying a particular field of substantive law. Laid down in a semi-open conflicts rule, the principle of functional allocation could be excepted in all situations in which application of another law is more appropriate. This would be the case, in particular, if a foreign *lex causae* embodies a substantive policy which is the reverse of the one from which the functional connecting factor has been derived. Functional allocation is by no means the only answer to the choice of law dilemma, nor is it necessarily the best. Yet, judged by its actual performance in European conflicts law, it would seem to be as valid as most other solutions discussed in this book, and definitely more convenient to use.

Having expounded my views on modern conflicts methodology by constant reference to multistate tort adjudication, I could not very well bring this book to a close without offering a suggestion on tort choice of law "beyond *lex loci delicti.*" Since there is hardly a decision I did not criticize for methodological shortcomings, I feel obliged to come up with an alternative solution which will hold out against at least some of the objections I have raised. For the benefit of the courts whose efforts I disparaged, and for the diversion of conflicts scholars whose theories I attacked, let me venture the following proposition. Considering what I wrote in the previous chapter and in the preceding paragraphs, I opt for a "rules approach". I have no faith in *ad hoc* adjudication, whatever the methodological structure on which the decision may be based. Thus, the allocation method will have to be my frame of reference. I reject *lex loci delicti* as a general rule because I fail to see what bearing the place of wrong could have on either the localization of the "seat" of a tort, the expectations of the parties, or the interest of the *locus* state, to name just a few choice-influencing factors. It is a territorial connecting factor which, at best, is supported by the notion that a potential tort-feasor subjects himself to local standards wherever he goes. In that respect, the *locus* criterion is premised on an admonitory rationale. The suggestion that deterrence is at least one of the major purposes of the substantive law of torts is still popular in the United States, as attested by many statements to that effect in the context of policy-oriented case law. Yet, in view of the social reality of the present day, this notion no longer holds true. The predominant function of modern tort law, most writers agree,[65] pertains to compensation or loss distribution, and if anything is left of the deterrence factor that once inhered in this civil offshoot from criminal law, it is in the premium rates we have to pay our liability insurer.[66] As a fact-oriented allocation criterion, the *locus delicti* is not very convincing either. If it is premised on the idea that multistate torts are likely to be most closely connected to the jurisdiction in which they occurred, judicial practice tends to contradict the validity of such a presumption. There are too many cases in which the tort occurred in a jurisdiction with which neither party had any connection, to relegate

65 F.H. Lawson/B.S. Markezinis, *Tortious Liability for Unintentional Harm in the Common Law and the Civil Law*, vol. I, Cambridge, 1982, p. 181: " . . . it is true to say that most writers in most countries nowadays accept that the prime purpose of the law of tort is the compensation of the injured plaintiff and that the admonitory function in the law of delict is attenuated, if not actually left to the criminal law." See also: Williams G. (1951), p. 144 ff. and *passim*; Hein Kötz, *Sozialer Wandel im Unfallrecht*, Karlsruhe/Heidelberg, 1976, p. 28 ff.; *id.*, *Deliktsrecht, Eine Einführung*, 2d. ed., Frankfurt a/M., 1979, p. 33 ff.; Bernd von Hoffmann, Behutsame Auflockerung der Tatortregel, *IPRax* 1986, p. 90.
66 *Cf.* P.S. Atiyah, *Accidents, Compensation and the Law*, 3d ed., London, 1980, p. 604: "Insurance operates as a method of distributing losses, and the varying premium rates operate as a form of general deterrence."

this type of situation to the category of atypical law-fact patterns. Since most multistate tort actions arise from traffic accidents – whether on the road, at sea, or in the air– it is not surprising that many judicial opinions refer to the place of wrong as a "fortuitous" factor.

I would prefer, therefore, a different connecting factor. Since there seems to be widespread consensus on the general function of the law of torts, functional allocation would appear to be a feasible approach. The expansion of tort law into the area of non-criminal behavior, the decreasing importance of fault, even the schemes for loss distribution through national insurance, all indicate that the emphasis of substantive law is on loss rather than wrong-doing, on compensation rather than deterrence, on the tort victim rather than the tort-feasor. As a functional allocation factor for torts, I submit, the domicile of the victim would be a most appropriate standard. Since it is a plaintiff-oriented criterion, it would support many of the actual decisions we encountered. Cases in which both parties are domiciled in the same state would be easily solved, and the results would generally be identical to those achieved by policy-oriented choice of law. On the other hand, since a non-resident plaintiff would not have the benefit of the forum's more generous law, functional allocation would not reward "resourceful forum-shopping", and in that respect its results would be different from quite a number of cases I discussed. In my opinion, there is no compelling reason why a tort victim in a multistate situation should be entitled to a "choice of law windfall", which the victim in a domestic case will never have. Application of the victim's domiciliary law would put both categories in the same position. To me, that is an advantage; others might consider it a valid reason to object.[67] At the risk of giving the impression that I am prejudiced against tort victims, I admit to being worried about the position of the tort-feasor in one particular situation: to him, application of the law of the victim's domicile might be unfair in case the victim is domiciled in a state which imposes a higher standard of financial protection than the state where defendant acted and has his home. I would be unpleasantly surprised, to say the least, if I were held to American standards of liability in case I had injured an American tourist in my home town Amsterdam. In that situation, an exception might be warranted, perhaps on account of the close connection principle, perhaps on account of the parties'

---

67 *Cf.* D. Kokkini–Iatridou, Book Review [De Boer (1982)], *NJB* 1983, p. 838.

expectations, perhaps on account of a predominant interest of defendant's home state. Therefore, I would append a proper law exception to my functional conflicts rule, to leave room for a judicious choice of law in special situations.

Much more could be said about the alternatives to *lex loci delicti*,[68] but I think I have said enough about that subject for the present. Throughout this book, my ruminations on tort choice of law were meant to demonstrate the nature, the operation and the viability of various policy-oriented choice of law approaches. Focusing on tort decisions, I wanted to submit the methodological validity of policy-oriented choice of law to the test of practice, not to discover an ideal solution to multistate torts. As I see it, I have accomplished what I set out to do. I have studied the new methodology, analyzed its results, appraised its performance, and measured its worth. In the end, unfortunately, I found it wanting, and that is all I had to know. To be sure, for a long time I kept secretly hoping that the philosopher's stone of conflicts methodology would be hidden somewhere in the multitude of policy-oriented cases I examined, and that everybody else had just missed its being there. Gradually, it dawned on me that I would never find it, and that no one ever will. It is in the nature of conflicts law that its solutions will always be found wanting. Since choice of law is ultimately a choice between the values, concerns, or interests embodied in the respective laws of the jurisdictions involved, concessions must be made to accommodate their differences. Any method of conflicts resolution, therefore, represents a way to justify the reductions each choice of law entails. The arguments may vary, and the motives may change, but as long as the international community comprises dissimilar legal systems, choice of law will have to make do with a methodology which is bound to rely on reduction and compromise. Until, of course, someone comes along with a better idea.

---

68 I did so in an earlier and more elaborate attempt at formulating conflicts rules for torts: De Boer (1982).

Summary

In most countries in the world today, the traditional *lex loci delicti* rule still determines which law applies to multistate torts. As a typical precept of the neutral allocation method, on which most systems of private international law rely, the rule blindly selects the applicable law by reference to the place of wrong, irrespective of the interests of the parties, or the policies underlying the tort laws of the jurisdictions involved. Since the 1950's, this approach has been subject to mounting criticism both in Europe and in the United States, and various methodological alternatives have been proposed. In the United States, a variety of radically new choice of law approaches has gained academic and judicial support. Their common denominator is *interest analysis*, a technique which calls for the identification and evaluation of the interests each of the jurisdictions involved may have in the application of its law. In Europe, these policy-oriented approaches, which are now being practiced in some form or another in a majority of American jurisdictions, have stirred much controversy among academic writers. Most of the criticism pertains to the difficulties inherent in any approach purporting to derive the spatial reach of a rule from its underlying policy. In this book, the validity of these objections is measured against the results the American courts have achieved thus far in applying the new approaches to multistate torts.

PART ONE focuses on the role of substantive law in the traditional choice of law process. Despite its postulated neutrality, the allocation method has been adapted in various ways to bridge the gap between its 19th century premises and contemporary ideas on the function and objectives of the law. In Europe, these adaptations have resulted in an ambivalent approach to choice of law, encompassing the determination of the "proper law" and "functional" allocation, as well as *favor* considerations and priority to so-called "rules of immediate application". These methodological features of modern European conflicts law are the subject of CHAPTER 1. Within the confines of the allocation method, several doctrines of traditional conflicts law, originally meant to solve some of the "pervasive problems" of conflicts law, have been used as manipulative devices to achieve justice in the individual case.

The question whether policy-oriented choice of law still has a need for these doctrines is considered in CHAPTER 2.

In PART TWO, the practical results of the American "conflicts revolution" are described. An analysis of multistate tort cases, chosen from various jurisdictions and grouped according to methodological characteristics, indicates that the modern approaches are no less conducive to result-selective manipulation than the traditional method. The "most significant relationship" test of the Restatement Second of Conflict of Laws is discussed in CHAPTER 3. CHAPTER 4, covering interests analysis, is divided into sections on no-conflicts, false conflicts, unprovided-for cases, and true conflicts, the latter category being subdivided according to the various attempts to solve the true conflict dilemma. In CHAPTER 5, judicial support for Robert Leflar's pragmatic choice-influencing considerations is surveyed, with some emphasis on the controversial better law consideration. Since New York was the first state to abandon the lex loci delicti rule, in 1963, CHAPTER 6 is devoted to the unhappy development of New York tort choice of law since then. Finally, the unabashed preference for forum law, marking judicial practice in Kentucky and Michigan, is discussed in CHAPTER 7.

In PART THREE, the viability of policy-oriented choice of law is evaluated. By way of example, special attention is given to one area in which the American courts have gained most of their experience with the new methodology: the adjudication of multistate guest statute controversies, examined in CHAPTER 8. While both the issue in these cases and the contents of a guest statute are relatively easy to determine, the choice of law conclusions reached by various courts in comparable situations are highly incompatible. The analysis of guest statute cases confirms the tentative conclusions of Part Two: since the policies of the substantive law of torts support various interpretations, the question whether the policy of a rule warrants its application to the case at issue cannot be answered unequivocally. While on the whole theoretically sound, the new approaches fail in their aspiration to provide standards which are both objective and practicable. As explained in CHAPTER 9, this implies that policy-oriented choice of law supports decisions which, in reality, are based on unarticulated notions of justice in the individual case. Compared with the "refurbished" allocation method, it has too many drawbacks to be adopted in Europe as a feasible methodological alternative. In the CON

CLUSION, the development of contemporary European conflicts law is set against the metamorphosis of its American counterpart. Undoubtedly, the American reform has greatly contributed to the European rediscovery of the interrelation of conflicts law and substantive law, resulting in the conception of a new type of conflicts rule in which the connecting factor is derived from the function of substantive law. Also, a more relaxed approach to allocation by way of "semi-open conflicts rules" and the judicious use of the doctrine of "priority rules" are apt to achieve substantially the same results that the American experiments "beyond lex loci delicti" have accomplished by a much more speculative and laborious process.

Samenvatting

Voorbij Lex Loci Delicti

Over methoden van internationaal privaatrecht en de rechtsvinding inzake de internationale onrechtmatige daad in de Verenigde Staten

Op vrijdag 16 september 1960 vond in de Canadese provincie Ontario een verkeersongeluk plaats dat grote gevolgen zou blijken te hebben voor de ontwikkeling van het internationaal privaatrecht in de Verenigde Staten en elders. Op die dag reden Mr. en Mrs. Jackson, in gezelschap van hun vriendin Miss Georgia Babcock, vanuit hun woonplaats Rochester (New York) naar Canada, alwaar zij gezamenlijk het weekend zouden doorbrengen. Rijdend in Ontario verloor Mr. Jackson de macht over het stuur, en botste tegen een muur. Bij dit ongeval raakte Miss Babcock ernstig gewond. Terug in haar woonplaats stelde zij Mr. Jackson als bestuurder aansprakelijk voor de financiële gevolgen van het ongeluk. De hoofdvraag in deze beroemd geworden actie uit onrechtmatige daad betrof het verschil tussen het recht van de provincie Ontario en dat van de staat New York: naar het recht van Ontario, dat een zgn. *guest statute* kende, had een gratis meerijdende passagier geen aanspraak op schadevergoeding, terwijl het New Yorkse recht geen onderscheid maakte tussen al dan niet betalende slachtoffer-passagiers en beide categorieën een recht op schadevergoeding toekende. Kortom, indien de New Yorkse rechter die dit geval te beoordelen kreeg New Yorks recht toepasselijk achtte, zou Miss Babcock haar schade volledig vergoed krijgen; zou het recht van Ontario haar vordering beheersen, dan zou de *host*, of diens verzekeraar, niet aansprakelijk gesteld kunnen worden.

De vraag naar het toepasselijke recht is een van de kernvragen waarmee het internationaal privaatrecht (kortweg "i.p.r.", of "conflictenrecht") zich bezighoudt. Hoewel de specifieke i.p.r.-regels van land tot land verschillen, wordt vrijwel overal ter wereld dezelfde methode ter oplossing van dit soort kwesties gehanteerd. Deze zgn. "verwijzingsmethode" berust op de gedachte dat internationale rechtsverhoudingen bij een bepaald rechtsstelsel "thuisgebracht" moeten worden aan de hand van een abstract plaatsbepalend criterium, zoals daar zijn: woonplaats, plaats van vestiging, nationaliteit, plaats van handelen, plaats van ligging e.d. Voor alle categorieën van privaatrechtelijke rechtsverhoudingen zijn dergelijke criteria bedacht en neergelegd in zgn. "verwijzingsregels" of "conflictregels". Dit zijn regels die aangeven welk rechtsstelsel een juridisch probleem van een bepaald type beheerst. Zo werd de vraag naar het op een onrechtmatige daad toepasselijke recht doorgaans beantwoord aan de hand van het criterium "plaats van het ongeluk". De traditionele verwijzingsregel voor deze categorie i.p.r.-problemen luidde dan ook: op een internationale onrechtmatige daad is toepasselijk het recht van het land waar die onrechtmatige daad plaatsvond. Met behulp van het Latijn kan men die regel kort samenvatten in de volgende formule: een onrechtmatige daad (een privaatrechtelijk "delict") wordt beheerst door de *lex loci delicti*. In de procedure *Babcock v. Jackson* zou de New Yorkse rechter derhalve op grond van deze klassieke regel het recht van Ontario moeten toepassen, met als gevolg dat Miss Babcock geen schadevergoeding zou ontvangen. Een groot bezwaar tegen de verwijzingsmethode, zeker op het terrein van de onrechtmatige daad, is de kans op een nogal willekeurige rechtsaanwijzing. Omdat het plaatsbepalend criterium abstract is, kan het verwijzen naar een omstandigheid die in het conrete geval van tamelijk ondergeschikt belang is. Maar ook dan is zo'n feit doorslaggevend voor de aanwijzing van het toe te passen recht. Als het ongeluk in de zaak *Babcock v. Jackson* nog net in New York had plaatsgevonden, en niet in Ontario, was het New Yorkse recht toepasselijk geweest.

De Court of Appeals, de hoogste rechterlijke instantie in de staat New York, ging echter voorbij aan de lex loci delicti-regel en kwam tot een tegengesteld resultaat. Geïnspireerd door de theorieën van een aantal vooruitstrevende Amerikaanse i.p.r.-geleerden, met name Professor Brainerd Currie, volgden de New Yorkse rechters een geheel andere methode ter beantwoording van de vraag naar het toepasselijk recht. Hun redenering luidde niet: "Dit is een internationale onrechtmatige daad, dus onderworpen aan de lex loci delicti-regel, dus beheerst door het recht van de staat waar het ongeval zich voordeed, in casu dus het recht van Ontario", maar zij stelden de geheel nieuwe vraag welke van de bij het ongeluk betrokken staten *belang* zouden kunnen hebben bij toepassing van hun recht. Daartoe werd eerst onderzocht waarom de wetgever van Ontario aan gratis meerijdende passagiers een recht op schadevergoeding had ontzegd. Vervolgens kwam de vraag aan de orde welk motief de New Yorkse wetgever had gehad om aan alle soorten passagiers, gratis meerijdend of niet, een aanspraak op vergoeding toe te kennen wanneer hun tengevolge van de onvoorzichtigheid van de bestuurder schade was overkomen. Uit onderzoek bleek, dat de Canadese bepaling, geldend in de provincie Ontario, was voortgekomen uit de idee dat gratis meerijdende passagiers doorgaans in een zo nauwe relatie tot de bestuurder staan, dat beide partijen wel eens zouden kunnen samenspannen om een hogere uitkering van de verzekeringsmaatschappij van de automobilist in de wacht te slepen dan het bedrag van de werkelijk geleden schade. In New York, daarentegen, was de wetgever meer begaan geweest met de positie van (bonafide) slachtoffers dan met die van de verzekeraar van de dader. De Court of Appeals vroeg zich vervolgens af, of het in dit concrete geval, waarin Mr. Jackson niet in Ontario maar in New York verzekerd was, zinvol zou zijn de *guest statute* van Ontario toe te passen. De conclusie lag voor de hand: omdat het niet bepaald aannemelijk was dat de wetgever van Ontario zich de belangen van New Yorkse verzekeringsmaatschappijen zou hebben aangetrokken, had Ontario geen belang bij toepassing van haar *guest statute* op dit "New Yorkse" geval. Technisch gezegd: er was hier sprake van een *false conflict* waarin slechts één rechtsstelsel, dat van de staat New York, gelding pretendeerde. Derhalve kon die geldingspretentie zonder bezwaar worden gehonoreerd.

In een notedop is met dit voorbeeld de thematiek van dit boek weergegeven. De methode die de New Yorkse Court of Appeals hanteerde is een van de materieelrechtelijk georiënteerde benaderingen van de vraag naar het toepasselijke recht. In de verwijzingsmethode komt de vraag naar de inhoud van het materiële recht (het eigenlijke antwoord op de vraag of Miss Babcock wel of niet schadevergoeding zou ontvangen) pas aan bod *nadat* is vastgesteld welk recht de vordering beheerst. In de materieelrechtelijke methode (*policy-oriented choice of law*), daarentegen, is de beantwoording van deze vraag bepalend voor de keuze van de toe te passen norm: de rechter onderzoekt de inhoud van de om toepassing dingende materiële regels teneinde de strekking van iedere norm en de daaruit af te leiden geldingspretentie te kunnen vaststellen. Deze benadering van wetsconflicten, die gebaseerd is op Currie's theorie van de *governmental interests analysis*, heeft sinds de uitspraak inzake *Babcock v. Jackson*, in 1963, een enorme vlucht genomen in de Verenigde Staten, met name op het terrein van de interstatelijke onrechtmatige daad. De methode is theoretisch bijzonder aantrekkelijk, omdat de keuze van het toepasselijke recht niet "in den blinde" wordt gemaakt op grond van een a priori bepaald en daarom abstract aanknopingspunt ("de" plaats van de onrechtmatige daad), maar door middel van een "rationele analyse" van het belang dat ieder van de betrokken rechtsgemeenschappen heeft (of niet heeft) bij toepassing van hun respectieve rechtsregels op het concrete geval. Het spreekt vanzelf dat deze methode hogere eisen stelt aan de rechtsvinding in het i.p.r., met name ook een gedegen onderzoek vergt naar de inhoud en achtergrond van de in aanmerking komende normen. In dit boek wordt onderzocht in hoeverre de Amerikaanse rechtspraktijk erin geslaagd is de nieuwe methode, in haar diverse varianten, gestalte te geven als bruikbaar alternatief voor de verwijzingsmethode.

In het EERSTE DEEL staat de toenemende invloed van materieelrechtelijke factoren op de traditionele verwijzingsmethode centraal. In Europa hebben zich de laatste decennia veranderingen in het i.p.r. voorgedaan die vrijwel alle hun oorsprong vinden in een hernieuwde belangstelling voor de wisselwerking tussen materieel recht en i.p.r. Deze heroriëntatie op het materiële (privaat)recht heeft het hedendaagse Europese i.p.r. een ambivalent karakter gegeven. De frictie tussen de abstracte, waardevrije rechtsaanwijzing van het traditionele i.p.r. en de tegenwoordig als dringend ervaren noodzaak rekening te houden met materiële belangen heeft tot allerlei aanpassingen van de verwijzingsmethode geleid. In HOOFDSTUK 1 wordt aandacht besteed aan de "half-open conflictregel", de "functionele verwijzing", de "favor"-noties, en het leerstuk van de "voorrangsregels", als de belangrijkste exponenten van een materieelrechtelijke evolutie binnen het nog steeds op de verwijzingsmethode gebaseerde Europese i.p.r.

In HOOFDSTUK 2 wordt de vraag behandeld in hoeverre bij toepassing van de zuiver materieelrechtelijke i.p.r.-methode, zoals die in de Verenigde Staten wordt gehanteerd, nog behoefte bestaat aan de algemene leerstukken van het traditionele conflictenrecht. Achtereenvolgens wordt aandacht besteed aan de kwalificatie, het renvoi, de openbare orde, en de processuele behandeling van conflictregels en buitenlands recht. Zowel in Europa als in de Verenigde Staten heeft men deze leerstukken nogal eens gebruikt als *escape devices*, ter vermijding van onaantrekkelijk geachte resultaten van de orthodoxe verwijzingsmethode, waarin voor een concrete belangenafweging geen plaats is. Het laat zich denken dat aan zulke "bijsturingsmechanismen" geen behoefte bestaat indien de gehanteerde i.p.r.-methode juist is toegespitst op een materiële belangenafweging. Een nader onderzoek van de Amerikaanse rechtspraak op dit punt laat zien dat het "misbruik" van algemene leerstukken aanzienlijk is afgenomen sinds de materieelrechtelijke i.p.r.-benadering in zwang is gekomen. De pogingen van sommige schrijvers nieuwe inhoud aan genoemde begrippen te geven zijn weinig overtuigend. In de nieuwe methode komt alleen aan de openbare orde een –overigens zeer beperkte– functie toe; de andere leerstukken zijn daarin overbodig. Een apart probleem vormt de processuele status van i.p.r. en buitenlands recht. Een methode waarin de respectieve geldingspretenties van botsende rechtsnormen centraal staan verliest aan overtuigingskracht indien het beroep op buitenlands recht en de vaststelling van de inhoud daarvan wordt overgelaten aan partijen.

Het TWEEDE DEEL is geheel gewijd aan de praktijk van de materieelrechtelijke methode in haar verschillende varianten. Het opent met de vraag of er, door de aanvaarding van nieuwe uitgangspunten, inderdaad een "crisis" is ontstaan in het Amerikaanse conflictenrecht, zoals sommige behoudende i.p.r.-deskundigen in Europa wel betogen. De argumenten voor deze stelling lijken niet zonder meer steekhoudend. De Europese bezorgdheid om de rechtszekerheid zou zich overigens evenzeer op de resultaten van de verwijzingsmethode kunnen richten als op die van het materieelrechtelijke i.p.r. Als eerste variant van de moderne Amerikaanse benadering wordt in HOOFDSTUK 3 de conceptie van de *Restatement Second of the Law of Conflict of Laws* besproken. Deze officieuze codificatie van het commune i.p.r. in de Verenigde Staten berust op een compromis tussen halfopen conflictregels en een tamelijk vrijblijvende verwijzing naar een aantal keuzebepalende factoren, waaronder met name de geldingspretentie van conflicterende normen. Gelet op het hybridische karakter van de Restatement's *most significant relationship approach* is het niet verwonderlijk dat de vlag van deze benadering in de praktijk een uiterst heterogene lading dekt: naast uitspraken waarin uitsluitend feitelijke factoren worden opgeteld en afgewogen, komen beslissingen voor waarin alleen aan geldingspretenties wordt gerefereerd. In HOOFDSTUK 4 wordt de *interest analysis* behandeld, de kern van alle Amerikaanse materieelrechtelijke benaderingen. Aan de hand van recente jurisprudentie worden kritische beschouwingen gewijd aan het verschil tussen *no-conflicts* en *false conflicts*, aan het verrassende, en volgens sommigen onbestaanbare fenomeen van de *unprovided-for case*, en tenslotte aan de verschillende oplossingen van de *true conflicts*, met name het "wegen" van geldingspretenties, de Californische *comparative impairment analysis* en de terugkeer naar territoriale, aan het verwijzingsmodel ontleende criteria. Op alle terreinen lijkt de rechtspraak de *interest analysis* als voorwendsel voor teleologische beslissingen te gebruiken, hetgeen de methodologische consistentie van de uitspraken niet ten goede komt.

Vervolgens komen drie andere varianten van het materieelrechtelijke i.p.r. aan de orde. In HOOFDSTUK 5 wordt de bruikbaarheid onderzocht van Robert Leflar's *choice-influencing considerations*, die oorspronkelijk bedoeld waren ter verklaring van de praktijk van de rechtsaanwijzing, maar inmiddels verheven zijn tot normatieve criteria. In de staten waar deze aanpak de conflictenrechtelijke rechtsvinding beheerst vertoont de rechtspraak, meer nog dan bij de voorgaande benaderingen het geval is, een tendens tot manipulatie van de keuzebepalende criteria. Het meest arbitrair is het beroep op de *better law consideration*, doorgaans ter rechtvaardiging van de toepassing van het eigen recht. HOOFDSTUK 6 betreft de ontwikkeling van het i.p.r. in de staat New York ná *Babcock v. Jackson*. De New Yorkse i.p.r.-rechtspraak op het terrein van de onrechtmatige daad wordt momenteel gekenmerkt door methodologische verwarring. Aanvankelijk leek de hoogste New Yorkse rechter, de Court of Appeals, bekeerd te zijn tot de *interest analysis*, maar allengs deed zich kennelijk toch weer de behoefte voelen aan vaste, simpel toe te passen regels. De door Chief Judge Fuld geformuleerde *principles*, waarin het traditionele lex loci delicti criterium weer enigszins in ere wordt hersteld, hebben echter geen vaste voet in de rechtspraak gekregen. Sindsdien verkeert het New Yorkse i.p.r. in een onloochenbare crisis, blijkend uit een groot aantal methodologisch tegenstrijdige uitspraken en zelfs inhoudelijk aanvechtbare beslissingen. HOOFDSTUK 7 behandelt een radicale ommezwaai in de rechtspraak van Kentucky en Michigan. In deze staten heeft men de traditionele verwijzingsmethode vervangen door een *lex fori*-benadering: in beginsel wordt het eigen recht toepasselijk geacht, tenzij er "voldoende reden" blijkt te bestaan voor toepassing van een ander recht. Onduidelijk is overigens door welke criteria een uitzondering op dit rechtsvermoeden bepaald wordt, met name ook of hierbij de geldingspretenties van conflicterende normen een rol kunnen spelen. In de praktijk lijkt men nogal snel geneigd "voldoende reden" aan te nemen voor toepassing van het eigen recht. De U.S. Supreme Court heeft inmiddels een positief oordeel gegeven over de constitutionaliteit van een i.p.r.-beslissing uit de staat Minnesota waarin de lex fori was toegepast op een casus die vrijwel integraal met Wisconsin verbonden was. Impliciet wordt de lex fori-benadering door deze uitspraak gesanctioneerd.

Het DERDE DEEL is gewijd aan een evaluatie van de Amerikaanse i.p.r.-vernieuwingen op basis van het in het tweede deel onderzochte materiaal. HOOFDSTUK 8 richt zich daartoe op het thema *guest statutes*, op welk terrein de Amerikaanse rechtspraktijk de meeste ervaring met de materieelrechtelijke benaderingen heeft opgedaan. Hier blijkt dat de ratio van een *guest statute*, een overigens betrekkelijk eenvoudig regeltype, niet eenduidig valt te bepalen. De *policy* van een en dezelfde regel wordt op de meest uiteenlopende wijzen geïnterpreteerd. Omdat het ruimtelijk werkingsbereik van de norm in het algemeen niet door de wetgever is aangegeven, derhalve afgeleid moet worden uit de ratio, is de vaststelling van geldingspretenties (*interests*) afhankelijk van een correcte uitleg van enerzijds de algemene strekking van de regel, anderzijds het daaruit af te leiden ruimtelijk werkingsbereik. Het lijdt geen twijfel dat in deze beide interpretatierondes allerlei teleologische factoren worden verdisconteerd. Een onmiskenbaar gevolg is dan ook, dat de bepaling van geldingspretenties gekleurd wordt door de normatieve voorkeuren van het forum, geheel in strijd met de objectieve pretentie van de methode. Gerangschikt naar identieke feitenconstellaties blijken de *guest statute*-beslissingen vooral hun materieelrechtelijk resultaat met elkaar gemeen te hebben: in vrijwel alle gevallen wordt de vordering tot schadevergoeding van de gratis meerijdende passagier gehonoreerd. De i.p.r.-argumentatie verschilt echter van geval tot geval, ook binnen dezelfde categorie.

In HOOFDSTUK 9 wordt aangegeven hoe het komt dat de materieelrechtelijke methode even manipulatief gebruikt wordt als de klassieke verwijzingsmethode. De grondleggers van de theorie nemen als vaststaand aan dat de bedoelingen van de wetgever bij het uitvaardigen van een rechtsnorm in alle gevallen duidelijk en ondubbelzinnig zijn, en dat de rechter hoe dan ook in staat zal zijn de *policy* van de norm, en daarmee zijn ruimtelijk werkingsbereik, te achterhalen, óók als het gaat om een buitenlandse norm. In de praktijk zijn de bedoelingen van de wetgever echter lang niet altijd helder en eenduidig. Tegenstrijdige belangen kunnen immers heel goed tot een legislatief compromis leiden, de functie van een regel kan in de loop der tijd veranderen, zelfs kan de norm een dode letter zijn geworden. Volgens sommigen berust de materieelrechtelijke methode dan ook op een ongeldige premisse: de *myth of legislative intent*. Omdat de theorie van de *interest analysis* geen criteria voor de vaststelling van *policies* en *interests* wil formuleren – de methode afficheert zich nadrukkelijk als een ad hoc benadering – wordt voorts een zware wissel getrokken op de internationaal privaatrechtelijke objectiviteit van de rechter. Het valt nauwelijks te verwachten dat de rechter in staat is zijn (door het eigen recht gekleurde) normatief besef geheel uit te schakelen wanneer hij zich bezig houdt met de vaststelling van de strekking en geldingspretentie van buitenlands recht. Zeker wanneer legislatieve bedoelingen niet zonder meer duidelijk zijn, dreigt het gevaar dat aan buitenlandse normen een fictieve ratio wordt toegedicht, aangepast aan het materiële resultaat dat de rechter wenst te bereiken. In het materieelrechtelijk i.p.r.-procédé komen meer keuzemomenten voor dan bij de verwijzingsmethode het geval is. Dit impliceert meer mogelijkheden tot selectieve interpretatie. Omdat de materieelrechtelijke methode zich vrijwel uitsluitend concentreert op de mogelijk conflicterende belangen van rechtsgemeenschappen bij toepassing van hun recht, en geen aandacht heeft voor onontkoombare systeemwaarden als rechtszekerheid, rechtvaardigheid, erkenbaarheid e.d., ligt het voor de hand dat deze waarden de uiteindelijke norm-keuze langs andere weg zullen beïnvloeden. Dit zou de aanzienlijke methodologische inconsistenties in de praktijk van het hedendaagse Amerikaanse i.p.r. goeddeels verklaren. Daarmee is echter tevens het oordeel over de materieelrechtelijke i.p.r.-benadering geveld: een methode die pretendeert een rationele aanpak van het conflictenrechtelijk keuzeprobleem mogelijk te maken, maar desondanks voornamelijk blijkt te fungeren als dekmantel voor *Kadi-Justiz*, kan geen deugdelijke grondslag voor de legitimatie van i.p.r.-beslissingen bieden.

In de CONCLUSIE wordt de verbinding gelegd met de in het eerste hoofdstuk besproken ontwikkelingen in Europa. De adaptaties van de traditionele verwijzingsmethode hebben de behoefte aan correctie van het verwijzingsresultaat door middel van "bijsturingsmechanismen" sterk doen afnemen. Omdat het ideaal van de beslissingsgelijkheid steeds minder als de centrale doelstelling van het i.p.r. wordt beschouwd, kunnen de waarde- en doelvoorstellingen van het materiële recht op meer directe wijze in het verwijzingsprocédé worden geïntegreerd dan vroeger het geval was. Aldus wordt de band tussen i.p.r. en materieel recht, die in het laat-negentiende-eeuwse i.p.r. verloren was gegaan, weer enigszins hersteld. De ontwikkelingen in de Verenigde Staten hebben onmiskenbaar bijgedragen tot het Europese compromis tussen waardevrije aanknoping en doelgerichte belangenafweging, en in dat opzicht heeft de aanvaarding van de materieelrechtelijke methode in de Amerikaanse rechtspraak en doctrine wel degelijk een heilzaam effect gehad op het Europese i.p.r. Als systeem van conflictenrechtelijke rechtsvinding biedt zij echter, zeker binnen de conceptualistische rechtscultuur van continentaal Europa, te weinig houvast en teveel interpretatie-vrijheid om een aanvaardbaar alternatief voor de verwijzingsmethode te kunnen zijn.

Bibliography

Akehurst (1984)	Michael Akehurst, A Modern Introduction to International Law. 5th ed., London, 1984.
Alexander (1975)	Gregory S. Alexander, The Application and Avoidance of Foreign Law in the Law of Conflicts. 70 N.W.U. L.Rev. 602–638 (1975).
Alexander (1979)	Gregory S. Alexander, The Concept of Function and the Basis of Regulatory Interests under Functional Choice-of-Law Theory: The Significance of Benefit and the Insignificance of Intention. 65 Va. L.Rev. 1063–1091 (1979).
Ariëns (1966)	W. Ariëns, Internationale verkeersongelukken. V.R. 1966, p. 153–159.
Atiyah (1983)	P.S. Atiyah, Law and Modern Society. Oxford/ New York, 1983.
Audit (1979)	Bernard Audit, A Continental Lawyer Looks at Contemporary American Choice-of-Law Principles. 27 Am.J.Comp.L. 589–613 (1979).
Baade (1967)	Hans W. Baade, Counter-Revolution or Alliance for Progress? Reflections on Reading Cavers, The Choice-of-Law Process. 46 Tex. L.Rev. 141–179 (1967).
Baade (1973)	Hans W. Baade, The Case of the Disinterested Two States: Neumeier v. Kuehner. 1 Hofstra L.Rev. 150–167 (1973).

Bartin (1897)	E. Bartin, De l'impossibilité d'arriver à la suppression définitive des conflits de lois. Clunet 1897, p. 225, 446, 720; reprinted in: E. Bartin, Etudes de droit international privé, Paris, 1899.
Basedow (1983)	Jürgen Basedow, Entscheidung: Das amerikanische Pipeline-Embargo vor Gericht: Niederlande: Pres. Rb. Den Haag 17.9.1982 (Fall Sensor). 47 RabelsZ. 141–172 (1983).
Batiffol/Lagarde (1983)	Henri Batiffol/Paul Lagarde, Droit international privé. 7th ed., 2 vols., Paris, 1981/1983.
Baxter (1963)	William F. Baxter, Choice of Law and the Federal System. 16 Stanf. L.Rev. 1–42 (1963).
Binder (1955)	Heinz Binder, Zur Auflockerung des Deliktsstatuts. 20 RabelsZ. 401–499 (1955).
Bourel (1961)	Pierre Bourel, Les conflits de lois en matière d'obligations extracontractuelles. Paris, 1961.
Brilmayer (1980)	Lea Brilmayer, Interest Analysis and the Myth of Legislative Intent. 78 Mich. L.Rev. 392–431 (1980).
Brilmayer (1984)	Lea Brilmayer, Methods and Objectives in the Conflict of Laws: A Challenge. 35 Mercer L.Rev. 555–563 (1984).
Bucher (1975)	Andreas Bucher, Grundfragen der Anknüpfungsgerechtigkeit im internationalen Privatrecht (aus kontinental-europäischer Sicht). Basel/Stuttgart, 1975.
Cavers (1933)	David F. Cavers, A Critique of the Choice-of-Law Problem. 47 Harv. L.Rev. 173–208 (1933).
Cavers (1963)	David F. Cavers, The Changing Choice-of-Law Process and the Federal Courts. 28 L. & C.P. 732–753 (1963).
Cavers (1965)	David F. Cavers, The Choice-of-Law Process. Ann Arbor, 1965.

Cavers (1970)	David F. Cavers, Contemporary Conflicts Law in American Perspective. 131 Rec. des Cours 75–308 (1970).
Cavers (1971-1)	David F. Cavers, Symposium: Conflict of Laws Round Table, The Value of Principled Preferences. 49 Tex. L.Rev. 211–223 (1971).
Cavers (1971-2)	David F. Cavers, Cipolla and Conflicts Justice. 9 Duquesne L.Rev. 360–372 (1971).
Cavers (1972)	David F. Cavers, A Critique of the Choice-of-Law Problem: Addendum 1972, in: Internationales Privatrecht (ed. Paolo Picone and Wilhelm Wengler). Darmstadt, 1974, p. 166–176. Reprinted in: 17 Harv. Int.L.J. 651–656 (1976).
Cavers (1976)	See: Cavers (1972), reprinted *sub nom.* A Critique of the Choice-of-Law Process: Addendum 1972. 17 Harv. Int.L.J. 651–656 (1976).
Cavers (1983)	David F. Cavers, A Correspondence with Brainerd Currie, 1957-1958. 34 Mercer L.Rev. 471–499 (1983).
Cheatham (1971)	Elliott E. Cheatham, Conflict of Laws: Some Developments and Some Questions. 25 Ark. L.Rev. 9–33 (1971).
Cheatham/Reese (1952)	Elliott E. Cheatham/Willis L.M. Reese, Choice of the Applicable Law. 52 Col. L.Rev. 959 (1952).
Cohen Henriquez (1980)	E. Cohen Henriquez, I.P.R. Trends, Ontwikkelingen op het gebied van het internationale personen-, familie- en erfrecht, zaken-, contracten- en vennootschapsrecht. Deventer, 1980.
Cook (1924)	Walter Wheeler Cook, The Logical and Legal Bases of the Conflict of Laws. 33 Yale L.J. 457 (1924).
Cook (1942)	Walter Wheeler Cook, The Logical and Legal Bases of the Conflict of Laws. Cambridge, Mass., 1942.

Couch (1970)	Harvey Couch, Choice of Law, Guest Statutes, and the Louisiana Supreme Court: Six Judges in Search of a Rulebook. 45 Tul. L.Rev. 100–113 (1970).
Couch (1978)	Harvey Couch, In Search of Justice: Torts Conflicts of Law. 61 Marq. L.Rev. 545–558 (1978).
Cramton/Currie/Kay (1981)	Roger C. Cramton/David P. Currie/Herma Hill Kay, Conflict of Laws, Cases – Comments – Questions. St. Paul, Minn., 1981.
Crombag/De Wijkerslooth/Cohen (1973)	H.F. Crombag, J.L. de Wijkerslooth, M.J. Cohen, Over het legitimeren van rechterlijke beslissingen, in: H.F. Crombag/J.L. de Wijkerslooth/M.J. Cohen/ F.H. van der Burg/J. ter Heide/G.E. Langemeijer, Het rechterlijk oordeel. Zwolle, 1973, p. 1–28.
Currie (1956)	Brainerd Currie, Law and the Future – Legal Education. 1956 N.W. U. L.Rev. 258 (1956).
Currie (1959)	Brainerd Currie, Notes on Methods and Objectives in the Conflict of Laws. 1959 Duke L.J. 171 (1959). Reprinted in: Selected Essays, Durham, N.C., 1963, p. 177–187.
Currie (1963-1)	Brainerd Currie, Selected Essays on the Conflict of Laws. Durham, N.C., 1963.
Currie (1963-2)	Brainerd Currie, The Disinterested Third State. 28 L. & C.P. 754–794 (1963).
Currie (1963-3)	Brainerd Currie, Comment on Babcock v. Jackson. 63 Col. L.Rev. 1233–1243 (1963).
De Boer (1974)	Th.M. de Boer, Subjectieve verwijzing: anomalie of grondbeginsel?, in: H.U. Jessurun d'Oliveira/ R. Kotting/Th.M. Bervoets/Th.M. de Boer, Partijinvloed in het internationaal privaatrecht. Deventer, 1974, p. 47–72.

De Boer (1979)	Th.M. de Boer, Buitenlands recht onder de loupe: problemen rond de toepassing van vreemd recht, in: Th.M. Bervoets/Th.M. de Boer/H.U. Jessurun d'Oliveira/ R. Kotting, Hoe vreemd is buitenlands recht? Opstellen over de positie van buitenlands recht in het burgerlijk proces. Deventer, 1979, p. 9–37.
De Boer (1980)	Th.M. de Boer, De vermaatschappelijking van het internationaal privaatrecht: ontwikkelingen in de jaren zeventig. N.J.B. 1980, p. 785–796. Reprinted in: Recente Rechtsontwikkelingen (1970–1980), Boekenreeks N.J.B., no. 8, Zwolle, 1983, p. 79–90.
De Boer (1982)	Th.M. de Boer, Alternatieven voor de lex loci delicti. Deventer, 1982.
De Boer/Kotting (1982)	Th.M. de Boer/R. Kotting, President Reagan vs. President Wijnholt, Kanttekeningen bij een uitspraak inzake het Amerikaanse gasleidingembargo (Pres. Rb. 's-Gravenhage 17 sept. 1982, RvdW/KG 1982, 167). N.J.B. 1982, p. 1177–1186.
De Boer/Kotting (1984)	Th.M. de Boer/R. Kotting, Der niederländische Richter und das US-Gasröhren-Embargo (Präsident der Rechtbank Den Haag 17.9.1982). 4 IPRax 108–112 (1984).
De Nova (1960)	Rodolfo de Nova, Conflits des lois et normes fixant leur propre domaine d'application, in: Mélanges offerts à Jacques Maury. Paris, 1960, vol. I, p. 377–401.
De Nova (1963)	Rodolfo de Nova, New Trends in Italian Private International Law. 28 L. & C. P. 808–821 (1963).
De Nova (1966)	Rodolfo de Nova, Historical and Comparative Introduction to Conflict of Laws. 118 Rec. des Cours 443–622 (1966).
De Nova (1977)	Rodolfo de Nova, Glancing at the Content of Substantive Rules under the Jurisdiction-Selecting Approach. 41/42 L. & C.P. 1–9 (1977).

De Winter (1940)	L.I. Barmat (= L.I. de Winter), De grenzen van de contractsvrijheid in het internationaal privaatrecht. W.P.N.R. 1940, p. 245-249; p. 257-261; reprinted in: Naar een sociaal I.P.R., Een keus uit het werk van L.I. de Winter. Deventer, 1979, p. 164-181.
De Winter (1947)	L.I. Barmat de Winter, De sociale functies der rechtsnormen als grondslag voor de oplossing van internationaal privaatrechtelijke wetsconflicten. R.M. Themis 1947, p. 101-166; reprinted in: Naar een sociaal I.P.R., Een keus uit het werk van L.I. de Winter. Deventer, 1979, p. 3-52.
De Winter (1964)	L.I. de Winter, Dwingend recht bij internationale overeenkomsten. N.T.I.R. 1964, p. 329-365; reprinted in: Naar een sociaal I.P.R., Een keus uit het werk van L.I. de Winter. Deventer, 1979, p. 182-217.
De Winter (1971)	L.I. de Winter, Enige beschouwingen over de wet van de karakteristieke prestatie, in: Met eerbiedigende werking, Opstellen aangeboden aan Prof. Mr. L.J. Hijmans van den Bergh. Deventer, 1971, p. 367-379; reprinted in: Naar een sociaal I.P.R., Een keus uit het werk van L.I. de Winter. Deventer, 1979, p. 236-249.
Deby-Gérard (1973)	France Deby-Gérard, Le rôle de la règle de conflit dans le règlement des rapports internationaux. Paris, 1973.
Deelen (1965)	J.E.J.Th. Deelen, Rechtskeuze bij internationale overeenkomsten, Een jurisprudentie-onderzoek. Amsterdam, 1965.
Deelen (1966)	J.E.J.Th. Deelen, De blinddoek van Von Savigny. Amsterdam, 1966.
Deelen (1971)	J.E.J.Th. Deelen, Internationale contracten. Med. N.V.I.R., no. 63, 1971, p. 69-80.
Deelen (1980)	J.E.J.Th. Deelen, Vreemd recht, Hoe kom je d'ran? Hoe kom je d'raf? in: J.E.J.Th. Deelen/ P.H.M. Gerver, De toepasselijkheid van materieel vreemd recht in de Nederlandse rechtssfeer. Preadvies Koninklijke Notariële Broederschap, Deventer, 1980, p. 1-30.

Dicey/Morris (1980)	Dicey and Morris on the Conflict of Laws (ed. J.H.C. Morris). 10th ed., 2 vols., London, 1980.
Drion (1949)	H. Drion, De ratio voor toepassing van vreemd recht in zake de onrechtmatige daad in het buitenland. R.M. Themis 1949, p. 3–66.
Drion (1964)	Huibert Drion, The Lex Loci Delicti in Retreat. A Foreigner's Remarks on Babcock v. Jackson, in: Festschrift für Otto Riese (ed. B. Aubin, E. von Caemmerer, P. Meylan, K.H. Neumayer, G. Rinck, W. Strausz). Karlsruhe, 1964, p. 225–238.
Drion/De Boer	H. Drion (ed.), Onrechtmatige Daad, loose-leaf publication; chapter III–C: Internationaal privaatrecht (ed. Th.M. de Boer). Deventer.
Drobnig (1975)	Ulrich Drobnig, Comments on Art. 7 of the Draft Convention, in: European Private International Law of Obligations (ed. Ole Lando, Bernd von Hoffmann, Kurt Siehr). Tübingen, 1975, p. 82–86.
Dubbink (1947)	C.W. Dubbink, De onrechtmatige daad in het Nederlandse internationaal privaatrecht. 's-Gravenhage, 1947.
Dubbink (1973)	C.W. Dubbink, Het rechtvaardigheidsgehalte van het internationaal privaatrecht, in: Speculum Langemeijer, 31 rechtsgeleerde opstellen. Zwolle, 1973, p. 63–72.
Duintjer Tebbens (1979)	Harry Duintjer Tebbens, International Product Liability, A study of comparative and international legal aspects of product liability. Alphen aan de Rijn/Germantown Md., 1979.
Egnal (1981)	John David Egnal, The 'Essential' Role of Modern Renvoi in the Governmental Interest Analysis Approach to Choice of Law. 54 Temple L.Q. 237–280 (1981).
Ehrenzweig (1960-1)	Albert A. Ehrenzweig, Guest Statutes in the Conflict of Laws – Towards a Theory of Enterprise Liability under 'Foreseeable and Insurable Laws'. 69 Yale L.J. 595–604 (1960).

Ehrenzweig (1960-2)   Albert A. Ehrenzweig, Products Liability in the Conflict of Laws – Toward a Theory of Enterprise Liability under 'Foreseeable and Insurable Laws'.
69 Yale L.J. 795–803 (1960).

Ehrenzweig (1960-3)   Albert A. Ehrenzweig, Vicarious Liability in the Conflict of Laws – Toward a Theory of Enterprise Liability under 'Foreseeable and Insurable Laws'.
69 Yale L.J. 978–991 (1960).

Ehrenzweig (1961)   Albert A. Ehrenzweig, Characterization in the Conflict of Laws: An Unwelcome Addition to American Doctrine, in: Twentieth Century Comparative and Conflicts Law, Legal Essays in Honor of Hessel E. Yntema (ed. Kurt Nadelmann, Arthur T. Von Mehren, John Hazard). Leyden, 1961, p. 395–408.

Ehrenzweig (1962)   Albert A. Ehrenzweig, A Treatise on the Conflict of Laws. St. Paul, Minn., 1962.

Ehrenzweig (1965)   Albert A. Ehrenzweig, A Proper Law in a Proper Forum: A 'Restatement' of the 'Lex Fori Approach'.
18 Okl. L.Rev. 340–352 (1965).

Ehrenzweig (1967-1)   Albert A. Ehrenzweig, Private International Law, A Comparative Treatise on American International Conflicts Law, Including the Law of Admiralty, General Part. Leyden/Dobbs Ferry N.Y., 1967.

Ehrenzweig (1967-2)   Albert A. Ehrenzweig, 'False Conflicts' and the 'Better Rule': Threat and Promise in Multistate Tort Law.
53 Va. L.Rev. 847–856 (1967).

Ehrenzweig (1971)   Albert A. Ehrenzweig, Symposium: Conflict of Laws Round Table, The Value of Principled Preferences.
49 Tex. L.Rev. 236–238 (1971).

Ehrenzweig (1974)   Albert A. Ehrenzweig, Choice of Law in California – A 'Prestatement'.
21 U.C.L.A. L.Rev. 781–796 (1974).

Ehrenzweig (1980)	Albert A. Ehrenzweig, Enterprise Liability, in: International Encyclopedia of Comparative Law, vol. III, Private International Law, chapter 32, nos. 1–53. Tübingen/Alphen a/d Rijn, 1980.
Ely (1981)	John Hart Ely, Choice of Law and the State's Interest in Protecting its Own. 23 W.&M. L.Rev. 173–217 (1981).
Erades (1960)	L. Erades, Het auto-ongeval in het internationaal privaatrecht. V.R. 1960, p. 93–95.
Erauw (1982-1)	J. Erauw, De onrechtmatige daad in het internationaal privaatrecht. Antwerpen/Apeldoorn, 1982.
Erauw (1982-2)	J. Erauw, Hoofdlijnen van de argumentatie voor een betere verwijzingsregel inzake de internationale gevallen van aansprakelijkheid. 45 R.W. 2520–2526 (1982).
Erauw (1985)	Johan Erauw, Beginselen van Internationaal Privaatrecht. Gent, 1985.
Ester (1962)	John W. Ester, Borrowing Statutes of Limitation and Conflict of Laws. 15 U.Fla. L.Rev. 33–84 (1962).
Falconbridge (1937)	John D. Falconbridge, Characterization in the Conflict of Laws. 53 L.Q.Rev. 235 (1937).
Fallon (1975)	Marc Fallon, Les dispositions de l'avant-projet C.E.E. relatives à la loi applicable aux obligations aquiliennes, in: European Private International Law of Obligations (ed. Ole Lando, Bernd von Hoffmann, Kurt Siehr). Tübingen, 1975, p. 87–98.
Felix (1968)	Robert L. Felix, Interspousal Immunity in the Conflict of Laws: Automobile Accident Claims. 53 Cornell L.Rev. 406–445 (1968).
Felix (1971)	Robert L. Felix, The Choice-of-Law Process at a Crossroads. 9 Duquesne L.Rev. 413–422 (1971).

Felix (1980)	Robert L. Felix, American Conflicts Law: *American Conflicts* Law (Leflar Symposium). 31 S.C. L.Rev. 423–433 (1980) = 34 Ark. L.Rev. 214–223 (1980).
Ferrer-Correia (1975)	A. Ferrer-Correia, Les problèmes de codification en droit international privé. 145 Rec. des Cours 57–203 (1975).
Fleming (1967)	John G. Fleming, The Role of Negligence in Modern Tort Law. 53 Va. L.Rev. 815–846 (1970).
Flessner (1970)	A. Flessner, Fakultatives Kollisionsrecht. 34 RabelsZ. 547–584 (1970).
Francescakis (1958)	Ph. Francescakis, La théorie du renvoi et les conflits de systèmes en droit international privé. Paris, 1958.
Francescakis (1966)	Ph. Francescakis, Quelques précisions sur les "lois d'application immédiate" et leurs rapports avec les règles de conflits de lois. Rev. Crit. d.i.p. 1966, p. 1–18.
Francescakis (1968)	Ph. Francescakis, Conflits de Lois (Principes Généraux), in: Répertoire de droit international, vol. I. Paris, 1968, p. 480 ff., nos. 122–149.
Freund (1946)	Paul A. Freund, Chief Justice Stone and the Conflict of Laws. 59 Harv. L.Rev. 1210–1236 (1946).
Friedmann (1967)	Wolfgang Friedmann, Legal Theory. 5th ed., New York, 1967.
Goodrich (1938)	Herbert F. Goodrich, Foreign Facts and Local Fancies. 25 Va. L.Rev. 26 (1938).
Goodrich (1950)	Herbert F. Goodrich, Yielding Place to New: Rest Versus Motion in the Conflict of Laws. 50 Col. L.Rev. 881 (1950).
Gutzwiller (1968)	Peter Max Gutzwiller, Von Ziel und Methode des IPR. 25 Schw.Jb.Int.R. 161–196 (1968).

Haak (1975)	W.E. Haak, Internationaal overeenkomstenrecht, Beschouwingen rondom en over het Voor-ontwerp E.E.G.-Verdrag nopens de wetten die van toepassing zijn op verbintenissen uit overeenkomsten en niet-contractuele-verbintenissen. Med. N.V.I.R. no. 71, 1975, p. 1–70.
Haak (1980)	W.E. Haak, Nieuw internationaal overeenkomstenrecht, Het E.E.G.-Verdrag inzake het recht dat van toepassing is op verbintenissen uit overeenkomst. W.P.N.R. 1980, p. 865–869; p. 881–888; p. 897–906.
Haak (1984)	W.E. Haak, Plaats en invloed van 'publiekrechtelijke' regels in het IPR. W.P.N.R. 1984, p. 669–674; p. 689–695.
Hancock (1961)	Moffatt Hancock, Three Approaches to the Choice-of-Law Problem: the Classificatory, the Functional and the Result-Selective, in: Twentieth Century Comparative and Conflicts Law, Legal Essays in Honor of Hessel E. Yntema (ed. Kurt Nadelmann, Arthur T. Von Mehren, John Hazard). Leyden, 1961, p. 365–379.
Hancock (1975)	Moffatt Hancock, Some Choice-of-Law Problems Posed by Antiguest Statutes: Realism in Wisconsin and Rule-Fetishism in New York. 27 Stanf. L.Rev. 775–789 (1975).
Hanotiau (1979)	Bernard Hanotiau, Le droit international privé américain, Du premier au second Restatement of the Law, Conflict of Laws. Paris/Bruxelles, 1979.
Hanotiau (1982)	Bernard Hanotiau, The American Conflicts Revolution and European Tort Choice-of-Law Thinking (Bologna Symposium). 30 Am.J.Comp.L. 73–98 (1982).
Hartley (1982)	T.C. Hartley, Consumer Protection Provisions in the E.E.C. Convention, in: Contract Conflicts, The E.E.C. Convention on the Law Applicable to Contractual Obligations: A Comparative Study (ed. P.M. North). Amsterdam/New York/Oxford, 1982, p. 111–141.

Hay (1981)	Peter Hay, Reflections on Conflict-of-Laws Methodology. 32 Hastings L.J. 1644–1677 (1981).
Heini (1962)	Anton Heini, Neuere Strömungen im Amerikanischen Internationalen Privatrecht. 19 Schw.Jb.Int.R. 31–70 (1962).
Herzog (1983)	Peter E. Herzog, Conflict of Laws (1983 Survey of New York Law). 34 Syr. L.Rev. 113–171 (1983).
Hijmans (1937)	I. Henri Hijmans, Algemeene Problemen van Internationaal Privaatrecht. Zwolle, 1937.
Hill (1960)	Alfred Hill, Governmental Interest and the Conflict of Laws – A Reply to Professor Currie. 27 U.Chi. L.Rev. 463–504 (1960).
Hogue (1978)	Lynn Hogue, Arkansas' New Choice of Law Rule for Interstate Torts: A Critique of Wallis, Williams, and the 'Better Rule of Law'. 1978 Wash.U. L.Q. 713–731 (1978).
Hohloch (1984)	Gerhard Hohloch, Das Deliktsstatut, Grundlagen und Grundlinien des internationalen Deliktsrechts. Frankfurt a/M., 1984.
Horowitz (1974)	Harold W. Horowitz, The Law of Choice of Law in California – A Restatement. 21 U.C.L.A. L.Rev. 719–780 (1974).
Jayme (1967)	Erik Jayme, Interspousal Immunity: Revolution and Counterrevolution in American Tort Conflicts. 40 So.Cal. L.Rev. 307–350 (1967).
Jayme (1974)	Erik Jayme, Zur Anwendung ausländischer Guest Statutes im Staate New York. 38 RabelsZ. 583–589 (1974).
Jayme (1977)	Erik Jayme, Zur Krise des 'Governmental-Interest Approach', in: Festschrift für Gerhard Kegel. Frankfurt a/M., 1977 p. 359–366.
Jessurun d'Oliveira (1965)	H.U. Jessurun d'Oliveira, Internationale verkeersongevallen, het slagveld van een grondslagenstrijd in het IPR. Amsterdam, 1965.

Jessurun d'Oliveira (1968)	H.U. Jessurun d'Oliveira, Een en ander over internationaal kinderalimentatierecht: Het Haags Verdrag van 1956, de exceptio plurium concubentium en de openbare orde. N.T.I.R. 1968, p. 266-306.
Jessurun d'Oliveira (1971)	H.U. Jessurun d'Oliveira, De antikiesregel. Een paar aspekten van de behandeling van buitenlands recht in het burgerlijk proces. Deventer, 1971.
Jessurun d'Oliveira (1973)	H.U. Jessurun d'Oliveira, De meerwaarde van rechterlijke uitspraken (Arrêts de règlement en precedenten). Geschr. N.V.R.V. no. 10, 1973.
Jessurun d'Oliveira (1975-1)	H.U. Jessurun d'Oliveira, Internationaal overeenkomstenrecht, Beschouwingen rondom en over het Voor-ontwerp E.E.G.-Verdrag nopens de wetten die van toepassing zijn op verbintenissen uit overeenkomsten en niet-contractuele verbintenissen. Med. N.V.I.R. no. 71, 1975, p. 71-136.
Jessurun d'Oliveira (1975-2)	H.U. Jessurun d'Oliveira, Die Freiheit des niederländischen Richters bei der Entwicklung des internationalen Privatrechts: zur antizipierenden Anwendung des Benelux-Einheitsgesetz über das Internationale Privatrecht – ein Requiem. 39 RabelsZ. 224-252 (1975).
Jessurun d'Oliveira (1975-3)	H.U. Jessurun d'Oliveira, Openbare orde en rechtsvergelijking, in: 't Exempel Dwinght, Opstellen aangeboden aan Prof. mr. I. Kisch. Zwolle, 1975, p. 239-261.
Jessurun d'Oliveira (1976)	H.U. Jessurun d'Oliveira, De ruïne van een paradigma: de konfliktregel. Deventer, 1976.
Jessurun d'Oliveira (1978)	H.U. Jessurun d'Oliveira, La pollution du Rhin et le droit international privé, in: R. Hueting/ C. van der Veen/A.Ch. Kiss/H.U. Jessurun d'Oliveira, Rhine Pollution, Legal, Economic and Technical Aspects/ La pollution du Rhin, aspects juridiques, économiques et techniques. Boekenreeks N.J.B. no. 5, Zwolle, 1978, p. 81-127.

Jessurun d'Oliveira (1979-1)	H.U. Jessurun d'Oliveira, Toepassing van het buitenlands recht en zijn marginale toetsing door de hoogste rechter. Geschr. N.V.R.V. no. 28, 1979.
Jessurun d'Oliveira (1979-2)	H.U. Jessurun d'Oliveira, Verdraaiing van vreemd recht, in: Th.M. Bervoets/Th.M. de Boer/H.U. Jessurun d'Oliveira/R. Kotting, Hoe vreemd is buitenlands recht? Opstellen over de positie van buitenlands recht in het burgerlijk proces. Deventer, 1979, p. 39–69.
Jessurun d'Oliveira (1979-3)	H.U. Jessurun d'Oliveira, De europese overeenkomst nopens het verstrekken van inlichtingen over buitenlands recht (Londen 1968) en art. 48 Rv., in: Th.M. Bervoets/Th.M. de Boer/ H.U. Jessurun d'Oliveira/R. Kotting, Hoe vreemd is buitenlands recht? Opstellen over de positie van buitenlands recht in het burgerlijk proces. Deventer, 1979, p. 87–119. Reprinted in N.J.B. 1979, p. 637–648.
Juenger (1969)	Friedrich K. Juenger, Choice of Law in Interstate Torts. 118 U.Pa. L.Rev. 202–235 (1969).
Juenger (1975)	Friedrich K. Juenger, Trends in European Conflicts Law. 60 Cornell L.Rev. 969–984 (1975).
Juenger (1980)	Friedrich K. Juenger, Leflar's Contributions to American Conflicts Law (Leflar Symposium). 31 S.C. L.Rev. 413–422 (1980) = 34 Ark. L.Rev. 205–213 (1980).
Juenger (1981)	Friedrich K. Juenger, Supreme Court Intervention in Jurisdiction and Choice of Law: A Dismal Project. 14 U.C.Davis L.Rev. 907–917 (1981).
Juenger (1982)	Friedrich K. Juenger, American and European Conflicts Law (Bologna Symposium). 30 Am.J.Comp.L. 117–133 (1982).
Juenger (1984)	Friedrich K. Juenger, Conflict of Laws: A Critique of Interest Analysis. 32 Am.J.Comp.L. 1–50 (1984).

Juste Ruiz (1976)	José Juste Ruiz, Interest-Oriented Analysis in International Conflicts of Laws: The American Experience. N.I.L.R. 1976, p. 5–42.
Kahn (1891)	Franz Kahn, Gesetzeskollisionen: ein Beitrag zur Lehre des internationalen Privatrechts, in: Franz Kahn, Abhandlungen zum Internationalen Privatrecht (ed. Lenel/Lewald). München/Leipzig, vol. I, 1928, p. 1–121.
Kahn (1896)	Franz Kahn, Der Grundsatz der Rückverweisung im deutschen Bürgerlichen Gesetzbuch und auf dem Haager Kongresz für internationales Privatrecht, in: Franz Kahn, Abhandlungen zum Internationalen Privatrecht (ed. Lenel/Lewald). München/Leipzig, vol. I, 1928, p. 124–160.
Kahn (1898)	Franz Kahn, Die Lehre vom ordre public (Prohibitiv-gesetze), in: Franz Kahn, Abhandlungen zum Internationalen Privatrecht (ed. Lenel/Lewald). München/Leipzig, vol. I, 1928, p. 161–254.
Kahn-Freund (1968)	O. Kahn-Freund, Delictual Liability and the Conflict of Laws. 124 Rec. des Cours 1–166 (1968).
Kanowitz (1978)	Leo Kanowitz, Comparative Impairment and Better Law: Grand Illusions in the Conflict of Laws. 30 Hastings L.J. 255–300 (1978).
Kay (1980)	Herma Hill Kay, The Use of Comparative Impairment to Resolve True Conflicts: An Evaluation of the California Experience. 68 Calif. L.Rev. 577–617 (1980).
Kay (1983)	Herma Hill Kay, Theory into Practice: Choice of Law in the Courts. 34 Mercer L.Rev. 521–592 (1983).
Kegel (1953)	Gerhard Kegel, Begriffs- und Interessenjurisprudenz im IPR, in: Festschrift Hans Lewald. Basel, 1953, p. 259–288.
Kegel (1964)	Gerhard Kegel, The Crisis of Conflict of Law. 112 Rec. des Cours 95–263 (1964).

Kegel (1974)	Gerhard Kegel, Wandel auf dünnem Eis, in: Friedrich K. Juenger, Zum Wandel des Internationalen Privatrechts. Karlsruhe, 1974, p. 35–44.
Kegel (1979)	Gerhard Kegel, Vaterhaus und Traumhaus, Herkömmliches internationales Privatrecht und Hauptthesen der amerikanischen Reformer, in: Festschrift für Günther Beitzke (ed. Otto Sandrock), Berlin/New York, 1979, p. 551–573. Reprinted *sub nom.* Paternal Home and Dream Home: Traditional Conflict of Laws and the American Reformers. 27 Am.J.Comp.L. 615–633 (1979).
Kegel (1985)	Gerhard Kegel, Internationales Privatrecht, Ein Studienbuch. 5th ed., München, 1985.
Keller (1983)	Max Keller, Schutz des Schwächeren im Internationalen Vertragsrecht, in: Festschrift fur Frank Vischer zum 60. Geburtstag (ed. Peter Böckli, Kurt Eichenberger, Hans Hinderling, Hans Peter Tsuchi). Zürich, 1983, p. 175–188.
Kelly (1969)	D.St.L. Kelly, Localising Rules and Differing Approaches to the Choice of Law Process. 18 I.C.L.Q. 249–274 (1969).
King (1973)	Josephine Y. King, Neumeier: Through the Eyes of Nullifidians (Neumeier Symposium). 1 Hofstra L.Rev. 178–182 (1973).
Kisch (1959)	I. Kisch, La loi la plus favorable, Réflexions à propos de l'article 9(3),2 de la loi uniforme Benelux, in: Ius et Lex, Festgabe zum 70. Geburtstag von Max Gutzwiller. Basel, 1959, p. 373–393; reprinted in: Uitgelezen opstellen, Een bloemlezing uit het werk van Prof. mr. I. Kisch (ed. H.U. Jessurun d'Oliveira). Zwolle, 1981, p. 223–241.
Kollewijn (1937)	R.D. Kollewijn, Geschiedenis van de Nederlandse wetenschap van het internationaal privaatrecht tot 1880. Amsterdam, 1937.
Kollewijn (1967)	R.D. Kollewijn [Book review Jessurun d'Oliveira (1965)]. N.T.I.R. 1967, p. 285–288.

Korn (1983)	Harold L. Korn, The Choice-of-Law Revolution: A Critique. 83 Col. L.Rev. 772–973 (1983).
Korthals Altes (1983)	A. Korthals Altes, Seamen's Strikes and Supporting Boycotts: Recent case developments abroad, in: Essays on International & Comparative Law in Honour of Judge Erades. The Hague, 1983, p. 104–121.
Kosters/Dubbink (1962)	J. Kosters/C.W. Dubbink, Algemeen deel van het Nederlandse internationaal privaatrecht. Haarlem, 1962.
Kotting (1979)	R. Kotting, Buitenlands recht: opgave of opgeven, in: Th.M. Bervoets/Th.M. de Boer/H.U. Jessurun d'Oliveira/R. Kotting, Hoe vreemd is buitenlands recht, Opstellen over de positie van buitenlands recht in het burgerlijk proces. Deventer, 1979, p. 71–85.
Kotting (1984)	Roelof Kotting, Extraterritoriale wetgeving en internationaal privaatrecht, in: P. Peters/ R. Kotting, Extraterritoriale wetgeving. Med. N.V.I.R. no. 89, 1984, p. 111–147.
Kotting (1985)	Roelof Kotting, Lex fori: zwerfkei of hoeksteen. N.J.B. 1985, p. 1345–1346.
Kozyris (1972)	P. John Kozyris, No-Fault Automobile Insurance and the Conflict of Laws – Cutting the Gordian Knot Home-Style. 1972 Duke L.J. 331–406 (1972).
Kozyris (1973)	P. John Kozyris, No-Fault Insurance and the Conflict of Laws – An Interim Update. 1973 Duke L.J. 1009–1034 (1973).
Kozyris (1981)	P. John Kozyris, Reflections on Allstate – The Lessening of Due Process in Choice of Law (Allstate Symposium). 14 U.C.Davis L.Rev. 889–906 (1981).
Kropholler (1969)	Jan Kropholler, Ein Anknüpfungssystem für das Deliktsstatut. 33 RabelsZ. 601–653 (1969).
Kropholler (1975)	Jan Kropholler, Internationales Einheitsrecht, Allgemeine Lehren. Tübingen, 1975.

Kropholler (1978)	Jan Kropholler, Das kollisionsrechtliche System des Schutzes der schwächeren Vertragspartei. 42 RabelsZ. 634–661 (1978).
Lando (1974)	Ole Lando, The EC Draft Convention on the Law Applicable to Contractual and Non-Contractual Obligations. 38 RabelsZ. 6–55 (1974).
Lando (1975)	Ole Lando, Les obligations contractuelles, in: European Private International Law of Obligations (ed. Ole Lando, Bernd von Hoffmann, Kurt Siehr). Tübingen, 1975, p. 125–154.
Leflar (1966-1)	Robert A. Leflar, Choice-Influencing Considerations in Conflicts Law. 41 N.Y.U. L.Rev. 267–327 (1966).
Leflar (1966-2)	Robert A. Leflar, Conflicts Law: More on Choice-Influencing Considerations. 54 Calif. L.Rev. 1584–1598 (1966).
Leflar (1972-1)	Robert A. Leflar, The 'New' Choice of Law. 21 Am.U. L.Rev. 457–474 (1972).
Leflar (1972-2)	Robert A. Leflar, The Torts Provision of the Restatement (Second). 72 Col. L.Rev. 267–278 (1972).
Leflar (1977-1)	Robert A. Leflar, American Conflicts Law. 3d ed., Indianapolis/New York/Charlottesville Va., 1977.
Leflar (1977-2)	Robert A. Leflar, Choice-of-Law Statutes. 44 Tenn. L.Rev. 951–974 (1977).
Leflar (1977-3)	Robert A. Leflar, Choice-of-Law: A Well-Watered Plateau. 41 L. & C.P. 10–26 (1977).
Leflar (1980)	Robert A. Leflar, A Response from the Author (Leflar Symposium). 31 S.C. L.Rev. 457–467 (1980) = 34 Ark. L.Rev. 243 (1980).
Leflar (1981)	Robert A. Leflar, The Nature of Conflicts Law. 81 Col. L.Rev. 1080–1095 (1981).
Lemaire (1968)	W.L.G. Lemaire, Nederlands internationaal privaatrecht (Hoofdlijnen). Leiden, 1968.

Lipstein (1977)	K. Lipstein, Interest Limitations in Statutes and the Conflict of Law. 26 I.C.L.Q. 884–902 (1977).
Lopez (1980)	Louis Lopez, The Law of the Domicile with Greater Compensation Rule: Toward Policy-Oriented Rules for Choice of Law. 17 Calif. Western L.Rev. 26–54 (1980).
Lorenz (1977)	Egon Lorenz, Zur Struktur des internationalen Privatrecht, Ein Beitrag zur Reformdiskussion. Berlin, 1977.
Lorenzen (1924)	Ernst G. Lorenzen, Territoriality, Public Policy and the Conflict of Laws. 33 Yale L.J. 736 (1924). Reprinted in: Selected Articles on the Conflict of Laws. New Haven, 1947, p. 1–18.
Lorenzen (1947-1)	Ernst G. Lorenzen, Territoriality, Public Policy and the Conflict of Laws, in: Selected Articles on the Conflict of Laws. New Haven, 1947, p. 1–18 = 33 Yale L.J. 736 (1924).
Lorenzen (1947-2)	Ernst G. Lorenzen, The Theory of Qualifications and the Conflict of Laws, in: Selected Articles on the Conflict of Laws. New Haven, 1947, p. 80–114 = 20 Col. L.Rev. 247 (1920).
Lorenzen (1947-3)	Ernst G. Lorenzen, The Qualification, Classification or Characterization Problem in the Conflict of Laws, in: Selected Articles on the Conflict of Laws, New Haven. 1947, p. 115–135.
Lorenzen (1947-4)	Ernst G. Lorenzen, Story's Commentaries on the Conflict of Laws – One Hundred Years After, in: Selected Articles on the Conflict of Laws, New Haven. 1947, p. 181–202 = 48 Harv. L.Rev. 15 (1934).
Loussouarn (1973)	Yvon Loussouarn, Cours général de droit international privé. 139 Rec. des Cours 271–385 (1973).
Lowenfeld/Silberman (1981)	Andreas F. Lowenfeld/Linda J. Silberman, Choice of Law and the Supreme Court: A Dialogue Inspired by Allstate Insurance Co. v. Hague (Allstate Symposium). 14 U.C.Davis L.Rev. 837–917 (1981).

Mann (1971)	F.A. Mann, Conflict of Laws and Public Law. 132 Rec. des Cours 107–196 (1971).
Martin (1984)	James A. Martin, An Approach to the Choice of Law Problem. 35 Mercer L.Rev. 583–593 (1984).
Mayer (1981)	Pierre Mayer, Les lois de police étrangères. Clunet 1981, p. 277–345.
McDougal (1979)	Luther L. McDougal III, Comprehensive Interest Analysis versus Reformulated Governmental Interest Analysis: An Appraisal in the Context of Choice of Law Problems Concerning Contributory and Comparative Negligence. 26 U.C.L.A. L.Rev. 439–483 (1979).
McDougal (1984)	Luther L. McDougal III, Toward Application of the Best Rule in Choice of Law Cases. 35 Mercer L.Rev. 483–533 (1984).
Milhollin (1975)	Gary L. Milhollin, Interest Analysis and Conflicts between Statutes of Limitation. 27 Hastings L.J. 1–53 (1975).
Morris, G. (1961)	G. Robert Morris Jr., Enterprise Liability and the Actuarial Process – The Insignificance of Foresight. 70 Yale L.J. 554–601 (1961).
Morris, J. (1951)	J.H.C. Morris, The Proper Law of a Tort. 64 Harv. L.Rev. 881–895 (1951).
Morse (1978)	C.G.J. Morse, Torts in Private International Law. Amsterdam/New York/Oxford, 1978.
Morse (1982)	C.G.J. Morse, Contracts of Employment and the E.E.C. Contractual Obligations Convention, in: Contract Conflicts, The E.E.C. Convention on the Law Applicable to Contractual Obligations: A Comparative Study (ed. P.M. North). Amsterdam/New York/Oxford, 1982, p. 143–184.
Morse (1984)	C.G.J. Morse, Choice of Law in Tort: A Comparative Study. 32 Am.J.Comp.L. 51–97 (1984).

Mühl (1982)	Margarete Mühl, Die Lehre vom 'besseren' und 'günstigeren' Recht im Internationalen Privatrecht, Zugleich eine Untersuchung des 'better-law approach' im amerikanischen Kollisionsrecht. München, 1982.
Nafziger/Dixon (1981)	James A. Nafziger/Steven Dixon, Oregon's Choice-of-Law Process. 60 Or. L.Rev. 219–248 (1981).
Neuhaus (1976)	Paul Heinrich Neuhaus, Die Grundbegriffe des internationalen Privatrechts. 2d ed., Tübingen, 1976.
Neumayer (1957)	Karl H. Neumayer, Autonomie de la volonté et dispositions impératives en droit international privé des obligations. Rev. Crit. d.i.p. 1957, p. 579–604; 1958, p. 53–78.
Neumayer (1963)	Karl H. Neumayer, Zur positiven Funktion der Kollisionsrechtlichen Vorbehaltsklausel, Ein Beitrag zur Geltung zwingender Rechtssätze und überpositiver Grundnormen im internationalen Privatrecht, in: Vom deutschen und europäischen Recht, Festschrift fur Hans Dölle (ed. Ernst von Caemmerer, Arthur Nikisch, Konrad Zweigert). Tübingen, 1963, vol. II, p. 179–208.
Odwald (1976)	Paul E. Odwald, Bernhard v. Harrah's Club: True Confusion in a True Conflict. 4 West St.U. L.Rev. 105–116 (1976).
Patocchi (1985)	Paolo Michele Patocchi, Règles de rattachement localisatrices et règles de rattachement à caractère substantiel: De quelques aspects récents de la diversification de la méthode conflictuelle en Europe. Genève, 1985.
Paulsen/Sovern (1956)	Monrad G. Paulsen/Michael I. Sovern, 'Public Policy' in the Conflict of Laws. 56 Col. L.Rev. 969–1016 (1956).
Peterson (1971)	Courtland H. Peterson, Weighing Contacts in Conflicts Cases: The Handmaiden Axiom (Cipolla Symposium). 9 Duquesne L.Rev. 436–445 (1971).

Peterson (1981)	Courtland H. Peterson, Proposals of Marriage between Jurisdiction and Choice of Law (Allstate Symposium). 14 U.C.Davis L.Rev. 869–887 (1981).
Philip (1982)	Allan Philip, Mandatory Rules, Public Law (Political Rules) and Choice of Law in the E.E.C. Convention on the Law Applicable to Contractual Obligations, in: Contract Conflicts, The E.E.C. Convention in the Law Applicable to Contractual Obligations: A Comparative Study (ed. P.M. North). Amsterdam/New York/Oxford, 1982, p. 81–108.
Posnak (1983)	Bruce Posnak, Choice of Law: A Very Well-Curried Leflar Approach. 34 Mercer L.Rev. 730–786 (1983).
Prosser (1984)	Prosser and Keeton on The Law of Torts (ed. W. Page Keeton). 5th ed., St. Paul, Minn., 1984.
Raape/Sturm (1977)	L. Raape/F. Sturm, Internationales Privatrecht. Vol. I, München, 1977.
Rabel (1931)	Ernst Rabel, Das problem der Qualification. Zeitschr. ausl. & intern. Privatr. 1931, p. 241–288.
Rabel (1958)	Ernst Rabel, The Conflict of Laws, A Comparative Study. 2d ed., 4 vols., Ann Arbor, Mich., 1958.
Ratner (1974)	Leonard G. Ratner, Choice of Law: Interest Analysis and Cost-Contribution. 47 So.Cal. L.Rev. 817–841 (1974).
Reese (1963)	Willis L.M. Reese, Conflict of Laws and the Restatement Second. 28 L. & C.P. 679–699 (1963).
Reese (1971)	Willis L.M. Reese, Chief Judge Fuld and Choice of Law. 71 Col. L.Rev. 548–566 (1971).
Reese (1972)	Willis L.M. Reese, Choice of Law: Rules or Approach. 57 Cornell L.Rev. 315–334 (1972).

Reese (1973-1)	Willis L.M. Reese, The Kentucky Approach to Choice of Law: A Critique (Foster Symposium). 61 Ky. L.J. 368–377 (1973).
Reese (1973-2)	Willis L.M. Reese, Dépeçage: A Common Phenomenon in Choice of Law. 73 Col. L.Rev. 58–73 (1973).
Reese (1977)	Willis L.M. Reese, Choice of Law in Torts and Contracts and Directions for the Future. 16 Col.J.Transn.L. 1–44 (1977).
Reese (1980)	Willis L.M. Reese, American Trends in Private International Law: Academic and Judicial Manipulation of Choice of Law Rules in Tort Cases. 33 Vand. L.Rev. 717–739 (1980).
Reese (1982)	Willis L.M. Reese, American Choice of Law (Bologna Symposium). 30 Am.J.Comp.L. 135–146 (1982).
Reese (1983-1)	Willis L.M. Reese, The Second Restatement of Conflict of Laws Revisited. 34 Mercer L.Rev. 501–519 (1983).
Reese (1983-2)	Willis L.M. Reese, The Influence of Substantive Policies in Choice of Law, in: Festschrift für Frank Vischer zum 60. Geburtstag (ed. Peter Böckli, Kurt Eichenberger, Hans Hinderling, Hans Peter Tsuchi). Zürich, 1983, p. 287–292.
Rehbinder (1973)	Eckard Rehbinder, Zur Politisierung des Internationalen Privatrechts. J.Z. 1973, p. 151–158.
Reilly (1974)	Jerrold B. Reilly, Tort Choice-of-Law in New York: The Fuldian Guest Statute Rules v. Professor Cavers' Principles in a Hypothetical Case. 25 Syr. L.Rev. 1005–1036 (1974).
Reppy (1983)	William A. Reppy Jr., Eclecticism in Choice of Law: Hybrid Method or Mishmash? 34 Mercer L.Rev. 645–708 (1983).

Rest (1980)	Alfred Rest, Die Wahl des günstigeren Recht im grenzüberschreitenden Umweltschutz, Stärkung des Individualschutzes?/The More Favourable Law Principle in Transfrontier Environmental Law, A Means of Strengthening the Protection of the Individual? Berlin, 1980.
Rheinstein (1944)	Max Rheinstein, The Place of Wrong: A Study in the Method of Case Law. 19 Tul. L.Rev. 4–31; p. 165–199 (1944).
Rheinstein (1962)	Max Rheinstein, How to Review a Festschrift. 11 Am.J.Comp.L. 632–668 (1962).
Richman (1982)	William M. Richman, Diagramming Conflicts: A Graphic Understanding of Interest Analysis. 43 Ohio St. L.J. 317–333 (1982)
Robertson (1940)	Arthur Henry Robertson, Characterization in the Conflict of Laws. Cambridge, Mass., 1940.
Rosenberg (1967)	Maurice Rosenberg, Kell v. Henderson: An Opinion for the New York Court of Appeals. 67 Col. L.Rev. 459–464 (1967).
Rosenberg (1980)	Maurice Rosenberg, A Comment on Neumeier (Leflar Symposium). 31 S.C. L.Rev. 443–456 (1980) = 34 Ark. L.Rev. 231–242 (1980).
Rosenberg (1981)	Maurice Rosenberg, The Comeback of Choice-of-Law Rules. 81 Col. L.Rev. 946–959 (1981).
Sauveplanne (1982)	J.G. Sauveplanne, New Trends in the Doctrine of Private International Law and their Impact on Court Practice. 175 Rec. des Cours 9–98 (1982).
Sauveplanne (1986)	J.G. Sauveplanne, Elementair internationaal privaatrecht. 8th ed., Deventer, 1986.
Savigny (1849)	Friedrich Carl Von Savigny, System des heutigen Römischen Rechts. Vol. 8, Berlin, 1849.
Schlesinger (1973)	Rudolf B. Schlesinger, A Recurrent Problem in Transnational Litigation: The Effect of Failure to Invoke or Prove the Applicable Foreign Law. 59 Cornell L.Rev. 1–26 (1973)

Schnitzer (1957)	Adolf F. Schnitzer, Handbuch des internationalen Privatrechts einschliesslich Prozessrecht, unter besonderen Berücksichtigung der Schweizerischen Gesetzgebung und Rechtsprechung. 4th ed., 2 vols. Basel, 1957/1958.
Schoordijk (1972)	H.C.F. Schoordijk, Oordelen en vooroordelen, Rede uitgesproken bij de vijfenveertigste herdenking van de dies natalis van de Katholieke Hogeschool te Tilburg op donderdag 28 september 1972. Deventer, 1972.
Schultsz (1983)	Jan C. Schultsz, Dutch Antecedents and Parallels to Article 7 of the EEC Contracts Convention of 1980. 47 RabelsZ. 267–283 (1983).
Schurig (1981)	Klaus Schurig, Kollisionsnorm und Sachrecht, Zu Struktur, Standort und Methode des internationalen Privatrechts. Berlin, 1981.
Schwander (1975)	Ivo Schwander, Lois d'application immédiate, Sonderanknüpfung, IPR-Sachnormen und andere Ausnahmen von der gewöhnlichen Anknüpfung im internationalen Privatrecht. Zürich, 1975.
Scoles/Weintraub (1972)	Eugene F. Scoles/Russell J. Weintraub, Cases and Materials on Conflict of Laws. 2d ed., St. Paul, Minn., 1972.
Sedler (1967)	Robert Allen Sedler, Babcock v. Jackson in Kentucky: Judicial Method and the Policy-Centered Conflict of Laws. 56 Ky. L.J. 27–138 (1967).
Sedler (1970)	Robert Allen Sedler, Characterization, Identification of the Problem Area, and the Policy-Centered Conflict of Laws: An Exercise in Judicial Method. 2 Rut.Cam. L.J. 8–100 (1970).
Sedler (1971-1)	Robert Allen Sedler, The Territorial Imperative: Automobile Accidents and the Significance of a State Line (Cipolla Symposium). 9 Duquesne L.Rev. 394–412 (1971).
Sedler (1971-2)	Robert Allen Sedler, Symposium: Conflict of Laws Round Table, The Value of Principled Preferences. 49 Tex. L.Rev. 224–228 (1971).

Sedler (1972)	Robert Allen Sedler, The Contracts Provision of the Restatement Second: An Analysis and a Critique. 72 Col. L.Rev. 279–328 (1972).
Sedler (1973-1)	Robert Allen Sedler, Judicial Method is 'Alive and Well': The Kentucky Approach to Choice of Law in Interstate Automobile Accidents (Foster Symposium). 61 Ky. L.J. 378–392 (1973).
Sedler (1973-2)	Robert Allen Sedler, Interstate Accidents and the Unprovided-for Case: Reflections on Neumeier v. Kuehner (Neumeier Symposium). 1 Hofstra L.Rev. 125–149 (1973).
Sedler (1977-1)	Robert Allen Sedler, The Governmental Interest Approach to Choice of Law: An Analysis and a Reformulation. 25 U.C.L.A. L.Rev. 181–243 (1977).
Sedler (1977-2)	Robert Allen Sedler, Rules of Choice of Law Versus Choice-of-Law Rules: Judicial Method in Conflicts Torts Cases. 44 Tenn. L.Rev. 975–1041 (1977).
Sedler (1979)	Robert Allen Sedler, On Choice of Law and the Great Quest: A Critique of Special Multistate Solutions to Choice-of-Law Problems. 7 Hofstra L.Rev. 807–832 (1979).
Sedler (1981)	Robert A. Sedler, Reflections on Conflict-of-Laws Methodology. 32 Hastings L.J. 1628–1643 (1981).
Sedler (1983-1)	Robert A. Sedler, Choice of Law in Michigan: Judicial Method and the Policy-Centered Conflict of Laws. 29 Wayne L.Rev. 1193–1221 (1983).
Sedler (1983-2)	Robert A. Sedler, Interest Analysis and Forum Preference in the Conflict of Laws: A Response to the 'New Critics'. 34 Mercer L.Rev. 593–644 (1983).
Seidelson (1973)	David E. Seidelson, Interest Analysis: For Those Who Like It and Those Who Don't. 11 Duquesne L.Rev. 283–312 (1973).

Seidelson (1981)	David E. Seidelson, Interest Analysis: The Quest for Perfection and the Frailties of Man. 19 Duquesne L.Rev. 207–244 (1981).
Shaman (1980)	Jeffrey M. Shaman, The Choice of Law Process: Territorialism and Functionalism. 22 W.&M. L.Rev. 227–257 (1980).
Shapira (1970)	Amos Shapira, The Interest Approach to Choice of Law, With Special Reference to Tort Problems. The Hague, 1970.
Shapira (1973)	Amos Shapira, 'Manna for the Entire World' or 'Thou Shalt Love Thy Neighbor as Thyself' – Comment on Neumeier v. Kuehner (Neumeier Symposium). 1 Hofstra L.Rev. 168–177 (1973).
Shapira (1977)	Amos Shapira, 'Grasp All, Lose All': On Restraint and Moderation in the Reformulation of Choice of Law Policy. 77 Col. L.Rev. 248–270 (1977).
Siehr (1975)	Kurt Siehr, General Report, in: European Private International Law of Obligations (ed. Ole Lando, Bernd von Hoffmann, Kurt Siehr). Tübingen, 1975, p. 42–79.
Siehr (1984)	Kurt Siehr, 'Forum Shopping' im internationalen Rechtsverkehr. Z.f.Rv. 1984, p. 124–144.
Siehr (1986)	Kurt G. Siehr, Die *lex-fori*–Lehre heute, in: Albert A. Ehrenzweig und das internationale Privatrecht, Symposium veranstaltet vom Institut für ausländisches und internationales Privat- und Wirtschaftsrecht der Universität Heidelberg am 17. Juli 1984 (ed. Rolf Serick, Hubert Niederländer, Erik Jayme). Heidelberg, 1986, p. 35–136.
Silberman (1981)	See: Lowenfeld/Silberman (1981)
Slagter (1961)	W.J. Slagter, Enige vragen van Nederlands internationaal privaatrecht met betrekking tot verkeersongelukken in het buitenland. V.R. 1961, p. 81–85; p. 101–105; p. 125–129; p. 145–151.

Steindorff (1958)	Erich Steindorff, Sachnormen im internationalen Privatrecht. Frankfurt a/M., 1958.
Story (1834)	Joseph Story, Commentaries on the Conflict of Laws. 1st ed., Boston, Mass., 1834.
Strikwerda (1978)	Luc Strikwerda, Semipubliekrecht in het conflictenrecht, Verkenningen op een kruispunt van methoden. Alphen aan de Rijn, 1978.
Strikwerda (1980)	L. Strikwerda, Kiest het Haags Verkeersongevallenverdrag voor verkeersslachtoffers? V.R. 1980, p. 25–31.
Strikwerda (1986)	L. Strikwerda, Naar een gereduceerd conflictenrecht? Iets over bescherming, begunstiging en better law in het internationaal privaatrecht. Groningen, 1986.
Strömholm (1961)	Stig Strömholm, Torts in the Conflict of Laws, A Comparative Study. Stockholm, 1961.
Ter Kuile (1983)	L.F.D. ter Kuile, International Issues on Collective Agreements of Seafarers, in: Essays on International & Comparative Law in Honour of Judge Erades. The Hague, 1983, p. 92–103.
Todd (1980)	John J. Todd, A Judge's View (Leflar Symposium). 31 S.C. L.Rev. 435–442 (1980) = 34 Ark. L.Rev. 224–230 (1980).
Toubiana (1972)	Annie Toubiana, Le domaine de la loi du contrat en droit international privé (contrats internationaux et dirigisme étatique). Paris, 1972.
Trautman (1967)	Donald T. Trautman, Kell v. Henderson: A Comment. 67 Col. L.Rev. 465–473 (1967).
Trautman (1979)	Donald T. Trautman, A Comment on Twerski and Mayer: A Pragmatic Step Towards Consensus as a Basis for Choice-of-Law Solutions. 7 Hofstra L.Rev. 833–855 (1979).
Trautman (1981)	Donald T. Trautman, Reflections on Conflict-of-Laws Methodology. 32 Hastings L.J. 1612–1627 (1981).

Traynor, M. (1961)	Michael Traynor, Conflict of Laws: Professor Currie's Restrained and Enlightened Forum. 49 Calif. L.Rev. 845–876 (1961).
Traynor, R. (1971)	Roger J. Traynor, Symposium: Conflict of Laws Round Table, The Value of Principled Preferences. 49 Tex. L.Rev. 239–242 (1971).
Traynor, R. (1976)	Roger J. Traynor, War and Peace in the Conflict of Laws. 25 I.C.L.Q. 121–155 (1976).
Trutmann (1973)	Verena Trutmann, Das internationale Privatrecht der Deliktsobligationen, Ein Beitrag zur Auseinandersetzung mit den neueren amerikanischen kollisionsrechtlichen Theorien. Basel/Stuttgart, 1973.
Twerski (1971)	Aaron D. Twerski, Enlightened Territorialism and Professor Cavers – The Pennsylvania Method (Cipolla Symposium). 9 Duquesne L.Rev. 373–393 (1971).
Twerski (1973-1)	Aaron D. Twerski, Neumeier v. Kuehner: Where Are the Emperor's Clothes? (Neumeier Symposium). 1 Hofstra L.Rev. 104–124 (1973).
Twerski (1973-2)	Aaron D. Twerski, To Where Does One Attach the Horses? (Foster Symposium). 61 Ky. L.J. 393–418 (1973).
Twerski/Mayer (1979)	Aaron D. Twerski/Renée G. Mayer, Toward a Pragmatic Solution of Choice-of-Law Problems – At the Interface of Substance and Procedure. 74 N.W.U. L.Rev. 781–802 (1979).
Vander Elst (1983)	Raymond Vander Elst, Droit international privé belge et droit conventionnel international, Tome Premier, Conflits de lois. Bruxelles, 1983.
Van Hecke (1977)	G. van Hecke, International Contracts and Domestic Legislative Policies, in: Internationales Recht und Wirtschaftsordnung/International Law and Economic Order, Festschrift für F.A. Mann zum 70. Geburtstag (ed. Werner Flume, Hugo J. Hahn, Gerhard Kegel, Kenneth R. Simmonds). München, 1977, p. 183–191.

Van Maanen (1981)	C.J.J. van Maanen, Het BBA en het internationaal privaatrecht. W.P.N.R. 1981, p. 793–796; p. 809–814.
Van Rooij (1976)	R. van Rooij, De positie van publiekrechtelijke regels op het terrein van het internationaal privaatrecht. 's-Gravenhage, 1976.
Van Rooij (1979)	R. van Rooij, De Haagse conferentie voor internationaal privaatrecht en het recht dat op de onrechtmatige daad van toepassing is. A.Ae. 1979, p. 255–264.
Van Rooij (1981)	R. van Rooij, Wetgeving internationale echtscheidingen. A.Ae. 1981, p. 420–429.
Van Schellen (1982)	J. van Schellen, Aspecten van internationaal stakingsrecht. Deventer, 1983.
Verheul (1978)	J.P. Verheul, De openbare orde als tweesnijdend zwaard. Leiden, 1978.
Verheul (1979)	Hans Verheul, Public Policy and Relativity. N.I.L.R. 1979, p. 109–129.
Vischer (1962)	Frank Vischer, Internationales Vertragsrecht: Die kollisionsrechtlichen Regeln der Anknüpfung bei internationalen Verträgen. Bern, 1962.
Vitta (1979)	Edoardo Vitta, Cours Général de Droit International Privé. 162 Rec. des Cours 9–243 (1979).
Vitta (1982)	Edoardo Vitta, The Impact in Europe of the American 'Conflicts Revolution' (Bologna Symposium). 30 Am.J.Comp.L. 1–18 (1982).
Vogel (1965)	Klaus Vogel, Der räumliche Anwendungsbereich der Verwaltungsnormen. Frankfurt a/M./Berlin,196
Von Hoffmann (1974)	Bernd von Hoffmann, Über den Schutz des schwächeren bei internationalen Schuldverträgen. 38 RabelsZ. 396–420 (1974).
Von Hoffmann (1975)	Bernd von Hoffmann, General Report, in: European Private International Law of Obligations (ed. Ole Lando, Bernd von Hoffmann, Kurt Siehr). Tübingen, 1975, p. 1–41.

Von Mehren (1961)	Arthur Taylor von Mehren, The Renvoi and its Relation to Various Approaches to the Choice-of-Law Problem, in: Twentieth Century Comparative and Conflicts Law, Legal Essays in Honor of Hessel E. Yntema. Leyden, 1961, p. 380–394.
Von Mehren (1974)	Arthur Taylor von Mehren, Special Substantive Rules for Multistate Problems: Their Role and Significance in Contemporary Choice of Law Methodology. 88 Harv. L.Rev. 347–371 (1974).
Von Mehren (1975)	Arthur Taylor von Mehren, Recent Trends in Choice-of-Law Methodology. 60 Cornell L.Rev. 926–968 (1975).
Von Mehren (1977)	Arthur Taylor von Mehren, Choice of Law and the Problem of Justice. 41 L. & C.P. 27–43 (1977).
Von Mehren/ Trautman (1965)	Arthur Taylor von Mehren/Donald Theodore Trautman, The Law of Multistate Problems, Cases and Materials on Conflict of Laws. Boston/ Toronto, 1965.
Von Overbeck (1982)	Alfred E. von Overbeck, Contracts: The Swiss Draft Statute Compared with the E.E.C. Convention, in: Contract Conflicts, The E.E.C. Convention on the Law Applicable to Contractual Obligations: A Comparative Study (ed. P.M. North). Amsterdam/New York/Oxford, 1982, p. 269–294.
Wasilczyk (1977)	John J. Wasilczyk, Choice of Law for True Conflicts. 65 Calif. L.Rev. 290–304 (1977).
Weintraub (1963)	Russell J. Weintraub, A Method for Solving Conflict Problems – Torts. 48 Cornell L.Q. 215–252 (1963).
Weintraub (1968)	Russell J. Weintraub, The Impact of a Functional Analysis upon the 'Pervasive Problems' on the Conflict of Laws. 15 U.C.L.A. L.Rev. 817–839 (1968).
Weintraub (1971)	Russell J. Weintraub, Commentary on the Conflict of Laws. 1st ed., Mineola, N.Y., 1977.

Weintraub (1972)	Russell J. Weintraub, Response to the Critiques of Professors Sedler, Twerski, and Walker. 57 Iowa L.Rev. 1258–1270 (1972).
Weintraub (1973)	Russell J. Weintraub, Finding a Substitute for the Place-of-Wrong Rule: The Kentucky Experience (Foster Symposium). 61 Ky. L.J. 419–428 (1973).
Weintraub (1977)	Russell J. Weintraub, The Future of Choice of Law for Torts: What Principles Should Be Preferred? 41 L. & C.P. 146–164 (1977).
Weintraub (1980)	Russell J. Weintraub, Commentary on the Conflict of Laws. 2d ed., Mineola, N.Y., 1980.
Weintraub (1984)	Russell J. Weintraub, Interest Analysis in the Conflict of Laws as an Application of Sound Legal Reasoning. 35 Mercer L.Rev. 623–646 (1984).
Wendels (1983)	A. Wendels, Internationale echtscheidingen, Rechtsmacht, Toepasselijk recht, Erkenning. 2d ed., Zwolle, 1983.
Westbrook (1975)	James E. Westbrook, A Survey and Evaluation of Competing Choice-of-Law Methodologies: The Case for Eclecticism. 40 Mo. L.Rev. 407–466 (1975).
Westen (1967)	Peter Kay Westen, False Conflicts. 55 Calif. L.Rev. 74–122 (1967).
Widger (1974)	Stanley W. Widger Jr., The Present Status of Automobile Guest Statutes. 59 Cornell L.Rev. 659–686 (1974)
Wilde (1968)	Christian L. Wilde, Dépeçage in the Choice of Tort Law. 41 S.Cal. L.Rev. 329–365 (1968).
Williams, G. (1951)	Glanville Williams, The Aims of the law of Tort. 4 Curr. Legal Probl. 137–176 (1951).
Williams, P. (1986)	Patrick Ross Williams, The EEC Convention on the Law Applicable to Contractual Obligations. 35 I.C.L.Q. 1–31 (1986).

Wurfel (1974)	Seymour Wurfel, Statutes of Limitation in the Conflict of Laws. 52 N.C. L.Rev. 489–574 (1974).
Yntema (1953)	Hessel E. Yntema, The Historic Bases of Private International Law. 2 Am.J.Comp.L. 297–317 (1953).
Yntema (1957)	Hessel E. Yntema, The Objectives of Private International Law. 35 Can. B.Rev. 721 (1957).
Zweigert (1973)	Konrad Zweigert, Zur Armut des internationalen Privatrechts an sozialen Werten. 37 RabelsZ. 435–452 (1973).

Names

References are either to pages or footnotes. References to footnotes, preceded by the number of the chapter concerned, have been printed in italics; *e.g.* chapter 1, footnote 21 = *1:21*.

Akehurst *1-42*, *8-97*
Aldricus 11
Alexander *2-267*, *2-270*
Allen *8-50*
Asser 21, *1-45*
Atiyah *9-18*, *9-66*
Audit *3-14*
Baade *1-21*, *4-20*, *4-23*, *4-25*, *4-100*, *4-121*, *4-128*, *4-278*, *4-295*, *4-298*, *6-32*, *6-33*, *8-40*, *8-49*, *8-50*, 423, *8-82*, *8-85*, *9-21*, 466, *9-29*, *9-43*
Bartin *2-8*
Bartolus *6-4*
Basedow *1-226*, *1-228*, *2-114*
Batiffol *1-144*, *2-172*
Baxter 5, *1-183*, 282, *4-188*, *4-190*, 283, *4-193*, *4-194*, *4-197*, 284, *4-198*, 285, *4-201*, *4-202*, *4-205*, *4-207*, *4-211*, *4-225*, 292, 293, 295, 299, *4-264*, *4-271*, 302, 388
Beale *1-2*, 198, *3-27*, 201, 225, *4-28*, 254, 324, 348, 400, 481, 487
Behr *1-41*
Bell *8-58*
Bentham *8-93*
Bergan *6-34*
Binder 29, *1-64*, *1-166*, *3-58*
Bloembergen *9-36*
Bourel 29, *1-65*, *2-172*
Brennan 390, 391
Brilmayer *2-78*, *3-8*, *4-155*, *8-6*, *8-81*, *8-98*, *9-22*, *9-30*, 469, *9-31*, *9-34*, 473, *9-39*, *9-40*, *9-42*, *9-52*, *9-59*, *9-61*
Broderick *6-74*
Bucher *1-202*, *1-206*
Burke *6-26*, 407, *8-29*, *8-122*
Burns *2-228*
Butler *1-1*, *1-3*, *2-30*
Cardozo *2-181*, 149, 152, *2-198*, *2-199*, *8-29*

Cavers 5, *1-15*, *1-44*, 125, *2-106*, *2-112*, *3-4*, *3-5*, *3-23*, 197, *3-26*, *3-27*, *3-102*, 228, *4-4*, *4-29*, 261, *4-126*, *4-143*, *4-157*, 273, 286, *4-218*, 302, 303, *4-274*, *4-275*, *4-276*, 304, *4-279*, *4-280*, *4-281*, *4-282*, *4-285*, 306, *4-288*, *4-290*, 307, *4-291*, *4-292*, *4-295*, *4-296*, 308, *4-298*, *4-299*, *4-301*, 309, *4-304*, 310, *4-308*, 311, *4-312*, 312, *4-313*, 313, 314, 316, 323, 324, 330, *5-35*, *5-41*, *8-5*, *8-10*, *8-17*, *8-30*, *8-39*, 417, *8-65*, *8-96*, 490
Cheatham *3-30*, *4-218*, 326, *5-14*, 482
Cohen *9-7*
Cohen Henriquez *1-116*
Cook *3-4*, *3-27*, *4-274*
Coscarelli *8-41*
Couch *8-58*, *8-102*
Cramton *1-44*, *2-2*, *2-52*, *2-72*, *2-81*, *2-106*, *2-189*, *2-210*, *4-3*, *4-29*, *4-92*, *4-157*, *4-190*, *4-325*, *5-44*, *8-89*
Crombag *9-7*
Currie, Brainerd 5, 6, *1-15*, 8, 11, *1-232*, 110, *2-53*, 125, *2-106*, *2-112*, *2-198*, *2-202*, *2-205*, 155, *2-210*, *2-211*, *2-214*, *2-253*, 171, *2-262*, *2-274*, *2-276*, *2-280*, *2-285*, *2-287*, 190, *3-4*, *3-5*, 191, *3-10*, *3-61*, *3-97*, *4-2*, 229, *4-5*, 230, *4-7*, *4-19*, 233, *4-21*, *4-24*, 234, *4-25*, *4-26*, *4-29*, 236, *4-33*, *4-34*, 252, *4-80*, 253, *4-81*, *4-86*, 254, 255, *4-87*, *4-100*, *4-118*, 271, 272, *4-149*, *4-150*, *4-151*, *4-152*, *4-153*, *4-154*, *4-155*, *4-156*, 273, *4-158*, *4-163*, 275, 282, 283, *4-197*, 285, *4-204*, 286, *4-207*, *4-211*, *4-225*, 293, *4-267*, *4-271*, *4-298*, 311, *4-322*, 323, 327, 330, *6-25*, 366, 374, 375, *7-4*, *7-6*, 377, *7-39*, *8-3*, 399, *8-8*, *8-90*, 428, *8-93*, *8-95*, *8-98*, *8-100*, 444, 455, 464, *9-14*, *9-16*, 465, *9-30*, 469, *9-32*, 473, *9-39*, *9-40*, 474, *9-43*, *9-50*, 479, *9-56*, *9-60*, 488
Currie, David *1-44*, *2-2*, *2-52*, *2-72*, *2-81*, *2-106*, *2-189*, *2-210*, *4-3*, *4-29*, *4-92*, *4-157*, *4-190*, *4-218*, *4-325*, *5-44*, *8-89*
Currie, Justice *4-49*
David *1-112*
De Boer *1-38*, *1-39*, *1-48*, *1-66*, *1-72*, *1-73*, *1-82*, *1-161*, *1-166*, *1-174*, *1-176*, *1-181*, *1-190*, *1-226*, *1-227*, *1-228*, *2-114*, *2-117*, *2-185*, *2-263*, *2-291*, *3-17*, *3-58*, *7-1*, *9-67*, *9-68*
De Nova *1-202*, *1-205*, *4-23*, *5-13*
De Wijkerslooth *9-7*
De Winter *1-20*, 21, 22, *1-85*, 44, *1-117*, *1-202*, 77, *1-203*, *1-204*, *4-191*
Deby Gérard *1-202*, *1-206*, *1-207*
Deelen 7, *1-17*, *1-110*, *1-202*, 77, *1-203*, *1-204*, *1-218*, *2-159*
Desmond 154, *2-206*, 407, *8-30*
Dicey *1-61*, *2-10*
Dixon *3-81*
Drion *1-26*, *1-38*, *1-73*, *1-174*, *7-6*, *8-7*
Drobnig *1-230*
Dubbink *1-43*, *1-44*, *1-72*, *1-166*, *1-167*, *1-175*, *2-3*, 96, *2-10*, *2-11*, 97, *2-14*, *2-80*, *2-81*, *2-126*, *2-154*, *2-169*, *2-172*, *4-293*

Duchek *1-100*, *1-101*, *1-102*
Duintjer Tebbens *1-66*, *1-165*, *1-168*, *1-223*, *2-131*, *2-172*, *4-221*, *4-223*
Ebener *8-47*
Egnal *2-93*, 127, *2-111*, *2-113*, 128, *2-115*, *2-119*, *2-120*, *2-121*, *2-122*, *2-123*, 134, *2-134*, *2-136*, 135, *2-138*
Ehrenzweig *1-7*, 6, *1-15*, *1-21*, *1-37*, *1-43*, *1-44*, *1-154*, *1-166*, *2-20*, 111, *2-56*, *2-131*, *2-188*, 150, *2-192*, 190, 197, *3-26*, 202, *3-36*, *4-18*, 234, *4-26*, *4-189*, *4-218*, *4-299*, 311, *4-312*, *4-322*, 323, *5-13*, 330, *5-35*, *6-4*, *7-5*, *7-6*, *7-39*, 410, *8-42*, *8-57*, *8-59*, 421, *8-77*, *8-114*
Ely *9-42*, 475, *9-46*
Erades *1-72*
Erauw *1-57*, *2-264*
Esser *9-7*
Ester *2-70*
Falconbridge *2-8*
Fallon *1-91*
Felix *4-68*, *4-307*, *4-312*, *4-322*, *5-1*
Ferrer-Correia *1-25*
Flessner *2-291*
Fletcher *1-124*
Francescakis *1-176*, *1-202*, 79, *1-207*
Franx 32, *1-118*, *1-209*, 85, *2-24*, 145, 146, *2-174*
Freund *2-108*, *4-251*
Fried *1-45*
Friedmann *1-146*, *8-93*
Fuld 164, *2-243*, *3-41*, 242, 244, *4-59*, 256, *4-95*, 257, *4-100*, 261, 309, *4-305*, 351, *6-15*, *6-16*, *6-24*, *6-30*, 356, *6-32*, *6-34*, 357, 358, *6-40*, 360, 369, 372, *8-5*, 417, 422, 423, 424, *8-86*, 443, *8-134*, 449, *8-152*, 452
Gamillschegg *1-123*, *1-132*
Giuliano *1-93*, *1-229*, *1-233*
Goldman *2-172*
Goodrich *2-7*, *2-97*, *2-188*
Gorman *4-218*
Grotius 20
Gutzwiller 7, 40, *1-107*, *1-183*
Haak *1-85*, *1-92*, *1-124*, *1-218*, *1-220*, *1-221*
Hancock *2-5*, *2-49*, 110, *2-54*, *2-181*, *6-33*, 416, *8-60*, *9-51*
Hanotiau *2-153*, *3-1*, *3-4*, *3-5*, *3-7*, *3-8*, *3-22*, *5-42*
Hartley *1-124*, *1-161*, *1-162*
Hay *3-29*, *4-105*, *4-265*, *5-79*, *6-18*, *6-43*
Heini 6, *1-15*
Herzog *6-45*, *6-55*
Hijmans 27, *1-58*, 28
Hijmans van den Bergh *1-81*, *1-87*, *1-123*, *1-203*, *1-213*

Hill *4-156*, *4-157*, *8-6*
Hogue *5-86*
Hohloch *1-165*, *1-166*, *1-170*, *1-193*, *5-43*, *6-6*
Holman *6-58*
Horey *6-37*
Horowitz *4-149*, 282, *4-189*, 285, *4-206*, 286, *4-211*, *4-218*, *4-221*, *4-224*, *4-225*, 295, *4-253*, *4-273*
Huber 20, 21, *1-43*, *1-44*, 348, *6-1*
Humphreys *2-234*
Ihering *8-93*
Jayme *1-25*, *1-150*, *3-22*, *4-68*, *4-69*, *4-99*
Jenard *1-90*
Jessurun d'Oliveira 6, *1-17*, *1-53*, *1-54*, *1-66*, *1-72*, *1-73*, *1-85*, *1-99*, *1-114*, 48, *1-129*, 66, *1-176*, *1-177*, *1-212*, 82, *1-218*, *1-219*, *1-220*, *1-221*, *2-157*, *2-167*, *2-251*, *2-263*, *2-264*, *2-266*, *2-291*, *4-27*, 235, *4-31*, *4-32*, *4-34*, *4-40*, *4-41*, *5-96*
Joerges 7
Joppe *5-96*
Juenger *1-21*, *2-3*, *3-1*, *3-36*, *4-265*, 330, *5-36*, *5-87*, *7-52*, *7-54*, *7-61*, 401, *8-9*
Kahn *2-8*, *2-8*, *2-171*
Kahn-Freund *1-66*, *1-88*
Kanowitz *4-265*
Kavanagh 384, *7-34*
Kay *1-44*, *2-2*, *2-52*, *2-72*, *2-81*, *2-106*, *2-189*, *2-210*, *4-3*, *4-29*, *4-92*, *4-157*, *4-189*, *4-190*, *4-191*, *4-197*, *4-202*, *4-203*, *4-204*, 286, *4-207*, *4-210*, *4-211*, *4-213*, *4-218*, *4-237*, *4-247*, *4-251*, *4-263*, *4-265*, *4-268*, *4-271*, *4-325*, *5-44*, *6-6*, *6-33*, *6-45*, *6-58*, *8-89*
Keating *6-15*, *8-43*, 417, 424, *8-86*
Keeton *8-23*
Kegel 6, *1-16*, *1-25*, *1-61*, *1-132*, *1-145*, *1-165*, *1-183*, *1-194*, *2-3*, *2-9*, *2-154*, *2-155*, *2-160*, *4-299*, *7-1*, *8-3*, *8-6*
Keller *1-115*, *1-137*, *1-138*, *1-183*
Kelly *1-205*
Kenison *5-58*
King *4-123*
Kisch 67, *1-179*
Kokkini-Iatridou *9-67*
Kollewijn *1-43*, *1-57*
Korn *2-212*, *2-217*, *3-29*, *6-18*, *6-24*, *6-28*, *6-30*, *6-31*, *6-34*, *6-35*, *6-55*, *6-58*, *6-63*, *6-76*, *6-85*
Korthals Altes *2-25*
Kosters *1-43*, *1-44*, *2-80*, *2-81*, *2-154*

Kotting *1-202, 1-209, 1-220, 1-221, 1-224, 1-226, 1-226, 1-227, 1-228, 1-226,*
2-111, 2-114, 2-117, 2-265, 2-284, 7-1, 7-2, 9-63
Kötz *9-65*
Kozyris 391, *7-52, 7-54, 7-55, 7-56, 7-58, 8-23*
Kreuzer *1-106*
Kropholler *1-66, 1-115, 1-126, 1-132, 1-160, 2-9, 2-81, 2-157, 3-58*
Lagarde *1-93, 1-229, 1-233, 2-172*
Lando *1-89, 1-115, 1-123, 1-136, 1-160, 3-1*
Lascher *8-46*
Lawson *9-65*
Leflar 5, *1-28, 1-29*, 11, *1-30*, 12, *1-31, 1-37*, 62, *1-163, 1-182, 1-232, 2-8, 2-36*, 106, *2-41, 2-52, 2-72, 2-81, 2-97, 2-147, 2-181, 2-182*, 152, *2-198*, 165, *2-255*, 172, *2-258*, 173, *3-5, 3-21, 3-25*, 200, *3-34, 3-35, 3-39, 3-47, 4-27, 4-28, 4-29, 4-41, 4-49*, 246, *4-130*, 273, 274, 286, 287, *4-218, 4-263*, 307, 311, 323, *5-2*, 324, *5-4, 5-5, 5-6, 5-7*, 325, *5-9, 5-10, 5-11, 5-12*, 326, *5-15, 5-16, 5-17, 5-18*, 327, *5-20, 5-21*, 328 *5-23, 5-24*, 329, *5-29, 5-32, 5-33, 5-34*, 330, 331, *5-56*, 337, *5-64, 5-66, 5-82*, 343, *5-86, 6-34, 6-39, 6-69, 6-86*, 370, 374, *7-38*, 388, 390, *8-5*, 407, *8-40*, 424, *8-88, 8-89, 8-90, 8-153, 8-162, 9-12*, 480, *9-57*, 482, 488, 489
Lehman 151, 153, *2-199*
Lemaire *1-85, 1-175, 2-159*
Levin 384, *7-34*
Lipstein *1-202*
Lopez *4-124*
Lorenz *5-43*
Lorenzen *1-44, 2-8*, 118, *2-83, 2-188*, 150, *2-192, 2-194, 3-27, 4-274*
Loussouarn *1-25*
Lowenfeld *3-1, 7-52*
Lubbers *5-96*
Mancini 21, *2-154*
Mann *1-202*
Markezinis *9-65*
Martin *9-32, 9-49, 9-50*
Mayer, Pierre *1-202*
Mayer, Renée 113, *2-63*, 116, *2-77*
McDougal *4-265, 8-2, 8-10, 8-15, 8-22, 8-39, 8-43, 8-46, 8-52, 8-57, 8-58, 8-69*, 421, *8-78*
Meijers 25, *1-52, 1-57, 2-263*
Milhollin *2-62, 2-77, 2-79*
Morris, G. Robert *8-59, 8-112, 8-113, 8-114*
Morris, J.H.C. 28, 29, *1-61, 1-63, 1-67, 1-68, 1-69*, 31, *2-10*
Morse *1-72, 1-124, 1-161, 1-164, 1-181, 2-126, 2-172, 2-181, 2-182, 2-193, 2-197, 4-29, 4-34, 4-63*
Mühl *1-154, 1-165, 1-166, 1-170, 1-194, 5-2, 5-3, 5-10, 5-12, 5-13, 5-44*

Nafziger *3-81*
Neuhaus *1-61*, *1-141*, *1-145*, *1-165*, *1-183*, *1-194*, *2-9*, *2-160*, *2-197*
Neumayer *1-202*
North *1-124*, *1-229*
Nussbaum *7-5*
O'Connell *8-23*
Odwald *4-240*
Offerhaus *1-88*
Oldenhuis *2-178*
Otis *3-59*
Palmer *1-112*
Patocchi *1-25*, *1-102*, *1-106*, *1-169*, *1-183*, *1-202*, *1-206*
Paulsen *2-170*, *2-181*, *2-187*, *2-188*, 150, *2-191*, *2-193*, *2-197*, *2-217*
Pelaez *4-312*, *4-322*
Peterson 311, *4-312*, *4-322*, 339, *7-52*, *7-56*, *7-57*, *7-60*
Philip *1-230*
Pillet *1-131*, *2-154*, *4-191*
Posnak *4-192*, 330, *5-40*, *5-89*
Pound *8-93*
Powell 391, *7-55*, 392
Prosser *4-163*, *8-14*, *8-15*, *8-17*, *8-21*, *8-22*, *8-23*, *8-25*, *8-37*, *8-39*, *8-40*, *8-47*, *8-49*, *8-50*, *8-62*
Quadri *4-23*
Quirico *4-76*
Raape *2-291*
Rabel *2-9*
Ratner 421, *8-79*, *8-90*, *8-94*
Reed *7-20*, *8-142*
Reese 5, *1-140*, *1-185*, *1-192*, *3-1*, 195, *3-20*, 199, *3-30*, *3-37*, *3-39*, *3-103*, *4-6*, 323, 326, *5-14*, *6-32*, *6-39*, *7-8*, *7-15*, *7-18*, *7-22*, 388, *7-43*, *7-45*, 423, *8-82*, *8-84*, *8-85*, 424, 482
Rehbinder *1-210*
Reilly *4-278*, *4-295*, *6-27*, *6-39*
Reppy *1-31*, *3-25*, *3-29*, *3-34*, *3-39*, 216, *3-79*, *4-207*, *4-221*, *4-226*, *4-265*, *4-266*, *4-272*, *4-273*, *5-5*, *5-8*, *5-25*, *5-34*, 337, *5-62*, *5-64*, *5-74*, *5-76*, *6-19*, *6-22*, *6-28*, *6-29*, *6-58*, *6-62*, *6-65*, *6-86*
Rest *1-166*, *1-176*, *1-186*, *1-193*
Rheinstein *2-35*, *2-48*
Rigaux *1-206*
Roberts 311, *4-311*, *4-326*, *8-66*, *8-109*, *8-113*, *8-143*
Robertson *2-8*, *2-39*
Robinette *8-82*
Rodenburg 20
Rolfe *8-15*

Rosenberg *1-31*, *4-218*
Sauveplanne *1-57*, *1-209*, *2-250*, *3-3*, *3-24*
Savigny *1-2*, 15, 41, *1-206*, 140, *2-217*, 201, 400, 487
Schlesinger *2-262*, *2-267*, *2-269*, *2-270*, *2-282*, *9-2*
Schnitzer 34, *1-85*, *1-87*, 48, *1-128*
Scholten *2-263*
Schoordijk *9-7*, *9-53*
Schultsz *1-76*, *1-77*, *1-202*, *1-214*, *1-220*, *1-223*, *1-228*, *2-17*, 100, *2-23*, *2-173*, *5-96*, *8-153*
Schurig *1-200*, *1-208*
Schwander *1-200*, *1-201*, *1-202*
Schwind, Fritz *1-100*, *1-101*, *1-102*
Schwind, Michael A. 7
Scoles *2-1*, *4-218*
Sedler *2-12*, *2-34*, 111, *2-57*, *2-59*, 112, *2-60*, *3-4*, *3-40*, *4-88*, *4-100*, *4-99*, 263, *4-120*, *4-122*, 264, *4-123*, *4-124*, *4-125*, *4-131*, *4-139*, *4-145*, *4-254*, *4-312*, 312, *4-319*, 313, *4-326*, *5-44*, *5-54*, *6-6*, *6-23*, *6-27*, *6-31*, *6-33*, *6-42*, *6-48*, *7-7*, *7-8*, 378, 379, *7-15*, *7-16*, *7-21*, *7-23*, 383, 384, *7-32*, *7-35*, 387, *7-40*, *7-42*, 388, *8-40*, *8-43*, *9-3*
Seidelson 130, *2-120*, *2-121*, 131, *2-122*, *2-125*, 132, *2-126*, 133, 134, 138, *4-312*, *4-322*, *6-30*
Selvin *8-47*
Shaman *6-2*
Shapira *3-31*, *3-35*, *3-102*, *4-100*, *4-146*, *4-156*, *6-33*, *6-34*, *7-41*, 400, *8-8*, *8-93*, 456, *9-1*
Siehr *1-89*, *1-90*, *1-91*, *3-1*, *7-6*
Silberman *7-52*, *7-55*
Slagter *1-72*
Smith *8-59*
Soek *2-265*
Sovern *2-170*, *2-181*, *2-187*, *2-188*, 150, *2-191*, *2-193*, *2-197*, *2-217*
Spaeth *4-330*, *8-148*
Sprecher *3-100*
Stafford *2-254*, *2-261*
Steiger *1-130*
Steindorff *1-20*
Stevens *7-53*, *7-61*
Story 21, *1-44*, 348, *6-1*, *6-4*
Strikwerda 8, 9, *1-23*, *1-48*, *1-109*, *1-116*, *1-134*, *1-141*, *1-146*, *1-149*, *1-152*, *1-172*, 68, *1-182*, *1-183*, *1-184*, 69, *1-202*, *1-203*, *1-204*, *1-206*, *1-207*, *1-208*, *1-210*, *1-218*, *1-236*, *2-51*, *2-114*, *2-154*, *2-253*, 171, *2-256*, *3-10*, *3-9*, 260, *4-108*, *4-119*, *4-153*, *4-158*, *4-197*, 286, *4-211*, *4-271*, *4-282*, *4-287*, *4-293*, *4-295*, *4-300*, *5-13*, *5-19*, *5-22*, *5-42*, *5-90*, *7-2*, *8-90*, *8-93*, *8-94*, *8-100*, *9-8*, *9-36*, *9-37*, *9-55*, *9-63*

Strömholm *1-165, 1-166, 1-167, 1-170*
Struycken *1-203*
Sturm *2-291*
Sullivan *4-191*, 286, *4-211*
Ter Kuile *2-25*
Tipton *8-61*
Todd *5-1*
Toubiana *1-202, 1-206, 1-207*
Trask *4-45*
Trautman 197, 245, *4-63, 4-218, 4-251*, 311, 404, *8-14, 8-40*, 423, *8-83, 8-84, 8-85*, 424, *9-8*, 466
Traynor, Michael *4-149, 9-43*
Traynor, Roger J. 241, *4-163*, 288, *4-301*
Twerski 113, *2-63*, 116, *2-77*, 253, *4-84, 4-98, 4-100*, 261, *4-112, 4-113, 4-114*, 262, 265, *4-127, 4-135, 4-312*, 312, *4-315*, 313, *4-323*, 353, *6-25, 7-8, 7-23*, 388, *7-43*, 474, *9-44*
Tyler *1-112*
Van Bynkershoek 20
Van Dievoet *1-57*
Van Hecke *1-202*
Van Maanen *1-212, 1-214, 9-64*
Van Oosten *1-219*
Van Rooij *1-149, 1-175, 1-176, 1-202, 1-209, 1-219, 1-220, 1-221, 1-234, 2-154*
Van Schellen *2-25*
Vander Elst *2-264*
Van der Grinten *1-203*
Van der Ploeg *5-96*
Veegens *1-112*
Verheul *2-158, 2-159, 2-161, 2-164, 2-164, 2-171, 2-191, 2-249*
Verwilghen *1-118, 1-120, 1-159*
Vischer 34, *1-85, 1-87*, 48, *1-128*
Vitta *1-25*, 189, *3-1, 3-2, 3-31*
Vlas *1-224*
Voet, Johannes 20, *1-43, 1-44*
Voet, Paulus 20, *1-43, 1-44*
Vogel *1-202*
Von Hoffmann *1-89, 1-96, 1-115, 1-160, 9-65*
Von Mehren *2-81*, 125, *2-108*, 126, *2-109*, 129, 137, *2-148*, 197, *4-251, 4-300*, 311, 331, *5-43, 6-33, 9-8*
Von Overbeck *1-162, 1-164, 1-181*
Walsh *3-41*
Wechsler *3-28*

Weintraub *1-29, 1-30,* 13, *1-34, 1-35, 2-1,* 95, *2-31, 2-32,* 110, *2-55, 2-61,* 126, *2-110, 2-115,* 129, *2-193, 2-199,* 153, *2-200, 2-252, 2-271, 2-288,* 197, *3-35, 3-40, 3-52, 4-6, 4-48,* 254, *4-88, 4-121, 4-125, 4-127, 4-129, 4-186, 4-218, 4-240, 4-263, 5-10,* 330, *5-37, 5-38, 5-39, 5-51, 5-79, 5-80, 5-89, 6-6, 6-18, 6-28, 6-34, 6-42, 6-45,* 369, *6-81, 7-7, 7-8,* 379, *7-16, 7-38, 7-39, 7-42,* 388, *7-56, 8-64, 8-89, 8-90, 8-132, 8-153*
Wendels *1-145*
Westbrook *1-31, 1-183, 3-25, 3-29, 5-7, 5-22, 5-36,* 330, *5-42, 5-94, 5-97*
Westen *4-6, 4-20, 4-26, 4-28, 4-29, 4-34*
Widger *8-12, 8-17, 8-20, 8-21, 8-22, 8-25, 8-39, 8-40, 8-46, 8-47, 8-49, 8-50, 8-52, 8-53, 8-61, 8-62, 8-110*
Wilde *4-6*
Williams, Chief Judge 377, 383, *7-31,* 384
Williams, Glanville *9-65*
Williams, Patrick Ross *1-98*
Wurfel *2-74, 2-76*
Yntema *1-44,* 324, 326, *5-14,* 482
Young *1-41*
Zweigert 53, *1-139,* 62, *1-163, 1-183, 1-186, 2-291*

Cases

References are to page numbers. In text and footnotes, the names of the decisions have been printed in italics.

1. United States

Abendschein v. Farrell 159, 160
Accusystems, Inc. v. Honeywell Information Systems 362
Acme Circus Operating Co., Inc. v. Kuperstock 110
Adams v. Buffalo Forge Co. 213, 320
Alabama Great Southern R.R. v. Carroll 29
Alaska Packers Ass. v. Industrial Accident Comm'n of California. 228, 390
Algie v. Algie 97
Allstate Ins. Co. v. Hague 321, 328, 337, 390, 391, 392, 393, 489
Amdur v. Zim Israel Navigation Company 178
Anderson v. The Milwaukee & St. Paul Railway Co. 349
Andrew Jackson Sales v. Bi-Lo Stores 350
Arbuthnot v. Allbright 244, 245, 247, 357, 358, 372, 452, 453
Ardoyno v. Kyzar 231, 274, 318, 319
Armstrong v. Armstrong 240, 241, 248
Arnett v. Thompson 163, 251, 377, 378, 379, 380, 381, 386, 387, 388, 389, 392
Aurora National Bank v. Anderson 103, 120, 136
Babcock v. Jackson 4, 9, 124, 132, 153, 161, 166, 189, 242, 244, 250, 256, 257, 277, 288, 315, 322, 351, 353, 363, 364, 365, 367, 369, 372, 397, 398, 407, 422, 423, 424, 442, 443, 445
Bailey v. Chattem, Inc. 349
Bain v. Northern Pac. Ry. Co. 349
Baird v. Bell Helicopter Textron 215, 235
Balts v. Balts 103, 338
Bankhaus Hermann Lampe K.G. v. Mercantile-Safe Dep. 230, 367
Barr v. Interbay Citizens Bank of Tampa, Fla. 270
Beasock v. Dioguardi Enterprises, Inc. 276, 364, 367, 368, 371
Beaulieu v. Beaulieu 213, 240, 243, 320
Beech Aircraft Corp. v. Superior Court 181, 235, 291
Belisario v. Manhattan Motor Rental, Inc. 360, 367, 371
Bell v. State Farm Fire & Cas. Co. 231, 280, 319
Bernhard v. Harrah's Club 282, 286, 287, 292, 293, 294, 296, 297, 299, 300

Bernkrant v. Fowler 288
Bigelow v. Halloran 339, 342
Bing v. Halstead 258, 259, 352, 359, 366, 367, 371
Bing v. Thunig 165
Bio/Basics Intern. v. Ortho Pharmaceutical Corp. 209
Bishop v. Florida Specialty Paint Co. 162, 204, 403
Blais v. Deyo 277, 364
Bolgrean v. Stich 338, 415, 449, 469
Bonfanti Industries, Inc. v. Teke, Inc. 295
Borst v. Borst 414
Bouchard v. DeGagne 251
Bournias v. Atlantic Maritime Co. 106, 107
Bowen v. United States 125, 135
Branyan v. Alpena Flying Service, Inc. 153, 160, 382
Bray v. Cox 245, 250, 252, 275, 352, 358, 372, 415, 418, 424, 453
Breeding v. Massachusetts Indemnity and Life Ins. Co. 382, 385, 389
Brickner v. Gooden 204
Brinkley & West, Inc. v. Foremost Insurance Company 318
Broudy v. United States 124
Brown v. Merlo 355, 406, 410, 413
Brown v. Riner 217, 218, 349
Browne v. McDonnell Douglas Corp. 297, 300
Bruck v. Eli Lilly & Co. 105, 148, 158
Byrn v. American Universal Ins. Co. 345, 409, 448
Caban v. United States 125
Cable v. Sahara Tahoe Corp. 291, 293, 294, 300, 301
Camp v. Forwarders Transport, Inc. 291, 296, 297, 300
Camporese v. Port Authority of N.Y. and N.J. 363
Cardillo v. Liberty Mutual Ins. Co. 390
Carver v. Schafer 215, 320, 321
Casey v. Manson Construction and Engineering Co. 4, 132, 217
Challoner v. Day & Zimmermann, Inc. 233
Champagnie v. W.E. O'Neil Construction Co. 150
Chance v. E.I. DuPont De Nemours & Company, Inc. 344, 360, 361
Chila v. Owens 359, 409, 415, 417, 450
Church of Scientology of California, Inc. v. Green 258
Cipolla v. Shaposka 269, 273, 310, 311, 312, 313, 314, 315, 316, 415, 417, 419, 433, 435, 448
Clark v. Celeb Publishing, Inc. 230, 275
Clark v. Clark 103, 242, 331, 332, 336, 338, 343, 406, 407, 408, 409, 410, 442, 444
Clay v. Sun Insurance Office, Ltd. 390
Conklin v. Horner 136, 243, 246, 247, 261, 266, 333, 337, 338, 352, 408, 419, 432, 435, 453

Conlin v. Hutcheon 214, 411, 438, 450, 451
Conservation Council of Western Australia v. ALCOA 315
Continental Oil Co. v. General American Transportation Corp. 218, 270, 278, 279
Cooper v. American Express Company 164
Cooperman v. Sunmark Industries Div. of Sun Oil 364, 367
Cousins v. Instrument Flyers, Inc. 166, 180, 258, 359, 360, 361, 362, 363, 366
Crawford v. Foster 409
Crim v. International Harvester Co. 215
Croft v. National Car Rental 362
Crossley v. Pacific Employers Ins. Co. 349
Danner v. Staggs 213, 214, 449
Dashiell v. Keauhou-Kona Company 207
Davenport v. Webb 154
Davis v. Cox 409
Day & Zimmermann, Inc. v. Challoner 192, 233, 299
Decker v. Fox River Tractor Co. 334, 335, 337, 342
De Foor v. Lematta 217, 218, 403
Delaney v. Moraitis 242
Delhomme Industries, Inc. v. Houston Beechcraft 149
DeMeyer v. Maxwell 213, 442
DeRoburt v. Gannett Co., Inc. 218, 219
DeVane v. United States 121
Dow v. Larrabee 444
DP Service, Inc. v. AM International 221, 317
Ducey v. United States 124, 204
Dym v. Gordon 9, 192, 278, 328, 351, 354, 398, 407, 408, 416, 417, 424, 435, 438, 439, 444, 445, 468
Edwards v. United States 124
El Cid, Ltd. v. New Jersey Zinc Co. 210
Emery v. Burbank 228
Emery v. Emery 151, 240, 241, 242, 248, 288, 419
Engine Specialties, Inc. v. Bombardier, Ltd. 275, 322
Equilease Corp. v. Smith Intern. Inc. 210
Erie Railroad Co. v. Tompkins 192, 223, 298
Erwin v. Thomas 132, 254, 256, 262, 270, 271, 363
Evra Corp. v. Swiss Bank Corp. 205
Ex Parte Archy 282
Fabricius v. Horgen 382
Farber v. Smolack 357
Farrier v. May Dep't Stores Co. 114
Felch v. Air Florida, Inc. 172
First National Bank in Fort Collins v. Rostek 204, 240, 403

Fisher v. Huck 3, 4, 403, 432
Flaiz v. Moore 147
Flammia v. Mite Corporation 232, 274
Fleury v. Harper & Row, Publishers, Inc. 236, 291
Flogel v. Flogel 103
Forsyth v. Cessna Aircraft Company 132, 135
Forty-Eight Insulations v. Johns-Manville Products 221, 278
Forward v. Cotton Petroleum Corp. 204
Fosen v. United Technologies Corp. 362
Fosillo v. Matthews 244, 245, 354, 358, 447, 452, 470
Foskey v. United States 123
Foster v. Leggett 163, 376, 379, 380, 381, 388, 389, 415, 447, 448
Fox v. Morrison Motor Freight, Inc. 157, 158, 266
Freund v. Spencer 243
Friday v. Smoot 349, 445
Frummer v. Hilton Hotels International, Inc. 178, 255, 256, 340
Fuerste v. Bemis 247, 344, 345, 419, 441, 445, 446
Gagne v. Berry 137, 246, 270, 331, 332, 352, 419, 453, 468
Gaither v. Myers 113, 309
Gallagher v. Koppers Co., Inc. 181, 215, 292
George v. Douglas Aircraft Co. 115
Girard Bank v. Mount Holly State Bank 274
Glenway Industries, Inc. v. Wheelabrator-Frye, Inc. 274, 277
Gordon v. Eastern Air Lines, Inc. 367, 369, 370, 371
Gordon v. Gordon 114, 237, 239, 251, 332, 343
Gordon v. Kramer 216, 419, 443
Gordon v. Parker 228, 229
Gore v. Northeast Airlines, Inc. 155, 157
Grancaris v. J.I. Hass Co. 364
Grant v. Bill Walker Pontiac-GMC, Inc. 381
Grant v. McAuliffe 240, 252, 287, 288, 398
Grass v. News Group Publications, Inc. 208
Gravina v. Brunswick Corporation 267, 323
Gray v. Gray 348
Griffith v. United Air Lines, Inc. 115, 123, 231, 269, 315, 382
Griggs v. Riley 135, 136, 214, 246, 453, 454
Gross v. McDonald 115, 450
Guillory on Behalf of Guillory v. United States 214
Gutierrez v. Collins 147, 148, 149, 205, 214
Hager v. Etting 315
Hague v. Allstate Ins. Co. 210, 337, 389, 390
Halstead v. United States 158, 350
Hamm v. Carson City Nugget, Inc. 292
Hanley v. Tribune Pub. Co. 204

Hansen v. Sears, Roebuck & Co. 107
Hardly Able Coal Co., Inc. v. International Harvester Co. 221, 279, 316, 317
Harkcom v. East Texas Motor, Etc. 221
Harris Corp. v. Comair, Inc. 376, 382, 385, 386, 389, 392
Harris v. Berkowitz 206
Hauch v. Connor 350
Haumschild v. Continental Casualty Co. 103, 111, 120, 151, 240, 241, 243, 248
Hawley v. Beech Aircraft Corp. 120
Hayden v. Krusling 204
Haynie v. Hanson 248
Heath v. Zellmer 332, 333, 337, 407, 408, 417, 419, 436, 456
Heavner v. Uniroyal 113
Heidemann v. Rohl 349
Henry v. Bauder 413
Hernandez v. Burger 260, 261, 262, 291, 432
Hilton v. Guyot 21
Himes v. Stalker 357, 358, 363, 371, 372
Hines v. Tenneco Chemicals, Inc. 114, 205
Holzer v. Deutsche Reichsbahngesellschaft 149
Home Ins. Co. v. Dick 390
Hopkins v. Lockheed Aircraft Corporation 162
Horvath v. Davidson 114, 397
Hotaling v. Smith 352
Huff v. LaSieur 248, 249
Hunker v. Royal Indemnity Co. 327, 334, 335, 336, 337, 341
Hurtado v. Superior Court of Sacramento County 110, 181, 259, 260, 261, 262, 266, 289, 290, 291, 297
In re "Agent Orange" Product Liability Litigation 158, 190, 231
In re Air Crash Disaster at Washington D.C. on January 13, 1982 238
In re Air Crash Disaster near Chicago, Ill. on May 25, 1979 223, 224, 298, 299, 301, 302, 364
In re Air Crash Disaster near Saigon, Etc. 158, 230, 231
In re Crichton 10
In re Pago Pago Aircrash of January 30, 1974 299, 301
In re Paris Air Crash of March 3, 1974 296
Ingersoll v. Klein 136, 210, 211, 212, 219, 220, 221, 222, 223, 279, 317, 382
Ins. Co. of North America v. United States 124
International Planning Ltd. v. Daystrom Inc. 330
Issendorf v. Olson 205, 206, 345
Jackson v. Koninklijke Luchtvaart Maatschappij, N.V. 266
Jackson v. Miller-Davis Company and v. Ceco Corporation 220, 221, 270
Jagers v. Royal Indemnity Company 240, 266, 318

James v. Bell Helicopter Co. 291
James v. Powell 180, 181
Jeffrey v. Whitworth College 149
John Hancock Mutual Life Ins. Co. v. Yates 390
Johnson v. Hertz Corporation 269, 270
Johnson v. Johnson 251, 282, 332
Johnson v. St. Paul Mercury Insurance Company 318, 431
Johnson v. Spider Staging Corporation 133, 214, 280
Johnston Associates, Inc. v. Rohm & Haas Co. 349
Kalmich v. Bruno 206
Kammerer v. Western Gear Corp. 170, 173
Karavorikos v. Indiana Motor Bus Co. 280, 281, 319
Kasel v. Remington Arms Co. 266, 290, 291, 292
Kell v. Henderson 244, 245, 250, 266, 354, 358, 423, 447, 452, 453, 470
Kennedy v. Dixon 242, 266, 420, 442
Kiehn v. Elkem-Spigerverket A/S Kemi-Metal 315
Kilberg v. Northeast Airlines, Inc. 105, 106, 153, 154, 156, 158, 167, 168, 211, 240, 361, 369, 407
Klaxon Co. v. Stentor Electric Mfg. Co. 192, 233, 285, 296, 299, 350
Kline v. Wheels by Kinney, Inc. 104, 270
Klingebiel v. Lockheed Aircraft Corporation 114
Knieriemen v. Bache Halsey Stuart Shields 364, 368, 371
Koplik v. C.P. Trucking Corporation 97, 103
Kopp v. Rechtzigel 243, 338, 415, 443
Kramer v. McDonald's System, Inc. 220
Krick v. Carter 315
Kruzie v. Sanders 404
Kuchinic v. McCrory 240, 242, 403, 442
LaBounty v. American Ins. Co. 336, 341, 343, 345
Labree v. Major 264, 266, 267, 268, 410, 419, 432, 449, 475
Lams v. F.H. Smith Co. 228
Lee-Hy Paving Corp. v. O'Connor 364
Leonard v. Columbia Steam Nav. Co. 147
Leschkies v. Playboy Club of Lake Geneva, Inc. 221
Lester v. Aetna Life Insurance Company 192, 233
Levy v. Daniels' U-Drive Auto Renting Co. 29, 104, 110, 270
Lewis v. Chemetron Corp. 213, 279, 315
Lichter v. Fritsch 335, 336, 337, 343
Lillegraven v. Tengs 107
Lin v. American Airlines, Inc. 298
Loebig v. Larucci 179
Long v. Pan American World Airways, Inc. 165
Loucks v. Standard Oil Co. of New York 147, 150, 152, 154, 168, 407
Loughan v. Firestone Tire & Rubber Co. 350

Lyons v. Lyons 249
Macey v. Rozbicki 192, 351, 398, 411, 423, 424
Machleder v. Diaz 278
Mager v. Mager 206, 345
Maguire v. Exeter & Hampton Electric Company 341
Marcano v. Offshore Venezuela 179
Marie v. Garrison 108
Maroon v. State, Dept. of Mental Health 120, 149
Masera v. Trans World Airlines, Inc. 97, 367, 371
Mason v. Southern New England Conf. Ass'n, Etc. 280, 281, 320, 321
Massaletti v. Fitzroy 405
McClaney v. Utility Equipment Leasing Corp. 363, 470
McConville v. State Farm Mutual Automobile Insurance Co. 405
McDaniel v. Sinn 105
McDermott v. Travellers Air Services, Inc. 185, 315
McGirl v. Brewer 149
McIntosh v. Magna Systems, Inc. 220
McMillan v. McMillan 349
McSwain v. McSwain 230, 231, 266
Mellk v. Sarahson 230, 231, 243, 442
Melville v. American Home Assur. Co. 213, 225, 257
Mentry v. Smith 404, 417, 443
Mertz v. Mertz 151, 152, 167
Mexican Nat. R.R. Co. v. Jackson 148
Michael v. Greene 204
Milkovich v. Saari 245, 335, 338, 339, 343, 390, 407, 408, 418, 419, 424, 454
Miller v. Gay 268, 269, 315, 316, 430, 449, 450
Miller v. Miller 361
Milliken v. Pratt 233, 398
Mitchell v. Craft 240, 340
Mitchell v. United Asbestos Corp. 212, 222
Mizell v. Eli Lilly & Co. 163, 351
Mosley v. United States 125
MPL, Inc. v. Cook 220
Mudd by Mudd v. Goldblatt Bros., Inc. 106, 113
Mullane v. Stavola 243, 277, 278, 443
Myers v. Cessna Aircraft 217
Myers v. Government Employees Insurance Company 339, 340, 341
Nelson v. Eckert 107
Neumeier v. Kuehner 166, 192, 196, 244, 253, 255, 256, 257, 258, 262, 263, 265, 268, 309, 352, 353, 354, 356, 357, 358, 359, 360, 361, 362, 363, 365, 366, 367, 369, 371, 398, 423, 424, 449, 451, 468
O'Brien v. Tri-State Oil Tool Industries, Inc. 350

O'Connor v. Lee-Hy Paving Corp. 364, 365, 367, 370, 371
O'Rourke v. Eastern Air Lines, Inc. 362, 365, 366, 367, 371
O'Shea v. Lavoy 405
Offshore Rental Co. v. Continental Oil Co. 239, 287, 294, 295, 296, 300, 301
Oltarsh v. Aetna Insurance Company 164, 266
Orawsky v. Jersey Cent. Power and Light Co. 315
Pacific Employers Ins. Co. v. Industrial Acc. Comm'n 228
Pahmer v. Hertz Corporation 355
Pancotto v. Sociedade de Safaris de Moçambique S.A.R.L. 167, 168, 170, 212, 221, 222, 279, 318
Panter v. Marshall Field & Co. 132, 133
Papizzo v. O. Robertson Transport, Ltd. 105
Parets v. Eaton Corp. 348
Patch v. Stanley Works (Stanley Chemical Co. Div.) 120, 158
Patton v. Carnrike 362, 367, 371
Pelinski v. Goodyear Tire & Rubber Co. 181, 221
People v. One 1953 Ford Victoria 282, 288
Perloff v. Symmes Hospital 239
Permagrain Products v. U.S. Mat & Rubber Co. 205, 315
Peters v. Peters 249, 261
Pevoski v. Pevoski 121, 250, 251, 322
Pfau v. Trent Aluminum Company 129, 130, 236, 237, 239, 411, 437, 438, 451
Pierce v. United States 123
Pittway Corp. v. Lockheed Aircraft Corp. 222, 317
Potlatch No. 1 Federal Credit Union v. Kennedy 133
President and Directors of Georgetown College v. Madden 107
Proprietors Ins. Co. v. Valsecchi 231
Pryor v. Swarner 353, 358, 359, 367, 371, 417, 447, 448
Purcell v. Kapelski 248, 251, 252
Pust v. Union Supply Co. 204
R & L Grain Co. v. Chicago Eastern Corp. 221, 317, 318
Rainsbarger v. Shepherd 409, 411
Rakaric v. Croation Cultural Club 166, 167, 170, 362, 364, 367, 371
Reich v. Purcel 19, 114, 181, 217, 259, 260, 288, 289, 293, 382
Resorts International, Inc. v. Zonis 150
Rhoades v. Wright 115, 349
Richards v. United States 122, 123, 124, 133, 138
Robertson v. McKnight 149, 248
Rogers v. U-Haul Co. 360, 363
Rohm & Haas Co. v. Adco Chemical Co. 234
Rolnick v. El Al Israel Airlines, Ltd. 181
Roman v. Delta Air Lines, Inc. 222

Rosenthal v. Warren 134, 135, 154, 328, 361, 364, 365, 367, 368, 369, 370, 371
Rozell v. Rozell 414
Rudin v. Dow Jones & Co., Inc. 207, 208
Rungee v. Allied Van Lines, Inc. 213
Ryan v. Clark Equipment Company 288, 289, 290, 291, 292
Rye v. Kolter 354, 358, 453, 470
Saalfrank v. O'Daniel 275, 276
Saharceski v. Marcure 121, 122
Saleem v. Tamm 452
Saloomey v. Jeppesen & Co. 350
Santana, Inc. v. Levi Strauss & Co. 204, 350
Schiltz v. Meyer 454
Schmidt v. Driscoll Hotel, Inc. 309, 338
Schneider v. Nichols 338, 448
Schulhof v. Northeast Cellulose, Inc. 270, 276, 322
Schwartz v. Consolidated Freightways Corp. of Del. 165, 173, 323, 339, 340, 341
Schwartz v. Schwartz 216, 240, 248
Semmelroth v. American Airlines 156, 220
Severine v. Ford Aerospace & Communications 385
Sexton v. Ryder Truck Rental, Inc. 159, 160, 349, 382, 383, 384, 385, 389
Shafarman v. Ryder Truck Rental, Inc. 470
Sharp v. Egler 230, 420
Shea v. Olson 409, 412
Siegelman v. Cunard White Star 178
Signs v. Signs 414
Silver v. Silver 405, 411
Simaitis v. Flood 350
Smith v. Cessna Aircraft Co., Inc. 350
Smith v. Pierpont 385, 389
Snow v. Bayne 104
Southern Pacific Transp. Co. v. United States 124
Stacey v. Greenberg 104
Stein v. Siegel 179
Storie v. Southfield Leasing, Inc. 159, 160, 382, 383, 384, 385, 389
Strassberg v. New England Mutual Life Ins. Co. 291, 297
Summers v. Interstate Tractor & Equipment Co. 240
Sweeney v. Sweeney 153, 158, 159, 160, 161, 382
Texas & Pacific Ry. Co. v. Richards 148
The Selma, Rome and Dalton RR v. Lacy 147
Thompson v. Thompson 240, 248
Tillett v. J.I. Case Co. 335, 340
Tolson v. Pan American World Airways, Inc. 178

Tooker v. Lopez 9, 192, 243, 244, 256, 257, 278, 351, 352, 353, 354, 357, 358, 364, 398, 404, 417, 424, 445, 447, 452, 467
Tower v. Schwabe 217, 345, 346, 420, 446
Towley v. King Arthur Rings, Inc. 359, 451
Trahan v. E.R. Squibb & Sons, Inc. 162
Tramontana v. S.A. Empresa de Viaçao Aérea Rio Grandense 113, 121, 131, 382
Trauth v. Northeast Airlines 155
Turcotte v. Ford Motor Company 266, 323
Turner v. Ford Motor Co. 160
Tyminski v. United States 133, 138
Val Blatz Brewing Co. v. Industrial Comm'n 228
Van Dusen v. Barrack 223, 298
Van Dyke v. Bolves 231
Veseley v. Sager 293
Vicon, Inc. v. CMI Corp. 205
Vrooman v. Beech Aircraft Corp. 133
W.H. Barber v. Hughes 114, 135, 397
Walkes v. Walkes 368, 370, 371
Wallis v. Mrs. Smith's Pie Co. 343
Walton v. Arabian American Oil Company 177
Watts v. Pioneer Corn Company 278
Wendelken v. Superior Court in and for the County of Pima 278
Wessling v. Paris 163, 240, 243, 377, 378, 380, 388, 442, 443
West v. Poor 404
Western Energy, Inc. v. Georgia-Pacific Corp. 209
White v. King 349, 445
White v. Trans World Airlines, Inc. 124
White v. White 204
Wilcox v. Wilcox 104, 213, 240, 243, 246, 418, 420, 436, 442, 443
Winters v. Maxey 163, 350, 406
Witherspoon v. Salm 97, 124, 210, 421, 446
Woodward v. Stewart 104, 323, 419, 442
Wuerffel v. Westinghouse Corp. 231
Wyatt v. Fulrath 10
Young v. Mitchell 349
Zelinger v. State Sand & Gravel Co. 248, 251, 333, 342

2. The Netherlands

HR 5 June 1915 (*Ehlers & Loewenthal v. Van Leeuwen*) 175
HR 31 January 1919 (*Lindenbaum v. Cohen*) 97
HR 8 April 1927 (*Benima v. Rohner*) 175
HR 13 March 1936 (*Bataafsche Petroleum Mij.* 142

HR 13 March 1936 (*Koninklijke*) 142
HR 11 February 1938 (*Dollar debentures Rotterdam*) 142
HR 2 April 1942 (*Jurgens Verbruggen v. Van Heesch*) 42, 43
HR 8 January 1943 (*Reijers v. Coert*) 118
HR 21 March 1947 (*Estonian succession*) 119
HR 18 april 1958 (*Nazi informer*) 146
HR 13 May 1966 (*Alnati*) 77, 80, 82, 83, 85, 86, 91
HR 8 January 1971 (*American Express v. Mackay I*) 80
HR 23 June 1972 (*W.A.M.*) 471
HR 27 October 1972 (*Neska v. De Beijer*) 35
HR 6 April 1973 (*Topsoe v. Del Prado*) 35
HR 8 June 1973 (*American Express v. Mackay II*) 35, 46, 80
HR 10 december 1976 (*Chelouche v. Van Leer*) 346
HR 26 May 1978 (*Gaasterdijk/Zuidpool*) 32
HR 12 January 1979 (*Sewrajsing Bros.*) 83, 84, 89
HR 16 March 1979 (*Free Enterprise/Brielle*) 32, 66
HR 4 May 1979 (*German/Dutch maintenance obligation*) 45
HR 18 December 1981 (*Hubers v. Kaak*) 85, 89
HR 3 December 1982 (*Levi v. Turkiye Seker*) 176
HR 15 April 1983 (*Balkema v. Van Münster*) 81
HR 16 December 1983 (*Saudi Independence*) 79, 97, 101, 145,

Hof Amsterdam 11 July 1946 (*Estonian succession*) 118, 119
Hof Amsterdam 6 June 1957 (*Nazi informer*) 146
Hof Amsterdam 9 June 1964 (*Child in Czechoslovakia*) 45
Hof Amsterdam 1 April 1970 (*NAP v. Christophery*) 34, 35
Hof Amsterdam 27 January 1984 (*Tanzanian father*) 59
Hof Arnhem 24 June 1980 (*Hubers v. Kaak*) 84
Hof The Hague 10 June 1955 (*De Beer v. De Hondt*) 30, 101
Hof The Hague 12 April 1973 (*German assignment*) 146
Hof The Hague 24 December 1976 (*Gaasterdijk/Zuidpool*) 32
Hof The Hague 11 May 1978 (*Cornelia Wilhelmina/Panter*) 32
Hof The Hague 23 April 1982 (*Saudi Independence*) 101, 145
Hof The Hague 10 September 1986 (*French Potassium Mines*) 67
Hof 's-Hertogenbosch 5 January 1932 (*Marriage promise*) 147

Rb. Alkmaar 20 December 1979 (*Matrimonial home*) 81
Rb. Alkmaar 17 April 1980 (*Joy-riding in Spain*) 99
Rb. Alkmaar 26 June 1980 (*Dutch/Swedish contract*) 176
Rb. Alkmaar 17 February 1983 (*B.B.A.*) 81
Rb. Alkmaar 16 February 1984 (*Spanish/Dutch bigamy*) 82
Rb. Amsterdam 30 November 1971 (*Open hatch*) 33
Rb. Amsterdam 13 October 1975 (*Tunesian child*) 82
Rb. Amsterdam 17 May 1978 (*Matrimonial home*) 82
Rb. Arnhem 31 January 1985 (*Kuipers-Denmark v. Van Wetten*) 37

Rb. Arnhem 27 June 1985 (*Hungarian Co-operative v. Saray*) 176
Rb. Breda 2 October 1962 (*Backx v. Franssen*) 30
Rb. Maastricht 11 January 1968 (*Belgian adultery*) 143
Rb. Maastricht 11 November 1982 (*Collision in Spain*) 33
Rb. Maastricht 1 November 1984 (*Fransbergen v. ENCI*) 37
Rb. Roermond 10 November 1983 (*Matrimonial home*) 82
Rb. Rotterdam 12 May 1922 (*Marriage promise*) 147
Rb. Rotterdam 27 July 1932 (*Marriage promise*) 147
Rb. Rotterdam 8 January 1979 (*French Potassium Mines*) 31, 32, 67
Rb. Rotterdam 5 February 1979 (*Levi v. Turkiye Seker*) 176
Rb. The Hague 14 January 1960 (*Calculation of damages*) 146
Rb. The Hague 19 April 1971 (*German assignment*) 146
Rb. The Hague 18 May 1972 (*Landhuis v. Zeeboormij.*) 81
Rb. The Hague 16 June 1976 (*Cornelia Wilhelmina/Panter*) 32
Rb. The Hague 17 December 1981 (*Balkema v. Van Münster*) 81
Pres. Rb. The Hague 17 september 1982 (*C.E.P. v. Sensor*) 37, 86, 87
Rb. The Hague 13 April 1983 (*B.B.A.*) 81
Rb. 's-Hertogenbosch 8 February 1980 (*Fallen tree*) 98, 100
Rb. Utrecht 14 March 1984 (*Matrimonial home*) 82
Rb. Zwolle 7 March 1983 (*American father*) 59

3. Other jurisdictions

International Court of Justice 28 November 1958 (*Elisabeth Boll*) 49
European Court 30 November 1976 (*French Potassium Mines*) 67, 452

Belgium

Cour de Cassation 17 May 1957 (*Bologne v. Sainte*) 27
Cour de Cassation 9 October 1980 (*Interpretation foreign law*) 175

France

Cass. Civ. 25 May 1948 (*Lautour v. Guiraut*) 144, 145
Cass. Civ. 30 May 1967 (*Kieger v. Amigues*) 144, 145

Germany

Reichsgericht 1882 (*J. v. H.*) 108
Reichsgericht 23 September 1887 (*Favor laesi*) 63
Reichsgericht 20 November 1888 (*Favor laesi*) 63
OLG Saarbrücken 22 October 1957 (*Favor laesi*) 63
BGH 26 October 1977 (*Lex fori interpretation*) 147

Great Britain

Lloyd v. Guibert 28
Sayers v. International Drilling Company N.V. 185, 186
Wilson v. Brett 404

Index

References are either to pages or footnotes. References to footnotes, preceded by the number of the chapter concerned, have been printed in italics, *e.g.* chapter 1, footnote 21 = *1-21*.

accessory choice of law *2-24*, 209, *3-58*, *3-59*, *3-83*
action directe → direct action
admonitory policy
  – generally 74, 75, 259, *4-131*, 266, 270, 276, 289, 334, 449, *9-48*
  – and guest statutes 418 ff., 431 ff. 434, 437, 444, *8-162*, 453
  – of locus state 184, 307, 310, 496
  – of tort law *3-38*, *3-71*, *3-99*, 246, 260, 264, 332, 333, 421, 453
alienation of affections → consortium
allocation method → jurisdiction-selection
"American" choice of law *3-6*, *3-84*, *7-54*, 491
anti-choice rule *2-94*, 235 ff.
apparent true conflicts → moderate and restrained interpretation
assumption of risk 405, 409
Austria, choice of law 38, 59, *1-162*, *3-16*
avoidable conflicts → moderate and restrained interpretation
basic policy
  – of the particular field of law 216, *3-92*, 224, *5-32*, 495
  – of tort law *8-129*, 453
  – see also: common policy approach
Belgium, choice of law 25, *1-57*, 98, *2-264*
Benelux Uniform Law on Private International Law
  – generally 25, 26, 34, *1-179*, *1-204*, 117
  – torts 26, 27, 29, 30, 31, *1-99*, 98, 99, 102, *3-18*
better law approach
  – generally 165, 172, 185, *3-47*, 265, 267, 311, *5-2*, 324, *5-10*, *5-12*, 333–347
  – and choice of law 53, 62, 68 ff., 136, *2-254*, 191, 307 ff., *5-330*, 369, *9-12*
  – criticism 329 ff., 338, 343 ff., *8-144*, 489
  – foreign law considered "better" 256, 294 ff., 341, *5-79*
  – forum bias 388, 390, 458, 480, 493
  – guest statutes *2-145*, 300, 407 ff., *8-144*, 456
  – in relation with public policy 139, *2-229*
  – see also: choice-influencing considerations
bilocal torts 63 ff., 66, *1-178*, 72, *1-198*
  – see also: place of wrong

borrowing statutes 114 ff.
Buitengewoon Besluit Arbeidsverhoudingen 80, *1-212*, 81, *9-25*, *9-64*
CIEC Conventions 59, *2-156*, *2-157*
California approach → comparative impairment analysis
capacity to sue 103, 111, 151, 179, *4-49*, 297
certainty and predictability
 – generally 40, 41, 53, 131, *5-8*, 329, 357, 383, 450, 452, 457, *9-32*, 482, 488
 – and choice of law methodology 189, 190, 191, 193 ff., 283, *4-193*
 – and principles of preference 303, 306, 316
 – Restatement Second 200, 224
 – and tort choice of law 195, *3-38*, 321 ff.
 – see also: expectations, justified; uniformity of result
characteristic performance theory 34, 35, *1-87*, 37, 48
characterization
 – generally 13, 24, 41, 85, 92 ff., 95–117, *2-196*, *2-197*, *2-251*, 350, 459, 492
 – and accessory choice of law *3-58*
 – contractual/delictual 103 ff., 121, *2-174*, 153, *3-58*, *7-27*
 – function 104, 109
 – modes 95 ff.
 – and policy-oriented choice of law 109–117, 460
 – primary 104, 105, 112, 146, *2-174*, 151
 – result-selective 102, 103, 108, 110, *3-58*, 240 ff., 287 ff.
 – secondary 104–109, *9-20*
 – substance/procedure *1-78*, 103, 104–117, *2-196*, *2-205*, 155, *3-83*, 460
choice of law policies 199 ff., *3-32*, 202 ff., 273, 324, 482, 493
 – system values 469, *9-34*, 482 ff.
 – see also: Restatement Second, principles of § 6
choice-influencing considerations
 – generally *2-147*, 165, 246, 323–347, 374, *7-27*, 390, *8-162*, 480, 482, 489
 – character 324 ff., 326 ff., *5-82*, *8-5*
 – and public policy 172 ff.
 – compared with Restatement Second 200, *4-41*, 328 ff.
 – as a solution to true conflicts 273 ff., 305
Civil Code (Netherlands) *1-52*, 81, *1-217*, *2-178*, 196
closest connection principle 26, 32, 34, 36, 38, 39, 44, 46, 102, 194, 201, 495
collisions at sea 32, 33, 66
collusion 412 ff., 414, 424
comity *1-43*, *1-44*, 326
common policy approach 254, 263 ff., *6-42*, *9-17*, 479
 – see also: basic policy
comparative impairment analysis 282–302, 388, *8-5*
comparative negligence → contributory negligence

compensatory policy 74, 184, *3-38*, *3-71*, 219, 246, 256, 263, 307, 333, 334, 387, *8-148*, 453, 471, 473, 496
conceptualism 193, 330, 477, 490
 – see also: jurisdiction-selection
conduct 30, 212, 220, 258, 315, 431, 437, 444, 473
 – and guest statutes *5-52*, 404 ff., 418 ff., 421, 444
 – interest of locus state 242, 244 ff., 250 ff. 258, 266, 269, 288, 322, 454
 – regulation 332 ff., *6-20*
conflicts justice 93, *2-3*, *2-4*, *2-155*, 183, *4-299*, 458
 – see also: choice of law policies
consortium *2-257*, 227, 254 ff., 369
Constitution
 – Illinois 167, *4-336*
 – New York 154, *2-204*
 – Ohio *2-218*
constitutionality
 – choice of law 68, 228, *4-346*, *7-6*, 376, 389–393
 – guest statutes 405, 406
construction and interpretation 127 ff., *2-147*, 138, 191, *4-2*, 425, 428, 464, 466 ff., 477 ff.
constructive intent → legislative intent
contacts-grouping 28, 29, 93, 165, 166, 173, 201 ff., 205, 208, 209, 238, 242, 275, 277 ff., *4-187*, *4-327*, 362, 364, 367, 380, *7-28*, *8-1*, *8-5*
contracts
 – generally 10 ff., 28, 34, *1-86*, 35, 36, 46, 48
 – choice of law approaches *1-126*, 192, 230, *4-164*, *4-277*, *8-1*
 – consumer contracts 36, 46, 47, 61, 73
 – employment *1-87*, 36, 46, *1-123*, 47, *1-132*, 61, *1-164*, 80 ff., 101, 145
contributory negligence *2-41*, 165, 205 ff., 255 ff., 334, 339, 340, *5-91*, 361 ff., *8-47*
damages 105, 167, *3-66*, 260, 277, 289 ff., *4-253*, 318, *5-79*, *6-71*, 368, 369, *9-17*
data, foreign law as 87, 100, *2-20*, 127, 128, 134
dépeçage *1-35*, 98 ff., *4-6*
decisional harmony → uniformity of result
defamation → libel
deterrence → admonitory policy
direct action 66, 164, 340 ff., *9-36*
disinterested forum 116, 164, *2-255*, 240, *4-109*, 288 ff., *7-4*, *8-149*
dissimilarity doctrine 139, 147 ff., 148, 152, *2-199*
divorce *1-108*, 55 ff., *1-189*, 81
domiciliary interests 261, 265, 266, 474, *9-44*, 481
Dramshop acts 292 ff., *4-266*, *4-303*, 320 ff., *5-67*, *3-75*

EEC Conventions
- Contractual Obligations 23, 36, *1-98*, 46, 48, 61 ff., *1-181*, *1-188*, 87 ff., 90 ff.
- Jurisdiction and Enforcement *1-177*, *2-12*, *8-153*

ease in determination and application 131, 225, *4-41*, 320, 328, 374
eclecticism *1-32*, 22, *2-228*, *3-25*, 199, 210, 216 ff., 285, 299, 324, 367, 376, 455
economic harm 222, 317 ff.
emotional harm *2-289*, 258
environmental torts 63, 66, 67, 70 ff., *1-191*
Erie doctrine 192, *3-96*, *4-259*
escape devices 24, 93, 119, *2-251*, 191, 198, 325, *6-14*, 373, 401, 488, 491 ff.
- see also: characterization, renvoi, public policy

European Convention on Information on Foreign Law *2-266*
"European" conflicts law
- generally *1-21*, 140, 189 ff., 193, *3-24*, 199, *2-281*, 491 ff., 495
- unification 23, 25

expectations, justified 214 ff., 219, 224, 307, 313, 319, 321, 329, *5-79*, 482, 496
- see also: certainty and predictability

Export Administration Regulations *1-205*, 86 ff., 89, *2-114*
fact/law dichotomy → notice and proof of foreign law
facultative choice of law *2-291*
failure to warn 207, 215, 220
false conflicts
- generally 52, 183, 191, 229, 233–252, 331 ff., 337, 340, 344, 370, *6-94*, 377, *9-43*
- interpretation *3-71*, 245 ff., 248 ff., 250 ff., 267 ff., *4-183*, 289 ff., *4-333*
- in policy-oriented choice of law 231, 308 ff., *5-18*, *5-40*, *5-56*, 352 ff., 355
- guest statute cases 442–445

family law *1-27*, *1-108*, 143
favor concepts
- generally 24, 53–75, 194, *5-22*, 493
- favor laesi 63 ff., 70, 265, 480
- favor negotii *1-30*, 42, 54, 55, *1-144*, *5-32*
- favor validitatis *1-30*, *1-144*

Federal Tort Claims Act *2-78*, 122–125, *2-133*, 137 ff., 365, *6-89*
foreign law
- ascertainment 148, 462 ff., 466 ff.
- and choice of law 92, 95, *4-32*, *4-35*
- and public policy 94, 149 ff., 158, *2-229*, 165, 167, 168, 170 ff.
- see also: notice and proof of foreign law

forum bias
- generally 479 ff., 489
- and escape devices 136 ff., 138, 168
- and lex fori approach 373 ff., 381, 389
- and policy-oriented choice of law 220, 230, 285, 367 ff., 370, 408, 455
- see also: forum preference

forum conveniens doctrine 386

forum interests 275, 327, 328, 331, 333, 337, 339, 340, 343

forum law
- prima facie applicability 170, *4-35*, 253 ff., *4-87*, 262, 291, 374, 380
- as a residuary solution 178 ff., 374
- as a true conflict solution 167, *7-6*
- see also: lex fori approach

forum preference
- generally 190, *3-63*, 230, 247, 374, 393, 481
- and Leflar approach *5-34*, *5-35*, 327, 331, 345, 347, 365, 374

forum shopping 116, 117, 138, 191, *3-11*, 211, 247, 254, 283, *4-221*, *5-16*, *5-72*, 370, 383 ff., 386 ff., *7-41*, 442, *8-136*, 481, 497

Fuld principles
- generally 196, 204, 244, 257, 258, 261, *4-120*, 268, 309, 352–372, 388
- exceptions *2-243*, 353, 356 ff., 359, 362, *6-63*, 366
- guest statutes 447, 449, *8-152*, 452
- and interest analysis 352 ff., 355, 356, 362, *6-74*

functional allocation
- generally 24, 42–52, 74
- torts 488, 494 ff., 496 ff.

Germany, choice of law 23, 29, *1-115*, 57, 63, 65, 72, *1-198*, 79, 84 ff., *2-47*, *2-160*, *2-263*

Gleichlauf 49, 386, 389, *7-57*

Great Britain, choice of law 28, *1-61*, 42, *1-162*

guest statutes
- generally 3, 115, 129, 131, 135 ff., *2-145*, *2-146*, *2-147*, 159, 162 ff., 204, 214, 216, 217, 331 ff., 338, 377, 379
- character 403 ff., 408 ff.
- and conduct 404, 444
- Fuld principles 351 ff., 357, 358, 360, 398
- policies 245, 265, *5-49*, *6-29*, 405, 408–426, 427, 437 ff., 443, *8-135*, 446, 453 ff., 461, *9-7*, 466, 473
- position of third parties 416, *8-123*, *8-141*, 453
- (potential) false conflicts 237, 242 ff., 247 ff., 442–446
- (potential) unprovided for case 256, 268 ff., 448–451
- principles of preference *4-285*, 310 ff., 315 ff.
- public policy 406 ff., 456
- spatial reach 426–440, 470

- true conflicts 278

Hague Conference on Private International Law 21 ff., 23, *2-157*

Hague Conventions
- on Maintenance Obligations 45, 59 ff., 69, *1-189*, *1-195*
- on Products Liability *1-73*, 64, *2-19*, 102
- on Traffic Accidents *1-73*, 65, *1-172*, 99 ff., 102
- other *1-142*, *1-143*, *1-147*, *1-231*, 44, 48 ff., 59 ff., *2-156*

homeward trend 135, 373 ff., 480
- see also: forum bias, forum preference, jurisdiction

identification of the issue 212, *4-6*, *4-12*, 459

immunity
- generally 263
- charitable 165 ff., *4-44*, 320, *9-48*
- interspousal *2-13*, *2-186*, 151 ff., *2-236*, 206, *4-51*, 248 ff., *4-190*, *4-285*, 315, *5-46*, *5-91*, 377, 388
- intrafamily 103, 112, 241, 288, 318, 413
- parental *2-13*, 159, *5-68*, *8-56*

insurance
- generally 389 ff., 406, 412 ff.
- interests 251, *4-168*, 313, 354, 405, *8-75*, 433
- and policy analysis 249 ff., *4-76*, *4-168*, 311, *4-311*
- rates *8-49*, 415 ff., *8-130*, 434 ff., *8-140*, 448, *8-145*, 496, *9-66*
- role of 85, *3-19*, 249, *4-121*, *4-125*, 297, 405, 410 ff., *8-43*, *9-7*, 476

interest analysis
- generally 129, 229–232, 233–321, *5-2*, 337, *7-28*, 398, *8-100*, 457, 488
- criticism *4-155*, *8-3*, *8-6*, 399, 439, 457 ff.
- false conflicts 239–252
- guest statute cases 398–483
- interest identification and evaluation 402, 463, 478, 487 ff.
- most significant relationship 243, 278 ff., 281
- other approaches 325, 327, 343 ff., *6-74*, 376 ff., 380, *7-23*, 400 ff.
- meaning of "public policy" 157 ff., 165 ff., 169 ff., *8-30*
- true conflicts 271–274, 363, 365, 367
- unprovided for case 252–271

interest-weighing
- generally 171, 191, 204, 227, 232, 242, 245, 247, 272 ff., 274–281, 283, *5-2*, 327, 364, 366, 375, 377, *7-23*
- and comparative impairment 284 ff., 291, *4-271*
- and guest statutes 447, 453
- and principles of preference 304
- and Restatement Second 278

invasion of privacy *2-238*, 267

issue-splitting → dépeçage

judicial method 190, 193, *4-120*, 376, 384, 386 ff.

judicial notice 177 ff., *2-282*, 185, *9-6*
- see also: notice and proof of foreign law

jurisdiction, adjudicatory
- generally 10, 49, 235, 255, 386, 389, 392 ff., 441, 451 ff.
- long arm statutes 2–128, 451

jurisdiction-selection
- generally 3 ff., 22 ff., 41, 43, 76, 79, 198, 201, *3-59*, 228, 232, 235, 488 ff.
- and escape devices 92 ff., 126, 140 ff., 159 ff., 169 ff., 350, 459
- as a methodological alternative 285, 301, 366, 383, 400 ff., 425, 458
- neutrality 53, *1-224*, 90, 191, 303, 373 ff.
- notice and proof of foreign law 182 ff., 463, *9-20*

justice in the individual case 94, 152, 190, 191, 193, *3-30*, 303, *4-275*, 328, 455, 457 ff.
- see also: choice of law policies, conflicts justice

Kadi-Justiz 40, 459, 489

Kentucky approach → lex fori approach

Klaxon doctrine 192, *4-22*, *4-202*, 296, *4-264*, 350

last event rule 63, 123, *2-97*, *2-33*, 222, 349
- see also: place of wrong

Leflar approach → better law approach, choice-influencing considerations

legal sphere 26, 27, 28, 29, 30–34, *1-99*, 40, 98, 99, *3-18*

legislative intent *4-155*, *8-81*, 428, 465 ff. 468 ff., 472 ff., 476 ff., 482 490

lex fori approach
- generally 325, 348, *6-4*, 387, 444, 488
- constitutionality 389–393
- Ehrenzweig 6, 190, *3-26*, *7-6*, *7-39*
- Kentucky *4-161*, *5-34*, 373–382, *8-5*, 448, 458, 480, 489
- Michigan 376, 382–389, *8-5*
- and policy-oriented choice of law 230, 254 ff., 272, 282, 295, 376–393, 455
- as a presumptive solution 254, 274, *4-225*, *5-75*, 381, 385 ff.
- as a residuary solution 32, 33, 148, 283
- see also: forum bias, forum law, forum preference, homeward trend

lex loci delicti rule
- generally *6-4*
- Fuld principles 355, *6-31*, 362, 366, 370
- and policy-oriented choice of law 302–322, 348–372
- presumption 220 ff., 257, *4-182*, 300, 302, 310, 318, 319, 321, *4-348*, 496
- as a residuary solution 274, 299

libel and defamation *3-55*, 208, 218, 258, 319

locus regit actum *1-113*, 54

maintenance 44, 45

maintenance of international/interstate order 326, 327, 328, 343
 – see also: choice-influencing considerations
malpractice 123, *2-101*, 134 ff., *4-44*, 275, 361, 385
moderate and restrained interpretation 223, *4-34*, 272 ff., 275, 286 ff., 291, 293, 300, *4-271*, 479 ff.
most favorable law 47, *1-157*, 62, 63, 66, 67, 70, 71, *4-173*, *5-13*, 367, 370
 – see also: favor concepts, plaintiff-favoring decisions
most significant relationship approach
 – generally 10, 132, *2-132*, 136, *2-215*, 169, 198–226, 237 ff., 349 ff., 374, 377, 380, *7-23*, *8-5*
 – and contacts-grouping 204–210
 – and policy oriented choice of law 210–226, 230, 243, 278 ff.
 – see also: Restatement Second
negligence
 – aggravated 404, *8-15*, 415
 – imputed 207, 360
 – see also: conduct, contributory negligence
neo-statutism 5, 8, 24, 169, 183, 430, 489
Netherlands, choice of law
 – generally 19 ff., 25 ff., 41, *1-127*, *1-145*, 56, 59, 65, *1-189*, 76, 79, 80 ff.
 – characterization 97–102, 146
 – notice and proof of foreign law 175, *4-32*
 – public policy 142 ff., 145–147, 492
 – renvoi 117–120
Neumeier rules → Fuld principles
New York, choice of law 11, 12, 244 ff., 363–372, 452
 – see also: Fuld principles
no-conflicts *2-94*, 129, *3-94*, *4-22*, 234–239, *4-171*, 288, 300, *5-18*, 359, *6-45*, 463
non-choice → anti-choice
notice and proof of foreign law
 – generally 95, 174–186, *4-86*, *4-222*, 373, 460
 – fact/law dichotomy 175, *2-266*, 182, *8-89*
 – and policy-oriented choice of law 460 ff., 462 ff.
 – status of choice of law rules *1-181*, 174 ff., 180 ff.
 – status of foreign law 14, 43, *1-114*, 174 ff., 424 ff.
 – see also: foreign law
party autonomy
 – generally 22, *1-115*, *1-121*, *1-149*, 61, *1-162*, 176, 326
 – contracts 10, 26, 36, *1-95*, 77, 209, 382
 – torts *1-73*, *1-177*, *2-24*, *6-61*
personal injuries 185, 221, 350
personalism and territorialism 430, 432, 443 ff., 449, 469, 473, 476
 – see also: territorial approach, territorial bias

place of wrong
- conduct/injury 63, 135, 222, *4-39*, 258 ff., 305, 321, 349, *8-55*, *8-434*
- see also: Federal Tort Claims Act, last event rule, lex loci delicti rule

plaintiff-favoring decisions
- generally 247, 254, *4-121*, *4-125*, *4-173*, 286, 307, 337, 341 ff., 354, 365, 369, 387, 441, 451, 479, 480
- see also: favor concepts

policy assessment 402, 422, 425 ff., 463 ff., 469–477
- see also: interest analysis

predictability of results 326, 335, *5-74*, *5-79*, 342
- see also: choice-influencing considerations, certainty, expectations

principles of preference 69, *3-23*, *4-4*, 261, *4-143*, 273, 302–316, 322, 324, *8-5*

priority rules 8, 24, 75–91, *2-20*, 194, *4-23*, 488, 493 ff., *9-64*

products liability 63 ff., 70 ff., 73, *1-197*, *2-233*, 205, *3-75*, 222, 284, 288 ff., 317 ff., 361

proper law 22, 24, 25–42, *1-136*, 56, 66, 93, 94, 102, *2-140*, 169, 194, 498

public/private law dichotomy 8, 49, *1-132*, 79, *2-154*, 194, 494

public policy
- generally 13, 24, 41, *1-169*, 84, *1-234*, 92 ff., 139–174, 406 ff. 492
- as a choice-influencing consideration 336, 370, 408
- of a foreign jurisdiction *2-220*, *2-257*
- of the forum state 168, 171, 173
- function 139 ff., 150, 157, 160 ff., 166, 168 ff., 173 ff.
- interest analysis 157 ff., 165 ff., 169 ff., *4-146*, 277, 280, *4-282*, 463
- minimum standard 141 ff., 144, 145, 149, 174
- negative 139, 160, 318, 347, *6-51*, 370, *7-28*, 383, *8-30*, 443
- positive *1-147*, 122, 139, 146, 158 ff.
- relativity 141–144, *2-158*, *2-160*, 146, *2-191*, *2-225*, *2-234*, 165, 166, 168 ff., *2-256*, 173 ff., *9-50*

punitive damages 164, *2-261*, 178, 223 ff., 276, *4-171*, 298 ff., 319, 367 ff.

règles d'application immédiate → priority rules

renvoi
- generally 13, 24, 41, *1-157*, *1-166*, 92 ff., 109–139, *2-196*, *2-208*, 492
- and policy-oriented choice of law 125–139
- purpose 117 ff., 119, 120, 121, *2-94*, 138
- and torts 119 ff., 125 ff., 137

Restatement First 4, *2-40*, *2-43*, 116, *2-97*, 198, 261, 348

Restatement Second
- generally 5, 10, 12, *1-83*, 50, *2-41*, *2-81*, *2-135*, 125, 135, *2-182*, 173, 198–226, 230, 237 ff., 278, *4-232*, 374, 379, *7-23*, 388, 489
- and policy-oriented choice of law 203, 273, 275, 278, 280, 305 ff., 316–322, *4-332*, 328 ff.

- principles of § 6 136, 192, 199 ff., *3-32*, 201 ff., 214 ff., *3-79*, 224, 325, 374, 482
- territorialism 238, 261, 316–322
- torts *3-21*, 200 ff., 242, 275, 278 ff., *4-327*, 350, *6-60*, 364, 377
- see also: most significant relationship approach

result-selective approach 33, 53, 65, 93, 105, 191, 194, 219, 228, 301, 330, 399, 455, 458, 459, 477 ff., 479, 481 ff., 491, 493
rule-selecting approach 109, 126, 185, 229, 372, 479, 490
scope rules *1-205*, 87, 127 ff., 427, *8-145*, 469–472
semi-open conflicts rules 24, 25–42, 199, 488, 492
semi-public law 8, 81, *1-236*, 494
simplification of the judicial task 72, 238, 326, *5-18*, 328, 343
- see also: choice-influencing considerations

social function of law *1-20*, 8, 45, 184, 399, 428
social values 53, 59, *7-2*, 493
sociological jurisprudence 28, 184, 428
spatial reach of substantive law
- generally 77 ff., *1-219*, 86, 128, 129, *2-154*, *4-2*, 271, *6-3*, *8-103*, 427 ff.
- guest statutes 426–440, 447
- identification 469–476
- and policies 246, 266 ff., 269 ff., 378, 426 ff., 436 ff., 473–477
- scope rules 469–472

special allocation → priority rules
standard of care → conduct
statutes of limitations 32, 106 ff., 113 ff., 120, *3-81*
statutism 108, *5-35*, 481
statutory construction → construction and interpretation
strict liability 132 ff., *2-233*, 218, 284, *4-131*
strike *2-13*, 101 ff., 145 ff., *2-174*
substance/procedure dichotomy → characterization
survival action 164, *4-80*, 287, *5-75*, *9-39*
Switzerland, choice of law
- generally 23, 57 ff., 61 ff., *2-157*, *2-263*
- method 39, *1-115*, 47 ff., *1-206*, 88 ff., *1-237*, *3-16*
- torts 64 ff., 67, 71 ff., *1-197*

territorial approach
- generally *2-154*, 302–322, 348, 360, 430, 432, 449, 454, 469
- enlightened territorialism 261 ff., 312, 353 ff.
- and policy-oriented choice of law *3-26*, 203, 221, 224, 266, 301, 353, 360
- see also: lex loci delicti rule, personalism and territorialism

territorial bias *3-26*, 261, 273, 302, 306 ff., 310, 312, 314
third parties 246, 252, 416, 435 ff., *8-123*, 444, *8-141*, 453
tolling statutes 115, *2-72*

torts
- and public policy 143 ff., *2-172*, 174
- substantive law 263 ff., 307, 308, 310, *5-80*, 421, 496 ff.

true conflicts
- generally 131, 155, 183, 191, 223, 229, 271–274, *5-10*, *5-56*, 474, 478 ff.
- comparative impairment solution 282–302
- guest statute cases 446–448, 453
- Leflar approach 327, 330, 332, 333, 335, *5-79*, 344 ff.
- lex fori solution 229 ff., 272, 282, 375, 380
- lex loci delicti solution 212, 302–322
- reinterpreted as false conflicts 133, *3-71*, 221, 251, 289 ff.
- various solutions 136, *4-25*, 302, 352, 377

unfair competition *1-167*, 349

uniformity of result 23, 26, 30, 53, 54, *2-33*, 117, 118, 119, 125, 138, 140, 182 ff., 198, 200, 215, 224, 303, 306, 316, 326, 328, 357, *7-41*, 469, 488

unilateral conflicts rules 52, *4-23*, 253, *7-13*, 495

unprovided-for case
- generally *1-135*, *2-6*, *3-71*, 229, 232, *4-221*, 252–271, 316, 334, 375
- solved as false conflicts 257 ff., 260 ff., 266, 267 ff., 291
- various solutions 254 ff., 261 ff., 263 ff., 302, 344, 352, 355, 478 ff.

validation, rule of → favor negotii

vested rights theory 115, 151 ff., 169, *2-267*, 196, 198, 211, 232, *4-274*, 348

vicarious liability 104, 210 ff., 269, *6-35*, 360, 363, 381, 382 ff., 423

workmen's compensation 121, *2-13*, 279, 335, *5-59*, 341, 350, 365, *7-27*, *8-138*

wrongful death
- generally *2-51*, 115 ff., 164, 204, 210, *3-75*, 223, 297, 350, *6-71*, 367, 368
- limitations 121, 152–157, *2-228*, 162, 217, *4-45*, 259 ff., 288, 320, *5-79*, 361